RESEARCH HANDBOOK ON GOVERNANCE
OF THE INTERNET

Research Handbook on Governance of the Internet

Edited by

Ian Brown

University of Oxford, UK

Edward Elgar
Cheltenham, UK • Northampton, MA, USA

Published by
Edward Elgar Publishing Limited
The Lypiatts
15 Lansdown Road
Cheltenham
Glos GL50 2JA
UK

Edward Elgar Publishing, Inc.
William Pratt House
9 Dewey Court
Northampton
Massachusetts 01060
USA

A catalogue record for this book
is available from the British Library

Library of Congress Control Number: 2012948841

This book is available electronically in the ElgarOnline.com
Law Subject Collection, E-ISBN 978 1 84980 504 9

MIX
Paper from
responsible sources
FSC   FSC® C018575
www.fsc.org

ISBN 978 1 84980 502 5

Typeset by Servis Filmsetting Ltd, Stockport, Cheshire
Printed by MPG PRINTGROUP, UK

Contents

Contents

Figures and tables

FIGURES

TABLES

Contributors

Johannes M. Bauer is a Professor of Telecommunication, Information Studies, and Media at Michigan State University.

Abbe Brown is a Lecturer in IT Law at Edinburgh University.

Ian Brown is a Senior Research Fellow at the Oxford Internet Institute.

Lee Bygrave is an Associate Professor in the Department of Private Law (Institutt for privatrett) at the University of Oslo.

Jonathan Cave is a Senior Tutor in Economics at Warwick University.

Nicholas Economides is Professor of Economics, Stern School of Business, New York University.

Lilian Edwards is Professor of Internet Law at Strathclyde University.

Michel van Eeten is a Professor of Public Administration in the School of Technology, Policy and Management, Delft University of Technology.

A. Michael Froomkin is the Laurie Silvers & Mitchell Rubenstein Distinguished Professor, University of Miami School of Law.

Graham Greenleaf is a Professor of Law at University of New South Wales.

Jeanette Hofmann is a Research Fellow at Wissenschaftszentrum Berlin für Sozialforschung (WZB).

Gus Hosein is a Visiting Fellow in the Information Systems and Innovation Group at the London School of Economics and Political Science.

Rikke Frank Jørgensen is Senior Advisor at the Danish Institute of Human Rights.

Christopher T. Marsden is a Professor of Media Law at Essex University.

Andrea Matwyshyn is Assistant Professor of Legal Studies and Business Ethics at the Wharton School of Business, University of Pennsylvania.

T.J. McIntyre is a Lecturer in Law at University College Dublin.

Milton Mueller is a Professor at Syracuse University School of Information Studies.

Alison Powell is Lecturer in Media and Communications at the London School of Economics and Political Science.

Joacim Tåg is an Associate of the Research Institute of Economics, Stockholm, Sweden.

Rolf H. Weber is Professor for Civil, Commercial and European Law at the University of Zurich Law School in Switzerland.

Malte Ziewitz is a Postdoctoral Fellow at the Department of Media, Culture, and Communication at New York University.

Abbreviations

APEC	Asia-Pacific Economic Cooperation
ARPA	Advanced Research Projects Agency
AS	autonomous system
ASEAN	Association of Southeast Asian Nations
BBS	bulletin board system
BCR	binding corporate rules
BGP	border gateway protocol
BRR	Books Rights Registry
CA	Certificate Authority
CAIC	child abuse image content
CBPR	cross-border privacy rules
ccTLD	country-code top-level domain
CDN	content delivery network
CIDR	classless inter-domain routing
CIR	country Internet registry
COE	Council of Europe
COPPA	Children's Online Privacy Protection Act
CWN	community wireless networking
DNS	domain name system
DOC	United States Department of Commerce
DPA	data protection authority
DPD	Data Protection Directive
DPI	deep packet inspection
DPO	data protection officer
DRMS	digital rights management system
ECOWAS	Economic Community of West African States
EULA	end-user license agreement
FCC	Federal Communications Commission
FD	Framework Directive
FTC	Federal Trade Commission
GAC	Government Advisory Committee (of ICANN)
gTLD	generic top-level domain/global top-level domain
IAB	Internet Architecture Board
IANA	Internet Assigned Numbers Authority
ICANN	Internet Corporation for Assigned Names and Numbers
ICCPR	International Covenant on Civil and Political Rights

ICESCR	International Covenant on Economic, Social and Cultural Rights
IETF	Internet Engineering Task Force
IGF	Internet Governance Forum
IP	Internet protocol
IPR	intellectual property rights
IPSS	International Packet Switching Service
IRPDC	Internet Rights and Principles Dynamic Coalition
ISOC	Internet Society
ISP	Internet service provider
ITU	International Telecommunication Union
IWF	Internet Watch Foundation
MMOG	massively multiplayer online game
NCP	network control program
NHRI	national human rights institutions
NPRM	notice of proposed rulemaking
NRA	national regulatory authority
NTIA	National Telecommunications and Information Administration
OBA	online targeted or behavioural advertising
PECD	Privacy and Electronic Communications Directive
PET	privacy-enhancing technology
PIA	privacy impact assessment
QoS	quality of service
RIR	regional Internet registry
ROA	route origin authorization
RPKI	resource public key infrastructure
SLA	service level agreement
SNS	social networking services/site
SPD	sensitive personal data
TCP	transmission control protocol
TLD	top-level domain
TRIPS	Agreement on Trade-Related Aspects of Intellectual Property Rights
UDHR	Universal Declaration of Human Rights
UDRP	Uniform Domain-Name Dispute-Resolution Policy
VOIP	voice over Internet Protocol
W3C	World Wide Web Consortium
WGIG	UN Working Group on Internet Governance
WIPO	World Intellectual Property Organization
WSIS	World Summit on the Information Society

PART I

INSTITUTIONS AND NETWORKS OF GOVERNANCE

1. A prehistory of internet governance
Malte Ziewitz and Ian Brown

What social, technical, economic and political developments played a role in constituting a field, in which the idea of 'Internet Governance' could thrive? What are the events, stories and ideas that preceded and made possible today's discussions about governance on, of and through the internet? In this chapter, we take a closer look at the prehistory of internet governance—the period from the mid-1960s to the mid-1990s before the internet became the mass phenomenon it is today.

As with every account that claims to give a comprehensive overview of the past, it is easy to foreclose analysis by hindsight rationalisations that make an initially complex set of uncoordinated interactions seem more planned and targeted than they actually were.[1] This is especially salient in the field of internet governance, which is not only very young by 'historical' standards, but also a highly contested area of policy and practice. Not surprisingly, historical accounts are often invoked to back up arguments or make laws or principles seem 'natural' or 'given'. We have tried to resist this temptation and maintain a working scepticism to such grandiose claims. Our goal is therefore not to give a definitive account of internet history, but to provide some background on the most common narratives that have informed debates about internet governance.

Our overview is based on a review and analysis of relevant literatures and other publicly available data and reports. Specifically, we draw on several existing accounts, especially Hafner and Lyon (1996), Abbate (2000), Castells (2001) and Leiner et al. (1997). Covering the period between the mid-1960s and the mid-1990s, we trace major developments and important milestones that are still influential in shaping current thinking about internet governance.

The remainder of this chapter is organised as follows. After sketching the evolution of networked computing from a technical perspective, we outline some of the main uses and users. Based on this analysis, we sketch the founding architectural principles and look at the emergence of different modes of governance and regulation. Our claim is that internet governance did not come about as a clearly defined concept, but rather as a process of searching and experimenting with an increasingly popular communications technology.

THE BIRTH AND GROWTH OF NETWORKED COMPUTING

Most narratives of the early history of the internet revolve around the formation of interconnected computer networks. While this process was complex and messy, four stages can be usefully distinguished.

The Idea of an 'Intergalactic Network'

In the 1950s, the main method of computing was batch processing, which allowed only one person at a time to use a computer system—widely considered a waste of valuable resources (Abbate 2000, pp. 24–25; Rheingold 2000b). A large research effort therefore went into developing new forms of computing like time-sharing that allowed more than one person to use a computer. A key goal was to facilitate access from a distance and transmit data accurately and efficiently between remote workstations. The leased telephone lines originally used for this purpose were expensive, and few connections were made at that time. Still, the idea of connecting machines into a more extensive network was a key concern among computer scientists in the early 1960s, famously articulated by J. C. R. Licklider, head of the Information Processing Techniques Office (IPTO) at ARPA, the Advanced Research Projects Agency of the U.S. Department of Defense, which would soon play a key role in the evolution of networked computing. It was Licklider who first documented the idea of an 'Intergalactic Computer Network', a globally interconnected set of computers through which everyone could access data from any site in the world (Licklider 1960; Licklider and Clark 1962; Licklider and Taylor 1968).

The Invention of Packet Switching in the U.S. and Europe

A major step towards such an 'intergalactic network' was marked by the development and uptake of packet switching (see, e.g., Kleinrock 1961). In the U.S., Paul Baran at RAND had worked for some time on new ways of organising communication networks that would survive a major military strike on infrastructure and came up with a new method called packet switching. In contrast to circuit switching, which required a direct and stable connection between hosts, packet switching split up all data into packets, which were then transmitted independently over the network and reassembled at their destination (see, e.g., Baran 1964). Almost simultaneously, a group of researchers in Europe were working on a very similar idea, albeit from a different perspective. Donald Davies and his team at the British National Physical Laboratory (NPL) were not so much concerned with the robustness of networks, but with the potential of packet-switched networks as commercial time-sharing devices, which would improve access to scarce capacity and provide affordable interactive computing for commercial and entertainment purposes (Abbate 2000, p. 27; see also Davies 2001). Even though the groups were motivated by different concerns, the idea of dynamic and distributed routing systems was developed independently on both sides of the Atlantic.

The implementation of packet switching, however, took very different paths on the two continents. In the U.S., the collective efforts of Baran and many other researchers resulted in the creation of ARPA's first packet-switched computer network (ARPANET). On 29 October 1969 at 10.30 p.m., the first link went live between terminals at UCLA and the Stanford Research Institute (SRI). Further nodes were added in the following weeks and months at other universities and institutions, leading to a cluster of 213 hosts by 1981. Implemented by the Boston firm Bolt, Beranek and Newman (BBN), the network was publicly demonstrated for the first time in 1972 at an international conference in Washington, D.C. The growth of ARPANET continued, and it became the major building block of the internet.

While Baran had been primarily concerned with the robustness of a decentralised packet-switched network against nuclear attacks, this had not been ARPA's original motivation to fund the research. As only a minor program in the ARPA portfolio, ARPANET was part of a more general effort in the IPTO to stimulate research in interactive computing and facilitate the sharing of computing time among various centres (Castells 2001, p. 10).

The European efforts were not quite as successful. In 1966, Davies had developed a plan for a national U.K. packet-switching network. In order to enable a range of commercial and entertainment services like remote data processing, point-of-sale transactions or online betting, his plan was to set up central nodes connected by high-speed telephone lines and provide local access points, to which users could connect their terminals, computers and printers (Abbate 2000, p. 29). Having neither the resources nor the authority to build such an infrastructure, Davies and NPL depended on the General Post Office (GPO) to realise the plan. Yet, not being convinced by the potential of data communications, GPO refused to collaborate and Davies had to settle for small in-house experimental networks later known as Mark I and Mark II. Only in 1977, long after ARPANET had gone live, did the GPO decide to build a data transmission network, the International Packet Switching Service (IPSS), by then using technologies from the ARPA spin-off Telenet instead of Davies' own creation (Castells 2001, p. 23).

TCP/IP and the Interconnection of Networks

While the military-funded researchers at ARPANET had pioneered networked computing, they were not the only ones to appreciate its potential. By the mid-1970s, the list of live computer networks included the Department of Energy's MFNET and HEPNET, NASA's SPN, the computer science community's CSNET and the academic community's BITNET (Leiner et al. 1997, p. 105). Besides these government or university-based networks, major commercial initiatives were based on technologies such as IBM's SNA, Xerox's XNS and Digital Equipment Corp.'s DECNET (Leiner et al. 1997, p. 105). Private companies like Compuserve and Tymnet started offering dial-up access to end-users. Another very successful application was the suite of Unix-to-Unix copy programs (UUCP) that became famous for distributing Usenet news and messages at low cost in computer-to-computer networks. UUCPnet expanded fast and also linked to the rapidly growing networked bulletin boards systems (BBS), among which FidoNet was particularly popular.[2]

Despite these initiatives, networks were still mostly run autonomously. Running on home-grown and often proprietary protocols, they were not able to communicate with each other. For example, while ARPANET had been built on the Network Control Program (NCP) protocol, the British IPSS was based on the X.25 standard that had been developed and fostered by the International Telecommunications Union (ITU).[3] X.25 also became the basis, among other things, for JANET—a government-funded network for education and research in the U.K. Other networks adopted and modified the X.25 standard for their own purposes, such as the Packet Radio Network with its AX.25 data link layer protocol. Further networks took advantage of both existing ARPANET and X.25 connections. In addition to UUCPnet and FidoNet, many other networks flourished, operating on a diverse range of incompatible standards and protocols.[4] However, a true 'network of networks' would require a standardised communication protocol that could accommodate the existing landscape.

Among the first to tackle this issue were Robert Kahn at ARPA and Vint Cerf at Stanford University. Rather than standardise existing specifications, their approach was to develop a protocol that could run on top of most other networks. A crucial element of their concept was to delegate responsibility for the reliability of transmission to the hosts and not the network itself. This suited the structure of ARPANET, which had evolved with the 'intelligence' located in the endpoints. In May 1974, Cerf and Kahn published a paper about their idea for 'A Protocol for Packet Network Intercommunication' (Cerf and Kahn 1974), which was formalised later that year in Request for Comments (RFC) 675. The document proposed a novel 'transmission control program' (TCP) to the community of engineers, which could run together with the 'internet protocol' (IP), and also coined the term 'internet', a short form of 'internetwork' (Cerf et al. 1974). With ARPA funding, a prototype system was developed and on 22 November 1977, for the first time, ARPANET, Packet Radio Network and Atlantic Packet Satellite Network were successfully interconnected to exchange data despite their heterogeneous designs. After further refinement, TCP/IP emerged as the final standard in 1978 and was declared the only approved ARPANET protocol on 1 January 1983. From the same year on, the Berkeley BSD 4.1c/2.8 Unix release was bundled with free TCP/IP code for hosts and simple routers. This version of TCP/IP could also be used for commercial applications. In 1985, NSF decided to make TCP/IP mandatory for NSFNET—a critical decision given the leading role of the NSF in the privatisation of the network infrastructure in the following years (Leiner et al. 1997, p. 105).

UCL, CERN and the 'International' Internet

As the account of packet switching suggests, European researchers had been involved in the development of the internet from the very beginning. In fact, the first link between a European network and the American ARPANET went live as early as 1973. Under the leadership of Larry Roberts, ARPA had had a strong interest in linking its 20-node ARPANET to Donald Davies' packet-switched network at NPL for research purposes. The original idea was to break an existing link between Washington and the NORSAR seismic array in Norway and add a drop-off point to include the NPL network. However, this plan proved unfeasible for both tariff implications and the political aspirations of the U.K. government to join the European Communities and thus avoid any major symbolic efforts to collaborate with the U.S. (Kirstein 1999, p. 4). In 1971, Roberts and Davies therefore involved Peter Kirstein, a computer scientist at University College London (UCL), which—unlike NPL—was not directly accountable to the government (Kirstein 2009, p. 20). The researchers agreed that ARPA would provide hardware for a UCL ARPANET node and allow use of the expensive transatlantic link if the U.K. established the link to Norway.

Despite some political resistance and funding problems, Kirstein and his team managed to establish the link, and on 25 July 1973 the first data packets passed via the new UCL ARPANET node from Norway to the Information Sciences Institute in California (Kirstein 1999, p. 1). This transatlantic link can be regarded as the first step towards a truly 'international' internet. However, despite this first and important connection, the U.S. and European networks continued to develop on quite different paths for some time.

While many institutions, governments and individuals were involved in the development of networked computing in Europe, some major impulses came from CERN, the European Organization for Nuclear Research in Geneva. During the 1970s CERN operated a number of smaller networks for its researchers, the main one being CERNET, which allowed fast file transfers between mainframes and minicomputers. While CERNET was similar to ARPANET in structure and approach, its protocols had been developed independently. CERN's protocol STELLA was inspired by ARPA's IP, but ran a different protocol on top of it. Purportedly, some of the designers had been in touch with Vint Cerf and his group, but a full transatlantic collaboration never materialised (Segal 1995).[5] In 1984 CERN researchers' proposal to introduce TCP/IP to interconnect the many smaller networks at CERN and TCP/IP was approved—but for internal connections only. According to Ben Segal, TCP/IP coordinator at CERN, the main reason for this hesitation was the political priority given to ISO-standard networking at that time (Segal 1995).[6]

This started to change in 1987 when CERN answered a request for support by Daniel Karrenberg, system administrator for the mcvax computer at the Amsterdam Mathematics Centre. With the mcvax acting as a gateway for all transatlantic traffic of the global USENET, Karrenberg's plan was to convert the European side (EUNet) into an IP-based network and connect it to its U.S. counterpart, which was also preparing itself for IP-based traffic at the time. Building on CERN's experience with internal IP filtering and routing, Karrenberg managed to set up a European TCP/IP-based 'internet' across existing UUCP networks and established internet connectivity via the mcvax. Only a year later, CERN opened its first external connection and later also operated the principal link between the European and American networks (see Segal 1995, for a comprehensive account).

Hence, it was not until the late 1980s that one could speak of a truly 'internetworked' global network of computers—or 'international' inter-net. In the following years, much activity was geared towards consolidating and expanding the existing networks and backbones as well as opening the infrastructure and its management to a much broader set of uses and users. The NSF played a leading role and was instrumental in managing the transition from a government-funded to a privately-managed internet. Despite increasing demand from non-academic users and private companies during the 1980s, NSF long prohibited backbone use for purposes 'not in support of research and education' in accordance with government regulations. Only regional networks were encouraged to seek commercial, non-academic customers.

This inevitably led to the building of competitive private long-haul networks by companies like UUNET, PSI or ANS CO+RE. It was only in 1995 that the NSF defunded its backbone and redistributed the recovered funds to the regional networks, which in turn bought connectivity from the new private providers (Leiner et al. 1997, p. 105). ARPANET had been decommissioned in 1990. Now built on modern commercial technologies, the internet had grown into a conglomerate of more than 50,000 networks worldwide by the mid 1990s (Cerf 1995).

EARLY USES AND USERS

While the history of networked computing is often told to illustrate the evolution of technical standards and specifications, in the next section we focus on the social context of this development. In contrast to authors who emphasise the role of a small number of 'internet pioneers' and their respective 'visions' (see, e.g., Slater III. 2002; for an opposite view, see Abbate 2000, p. 3), we adopt a broader approach and include all those, who—in one way or another—have played a crucial role as early users of the emerging networks. In doing so, we draw on the taxonomy proposed by Castells (2001).

Researchers, Grad Students and Engineers

The earliest users of computer networks were those who had created them: scientists and engineers at universities and government-funded R&D projects. Already in the 1950s, RAND had supported researchers like Herbert Simon in Pittsburgh in connecting computers via long leased lines. Beginning in the 1960s, computer scientists became increasingly interested in networked computing and began to form a growing community, connecting individuals in public research organisations like ARPA and CERN, major universities like UCLA, Harvard and MIT, and private think tanks like RAND, the Stanford Research Institute (SRI) and Bolt, Beranek and Newman, Inc. (BBN). Most of the people thought of as 'Fathers of the internet' (see, e.g., Harvey 2008) today were grad students at the time. Vint Cerf, Steve Crocker and Jon Postel were all studying with Kleinrock at UCLA when they started working on internet protocols. As part of the 1970s U.S. university culture, these students and their advisers used ARPANET for many activities—including those that cannot be straightforwardly considered research. For example, networked computers were heavily used for chats or private messaging. The first e-mail was reportedly sent from LA to the University of Sussex,

U.K., to retrieve somebody's razor left at a conference (Hafner and Lyon 1996, pp. 187–88). One of the most successful thematic mailing lists at the time was 'SF-Lovers', where science fiction fans shared their passions for cyborgs and robots rather than papers and protocols (Castells 2001, p. 19). In other words, the early computer networks constituted both the object of research and a platform for doing this research and socialising.

In this context, an important role is often attributed to the conditions under which at least U.S.-based researchers worked. Despite receiving extensive funding from the Department of Defense (DoD), they enjoyed a considerable amount of financial and intellectual freedom. ARPA and IPTO were largely autonomous in structuring their initiatives and research agendas. Researchers were not expected to produce any immediate results of military use. Rather, the goal was to stimulate research and innovation in the field of cutting-edge technologies without stifling creativity. The results of this policy were highly experimental projects like ARPANET, 'whose actual content was never fully understood by the overseeing committees' (Castells 2001, p. 19). Thus, by granting researchers a great deal of autonomy and letting them choose what they perceived as the most promising lines of inquiry, the U.S. government had created an environment in which creativity and experimentation could flourish.

In many ways, the design of the internet reflected the spirit of its creators. The researchers and grad students did not aim at building a carefully planned and standardised global network or exercising control over users' behaviour. Network management was largely seen as a burden to be avoided by elegant protocols that could run effortlessly on the network (Zittrain 2006, p. 1989). It also seemed reasonable to these researchers to keep the options open for future growth and innovation (National Research Council (U.S.) Committee on the Internet in the Evolving Information Infrastructure 2001, pp. 40–41). Abuse and anti-social behaviour was not a concern, since all users at the time were part of a rather close-knit and trusted network of researchers and scientists from the same cultural background with a shared set of values and beliefs.

Hobbyists, Sysops and Virtual Communitarians

A further group of users joined the internet once networked computing became accessible beyond academic circles in the late 1970s. Attracted by the new possibilities of computer-mediated communication, a large number of hobbyists and 'virtual communitarians' (Castells 2001, p. 52) connected their machine at home or work first into local networks and later to the internet.

Some of the earliest and most popular services in networked computing were Bulletin Board Systems (BBS). Arguably the first of its kind was the Computerised Bulletin Board System (CBBS), which had been developed by two Chicago students, Ward Christensen and Randy Suess, in January 1978 and allowed hobbyists to remotely leave messages in a central database (cf. Christensen and Suess 1989). Initially, bulletin board systems allowed users to connect and log in to local systems via telephone lines and modems, later via other means like Telnet, packet-switched network connections, or packet radio. Logged in to a BBS, users could exchange messages with other users via e-mail or public message boards, read and contribute news, download or upload software, or even play early text-based online games. Most BBSes at the time were run free of charge by computer hobbyists, many with strong ties to the amateur radio community. Later, fee-based BBSes like The Well, Mindvox and Echo NYC emerged and supported close-knit communities of dedicated users. While most BBSes were initially run as stand-alone systems that provided self-contained platforms with no direct exchange with other systems, this changed when users started to experiment with interconnecting BBSes. The first and best-known of these systems was the non-commercial FIDONET. Founded in 1984 by Tom Jennings, it allowed operators of FIDO-based BBS software to connect into a network so that electronic messages between users could be conveniently exchanged beyond the narrow confines of a single BBS.

Many of these early grassroots networks developed into 'virtual communities' and are often linked to the countercultural movements of the late 1960s (see generally Rheingold 2000a). Many of the early BBSes like The Well had a dedicated followership of 'people who had tried life in rural communes, PC hackers, and a large contingent of the Deadheads, the followers of the Grateful Dead rock band' (Castells 2001, p. 54; see also Hafner 1997). Soon, these communities spread and grew around whatever users had a shared interest in, including Kinky Komputer, the Catholic Information Network, Zen Connections and BBS communities specialised on earthquakes, weapons, photography, Star Trek fandom, Zionism, feminism, environmental issues and much more (Rheingold 2000a, ch. 4).

Besides BBSes, people used a number of other ways to connect in grassroots organisations. Very similar to bulletin board systems was Usenet with its equally anarchic and diverse newsgroups. The main difference between a Usenet group and a BBS is that Usenet does not rely on a central server, but on a meshed network of many constantly changing servers through which messages are stored and forwarded (Wikipedia 2011b). In contrast to the home-grown cultures of BBSes and Usenet, a number of large-scale networks were run as commercial online services.

Finally, further points of access to networked computing were the so-called free-net community networks. Networks like Cleveland FreeNet or Blacksburg Electronic Village provided public access to community information and other resources via dial-up connections. While many of these early users did not consider themselves as researchers, they often had connections with academic institutions. Most community networks and applications depended on powerful backbones, which could only be found at universities.

Hackers, Geeks and Open Source Advocates

Often portrayed as a subset of the emerging online community culture, the technology-savvy geeks and hackers deserve special attention. While the concept is contested, hackers are commonly understood as members of 'a community, a shared culture, of expert programmers and networking wizards that traces its history back through decades to the first time-sharing minicomputers and the earliest Arpanet experiments' (Raymond 2001, para 7). Castells defines hacker culture more specifically as 'the set of values and beliefs that emerged from the networks of computer programmers interacting on-line around their collaboration in self-defined projects of creative programming' (Castells 2001, p. 42). He emphasises two features: the autonomy of projects vis-à-vis institutional and corporate arrangements and the use of networked computing as the technological basis for this autonomy (Castells 2001, p. 42).

Hacker culture played an important role in the development of new applications and platforms on the internet. A case in point was the struggle to defend the openness of UNIX, an operating system originally developed in 1969 by a group of AT&T employees at Bell Labs. Members of the hacker culture had worked early on with UNIX. For example, the software underlying Usenet drew heavily on UNIX and UUCP by allowing UNIX computers to communicate outside the ARPANET backbone. However, when AT&T decided to claim proprietary rights in the UNIX operating systems in 1985, Richard Stallman, then a programmer at MIT's Artificial Intelligence laboratory, decided to found the Free Software Foundation.

Unhappy with the control of big corporations over the source code of UNIX, Stallman proposed to substitute the existing proprietary copyright in software with what he called 'copyleft'. Copyleft—or 'free'—software would be licensed in a way that required future users to require others to adopt the same licence terms for work derived from copyleft code.[7] The idea became known as the General Public License (GPL) and enabled programmers to develop software without the constraints of traditional copyright.[8]

As a starting point, Stallman and his colleagues began to develop an alternative operating system called GNU under the GPL.[9] In 1991, Linus Torvalds, a student at the University of Helsinki, released the source code for an operating system kernel under the same terms. The kernel could be complemented by existing work on GNU and soon became the core of the new Linux operating system. Thousands of volunteer programmers have been working on the open source code of Linux since and developed it into a powerful piece of software, used on a large number of servers and home computers today.

In the following years, many other open source projects formed and became technically and commercially successful. Examples are the Apache HTTP Server, the Mozilla project and even the protocol stacks implementing the Internet Protocol.

Entrepreneurs and Network Operators

A further group of early users consisted of entrepreneurs and business people that saw the commercial potential of the internet. While networked computing had early been identified as an opportunity for businesses and private households, initiatives were long held back because of the funding arrangement behind the early internet architecture. While the European vision of an internet had included commercial interests from the very beginning, at least on ARPANET this had been highly problematic. Since ARPANET was funded from public sources, any commercial exploitation was prohibited. Until 1995, NSF insisted that commercial access to the internet should only be granted at the level of regional networks, but not the backbone.[10]

As a consequence, a number of commercial companies developed businesses that operated outside of the ARPANET backbone. Early examples were online services like CompuServe, The Source or Prodigy that offered fee-based access to their servers. Cut off from existing internet technologies, these companies developed their own applications and business models for audiences broader than just researchers and hobbyists. As early as 1978, for instance, CompuServe started to offer e-mail services and technical support to subscribers (Wikipedia 2011a). Later, the company pioneered the development of real-time chat systems with CB Simulator, a multi-channel chat service introduced in 1983. Centrally managed content platforms and later also internet connectivity followed.

Since these companies understood themselves primarily as commercial providers of a new online experience with graphical user interfaces and innovative services, they mostly operated on proprietary protocols and restricted access to subscribers. Many of these services were quite costly.

In 1985, for instance, a user had to pay $12.50 per hour to connect to CompuServe services on non-holiday weekdays between 8 a.m. and 6 p.m., and $6 per hour at all other times (Pierce 1985, p. 19). Still, for many users these companies provided a convenient way of taking part in the new online experience. By 1987 CompuServe had 380,000 subscribers, compared to 320,000 at Dow Jones News/Retrieval and 80,000 at The Source (Pollack 1987).

Another case of commercial activity outside the existing backbone was investment into alternative long-haul infrastructure made by Internet Service Providers (ISP) like PSINet or UUNET in the 1980s. Building their own, technologically superior networks alongside existing lines, they could offer alternative network access to paying customers, building the basic infrastructure for today's internet.

The Anonymous User

A final contributor to internet development is rarely mentioned in analyses: the anonymous user. By testing applications, giving feedback, participating in discussions and choosing between competing services, a large number of nameless people participated in the 'production' of technologies, services and content (see, e.g., Fischer 1994). Many open source projects, for example, critically depended on feedback from the so-called periphery of users for bug reports and suggestions of new features. Companies often responded to these user demands and managed to improve their services. While such user-driven innovation was already observed and discussed in the 1970s, it later became a key theme among analysts of the emerging web (cf. Von Hippel 1976; Von Hippel 2005).

As this section has shown, the evolution of the internet cannot be understood as a merely technical phenomenon. Rather, the network of networks emerged as a set of complex social dynamics, involving millions of people around the globe. Engineering-minded researchers and grad students, amateur sysops and hobbyists, libertarian hackers and open source advocates, resilient entrepreneurs and businesspeople, as well as an army of anonymous users—all these people have been critically involved in the evolution of the internet.

FOUNDING ARCHITECTURAL PRINCIPLES

Based on the developments sketched above, both scholars and practitioners have tried to deduce a number of architectural principles to characterise this early phase of networked computing. Principles, in this context, should not be viewed as fixed or authoritative rules, but rather as shared beliefs and guidelines that are invoked at various points in debates about appropriate design and behaviour in relation to the internet.

Locating Architectural Principles

While there is no single 'official' or authoritative code or constitution stipulating rules for the internet's architecture, a number of authors have tried to pin down a set of principles that help understand the characteristics of the early internet.

A good first indication can be found among the original design community itself in the Internet Architecture Board's (IAB) Network Working Group. Titled 'Architectural Principles of the Internet', this document suggests that there are certain shared beliefs about the internet's architectural design. Among other things, it states the community's belief 'that the goal is connectivity, the tool is the Internet Protocol, and the intelligence is end to end rather than hidden in the network' (Carpenter 1996). The Request for Comments document describes in further detail why it is important that devices are interoperable and how this is achieved through an open universal protocol and related standards.

Numerous other authors have expressed these ideas in different ways. For example, Castells points to three aspects he sees exemplified in Baran's conception of packet switching: a decentralised network structure that is easy to expand; distributed computing power throughout the network so that no node is essential for the functioning of the whole; and redundancy in functions to minimise risk of disconnection (Castells 2001, p. 17). Another metaphor that has frequently been used to describe the architecture of the internet more generally is that of an hourglass. The technical infrastructure of the internet is conceptualised in layers, at the core of which a single and narrow Internet Protocol (IP) is located. This is assumed to maximise interoperability and minimise the number of service interfaces, demanding only little from service providers and users to connect at the narrowest point (Deering 2001).

Openness, Interoperability, Redundancy and End-to-end

Four key architectural principles can be summarised from these analyses: openness, interoperability, redundancy and end-to-end.

Openness has come to denote the absence of centralised points of control—a feature that is assumed to make it easy for new users to join and new uses to unfold. Consequently, people talk about 'open networks', 'open source software', 'open identity', or 'open standards', or call for an 'open internet policy' and 'open democracy' in 'open internet coalitions', 'open net initiatives' or 'open rights groups'. In many ways, the attribute has come to be a general icon for a commitment to a culture of distributed authority, cheap and easy access to infrastructure, and widespread and 'democratic' user participation.

As a political concept, it may be of limited use for technical network design. However, it has certainly shifted the focus from technical standards to the far-ranging social implications of basic architectural decisions, framing many of the contemporary debates about the internet's architecture. At any rate, using 'openness' as an architectural principle requires careful specification of who, which, or what exactly is open to what, which, or whom under which circumstances.

Interoperability requires that new devices can be easily connected to the network and communicate seamlessly with existing ones. A rough working definition would treat interoperability as 'the ability to transfer and render useful data and other information across systems (which may include organisations), applications, or components' (Gasser and Palfrey 2007, p. 4). Sometimes discussed under the rubric of 'connectivity' or 'compatibility', interoperability is often regarded as crucial for expanding a network. Clear and transparent standards for connectivity allow independent actors to add nodes to a backbone without central planning.

Interoperability is also viewed as one of the main drivers behind, though not necessarily a condition of innovation (Gasser and Palfrey 2007, p. 18). For example, it has been noted that interoperability favours network economies of scale and should therefore be seen as crucial for connectivity, cooperation and reach. At the same time, it could be argued that firms have an even stronger incentive to innovate when lower levels of interoperability promise higher returns.

Redundancy refers to the idea that the same network function can be carried out by more than one element. This principle may be most clearly articulated in Baran's and Davies' idea of packet switching. Instead of having to rely on a single, stable connection between two points to transmit data, alternative nodes would route packets through the network and compile the full message only at the destination. While redundancy does not lead to the most efficient use of network resources, it renders the network more robust and reliable. Best-effort routing can easily circumvent obstacles or defective nodes as envisioned by Baran under the scenario of a major military strike. Similarly, the redundancy built into the network can also act as an insurance against interventions at the content level, such as in the case of censorship. Sometimes these ideas are also summarised under the rubric of 'robustness' (National Research

Council (U.S.) Committee on the Internet in the Evolving Information Infrastructure 2001, pp. 39–40).

End-to-end: the most famous early architectural principle is the end-to-end principle. First articulated by Saltzer, Reed and Clark, it stipulates in its technical form that 'certain end-to-end functions can only be performed correctly by the end-to-end systems themselves' (Saltzer et al. 1984). A more simple version is offered by RFC 1958: 'The network's job is to transmit datagrams as efficiently and flexibly as possible. Everything else should be done at the fringes' (Carpenter 1996). Thus the end-to-end principle assumes that the network itself performs no function beyond transmitting data packets efficiently while all additional functionality is to be done at the end points. In this regard, the internet differs fundamentally from other technical networks such as the telephone network, where telephones remain relatively 'stupid' while major functions are executed in the network (Isenberg 1998).

Again, this design feature is not just a technical phenomenon, but also has far-ranging social implications. For example, if a network acts as a mere transport facility, it is less likely that points of control will emerge at the level of infrastructure, but rather at the endpoints, on the machines and devices of users and their access points to the internet. Recently the end-to-end principle has been criticised as too narrowly focused on a macro perspective on network structure. The argument is that the original end-to-end argument neglects the endpoints themselves, which may be of little use when locked down and not inviting user-driven innovation (Zittrain 2006, pp. 2029–36).

Some Exemplary Cases

Many of the milestones in the development of networked computing discussed above exemplify these principles and the many ways they are interrelated. For example, TCP/IP was designed to be agnostic to the underlying network, positioning all major data processing functions at the endpoints of the network in the spirit of the end-to-end principle. At the same time, this allowed users to connect relatively easily across heterogeneous infrastructures and thus contributed to interoperability. By the mid-1980s, all those with basic technical skills could join the network, which allowed it to grow without central planning or investments. In combination with packet switching, the best-effort approach embodied in TCP/IP also made specific nodes in the network redundant and therefore robust against local disruptions of or attacks on network infrastructure.

Architectural principles also can help us understand how and why certain design approaches and initiatives succeeded or failed. Many of the most successful technologies in terms of distribution and uptake were created by amateurs and geeks, who benefited from the open architecture of the internet. Chat rooms, BBSes and e-mail were all developed on top of an interoperable and 'stupid' infrastructure that allowed them to flourish. This was not the case for other network protocols and standards, most prominently X.25 (Castells 2001, p. 25). Developed by the post and telecommunications offices of major European governments and officially standardised in 1976 by the International Telecommunications Union (ITU), X.25 was based on virtual circuits. Network functions were largely under the control of a small number of providers, operating centralised and homogeneous communications infrastructures like the French Minitel managed by the French PTT. As indicated above, this approach had considerable implications. Trying to safeguard their investments, state-owned telecommunications carriers were naturally reluctant to let private companies connect to their networks. X.25 thus stood in sharp contrast to ARPANET's TCP/IP, which could accommodate many different protocols and run on heterogeneous networks. Ultimately, this led to the X.25 protocols being overtaken by TCP/IP, the code of which was open and freely available for everyone to use.

In sum, the internet's early infrastructure is best characterised as an hour-glass architecture aimed at facilitating real-time and best effort communications over lossy networks. Besides the rather general notion of 'openness', key principles include interoperability, redundancy, and the end-to-end principle, exemplified and enacted by a number of protocols and standards like TCP/IP and packet switching. Though often discussed in rather abstract terms, these principles have important policy implications by limiting control over information flows and providing guidelines for designing scalable and adaptable communications networks. As such, these principles are themselves negotiated and contested and can inform the more recent debates about IPv6 and other standards discussed later in this chapter.

EMERGING GOVERNANCE AND INSTITUTIONALISATION

While architectural principles are useful for describing a complex network infrastructure from a technical perspective, they cannot capture the broader dynamics of coordination and control that take place in and around computer-mediated communication. In this section we describe the different forms of governance that emerged on the early internet at different levels of the network. Governance here refers generally to the dynamics of coordination and control in specific social settings. In order to better understand emerging governance regimes on the internet, it seems useful to trace processes of institutionalisation rather than describe the field as a static arrangement of organisations, procedures, and committees. 'Internet governance' is a field in flux that has continuously changed its focus with new users, uses and technology (Hofmann 2005, p. 2).

Network Management: RFC and Consensus-based Decision-making

One of the earliest governance regimes can be found in the area of network management. Exchanging data on a common infrastructure required a minimum of coordination and control at the level of technology and standards. The early patterns of interaction emerging in this area have sometimes been described as 'ad hoc governance' (Castells 2001, p. 31). Given the rather small and close-knit group of engineers and academics who were involved in the early internet, coordination and control took place largely on an interpersonal basis wherever a problem was identified. Problems were conceptualised as mostly 'technical' ones, which just needed to be 'engineered' with the tools and approaches people used in their day-to-day professional work.

A good illustration of such an engineering approach is the informal Request for Comments (RFC) procedure that the early engineers used to exchange and coordinate their views on internet architecture and design. Under RFC, an author or a group of authors publish a document very similar to an academic paper, in which they sketch a new idea for a standard or specification, or just share an insight they think would be valuable for others. The goal is to receive comments and feedback on an RFC document so that it can be revised, improved, or abandoned if needed and get a sense of the dominant opinion in the community. From the beginning, RFC was not designed as a formal governance instrument, defined by a set of rules or mechanisms for oversight and enforcement. Instead, RFC was first used by a group of Stanford grad students around Steve Crocker and Vint Cerf as a way to get feedback on a new idea. The junior researchers were unsure about the potential and implications of some new network elements they had developed. So instead of single-handedly implementing their ideas, they posted their proposal as RFC 1 and received valuable feedback from the community. The procedure, which did not involve any membership, procedures, or formal voting, proved useful in the eyes of those involved and became an early institution of governance on and of the internet. Anyone could post or comment on an RFC, no special membership or formal qualifications were required. The documents provided a focal point for the concerns and communications of a group of technologically-inclined people and allowed for cheap and easy participation of a potentially large number of people.

Later, the RFC process was adopted by the Internet Engineering Taskforce (IETF), which started in 1985 as a quarterly meeting of researchers and engineers. An informal community without a legal form, it was open to anyone and became the primary institution for standard-setting at the network level.[11] A good example of the unconventional practices employed by the IETF, which differ substantially from those of other standard-setting organisations, was the mode of decision-making used in face-to-face meetings. IETF participants do not simply vote on standards and specifications but hummed to indicate their approval or disapproval; the option with clearest humming would win, if not overruled by the parallel discussion on the IETF mailing list (Hoffmann 2001). While this may not be recommended as a universal model for group decision-making, it proved useful in the context of the culture and ethos of the IETF engineers and researchers. To illustrate the commonly held beliefs of IETF, authors often quote MIT's David Clark, an early participant: 'We reject kings, presidents and voting. We believe in rough consensus and running code'.[12]

Community Governance: from Netiquette to Open Source

However, reducing early internet governance to technical standard-setting and engineering meetings would be too narrow a perspective. As already mentioned, a large number of more or less 'virtual' communities had developed on the network, centred around shared interests and activities. As a result, new forms of governance emerged. Many mailing lists and Usenet discussion groups, for example, had developed sets of norms in response to new forms of anti-social behaviour. A common occurrence in e-mail communications was so-called 'flaming', i.e. increasingly hostile and insulting interactions among participants, which usually killed off the discussion (cf. Kruger et al. 2005). In this context, a set of conventions for good behaviour in text-based online discussions emerged called 'netiquette'.[13] Another element of such early governance regimes were moderators, who held authority or technical capacities to ban or approve individual users on mailing lists or discussion boards.

While these cases reflect comparatively simple governance regimes, more advanced arrangements have been described in areas where users collaborated on a common project. A prime example was the emerging open source projects, in which programmers worked together on a piece of software in loosely coupled and computer-mediated networks. The key feature of these collaborations was full disclosure of the code produced by a participant for a specific module of the project in order to allow others to spot bugs and build upon that work to create the next best version. Significantly larger open source projects developed complex governance arrangements (Weber 2004). For example, participants in large projects tend to be divided into core and periphery. While the periphery comprises a large number of users who can test pieces of software and spot bugs, the core consists of a small number of leaders with responsibility for certain parts of the project (cf. Crowston and Howison 2005). The decision-making processes within the core can differ substantially across projects. The Mozilla community, for example, is supported by a foundation and has developed a complex system of formal and informal roles and responsibilities including module owners, peers, super-reviewers, staff, and many more.[14] The Apache community has developed a formal system of e-mail voting for its membership (Weber 2004, p. 187).

Another more general mechanism stemmed from the dependence of most projects on a large number of contributors. Since under most open source licences nothing prevented a group of users at least in principle from taking the code and starting their own project (a process called 'forking'), there was a basic incentive to reach consensus and comply with the dominant governance regime.

These examples indicate that governance regimes emerged in many forms and contexts on the internet—not just at the level of network management, but in a variety of likely and unlikely areas.

The Beginning of 'Internet Governance' as an Area for Policy and Research

A feature frequently attributed to the early internet was its ability to undermine traditional forms of governance, particularly state-based law and regulation. While the jurisdictional challenges that 'virtual' computer networks posed to territorially constituted nation states were more or less intuitive, many early users experienced and conceptualised computer-mediated communication as a 'space', also referred to as 'cyberspace'. This cyberspace was regarded as egalitarian by design, defying the authority of traditional political institutions (cf. Johnson and Post 1995; Goldsmith 1998). This view is perhaps best illustrated in John Perry Barlow's Declaration of the Independence of Cyberspace (1996), which famously proclaimed:

> Governments of the Industrial World, you weary giants of flesh and steel, I come from Cyberspace, the new home of Mind. On behalf of the future, I ask you of the past to leave us alone. You are not welcome among us. You have no sovereignty where we gather.

Academics argued that the internet 'radically subverts a system of rule-making based on borders between physical spaces, at least with respect to the claim that cyberspace should naturally be governed by territorially defined rules' (Johnson and Post 1995, p. 1370). The internet was perceived 'ungovernable' in the sense that state sovereignty could not effectively be exercised. In the absence of borders and clearly enforceable rules, it was asked what other institutions or actors would take the place of the traditional forms of political authority—if any.

In contrast to such libertarian ideas, others argued that the role of national and international law and regulation should not be underestimated and was in fact a necessary element of governance in digitally networked environments (see, e.g., Goldsmith 1998). Some even questioned whether the internet constituted a special field of regulation at all and suggested that a 'law of the internet' was as useless as a 'law of the horse' (Easterbrook 1996, pp. 212–13).

New models of internet governance were proposed, grounded in layered network architecture (Benkler 2006, ch. 12) or legal domains (Mayer-Schoenberger 2002, p. 617). In an influential book, Lawrence Lessig pointed out the normative role of code, i.e. the software and hardware that regulates behaviour or at least makes behaviour regulable (Lessig 1999). Similarly, the notion of *lex informatica* became popular, drawing an analogy to *lex mercatoria*, the non-state-based cross-border merchant law that had developed in the Middle Ages (Reidenberg 1997).

A key insight from these debates was that network infrastructures should not just be seen as objects of regulation, but also as regulating entities themselves that enabled or prevented certain forms of behaviour. It can be argued that it was these academic and policy debates over a perceived vacuum of political authority that marked the beginning of internet governance as a dedicated field of study in the 1990s (cf. Hofmann 2005, p. 6).

CONCLUSION

As this brief overview has shown, there has always been governance of, on and through the internet—albeit in many different forms. The moment people start interacting and cooperating in whatever socio-technical arrangement, they come up with and imitate practices that may develop into fully-fledged governance institutions. While analyses of early internet governance often focus on the institutional ecosystem of network management, it is important to keep in mind that a majority of governance arrangements emerged in the shadow or the absence of law and state regulation in highly specific areas of activity.

Three aspects seem particularly important. First, various groups of users have played a crucial role in the development of the internet. From the early days of networked computing, the largely uncoordinated interactions in and among cliques of researchers, policy-makers, business people and the many individual users have shaped the development and uses of the internet. The diverse and not always research-related motivations of computer scientists at ARPA, UCL, CERN and other institutions turned out to be as relevant as the many smaller communities of hackers and hobbyists that formed around BBSes and university networks. It therefore seems appropriate to characterise the internet not as a technical network or infrastructure, but as a cultural creation, which is 'as much a collection of communities as a collection of technologies' (Leiner et al. 1997). Not surprisingly, accounts that focus on technological design and standard setting tend to miss important aspects and run the risk of underestimating the complex mix of socio-technical interactions that generated the internet as we know it.

Second, even though a historical account of the evolution of the internet appears necessarily ordered, it is important to acknowledge the overall messiness and contingency of the process. What 'the internet' was at any given point in time has changed radically over the decades. Originally conceptualised as a solution to the rather narrowly defined problem of time-sharing in view of scarce computing resources, it soon became a medium for file exchange between trusted parties, developing into the pervasive multimedia platform of the World Wide Web. As many observers pointed out, this development was not so much driven by the 'vision', 'foresight' and 'planning' of a small number of chosen experts, but by accidents, coincidence, boredom, procrastination, tinkering and trial-and-error of a large and uncoordinated group of people. As the success of ARPA illustrates, governments were instrumental in funding some of the key technologies from packet switching to TCP/IP, but did well to resist the temptation to pick a winner early on.

Third, this overview has shown that ideas of social and organisational openness were crucial in the evolution of the internet. Often described in terms of architectural principles like interoperability, redundancy and the end-to-end principle, this openness allowed a large number of people to experiment and tinker with the new technologies for whatever purpose (or non-purpose) they pursued. As a consequence, business-minded entrepreneurs could come up with the first commercially viable internet services, tech-savvy nerds and hackers developed killer applications like e-mail or bulletin board systems, and network operators built their own backbones to allow commercial uses outside the restrictions of a government-funded infrastructure.

A key challenge will therefore be to understand how best to harness and preserve this creativity, growth and collaboration while mitigating the risks and problems it entails. This will be especially important as with the growth of the internet the discourse on 'internet governance' has moved from specific, situated and local practices to 'the internet' as a rather general and unspecified whole.

NOTES

1. The power of hindsight rationalisations in historical accounts is often signalled by language like 'this decision turned out to be essential later': Cf Wilcks (2010).
2. See, e.g., Fidonet, http://www.fidonet.org/ (last visited 23 April 2011).
3. One exception could be found in Norway, where NORSAR, the Norway Seismic Array, was developed and linked to ARPANET in 1972.
4. Among these was, for instance, the mainly university-based BITNET, an experimental network on the basis of IBM's RJE protocol (Castells 2001, p. 13).
5. Ironically, the network that would have facilitated that collaboration had not yet been established. But also political reasons are said to have played a role here (Segal 1995).
6. The only major exception had been made for DECnet (Segal 1995).
7. The most common copyleft licence is the General Public License (GPL). The latest version 3 can be found at http://www.gnu.org/licenses/gpl.html (last visited 23 April 2011).
8. While there is considerable argument over the meaning and correct use of the terms 'free software', 'open source software' and the respective acronyms F/OSS or FOSS, we will use the term 'open source software'.
9. GNU is a recursive acronym for 'GNU's Not Unix'. For an overview and analysis of the Linux project, see Raymond (2001).
10. This was also the reason why UUCP had not been allowed to use ARPANET or NSFNET connection, with a few tolerated exceptions.
11. In 1992, IETF was incorporated under the umbrella of the newly founded Internet Society, but maintained its authority in the area of Internet standards (cf. Brown 2008).
12. Quoted in Hoffmann (2001, Section 3). Another famous quote describing the culture of the IETF is attributed to Jon Postel: 'Be conservative in what you send and liberal in what you accept.'
13. For a rough summary, *see* RFC 1855, 'Netiquette Guidelines', http://tools.ietf.org/html/rfc1855 (last visited 23 April 2011).
14. *See* http://www.mozilla.org/ (last visited 23 April 2011).

BIBLIOGRAPHY

Abbate, J. (2000), *Inventing the Internet*, Cambridge, MA: MIT Press.
Baran, P. (1964), 'On distributed communications: Twelve volumes', *RAND Report Series*.
Barlow, J. P. (1996), 'A Declaration of the Independence of Cyberspace', http://homes.eff.org/~barlow/Declaration-Final.html, accessed 23 April 2011.
Benkler, Y. (2006), *The Wealth of Networks: How Social Production Transforms Markets and Freedom*, New Haven, CT: Yale University Press.
Brown, I. (2008), 'Standards (Global): Internet Engineering Task Force', in Marsden, C. (ed.)

Options for and Effectiveness of Internet Self- and Co-regulation, Brussels: European Commission, pp. 51–60.

Carpenter, B. (1996), 'RFC 1958: Architectural Principles of the Internet', http://www.ietf.org/rfc/rfc1958.txt, accessed 23 April 2011.

Castells, M. (2001), *The Internet Galaxy: Reflections on the Internet, Business, and Society*, Oxford: Oxford University Press.

Cerf, V. (1995), 'Computer Networking: Global Infrastructure for the 21st Century', http://www.cs.washington.edu/homes/lazowska/cra/networks.html, accessed 23 April 2011.

Cerf, V. et al. (1974), 'RFC 675—Specification of Internet Transmission Control Program', http://www.faqs.org/rfcs/rfc675.html, accessed 1 March 2011.

Cerf, V. and R. Kahn (1974), 'A protocol for packet network intercommunication', *Communications, IEEE Transactions on*, **22**(5), 637–48.

Christensen, W. and R. Suess (1989), 'The Birth of the BBS', http://chinet.com/html/cbbs.php, accessed 23 April 2011.

Crowston, K. and J. Howison (2005), 'The social structure of free and open source software development', *First Monday*, **10**(2), http://firstmonday.org/htbin/cgiwrap/bin/ojs/index.php/fm/article/view/1478/1393, accessed 6 November 2012.

Davies, D. W. (2001), 'An historical study of the beginnings of packet switching', *Computer Journal*, **44**(3), 152–62.

Deering, S. (2001), 'Watching the waist of the protocol hourglass', *IETF* 51, London.

Easterbrook, F. (1996) 'Cyberspace or the law of the horse', *U. Chi. L. Forum*, 207–16.

Fischer, C. S. (1994), *America Calling: A Social History of the Telephone to 1940*, Berkeley and Los Angeles, CA: University of California Press.

Gasser, U. and J. G. Palfrey (2007), Breaking Down Digital Barriers: When and How ICT Interoperability Drives Innovation. *Berkman Publication Series*, Cambridge, MA: Berkman Center for Internet & Society, Harvard Law School.

Goldsmith, J. L. (1998), 'Against cyberanarchy', *U. Chi. L. Rev.*, **65**, 1199.

Hafner, K. (1997), 'The Epic Saga of the Well', http://www.wired.com/wired/archive/5.05/ff_well_pr.html, accessed 23 April 2011.

Hafner, K. and M. Lyon (1996), *When Wizards Stay Up Late: The Origins of the Internet*, New York: Simon and Schuster.

Harvey, M. (2008), 'Who were the "Fathers of the Internet"?', *The Times*, 25 September.

Hoffmann, P. (2001), 'The Tao of IETF: A Novice's Guide to the Internet Engineering Task Force', http://www.ietf.org/tao.html, accessed 23 April 2011.

Hofmann, J. (2005), *Internet Governance: A Regulative Idea in Flux*, Berlin: Social Science Research Centre.

Isenberg, D. (1998), 'The rise of the stupid network', *ACM Networker*, **2**.1, 24–31.

Johnson, D. R. and D. Post (1995), 'Law and borders: The rise of law in cyberspace', *Stan. L. Rev.*, **48**, 1367.

Kirstein, P. T. (1999), 'Early Experiences with ARPANET and INTERNET in the UK'. http://nrg.cs.ucl.ac.uk/mjh/kirstein-arpanet.pdf, accessed 28 July 2009.

Kirstein, P. (2009), 'The early history of packet switching in the UK', *Communications Magazine, IEEE*, **47**(2), 18–26.

Kleinrock, L. (1961), 'Information flow in large communication nets', *RLE Quarterly Progress Report*.

Kruger, J. et al. (2005), 'Egocentrism over e-mail: Can we communicate as well as we think?', *Journal of Personality and Social Psychology*, **89**(6), 925.

Leiner, B. M. et al. (1997), 'The past and future history of the Internet', *Communications of the ACM*, **40**(2), 102–08.

Lessig, L. (1999), *Code, and Other Laws of Cyberspace*, New York, NY: Basic Books.

Licklider, J. C. R. (1960), 'Man-computer symbiosis', *IRE Transactions on Human Factors in Electronics*, **HFE-1**, 4–11.

Licklider, J. C. R. and W. E. Clark (1962) On-line man-computer communication. *Spring Joint Computer Conference*, IEEE Computer Society, 113.

Licklider, J. C. R. and R. W. Taylor (1968), 'The computer as a communication device', *Science and Technology*, **76**, 21–31.

Mayer-Schoenberger, V. (2002), 'The shape of governance: Analyzing the world of Internet regulation', *Va. J. Int'l L.*, **43**, 605.

National Research Council (U.S.) Committee on the Internet in the Evolving Information Infrastructure (2001), *The Internet's Coming of Age*, Washington, DC: National Academies Press.

Pierce, J. W. (1985), 'Computer network', *Educational Researcher*, **14**(8), 19.

Pollack, A. (1987), 'Ruling may not aid videotext', *N. Y. Times*, 15 September.

Raymond, E. S. (2001), 'How to become a hacker', http://www.catb.org/esr/faqs/hacker-howto.html, accessed 6 November 2012.

Reidenberg, J. R. (1997), 'Lex informatica: The formulation of information policy rules through technology', *Tex. L. Rev.*, **76**, 553.

Rheingold, H. (2000a), *The Virtual Community: Homesteading on the Electronic Frontier*, Cambridge, MA: MIT Press.

—— (2000b), *Tools for Thought: The History and Future of Mind-expanding Technology*, Cambridge, MA: MIT Press.

Saltzer, J. H. et al. (1984), 'End-to-end arguments in system design', *ACM Transactions on Computer Systems*, **2**, 277.

Segal, B. (1995), 'A Short History of Internet Protocols at CERN', http://ben.home.cern.ch/ben/TCPHIST.html, accessed 23 April 2011.

Slater III., W. F. (2002), 'Internet History and Growth', http://www.docstoc.com/docs/297578/Internet-History-and-Growth, accessed 23 April 2011.

Von Hippel, E. (1976), 'The dominant role of users in the scientific instrument innovation process', *Research Policy*, **5**(3), 212–39.

—— (2005), *Democratizing Innovation*, Cambridge, MA: MIT Press.

Weber, S. (2004), *The Success of Open Source*, Cambridge, MA: Harvard University Press.

Wikipedia (2011a), 'CompuServe', http://en.wikipedia.org/wiki/CompuServe, accessed 23 April 2011.

—— (2011b), 'Usenet', http://en.wikipedia.org/wiki/USENET, accessed 23 April 2011.

Wilcks, Y. (2010), 'Happy surprises? The development of the WWW and the semantic web', in H. Margetts, P.6 and Hood C. (eds), *Paradoxes of Modernization*, Oxford: Oxford University Press, pp. 101–18.

Zittrain, J. (2006), 'The generative Internet', *Harv. L. Rev.*, **119**, 1974.

2. ICANN and the domain name system after the 'Affirmation of Commitments'
A. Michael Froomkin

On September 30, 2009, the United States Department of Commerce (DOC) and the Internet Corporation for Assigned Names and Numbers (ICANN) signed an "Affirmation of Commitments" (U.S. Department of Commerce and ICANN 2009) that purports to recast the public–private relationship at the heart of the management of the domain name system ("DNS"). ICANN trumpeted this document as a culmination of the move from public to private control of the DNS, one that ICANN said "completes a transition that started 11 years ago" and "places beyond doubt that the ICANN model is best equipped to coordinate" the DNS (ICANN 2009c). The DOC treated it as a major milestone (U.S. National Telecommunications and Information Administration 2009b).

In fact, while the Affirmation is significant, its significance is more political than legal. As a legal matter, the DOC allowed one of its main agreements with ICANN to lapse, thus surrendering the most formal and visible legal control the DOC had over ICANN. In so doing, the DOC gave up its reversionary interests in contracts ICANN had with third parties—the DOC's right to require ICANN to assign those contracts to someone else were the DOC ever to lose faith in ICANN. In exchange, ICANN promised to remain located in the U.S., thus remaining subject to U.S. jurisdiction. ICANN also committed itself to a lengthy round of accountability exercises, although whether these will amount to anything substantive is not obvious. Furthermore, ICANN again expanded the role of its Government Advisory Committee (GAC), a committee of government representatives open to every nation, which has a direct channel to the ICANN Board as well as some agenda-setting powers.

These changes are less legally earthshaking than the parties might have sought to make them seem, but their political importance is real. By allowing its most visible agreement with ICANN to expire, the DOC made a tangible—if still incomplete—response to growing international pressure for the U.S. to abandon the control over ICANN that other nations feared gave the U.S. a dominant role over the DNS. Due to the lapse of the agreement the Affirmation replaces, ICANN enjoys significantly more independence after the Affirmation than it has ever had before. And the

GAC, the only direct means by which non-U.S. governments can influence ICANN, emerges from the Affirmation stronger as well.

Who controls the DNS matters to all internet users because every web page access, e-mail, or exchange of data online that uses a human-friendly domain name address relies on the DNS to translate that address to the right Internet Protocol (IP) number: save for the rare user who inputs an IP number directly, that DNS translation is necessary for every internet communication to find its target. Hierarchy and caching ensure that most DNS lookups happen without ICANN's involvement. But ICANN's ability to determine the content of the root zone file in the DNS gives it the power to determine which top-level domains (TLDs) will work for the vast majority of internet users and also who will control the registries and registrars that determine who has which domain name. ICANN sets rules for the acquisition, retention, and removal of internet domain names.

ICANN's increased independence from the U.S. Government provides an occasion to revisit two underlying issues that the Affirmation papers over: what standby or fail-safe control the United States retains over the DNS, and to what extent that (or any) control over the DNS matters. Here the picture is less clear, but some of the answers are surprising: the U.S. retains a lessened, but still real, degree of control over the DNS—but it may not matter as much as many of us think. There are some real economic risks. Most notably, control of the DNS may allow the exercise of market power over domain name registries, registrars, and registrants. But other dangers—in particular the geo-strategic risk of misuse of the DNS—has, it will be argued, been greatly exaggerated.

KEY ASPECTS OF THE AFFIRMATION

"U.S. Cedes ICANN Control to the World" read the headline at Internetnews.com (Kerner 2009). Yet, from a legal standpoint, the Affirmation of Commitments is, on the whole, quite vacuous. The Affirmation's greatest significance may lie in what it is not.

By the time the Affirmation was inked in 2009, ICANN had been managing the DNS for over a decade under the auspices of the DOC. The legal basis of the original ICANN–DOC relationship rested on three agreements: (1) a Memorandum of Understanding (MOU) (U.S. Department of Commerce and Internet Corporation for Assigned Names and Numbers 1998), later replaced by a Joint Project Agreement (JPA) (U.S. Department of Commerce and Internet Corporation for Assigned Names and Numbers 2006); (2) ICANN's Cooperative Research and Development Agreement (CRADA) with the U.S. Government (ICANN

2003b); and (3) a contract between ICANN and the U.S. Government for performance of the Internet Assigned Numbers Authority (IANA) function relating to the operational management of the root zone file, the assignment of IP numbers, and certain other standards-related functions (U.S. National Telecommunications and Information Administration 2003).

Over the course of the decade before the Affirmation, each of these agreements was amended numerous times; the amendments gradually gave ICANN more authority and more independence. Full independence from the U.S. was ICANN's goal. But the U.S. retained leverage over ICANN for several reasons. Some were contractual and are discussed below. Others were political or institutional. Of the institutional constraints, the most important was the role played by Network Solutions, Inc. ("NSI," later acquired by VeriSign, then hived off as NSI again, see Network Solutions (undated)), a private, for-profit company. The actual root zone file, sometimes abbreviated as "the root", was and is housed on a computer run by NSI/VeriSign, not ICANN. This allowed the U.S. Government significant leverage because there was little chance that someone at NSI/VeriSign would take orders from ICANN if the U.S. Government told them not to.

The MOU was repeatedly amended during its life. Ultimately, in September 2006, the DOC and ICANN rebadged the MOU as a "Joint Project Agreement" (JPA). The JPA significantly reduced ICANN's obligations to perform specific work items (compare JPA, s. II with MOU s. V.C.). In contrast, the legal relationship between ICANN and the U.S. did not change significantly. Meanwhile, ICANN continued to press for full independence. Although the U.S. Government may have had some concerns about its legal authority to cut ICANN free, the political ramifications of being accused of "losing" the internet (see Rabkin and Eisenach 2009) likely loomed larger. Despite this, ICANN's case for independence continued to gather steam.

Meanwhile, the U.S. Government's residual authority over ICANN came under increasing assault in the international political realm. Non-U.S. governments and interest groups increasingly asked why it should be that the U.S. Government should have unique control over the DNS when the internet was becoming increasingly global. The bulk of internet users were no longer in the U.S. Influential voices in the European Union and Japan, soon joined by others from every continent and region, began to push for the U.S. to divest itself of its controlling position or for ICANN's role to be turned over to a more international body.

In response, ICANN gradually expanded the role of non-U.S. governments by empowering the GAC. ICANN's GAC began in 1998 as an advisory organ consisting of one representative of each participating national government, and selected international governmental organizations (ICANN 1998, art. VII s. 3(a)). In 2002, the first of a series of new ICANN Bylaws (ICANN 2002, art. XI s. 2(1)) considerably expanded the GAC's powers. In the event of a conflict between a GAC "comment" and the Board's decision, the Bylaws mandated negotiation towards mutual resolution (ICANN 2002, art. XI s. 2(1)(j)). However, the Board maintained the power to take action notwithstanding conflicting advice, so long as its reasoning was included in the final decision (ICANN 2002, art. XI s. 2(1)(k)). The 2002 Bylaws gave the GAC unilateral power to put items on the Board's agenda (ICANN 2002, art. XI s. 2(1)(i)). The GAC was given additional representation in ICANN governance through participation in Board meetings (ICANN 2002, art. VI ss. 9(1)(a), 9(5)) and in Generic Names Supporting Organization policy recommendations (ICANN 2002, art. X s. 3(1)), and in 2003 in the country-code Names Supporting Organization also (ICANN 2003a, art. IX s. 3(2) and annex B s. 5(a)).

In enhancing the GAC's power, ICANN achieved a trifecta. It made friends in foreign governments and created constituencies in the ministries that sent delegates to ICANN GAC meetings. Often these ministries were commerce-and-trade-based, and thus, internal competitors to the communication ministries that attended International Telecommunications Union (ITU) plenaries. Having a different ministry invested in ICANN created a constituency for the proposition that even if ICANN was not perfect, an ICANN with a strong GAC was a good deal. Even without this piece of internal politics, many non-U.S. governments concluded that an independent ICANN was better than the status quo in which the U.S. had a dominant role (Kleinwaechter 2003). Those governments in turn became more likely to pressure the U.S. to overcome its vacillation and doubt and honor its promise in the 1998 White Paper to make ICANN independent (Froomkin 2000).

The Affirmation is thus the U.S. Government's response to pressure from ICANN and from many world governments. It requires much less of ICANN than did the MOU or JPA.

WHAT'S THERE

The most important aspect of the Affirmation appears in its first paragraph: the Affirmation recognizes the lapsing of the JPA—and unlike the many amendments to the MOU that preceded it, this time ICANN and the DOC were not extending the agreement. Instead, in the subsequent sections ICANN and the DOC recited some commitments. The parties described these commitments in broad and ringing terms:

> This document affirms key commitments by DOC and ICANN, including commitments to: (a) ensure that decisions made related to the global technical coordination of the DNS are made in the public interest and are accountable and transparent; (b) preserve the security, stability and resiliency of the DNS; (c) promote competition, consumer trust, and consumer choice in the DNS marketplace; and (d) facilitate international participation in DNS technical coordination (Affirmation, para. 3).

Sounds great. But, in fact, the DOC didn't really promise anything enforceable, and neither, in the main, did ICANN.

DOC's Promises

The Affirmation contains no binding promises by the U.S. Government. Given the history of the agreements it replaced, which consisted of commitments almost solely by ICANN, the absence of explicit statutory authority for the DOC's management of ICANN and of the root, and the equal nonexistence of any formal rulemaking or adjudicatory process, it is hardly surprising that the U.S. Government was not in a position to promise much.

Instead, the DOC "affirm[ed] its commitment" to the internet equivalent of Motherhood, "a multi-stakeholder, private sector led, bottom-up policy development model for DNS technical coordination that acts for the benefit of global Internet users." (Affirmation, para. 4). The DOC also affirmed its commitment to the GAC and (in principle, subject to more on the details) to multinational character sets for internationalized TLDs (Affirmation, paras. 4–6).

And that's it. The rest of the Affirmation consists of statements about what ICANN will do.

ICANN's Promises

ICANN makes some sweeping promises in the Affirmation. ICANN promises:

> to adhere to transparent and accountable budgeting processes, fact-based policy development, cross-community deliberations, and responsive consultation procedures that provide detailed explanations of the basis for decisions, including how comments have influenced the development of policy consideration[;] . . . to provide a thorough and reasoned explanation of decisions taken, the rationale thereof and the sources of data and information on which ICANN relied[;]

(Affirmation, para. 7) . . . [to] remain a not for profit corporation, headquartered in the United States of America with offices around the world to meet the needs of a global community; . . . to operate as a multi-stakeholder, private sector led organization with input from the public, for whose benefit ICANN shall in all events act[;] (Affirmation, para. 8) . . . to maintain and improve robust mechanisms for public input, accountability, and transparency so as to ensure that the outcomes of its decision-making will reflect the public interest and be accountable to all stakeholders . . . . (Affirmation, para. 9.1).

These are significant-sounding commitments about almost every aspect of ICANN's operations. Fully realized, they would likely defang all but the most overly zealous or nationalistic of ICANN's critics. But any jaundiced veteran of the DNS wars will immediately notice two things about this list: almost nothing on this list is new, and none of it is enforceable.

All but one of these commitments could have been lifted from any of a number of previous similar documents that ICANN has produced. With the exception of its explicit promise to stay headquartered in the USA—which is significant—ICANN not only has made these or similar commitments many times in the past (see for example ICANN 2008c, ICANN 2008d, ICANN 2008e, ICANN, 2008f), it has also congratulated itself for making good on these or similar objectives (McCarthy 2009).

Many of ICANN's commitments in the Affirmation turn out to be less binding than they might seem, although that certainly does not prevent ICANN from following through with them. For example, the promise "to maintain and improve robust mechanisms for public input, accountability, and transparency so as to ensure that the outcomes of its decision-making will reflect the public interest and be accountable to all stakeholders" turns out to have four sub-parts describing implementation. Each of these sub-parts commits ICANN to actions with words like "assessing and improving," "assessing . . . and making recommendations," "continually assessing and improving," and "continually assessing". As if that were not enough, ICANN commits to "organize a review of its execution of the above commitments no less frequently than every three years" to make sure that all the assessing and improving is proceeding (Affirmation, para. 9.1).

The means by which the triennial assessment teams are constituted does say something about where ICANN sees its future. The teams are made up of ex officio members and "volunteer community members" selected by ICANN's Board Chair and the Chair of the GAC. It is possible that the triennial assessments may matter, because delivery of the reports will provide an occasion for ICANN to agenda their recommendations. Indeed, in the Affirmation, ICANN promises that "[t]he Board will take action within six months of receipt of the recommendations" (Affirmation, paras 9.1–9.3). Of course that is carefully vague as to what sort of action the Board might take; it is certainly not a promise to agree with the teams or implement their recommendations.

One thing is clear: in contrast with the MOU and JPS regime, no more will ICANN's reports be directed to the DOC, playing the role of ICANN's master, but instead to the internet community at large. Whatever its practical import, this is high symbolism and thus may have a political importance of its own.

Symbolism may indeed be the strongest affirmative characteristic of the Affirmation: nothing in the Affirmation, nor anything else ICANN has said on the subject, suggests that any of these promises are enforceable by the U.S. Government, much less by an interested third party. Either party can terminate the Affirmation on 120 days' notice (Affirmation, para. 11). However, termination is an empty threat because the MOU and the JPA are non-existent. There is nothing to revert to if the Affirmation bites the dust. As ICANN CEO Rod Beckstrom noted, "The Affirmation is effectively a perpetual agreement." (ICANN 2009d).

WHAT'S NOT THERE

The most interesting aspects of the Affirmation are not what it says, but rather the parts of ICANN's relationship with the U.S. that are not addressed explicitly. Some remain unchanged; for others the change in political relations symbolized by the Affirmation may make a difference. And, in one case, the lapse of the MOU/JPA regime creates a legal opening for ICANN to further liberate itself from any threat the U.S. Government might make to displace it.

Final Authority over Changes to the Root Zone File

Prior to the Affirmation, the U.S. Government, not ICANN, had final authority over changes to the key root zone file. The physical root zone file resides on a computer controlled by VeriSign (formerly NSI), a U.S. Government contractor. The contractual relationship between the U.S. and NSI/VeriSign was itself fraught with conflict, but while the U.S. Government generally prodded NSI/VeriSign to cooperate with and even obey ICANN, there was one key exception. As spelled out in Amendment 11 to the U.S.–NSI contract, NSI (as it then was called) could not change the root file on ICANN's instructions without a counter-signature from a federal official.

Before the Affirmation, ICANN could not add, change, or remove a

TLD without the DOC's permission or at least acquiescence. This is still true after the Affirmation: in 2000, NSI was acquired by VeriSign, Inc. (Network Solutions undated). The Cooperative Agreement remained in effect between the DOC and VeriSign (ICANN 2001b). No subsequent amendments have expressly changed the Amendment 11 provision. The core responsibilities of Amendment 11 have been referred to in other subsequent contracts, which is evidence of their continued validity at least as late as August 2006 (see U.S. National Telecommunications and Information Administration, 2006 at s. C.4.1). As a practical matter, it remains true unless the U.S. amends its contract with VeriSign or changes the technical means by which the root zone file is authenticated in a way that would make ICANN the only party controlling the cryptographic certification process. Such a change does not seem likely. After the Affirmation was signed, ICANN and the DOC did alter the procedure for authenticating and thus, perforce, for changing the content of the root. ICANN had originally proposed to manage the whole security procedure for the root, including editing, signing, and publishing the zone file (ICANN 2008a). VeriSign objected to this plan (Kuerbis 2008), and the U.S. Government chose not to give ICANN the sole power to define the root (U.S. National Telecommunications and Information Administration, 2009a). As a result, ICANN still cannot change the content of the root unilaterally; it must get cooperation from an outside party—at present, VeriSign.

U.S. Government Power to Make a Unilateral Change in the Root

A re-delegation of a TLD is a change in control (from one registry to another) of the master file that defines who is registered in it. Re-delegations are by no means unheard of among the country-code top-level domains (ccTLDs). Since the registry that controls a TLD's master database has in effect total power over who can register in it, ICANN has a moderately involved process, run through its IANA subsidiary, for determining whether to accept a re-delegation application (for current procedures see IANA 2007). The process for re-delegating a ccTLD involves a period of consultation with local stakeholders although, oddly, the process is not very public as well as being far from instantaneous.

In 2001, the U.S. Government decided to put the Neustar Corporation in charge of the .us ccTLD. The change was not especially controversial by ICANN standards, but it happened in a very rushed manner and bypassed the usual IANA procedures (see ICANN 2001c, admitting that "redelegation occurred before the completion of the normal IANA requirements"), thus demonstrating the U.S. Government's unilateral power over the root (Schneiders and Higgs 2002). Nothing has formally changed as a result of the Affirmation that would alter the U.S. Government's ability to order or persuade VeriSign to insert a change into the root without a recommendation from ICANN (acting through IANA). On the other hand, the U.S. Government's participation in the Affirmation, and especially its statements about ICANN's independence, may be seen as a promise not to take any such action. Plus, the one example of U.S. unilaterally forcing a re-delegation involved the .us TLD. Despite arguments to the contrary (Froomkin 2004), many governments see management of the ccTLD bearing their country code as something that is or should be primarily an internal matter. Therefore, the precedent set by the U.S. actions relating to .us may be of little value were the U.S. to try similar tactics with any other non-proprietary TLD in the future.

The U.S. Government's Reversionary Interest in ICANN's Contracts with Key Third Parties

Amendment 3 to the MOU specified that the U.S. Government kept the right to replace ICANN, and if it did, NSI/VeriSign, the other registrars, and the other registries—the people who run the mechanics of the DNS—must terminate their relationships with ICANN, thus allowing them to substitute the Government's new choice (ICANN 2001a). In furtherance of this duty, ICANN's early standard contract with, for example, registries, terminated if the DOC "withdr[ew] its recognition of ICANN." (ICANN 1999, p. 24). However, there is no evidence that the U.S. Government contemplated using this nuclear option or even threatened to do so. These contractual terms between ICANN and others remain in effect after the Affirmation; there remains no way other than perhaps terminating the Affirmation itself for the U.S. to "withdraw its recognition of ICANN." Furthermore, there appears to be no reason why ICANN could not, if it chose, now amend its standard form agreement to remove the clause and gradually amend the agreements in place as they come up for renewal. The lapse of the U.S. Government's pre-existing ability to credibly threaten to replace ICANN and force it to assign its contracts with the registries and registrars may be the most significant legal consequence of the Affirmation.

The IANA Agreement is a Separate Agreement from the MOU

Many of ICANN's most important powers—such as the ability to re-delegate domains and its control over IP number block allocations—derived not from the MOU but from a separate, most peculiar, purchase order by which ICANN contracted to provide the "IANA function" to the U.S. Government for an annual fee of $0 (Froomkin 2000, p. 86). The IANA agreement is unaffected by the Affirmation, and was then due to expire on March 31, 2012 (U.S. Department of Commerce 2011). So long as the agreement remains in force, however, the U.S. retains the ability to threaten, albeit less credibly than before, to shift those powers to a different organization if ICANN acts in a manner the U.S. views as an attempt to wrest control from it.

What would happen if the U.S. were to attempt to assign the IANA function to a new body is a complicated question. On the one hand, if the U.S. had the authority to enter into the IANA agreement with ICANN, then it ought logically to have the same authority to enter into a successor agreement with some other party. On the other hand, IANA's most important functions depend on the consent and cooperation of many third parties who all agree to treat IANA's decisions as authoritative. Thus, for example, with regard to IP numbering, any new IANA's ability to act meaningfully depends in large part on being recognized by the five Regional Internet Registries (RIRs).

WHAT THE AFFIRMATION TELLS US ABOUT ICANN'S LEGAL STATUS AND ABOUT ITS FUTURE

The Affirmation explicitly states that ICANN is a private body (Affirmation, para. 8). Indeed, whatever the case a decade ago, the lapse of the MOU–JPA certainly strengthens the case for ICANN as a non-governmental actor under U.S. law, although ironically ICANN looks increasingly like an inter-governmental entity at the international level. ICANN's growing independence from the U.S.—even if it is not yet complete—fatally weakens any case for labeling ICANN a state actor under U.S. law in the future.

To date, criticisms of the Affirmation have tended to focus on accountability concerns. Some argue that the lack of defined criteria and standards of measurement for ICANN's performance are likely to diminish the effectiveness of the review panels (Gross 2009). The power to select the review panels is concentrated in the hands of insiders—ICANN's CEO, the leader of the body being reviewed, chief among them. This led the Coalition Against Domain Name Abuse to criticize the Affirmation as making ICANN "a regulator that has been captured from within" (CADNA 2009). Others note that the review panels' recommendations are not binding, leaving the ICANN Board with the same decision-making autonomy it has enjoyed since it revised its Bylaws to dispense with the need for community consensus (Mueller 2009, p. 17).

Another line of critique has focused on who gained power as the U.S. gave some up: the GAC and insider business interests. The GAC's increasing ascendency is somewhat ironic as ICANN was originally founded as a means to *privatize* the DNS. Version 1.0 of the ICANN Bylaws imagined an international board, but one drawn entirely from the private sector—government officials were not allowed to be Board members (ICANN 1998, art. V s. 5). As described above, over time ICANN allied itself with non-U.S. governments as a way to extract the U.S. from its directly controlling role, and also as a way to head off non-U.S. support for alternatives to ICANN based in the ITU or the United Nations. In ICANN's latest evolution, rather than being fully privatized, the DNS is instead semi-internationalized (compare: Doria 2009) although the role of business interests remains strong (Kovacs 2009).

The Affirmation gives ICANN the freedom to decide what sort of organization it wants to be. The question is whether, now that it is freed from many of the political constraints that have shaped, or perhaps even deformed it, ICANN sees a need to change or is happy as it is (Botzem and Hofmann 2010; Weinberg 2011).

As for the U.S. Government, its future influence over ICANN will be diminished. This can be seen from the largely unsuccessful attempt by the National Telecommunications and Information Administration (NTIA), the agency within the Department of Commerce charged with interacting with ICANN, to protest ICANN's restart of the new generic top-level domain (gTLD) application process (Strickling, 2010).

After years of delay, ICANN took significant steps in 2010 towards restarting the gTLD application process, most notably by proposing a new gTLD Applicant Guidebook (ICANN 2010b) and opening it up for public comment. In a letter from Assistant Secretary of Commerce Lawrence E. Strickling (2010) the U.S. protested ICANN's plan, igniting the U.S. Government's first public post-Affirmation dispute with ICANN.

The Strickling letter contained a specific complaint about the new gTLD process and a more general complaint about ICANN's failure to re-engineer its decision-making processes "to meet the obligations identified in the Affirmation (e.g., transparency, accountability, fact-based policy development)" (Strickling 2010, p. 2). The specific complaint was that NTIA had previously emphasized the importance of doing a full economic analysis of the possible impact of new gTLDs and that ICANN had failed to complete these studies and make them available for public comment. In his letter, Assistant Secretary Strickling asked ICANN to further delay the opening of the new gTLD application process until all the economic studies were complete. Notably absent from the Strickling letter was any suggestion about what, if anything, NTIA planned to do about its complaint other than to discuss them within the GAC (Strickling 2010, p. 2).

The ICANN Board met in December 2010, a few days after the Strickling letter, and voted to delay action on key aspects of the gTLD proposal pending further discussions with the GAC. The U.S. then attempted to get the GAC to adopt its objections to the new gTLD process, but with at best partial success (McCullagh 2011). ICANN agreed to some modifications in the new gTLD process, and adopted a revised application template and timeline (ICANN 2011).

At risk of being lost in this debate was Assistant Secretary Strickling's more specific complaint about the availability of the economic studies, a complaint which has some formal procedural validity, and ties in to his more general complaint about transparency and regularity in ICANN's decision-making. ICANN's decision-making is substantially improved from its rocky past. That does not mean, however, that ICANN's process has achieved the regularity of a U.S. government agency in which an agency limits its decisions to the record before it and discloses all the facts on which the agency plans to rely when setting out a proposed rule. ICANN works on a much more relaxed system in which it has not always been easy to identify all the relevant facts on which a decision may be based. Additionally, there is always the possibility that the Board or the staff will emerge from their private deliberations with an unexpected result—the so-called "bolt from the blue" forbidden by U.S. administrative law. Flexibility is a virtue of privatized decision-making but also its bane.

DOES THE DNS MATTER?

The possible risks of having a public or private body in charge of the DNS can be grouped into four categories: (1) primarily economic issues involving market power over DNS service providers (registrars and registries), (2) economic power exercised over registrants and other third parties, (3) more general political power over speech or other uses of the internet, and (4) geo-strategic. (Other issues, not considered here, have to do with the specification of technical parameters such as new character sets (IDNs), DNSSEC, and IPv6.) It turns out that some of these are much more real dangers than others.

Many concerns regarding who controls the root remain valid, particularly those relating to the ability to shape or control the market for domain names, and a number of trademark-related issues or issues arising from attempts to solve the trademark issues. In contrast, some other worries about the DNS now seem somewhat inflated. Still others, perhaps like the DNS itself someday, may be falling victim to technical change.

ECONOMIC AND MARKET POWER OVER DOMAIN-NAME SERVICE PROVIDERS

Most obviously, the power to control the root includes the ability to decide which TLDs are visible to the vast majority of internet users who rely on the legacy root. The power to create is also, largely, the power to destroy. Thus, ICANN can make visible and usable—or nearly invisible and largely useless—TLDs such as .com or .ibm. It can re-delegate a TLD from one registry to another.

TLDs are valuable and people want them. Further, the power to control TLDs can be leveraged into power over registries, and through them registrars. ICANN has used its power to limit the number of new TLDs, pick winners (or, some would claim, play favorites), and determine business models and domain name market structure (in both pro- and anti-competitive fashions). Since ICANN reserves the right to pass on the semantic validity of names, it has also been drawn into controversies about what terms are suitable for registration.

As it creates new TLDs, ICANN has also imposed various limits on what names they can register and to whom they can be offered. ICANN requires new global top-level domains (gTLDs) to use a "landrush" system in which trademark holders get first dibs on names matching their trade-marked character strings—even if the term has multiple meanings or is generic for some other use. It also has a list of reserved words that new gTLDs are not allowed to allocate to anyone—primarily reserved country names (Draft Applicant Guidebook, ICANN 2010a; Denton and Chango 2007; see also ICANN 2009b). This is an exercise of real power, and it is being exercised in service to the interests represented in GAC even though there is no relevant law in most countries, nor at the international level, that requires the owner of the TLD to withhold those potentially valuable names from the market (Froomkin 2004, p. 840).

ICANN also uses its power over the root to "tax" (require contractual payments from) the registrars and registries, costs that in most cases are passed on to the end-user. In the 2009 fiscal year, ICANN raised $60 million, $54.8 million of which came from domain name registry and registrar fees, a $10 million revenue increase over 2008 (ICANN 2009a, p. 58). That ICANN determines the market structure for domain names is not a critique, but rather a design feature—something built into its DNA from the seminal 1998 White Paper that called ICANN into being. And while ICANN has not created nearly as much competition among registry terms of service as one might hope for, its early moves in particular broke NSI/VeriSign's monopoly as the only commercial domain registrar that mattered. There is now a flourishing competitive market in new domain name registrations, albeit one marked by a certain lack of attractive new stock and by various technology-based attempts to corner the market in abandoned names (Zittrain and Edelman 2003; McCullagh 2004; ICANN Sec. & Stability Advisory Comm. 2007).

One economic risk is that ICANN might abuse its power by seeking extortionate payments (rents) from the registrars or registries. As ICANN's status as a nongovernmental body becomes increasingly solidified, it should become increasingly uncontroversial that the appropriate constraints on these negotiations come from private law and ordinary regulation, particularly anti-trust law (see for example *Coalition for ICANN Transparency v. VeriSign* at 505–07). In this context, ICANN's promise to remain in the U.S., and thus remain subject to U.S. anti-trust law is significant. So too is its promise to have offices around the globe, potentially making it subject to local private law remedies where it has offices, and also to the competition law jurisdiction of the EU.

Another economic risk is that control of the DNS could be abused to erect anti-competitive barriers to entry to the market for new domain names, thereby creating an oligopolistic market. The registry market does not currently have significant barriers to entry, but there are some obstacles to price and service competition. ICANN's levies on market participants put a floor on prices. And ICANN's requirement that registrars impose some standard contract terms on registrants limits service competition in the service of third parties, that is, trademark holders (Froomkin 2002). This in turn creates the possibility that, as a result of limitations in the domain names available, late entrants to the internet and especially smaller businesses and startups might find it more difficult to market online due to the shortage of semantically attractive domain names (Manheim and Solum 2003; Koppell 2005, p. 101).

REGULATORY POWER OVER REGISTRANTS AND OTHER END-USERS

More importantly, ICANN's power over the end-user extends well beyond the economic realm in which it can set a fee of a dollar or more per domain name. By requiring the registries—as a condition of being listed in the root—to require the registrars to include standard form terms in their contracts with registrants, ICANN gains a degree of control over registrants, at least to the extent that a registrar could impose terms in a contract with the end-user. To date, ICANN has used this power only for matters relating to trademark issues raised by domain name registrations, most notably its imposition of the Uniform Domain-Name Dispute-Resolution Policy (UDRP) (Froomkin 2002, pp. 651–52) and retention of anti-privacy rules relating to the "whois" function (see for example Letter from EPIC & NGO to ICANN Board 2007).

The interesting question is how much this ability to impose contractual legal duties on domain name registrants could be used for other things. ICANN (or any other entity controlling the root) could attempt to leverage that control in either of two ways. First, and more plausibly, control over the root could be used to impose additional contract terms on registrants in service of social goals. Over the past decade ICANN has been urged to require registrants to enforce copyright laws, remove some classes of hate speech, agree to takedown provisions, or otherwise assist law enforcement or others in the enforcement of legal or social policies. These suggestions have all differed from the UDRP in one critical fashion: the UDRP is designed to combat an ill—cybersquatting—that is a direct result of the structure of the DNS. In contrast, all of the other proposals that have bubbled up from time to time involve harms that are not direct results of the DNS; they may be torts or crimes that result from use of the internet, but they are not specific to the DNS and so far ICANN, to its credit, has shown no appetite for taking them on.

Somewhat less plausibly, control over the root also might be used to require that registrants themselves impose terms on parties with whom they contract either directly or indirectly via "web wrap" contracts (in which the consumer is said to be bound by viewing the agreement) with people who visit their websites or read their e-mails. Thus, everyone registering a domain name would have to agree, for example, that it would never be used to infringe a copyright or send a threatening e-mail from a user address at that domain. In theory, this obligation on the registrant to bind his customers or readers would work in a manner akin to the way that ICANN requires registrars to impose contracts on their registrants. But in fact, the scope for such terms in domain name agreements must be extremely limited. For starters, it is far from obvious that such terms would be effective, especially in consumer contracts, in many parts of the globe. More fundamentally, there is only so much that most registrants would put up with before walking away from domain names and towards some alternative. Many social networks flourishing online already use addressing schemes independent of the DNS. Twitter, for example, handles message traffic between millions of users within its single domain.

POLITICAL POWER OVER SPEECH AND OTHER USES OF THE INTERNET

Control of the root arguably might translate into political power. In particular some have warned that control of the root could be used to limit freedom of expression (Schiavetta and Komaiti 2003; Froomkin 2002, p. 664; Schwartz 2006, p. 78), while others have sought to harness the power conferred by the root for what they see as the good (e.g., Preston 2008), in turn causing others to warn of ICANN-enforced domination of the internet:

> Down the road, one can imagine demands from Brussels that ICANN cooperate with EU efforts to tax commercial sales negotiated over the Internet. Or perhaps it will demand a new understanding aimed at forcing top level domain managers to uphold EU privacy standards against U.S. government security measures (J. Rabkin 2009).

Control over the DNS can clearly be used to restrict the semantic content of TLDs—and as noted above, it is being used that way today. Under the current ICANN regime there is never going to be a .god or .satan domain name because too many people would find it offensive or at least controversial, and because the process of picking the body to run them would be highly contentious.

But even if deities and demons will not be TLDs, they can be, and are, second-level domains. For example, god.com and satan.com both exist and are registered to a party protecting its identity. (This information can be obtained by running the "whois" command on any UNIX computer connected to the internet; i.e. by typing "whois satan.com.").The lost expressive value of a TLD seems quite small when so many second-level alternatives are available. As for the suggestion that the DNS could be leveraged to work a major change in privacy law, it is hard to see how the controller of the root would pull this off—other than an end-user's contract with a registrar possibly being used as a jurisdictional hook by which a national government would seek extraterritorial application of a local law.

So much then for what a rational master of the root could do. But there is no certainty that the master will always be rational. The Affirmation states that "ICANN is a private organization and nothing in this Affirmation should be construed as control by any one entity" (Affirmation, para. 8). ICANN itself seems concerned about the dangers of capture (ICANN 2008b). Yet independence from capture is not achieved by fiat. Suppose that some interest group—political, religious, or economic—were able to capture ICANN and then attempted to make the most of their control of the root without regard for long-term political or economic consequences. At present, the danger of most forms of political or religious capture seems somewhat remote if only because the U.S. Government retains some leverage over ICANN as described above. The risk of capture by an economic interest group seems more plausible, but as noted previously the remedy for this sort of abuse remains a reference to anti-trust law.

What then might a fanatical political or religious group be able to do? As noted earlier, there are opportunities for financial gain. And there are ways to twist the future growth of the domain system to support, or avoid hurting, beliefs about offensive semantic content of TLDs. Onerous contracts with new TLDs might limit their registrations only to approved names, or perhaps attempt to require that they police their users, but it would be no simple matter to enforce similar rules on either the existing gTLDs or ccTLDs. The gTLDs have contractual rights in their delegations, and so long as courts remain open to enforce them, ICANN is subject to their jurisdiction, and the physical root is in VeriSign's control, the ordinary procedures of the courts should be fully adequate to guard against any chicanery. The ccTLDs often have a government behind them. Short of pulling the plug or re-delegating the domain to someone else—the nuclear option—in the current contractual regime there may be little that ICANN could do to seriously damage a ccTLD.

At the end of the day, the greatest risk to the domain system from control of the root comes only if governments act in concert with the root's controller. At that point, instead of civil law and diplomatic pressure working to counter-balance an attempt to leverage control of the root to achieve a social or political aim, both the technical and legal arms would be working together. That might be bad. And that is why the increasing power of the GAC might give one a slight pause. On the one hand, the existence of the GAC provides a source of limited external supervision over ICANN's activities; on the other hand, the GAC also provides a route by which governments might be able to harness the root to some extraneous end. If, for example, governments around the globe were to decide that internet anonymity was a bad thing that needed to be stamped out, and if they passed domestic laws prohibiting it, the field might then be open to use the root to make life difficult for Internet Service Providers ("ISPs") and website operators who provided anonymizing services.

The real prize, and the real danger here, is not the DNS: it is the IP numbering system. It is not complex to exist online without a domain name. It is impossible to exist online in today's internet without the use of an IP number. The power over IP numbers comes with the IANA function. It is IANA that hands out blocks of IP numbers to the RIRs, who in turn hand them out to ISPs and to others who demonstrate a need for them. And recall that IANA, at least at present, remains in ICANN's hands through a separate contract from the U.S. Government. So long as the U.S. keeps at least a reversionary interest in IP numbers by having contracts with ICANN that require routine renewal and that contain a termination clause, this danger remains fairly small. In any case, the RIRs are independent of ICANN, so there is not much ICANN can do to them except not give them new numbers. There are only five RIRs and they could act together in self-defense if ICANN were ever to try to starve them or worse, attempted to destroy the internet by giving the same number blocks to multiple recipients in an attempt to create IP number conflicts.

The Affirmation is silent on IANA's fate, but there are powerful reasons why both the U.S. Government and ICANN might wish to preserve the status quo. On the U.S. Government's side, the IANA arrangement remains a less controversial fail-safe against the eventuality that if ICANN were ever to be captured by fanatics or otherwise go off the rails, the theoretical ability to reassign the IANA function creates a lever that the DOC could use to cripple a runaway ICANN. On ICANN's side, its status as a government contractor supplying numbers in accordance with U.S. federal policy provides a valuable shield against what might otherwise be plausible anti-trust risks.

THE MYTH OF THE DNS'S GEO-STRATEGIC POWER

Perhaps the strangest canard about the DNS is that control over it confers some sort of geo-strategic power (Von Arx and Hagen 2002, pp. 26–28; Barker 2001, p. 39; A. Rabkin 2009, p. 14; Sonbuchner 2008, p. 207). From time to time writers have suggested that by controlling the DNS the United States enjoys some potential advantage that might be deployed in case of real war or cyber-war. The first assertion is clearly wrong; the second seems implausible also.

The scenario seems to go something like this. The United States gets into a shooting war with Ruritania. The Ruritanians rely on the internet for critical military and civilian communications. If the U.S. could knock out Ruritanian internet communications, it would secure a material military advantage. So far, so good. But how is control of the DNS supposed to achieve this? Apparently by the U.S. using its power over the DNS to delete Ruritania's ccTLD, bringing the nation to its virtual knees.

Like every nation, the Ruritanians have a ccTLD, which we will imagine is .rt. There is no question that whoever controls the root can delete .rt from it. Then, in the ordinary course of things, as the new root zone file propagates across the net, addresses ending in .rt will stop functioning because computers no longer know where to find the .rt registry's file that would tell them where to send packets destined for .rt domains. Ruritania is in chaos! U.S. forces are met with flowers . . . wait, wrong movie . . .

The scenario gains some potential plausibility due to the location of the root zone file in the U.S. Even if ICANN has rules prohibiting political deletions or surreptitious change of control of a domain, it is possible that if faced with a claim of national emergency, VeriSign or whoever was running the server hosting the root zone file would allow the U.S. to do whatever it asked. That at least appears to be what several U.S. phone companies did when asked to allow illegal wiretaps in the name of national security (see *In re Nat'l Sec. Agency Telecomms. Records Litig.* for examples of the allegations).

Even so, it could never work that way, and it certainly could never work that way twice.

For starters, unless the government of Ruritania is technically clueless, it will have taken two simple steps that will protect it against the disappearance of the .rt domain. First, it will have registered many names in .com or some other TLD and pointed those names to its critical sites as backups. Second, it will have recorded the IP numbers of the most critical sites, burned them to CDs, and distributed those disks to its military and critical infrastructure. If the .rt domain suddenly starts disappearing, then forewarned internet users in Ruritania will start using the alternate domain names or will fire up the emergency CD and write over their cached copy of the zone file.

More insidiously, the U.S. could quietly enter a re-delegation into the root, grabbing control of .rt. Then the U.S. would mirror the old .rt information on its new machine and use its control to enable traffic analysis and perhaps even eavesdropping. As the U.S. built up a database of .rt second-level domains from the queries it received, or by other national technical means, it could quietly insert some changes in the .rt second-level records that would send all traffic to a U.S. machine before being sent on to its original destination. This attack is subtler, but Ruritanian technologists should be able to detect it almost instantly by monitoring the root which, after all, is public and must be visible in order to achieve its function. If the delegation of .rt changed, they could sound the alarm and apply the same counter-measures as in the more direct deletion scenario.

Next, consider the reaction of key internet players such as major civilian ISPs. Ordinarily they set their computers to mechanically copy alterations in the master zone file and to use the most recent file to serve their users. But if they become aware that the file has been intentionally tampered with for political reasons, at least some of them will go to their backup copies and manually restore .rt to their cached copies of the root. Certainly any

ISPs in .rt will be forced to restore it, and internal .rt communications will recover quickly; how much the outside world will be able to send in data will depend on how the world internet technical community responds initially.

But that's not all. Even if the disruption were effective for a day or two due to the Ruritanian failure to anticipate and plan for the problem, the international community would ensure that it never happened again by switching to an alternate system that no longer relied on a file that the U.S. could manipulate single-handedly (Froomkin 2000, p. 49). The bottom line is that whatever geo-strategic power exists over the root, it can only be exercised once, if at all.

CONCLUSION

As a legal document, the Affirmation itself is a paper tiger. It may not be a contract; even if it is a contract, there is no practicable way for either of the parties to enforce it (and almost no promises by the U.S. Government). Although both parties have a right to cancel the Affirmation upon notice, it is difficult to imagine circumstances in which either party would have anything to gain by such an act—and is also not that easy to imagine circumstances in which the cancellation would actually make a legal difference to either party. Indeed, the most important legal aspect of the Affirmation is that it is not the JPA it replaced, for the JPA had some teeth.

In contrast, the Affirmation likely will be much more meaningful as a political document. By announcing in the Affirmation that it would allow the JPA to lapse, the U.S. signaled that it was giving up the most visible of its claims to direct control of ICANN. In so doing, it gave up powers that it could reasonably have calculated it would be unlikely to use. By further enhancing the power of the GAC, the U.S. DOC sought, with it appears some success, to meet the most vociferous critics of the unique U.S. role in the governance of the DNS more than half way, yet without completely giving up its fail-safe powers, those deriving from the IANA contract and from ICANN's domicile in California.

If the U.S. won some breathing room from its critics, and the international community achieved a large step towards its agenda of internationalizing the control of the governance of the DNS, the biggest winner from the Affirmation undoubtedly remains ICANN itself. ICANN is now largely free of U.S. Government control and yet still substantially free of direct control by other governments. World governments must channel their influence via the GAC. The GAC has real influence over ICANN, but it does not have control. This fact, and the fact that the residual U.S. influence is not totally eradicated, has caused some non-U.S. leaders to call for yet more divestment by the U.S. (Kroes 2010, but so far these calls have been rare).

Newly unchained, or at least on a very long leash, ICANN enjoys unprecedented freedom to shape its own fate and to decide what sort of body it wants to be. In losing the specter of undue U.S. influence, ICANN has also lost its major excuse for failing to live up to its professed ideals of transparency and accountability to the wider internet community. What will happen next depends in large part on the extent to which ICANN's struggle for autonomy has shaped its DNA, and to what extent ICANN is ready to transcend its past.

The DOC's next big decision will come when the DOC decides the fate of the IANA contract (U.S. NTIA 2011). The fear that ICANN might attempt to expand its reach, either on its own or if captured by some outside group, remains the major argument for the U.S. to retain its hold on the IANA function. On the other hand, if the U.S. accepts that, as argued above, the DNS lacks geo-strategic value, the U.S. may be more willing to let go.

In time, geo-strategy may not be the only arena in which the DNS's centrality diminishes. If it is true that "[e]ighty percent of all online sessions begin with search," (Richman 2009) then the DNS's importance to the World Wide Web is well into its decline. Of course, the Web is not the internet; many other services from e-mail to video transport rely on the DNS also. But the example of search, combined with the growth of "walled garden" discursive communities such as MySpace and Facebook, plus virtual worlds such as Second Life and World of Warcraft, all suggest that the long-predicted moment when the DNS's human-readable naming system begins to lose its importance actually will arrive some day.

Until then, however, ICANN remains important because even if control of the DNS has limited political relevance, that control still has substantial economic importance—so long as the DNS's hegemony of convenience continues.

***

As this chapter went to press in March 2012, the U.S. Government made a terse announcement that it would not accept ICANN's bid to renew the IANA contract on the ground that "we received no proposals that met the requirements requested by the global community". The two-paragraph announcement noted that the latest solicitation for the IANA functions had added requirements to IANA's statement of work in response to international comments "including the need for structural separation of policymaking from implementation, a robust companywide conflict of interest policy, provisions reflecting heightened respect for local country laws, and a series of consultation and reporting requirements to increase transparency and accountability to the international community" (NTIA 2012a). The U.S. Government extended ICANN's IANA contract to September 30, 2012 to preserve the status quo, pending reissuance of the U.S. Government's request for proposals to run the IANA functions (U.S. NTIA 2012b).

Whatever the reasons for rejecting ICANN's seemingly routine renewal of its bid for the IANA function, this action supports the claims made above that the U.S. Government retains a degree of leverage over ICANN notwithstanding the Affirmation of Commitments.

BIBLIOGRAPHY

Barker, L. (2001), 'Information Assurance: Protecting the Army's Domain-Name System', http://www.signal.army.mil/ocos/ac/Edition,%20Summer/Summer%2001/dnsia.htm.
Botzem, S. and J. Hofmann (2010), *Transnational Governance Spirals: The Transformation of Regulatory Authority in Internet Governance and Corporate Financial Reporting*, unpublished manuscript, http://duplox.wzb.eu/people/jeanette/pdf/BotzemHofmann_2010_draft.pdf.
CADNA (2009), 'Press Release, Coal. Against Domain Name Abuse, CADNA Asserts That the ICANN Affirmation of Commitments Falls Short', http://www.cadna.org/en/newsroom/press-releases/iccan-affirmation-of-commitments-falls-short.
Coalition for ICANN Transparency, Inc. v. VeriSign, Inc., 611 F.3d 495 (9th Cir. 2010).
Denton, T. and M. Chango (2007), *ICANN and IANA Reserved Names*, http://gnso.icann.org/drafts/ICANNandIANA-reserved-names-v.12.pdf.
Doria, A. (2009), 'Post JPA: Tempered Happiness', http://www.circleid.com/posts/post_jpa_tempered_happiness.
EPIC and NGO (2007), 'Letter to ICANN Board on Need for Whois Reform', http://ipjustice.org/wp/2007/10/30/epic-ngo-letter-to-icann-board-on-need-for-whois-reform.
Froomkin, A.M. (2000), 'Wrong Turn in Cyberspace: Using ICANN to Route Around the APA and the Constitution', *Duke L.J.*, **50**, 17–186.
Froomkin, A.M. (2002), 'ICANN's "Uniform Dispute Resolution Policy"—Causes and (Partial) Cures', *Brook. L. Rev.*, **67**, 605–718.
Froomkin, A.M. (2004), 'When We Say US™, We Mean It!', *Hous. L. Rev.*, **41**, 839–84.
Froomkin, A.M. and M.A. Lemley (2003), 'ICANN & Antitrust', *U. Ill. L. Rev.* **2003**, 1–76.
Gross, G. (2009), 'New ICANN Agreement Runs Into Criticism', http://www.techworld.com.au/article/320747/new_icann_agreement_runs_into_criticism.
IANA (2007), 'Understanding the ccTLD Delegation and Redelegation Procedure', http://www.iana.org/domains/root/delegation-guide.
ICANN (1998), 'Bylaws as effective 6 November 1998', http://www.icann.org/en/general/archive-bylaws/bylaws-06nov98.htm.
ICANN (1999), 'ICANN-NSI Registry Agreement', http://www.icann.org/en/nsi/nsi-registry-agreement-04nov99.htm.
ICANN (2001a), 'Amendment 3 to ICANN/DOC Memorandum of Understanding', http://www.icann.org/en/general/amend3-jpamou-25may01.htm.

ICANN (2001b), 'Amendment 24 to Cooperative Agreement Between NSI and U.S. Government', http://www.icann.org/en/nsi/coopagmt-amend24-25may01.htm.

ICANN (2001c), 'Redelegation of .us Country-Code Top-Level Domain', http://www.icann.org/en/announcements/announcement-19nov01.htm.

ICANN (2002), 'Bylaws as adopted effective 15 December 2002 (the "New Bylaws")', http://www.icann.org/en/general/archive-bylaws/bylaws-15dec02.htm.

ICANN (2003a), 'Bylaws as amended effective 26 June 2003', http://www.icann.org/en/general/archive-bylaws/bylaws-26jun03.htm.

ICANN (2003b), 'Cooperative Research and Development Agreement Between ICANN and US Department of Commerce', http://www.icann.org/committees/dns-root/crada.htm.

ICANN (2008a), 'ICANN Proposal to DNSSEC-Sign the Root Zone', http://www.icann.org/en/announcements/dnssec-proposal-09oct08-en.pdf.

ICANN (2008b), 'Improving Institutional Confidence', http://www.icann.org/en/jpa/iic/improving-confidence.htm.

ICANN (2008c), 'Accountability and Transparency Frameworks and Principles: Accountability in the Public Sphere', http://www.icann.org/en/accountability/frameworks-principles/public-sphere.htm.

ICANN (2008d), 'Accountability and Transparency Frameworks and Principles: Legal and Corporate Accountability', http://www.icann.org/en/accountability/frameworks-principles/legal-corporate.htm.

ICANN (2008e), 'Accountability and Transparency Frameworks and Principles: Accountability to the Participating Community', http://icann.org/en/accountability/frameworks-principles/community.htm.

ICANN (2008f), 'Accountability and Transparency Frameworks and Principles', http://www.icann.org/en/transparency/acct-trans-frameworks-principles-10jan08.pdf.

ICANN (2009a), 'Complete Report: Addressing the Global Internet', 58, http://www.icann.org/en/correspondence/beckstrom-to-disspain-07apr10 en.pdf.

ICANN (2009b), 'AERO Agreement Appendix 6 Schedule of Reserved Names', http://www.icann.org/en/tlds/agreements/aero/aero-appendix-6-11jun09-en.htm.

ICANN (2009c), 'The Affirmation of Commitments – What it Means', http://www.icann.org/en/announcements/announcement-30sep09-en.htm.

ICANN (2009d), 'ICANN CEO Talks About the New Affirmation of Commitments', http://www.icann.org/en/announcements/announcement-30sep09-en.htm.

ICANN (2010a), 'Draft Applicant Guidebook, Version 4 annex Separable Country Names List', http://www.icann.org/en/announcements/announcement-4-31may10-en.htm.

ICANN (2010b), 'gTLD Applicant Guidebook: Proposed Final Version', http://www.icann.org/en/topics/new-gtlds/draft-rfp-clean-12nov10-en.pdf.

ICANN (2011), 'Adopted Board Resolutions #3, Process for Completion of the Applicant Guidebook for New gTLDs', http://www.icann.org/en/minutes/resolutions-18mar11-en.htm#3.

ICANN Sec. & Stability Advisory Comm. (2007), 'SAC 022: SSAC Advisory on Domain Name Front Running', http://www.icann.org/en/committees/security/sac022.pdf.

In re Nat'l Sec. Agency Telecomms. Records Litig., 700 F.Supp.2d 1182 (N.D. Cal. 2010).

Kerner S. (2009), 'U.S. Cedes ICANN Control to the World, InternetNews.com', http://www.internetnews.com/infra/article.php/3841671/US+Cedes+ICANN+Control+to+the+World.htm.

Kleinwaechter, W. (2003), 'From Self-Governance to Public-Private Partnership: The Changing Role of Governments in the Management of the Internet's Core Resources', *Loy. L.A. L. Rev.*, **36**, 1110–11.

Koppell, J.G.S. (2005), 'Pathologies of Accountability: ICANN and the Challenge of "Multiple Accountabilities Disorder"', *Pub. Admin. Rev.*, **65**, 101.

Kovacs, A. (2009), 'The ICANN-US DOC "Affirmation of Commitments"—A Step Forward?', http://ncdnhc.org/profiles/blogs/the-icannus-doc-affirmation-of.

Kroes, N. (2010), 'Vice-President, European Comm'n Responsible for the Digital Agenda,

The Need for Accountability in Internet Governance', ICANN's 38th International Meeting, http://europa.eu/rapid/pressReleasesAction.do?reference=SPEECH/10/323.

Kuerbis, B. (2008), 'ICANN's DNSSEC Root Signing Proposal D.O.A.?', http://blog.inter netgovernance.org/blog/_archives/2008/10/3/3899192.html.

Manheim, K. and L. Solum (2003), 'An Economic Analysis of Domain Name Policy', *Hastings Comm. & Ent L.J.*, **25**, 359.

McCarthy, K. (2009), 'Leaving Report of General Manager of Public Participation', http://www.icann.org/en/participate/gmpp-leaving-report-25nov09-en.pdf/.

McCullagh, D. (2004), 'ICANN Approves Wait List for Desired Domains', *CNET News*, http://news.cnet.com/ICANN-approves-wait-list-for-desired-domains/2100-1038_3-517 1809.html.

McCullagh, D. (2011), 'No Support for U.S. Proposal for Domain Name Veto', http://news.cnet.com/8301-31921_3-20037090-281.html.

Mueller, M. (2009), *IGP, ICANN, Inc.: Accountability and Participation in the Governance of Critical Internet Resources*, Syracuse, NY: Syracuse University.

Network Solutions (undated), 'Company History: Network Solutions', http://about-networksolutions.com/corporate-history.phphttp://about-networksolutions.com/corporate-history.php.

One World Trust (2007), 'Independent Review of ICANN's Accountability and Transparency—Structures and Practices', http://www.icann.org/en/transparency/owt-report-final-2007.pdf.

Preston, C.B. (2008), 'Internet Porn, ICANN, and Families: A Call To Action', *J. Internet L.*, **12** (October) 3–15, http://papers.ssrn.com/sol3/papers.cfm?abstract_id=1285270.

Rabkin, A. (2009), 'Who Controls the Internet?', *Weekly Standard*, **14** (34), http://staging.weeklystandard.com/Content/Public/Articles/000/000/016/515zoozk.asp.

Rabkin, J. (2009), 'Careful What You Wish For: Why ICANN "Independence" is a Bad Idea', http://www.circleid.com/posts/20090622_careful_what_you_wish_icann_independ ence_bad_idea.

Rabkin, J. and J. Eisenach (2009), 'The U.S. Abandons the Internet', *Wall Street Journal* (Oct. 3, 2009), at A13.

Richman, J. (2009), '4 Technologies That Are Killing the URL', *iMedia Connection*, http://www.imediaconnection.com/content/23912.asp.

Schiavetta, S. and K. Komaitis (2003), 'ICANN's Role in Controlling Information on the Internet', **17** (3), 267–84.

Schneiders, M. and S. Higgs (2002), 'Root Fix for the .US Top Level Domain', http://tools.ietf.org/id/draft-higgs-schneiders-root-fix-us-00.txt.

Schwartz, J.L. (2006), 'Making the Consumer Watchdog's Bark As Strong As Its Gripe: Complaint Sites and the Changing Dynamic of the Fair Use Defense', *Alb. L. J. Sci. & Tech.*, **16**, 78.

Sonbuchner, S.P. (2008), 'Master Of Your Domain: Should the U.S. Government Maintain Control Over the Internet's Root?', *Minn. J. Int'l L.*, **17**, 207.

Strickling, L.E. (2010), 'Letter from Assistant Secretary for Communications and Information Larry Strickling to Rod Beckstrom, ICANN President and CEO', http://forum.icann.org/lists/5gtld-guide/pdf9gaUJneTz8.pdf.

U.S. Department of Commerce and Internet Corporation for Assigned Names and Numbers (1998), 'Memorandum of Understanding Between the U.S. Department of Commerce and Internet Corporation for Assigned Names and Numbers', http://www.icann.org/general/icann-mou-25nov98.htm/.

U.S. Department of Commerce and Internet Corporation for Assigned Names and Numbers (2006), 'Joint Project Agreement Between U.S. Department of Commerce and the Internet Corporation for Assigned Names and Numbers', http://www.icann.org/en/general/JPA-29sep06.pdf.

U.S. Department of Commerce and Internet Corporation for Assigned Names and Numbers (2009), 'Affirmation of Commitments by the United States Department of Commerce and the Internet Corporation for Assigned Names and Numbers', http://www.ntia.doc.gov/files/ntia/publications/affirmation_of_commitments_2009.pdf.

U.S. Department of Commerce (2011), 'Amendment of Solicitation/Modification of Contract', http://www.icann.org/en/about/agreements/iana/iana-contract-14jun11-en.pdf.

U.S. National Telecommunications and Information Administration (2003), 'IANA Functions Contract', http://www.ntia.doc.gov/files/ntia/publications/ianaorder_03142003. pdf.

U.S. National Telecommunications and Information Administration (2006), 'IANA Functions Contract', http://www.ntia.doc.gov/files/ntia/publications/ianacontract_0814 06.pdf.

U.S. National Telecommunications and Information Administration (2009a), 'Testing and Implementation Requirements for the Initial Deployment of DNSSEC in the Authoritative Root Zone (2009)', http://www.ntia.doc.gov/dns/DNSSEC_Requirements_102909.pdf.

U.S. National Telecommunications and Information Administration (2009b), 'Press Release: Commerce's NTIA and ICANN Establish a Long-Lasting Framework for the Technical Coordination of the Internet's Domain Name and Addressing System', http://www.ntia. doc.gov/press/2009/ICANN_Affirmation_090930.html.

U.S. National Telecommunications and Information Administration (2011), 'Request for Comments on the Internet Assigned Numbers Authority (IANA) Functions', 76 Fed. Reg. 10569-01.

U.S. National Telecommunications and Information Administration (2012a), 'Notice— Cancelled Internet Assigned Numbers Authority (IANA) Functions—Request for Proposal (RFP) SA1301-12-RP-IANA', http://ntia.doc.gov/other-publication/2012/ notice-internet-assigned-numbers-authority-iana-functions-request-proposal-rf.

U.S. National Telecommunications and Information Administration (2012b), 'Notice— Extension of the Internet Assigned Numbers Authority (IANA) Functions Contract', http:// www.ntia.doc.gov/other-publication/2012/notice-extension-internet-assigned-numbers- authority-iana-functions-contract.

Von Arx, K.G. and G.R. Hagen (2002), 'Sovereign Domains: A Declaration of Independence of ccTLDs from Foreign Control', *Rich. J.L. & Tech.*, **9**, 26.

Weinberg, J. (2011), 'Non-State Actors and Global Informal Governance—The Case of ICANN', Christiansen T. and C. Neuhold (eds), *International Handbook On Informal Governance*, forthcoming, http://papers.ssrn.com/sol3/papers.cfm?abstract_id=1621862.

Zittrain J. and B. Edelman (2003), 'Technical Responses to Unilateral Internet Authority: The Deployment of VeriSign "Site Finder" and ISP Response', http://cyber.law.harvard. edu/tlds/sitefinder (last updated Oct. 7, 2003).

3. Internet addressing: global governance of shared resource spaces
Milton Mueller

Internet protocol addresses are the unique numbers that identify the origin and destination of information flows on the internet. The addressing scheme, when combined with the method for formatting data into packets, is one of the core features of the Internet Protocol (IP). The address blocks themselves can be considered critical resources, a kind of virtual real estate the possession of which is a requirement for participation in the internet economy. And the inter-domain routing of IP packets, a process which depends heavily upon the way IP addresses are allocated and assigned, is at the center of the day-to-day functioning of the internet.

Routing, as we shall see, raises many economic and policy issues of a highly interdependent resource system, such as tragedy of the commons, externalities, etc. IP addresses also serve as a control point or identification method for internet users, raising issues of privacy, surveillance and freedom. Thus, even though the controversies surrounding domain names have attracted much more attention, IP addressing and routing are far more central to internet operations. In the coming decade, the public policy issues associated with addressing and routing are likely to occupy more attention than they have before (Mueller 2006).

In IP addressing, public policy and technical knowledge are intimately intertwined. This fact prevents many people from understanding what is at stake in debates over the topic, much less participating in them. For better or worse, the steep technical learning curve has left most of the discourse in the hands of a relatively small community of technical experts (Hain 2005; Huston 2005; Meyer, Zhang et al. 2007; de Velde, Popoviciu et al. 2008).

This chapter tries to make the addressing and routing aspects of internet governance more accessible to those interested in communications policy and economics. It begins by analyzing the characteristics of IP addresses as a resource, using the theoretical tools of institutional economics. Next, it looks at the institutions that currently govern the allocation and assignment of IP addresses; specifically, the Regional Internet Registries and ICANN. The next section explains the three political economy factors driving change in this area. They are: 1) the depletion of the IPv4 address space; 2) the attempt to migrate to a new Internet Protocol, IPv6, with a larger address space; and 3) the push to make internet-based communications more secure. Next, the chapter explains some of the policy debates that are occurring as a result of the changes set in motion by those forces.

IP addressing is now attracting more attention among social scientists, but one can still tick off the main contributions in a short paragraph. DeNardis (2009) explained the role of the address space in internet protocol and documents some of the history and hopes surrounding the development of a new internet protocol. Mueller (2010) applied theories of institutional economics to the governance of the IP address-routing resources. A policy analysis by Mueller and Kuerbis (2008) flagged some of the high-level institutional issues raised by IP addressing. Other recent literature focused on the heated debate over the possibility of establishing a trading market for scarce IPv4 addresses (Edelman 2008; Lehr, Vest et al. 2008; Mueller 2008; Hofmann 2009; Dell 2010). There are also a few reports on IP addressing commissioned by intergovernmental agencies such as OECD and ITU (Perset 2007; Ramadass 2009). This chapter draws on this prior work to provide a survey and overview of the relevant policy issues.

THE TECHNO-ECONOMICS OF IP ADDRESSING/ ROUTING

Internet protocol creates a virtual resource, the IP address space, of finite dimensions. The size of the address space is fixed by the technical standards defining the internet protocol. The internet standard we currently use, IP version 4 (IPv4), specified a 32-bit address space that allowed for about 4 billion unique addresses. IPv4 addresses are scarce in the strict sense that economic theory defines scarcity: it is not possible for all of us to have all of the addresses we would like at zero cost.

As a virtual resource, however, they are not consumed when put into production; rather, they are *occupied* just as land or radio spectrum is occupied. When the occupation of one party ends, the resource is not "used up" but could be available for others to occupy. In internet discourse, the reservation of an address block to a single network or administrator for direct use is called an *assignment*; the occupation of a larger contiguous block of addresses by an intermediary for assignment to others is called an *allocation*. To function properly in a network, IP addresses must be uniquely assigned. In other words, the same address cannot be given to two or more different networks on the public internet.

This creates a need for registration authorities to coordinate the distribution of address blocks and to keep track of which user is holding which blocks.

Superficially, IP addressing policy might be seen as a simple resource allocation problem. Property rights to IP address blocks could be transferred to private parties and their allocation governed by trading and the price system. But this simple picture breaks down when routing is brought into the picture. Routing is the process that guides the movement of internet protocol packets from their origin to their destination. IP address blocks are useful only insofar as the addresses can be used to successfully route packets on the public internet. The policy problem of efficiently allocating IP address resources is conditioned by the efficiency and scalability of internet routing.

Routing protocols rely upon globally unique IP addresses to define pathways that can guide packets to their destination. Routing protocols consider the IP address to be composed of two parts: the address of the network (the *prefix*) and the address of the connected computer (the *host*). Routing through the internet is based on the network portion of the address. A router stores its best and alternate routes for each prefix and uses this information to construct a forwarding table (the routing table) that controls the movement of each incoming packet to the next hop in its journey. Routers also transmit announcements to other routers about the address prefixes to which it is able to deliver packets, and this information is incorporated into the tables of other routers. Currently, interactions among routers are based on an internet standard known as Border Gateway Protocol (BGP) (Rekhter and Li 1995; Rekhter, Li et al. 2006). Thus, routers are engaged in constant, automated conversations with each other that exchange network prefixes and other information to keep every router informed about how to reach hundreds of thousands of other networks on the internet.

If no policy limits are placed on the number of route advertisements, it is possible that the size of the routing table in the largest and most interconnected internet service providers (known as the *default-free zone*[1]) could grow until it exceeds the processing power of their routing equipment. This is an externality because when one network adds announcements of many different fragments of an address block to the routing space it does not make its own operations much more expensive (and may make them less expensive), but when such behavior is repeated across many other actors it makes the size of the table in the BGP routers used by ISPs larger and larger, making routing equipment more expensive. Some have described this problem as a tragedy of the commons (Rekhter, Resnick et al. 1996; Huston 2001).

The interdependence of routing and addressing means that ISPs must trade off efficient routing against efficient use of the IP address space. Thus, one should refer to the relevant resource as the "routing-addressing space" rather than as "IP address resources" solely. That term recognizes the interdependency of the two while also maintaining addresses and routes as distinguishable parts of the resource space.

The basic trade-off between address conservation and routing table size plays a major role in the history of internet management. During the early to mid-1990s, as the internet took off as a public medium, the scalability of the internet was called into question. The number of prefixes listed in routing tables began to grow at an alarming pace and it was feared that router technology would not be able to cope with it. At the same time, the IPv4 address pool was being occupied at a pace that seemed to allow for only a few more years of growth. In an attempt to control this problem, the IETF instigated a mixture of technical and policy adjustments that established *provider-based route aggregation* and *classless address allocation* as basic principles for address-routing governance.

Classless Inter-Domain Routing (CIDR) was implemented as a way to make more efficient use of the diminishing IPv4 address pool (Fuller, Li et al. 1993). Instead of allocating address blocks in three arbitrary, pre-defined sizes,[2] CIDR allowed allocations to be more granularly matched to an ISP's actual needs. Provider-based route aggregation was developed around the same time and codified in RFC 2008 (Rekhter and Li 1995). It gave network service providers (ISPs) large, contiguous address blocks and encouraged most other internet users to use sub-allocations from these larger address blocks because they can be aggregated by the ISP into a single route announcement. This was intended to minimize the number of entries in the routing tables, and reduce the amount of traffic exchanged among routers – two very important economic efficiency benefits.

But provider-based route aggregation had two other economic consequences. First, it increased end user switching costs in the market for internet services. The customers of ISPs cannot take their address blocks with them when they change service providers. Second, it militates against trading, subdividing or other uncontrolled transfers of address blocks among ISPs and end users. The ability to move unused address blocks or portions of a block from one user to another would greatly increase the efficiency of address space utilization. But such transfers would also require breaking up contiguous blocks of addresses into separately routed parts, undermining the efficiency of routing. Since the mid-1990s, the efficiency of route aggregation has been deemed more important than address utilization efficiency.

THE GOVERNANCE REGIME

The institutional framework for governing IP address-routing resources is organized around Regional Internet Registries (RIRs). As noted above, IP address assignments must be unique to function properly on the public internet. This uniqueness is maintained by address registries. Registries keep track of which parts of the address space have been assigned to which organization. The first address registry was a centralized function performed by U.S. research and military contractors. As the internet grew and became internationalized and privatized, the registry function was delegated to nonprofits serving different world regions. The rationale for RIRs was first set out in RFC 1174 (Cerf 1990). The first regional registry, RIPE-NCC, was established in 1991 to serve the European region.

There are now five RIRs. In addition to RIPE-NCC, APNIC (established 1995) is the institution for the Asia-Pacific region (which includes India). North America's ARIN was established in 1997 through the privatization of the old centralized registry operated by Jon Postel and other U.S. government contractors since the early 1980s. As part of this privatization process, the top of the number allocation hierarchy was delegated to ICANN, which performs the Internet Assigned Numbers Authority (IANA) function under contract to the U.S. Department of Commerce. LACNIC (established 2002) serves the South American continent. The newest RIR, AFRINIC (established 2005), serves the African continent.[3] Figure 3.1 illustrates the delegation hierarchy and the place of the RIRs

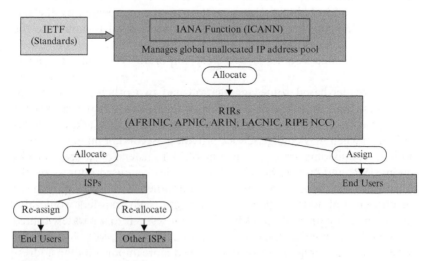

Figure 3.1   IP address allocation and assignment hierarchy

in it. Beginning in the mid-1990s, the RIRs' policies and practices incorporated CIDR and provider-based aggregation, and their role was formalized in RFC 2050 (Hubbard, Kosters et al. 1996). The RIRs created a more formal contractual regime, and fee structures for membership/address blocks were put into place.

Various discussions of IP addresses, including statements by the internet address registries themselves, assert that addresses are "public resources." "Public resource" is an unscientific term, however; its meaning varies and the differences in usage often reflect ideologies and political agendas.[4] Institutional economics provides a more precise and useful distinction between four broad classes of goods: public goods, private goods, club goods, and common pool resources. The distinctions hinge on the degree to which resources are *rival in consumption* (i.e., one person's consumption does not prevent anyone else from using it) and *exclusive* (i.e., the degree to which an owner or appropriator of the resource can prevent others from appropriating it).

With public goods, consumption is nonrival and exclusion is difficult or impossible. With private goods, consumption is rival and exclusion is relatively easy. Thus for private goods, market allocation is the most common option (although it is usually shaped by government regulations or subsidies in some way). The resource is allocated by means of exchanges of property rights among private owners; as supply goes down prices go up, and conservation incentives adapt accordingly. Resources do not fall unambiguously into these categories, and their status can change. Encryption technology, for example, made it possible to exclude owners of a radio receiver from access to a broadcast signal, transforming it from a public good situation to more of a toll good.

Common pool resource management regimes are responses to a unique set of economic conditions. Consumption is rival, and thus private appropriation must be rationed or limited in some way. But if exclusion is too costly, or interdependencies among users of the resource make it too difficult to define and enforce tradable property rights, then a private market may not work. An example of a resource which faces difficulty of exclusion is a school of fish in the ocean, which cannot easily be fenced in. In these cases collective governance rules can take the place of market prices as the allocator of the resource.

It is illuminating to apply the framework in Table 3.1 to IP addresses. Clearly, address assignments and allocations are rival. If one network occupies an address block, another network cannot also use it on the global internet without creating conflicts in routing. Addresses must be exclusive and globally unique to function properly. Exclusion is also possible, although not in a straightforward way. When a user appropriates a natural

Table 3.1   Classification of goods

Difficulty of excluding users		Subtractability of use (Rival occupation or consumption)	
		Low	*High*
	Low	Toll goods	Private goods
	High	Public goods	Common pool goods

Source: adapted from Ostrom (2005).

resource like a mineral or a fish from the ocean, the mere act of possession and consumption by one person physically prevents others from also
appropriating the resource. The act of assigning numbers to host computers on a network, however, does not by itself prevent anyone else from also
assigning the same numbers to their own hosts. To maintain the exclusivity
of assignments requires collective action in the form of a registry accepted
by internet network operators as an authoritative coordination instrument.

IP address registries meet this need. They keep track of which organizations are using which address blocks and ensure that the allocations are
unique and exclusive. But the registry's ability to maintain exclusivity
depends heavily on its acceptance and recognition by internet service providers as a guide to their routing decisions. To enforce exclusive assignments of IP addresses, ISPs must refuse to route traffic to another network's
address if it is not registered as the legitimate holder of that address. The
governance power of the registry, in other words, depends heavily on
the assent and participation of the ISPs who operationalize routing. An
address registry cannot simply take back an assignment or allocation in the
way that physical property is repossessed; it can only eliminate a party from
the list of authorized holders and hope that ISPs adjust their routing practices accordingly. (This lack of central control could be changed by technology, however (see the discussion of "Resource Public Key Infrastructure
(RPKI)" below). Despite these complications, it is obvious that it is per-
fectly feasible to maintain exclusivity in the occupation of IP addresses.
Laws, regulations or contracts could give registered address block holders a
right to take legal action against "trespassers" who occupied address blocks
that conflicted with those of a registered user. Thus we are left with a key
theoretical puzzle: why don't we treat IP addresses as private goods?

The answer is that the choice of a common pool regime and its restrictions on address ownership and trading were motivated *neither* by difficulties of exclusion *nor* by the absence of rival consumption. Rather, common
pool governance emerged because of concerns about routing. If there were

free market trading of address blocks, the RIRs (and by extension, the interacting community of ISPs) would lose their ability to enforce route aggregation policies. It is the interaction between routing announcements and the structure of address block allocations that pushes the industry into a common pool governance regime.

The technical community's decision to prioritize route aggregation prevented market trading of addresses. In the absence of a market price system, some other method had to be used to limit appropriation of scarce number resources. The existing IP address regime rations and conserves the resource by leveraging the IP address registry function. The registry is more than a mere coordinative device; it also acts as a gatekeeper to the address space. The RIRs grant of an exclusive, legitimate "title" to an address block is linked to administrative limits on the size of the address block any appropriator can claim. Applicants for address space submit network plans and information about utilization levels; the RIRs review these plans and award address blocks accordingly. These limits are known in the industry as "justified needs assessments." This bears more than a passing resemblance to a centrally planned economy. But this feature of the regime could also change. As the IPv4 address space becomes fully occupied, pressures to allow market trading of address blocks intensify (see discussion below in "TRANSFORMATIONAL PROBLEMS IN ADDRESSING-ROUTING").

The problem of resource reclamation is an important and neglected topic in address governance. Those who have been allocated addresses but no longer use them are, in principle, supposed to return them to the common pool to make them available for use by others. This is supposed to be one of the primary efficiency benefits of a common pool regime. But resource reclamation has been a persistent weak point of the current regime. Address block holders have few positive incentives to return unused blocks voluntarily. RIRs have no contractual authority over the so-called "legacy" holders who received their allocations before the contractual regime was put into place. Legacy holders account for about 40 percent of the IPv4 address space. For the other users, RIRs have contractual authority to reclaim IPv4 resources from those who do not need them but their ability to monitor the actual use of addresses and reclaim resources from current holders is weak. The scalability of detailed monitoring or auditing of thousands of individual organizations is questionable. Even the definition of what constitutes "use" of an address block is far from clear. Thus, huge portions of the IPv4 address space are thought to be unused or underutilized, and, contrary to the communitarian ethic underlying the common pool regime, hardly any organizations return them to the common pool.

To summarize the analysis of the institutional framework, by 1997 the IP address governance regime had converged around three principles: registration (maintaining the uniqueness of addresses), route aggregation and address conservation through "needs assessment." Aside from growing and becoming more professional, little changed for a decade. By 2007 the RIRs had become a mature transnational governance regime composed of nonprofit, private sector membership organizations that govern primarily through private contract. The membership is composed of autonomous systems; i.e., organizations that operate networks and utilize internet addresses.

But today three radical changes in the economic and technical environment threaten to change some of the key foundations of IP address governance.

TRANSFORMATIONAL PROBLEMS IN ADDRESSING-ROUTING

Three transformational changes in the political economy of IP addressing now confront the governance of the address-routing space. One is the depletion of the IPv4 address space; i.e., all of the space will be occupied and there will be no more "free pool" of addresses available for the RIRs to give to applicants based on needs assessment. The second, directly related, problem is the need to migrate to a new internet protocol, known as IPv6, which has a larger address space. The third is the perceived need to make internet routing more secure, in order to protect internet operations from mistaken configurations and malicious conduct.

The most immediate problem is the depletion of the IPv4 address space. Created 30 years ago, its 32-bit address space seemed to provide an inexhaustible supply. But the rate of growth in the number of internet users and of devices capable of networking has exceeded everyone's expectations. The so-called "free pool" of unoccupied IPv4 addresses was depleted in the Asia-Pacific region in 2011, and in Europe in 2012. Projections show that North America will reach the threshold some time in 2013.

The full occupation of the IPv4 address space was not unanticipated. The internet technical community developed a new internet protocol in the late 1990s, known as IP version 6 (IPv6). IPv6 has a vastly expanded address space (2^{128} addresses). But there is a serious problem with it. In one of the most magnificent and costly blunders in modern technological history, the savants of the IETF designed a new internet protocol that is not backwards compatible with the old one. Any network that simply switches to the IPv6 protocol would be cut off from the rest of the internet; compatibility must be maintained by running both protocols (known as "dual stack") or by costly and slow tunneling and Network Address Translation techniques, which add to the cost and complexity of the transition. Moreover, dual stack – the method most organizations will use during the transition – requires continued utilization of scarce IPv4 addresses.

While IPv6 introduces some marginal improvements, it adds few new features and capabilities to the current internet protocol. Thus, the exhaustion of the IPv4 address space is the only major incentive to migrate to the IPv6 standard. The lack of any "killer application" available exclusively through the new protocol, added to the switching costs and incompatibility risks inherent in the transition, has severely limited migration to IPv6. Current estimates show that only about 1 percent of the internet is running IPv6, and most of that traffic is outside the market economy, being centered in educational and governmental institutions. (Colitti, Gunderson et al. 2010). There is still some uncertainty about whether the migration to the new IPv6 standard will succeed at all (Elmore, Camp et al. 2008; DeNardis 2009).

It is now evident that full migration to IPv6, if it happens at all, will take a decade or more. This means that active competition for scarce IPv4 address resources will remain a feature of the internet governance landscape for some time. This will have transformational effects on governance practices. As the IPv4 free pool runs out, the "justified need" approach to IPv4 addresses cannot solve address allocation problems. As the number of unallocated blocks approaches zero, the demand for IPv4 addresses can only be satisfied through transfers from one holder of address resources to another – not through initial appropriation from a free pool. It is possible for dozens or even hundreds of prospective users to demonstrate a legitimate technical "need" for IP address resources, so performing a needs assessment cannot say which one should get the scarce resource. To allocate the resource under these new circumstances, an RIR would have to decide which plan was more important or more valuable, and remove addresses from one user to give them to another.

Another transformational change is created by attempts to make routing more secure. In the original BGP protocol, all routers in all Autonomous Systems (ASs) were assumed to be trustworthy. As the internet grew, the assumption of ubiquitous trust made less and less sense. The existence of malicious actors on today's internet is a given. But the internet's routing infrastructure is also vulnerable to unintentional misconfigurations that can cause harmful results. (Barbir, Murphy et al. 2006; ENISA 2010). Extensive work has been done in the technical community exploring the issue of routing security and proposing various solutions to improve it (Butler, Farley et al. 2010). One of the security flaws in BGP was illustrated vividly in 2008 when a Pakistani ISP's attempt to block YouTube in that country affected ISPs around the world, effectively knocking YouTube off the internet for most users for an hour. Several other well-known misconfigurations leading to temporary routing outages have occurred in the past, although the overall extent and severity of the routing security problems network operators' deal with is not publicly known.

FUTURE POLICY, ECONOMIC AND INSTITUTIONAL ISSUES

Each of the transformational problems identified above sets in motion important changes in the political economics of addressing and routing. Institutional economics suggests two distinct perspectives that can be taken to analyzing such changes. One emphasizes the role of inertia and path dependency as an explanatory factor in institutional evolution (North 1990). The other emphasizes the way major discontinuities in supply and demand and in the incidence of costs and benefits can produce radical qualitative shifts in institutional regimes (Mueller 2002). In this case both pressures will play an active role.

IPv4 address scarcity generates discontinuous, qualitative change. It is already generating important changes in norms, procedures and policies. As noted above, once the free pool of IPv4 addresses is fully occupied, addresses can only be gained by transferring them. To justify transferring address resources from one user to another, one must make judgments about the social value of the resource in alternate uses.

The normal and generally most feasible way to discover how valuable the address resources are in alternate uses is to institute competitive bidding for them. The alternative to competitive bidding is a central planning regime; i.e., ongoing beauty contests in which a centralized agency tries to assess the relative merit of every internet-related business in their region. In addition to empowering themselves to more actively scrutinize existing uses and users, RIRs would also have to give themselves more power to take away resources from parties who they decided didn't really need them. Such a policy would make RIRs central planners for the internet economy. Any attempt to make and enforce such judgments would likely become ensnared in controversies and litigation.

Future resource allocation should rely instead on decentralized judgments about the value of resources by the actual holders of address resources. RIRs should act more as title agencies than resource managers and let market transactions take over the process of moving the resources to their most appropriate uses. To their credit, the RIRs have attempted to institute new policies to permit the transfer of address resources in response to market demand. The implementation of these policies, however, has been constrained by ideological commitments to old methods and norms. RIRs have tried to graft needs assessment onto the market transfer process, forcing anyone who acquires address resources by means of market transfers to prove that they "need" them using the old technical criteria. This may limit utilization of the new transfer policies and stifle valuable forms of intermediation and brokerage. More importantly, these constraints could prove to be ineffective. Organizations who received their IPv4 address blocks prior to the maturation of the RIR regime (known as "legacy holders") have no contractual obligations to the RIRs. It is these legacy holders who are most likely to release unused or underutilized IPv4 address blocks onto the market to alleviate the shortages, and they could trade address resources outside of the RIR-set rules. The business opportunities presented by this prospect have already provoked demands for a new regulatory structure that separates the address allocation process from "post-allocation services" such as Whois, account maintenance and the like (Thimmesch September 14, 2010). Just as the U.S. Commerce Department introduced a vertical separation between domain name registry services and domain name registrars, a similar split could occur between IP address allocation and assignment, further strengthening the role of market forces in IP addressing. Some people in the industry believe that IPv4 address resources are vastly underutilized and that an efficient market price system will actually alleviate the need to migrate to IPv6. Others emphatically dispute this. Only time will tell who is right.

As noted earlier, there is still some uncertainty about whether the migration to the new internet standard will succeed completely. The basic problem is that migrating to IPv6 imposes significant costs on organizations and yields no corresponding immediate benefits. Costs of training, weeding out compatibility problems, and software and hardware upgrades could be substantial. Moreover, an IPv6-capable internet service provider will have to keep running both protocol stacks (both IPv4 and IPv6) for some time. After all these expenditures the end result will be, at best, an internet that functions almost the same as it did before, albeit with an expanded address space. Aside from the larger address space, IPv6 has few superior capabilities (better support for mobility is one of them). For large ISPs with growing customer bases, the expanded address space does yield important benefits, but for many organizations whose current assignments are sufficient, there is no incentive to move. There are few first-mover advantages to adopting IPv6; indeed, for many organizations the rational strategy is to stall the migration as long as possible and only shift when one is forced to by the prospect of incompatibility with others.

Assuming that IPv6 does take hold, the movement from an environment of address-routing scarcity to one of address abundance with continued constraints on routing promises to have transformational effects on the policies and institutions for critical internet resource management. The large size of the IPv6 address space challenges the very basis of "needs assessment" as the basis for address block allocations. As noted earlier, the IETF allocation standards already constitute a major departure from classical needs-based methods. Users are assigned blocks more on the basis of their status and the number of "sites" they have than on "demonstrated need." Many holders of allocations will be given address blocks that vastly exceed their immediate needs. Only when organizations ask for additional addresses will actual utilization levels be assessed. Currently, a lot of the RIRs' regulatory leverage comes from their status as being the only source for new address allocations. In the IPv6 world, the initial allocations will be so large that RIRs may have less continuing leverage on user organizations, because they will not need to come back asking for more addresses very often. IP address abundance may make it more difficult for internet registries to prevent those holding capacious allocations to reassign all or part of their blocks for use by third parties. Portions of that address space might be leased out to those who want them but consider the RIR process too costly or bureaucratic. As long as an internet service provider can be found who will route that address space, it would be difficult for address assignment authorities to keep track of, much less prevent, such sub-delegations or leasings.

Resource Public Key Infrastructure (RPKI)

On the other hand, the RIRs could actually strengthen and rigidify their control over address allocation. The attempt to make routing and address allocation more secure could lead to the creation of a Public Key Infrastructure capable of authenticating possession of internet protocol addresses and route announcements. Resource Public Key Infrastructure (RPKI) is a security technology that would create a hierarchy of digital certificates which would be used to authenticate the allocation of address blocks, and any route announcements using those blocks.

RPKI uses digital resource certificates to authenticate the assignment of IP address blocks, Autonomous System (AS) numbers, and route announcements. (Kent 2006). These certificates bind a resource holder to its public cryptographic key, as well as information about the IP address block prefixes and Autonomous System (AS) numbers allocated to them.

Subsequently, resource holders can create Route Origin Authorization (ROA) statements, or standardized verifiable attestations that the holder of a certain prefix authorizes a particular Autonomous System (AS) to announce that prefix. Using this information in the RPKI, network operators (e.g., ISPs) can validate that 1) a specific network, as indicated by a unique AS, is the legitimate holder of an IP address block, and 2) the AS that originates a route announcement using a particular prefix is authorized to do so. Like all PKIs, authenticating certificates therein (and subsequently the associated allocation and routing information) would rely on the system having one or more Certificate Authorities (CAs), which would publish a public key(s) or "trust anchor" to be used to authenticate other certificates.

While RPKI would add some security to what is now a loosely organized routing system and prevent address hijacking, it would also provide the RIRs with a greater level of direct control over ISP operations and their use of address resources. A fully automated RPKI system applied to both address assignments and routing could give the RIRs the ability to disable the routing of ISPs who do not conform to their policies. This, along with the issue of who stands at the apex of the trust anchor hierarchy, poses a host of new governance problems. Thus, RPKI could challenge the independence of internet service providers, alter the governance role of the regional internet address registries (RIRs) and change the relationship between IANA and the RIRs. (Mueller and Kuerbis 2010). At best, RPKI implementation can prevent deliberate and unintentional routing problems and enable a more efficient and flexible use of address resources. A market transfer process for address resources could, for example, be greatly facilitated by accurate titling and control via RPKI. At worst, it could greatly centralize power over the internet, creating political struggles to seize or capture the leverage over internet users and suppliers it produces.

Insofar as one uses a centralized, strictly hierarchical trust model, one is also creating the potential for centralizing political and regulatory authority over the internet. We have already seen this drama play out in the domain name system. The DNS is a hierarchical name space. From a purely technical standpoint, all the administrator of the root has to do is coordinate top level domain name assignments to ensure that all names are unique and there are no duplications. But the concentration of power at the root creates a big, fat target for political, military and business actors. Almost inevitably, control of the DNS root will be extended beyond coordination of uniqueness to achieve other political and economic objectives. ICANN, for example, regulates the dispensation of top level domains (as well as second level domains) in ways that respond to political demands for trademark and copyright protection, economic competition policy objectives, nation-state control of geographic names, etc.

The RIRs are taking aggressive steps to implement their own RPKI solutions, and the Internet Architecture Board (IAB) has announced that RPKI should be organized into a single, hierarchical, global trust anchor (IAB February 12, 2010). Strictly applied, the IAB's principle that "th[e] trust anchor should be aligned with the registry of the root of the allocation hierarchy" means that ICANN, which controls the root of the IP address allocation hierarchy, should be the supreme certificate authority over addressing. If ICANN held this authority, however, it would add yet another revenue stream and its authority over internet governance would grow. It might even be possible to disintermediate the RIRs completely, and issue certificates and address blocks directly to organizations and end users. It is notable that despite all the support expressed by the RIRs and the IAB for a single trust anchor for RPKI, neither organization explicitly proposes to make ICANN the root. This provides a very interesting clue to the institutional competition going on between ICANN and the RIRs.

The shift to IPv6 also raises questions about the proper geographic scope of an address governance regime (i.e., should it be global, national or regional?). The regional nature of RIRs is something of a historical artifact, driven more by political concerns than by technical ones. There are tensions between the regional status quo, the technical imperatives of governing the internet (which lead toward global governance), and political imperatives (which sometimes lead to a reassertion of national arrangements).

Address abundance undermines the rationale for localized needs assessments. While the problem of route aggregation remains, routing externalities respond to global interactions among ISPs and are based on the topology of the network, not on geography per se. Many of the policies and problems associated with IPv4 scarcity also require globally coordinated responses, such as shifting reclaimed address space from one region to another. So far, the RIRs have not been able to establish coordinated policies to attack these problems. It is possible that various forms of arbitrage will emerge and take advantage of the differences among the regional IRs' policies.

Furthermore, the possibility of a new routing technology, emerging either from the IETF or from de facto adjustments to the v4–v6 migration, could lead to major institutional changes. In the past 15 years, route aggregation has provided one of the key rationales for the RIRs' central management of address resources. Defenders of the address-routing status quo have basically lost most of the arguments against market transfers as a form of rationing address resources. The only credible reason they can provide for preventing market transfers and for centralized coordination of allocations is the need to maintain hierarchical aggregation. What happens to the RIR regime if a new routing architecture evolves and BGP and its peculiar problems go away?

In contrast to these technical pressures, it is evident that some nation-states, working through the International Telecommunication Union (ITU), want to reassert a traditional nation-based governance model for internet addresses (Karlin, Forrest et al. 2009). A recent report commissioned by the ITU explicitly advocates a parallel system of Country Internet Registries (CIRs) managed by the ITU as a competitive alternative to the existing RIR regime (Ramadass 2009). Many ITU members prefer a CIR arrangement not because of any real or imagined benefits of competition, but because they are concerned about resource depletion and political control. Developing countries fear a replay of the address land rush that characterized the early days of IPv4; reserving a substantial block of IPv6 addresses to each national government not only secures their access to the resource but also makes it easier for them to exert policy control over the internet industry. Critics of this proposal fear that national governments would abuse that power to censor, over-regulate or even partition the internet. They also believe that aggregation requires a globally coordinated approach and do not trust the national governments and ITU to follow the appropriate policies.

Combining issues of nation-states and security, many regulatory entities now view IP addresses as a form of leverage that can be used to facilitate law enforcement and security on the internet. Copyright interests have been using IP addresses collected from peer to peer file sharing activities as a form of identification for many years. They have created transnational pressures to require ISPs to reveal the identity of customers associated with IP addresses. Law enforcement agencies have also used IP addresses as part of their forensics in tracking cyber-crimes. Within the RIRs, debates are ongoing about how much information about users should be revealed through the IP address "Whois" service, which links specific IP addresses or blocks to specific organizations. Like the domain name system, the tradeoff between network transparency and privacy must be negotiated in these controversies. Governments have also become more interested in, and to some extent more involved in, the RIRs.

To conclude, despite the highly technical subject matter a number of critical values are at stake in IP address allocation. The future of global compatibility is implicated by the apparent need to migrate to a new internet standard that is not backwards-compatible. We do not know exactly how liberal or conservative to be in the initial allocation of the new address resources, but the decisions we make now will have a major impact on the costs and accessibility of internet resources decades from now. The future of the end to end principle is implicated by the numerous gateways, network address translators and kludges that might be required to extend the life of the IPv4 space or to maintain connectivity between the IPv4 and IPv6 internets. There are also weighty geopolitical and political economy issues involved in the governance of the new IPv6 address-routing space. The IPv6 address-routing space can be compared to the opening of a vast new continent. It is inevitable that political and institutional authorities would compete over the control of that resource space. The scalability of the internet – its continued growth – cannot be taken for granted unless these problems are solved.

NOTES

1. "Default-free zone" refers to the collection of all internet autonomous systems (ASs) that do not require a default route to send a packet to any destination. A default route is used by a router when no other known route exists for a packet's destination address. Typically, defaults are used by smaller networks which rely on larger internet service providers to find the destination. ASs in the default-free zone are generally the largest and most interconnected networks.
2. Class A addresses contained about 16.777 million unique IPv4 addresses; Class B's contained about 65,500 unique addresses, and Class C's contained 256 unique addresses.
3. Until then, Africa was served by ARIN.
4. It can be used to mean state-owned resources; or privately owned but state regulated; or it can simply mean a resource that is publicly shared; or it can mean a public good in the strict economic definition of nonrival consumption, or it can mean an essential facility as the term is used in antitrust law.

REFERENCES

Barbir, A., S. Murphy et al. (2006), 'Generic Threats to Routing Protocols', *Network Working Group*, **RFC 4593**, Reston, VA: Internet Society.
Butler, K., T. R. Farley et al. (2010), 'A Survey of BGP Security Issues and Solutions', *Proceedings of the IEEE*, **98**, 100–22.
Cerf, V. (1990), 'IAB Recommended Policy on Distributing Internet Identifier Assignment', **RFC 1174**, Internet Engineering Task Force.
Colitti, L., S. Gunderson et al. (2010), 'Evaluating IPv6 Adoption in the Internet, PAM 2010', Passive and Active Measurement Conference, Zurich, Switzerland.
de Velde, G.V., C. Popoviciu et al. (2008), 'IPv6 Unicast Address Assignment Considerations', *Network Working Group*, **RFC 5375**, Reston, VA: Internet Society.
Dell, P. (2010), 'Two Economic Perspectives on the IPv6 Transition', *Info – The Journal of Policy, Regulation and Strategy for Telecommunications, Information and Media*, **12**(4), 3–14.
DeNardis, L. (2009), *Protocol Politics: The Globalization of Internet Governance*, Cambridge, MA: MIT Press.
Edelman, B. (2008), *Running Out of Numbers: The Impending Scarcity of IP Addresses and What To Do About It*, Cambridge, MA: Harvard Business School.

Elmore, H., L. J. Camp et al. (2008), 'Diffusion and Adoption of IPv6 in the ARIN Region', *Workshop on the Economics of Information Security*, 25–28 June 2008, Hanover, NH.

ENISA (2010), 'Report on Secure Routing Technologies, Crete, Greece, European Network and Information Security Agency and Institute of Communications and Computer Systems (ICCS)'.

Fuller, V., T. Li et al. (1993), 'Classless Inter-Domain Routing (CIDR): an Address Assignment and Aggregation Strategy', *Network Working Group*, **RFC 1519**, Reston, VA: Internet Engineering Task Force.

Hain, T. (2005), 'A Pragmatic Report on IPv4 Address Space Consumption', *Internet Protocol Journal*, **8**(3).

Hofmann, J. (2009), 'Before the Sky Falls Down: a "Constitutional Dialogue" over the Depletion of Internet Addresses', 4th Annual Giganet Symposium, Sharm el Sheikh, Egypt.

Hubbard, K., M. Kosters, D. Conrad, D. Karrenberg, J. Postel (1996), 'Internet Registry IP Allocation Guidelines', *Best Current Practice*, **RFC 2050**, Internet Engineering Task Force.

Huston, G. (2001), 'Analyzing the Internet BGP Routing Table', *The Internet Protocol Journal*, **4**(1), 2–15.

Huston, G. (2005), 'Just How Big Is IPv6? Or Where Did All Those Addresses Go?', **2009**, *www.potaroo.net/papers/isoc/2005-07/ipv6size.html*.

IAB (12 February 2010), *IAB statement on the RPKI, Internet Architecture Board, Internet Engineering Task Force*, http://www.ietf.org/mail-archive/web/ietf-announce/current/msg07028.html.

Karlin, J., S. Forrest et al. (2009), 'Nation-State Routing: Censorship, Wiretapping, and BGP', ARXIV: 0903.3218v1 [cs.NI] 18 Mar 2009 http://arxiv.org/pdf/0903.3218.pdf.

Kent, S. (2006), 'An Infrastructure Supporting Secure Internet Routing. Public Key Infrastructure', Third European PKI Workshop, A. S. Atzeni and A. Lioy, **4043**, 116–29.

Lehr, W., T. Vest et al. (2008), 'Running on Empty: The Challenge of Managing Internet Addresses', 36th Annual Telecommunications Policy Research Conference, 27 September 2008, Arlington, VA: TPRC.

Meyer, D., L. Zhang et al. (2007), 'Report from the IAB Workshop on Routing and Addressing', *Network Working Group*, **RFC 4984**, Reston, VA: Internet Engineering Task Force.

Mueller, M. (2002), *Ruling the Root: Internet Governance and the Taming of Cyberspace*, Cambridge, MA: MIT Press.

Mueller, M. L. (2006), 'IP Addressing: The Next Frontier of Internet Governance Debate', *Info – The Journal of Policy, Regulation and Strategy for Telecommunications, Information and Media*, **8**, 3–12.

Mueller, M. L. (2008), 'Scarcity in IP Addresses: IPv4 Address Transfer Markets and the Regional Internet Address Registries', *Internet Governance Project*.

Mueller, M. L. (2010), 'Critical Resource: An Institutional Economics of the Internet Addressing-routing Space', *Telecommunications Policy*, **34**(8), 405–16.

Mueller, M. L. and B. N. Kuerbis (2008), 'Regional Address Registries, Governance and Internet Freedom', *Internet Governance Project*, **24**, Paper IGP08-004, http://www.internetgovernance.org/pdf/RIRs-IGP-hyderabad.pdf.

Mueller, M. and B. Kuerbis (2010), 'Building a New Governance Hierarchy: RPKI and the Future of Internet Routing and Addressing', *Internet Governance Project*, Paper IGP10-001, http://internetgovernance.org/pdf/RPKI-VilniusIGPfinal.pdf.

North, D. C. (1990), *Institutions, Institutional Change and Economic Performance*, Cambridge, UK: Cambridge University Press.

Ostrom, E. (2005), *Understanding Institutional Diversity*, Princeton, NJ: Princeton University.

Perset, K. (2007), 'Internet Address Space: Economic Considerations in the Management of IPv4 and in the Deployment of IPv6', Organisation for Economic Co-operation and Development (OECD), *Ministerial Background Report*, Paris: DSTI/ICCP.

Ramadass, S. (2009), *A Study on the IPv6 Address Allocation and Distribution Methods*, Geneva: International Telecommunication Union.
Rekhter, Y. and T. Li (1995), 'A Border Gateway Protocol 4 (BGP-4)', *Network Working Group*, **RFC 1771**, Internet Engineering Task Force.
Rekhter, Y., T. Li et al. (2006), 'A Border Gateway Protocol 4 (BGP-4)', *Network Working Group*, Reston, VA: Internet Society.
Rekhter, Y., P. Resnick et al. (1996), 'Financial incentives for route aggregation and efficient utilization in the Internet', in B. Kahin and J. Keller (eds), *Coordinating the Internet*, Cambridge, MA: MIT Press.
Thimmesch, P. (14 September 2010), 'Competition to Regional Internet Registries (RIR) for Post-Allocation Services?', *CircleID*, http://www.circleid.com/posts/competition_to_regional_internet_registries_rir_for_post_allocation_service/.

4. Information governance in transition: lessons to be learned from Google Books
Jeanette Hofmann

INTRODUCTION

In its early days, governance of the internet focused on the logical infrastructure, particularly the domain name system and the numerical address space. With the growth of information services and digital content online, a range of regulatory policies are now seeking to shape the evolution of the internet. Terms such as the "networked information society" indicate the expanding overlap between internet governance and information governance. The regulation of the network infrastructure and that of digital content are becoming increasingly intertwined.

Information governance in this context should be understood in a broad sense encompassing statutory rules such as copyright law but also private contracts, technical standards or social norms and practices, all of which aim to govern the creation and circulation of information. This chapter addresses the regulation of information goods, assuming that information governance has a growing impact on the development of the internet.

The information economy is undergoing a period of fundamental change. These changes concern the ways information goods are owned and traded, and how they are regulated through public and private rules. Thus, they pertain to core institutions of the digital information landscape. Prompted by the juristic discussion on the role and impact of the copyright regime in the information age, this chapter offers a regulatory perspective on the evolving governance arrangements that shape the market for cultural goods. Without privileging either one, this approach includes public ordering through copyright law and private ordering through license contracts. Furthermore, it discusses proliferating strategies of selling access to information and the impact of those strategies, both on the use of literature and the constitution of cultural works.

Google Books, the unsuccessful but very well documented attempt to reutilize the vast amount of out-of-print works, serves as an example to illuminate the ongoing transformation of information governance. Google Books is the outcome of a settlement agreement of a lawsuit that the Authors Guild of America and five large members of the Association of American Publishers each had filed against Google on the grounds of copyright infringement. While "Google Print", the subject of the original lawsuit, merely intended to integrate ink and print works into Google's search service, the objectives of the settlement went a significant step further. Google Books intended to sell access to out-of-print works and thus infuse new value into works deemed worthless in the past. In a sense, this business model blurs the distinction between the services offered by public libraries and the products of commercial bookshops. It planned to offer for a fee what public libraries provide for free: access to works. Such a project requires the scanning and indexing of millions of texts. In other words, it demands mass digitization – a venture neither anticipated nor covered by copyright law.

Google Books made many observers hold their breath. Its business model could have changed the global book economy in profound ways. Samuelson (2010, p. 1308), for example, has portrayed Google Books as "one of the most significant developments in the history of books, as well perhaps in the history of copyright". Likewise, von Lohmann (2008) predicted that it is "likely to change forever the way we find and browse for books". Grimmelmann (2009, p. 1) found it "difficult to overstate the importance of the settlement" and Google itself referred to the digitization of books as its "moon shot" (Toobin 2007).

A central element of the present transformation affecting the information sphere concerns access to digital works. Starting with the sale of software as a mass commodity in the 1980s, license contracts have begun replacing the traditional sale of information goods. Instead of purchasing an information artifact, users are now more often buying *rights to use*. Carefully circumscribed terms and conditions, the *fine print*, form a crucial element in the commodification of access to information goods and, to a growing extent, substitute the transfer of property.

At first glance, license contracts appear as a mere implementation of copyright law. Yet they have the potential to sidestep or modify copyright law and thereby reshape the rules of the game. Embedded in an evolving mode of industry self-regulation, a whole new set of information assets is emerging that requires close monitoring of users in order to unfold its economic potential. As the case of Google Books shows, this contract-based regime involves a redistribution of the rights that used to structure the information economy (see also Gasser 2004). Although the competent court rejected Google Books in early 2011, it is worth studying this case as a possible blueprint of the future information economy. Its business model indicates how books and other cultural commodities could be traded and how public and private regulation interact to enable such markets.

The next section of this chapter outlines a governance perspective on Google Books emphasizing the transformation of both information markets and respective modes of regulation. The third section provides an overview of Google Books, its regulatory framework and business model. The fourth section discusses three aspects of relevance beyond the specific case of Google Books: (1) the intended private reform of copyright, (2) the commercial exploitation of access to information goods and (3) the rise of license contracts as a means of ordering the information economy.

CHANGING BUNDLES OF ENTITLEMENTS: A GOVERNANCE PERSPECTIVE ON COPYRIGHT REFORM

Due to its legal, commercial and geographical scope, Google Books has triggered a major international controversy encompassing three class action lawsuits, a proposed and subsequently amended settlement by the litigating parties, more than 400 filings by class-members and "friends of the court" (among the latter the French and German governments), two court hearings, various conferences, innumerable blog entries, articles and a still growing amount of academic publications, all covered by a special online-bibliography.[1] The academic debate has focused on the legal dimension of Google Books. The predominantly juridical literature has addressed copyright infringement (Samuelson 2011, 2010), competition concerns (Picker 2009) and procedural matters pertaining to the class action nature of the settlement agreement (Grimmelmann 2010).[2]

This chapter approaches Google Books from a governance perspective with an emphasis on its regulatory implications for the book trade and the information economy at large. The analytical value of the governance approach lies in its ability to "decenter" rule-setting authority within a given regime (Bevir and Rhodes 2006). Instead of privileging ex ante statutory norms and the legislator, it aims to take all relevant actors and means of regulation into account (Botzem et al. 2009). Notwithstanding the common assumption of the growing importance of copyright law, the governance approach suggests treating the relationship between public and private ordering as one of the research questions. An advantage of such a "low-presupposition" perspective is that it is particularly sensitive to shifts between various forms of regulation and thus well-suited to study the transformation of the copyright regime.

Yet, studying Google Books from a governance perspective is less self-evident than it may appear. Many, if not most, observers have condemned the commercial library project as a case of copyright infringement, pure and simple. In more or less drastic terms, Google Books has been accused of "trampling on property rights" (Nimmer 2009), causing a "copyright meltdown" (Vaidhyanathan 2007, p.1221; see also Newitz 2010) or turning copyright on its head (Peters 2009, p.70). In the view of the latter, the then U.S. Register of Copyrights, Google Books "would alter the landscape of copyright law – which is also the role of Congress and not the courts – for millions and millions of rights holders of out-of-print books. The out-of-print default rules would flip copyright on its head by allowing Google to engage in extensive new uses without the consent of the copyright owner, in my view making a mockery of Article 1 of the Constitution that anticipates that authors shall be granted exclusive rights." In sum, many copyright experts have assessed Google Books against statutory copyright rules, coming to the conclusion that it deviates both from U.S. and European copyright law.

The allegation of copyright infringement raises the question as to how this perspective relates to the governance approach and its effort to decenter rule making authority. According to Elkin-Koren (2004, p.252), the verdict of copyright infringement can be attributed to one of the two concepts that currently shape the discourse on the internet and the information regime. The more traditional model of the regulation of information reflects the idea of property rules "created by centralized institutions of the territorial state". According to this understanding, only the legislator has the authority to alter the norms that constitute intellectual property law, which is why Google Books clearly constitutes a case of copyright violation. Elkin-Koren's (2004, pp.252–53) second model refers to the "emerging regime of standard contracts" shaping the markets for copyrighted works. Against the backdrop of this latter concept, Google Books appears as a case of private ordering loosely defined as "decentralized processes by which norms are formulated".

The second model suggests that non-governmental practices, for instance market-based transactions in the form of contracting, may assume a regulatory role to the extent that such transactions prove to contribute to the change of rules and expectations. Instead of confining itself to the question of whether or not Google Books infringes on copyright laws, the private ordering approach may be more interested in the proposed or practiced modifications of existing norms and in their consequences for the information economy. That said, Samuelson (2011, p.482) recently discussed Google Books as a private act of rewriting copyright. It is "intriguing", she wrote, to view the settlement as a "mechanism through which to achieve copyright reform that Congress has not yet and may never be willing to do".

The governance perspective on the information economy does not neglect the role of statutory property rights for information markets, but it adopts a dynamic stance on the property regime by paying close attention to its ongoing reinterpretations and modifications. These changes concern the distribution of rights in the information sphere but they may also affect the regulatory weight of copyright law relative to other, private, forms of ordering (see Bakardjieva Engelbrekt 2007, p. 72). Referring to Hohlfeld's conception of property as a changing and relational "bundle of entitlements",[3] Bracha (2007, p. 1807) argues that copyright is neither absolute nor invariant. Instead of one ontological form, "property rights involve a multitude of choices among various institutional forms". While there is broad agreement that intellectual property rights change over time, Carruthers and Ariovich (2004, p. 25) emphasize that they do not always expand. One of the most controversial aspects of Google Books, for example, pertains to a provision that would curtail the control of right owners (see discussion below in the section "GOOGLE BOOKS: REUTILIZATION OF OUT-OF-PRINT LITERATURE"). Likewise, although the legal system may be the most important source of property rights, the governance perspective casts into doubt if it is indeed the only one. Market transactions, for example, can manifest themselves in the transformation of a property regime. Carruthers and Ariovich (2004, p. 25) describe this development as a decoupling of commercial practices from formal institutions resulting in the emergence of (perhaps temporary) "informal property rights". License contracts between creators and publishers or between information producers and customers offer numerous examples for the emergence of such informal property rights. An albeit rather generic economic explanation for this phenomenon can be found in the inefficiency of a given property regime (Salzberger 2006, p. 48).[4] In order to exploit new business opportunities such as the re-exploitation of discontinued works, private actors may test the boundaries of a given regulatory framework.

Taken together, the contrary perceptions of copyright infringement versus privately enacted copyright reform differ in terms of the legitimacy they ascribe to the Google Books agreement. More generally, they imply different ideas about the type and location of rule making authority in the information economy. The diagnosis of copyright infringement reflects the common view of copyright as a fixed set of property rights granted by statutory law whose scope and boundaries are exclusively to be defined by the legislator. The private ordering perspective, on the other hand, adds, and emphasizes the regulatory dimension of copyright law, which allows public and private ordering as concurrent or complementary forms of governance.[5] Exemplified by Samuelson's work (2011, 2010), the latter approach primarily focuses on the regulatory ramifications of Google Books and assesses them against the benchmark of public ordering – or more precisely: the actual mission attributed to copyright legislation.

If the allocation of entitlements is the exclusive domain of the state, modifications of such entitlements also fall under the exclusive scope of the legislator. Other forms of modification, by definition, must be infringement. By contrast, copyright understood as a regulation of information markets can be the subject of public and private interventions. A redistribution of property rights could thus result from various, more or less formal and coordinated actions and means. The governance approach escapes the narrow debate on whether or not Google Books constitutes a copyright infringement and opens up additional analytical avenues for studying the development of such arrangements. Specifically, it allows studying Google Books as one significant instance within the larger interplay of public and private ordering in the emerging information economy.

The next section will describe in more detail the genesis and business model of Google Books.

GOOGLE BOOKS: REUTILIZATION OF OUT-OF-PRINT LITERATURE

The Regulatory Framework

The key element of Google Books is the commodification of access to the vast amount of out-of-print literature. Somewhat similar to digital subscription models for music, Google Books meant to make available present and past works of literature as a commercial service. The reutilization of information goods is not specific to digitization, however. New technologies regularly create secondary markets for cultural goods. Examples are TV broadcasting that "breathed new life" into cinematographic works or video recorders that had the same effect on television series (van Gompel and Hugenholtz 2010, p. 61). Yet, digitization does not only enable new markets for out-of-print works, it also transforms the valuation principles of cultural goods.

According to Anderson's (2004) theory of the "long tail" we are moving from a world of scarcity governed by limited shelf space, TV channels or screen time towards a world of abundance. The world of abundance implies that, due to reduced costs of digital storage and online distribution, there is no longer a need for the cultural industries to solely focus on high volume mainstream taste. Instead it becomes economically feasible to offer access to all types of available cultural works.[6] It is estimated that roughly 5–10 percent of all books ever printed are commercially available. The rest are out of print. The "long tail" for books may thus consist of an enormous amount of unavailable works gathering dust on library book shelves.

Google Print, also called Google Book Search, began as a large-scale digitization project aiming to expand Google's search service into the analogue world of ink and print. The original idea was that books should become searchable just like any other content on the internet. However, Google Print has been neither the first nor the only project aspiring for a digital library on the internet. What sets Google Print apart from other digitization efforts such as "Project Gutenberg"[7] or the "Open Content Alliance"[8] is its magnitude and audacity (Johnson 2007). While most digitization projects make sure they stay within the boundaries of copyright law, typically by focusing on books or collections whose copyright has expired, Google boldly envisions digitizing each and every book: "Imagine sitting at your computer and, in less than a second, searching the full text of every book ever written. (. . .) Imagine one giant electronic card catalog that makes all the world's books discoverable with just a few keystrokes by anyone, anywhere, anytime" (Schmidt 2005). Reaffirming its mission to "organize the world's information", Google Books seeks to assemble the world's entire literature in an electronic, full-text searchable database.

In 2004 Google announced, as a first step, its plan to digitize 17 million books within ten years.[9] By late 2009, half way through, Google had scanned 12 million books,[10] in autumn 2010 the number had risen to 15 million (Crawford 2010). The book database is compiled from two sources: a partnership program with publishers, and the library project. The partnership program, which accounts for about 15 percent of the database, gives Google access to works in print. It includes approximately 30,000 publishers from roughly 100 countries (von Lohmann 2010) who expressly authorize Google to include their publishing program in the database and display portions of it, to an extent they choose, as search results. Publishers thus enjoy an *opt-in* relationship with Google Books: only works they make available will be searchable through Google Books.

The library project, the contentious part of Google Books, is based on agreements with major university and research libraries mostly in the U.S. and Europe. According to the general arrangement, Google bears the costs of digitizing and indexing the books while the libraries, in exchange for making their collection available, get a copy of the database generated from their individual corpus if they so choose.[11] In 2010, 42 libraries cooperated with Google.[12] Most libraries have restricted their collaboration to collections in the public domain. There have been a few noticeable exceptions, however. The libraries of the University of Michigan and Stanford University (holding 7.8 and 8 million books respectively) have given

Google permission to digitize their complete collection, including works still protected by copyright law.

Depending on the legal status of a queried text, Google's book search service shows, in addition to bibliographical information, snippets of a few lines surrounding the search term for copyrighted works or entire documents in case of works in the public domain. Copyright experts have regarded, and in many cases welcomed, Google book search as a test case for the future regulation of information goods. It is still unclear whether or not the scanning and indexing of books and the online display of text snippets, as a response to search queries, is protected by limitations and restrictions of copyright (CRS 2007; Samuelson 2011, p. 490). Google itself has argued that it modeled the library project after its search engine and if its search service is considered fair use, the new book search service should be as well.[13] Perhaps unsurprisingly, the rightsholders' associations failed to find Google's point of view convincing.

In 2005, the Authors Guild of America and five large members of the Association of American Publishers each filed lawsuits against Google on the grounds of copyright infringement. However, instead of following the lawsuits through, and clarifying the rights to indexing the world's literature, the litigating parties sounded out a private settlement. For more than two years, incidentally while legislation on orphan books was pending in the U.S., they negotiated behind closed doors (for details see Samuelson 2011). The resulting agreement between the Authors Guild, the Association of American Publishers and Google did not resolve the contested issue. In fact, it did not even touch on the question as to whether or not an indexing of copyrighted books deserves exemption from copyright.

Apparently driven by the plaintiffs,[14] the scope of the settlement agreement grew far beyond the original cause of the lawsuits. Google Books, the outcome of the negotiations, fundamentally differs from the original book search engine, the actual bone of contention for which Google was sued. Whereas Google Book Search intended to display mere text snippets of copyrighted works, the settlement agreement planned to offer access far beyond the 20 words once regarded as a violation of copyright (von Lohmann 2008). Instead of awaiting a legislative solution, the litigating parties "thought big" and developed a private regulatory framework for the reutilization of discontinued literature. Announced in autumn 2008, the settlement agreement includes a detailed licensing architecture and business plan for selling access to out-of-print works. The costs for establishing this new exploitation system are borne by Google. Google agreed to bear the costs for the litigation, to compensate the rightsholders (not to be confused with the authors) for the indexing of their works and provide a start-up fund for the new Books Rights Registry (see below). All in all, Google agreed to contribute a total of $125 million to the settlement.

In return for Google's investment, the settlement agreement endorses the digitization of books and protects Google – and exclusively Google – against the potentially enormous liability for copyright infringement in the U.S. (Picker 2009, p. 229). On behalf of the affected publishers and authors, oddly enough including missing rightsholders, it authorized Google to digitize and index out-of-print in-copyright books published before 5 January 2009, both in and outside the United States. The rights-holders' authorization for a re-exploitation of the millions of works digi-tized by Google was to be derived from a body that first had to be created: the "Books Rights Registry" (BRR), a new type of collecting agency designed to represent all authors and publishers with a stake in the Google Books database. Initially funded by Google with $34.5 million, the BRR was supposed to form the institutional core of Google Books. Among other tasks, the BRR would be responsible for locating rightsholders, distributing royalty payments earned through Google Books, negotiating prices and creating a voluntary copyright database to provide information on copyright ownership. The BRR was to be set up as an independent nonprofit organization governed by copyright owners, equally divided between publishers and authors. It acts as the clearing house between all copyright owners and Google.

Members of the BRR would transfer their rights in discontinued works to the BRR which would license them to Google, thereby authorizing the company to sell access to these books. Membership in the BRR was designed by default rule. In other words, the settlement stipulates that copyright owners must expressively opt out if they do not wish to par-ticipate in Google Books. By assembling all publishers and authors under one umbrella agency, the settlement sought to mitigate the fragmentation of rights preventing the reutilization of discontinued cultural goods. As a result of its opt-out mechanism, the costs of clearing rights would signifi-cantly decrease. Simultaneously, however, the private settlement would create a powerful new stakeholder group which would act in the name of "an entire industry, more or less" (Grimmelmann 2009, p. 7) – including its absent members.

The sweeping, all copyright owners encompassing scope of this licens-ing regime was due to the class action nature of the legal dispute.[15] The Authors Guild and the Association of American Publishers claimed to represent, and act on behalf of "all persons or entities having a U.S. copyright interest in one or more books as of January 5, 2009" (Samuelson 2010, p. 1316). Importantly, the U.S. copyright interest is not confined to American authors but applies to all authors whose country has signed the

Berne Convention (Band 2009, p. 263). Hence, the class action law suit had the potential to create a global regime for the re-commodification of out-of-print literature.[16]

As a response to the massive criticism of the settlement, particularly the anti-trust concerns brought forth by the U.S. Department of Justice, the litigating parties presented an amended settlement in November 2009 (ASA 2009).[17] The revised settlement was the subject of a fairness hearing held in February 2010.[18] In March 2011, the competent court rejected the settlement on the grounds that it was not "fair, adequate, and reasonable".[19]

The Business Model

Based on its licensing framework, the settlement outlines a business model aiming to establish a secondary market for digitized out-of-print books. Interestingly, Google Books was to create not only new sources of revenue for existing works, it also gave rise to new categories of information goods. Stripped of their physical container, literary works can be easily modified and merged into new information artifacts or "content" such as a subscription database, a reader for students or a research corpus. Specifically, the settlement outlines three forms of commercial exploitation (the settlement speaks of "revenue models"): (1) a free preview of portions of texts (supplemented by advertisements), (2) purchases of individual works and (3) institutional subscriptions. The rules governing the business model are, as many commentators have pointed out, exceedingly complex – so complex indeed that they can only be grasped by way of radical simplification. Most rules vary with the category and status of works and, at times, with the type of users.

In order to achieve this level of differentiation, the settlement introduced a number of classifications such as types of libraries (varying with their level of collaboration with Google),[20] digital file collections (varying with their purpose and comprehensiveness)[21] or market segments for institutional subscriptions (varying with the type of subscriber (ASA 2009, pp. 53–54). The definition of terms used in, and partly created for, the settlement agreement alone accounts for more than 20 pages. A glance at these definitions shows that the market envisioned by the architects of Google Books did not have much to do with the traditional book trade. Many established terms acquired a new meaning; a meaning negotiated between the lawyers involved. A telling example is the settlement's definition of a book.[22] It is nonetheless worthwhile studying this thicket of rules and classifications in some detail because, in one way or another, it is likely to influence the future book economy including practices of accessing and using literary works.

Google Books plans to offer users a free preview of up to 20 percent of copyrighted out-of-print works. The "standard preview" for non-fiction works implies that American users (more precisely, users with a North American IP address) can access and read, in response to a search query, up to five adjacent pages of a book. The two preceding and following pages will be blocked from view. The net revenues generated through advertising on the preview pages will be divided between Google (30 percent) and the rightsholders (70 percent) (ASA 2009, p. 70). Different rules govern access to other text genres.[23] Such detailed restrictions notwithstanding, public access (in the U.S.) to the world of out-of-print literature would be infinitely greater than the snippets offered under the rules of the original book search project (Lessig 2008; Samuelson 2010, p. 1358).

"Consumer purchase", the second revenue model of Google Books, offers full access to texts. The settlement defined this service in the following way: "consumer purchases mean a service provided by Google that allows a user, for a fee, to *access* and *view* Online the full contents of a Display Book" (ASA 2009, p. 6; highlighted by J.H.). Unlike what the term "purchase" suggests, the customer does not buy an electronic copy of a book, s/he buys a specific service. The electronic copy itself won't change hands; it will remain in the "cloud", i.e. on an individualized virtual shelf provided by Google to its customers who are buying a perpetual right to access their books from any computer. Google expects this service to "revolutionize the way some people read books [. . .] in an open cloud-based platform" (Drummond 2009). The business model of Google Books thus replaces the common exchange of ownership between bookseller and buyer by an end user license that carefully prescribes what the consumer is allowed to do with her acquisitions.[24] Preventing users from reassembling books in the form of hard copies or electronic files seems to be one of the common objectives underlying the constraints that characterize the consumer purchase model (Picker 2009, p. 18). Considering all these restrictions, Samuelson (2010, p. 1349) suggests "single-user access license model" as a more adequate description of this revenue approach.

Institutional subscriptions, the third "contemplated rightsholder service", represent a new type of information good consisting of a blanket license to a collection of copyrighted texts (Grimmelmann 2010, p. 114). The settlement refers to this collection as the "Institutional Subscriber Database", redundantly defined as "all Books available for Institutional Subscription" (ASA 2009, p. 54). Institutional subscriptions target organizational users such as universities, public libraries or corporations. "Appropriate individuals" (defined, for example, as students, faculty or library patrons) will have access to all documents included in the subscription database or discipline-specific subsets thereof. Not unlike a subscription service for music or video, access to the database is limited to the duration of the subscription. The rules for copying, pasting and printing text are the same as those for "consumer purchases".

In addition to these revenue models, the settlement agreement also envisioned so-called "non-display uses" of the book database. These uses include research and development-related forms of data mining that could lead to new services and products such as improved search or translation algorithms. Non-commercial researchers may be granted access to the database for "non-consumptive" purposes. As Samuelson (2010, pp. 1324–25) notes, a searchable digital corpus of millions of books would enable novel lines of research: "Linguists could discover the origins of words, concepts, and principles, or learn new things about usage patterns over time. (. . .) A digital corpus such as GBS thus opens up opportunities to explore knowledge embodied in books in ways that today can only be imagined." Some observers expect that such non-display uses of the database could end up being more important than the sale of access to books (von Lohmann 2008).

The settlement specifies two, in the litigants' view, compatible objectives for the commercial exploitation of the Google Books database, "(1) the realization of revenue at market rates for each Book and license on behalf of Rightsholders and (2) the realization of broad access to the Books by the public, including institutions of higher education" (ASA 2009, pp. 52–53). Prices for individual books will either be set by the rightsholders or a pricing algorithm developed by Google will be used to determine the optimal price of a work "in order to maximize revenue for each rightsholder" (ASA 2009, p. 61).[25] Not much is known about the pricing for the institutional subscriptions (Band 2009, pp. 269–72). Assuming that the authors and publishers represented in the BRR are likely to privilege the first of the two official objectives, observers fear that prices could become very high (Band 2009, pp. 299–301; Samuelson 2010, pp. 1333–34).

The business model of Google Books is based on a strikingly dense web of rules defining a range of authorized services, appropriate uses and users. The most detailed section of the settlement, however, concerns precautions to prevent unauthorized users and uses (Samuelson 2011, p. 537; ASA 2009, Attachment D). Like a reverse image of the rules governing access to the book database, the settlement outlined an equally comprehensive web of monitoring techniques to enforce its terms and conditions and, above all, to secure that leakages of files or violations of rules can be traced back to the transgressor. Its control apparatus affects all services, including the free preview of book sections. In order to ensure, for instance, that individual users cannot read free of charge more than five adjacent pages or more than 20 percent of a work altogether, all access, browsing and reading activities related to display files of books need to be recorded. In light of the restrictions placed on the sale of access, the actual use of purchased books will also require close and permanent observation.

To that end, Google Books implies collecting numerous data about its readers and their activities, their hardware and software. The methods concerned have been described as "some unstated combination of cookies, IP addresses, referrer logs"[26] (Privacy Authors 2009, p.8). On the basis of this data Google can identify "unique access points", i.e. the computers used for accessing texts, link them to the specific texts and pages and monitor the browsing activities. Furthermore, all digital files available to users will include a trackable "identifying mark". Watermark technology will collect encrypted session identifying information enabling Google to trace each copy of the text and log the authorized users' printing activities including their printing devices (ASA 2009, p.57). In other words, Google will be able to store information about each user in the following form: "Fred von Lohmann entered the store at 19:42:08 and spent 2.2 minutes on page 28 of 0-486-66980-7, 3.1 minutes on page 29, and 2.8 minutes on page 30" (von Lohmann 2008). The tight coupling of the commodification of access with available monitoring technologies will mean the end of online reading as a private activity. On the contrary, the monitoring entity will sooner or later know more about the customers' browsing and reading habits than the individuals themselves.

Libraries that choose to keep a copy of the digital text corpus that Google generated from their collection will also undergo extensive security provisions. They are required to develop a "security implementation plan" that complies with the settlement's "security standard". The settlement's 17 pages of security standard specifies security-critical objects (for instance systems containing "sensitive copyrighted material"), places, processes and people as well as security-ensuring management positions, responsibilities, awareness programs and practices subject to external control through annual audits by third parties (ASA 2009, Attachment D; Band 2009, p.281). In addition, the library digital copies will have identification marks indicating the hosting library so that potential leakages can be traced to the source. Breaches of the security implementation plan may result in harsh monetary remedies, depending on the extent of the damage.

While the privacy provisions of the settlement can probably be improved and the monitoring of individual customers somewhat scaled down,[27] the "securitization" of the digital book trade as such is likely to remain an essential part of Google Books. More generally, the non-stop watching of customers and the transformation of reading, browsing or sharing activities into potentially criminal acts appears to be the flip side of a business model intending to commodify access and to prescribe in greatest detail

what users are and are not allowed to do with digital works. If the ownership of the digital copy remains in the hands of the rightsholders, terms
and conditions including various enforcement techniques will govern the
individual use.

REALIGNING THE DIGITAL BOOK TRADE: RIGHTS, ASSETS, CONDITIONS

Private Copyright Reform

Google Books exemplifies the growing supply of online services surrounding digital content. Streaming services for video or music, for instance,
involve complicated negotiations with national collecting agencies and
rightsholders. Licensing agreements are the proverbial eye of the needle
that every reutilization effort has to pass through. Due to differing
national laws and multiple rights owned by differing actors, clarifying the
rights is often a costly process (see also Hargreaves 2011, pp. 28–29). The
cost of identifying, locating and contacting all rightsholders assembled in
a single book can easily total a three- or four-digit amount (Vuopala 2010,
p. 36; Band 2009, p. 228–29). In case of so-called orphan works whose
rightsholders are unknown, digitization and related forms of reutilization may be entirely out of the question. Estimating that approximately
40 percent of all copyrighted works could be orphans, the British Library
(2009) characterizes the resulting situation as the "information black
hole of the twentieth century" (for different figures see Vuopala 2010,
pp. 17–21).

Heller and Eisenberg (1998) have dubbed the high costs of clearing
rights to cultural works the "tragedy of the anticommons". Reflecting on
Hardin's (1968) "tragedy of the commons" which denotes an overutiliza-
tion of scarce resources, the "anticommons" refer to an underutilization
of resources due to the fragmentation of property rights. If rights in
resources are widely dispersed, coordination may prove to be prohibitively
expensive. Out-of-print works whose reutilization is blocked by high costs
of clearing copyrights are cases in point. Ironically, a comprehensive reutilization of literary works thus seems to call for a reversing of the rights
deemed indispensable for generating markets for literature in the first
place. As Hodgkin (2009) concludes, the introduction of new information services would require "something like a new Berne convention on
copyright".

In fact, orphan works have been on the political agenda in Europe and
the U.S. for at least a decade (Hugenholtz and van Eechoud et al. 2006,

p. 163). Commencing in 2003, several attempts have been made in the U.S. to address the issue of increasing rights clearing costs through a reform of copyright law; so far without sufficient political support.[28] In Europe, the problem of orphan works has been discussed both on the national and the European level. Yet with the exception of the Nordic countries[29] most member states have not taken any concrete measures to address the information black hole (EC 2008, p. 11). Following a recommendation of the European Commission (EC 2006), a High Level Expert Group was established to develop a set of European guidelines. The resulting non-binding Memorandum of Understanding on "Diligent Search Guidelines for Orphan Works" (HLEG 2008) specifies minimum standards for the identification of orphan works. The search guidelines have been criticized for their single work approach that does not take into account, let alone offer a solution for, large-scale digitization projects (EC 2009, p. 6).

While mass digitization of out-of-print literature is technically feasible, generally desirable and perhaps a commercially viable undertaking, a legal framework for such a market has yet to be established. The present "opt-in regime" mandates a clearing of rights for each work involved. On the surface, the issue of opt-in versus opt-out may look like a negligible detail of the overall property regime. In practice, however, the question of rights distribution goes "to the core of the role played by copyright in the digital age" (Bracha 2007, p. 1802) with far-reaching consequences for the accessibility of information goods in general. Lessig (2010) has characterized the opt-in rule as "a digital death sentence" to the majority of library works: "to require permission first is to guarantee invisibility".

From a library's as well as a user's standpoint, the present property regime blocks access to and reutilization of a substantial amount of the cultural heritage. From a commercial information distributer's point of view, the property regime causes market failure due to high transaction costs. From the perspective of the authors of the settlement, however, it may epitomize both market and policy failure. The inactivity of the legislator, according to some observers, may have encouraged the litigants' choice of a private solution (Grimmelmann 2010, p. 112). "The settlement", as Samuelson (2011, p. 482) quotes Dan Clancy, engineering director of the Google Books project at Google, is the "only way to free up access to digital copies of millions of out-of-print books because Congress [is] dysfunctional in dealing with copyright issues."

Samuelson (2011) suggests interpreting Google Books as an attempt to assert copyright reform by means of private ordering. The settlement amounts to "quasi-legislation" (op cit, p. 529) because it would have been binding for many millions of copyright owners. What is more, it intended to establish regulatory solutions to problems believed to be in need of copyright legislation with orphan works as the obvious example. The most significant reform of copyright law concerns the licensing system allowing Google to digitize, store and commercially exploit copyrighted books. It involves a modification of copyright law by shifting some of the costs of clearing rights to the copyright owners (Band 2009, p. 236). Specifically, it would have narrowed down the control over works past their exploitation period. However, according to Sag (2010, p. 75) it would have done so in ways "likely to benefit authors, publishers and readers alike". Due to their opt-out-character, these are in effect compulsory licenses that normally require legislation (see Samuelson 2011, p. 519).

Hargreaves (2011, p. 32) makes a similar point by portraying Google Books as an effort to introduce a still lacking digital licensing system "complete with stakeholder governance and dispute procedures". Sooner or later, he argues, a global licensing infrastructure will emerge in order to facilitate the global trade of digital content. The open question is who will initiate and govern such a transnational arrangement? Will it be governments or a group of private actors with enough power to set the rules and thereby reorganize the global markets for information goods (ibid)? In either case, one may add, a licensing system that enables a global market for cultural works requires a reaggregation of the property rights dispersed by copyright.

While many aspects of Google Books would have indeed advanced the public interest in access to out-of-print works, all in all, the settlement agreement clearly bears the hallmark of industry self regulation. One indication of private ordering is the equal weight the settlement gives to the goals of public access and revenue maximization for rightsholders. Even orphan works whose rightsholders by definition cannot benefit from a secondary market are subjected to the maxim of profit making. However, the most obvious evidence for a private copyright reform can be found in the fact that the settlement agreement primarily serves the negotiating parties instead of seeking a solution for the entire book market. The license for indexing books applies to Google only and would thus have established a monopoly over the indexing of out-of-print literature. Google Books offers a hint of the possible services and uses given a supportive legal framework, but it does not provide that framework itself.

Replacing Transfer of Ownership with Selling Access

Unlike currently available "print on demand" or "ebook" products which more or less replicate the trade of physical books, Google Books intends to sell services rather than copies of a work. Neither the envisioned "consumer purchase" nor the "institutional subscription" model involves transfers of property between sellers and buyers. As Duguid (2007, p. 8) puts it, Google treats printed literature "as a storehouse of wisdom to be opened up with new tools". These new tools, in the settlement agreement referred to as "contemplated rightsholder services" consist of *access* to the digital book database.

Access-based business models for information goods are not entirely new. The movie industry, for example, generates revenues by selling, and controlling, access to films, as Gillespie (2004, p. 241) shows: "By controlling access to the theater rather than reproduction of the work, the movie industry has developed ways to monetize each viewing experience, rather than possession." Although the commodification of access or experience is not limited to information goods (see Rifkin 2000), digitization has clearly broadened its possibilities. In the 1980s, the software industry paved the way towards novel types of information services with "shrink wrap", "click" or "browse wrap" licenses for computer programs (Benkler 2006; Lemley 2007; Madison 2003). User licenses for software have since more or less replaced the traditional exchange of property.

As long as texts were linked to physical containers, access to works was a rather unproblematic matter. Given its print and ink legacy, copyright law does not even mention access as a regulatory issue (Picker 2008, pp. 3–5; Heide 2001; Goldstein 1997). Before the advent of electronic publishing, books could not be read without accessing a physical copy, the latter of which would typically take place in regulated spaces such as bookshops, public libraries or someone's house. Unlike their physical counterparts, digital information goods are no longer self-regulating (Madison 2003, p. 290) and legally significant actions such as accessing, copying or reading works have become difficult to tell apart. In a famous article Ginsberg (2003) describes the consequences the information industry has drawn from the challenges that digitization poses for the sale of copyrighted works: "from having copies to experiencing works". Such access-centered distribution arrangements will only succeed, according to Ginsberg (2003), if the state of "experiencing" a copy will not turn into an unauthorized "having" a copy, or, worse yet, an unauthorized "sharing copies".

Google Books exemplifies in detail how access-based forms of commercial exploitation can be applied to the book trade. The settlement agreement anatomizes potential uses of books into discrete activities such as browsing, sharing, copying, annotating and printing; it translates these practices into single exclusive rights of the copyright owner and thereby ascribes economic value to each of these actions. Additional value is created by qualifying these rights according to various parameters such as the number and type of books, the number and type of users, perhaps the duration of the users' rights, the geographic region and other criteria (see also Kretschmer et al. 2010, p. 14). In an access-centered regime, the once unregulated, if not altogether undefined practice of making use of texts becomes an economically valuable action that can and, in fact is likely to be measured – for instance in terms of the absolute or adjacent number of pages viewed – calculated, priced and sold.

The substitution of access for the exchange of information goods affects the relationship between seller and buyer in various ways. To begin with, customers lose some of the rights and liberties linked with taking possession of a book. The practice of selling access sidelines the exhaustion principle inherent to copyright, which stipulates that the exclusive rights over a copy end with its sale. The purchasers of printed works "can lend their books to friends; the latter [purchasers of Google Books, J.H.] cannot. The former can resell their books or give them away; GBS e-book purchasers can do neither. (. . .) GBS e-book purchasers cannot, in fact, even take possession of their books" (Samuelson 2010, p. 1348). The subject of control in this regime is no longer the duplication of copyrighted works but access to or the "experience" of it. Access-based exploitation models imply a redistribution of property rights and control between rightsholders and users at the expense of the latter (Kretschmer et al. 2010, p. 115).

However, selling access instead of tangible copies does affect the constitution or ontology of books themselves. Recalling that texts purchased from Google Books remain on the supplier's virtual shelf, books cease to be goods in the traditional sense and acquire features usually associated with services. Not unlike the service of a library, Google offers varying forms of access to literature. Furthermore, like a service, access to texts is specifically generated at the request of the buyer and confined to her. The purchased access can neither be sold nor returned. Also, the relationship between the supplier and the customer continues throughout the "experience" of the good. Finally, each version of a purchased text will be individualized and thus, to some extent, be unique – thanks to the watermark technologies appended to each single file in order to identify users and monitor their actions. Hence, digitized books and other information goods may become hybrids that lean towards services rather than ordinary goods, and publishers may turn into "service-delivery enterprises" (Cohen 2011, p. 141). Consequently, as Rifkin (2000) noted, customers would be spending more and owning less. The freedom of use linked to ownership in information goods would be largely lost.

Critical observers therefore fear that the emergence of an access-centered regime would have profound consequences for the future circulation and availability of information goods or, more broadly speaking, the order of the "networked information society" (Cohen 2006). Reflecting on the Google Books settlement, Grimmelmann (2010, p. 121) has predicted that cultural works will be wrapped up "in endless, needless layers of red tape, DRM, and legal restrictions". Likewise, Lessig (2010, pp. 5–6) concludes that Google Books "constructs a world in which control can be exercised at the level of a page, and maybe even a quote. It is a world in which every bit, every published word, could be licensed. It is the opposite of the old slogan about nuclear power: every bit gets metered, because metering is so cheap".

As the security provisions of the settlement show, the commodification of access also affects the privacy of reading. Cohen (2006, pp. 2–3) observes a disruption and "casual" rearrangement of "the boundaries of personal spaces and of the intellectual and cultural activities played out within those spaces". New forms of authorizing access and use assume that customers will come to regard these regime changes as necessary and the involved restrictions "as natural attributes of the information environment". In this respect, Google Books and the changes in the information economy it represents also implies a dimension of "social ordering" (Cohen 2006, p. 3).

Governing Information by License Contracts

Google Books is based on a licensing framework. License contracts have become the principle means to control access, to tailor and commodify types of use, in short, to shape markets for end-user information goods. Licenses belong to the world of contract law. Private actors, according to the theory, agree on the terms of a transaction which involves the transfer of some rights or permissions. Crucially, the purchase of a license does not imply a transfer of ownership but rather resembles that of a lease which specifies how a good can be used. In the information economy, licenses represent the legal instrument to "apportion, by granting or withholding, rights given to the transferee to use information or related products" (Nimmer 2007, p. 4). Copyright law and license contracts meet where the authority to license a good is rooted in the ownership of copyright. Whereas copyright creates and defines the entitlement to be leased, the contract specifies its conditions.

License contracts are used to regulate the relationship between creators and publishers or among rightsholders. In the course of digitization, the domain of licenses has significantly expanded. License contracts now increasingly shape the relationship between rightsholders and end-users – and thus the workings of mass markets. Licenses owe their rising regulatory power to no small extent to recent copyright reforms. Following the 1996 WIPO copyright treaty, which prohibits the circumvention of technical protection measures, a new governance arrangement has emerged. This regime exercises control through the "tight coupling of technology and law, each sharing the task of regulation of not only copying, but access, use, and purchase" (Gillespie 2004, pp. 240–41). Without digital protection measures designed to enforce compliance, the fine print in license contracts would arguably lack the clout to effectively govern the behavior of customers.

From the perspective of copyright owners, licensing cultural goods provides clear advantages over the traditional sales model. First, licenses blur crucial distinctions between "the work of authorship protected by copyright law and the tangible artifact in which a work is embodied" (Madison 2003, p. 281) with the effect that statutory limits of the rights-holders' control are undermined and binding restrictions on users can be imposed (Elkin-Koren 2010, p. 9). What is more, licenses imply nearly unlimited flexibility for the design and differentiation of products or services. Identical information objects such as the Google Books database can be exploited in various ways by modifying the terms of use along simple parameters such as the number of users and type of usages. Since the value of information goods no longer lies in physical objects, digitization "amplifies the capability to tailor products by contract" (Nimmer 2007, p. 12). Hence, contracts do more than stipulate particular forms of use; they increasingly constitute information goods as such: "The license, in effect, defines the product" (Nimmer 2007, p. 11).

Compared to copyright law with its regulatory focus on duplication and dissemination, licenses allow governing, and commercially exploiting a much wider array of uses. Put differently, the regulatory impact of end-user licenses unfolds where that of copyright law used to end: after the purchase of information goods. Hence, licenses establish new forms of "information propertization" (Radin 2006; Salzberger 2006; Siegrist 2006) able to inject additional value also in abandoned cultural works. While licensing contracts necessarily remain anchored in copyright law, the small print is emancipating itself from the norms and principles of copyright regulation. As Radin (2004, p. 145) observes, mass market contracts create their "own regime of liberties and obligations, in which the constitutional, legislative or judicial rules engendered by the state are superseded by the contractual regime". Although copyright law is still vital for creating property rights in informational works, its regulatory power beyond this basic function seems to fade. Neither statutory limitations of intellectual property rights nor their underlying concept of balancing commercial and public interests show much regulatory impact on the information sphere.

Commenting on Google Books, Madison (2008) wonders if we are witnessing the demise of copyright as we know it. Copyright, in his view, is increasingly replaced by other governance arrangements that are moving "the statute to a place where it negotiates for attention as a normative landmark". Paradoxically, the authority of statutory copyright rules seems to shrink at times when the information economy is expanding and the scope of information governance rising. Google Books, with its intricate rules and restrictions, exemplifies the overall trend towards private ordering of the information economy. Empowered by legal anti-circumvention provisions, private licensing norms and practices are aligning themselves to an evolving governance arrangement in the shadow of copyright law.

Information governance has been the principal domain of legal and, to a lesser degree, economic scholarship. Seen through the lens of copyright law, the advent of end-user license arrangements presents itself as an extension of the control that rightsholders, empowered by copyright law, are exercising over the information sphere. If in analogue times copyright law used to focus on the commercial use of cultural goods, beginning with the digital age it is regulating nearly all conceivable forms of use. As Lessig (2010) describes this situation, "we are about to make every access to our culture a legally regulated event, rich in its demand for lawyers and licenses, certain to burden even relatively popular work". In this spirit, legal scholars have analyzed, and explicitly criticized, the rise of license contracts as processes of increasing and continuous propertization, privatization, commodification and judicialization of knowledge and information (for instance Boyle 2008; Lessig 2010; Lucchi 2007).

The image of the hypertrophic copyright regime has framed nearly every critical account of information governance against the backdrop of digitization. Like an octopus, intellectual property rights seem to wrap themselves around more and more information resources and thereby dry up the public domain. Boyle (2004) even referred to copyright laws as the "legal sinews of the information age". Despite all its intuitiveness, however, this linear account is not without biases. The narrative of ever expanding propertization and control emphasizes political continuities at the expense of discontinuities. Moreover, it does not distinguish between statutory norms and contract-based norms and therefore underrates the shifts between public and private regulation in information governance.

CONCLUSION: CONTINUITIES AND DISCONTINUITIES IN INFORMATION GOVERNANCE

Studying the information economy as governance arrangements facilitates a de-centering of regulatory authority. Instead of privileging copyright law as the central point of reference, the governance perspective also considers other relevant actors, norms and means that order information markets. This chapter has looked at Google Books as an, albeit, unsuccessful attempt at private regulation in the face of assumed policy failure. The guiding assumption was that Google Books can be understood as a blueprint that anticipates and drives the transformation of the book trade and possibly the market of other digital consumer goods as well. Even though the competent court rejected the private settlement, some of its features are likely to resurface as part of standard business practices. Three aspects of Google Books seem particularly emblematic in the context of information governance.

The first concerns the modification and re-distribution of property rights inherent to the Google Books settlement. Exclusive rights deemed necessary to enable markets for information goods to begin with are now effectively inhibiting the formation of new markets and, thus, additional ways of exploitation. Expressed in terms of the "tragedy of the anti-commons" (Heller and Eisenberg 1998), copyright causes a fragmentation of property rights which makes coordination difficult if not impossible. The settlement agreement suggested a private solution to this dilemma. While this solution would have greatly enhanced public access to the print heritage, it clearly bears the signature of its authors. Google Books' licensing framework privileges the founding organizations over other stakeholders. Even if the private rewriting of copyright makes sense per se, its results do not live up to the standards of a common welfare concept; a shortcoming which perhaps can be attributed to the tightly-knit circle of actors involved.

A second aspect, the significance of which exceeds the scope of Google Books, refers to the transformation of the book trade. Following the business model of the software industry, Google intended to sell rights of use instead of titles in actual copies of books. The settlement agreement intended to decompose the use of books into single activities, translating them into rights and thereby ascribing economic value to them. In this new regime, the focus of control is no longer on the duplication of works but on access and therefore would cover all types of usage. To the degree that digital access is becoming subject to commodification, reading may lose some of its private character and turn into a monitored and measured activity regulated by license contracts. What is more, without the transfer of property rights, books are transformed into hybrids between goods and services, thereby giving rise to a permanent relationship between information providers and customers.

A third aspect pertains to the evolving governance arrangement for information goods. As a response to digitization, license contracts have become a means to tailor products in the form of rights to use. Given that in this scenario the exhaustion of copyright no longer takes place, license contracts control the use of information beyond the time of sale and establish long-term relationships between rightsholder and users. The rise of mass licensing as a new distribution model also changes the division of labor between copyright and private contracts. While statutory copyright remains necessary to create exclusive rights in information goods, its regulatory authority beyond this task seems to decline. This is evident from the diminishing importance of its exceptions and limitations. Supported by legal anti-circumvention rules, private contracts are emancipating themselves from statutory principles and are bringing about a new regime. Google Books exemplifies this shift in information governance towards private ordering.

It is true the commodification of usage rights adds up to a continuous propertization of information goods. However, this continuity is closely linked to fundamental discontinuities in the development of information markets. Some examples of such discontinuities are the transformation of books into services, the shift from public to private regulation and the declining authority of copyright law. Hence, information governance is undergoing a profound transformation and the narratives of the information society should reflect this process.

NOTES

1. http://digital-scholarship.org/gbsb/gbsb.htm.
2. Specifically, observers address ramifications relating to (market) power (Grimmelmann 2009), price setting (Band 2009), privacy (von Lohmann 2008), privatization (Sag 2010), propertization (Vaidhyanathan 2007, p.1218). Some of the authors weigh them against the opportunities of an unparalleled access to the vast amount of out-of-print literature (Picker 2009, p.2).
3. See for example Carruthers and Ariovich (2004) and Stepanians (2005, p.236) for a more detailed account on this interesting subject.
4. See also Cohen (2011, pp.153–55) who raises the question if copyright law provides an adequate framework for the "post-industrial resource-coordination problems" that a property regime is expected to handle.
5. I thank Mike Madison, University of Pittsburgh, School of Law, for pointing out these different ideas of copyright to me. See also Liu (2004).
6. Anderson (2004) describes the implications for books: "The average Barnes & Noble carries 130,000 titles. Yet more than half of Amazon's book sales come from outside its top 130,000 titles. Consider the implication: If the Amazon statistics are any guide, the market for books that are not even sold in the average bookstore is larger than the market for those that are".
7. http://www.gutenberg.org/wiki/Main_Page.
8. http://www.opencontentalliance.org/.
9. It is difficult to assess this figure since there are no reliable statistics about the number of all books ever printed world wide. In the course of its digitization project, Google

has identified roughly 130 million unique books (Taycher 2010). WorldCat, the largest international library catalogue, listed in 2009 roughly 85 million manifestations of works (Lavoie and Dempsey 2009).

10. Of the 12 million books digitized by 2009, at least two million were in the public domain and another two million derived from the partner program with publishers (Dan Clancy, Chief Engineer of Google Books quoted after Samuelson (2010, p. 1310)). The remaining number of books is likely to be protected by copyright and thus subject of the lawsuits filed against Google.

11. The specific conditions depend on the type of agreements with Google (for details see Band 2008).

12. For details see: http://www.google.com/googlebooks/partners.html.

13. "We really analogized book search to Web search, and we rely on fair use every day on Web search (. . .) Web sites that we crawl are copyrighted. People expect their Web sites to be found, and Google searches find them. So, by scanning books, we give books the chance to be found, too" (Drummond 2009).

14. According to Alexander Macgillivray, then Deputy General Counsel for Products and Intellectual Property at Google (see his presentation at the Berkman Center http://cyber.law.harvard.edu/events/luncheon/2009/07/macgillivray at min 14 and the corresponding blog entry on the talk: "Google usually thinks very big – this, he says, is one of the few times that other parties at the table were thinking bigger than Google was", http://www.ethanzuckerman.com/blog/2009/07/21/alex-macgillivray-ex plains-the-google-books-settlement/).

15. Class actions are law suits specific to U.S. law that allow collective actors to sue on behalf of the class, i.e. all affected people. Band (2009, p. 263) characterizes class actions as "legal fiction (. . .) where a handful of class representatives bring an action on behalf of all members of a defined class".

16. The amended settlement from November 2009 considerably narrowed down this broad scope to books registered in the U.S. or published in the U.S., Canada, Australia and United Kingdom (Band 2009).

17. In addition to the downsizing of the class, the amended settlement created a fiduciary to represent the interests of missing rightsholders. Also, it offered competitors the possibility to resell access to the Google Books database (ASA 2009).

18. For the transcript see http://thepublicindex.org/docs/case_order/fairness-hearing-transcript.pdf.

19. For the opinion of the judge see [http://thepublicindex.org/docs/amended_settlement/opinion.pdf].

20. Fully participating libraries, host sites, cooperating libraries, public domain libraries, other libraries. For details, see Band (2009, pp. 275, 284).

21. Digital copies of a book, library digital copies consisting of copies Google created from a given library, display books (electronic books authorized for commercial services), the institutional subscription database and the research corpus (set of all digital copies generated as part of Google's library project) (ASA 2009, pp. 8–21).

22. Since the definition runs over 21 lines, I only quote what is *not* considered a book: "The term 'Book' does not include: (i) Periodicals, (ii) personal papers (e.g. unpublished diaries or bundles of notes or letters), (iii) written or printed works in which more than twenty percent (20%) of the pages of text (not including tables of contents, indices, blank pages, title pages, copyright pages and verso pages) contain more than twenty percent (20%) music notation, with or without lyrics interspersed (for purpose of this calculation, "music notation" means notes on a staff or tablature), (iv) written or printed works in, or as they become in, the public domain under the Copyright Act in the United States, (v) Government Works, or (vi) calendars." (ASA 2009, p. 4).

23. In case of fiction, Google may show up to 20 percent of a text but not more than 5 percent of adjacent pages and the final 15 pages or 5 percent of a book are blocked. No preview is available for poetry, short stories and anthologies. For dictionaries, encyclopedias etc, no queries but a fixed preview of 10 percent is available.

24. "Consumer Purchase will enable purchasers to view, copy/paste and print pages of a Book, and may enable Book Annotations. With respect to copy/paste, the user will not be able to select, copy and paste more than four (4) pages of the content of a Display Book with a single copy/paste command. Printing will be on a page-by-page basis or a page range basis, but the user will not be able to select a page range that is greater than twenty (20) pages with one print command for printing" (ASA 2009, pp. 60–61). More and different rules apply to works of fiction, poetry, anthologies, encyclopedias and dictionaries (ASA 2009, p. 65).
25. The algorithm consists of several pricing bins between US\$ 1.99 and US\$ 29.99. All books will be distributed among these bins whereby 5 percent of the books will be offered at US\$ 1.99 and 29.99. The majority of books will range between US\$ 2.99 and 9.99 and thus fairly close to commercially available hard copies.
26. "Referrer logs" identify the website from which a user is coming.
27. Experts have made concrete proposals to that effect; see, for example, Jones and Janes (2010).
28. See: http://en.wikipedia.org/wiki/Orphan_works_in_the_United_States.
29. The Nordic countries' extended collective license scheme authorizes collecting societies to sell licenses not only on behalf of their members but also non-member rightsholders, thereby significantly reducing transaction costs for clearing rights of cultural works (van Gompel and Hugentholtz 2010; Riis and Schovsbo 2010).

BIBLIOGRAPHY

Anderson, C. (2004), 'The Long Tail', *Wired*, http://www.wired.com/wired/archive/12.10/tail.html?pg=2&topic=tail&topic_set=.

ASA (2009), 'Authors Guild, I., I. Association of American Publishers, Google Inc. Amended Settlement Agreement', http://www.googlebooksettlement.com/r/view_settlement_agreement.

Bakardjieva Engelbrekt, A. (2007), 'Copyright from an Institutional Perspective: Actors, Interests and Institutional Design', *Review of Economic Research on Copyright Issues*, **4(2)**, 65–97.

Band, J. (2009), 'The Long and Winding Road to the Google Books Settlement', *The John Marshall Review of Intellectual Property Law*, **9(227)**, 227–329.

Benkler, Y. (2006), *The Wealth of Networks: How Social Production Transforms Markets and Freedom*, New Haven: Yale University Press.

Bevir, M. and R. A. W. Rhodes (2006), 'Interpretive Approaches to British Government and Politics', *British Politics*, **1**, 84–112.

Botzem, S. and J. Hofmann, et al., eds (2009), *Governance als Prozess. Koordinationsformen im Wandel, der Reihe Schriften zur Governance-Forschung*, Baden-Baden: Nomos.

Boyle, J. (2008), *The Public Domain. Enclosing the Commons of the Mind*, New Haven: Yale University Press, http://thepublicdomain.org/thepublicdomain1.pdf.

Boyle, J. (2004), 'A Manifesto on WIPO and the Future of Intellectual Property', *Duke Law and Technology Review*, **9**, 1–12.

Bracha, O. (2007), 'Standing Copyright Law on Its Head? The Googlization of Everything and the Many Faces of Property', *Texas Law Review*, **85**, 1799–869.

British Library (2009), 'Copyright in the Knowledge Economy', *Response from the British Library to the Green Paper on Copyright in the Knowledge Economy*, London.

Carruthers, B. G. and L. Ariovich (2004), 'The Sociology of Property Rights', *Annual Review of Sociology*, **30**, 23–46.

Cohen, J. E. (2011), 'Copyright as Property in the Post-Industrial Economy: A Research Agenda', *Wisconsin Law Review*, **2011(2)**, 141–65.

Cohen, J. E. (2006), 'Pervasively Distributed Copyright Enforcement', *Georgetown Law Journal*, **95(1)**, 1–48.

Crawford, J. (2010), 'On the Future of Books', October 14, 2010, *Inside Google Books*, http://booksearch.blogspot.com/2010/10/on-future-of-books.html.
CRS [Congressional Research Service] (2007), 'The Google Book Search Project: Is Online Indexing a Fair Use Under Copyright Law?', *CRS Report For Congress, Washington, D.C.*, http://www.ipmall.info/hosted_resources/crs/RS22356-070122.pdf.
Darnton, R. (2011), 'Six Reasons Google Books Failed', http://www.nybooks.com/blogs/nyrblog/2011/mar/28/six-reasons-google-books-failed.
Darnton, R. (2009), 'Google & the Future of Books', *The New York Review of Books*, **56(2)**, http://www.nybooks.com/articles/22281.
Drummond, D. C. (2009), 'Competition and Commerce in Digital Books. U.S. House of Representatives Judiciary Hearing', http://judiciary.house.gov/hearings/pdf/Drummond090910.pdf.
Duguid, P. (2007), 'Inheritance and Loss? A Brief Survey of Google Books', *First Monday*, **12(8)**, 8.
EC [European Commission] (2009), 'Communication from the Commission', *Copyright in the Knowledge Economy Com*, **532**, Brussels: Commission of the European Communities.
EC [European Commission] (2008), 'Copyright in the Knowledge Economy', *Green Paper*, Brussels, http://ec.europa.eu/internal_market/copyright/docs/copyright-infso/greenpaper_en.pdf.
EC [European Commission] (2006), 'Commission Recommendation of 24 August 2006 on the digitisation and online accessibility of cultural material and digital preservation', Brussels.
Elkin-Koren, N. (2010), 'Governing Access to Users-Generated-Content: The Changing Nature of Private Ordering in Digital Networks', M. Marzouki Brousseau, and C. Méadel (eds), *Governance, Regulations and Powers on the Internet*, Cambridge, UK: Cambridge University Press, http://ssrn.com/abstract=1321164.
Elkin-Koren, N. (2004), 'The Internet and Copyright Policy Discourse', in H. Nissenbaum and M. Price (eds), *Academy and the Internet*, New York: Peter Lang, pp. 252–74.
Gasser, U. (2004), *iTunes: How Copyright, Contract, and Technology Shape the Business of Digital Media. A Case Study*, Berkman Center for Internet & Society at Harvard Law School.
Gillespie, T. L. (2004), 'Copyright and Commerce: The DMCA, Trusted Systems, and the Stabilization of Distribution', *The Information Society*, **20(4)**, 239–54.
Ginsberg, J. C. (2003), 'From Having Copies to Experiencing Works: The Development of an Access Right in U.S. Copyright Law', *Journal of the Copyright Society of the USA*, **50**, 113–30.
Goldstein, P. (1997), 'Copyright and Its Substitutes. The Kastenmeier Lecture', *Wisconsin Law Review*, 865–71.
Grimmelmann, J. (2010), 'The Elephantine Google Books Settlement', *Buffalo Intellectual Property Law Journal*, forthcoming, 101–22, http://papers.ssrn.com/sol3/papers.cfm?abstract_id=1607423.
Grimmelmann, James (2009), 'The Google Book Search Settlement: Ends, Means, and the Future of Books', *American Constitution Society*, http://works.bepress.com/cgi/viewcontent.cgi?article=1024&context=james_grimmelmann.
Hardin, G. (1968), 'The Tragedy of the Commons', *Science*, **162**, 1243–48.
Hargreaves, I. (2011), 'Digital Opportunity. A Review of Intellectual Property and Growth', *An Independent Report*, London, http://www.ipo.gov.uk/ipreview-finalreport.pdf.
Heide, T. (2001), 'Copyright in the EU and U.S.: What "Access-Right"?', *Journal of the Copyright Society of the USA*, **48(3)**, 363.
Heller, M.A. and R.S. Eisenberg (1998), 'Can Patents Deter Innovation? The Anticommons in Biomedical Research', *Science*, **280(5364)**, 698–701.
HLEG [High Level Expert Group–Copyright Subgroup] (2008), 'Final Report on Digital Preservation, Orphan Works, and Out-of-Print Works', i2010: Digital Libraries, Brussels, http://ec.europa.eu/internal_market/copyright/docs/copyright-infso/greenpaper_en.pdf.

Hodgkin, A. (2009), 'Google Book Search and the Tragedy of the Anti-Commons', http:// exacteditions.blogspot.com/2009/02/google-book-search-and-tragedy-of-anti.html.

Hugenholtz, B. and M. van Eechoud et al. (2006), 'The Recasting of Copyright & Related Rights for the Knowledge Economy', Amsterdam: Institute for Information Law, University of Amsterdam, http://ec.europa.eu/internal_market/copyright/docs/studies/ etd2005imd195recast_report_2006.pdf.

Johnson, R. K. (2007), 'In Google's Broad Wake: Taking Responsibility for Shaping the Global Digital Library', ARL (Association of Research Libraries), **250**, 1–15.

Jones, E. A. and J. W. Janes (2010), 'Anonymity in a World of Digital Books: Google Books, Privacy, and the Freedom to Read', *Policy & Internet*, **2(4)**, 43–75.

Kretschmer, M., E. Derclaye et al. (2010), 'The Relationship Between Copyright and Contract Law', Research commissioned by Strategic Advisory Board for Intellectual Property Policy, London, http://eprints.bournemouth.ac.uk/16091.

Lavoie, B. and L. Dempsey (2009), 'Beyond 1923: Characteristics of Potentially In-copyright Print Books in Library Collections', *D-Lib Magazine*, **15 (11/12)**, http://www.dlib.org/dlib/ november09/lavoie/11lavoie.html.

Lemley, M. A. (2007), 'Should a Licensing Market Require Licensing?', *Law & Contemporary Problems*, **70(2)**, 185–203, http://www.law.duke.edu/shell/cite.pl?70+Law+&+Contemp. +Probs.+185+%28spring+2007%29+pdf.

Lessig, L. (2010), 'For the Love of Culture. Google, Copyright, and our Future', *The New Republic*, **26.01.2010**.

Lessig, L. (2008), 'On the Google Book Search agreement', http://lessig.org/blog/2008/10/ on_the_google_book_search_agre.html.

Liu, J. P. (2004), 'Regulatory Copyright', *Boston College Law School Public Law and Legal Theory Research Paper Series*, **No.37**, Boston, http://papers.ssrn.com/sol3/papers. cfm?abstract_id=558681&.

Lohmann, F. von (2008), 'Google Book Search Settlement: A Reader's Guide', http://www. eff.org/deeplinks/2008/10/google-books-settlement-readers-guide.

Lucchi, N. (2007), 'The Supremacy of Techno-Governance: Privatization of Digital Content and Consumer Protection in the Globalized Information Society', *International Journal of Law and Information Technology*, **15(2)**, 192–225.

Madison, M. J. (2008), 'On Google Book Search', http://madisonian.net/2008/10/29/ on-google-book-search/.

Madison, M. J. (2003), 'Reconstructing the Software License', *Loyola University Chicago Law Journal*, **35**, 275.

Newitz, A. (2010), '5 Ways The Google Book Settlement Will Change The Future of Reading', io9 http://www.libraryjunction.net/blogs/item/5-ways-the-google-book-settlement-will- change-the-future-of-reading.

Nimmer, R. T. (2009), 'Google Book "Settlement" is Bad for Law, Copyright Owners and Users', http://www.ipinfoblog.com/archives/intellectual-property-google-book-settlement- is-bad-for-law-copyright-owners-and-users.html.

Nimmer, R. T. (2007), 'Licensing Information Assets in the New Economy: A Pro-Rights Perspective', *The Indian Journal of Law & Technology*, **3**, 1–24.

Peters, M. (2009), 'Competition and Commerce in Digital Books', **Serial No. 111-31**, Committee on the Judiciary House of Representatives, One Hundred Eleventh Congress.

Picker, R. C. (2009), 'The Google Book Search Settlement: A New Orphan-Works Monopoly?', *Olin Law and Economics Program Research Paper Series*, http://papers.ssrn. com/sol3/papers.cfm?abstract_id=1387582#.

Picker, R. C. (2008), 'Fair Use v. Fair Access', *John M. Olin Law & Economics Working Paper*, **No. 292**, http://www.law.uchicago.edu/Lawecon/index.html.

Privacy Authors and Publishers (2009), 'Privacy Authors and Publishers' Objection to Proposed Settlement', https://www.eff.org/files/filenode/authorsguild_v_google/File%20 Stamped%20Brf.pdf.

Radin, M. J. (2006), 'A Comment on Information Propertization and its Legal Milieu', *Cleveland State Law Review*, **54(1)**, 23–39.

Radin, M. J. (2004), 'Regulation by Contract, Regulation by Machine', *Journal of Institutional and Theoretical Economics*, **160**, 142–56.

Rifkin, J. (2000), *The Age of Access. How the Shift from Ownership to Access is Transforming Modern Life*, London: Penguin.

Riis, T. S. and J. Schovsbo (2010), 'Extended Collective Licenses and the Nordic Experience – It's a Hybrid but is it a VOLVO or a Lemon?', *Columbia Journal of Law and the Arts*, **33(4)**, http://papers.ssrn.com/sol3/papers.cfm?abstract_id=1535230.

Sag, M. (2010), 'The Google Book Settlement and the Fair Use Counterfactual', *New York Law School Law Review*, **55**, 19–75, http://www.nyls.edu/user_files/1/3/4/17/49/1080/551%20Final%20Sag%2011.17.10.pdf.

Salzberger, E. M. (2006), 'Economic Analysis of the Public Domain', in L. Guibault and B. Hugenholtz (eds), *The Future of the Public Domain: Identifying the Commons in Information Law*, Alphen an den Rijn: Kluwer, pp. 27–58.

Samuelson, P. (2011), 'The Google Book Settlement as Copyright Reform', *Wisconsin Law Review*, **2011(2)**, 479–562, http://ssrn.com/abstract=1683589.

Samuelson, P. (2010), 'Google Book Search and the Future of Books in Cyberspace', *Minnesota Law Review*, **94(5)**, 1308–74, http://ssrn.com/abstract=1535067.

Schmidt, E. (2005), 'Books of Revelation', *The Wall Street Journal*, A18.

Siegrist, H. (2006), 'Die Propertiserung von Gesellschaft und Kultur. Konstruktion und Institutionalisierung des Eigentums in der Moderne', *Comparativ. Leipziger Beiträge zur Universalgeschichte und vergleichenden Gesellschaftsforschung*, **16(5/6)**, 9–52.

Stepanians, M. (2005), 'Die angelsächsische Diskussion: Eigentum zwischen "Ding" und "Bündel". Was ist Eigentum?', A. Eckl and B. Ludwig (eds), *Philosophische Positionen von Platon bis Habermas*, München: C. H. Beck, pp. 232–45.

Taycher, L. (2010), 'Books of the World, Stand up and be Counted! All 129,864,880 of you', http://booksearch.blogspot.com/2010/08/books-of-world-stand-up-and-be-counted.html.

Toobin, J. (2007), 'Google's Moon Shot. The Quest for the Universal Library', *The New Yorker*, http://www.newyorker.com/reporting/2007/02/05/070205fa_fact_toobin.

Vaidhyanathan, S. (2007), 'The Googlization of Everything and the Future of Copyright', *University of California Davis Law Review*, **40**, 1207–31.

van Gompel, S. and B. Hugenholtz (2010), 'The Orphan Works Problem: The Copyright Conundrum of Digitizing Large-Scale Audiovisual Archives, and How to Solve It', *Popular Communication*, **8(1)**, 61–71.

Vuopala, A. (2010), 'Assessment of the Orphan Works Issue and Costs for Rights Clearance. Brussels', European Commission, DG Information Society and Media, http://ec.europa.eu/information_society/activities/digital_libraries/doc/reports_orphan/anna_report.pdf.

5. The legitimacy and accountability of the internet's governing institutions
Rolf H. Weber

INTRODUCTION

Internet governance tackles central questions such as: who rules the internet, in whose interest, by which mechanisms and for which purposes? These questions are of importance since internet regulations do not follow the traditional pattern pursuing an approach strictly distinguishing the state (public law) from the society (civil law) (Weber/Grosz 2007, pp. 119–20). Moreover, private organizations such as the Internet Corporation of Assigned Names and Numbers (ICANN), the Internet Society (ISOC) and the World Wide Web Consortium (W3C) play a crucial role in the governance structures of the internet.

Being the organizational home for entities responsible for internet infrastructure standards, including the Internet Engineering Task Force (IETF) and the Internet Architecture Board (IAB), the non-profit, non-governmental membership society ISOC's aim is to promote the development, availability and the associated technologies of the internet (Grosz 2009a, p. 621). Following its mission to lead the internet to its full potential the W3C as the main international standards organization for the World Wide Web is engaged in the development of common technical Web standards and promotes the harmonization of the Web's technologies (Grosz 2009b, p. 633). Since legitimacy and accountability problems of ISOC and W3C are of little importance, the chapter focuses on ICANN as the most important and most debated organization.

In this chapter, the framework of governance structures will be tackled from the perspectives of legitimacy of ICANN's constitution and the accountability of its officers for activities taken in the execution of the functions. The two key pillars are not identical, only interrelated, however, legitimacy and accountability are the core themes of the ongoing discussions.

(1) **Criteria for assessing states' legitimacy** need to be evaluated in the light of the existence of private international entities in the field of the internet. Furthermore, the realization of a concept of "multi-stakeholderism" as developed in the context of the World Summit on

the Information Society (WSIS) also influences the notion of legitimacy. Relevant aspects are the potential connections between private organizations and political institutions; in the case of ICANN the representative composition of ICANN's Board of Directors, the consent of the governed, and the establishment of a procedural framework related to the decision-making processes of the relevant private bodies (Malcolm 2008, pp. 3, 9, 20).

(2) **Accountability** stems from the latin word *accomptare* (to account), a prefix form of *computare* (to calculate), used in the money lending system developed in Ancient Greece and Rome (Weber 2009, p. 133). Accountability is the acknowledgement and assumption of responsibility for actions, products, decisions, and policies within the scope of the designated role. Accountability is a pervasive concept, encompassing political, legal, philosophical, and other aspects. Each context casts a different shade on the meaning of accountability; nevertheless, a general definition incorporating the main elements of accountability is directed to the obligation of a person (the accountable) to another person (the accountee), according to which the former must give account of, explain and justify his/her actions or decisions in an appropriate way.

Together with checks and balances, accountability is a prerequisite for legitimacy and a key element of any governance discussion. While checks and balances take place by providing established mechanisms to prevent the abuse of power, accountability steps in to do so by providing for or accessing actions with mechanisms such as non-judicial remedies, or judicial review. In particular, accountability implies that the stakeholders who form part of the governance mechanisms should be obliged to answer to anyone (Weber 2011, p. 134).

Accountability of internet governing bodies is not only important for the public to oversee the organizations' activities, but also serves the self-interest of the respective entities. A clear definition of the authority of each governing body and a justification for actions taken contributes to their respective effectiveness and credibility. Therefore, accountability has become an important topic in the discussion about the legitimacy of international bodies. Due to the lack of a "global democracy" to which organizations must abide, global administrative bodies are confronted with requests to overcome accountability gaps. In particular, accountability of internet governance organizations would require the disclosure of actions and information, evidencing whether the respective body has met the stated standards of conduct, and the correction or sanction of a person not complying with the standards.

LEGITIMACY

Present Situation and Criticisms

Notwithstanding the fact that ICANN is neither an international nor a legislative body, but a privately organized body, this organization is in charge of running the Domain Name System (DNS) and therefore responsible for deciding which devices can connect to the internet and under which names. ICANN's organizational structure, however, does not grant it the authority to issue legal norms; the chosen structure places the DNS outside the scope of sovereign legislative powers, i.e. beyond institutional review and without the public having any legitimizing influence.

During recent years, the organization of the DNS by ICANN has been subject to various objections in view of its quasi-legislative functions (Malcolm 2008, pp. 52–57). Also other internet organizations such as the World Wide Web Consortium (W3C) and Internet Engineering Task Force (IETF) have been criticized, both having the mandate to develop standards for the World Wide Web, and thus fulfilling a predominantly technical task without having a government mandate to develop the respective policies; both organizations lack the consensus of a broad community which could endorse such decisions, even if it is considered that boundaries between standard setting and public policy decisions are rather blurred.

Another important objection against ICANN's structure is related to the substantial influence that the United States possesses within the organization (Froomkin 2000, pp. 93–165; Weinberg 2000, pp. 187–260). Based on the standing other countries have within the organizational structure, much of the expressed criticism is based on the claim that ICANN lacks a democratic basis, which culminated in the challenge of ICANN's legitimacy to regulate the DNS. ICANN has responded to such objections by initiating different reforms, which particularly tackled the enhancement of democratic processes within the corporation, by supporting individual internet users' participation within ICANN's activities and particularly their role as an electing body of ICANN's Board Members.

Notwithstanding the mentioned developments, the claim that ICANN lacks democratic legitimacy has persisted. The multi-stakeholder approach does not directly apply in the decision-making processes of ICANN. Furthermore, the example of ICANN's At-Large Members Initiative reveals some particular problems with regard to democracy (Weber 2009, p. 108): the practicability of internet-wide elections with the aim of leading to a representative result by reflecting the shared will of the internet users world-wide is brought into question by the low number of participating electors. Although participation may have been increased through improved information of the potential internet users via additional communication channels on the internet, the question as to how world-wide representation can be achieved remains to be answered.

Furthermore, as long as the digital divide persists, global participation is a very ambitious objective, due to the fact that particularly developing countries do not have the same technical know-how or infrastructure which provides them with the same opportunities to engage in the information society. In addition, in the specific field of the internet, the question of how the election of specialized Board members can be secured and populist, symbolic results avoided remains paramount.

Elements of Increased Legitimacy – Right to Rule

Legitimacy can be perceived as a justification of authority, i.e. as establishing an authority's "right to rule". This interpretation can also be traced back to a translation of the Latin word *legitimus* as meaning "lawful, according to law". Particularly after the French Revolution in 1789, different theories attempted to explain legitimacy as a general concept regarding state authority, thereby aiming at filling the notion with more content.

The sociological doctrine on states' legitimacy goes back to Max Weber; by analyzing the general reasons why state authority is factually accepted, he distinguished three ideal types of governance, namely rational or legal, traditional and charismatic authority. Legitimacy may further be understood in a wider sense, encompassing an ethical-philosophical dimension, which heaves legitimacy above positive law. A similar differentiation has been adopted by Ian Clark, distinguishing between "normative theories" of legitimacy, which set out general criteria for evaluating the right to rule, and "empirical theories", which focus on belief systems of those subject to government (Clark 2005, pp. 18–19). Consequently, legitimacy can either be justified by formal ideas as the rule of law (legality) or by substantial value rationality based on morality and justice (Weber 2009, pp. 110–11).

According to a source-oriented perception of legitimacy, an authority may be qualified as legitimate when referring to democratic states which base their authority on the "*demos*", the public. The legitimacy of policy-making decisions on the internet may also be enhanced by procedural aspects within the different governing entities. This comprehension of legitimacy can be traced back to Niklas Luhmann (1975, pp. 9–53), who founded the doctrine on the effects of adequate procedures. In this tradition Thomas Franck described legitimacy as "the aspect of governance that validates institutional decisions as emanating from a right process.

What constitutes right process is described in a society's adjectival constitution of rules of order, or is pedigreed by tradition and historic custom" (Franck 1995, p. 1).

The procedural approach can be complemented by a result-oriented type of legitimacy, i.e. a substantive conception which looks at the outcome of the legitimizing procedures. This result-oriented approach depends on the values deemed as "right" by the stakeholders concerned, thus, in part leading back to the legitimizing sources which reveal a particular difficulty, because this idea relies on subjective perceptions of values which depend on cultural and societal differences and evolve over time. In view of the difficulty of operationalizing this approach, Jürgen Habermas (1992, p. 161) tried to link the procedural aspects with the "discourse principle", assuming that just those norms can claim validity which receive the approval of potentially affected people, insofar as they participate in a free rational discourse.

Such perceptions of legitimacy emphasize the concept's origin in the political sciences, i.e. the concept's primary applicability to nation states. Legitimacy in internet governance is confronted with the fact that not states, but private organizations are regulating bottom-up and that the technical policy-making standing is further challenged by the role such bodies play in international law.

Perception of Democracy

Legitimacy is often linked to democracy: the legitimizing basis of democratically appointed bodies is the mandate given by the public or any other competent body. Nevertheless, it cannot be overlooked that democracy, throughout history, has been differently shaped and framed. From the origins in Ancient Greece via the democracy elements proposed by Jean-Jacques Rousseau in his opus "Du contrat social ou principes du droit politique" (Amsterdam 1762) to modern democracies, different approaches have been chosen and scholars have shed light on the question whether democracy entails particular values and principles. At any rate, however, consent must be achieved from the governed; "deliberative democracy" focuses on the existence of "free, inclusive, rational debate" among citizens which determines the underlying point of public policy. As a consequence, democracy is perceived as hinging on the open exchange of views and informed debates (Weber 2009, pp. 112–13).

Nevertheless, the brief overview reveals particular difficulties in crystallizing a generally acknowledged content common to the different understandings and characteristics inherent in the rather heterogeneous concept of democracy. Therefore, the application of state-based principles to multi-stakeholder actors in internet governance encompassing both states and non-state actors, is not a panacea but a rather complicated venture (Weber/Grosz 2009, pp. 316–30). In a nutshell, relying on democracy and democratic principles in order to enhance legitimacy in internet governance increases risks that one very complex and vague generic word could merely be replaced by another, without much contribution having been made to the actual content of the terms. Furthermore, dependence on individual theories alone, e.g. the source-based approach to legitimacy, for the enhancement of the legitimate governing of the internet as a whole poses the risk of adopting a too narrow perception and thus of not corresponding to the broad and manifold notion legitimacy implicates (Weber 2009, pp. 114–15).

Possible Improvements of Legitimacy – Personal Approach

As outlined, state-based democracy cannot be applied one-to-one to internet governing entities; moreover, an adequate approach endorses the idea of adopting particular elements – commonly perceived as "democracy" – that provide for valuable inputs. Such constituents should include transparency obligations and the implementation of accountability mechanisms, as well as procedures enabling consensus making. Along with the so-called "disaggregation" of states, coordination among the different entities of private and public nature across borders, between and among like agencies could create a new web of relations and thus a new transgovernmental (horizontal) order (Slaughter 2004, pp. 12–15). Besides the fact that such government networks are deemed more flexible and efficient in contrast to centralized, hierarchical procedures of international institutions, this form of transnationalism is also regarded as enjoying greater legitimacy.

In order to give the governed the assurance that their own values are being represented in the decisions made, it must be decided who would be the governed stakeholders of the internet governing organizations. Only clarity about the different actors involved can be the starting point for enhancing legitimacy. The heterogeneity of the different actors in the field of the internet has been addressed by the concept of "multistakeholderism", which encompasses governments, the private sector, civil society and international organizations. The sources of the different stakeholders' legitimacy deserve particular analysis: whilst democratic entitlement may suffice for state government, the private sector might generally derive its legitimacy from superior efficiency characteristics. Civil society could be perceived as a stakeholder due to the mere fact of being particularly affected by decisions about the governance of the internet or by the substantive values it promotes. Nevertheless, the question arises as to whether this suffices to make civil society a legitimate actor or whether particular experience and expertise can be demanded (Weber 2009, pp. 116–17).

Shifting the focus to the different organizational bodies involved in the manifold aspects of the internet helps channel the very broad stakeholder basis into an intermediate level of representatives within the organizational structures. For example, standard-setting organizations such as the IETF probably involve more technically specialized stakeholders than the Internet Governance Forum (IGF), which was established as a public policy forum.

Consequently, legitimate "representatives" would result from responsible entities on the national and international level. In terms of multi-stakeholderism, civil society, i.e. citizens alone, would not form a legitimate basis, but would have to be complemented by all the people affected by the governance of the internet.

Procedural Approach

Effective techniques of consensus-building could improve the organizations' legitimacy in terms of Niklas Luhmann's approach to legitimacy through process. Procedures are to be established which give bargaining power to all the participants and thus ensure equal opportunities, also for stakeholders with less powerful interests (Weber 2009, p. 118). Indeed, multi-stakeholderism is a general concept taking into account the substantial differences among the players in internet policies. Reasonable mechanisms should enable participation and interaction to take place on fair terms, so as to give different stakeholders a real voice. Fairness can be framed as embracing both legitimacy and justice, and as establishing the term "fairness doctrine" as a way forward in enhancing legitimacy of international law and its institutions. Generally, it is crucial that organizations governing the internet inform their stakeholders and make effective use of the often bespoken "facilitated information flow" on the internet. As a consequence, the involvement in decision-making processes should strengthen public confidence in the decisions taken and enhance their legitimacy (Weber/Weber 2009, pp. 9, 13).

On top of procedural "fairness" rules, human rights can be perceived as fundamental principles for implementing good governance. The establishment of consensus on such core values – either for the internet as a whole or for the governance of specific sectors of the internet – should be a main issue in the field of internet governance. Architectural principles could be compiled in an international legal framework for the internet as a general statement with soft law implications (Weber 2009, p. 119).

Not surprisingly, the acknowledgement prevails more and more that legitimacy for ICANN consists of the consent of the government, a fair process, and fidelity to mission (Gunnarson 2010, p. 20). These virtues, more commonly attributed to governments than corporations, seem to fit the description of an organization with ICANN's government-like control of the internet DNS. Process and mission should not be too difficult to reform. The kind of fair process most commonly referred to in this context involves "strong provisions for checks and balances, and avenues of recourse" as well as "provisions for evaluation and oversight and/or mechanisms for appeal". ICANN's legitimacy depends on whether it can obtain the consent of those it governs, establish fair procedures by which to act and settle the long-simmering debate over its proper mission.

ACCOUNTABILITY

Present Situation and Criticisms

During the last few years, debates about accountability of ICANN[1] and other internet organizations have been quite intensive. The tasks to be fulfilled by ICANN are described in the Affirmation of Commitments (AoC) between ICANN and the US Department of Commerce (DoC) as being in place since October 2009, as well as in ICANN's corporate documentation. All in all, however, the self-regulatory legal framework is relatively meager. Nevertheless, the fact that ICANN has realized the importance of accountability provisions is – at least indirectly – reflected in the following documents:

(1) In Article III Section 1, the bylaws of ICANN state that the corporation "shall operate to the maximum extent feasible in an open and transparent manner and consistent with procedures designed to ensure fairness". Furthermore, Article I Section 2 includes several objectives such as "remaining accountable to the Internet community through mechanisms that enhance ICANN's effectiveness" (No. 10).
(2) In its Annual Reports, ICANN regularly emphasizes the need to uphold and improve accountability standards. In order to comply with this objective it is stated that "a regular review of performance is an important aspect of seeking continuous improvement in effectiveness and accountability" (ICANN, Annual Report 2009, p. 76).
(3) The President's Strategy Committee proposed in its Report of February 2009, 24 "detailed recommendations", encompassing, for example, measures to enhance the public consultation process and to manage its revenue growth in line with its core mission and mandate.

(4)   The Affirmation of Commitments (AoC) with the US Department of Commerce contains the following provisions: ICANN and the US DoC envisage with the AoC to (i) ensure the outcome of ICANN's decision-making as being accountable, transparent, and in the global internet users' interest, (ii) preserve DNS's security and stability, (iii) promote competition, consumer trust, and consumer choice in the DNS market place and (iv) advance DNS's international participation. Particularly, the AoC highlights the importance of ICANN's decisions being in the public interest and not just the interests of a particular set of stakeholders. The AoC's intention is that ICANN shall no longer be subject to unilateral oversight by the US DoC, but reviewed constantly by independent panels, consisting of inter alia volunteer community members, the Chair of ICANN's Governmental Advisory Committee (GAC), the Chair of the Board of ICANN, and representatives of the relevant ICANN Advisory Committees. Subsequently, the review's output shall be published for public comment. In order to promote the ongoing internet governance process, the AoC contains no time limit, even if it can be amended at any time by mutual consent of the parties.

Although the AoC states that the headquarters of ICANN will remain in the United States, which means that the problem of legitimacy of a private not-for-profit body under Californian law acting as a technical coordinator of the critical internet resources of the global community is not changing, the AoC seems to be a step into the right direction. The principles of acting in the public interest, of transparency and accountability – if duly implemented – will help to strengthen the legitimacy of ICANN to continue its role as coordinator of the DNS system for the global community.

During the last few years, governments and government-affiliated organizations characterized ICANN's accountability as hardly far-reaching (Gunnarson 2010, pp. 13–15 with further references). Many countries refer to the need to address several fundamental accountability questions. Registrars and registries seem to be even more critical of ICANN's lack of accountability by referring to the fact that "absent (i) additional accountability mechanisms, (ii) appropriate oversight mechanisms, and (iii) a greater commitment to contract enforcement, ICANN remains at risk of failing to maintain the core principle of stability, competition, private-sector coordination and representation". Trade associations, public interest groups, and individual businesses likewise singled out ICANN's lack of accountability.

Recently, as mentioned, ICANN took more and more note of the criticisms aimed at its accountability. Therefore, the organization accepted in the Affirmation of Commitments that a review of the accountability and transparency matters should be executed; in the meantime, the final recommendations of the Accountability and Transparency Review Team (ATRT) are available (ATRT 2010).

ICANN's Elements of Increased Accountability – Objectives of Accountability

In its own documentation, ICANN distinguishes three types of accountability which encompass three ways of actions (Accountability & Transparency Frameworks and Principles 2008, p. 4):

- *Public sphere accountability* deals with mechanisms for assuring stakeholders that ICANN has behaved responsibly;
- *Corporate and legal accountability* covers ICANN's obligations under the legal system and its bylaws;
- *Participating community accountability* ensures that the Board and the executive perform functions in line with the wishes and expectations of the ICANN community.

Obviously, inherent tensions exist among the three types of accountability, making it necessary to establish effective navigation mechanisms which allow for a careful weighing and balancing of the diverging interests involved (Weber 2009, p. 136). In particular, ICANN is accountable to the global community or the public at-large rather than to any specific "member" or group of "members". Therefore, accountability can be framed along the following three elements (Weber 2011, p. 134):

- Standards need to be introduced that hold governing bodies accountable, at least on the organizational level; such standards help to improve accountability.
- Information should be made more readily available to the concerned governed, enabling them to apply the standards in question to the performance of those who are held to account; in order to make information flow active rather than passive, consultation procedures are to be established.
- Beneficiaries of accountability must be able to impose some sort of sanction, thus, attaching costs to the failure to meet the standards; such "sanctioning" is only possible if adequate participation schemes are devised through direct voting channels and indirect representation schemes.

Generally, any form of accountability is based on the assumption that objectives and standards exist against which an action or decision may be assessed. Such improved accountability, be it ex ante (a priori) or ex post (a posteriori), would also help to overcome the already discussed problem of legitimacy of internet governing bodies and to increase the effectiveness of activities (Weber 2009, p. 140).

Furthermore, an important feature of accountability is the criterion of control. Any debate regarding accountability occurs in relation to the measures taken to improve representativeness and transparency and also in relation to the exercise of power and the legitimacy of the measures adopted as well as the standards defined (Senn 2011, p. 262). In a way, accountability can be interpreted as a means to achieve legitimacy even if the extent of accountability and its formalization can vary.

Levels of Accountability

Accountability can be improved on several levels, namely the organizational level, the project level and the policy level (Weber 2009, pp. 137–40):

(1) *Organizational level*: In terms of a democratic governance understanding, the most important element of the decision-making processes should lie in the hands of the body establishing the constitutional level or international agreements, respectively. Addressing the roots of a voting system, the extent of adequacy of the traditional "one-person = one-vote" principle in internet governance can be questioned.

Accountability is further affected by the partial lack of transparency with respect to deliberations of the decision-making bodies in internet governance. Obviously, secrecy provisions for statements made by individuals in established bodies of an organization play a certain role; however, secrecy provisions should not be used as pretext for not revealing how decisions were made, i.e. on what grounds and with which objectives. In democratic states, governments typically bolster public accountability through measures of institutional checks and balances in which certain branches or agencies of the government are empowered to oversee and sanction others. No such "horizontal" mechanism exists in the context of internet governance and ICANN in particular: external review bodies have not been available so far and traditional control does not exist in respect of policy decisions by the highest bodies of the internet. Furthermore, virtually no judicial review is available in internet governance matters; governance rules do not fall under courts' judicial competences.

(2) *Project level*: The technological changes and business needs in the use of the internet require substantial project work to be performed by the internet's governing bodies, mainly ICANN. Many working

groups exist, each of them engaged in the elaboration of techniques and technical models. In principle, it would be possible to design specific information disclosure or other safeguard policies, which could contribute to the information of the public on such developments and thereby increase accountability. Yet, such a compliance regime does not exist in ICANN.

So far, the Board of ICANN has not established quality assurance bodies to address the manifold aspects of accountability. Therefore, it is quite difficult for civil society to evaluate conduct (and misconduct) of the project working groups and to hold to account the respective bodies. An additional problem consists in the fact that civil society does not play a role in the more technical steering groups and therefore does not have a direct influence on the technical expertise; as a result, cooperation between the institutionalized "technical" bodies and civil society is not encouraged and also not seen as a reasonable option, instead perceived as investment of time and capacity.

(3)   *Policy level*: The policies chosen by the competent bodies of the internet have a major impact on the future of infrastructural networks; therefore, such policies should be checked in view of the needs and wishes of the netizens. Practically, this objective could be achieved through feedback mechanisms designed to play an important role, also regarding accountability. Policy processes need to be consultative in the sense that civil society is invited to comment on policy proposals.

A first possibility to observe the feedback approach could consist in the distribution of interactive drafts of policy provisions prior to their release for comments from civil society. According to its own documentation, the Board of ICANN is indeed asked to look for comments from civil society: Article I Section 2 of the bylaws provides for consultation processes in order to achieve the aim of "seeking and supporting broad, informed participation reflecting the functional, geographic and cultural diversity of the Internet at all levels of policy development and decision-making" (No. 4) as well as "employing open and transparent policy development mechanisms that (i) promote well-informed decisions based on expert advice, and (ii) ensure that those entities most affected can assist in the policy development process" (No. 7).

Another mechanism could consist in the publication of a matrix which compiles all comments and explains how each input was addressed within the policy review, or why it was not approved of. Thereby, civil society would become aware of its input's potential effect on the reasoning of the competent bodies in accepting or rejecting comments; such an approach would establish a high level of accountability (Weber 2009, p. 140).

Accountability and Transparency Review Team

Subsequent to the signing of the Affirmation of Commitments, the Accountability and Transparency Review Team (ATRT) was established (Para. 9.1 of the AoC) and has conducted extensive interactions with the ICANN authorities as well as with non-governmental organizations and the public in order to prepare final recommendations which should allow consideration of future improvements of the accountability mechanisms. The ATRT created four Working Groups addressing the following subjects, respectively (ATRT 2010):

- *Working Group 1*: ICANN Board of Directors governance, performance and composition;
- *Working Group 2*: Role and effectiveness of the GAC and its interaction with the Board;
- *Working Group 3*: Public input processes and the policy development process;
- *Working Group 4*: Review mechanisms for Board decisions.

Together with its appendices, the Final Recommendations of the ATRT encompass 200 pages (published as of December 31, 2010); apart from its own work, the ATRT selected the Berkman Center for Internet & Society at Harvard Law School to act as Independent Expert for the review; the Berkman Center delivered an extensive expert report on October 20, 2010 being now a part of the ATRT Final Recommendations.

(1) Working Group 1 looked at two broad areas, namely the composition of the Board, skill-set requirements for the Board and the roles of several committees in respect of the Board composition as well as the transparency of the Board's decision-making process and the explanation of its decisions to the ICANN community. Concerns expressed were the relative weight of some stakeholder groups in the Board, the lack of transparency in certain special committees and the skill-set of the Board. The recommendations of the ATRT encompass the benchmarking of Board skill-sets against similar corporate and other governance structures, the tailoring of the required skills to suit ICANN's unique structure and mission, mainly through an open consultation process, including direct consultation with the leadership of committees, the review of these requirements annually, and the increase of transparency in the nomination process. The specific recommendations submitted by the ATRT are to be fulfilled within the year 2011 (ATRT 2010, p. 19). Since then the ICANN Board has approved them in full (ICANN 2011, para. 2) but has so far failed to solicit the expert study of Board review mechanisms called

for by the ATRT (Gunnarson 2012). Furthermore, the Board should be responsible for a thorough and reasoned explanation of decisions taken, the rationale thereof and the sources of data and information on which the ICANN relied (ATRT 2010, p. 29).

(2)   Working Group 2 came to the conclusion that the current Board–GAC relationship is dysfunctional and should be improved, for example by clarifying what GAC "advice" would constitute, by improving cooperation based on GAC advice in a more timely manner, by developing and implementing a process to engage the GAC earlier in the policy development process and by increasing the level of support and commitments of governments to the GAC process (ATRT 2010, pp. 37, 38).

(3)   Working Group 3 pointed to the timeliness and effectiveness of policy-making as major concern and invited the Board to adopt and to specify a timeline for the implementation of public notice and comment processes (ATRT 2010, p. 44).

(4)   Working Group 4 questioned whether the existing accountability review mechanisms would satisfy the criteria to be expected under the given circumstances. This part relies quite substantially on the Expert Report of the Berkman Center which contains very valuable research results (ATRT 2010, pp. 53–55). Thereby, the Berkman Center analyzes mechanisms for accountability, transparency, public participation, and corporate governance, based on a so-called issues cluster, encompassing structural issues (related to what is described as the "DNA" of ICANN), procedural issues (related to procedures within a given institutional framework), and substantive issues (related to substantive ICANN activities and decisions) (ATRT 2010, pp. 81–86 and 91).

Based on the findings related to the need for increased transparency, the Berkman Center submits the recommendation that ICANN should create and implement policies and processes for conducting and communicating regular transparency audits due to the lack of a comprehensive audit of ICANN's information activities which makes it difficult to assess its practices across active, passive, and participatory transparency. Furthermore, the Berkman Center invites the ICANN Board to better delineate areas of high, medium, and limited disclosure of Board inputs, deliberations, and decisions, and the rationale for each, as well as to offer detailed explanations of the reasons for taking various decisions, including the manner in which expert opinion and community input are factored into these decisions (ATRT 2010, pp. 93–113).

For the time being, ICANN provides three avenues for review of Board and staff decisions, namely the Ombudsman, the Reconsideration Requests, and the Independent Review Panel (IRP); to varying degrees, each mechanism is aimed at increasing ICANN's accountability. According to the bylaws, the Ombudsman "shall serve as an advocate for fairness" (Article V Section 2 ICANN Bylaw) in cases in which the Reconsideration Request and the IRP procedures have not been invoked. The Reconsideration Request and IRP "are intended to reinforce the various accountability mechanisms otherwise set forth" (Article IV Section 1 ICANN Bylaw). The Berkman Center mainly looks at the IRP, considering the design of the existing process in general and the current (broad) scope of IRP review as provided in the bylaws in particular; thereby, the Berkman Report concludes that it is not advisable to implement such a broad-reaching binding third-party review of any Board decisions and actions, arguing with normative policy and governance perspective reasons as well as reasons of Californian corporate law (ATRT 2010, p. 115). Rather, the creation of more robust and better-defined processes upfront for policy and other decision-making is proposed. Thereby, the Berkman Center submits the recommendation to better define the scope of the IRP processes, with an eye not only on better access and fairness, but also on cost containment and early identification of issues that should be fully argued and briefed and those that can be resolved at the more summary level. For the time being, *ICM v. ICANN* is the only request for independent review that has been heard by an IRP on the merits; in this case, the IRP consisted of a three-member panel of arbitrators contracted by the International Centre for Dispute Resolution; the Berkman Center Report analyzes in detail the respective procedures and the questions which had to be tackled in these proceedings (ATRT 2010, pp. 181–89).

During the next months, the ICANN Board is supposed to take action regarding the implementation of the recommendations of the ATRT. Expecting the recommendations' full adoption and implementation, the ATRT asked the Board to prepare a first status report on all recommendations to be presented at the ICANN meeting no. 40 in San Francisco, 13–18 March 2011. Within the frame of this meeting the ICANN Board found that "all 27 of the recommendations have the potential to advance ICANN's transparency and accountability objectives and may be implemented by ICANN following careful and transparent consideration". Since the ATRT recommendations do not appear to have a negative impact on the security and stability of the DNS, the Board pledged to develop final implementation plans in a timely manner (ICANN, Adopted Board Resolutions). Furthermore, the ATRT asked the Board to prepare a more formal report to be presented at the ICANN meeting no. 41 in Singapore, 19–24 June 2011.

Possible Improvements of Accountability – Consultation and Inclusion of Civil Society

In democratic nation states, governments typically bolster public accountability through institutional checks and balances based on transparent information; in the field of the internet, corresponding procedures do not yet exist. Therefore, consultation processes should be put into effect to help streamline the establishment and the implementation of policies; consultation with civil society allows potential disputes to be addressed at an early stage and looking for solutions within due time.

The design of consultation processes depends on the matters involved and on the availability of active groups. However, users of the internet should not only be consulted in the preparatory phase of any project, but also be informed after its implementation. Feedback mechanisms concerning reviewing processes need to be consistently utilized – an aspect which would also allow the participants in the process to understand how their insights and expertise have influenced the policy outcomes. By presenting the results of negotiations, communications and dialogues to civil society, accountability would be enhanced and facilitated (Weber/Weber 2009, p.91).

Consultation processes require the disclosure of information. Concerns of civil society regarding accountability, in particular at the project level, usually address transparency issues. In the meantime, ICANN has realized the importance of transparency and has initiated certain measures to improve the situation. The open communication of governing bodies improves stakeholders' confidence, and transparent minimum quality standards enhance the internet's conditions and the assessment of performance and accountability as well as facilitating the coordination of internet governance-related regulations. Transparent procedures allow for a certain level of "democratic" legitimization and credibility through active involvement of citizens as well as through a certain control over the decision-making processes. Since a transparent methodology for rulemaking processes based on revisable procedures reduces mistrust and can have a legitimizing effect, transparency should become a persistent objective of governance mechanisms (Weber 2009, p.132).

Making activities and achieved results accountable to the "public" is particularly important in respect to participation of civil society. The internet governing bodies can only be held to account if their activities are visible and subject to evaluation. Therefore, accountability should also extend to monitoring stages related to actual efforts and empower the development of effectiveness through citizen participation. Different kinds of capacities need to be made available in order to meaningfully improve participation during a decision-making process (Weber 2009, p. 142), namely (1) the ability to understand and criticize technical issues, (2) sufficient knowledge on the given structures and potentials, and (3) the skills necessary to negotiate with more powerful actors. Therefore, respective assistance to civil society has to be provided by the competent bodies. If the participatory processes are considered to be insufficient or if concerns and comments by the public have not been adequately addressed by the competent internet bodies, civil society should also be able to get redress.

According to its Management Operating Principles on Accountability and Transparency Frameworks and Principles (2008, pp. 25, 26), ICANN aims at maximizing participation in any consultation by:

- Providing information on upcoming issues as far as possible in advance to give the internet community time to respond;
- Maintaining a calendar of current consultations and, where practicable, forthcoming consultations;
- Using online fora as the basic mechanism for conducting consultation;
- Providing sufficient context and background material to enable participants to understand the issues on which they are being asked to comment;
- Making clear the purpose of the consultation and the way in which comments will be used;
- Using developments in technology to enhance the consultation process;
- Maintaining a public participation site that encourages the community to discuss particular issues ahead of time and to clarify arguments and positions in advance.

A specific approach adopted from national democratic frameworks consists in the implementation of direct elections. Generally, direct elections are seen as a mechanism to reduce the accountability deficit and the legitimacy problem. However, ICANN's original attempt to integrate direct elections of (a part of) its Board of Directors into its organizational structure was deemed a failure and consequently stopped, particularly due to the very small percentage of voting internet users who actually participated in the elections (De Vey Mestdagh/Rijgersberg 2007, p. 29).

However, whether the decision to terminate that experiment was in fact the right one remains doubtful (Weber 2009, p. 143), especially because the other option of encouraging the public to vote was not even given a chance. The untried option would admittedly have contributed to an improvement of accountability. Information about the possibility to vote could have been disseminated on the internet itself, but also through other channels such as newspapers, radio and television. Therewith, a broader public might have been approached. If individuals only use the internet for specific purposes or very infrequently, they most probably will not visit ICANN's webpage and therefore will not have known about the elections. However, these individuals might still be interested in the subject and be likely to vote if they were informed of the possibility.

Monitoring, Supervision and Sanctioning

The design of consultation processes involving internet users and their participation in decision-making processes makes it desirable to establish a monitoring process. A possible solution to this problem could be seen in the establishment of an overseeing board on the operations of the internet governing bodies, being also charged with the task of balancing the confidentiality interests of the Board of Directors and the accountability to be provided to internet users (Weber 2011, p. 137).

A "natural" approach for monitoring governing bodies' accountability would consist in strengthening the market accountability by being based on informal economic mechanisms rather than on highly formal hierarchical control types (De Vey Mestagh/Rijgersberg 2007, p. 32). The implementation of accountability mechanisms reflecting the responsiveness to customer needs would imply that the internet governing bodies should more strongly assume the role of private enterprises, focusing on the wishes and desires of internet users. Since the needs of market participants might not always be easily understandable and the definition of relevant markets difficult to achieve in a global framework, participation of civil society and the "customer side" in decision-making bodies should be increased to help crystallize the different market participants' needs and interests. The At-Large Advisory Committee (ALAC) stands out as a suitable body to collect the ideas and inputs of the internet community since it is the ALAC's primary role to consider and provide advice on the activities of ICANN, insofar as the advice relates to the interests of individual internet users.

The market-oriented accountability model could also benefit from the potential availability of alternative root server systems and competing TLD provisions. However, rules need to be established in this context to avoid the occurrence of market abuses in case a few providers of the technical infrastructure take control of access to the network without regard to the basic "checks and balances" principles (Weber 2009, p. 146).

A slightly more work-intensive possibility to increase the accountability of the internet governing bodies and to tackle the apparent legitimacy problem consists in the introduction of some kind of supervision. This topic has been intensively discussed in the UN Working Group on Internet Governance (WGIG) as well as during the UN World Summit on the Information Society (WSIS) in November 2005 (Tunis). The establishment of the Internet Governance Forum (IGF) was the outcome of this process; the IGF should facilitate the collection of voices of civil society and bring forward proposals for the improvement of internet governance. Nevertheless, certain limitations to the mechanisms of the IGF are not to be overlooked. First, reports should be prepared better and contributions synthesized in order to give the public a better understanding of the content of consultations. Second, more detailed documents and the precise reasons leading to a particular decision should be provided to the public. Third, ways for the public to object to decisions of the Secretariat or Advisory Group which are not in accordance with the consensus of the plenary body need to be established (Malcolm 2008, pp. 498–99).

Accountees must be able to impose some sort of disciplinary and enforcement powers, thus attaching costs to the failure to meet the standards. Such "sanctioning" is only possible if adequate participation schemes allow the concerned persons to get hold of the relevant information constituting the basis for redress (Weber 2011, p. 137):

- Sanctions can be of a civil or criminal nature. Civil law accountability mechanisms encompass legal remedies to claim compensation for losses; as a rule, such remedies will be provided for by the applicable national civil law framework. From a governance and policy perspective, providing effective grievance mechanisms for those who believe that they have been harmed contributes to restoring trust in the business system. Yet, traditional remedies are not easily available to everybody, and additionally, they may be cost and time intensive. A minimum framework, which could be established by the legislator, would have to include legitimacy with regard to the decision-making courts, fair and equitable procedures, accessibility of courts and predictability of judicial outcomes.
- The legislative approach must also include criminal sanctions that can be imposed on those accountable in the case of non-compliance with accountability criteria. Widely accepted criminal standards could help implement legitimizing structures and the guideline for governance principles. Experience shows that compliance with standards is generally increased by the threat of criminal sanctions in the case of violations.

In a nutshell, responsibility should be commensurate with the extent of the power possessed, i.e. accountability concerns itself with power and power cannot be divorced from responsibility.

OUTLOOK

Enhanced legitimacy in internet governance is a daunting task; therefore, different approaches to advance legitimacy should be scrutinized. The crucial question reads as follows: which governed "demos" forms the basis that is in a position to decide on legitimacy? Based upon this first appreciation, consensus should be secured as to how the players can effectively receive a legitimizing background in order to represent the multi-stakeholders within the different organizational structures. Thereby, differentiation is needed: whilst valuable inputs deriving from prominent concepts should be adopted, new approaches that challenge existing international internet governing entities and actors and at the same time freshly address aspects of legitimacy are not to be eschewed (Weber 2009, p. 120). In a nutshell, ICANN's form does not follow its function (Gunnarson 2011, p. 22). Legitimacy for ICANN in particular must encompass the consent of the governed, a fair process, and fidelity to the mission as basic virtues (Frankel 2002, p. 1; Gunnarson 2011, p. 21).

Accountability is regularly called for to improve the governance regimes of organizations in the field of the internet in terms of enhancing their legitimacy. Accountability has been principally addressed and developed within ICANN as the pre-eminent organization in the field of internet governance. However, the difficulties in establishing accountability principles as part of an adequate internet governance model for the virtual sphere should not be underestimated. Improvements of the accountability elements are possible, but the details need thorough discussion.

For the enhancement of accountability in internet governance, it is helpful to frame accountability to include the following three elements (Buchanan/Keohane 2008, p. 51; Weber 2009, p. 147):

- Standards need to be introduced which hold governing bodies accountable, at least at the organizational level; such standards help to improve accountability.
- Information should be made more easily available to accountability-holders, enabling them to apply the standards in question to the performance of those who are held to account; in order to make information flow rather active than passive (seen from a recipient's point of view) consultation procedures are to be established.

● Accountability-holders must be able to impose some sort of sanction, thus, attaching costs to the failure to meet the standards; such kind of "sanctioning" is only possible if adequate participation schemes are realized, for example through direct voting channels or indirect representation schemes, but also through the implementation of judicial review bodies.

In particular the establishment of standards in terms of specific values that lay the foundation of accountability could provide for a viable way forward. Similarly to a Magna Charta, such standards could help implement a legitimizing structure and a guideline for internet governance. Furthermore, they would be suitable to entail significant self-constraints for the policy-making institutions, and hence, move towards substantiating the realistic implementation of accountability (Weber 2009, p. 147).

NOTE

1. For an overview see Weber and Gunnarson (2012).

REFERENCES

Accountability and Transparency Review Team (ATRT) (2010), 'Final Recommendations of the Accountability and Transparency Review Team', http://www.icann.org/en/reviews/affirmation/atrt-final-recommendations-31dec10-en.pdf, accessed 29 March 2011.

Buchanan, A. and R. O. Keohane (2008), 'Legitimacy of Global Governance Institutions', in R. Wolfrum and V. Röben (eds), *Legitimacy in International Law*, Berlin/Heidelberg, Germany and New York, US: Springer, 25–62.

Clark, I. (2005), *Legitimacy in International Society*, Oxford: Oxford University Press.

De Vey Mestdagh, K. and R. W. Rijgersberg (2007), 'Rethinking Accountability in Cyberspace: A New Perspective on ICANN', *International Review of Law, Computers & Technology*, **21**, 27–38.

Franck, T. (1995), *Fairness in International Law and Institutions*, Oxford: Oxford University Press.

Frankel, T. (2002), 'Report to the Markle Foundation, Accountability and Oversight of the Internet Corporation for Assigned Names and Numbers (ICANN)', http://papers.ssrn.com/sol3/papers.cfm?abstract_id=333342, accessed 29 March 2011.

Froomkin, A. M. (2000), 'Wrong Turn in Cyberspace: Using ICANN to Route around the APA and the Constitution', *Duke Law Journal*, **50**, 17–184.

Grosz, M. (2009a), 'Internet Society', in C. Tietje and A. Brouder (eds), *Handbook of Transnational Economic Governance Regimes*, Leiden: Martinus Nijhoff Publishers, 622–31.

Grosz, M. (2009b), 'World Wide Web Consortium', in C. Tietje and A. Brouder (eds), *Handbook of Transnational Economic Governance Regimes*, Leiden: Martinus Nijhoff Publishers, 633–41.

Gunnarson, R. S. (2010), 'A Fresh Start for ICANN', http://forum.icann.org/lists/atrt-questions-2010/pdfORuEyja140.pdf, accessed 29 March 2011.

Gunnarson, R. S. (2012), Failing to act on Accountability, 24 January 2012, available at http://www.circleid.com/posts/failing_to_act_on_accountability/.

Habermas, J. (1992), *Faktizität und Geltung, Beiträge zur Diskurstheorie des Rechts und des demokratischen Rechtstaats*, Frankfurt a.M.: Suhrkamp.

ICANN, Accountability & Transparency Frameworks and Principles, January 2008, available at: http://www.icann.org/en/transparency/acct-trans-frameworks-principles-10jan08.pdf.

ICANN, Annual Report 2009, available at http://icann.org/en/about/annual-report/annual-report-2009-en.pdf.

ICANN, Adopted Board Resolutions, 24 June 2011, available at http://www.icann.org/en/minutes/resolutions-24jun11-en.htm#2.

Luhmann, N. (1975), *Legitimation durch Verfahren*, 2nd ed., Darmstadt and Neuwied: Luchterhand.

Malcolm, J. (2008), *Multi-Stakeholder Governance and the Internet Governance Forum*, Perth: Terminus Press.

Senn, M. (2011), *Non-State Regulatory Regimes*, Berlin and Heidelberg: Springer.

Slaughter, A.-M. (2004), *A New World Order*, Princeton, NJ: Princeton University Press.

Weber, R. H. (2009), *Shaping Internet Governance: Regulatory Challenges*, Zurich: Schulthess.

Weber, R. H. (2011), 'Accountability in the Internet of Things', *Computer Law & Security Review*, **27**, 133–38.

Weber, R. H. and M. Grosz (2007), 'Internet Governance – From Vague Ideas to Realistic Implementation', *Medialex*, **3**, 119–35.

Weber, R. H. and M. Grosz (2009), 'Legitimate Governing of the Internet', *International Journal of Private Law*, **2**, 316–30.

Weber, R. H. and R. S. Gunnarson (2012), 'A constitutional solution for internet governance', SSRN, http://papers.ssrn.com/sol3/papers.cfm?abstract_id=2076780.

Weber, R. H. and R. Weber (2009), 'Social Contract for the Internet Community? Historical and Philosophical Theories as Basis for the Inclusion of Civil Society in Internet Governance?', *SCRIPT-ed*, **6**, 90–105.

Weinberg, J. (2000), 'ICANN and the Problem of Legitimacy', *Duke Law Journal*, **50**, 187–260.

6. Network neutrality and network management regulation: quality of service, price discrimination, and exclusive contracts
Nicholas Economides and Joacim Tåg

INTRODUCTION

The topic of network neutrality regulation is both important and controversial. The issue concerns mainly two questions. First, should the networks that provide last mile access to residential users be able to manage or restrict the packets of data flowing through their networks in a way so that some types of packets or packets from certain content providers are favored? Second, should the network operators be allowed to charge content and applications providers' fees for faster access to consumers (either through a dedicated last mile line or through obtaining prioritized access)? Proponents of network neutrality regulations fear that without regulation, network operators will be in a position to favor their own content, pick the winners among content providers, create artificial congestion in the last mile, reduce the availability of content and negatively affect innovation incentives for content providers "at the edge" of the internet.[1] Opponents of network neutrality regulations argue that the ability to manage and restrict traffic on their lines is needed to ensure efficient use of the network and to ensure Quality of Service (QoS). They also state that revenue from charging content providers for faster access is needed to encourage new investments in network infrastructure.

In the United States, the Federal Communications Commission (FCC) proposed in October 2009 a Notice of Proposed Rulemaking (NPRM), a strict non-discrimination rule that imposed non-discrimination, defined in paragraph 104 as follows: "We understand the term 'nondiscriminatory' to mean that a broadband Internet access service provider may not charge a content, application, or service provider for enhanced or prioritized access to the subscribers of the broadband Internet access service provider".

In its final rule on network neutrality adopted in December 2010, the FCC retreated considerably from its NPRM proposal and imposed (1) Transparency: Fixed and mobile broadband providers must disclose the network management practices, performance characteristics, and terms and conditions of their broadband services; (2) No blocking: Fixed broadband providers may not block lawful content, applications, services, or non-harmful devices; mobile broadband providers may not block lawful websites, or block applications that compete with their voice or video telephony services; (3) No unreasonable discrimination: Fixed broadband providers may not unreasonably discriminate in transmitting lawful network traffic; (4) Exempted wireless networks from the last rule.[2] Even though this regulation is weak, Verizon sued to stop it, claiming that the FCC does not have legal authority to impose any rules on internet traffic.[3] Additionally, on April 11, 2011, the House passed, along party lines, a Republican-sponsored resolution reversing the FCC's "network neutrality" rules. The resolution was rejected by the Senate.[4]

Since the topic of network neutrality covers a wide range of issues, and means different things to different people, it is not surprising that several approaches to network neutrality regulation have been discussed by policy makers. In this chapter we formally compare three such approaches to the alternative of no regulation. We highlight how each of these regimes can be interpreted to either allow or restrict (1) variations in guaranteed QoS levels (non-discrimination), (2) tariff-based price discrimination, where tariff-based fees are imposed on content providers without identity-based discrimination, and (3) exclusive contracts where identity-based discrimination can be used to block content providers from reaching consumers. The regimes we compare are the following.

- *Absolute Non-Discrimination (No QoS)*. In this regime is the strongest form of regulation and is in line with the definition of network neutrality put forth by Tim Wu: "Network neutrality is best defined as a network design principle. The idea is that a maximally useful public information network aspires to treat all content, sites, and platforms equally. This allows the network to carry every form of information and support every kind of application."[5] In this regime, offering separate guaranteed levels of QoS to different content providers is not permitted, even if offered without price discrimination. Neither price discrimination nor exclusive contracts are allowed in this regime.
- *Limited Discrimination without Quality of Service Tiering (No Fees)*. This regime is in line with the fifth principle suggested as a regulatory proposal for the internet in the FCC NPRM (FCC 2009, para. 104)[6]: "Subject to reasonable network management, a provider of broadband Internet access service must treat lawful content, applications, and services in a nondiscriminatory manner." In this

regime, it is possible for the network operator to offer different guaranteed levels of QoS to different content providers depending on what level of QoS they demand (e.g. a VOIP provider needs a higher level of QoS than a standard-text-based search engine). This is captured by the phrase "reasonable network management" in (FCC 2009, para. 135): "Reasonable network management consists of: (a) reasonable practices employed by a provider of broadband Internet access service to (i) reduce or mitigate the effects of congestion on its network or to address quality-of-service concerns; (ii) address traffic that is unwanted by users or harmful; (iii) prevent the transfer of unlawful content; or (iv) prevent the unlawful transfer of content; and (b) other reasonable network management practices." However, in this regime, neither charging content providers for access to higher guaranteed levels of QoS nor exclusive contracts are allowed (FCC 2009, para. 104): "We understand the term 'nondiscriminatory' to mean that a broadband Internet access service provider may not charge a content, application, or service provider for enhanced or prioritized access to the subscribers of the broadband Internet access service provider").

- *Limited Discrimination and QoS Tiering (No Exclusivity)*. This regime is inspired by the FCC Broadband Policy Statement released in September 2005[7] and is also in line with the Internet Consumer Bill of Rights. In this regime, exclusive contracts and identity-based discrimination are banned, but the network operator can offer various guaranteed levels of QoS (tiers), each at a different price to content providers. A content provider can choose not to pay for a higher guaranteed level of QoS, in which case only a basic level of access to consumers is provided (for free).
- *No Regulation*. In this regime, any discrimination is allowed, including identity-based discrimination and exclusivity. A network operator can choose to sell exclusive access to one content provider instead of only selling various guaranteed levels of QoS to all providers. A content provider not obtaining exclusive access has no way to reach consumers and exits the market leading to less content provider variety available for consumers.

We compare these regimes in the context of a stylized model with a monopolist network operator and two competing content providers. Specifically, we aim to answer the following questions. Which form of regulation yields the highest guaranteed levels of QoS? What is the market outcome in case of no regulation? Is regulation needed to maximize social welfare?

We establish the following results. First, in relation to incentives of the network operator to improve guaranteed levels of QoS, we find that QoS offered to the two content providers will be highest if the network operator is allowed to price discriminate and charge content providers for access to better QoS. With an exclusive contract, the level of QoS offered to the exclusive content provider may still be higher than with price discrimination if content providers do not profit much from increases in QoS but consumers value QoS highly. Hence, regulation to restrict exclusive contracts and price discrimination is likely to lead to lower levels of QoS. Further, the difference in QoS offered to content providers is highest under exclusive contracts or price discrimination. It is only equal when QoS improvements are banned and is likely to differ even when price discrimination is not allowed but variations in QoS are. The reason is heterogeneity in the valuation of QoS among consumers and content providers and that QoS provision is costly for the network operator (Proposition 1).

Second, a private monopolist network operator will always prefer price discrimination to only variations in QoS or to no QoS improvements. The network operator will prefer to implement exclusive contracts if consumers view content providers as similar and if there is a large difference in content providers' ability to profit from consumers, thereby implying that exclusive access is very valuable for the content providers (Proposition 2).

Third, though ranking of the private profitability of the regimes is unambiguous, ranking social welfare to determine optimal regulation yields different results depending on parameter values. We identify four channels through which regulation affects total welfare: 1) through the effect of QoS variations on consumer common valuation of the content providers, 2) through affecting total transportation costs determined by consumer preferences over content providers, 3) through redistributing consumers among content providers and thereby changing total surplus created on the content provider side and 4) through changing the total costs of QoS provision (Proposition 3).

The policy implication from these results is that we should expect that network operators will have incentives to implement price discrimination and possibly also to exclude some content providers from reaching consumers absent any regulatory intervention. This can be prevented by implementing regulation, but it can come with costs in terms of reducing the network operators' incentives to invest in upgrading their network to achieve better guaranteed Quality of Service. A balanced path, for example as suggested by the FCC NPRM (FCC 2009), may be one way forward as it allows some quality of service variations and investment in improving quality of service that is driven entirely by payments from consumers, but shies away from allowing investments in quality of service to be driven by payments from content providers as well.

The rest of the chapter proceeds as follows. The next section provides a literature review. In section 3, we present the model that we utilize to compare the regimes. Section 4 solves the model and presents our main results. Section 5 discusses our model. We conclude in section 6.

LITERATURE REVIEW

Despite a considerable literature discussing legal issues of network neutrality regulations and net management regulations, the literature on economic analysis of these issues is not extensive.

An early paper, Hermalin and Katz (2007), analyzes a model where network neutrality is equivalent to the imposition of a single product quality requirement. They analyze a monopoly platform facing heterogeneous content providers and homogeneous consumers. A key result of imposing a single product quality requirement is that the number of content providers available to consumers is reduced, as some low valuation content providers choose not to sell when only one price is offered (exclusion effect). This reduces welfare. Welfare is also reduced because some high valuation providers sell lower and less efficient qualities (reduced quality effect). However, medium valuation providers end up selling higher and more efficient qualities which increase welfare (improved quality effect). Total welfare may thus increase or decrease, but the authors suggest that total welfare will increase only if the marginal types served under the restriction obtain a much higher quality than they would obtain absent the restriction. From a welfare perspective some low valuation content providers should be excluded if the costs of providing quality exceed the benefit they bring to the platform. Further, an unrestricted platform will exclude even more content providers since it has to give information rents to higher quality content providers. Hermalin and Katz (2007) also analyze the case where the ISP is forced to quote a zero price to content providers and show that then only one quality level is offered, and that the level of this quality is lower than the socially efficient level as well as the level that would be offered under a single quality level requirement. The reason is that the IPS ignores the preferences of the content providers because they do not pay for access to consumers.

Another early formal analysis of network neutrality is Hogendorn (2007), who analyzes the differences between open access and network neutrality and emphasizes that these are different policies that may have different implications. Hogendorn interprets network neutrality in a slightly different way than most of the literature. In Hogendorn (2007), open access refers to allowing intermediaries access to conduits so that intermediaries such as AOL and MSN can access conduits like AT&T at a nondiscriminatory price, while full network neutrality is interpreted to mean that content providers have unrestricted access to intermediaries so that e.g. Yahoo cannot restrict which content providers can be reached through its portal, in addition to open access between conduits and intermediaries. He studies a three-stage game: entry of conduits and intermediaries, negotiations between intermediaries and content firms, and finally consumers' subscription to conduits and intermediaries' consumption of content. There is free entry of conduits and intermediaries, while there is monopolistic competition between content providers. He then analyzes the differences between open access and network neutrality and emphasizes that these are different policies that may have different implications. In particular, he finds that under network neutrality, a smaller number of intermediaries enter the market due to decreased profits (so this would mean fewer AOLs, Yahoos and MSNs). The reason profits decrease under network neutrality is that they cannot charge high fees to content providers. Open access, on the contrary, increases the entry of intermediaries since they now have free access to conduits, and can also charge content providers. However, open access is not a substitute for network neutrality regulation. Network neutrality reduces the number of intermediaries, implying that network neutrality reduces content on the internet. He argues that the effect on restricting content is likely to be larger now than it would have been a decade ago, since profits for content providers are larger now implying that incentives to extract these profits also are larger. The overall total welfare results are ambiguous and depend on parameter values.

Economides and Tåg (2012) explicitly study two-sided pricing in the context of network neutrality on the internet and abstract from issues related to price discrimination, dynamic innovation incentives or prioritization. Network neutrality is interpreted to mean zero prices to one side of the market (the content side). The paper considers both a setting with a monopolist platform and a setting with two duopolistic platforms and multi-homing content providers. Consumers are horizontally differentiated and buy from either of the platforms. The central argument in the paper is that Internet Service Providers must be seen as platforms in a two-sided market intermediating transactions between consumers and content providers. In such a market, private ISPs may not internalize the externalities across sides (between consumers and content providers). This gives a rationale for government intervention. Depending on parameter values, network neutrality regulations that implicitly impose a price of zero towards content providers may bring the price balance closer to the socially optimal price balance and thereby increase social welfare. However, for other parameter values the opposite is true.

Focusing on the long run effects of network neutrality regulations, Choi and Kim (2010) study both a static and a dynamic setting focusing on how innovation incentives are affected by network neutrality. The authors use a Hotelling model to study two aspects of network neutrality regulation: congestion and innovation incentives (both for the ISP and the content providers). There is a monopoly ISP and two competing content providers. Network neutrality implies that the ISP cannot sell prioritized access to consumers to one of the content providers. They find ambiguous results regarding the impact of network neutrality regulations on welfare; however, they underscore that in a static setting social welfare is higher under network neutrality if content providers are sufficiently similar. In a dynamic setting they underscore two trade-offs. First, network neutrality regulation affects the investment incentives of the ISP by either allowing the ISP to charge more/less for access (network access fee effect) or by allowing the ISP to sell rights to prioritized delivery of content (rent extraction effect). Investing in improving capacity implies that the ISP must charge less for prioritized delivery, so incentives to expand capacity can possibly be lower without network neutrality regulation (contrary to what opponents of network neutrality regulation claim). Further, to achieve better rent extraction the ISP may have incentives to degrade the non-priority packets in order to restore incentives to invest (though the authors do not formally show this). Second, since the ISP can extract rents from content providers through selling first priority access, network neutrality regulation improves investment incentives for content providers by removing the rent extraction possibility. However, it is not clear that the ISP wishes to extract all rents from content provider investments since he has incentives to encourage some investment by content providers and might thereby be willing to commit to network neutrality. In sum, the authors find ambiguous results regarding the impact of network neutrality regulations on welfare, but highlight that, in a dynamic setting, network neutrality regulation affects the incentives of the network operator by either allowing the network operator to charge more/less for access or by allowing the network operator to sell rights to prioritized delivery of content.

Focusing on congestion effects in the short run, Cheng, Bandyopadhyay and Guo (2010) model two content providers who can avoid congestion by paying ISPs for preferential access. The model is similar to Choi and Kim (2010) since the authors use a monopoly ISP model with two content providers. They find that abolishing network neutrality will benefit ISPs and hurt content providers. Depending on the parameter values, consumers are either unaffected or better off. In particular, social welfare increases when network neutrality is abandoned and one content provider pays for access; but it remains unchanged when both content providers pay. The reason why the consumer surplus may increase is that it is always the more profitable content provider that pays for access and hence, gets preferential treatment. This benefits consumers of the more profitable content provider because congestion is reduced. However, it results in a loss for consumers of the less profitable content provider that does not pay for preferential access, since there is an increase in the congestion costs. Further, incentives for the broadband provider to expand its capacity are higher under network neutrality regulation since more capacity leads to less congestion. Since congestion decreases, internet services become more valuable (to the benefit of ISPs). If network neutrality is abolished, their model predicts reduced investment incentives because congestion becomes less of a problem.

Emphasizing that the quality of the ISP's network affects trade across the platform, Cañón (2009) studies active discrimination between buyers and sellers in a fully two-sided market by generalizing the Hermalin and Katz (2007) approach and the Economides and Tåg (2012) paper by considering dynamic investment incentives in a two-sided market with heterogeneous consumers. The formal model has two stages: investment by the ISP and entry/trade between buyers and sellers on the platform. The ISP invests without knowing the private benefits for trade for the buyers and the sellers. Investment benefits end users as the marginal utility of consumption of the content provider's goods is higher. The users enter the platform to trade only if their expected utility of trade with the sellers is higher than the access fee. Sellers design an optimal non-linear tariff for all end users. The results support network neutrality regulation by underscoring that imposing zero fees to content providers will lead to more content providers and users entering the platform. More investment will be made by the ISP since more users join the platform when their value from trade increases for each content provider. While imposing regulation leads to higher welfare costs in terms of ISP investment costs and end user entry costs, the benefits from increased total trade surplus on the platform tend to outweigh the costs.

Creating lanes with prioritized delivery of content may help small content providers who are sensitive to the quality of service. Jamison and Hauge (2008) set up a model of a monopolist ISP intermediating heterogeneous content providers to consumers and study the innovation incentives of content providers and ISPs. Their main arguments are that offering differential levels of quality of service helps smaller content providers (with lower quality) because they can purchase premium access and thereby better compete with higher quality content providers (because total quality depends on both transmission speed and underlying quality). The reason is that in their setup the marginal value of increased speed is higher for low quality content providers than for high quality content providers. Without premium access, it would not be profitable for them to enter the market. Abandoning network neutrality will thus decrease innovation among content providers. Hence, offering premium service to content providers will increase demand for broadband and thereby give the ISP more revenues from consumers as well.

Departing from network neutrality could potentially give an ISP a way of degrading the services of competitors who rely on high levels of quality of service. Chen and Nalebuff (2007) analyze competition between complements and briefly touch upon the issue of network neutrality. Some services that are offered by an ISP may also be offered over the internet (such as Vonage or Skype). There is a concern that the ISP would like to disrupt the quality of the services of its competitors to further its own product. However, the authors show that this would not be profit maximizing in their model since a monopolist ISP benefits from valuable complements such as VOIP services (a higher price for internet access could be charged instead of trying to force consumers to its own VOIP service).

More recently, two papers have emerged indicating that network neutrality regulation is likely to be beneficial if it leads to entry of more content providers. Krämer and Wiewiorra (2009) study a two-sided monopoly market model that focuses on congestion and prioritization of access. Content providers are vertically differentiated and consumers are homogeneous. Network neutrality implies that the ISP cannot build a "fast-lane" that gives prioritized access over best-effort delivery at a price. Hence, without network neutrality the ISP charges only for prioritized access and not for best-effort access. The ISP faces a tradeoff in that reducing congestion draws in more content providers and consumers (the expansion effect), but on the other hand more content providers and consumers in turn drive up congestion (the congestion effect). In the short run, prioritization degrades performance on the best-effort line, and this hurts non-paying content providers. However, it allows content providers with business models that are sensitive to quality of service to enter the market. Hence, from a welfare perspective, discrimination harms all content providers in the short run since some pay and some face increased congestion. However, welfare is increased since congestion is better allocated. Content providers are worse off because the ISP extracts surplus from them through the fee for prioritized access. In the long run, however, ISP investments will be lower under network neutrality and less content will be available. ISP investments are lower under network neutrality because they cannot charge content providers. Lower investments lead to higher congestion and less content is available.

Economides and Hermalin (2012), despite assuming network congestion, find that network neutrality is welfare-superior to bandwidth subdivision and prioritization. They also find that the incentive to invest in bandwidth is greater when the ISPs can price discriminate, and investment in bandwidth may mitigate the welfare losses of departures from network neutrality. A central assumption is that content and applications providers differ in how valuable their content or application is perceived to be by consumers. As such, high value content generates higher revenues, gets more traffic and therefore congests the network more even when capacity is expanded.

In sum, though several aspects of network neutrality regulation have been considered, no work has so far been done on comparing the effects of different degrees of regulation within the framework of the same model. The formal model in this chapter provides such an analysis. It is related to Cheng, Bandyopadhyay and Guo (2010), Choi and Kim (2010) and Krämer and Wiewiorra (2009), in that we use a similar setup of a monopolist network operator (ISP) in a two-sided market connecting two competing content providers with consumers. One important difference is that we specifically allow for different "lanes" with different levels of QoS and for pricing each lane separately. We assume that providing QoS is costly to the network operator and because of differences in consumers' valuation of content providers and content providers' valuation of QoS, we typically get different equilibrium levels of QoS for different content providers. This approach assumes that potential congestion effects are completely captured in the cost function for guaranteeing a specific combination of QoS. Our research is complementary to Jamison and Hauge (2008), Hermalin and Katz (2007), Cañón (2009), Economides and Tåg (2012) and Economides and Hermalin (2012) as we do not specifically here focus on price balance between consumers and content providers or on the effects of restricting the product line offered to content providers.

THE MODEL

There are three types of actors in our model: consumers that buy internet access, a monopolist network operator (Internet Service Provider, "ISP"), and two content providers: A and B. The monopolist network operator sells internet access to consumers at price P and can also charge prices s_A and s_B to content providers A and B respectively for access to better

QoS. The network operator can also decide to sell to one content provider exclusive access to consumers, in which case s_E denotes the price for exclusivity. The timing is the following.

1. The regulator chooses among the four possible regimes.
2. The network operator observes the regulatory regime and, if possible, decides on whether to invest in QoS, whether to charge A and B for access to better QoS, or whether to sell only exclusive access. Then, if the network operator chose to improve QoS, it chooses the level of QoS to provide to A and B.
3. The network operator sets price for internet access and either sets individual fees for QoS improvements or the fee for exclusivity. Content providers decide on buying better access or on buying exclusive access.[8]

Consumers are differentiated in their preferences for content providers. Our model has a continuum of consumers distributed on the interval [0, 1] according to their location x with cumulative distribution function F(.) with density f(.). There are two content providers, A and B, located at each end of the interval (A at 0 and B at 1). The loss of utility or "transportation cost" faced by a consumer located at x_i for using the services of A is tx_i and for using the services of B is $t(1 - x_i)$. To gain access to content providers, a consumer must pay the network operator the price P. We assume that all consumers buy content either from A or B, so that there are no demand expansion effects. The levels of QoS provided by the network operator to content provider A and B are denoted by q_A and q_B. Content providers are valued by consumers at $v_A(q_A)$ and $v_B(q_B)$, excluding transportation costs.[9] Since higher QoS is desirable, we have that $v'_A(q_A) > 0$, and $v'_B(q_B) > 0$. We impose the following assumption.

Assumption 1: $v_A(q) > v_B(q)$ and $v'_A(q) > v'_B(q)$.

This assumption says that for a given level of QoS, consumers value the content from A higher than the content from B, absent transportation costs. Additionally, A offers services that rely more on real-time transmission of packets and thus A benefits relatively more from an improvement in QoS than B does. This assumption is imposed in order to account for diversity in the services that are provided on the internet. In particular, regulation is likely to affect latency sensitive services such as video, voice over IP and streaming music services differently than it impacts text-based services such as simple web pages and email services. By allowing one content provider (provider A) to be more sensitive to QoS than the rival (provider B), we account for this difference in our model and allow for different effects of regulation on different content providers.

Given the above specification, the utility of a consumer located at x_i is given by

$$u_i(q_A, q_B, P) = \begin{cases} v_A(q_A) - tx_i - P \\ v_B(q_B) - t(1-x_i) - P. \end{cases} \tag{6.1}$$

The location of the consumer who is indifferent between A and B is thus

$$x^*(q_A, q_B) = \frac{1}{2} + \frac{v_A(q_A) - v_B(q_B)}{2t}, \tag{6.2}$$

and the resulting mass of consumers at each content provider is $n_A = F(x^*)$ and $n_B = 1 - F(x^*)$.

Each content provider profits from selling advertising space. For each content provider, profit from advertising is an increasing function of the mass of consumers using its services, $\pi'_A(n_A) > 0$, $\pi'_B(n_B) > 0$. Content providers' total profits are $\Pi_A = \pi_A(n_A) - s_A$ and $\Pi_B = \pi_B(n_B) - s_B$, where s_A and s_B denote fees the content provider must pay for access to consumers in the case the network operator charges content providers for access to better QoS. If the network operator sells exclusive access only, then price s_A or s_B is replaced by s_E. We further impose the following assumption:

Assumption 2: $\pi_A(n) > \pi_B(n)$.

This assumption states that for a given mass of consumers (market share), A is more efficient at turning users' attention into profits through advertising than B is. Again, this allows us to account for the fact that depending on the content provider's ability to profit from users, regulation may affect one content provider more than the other.

The network operator has a cost function of improving QoS given by $c(q)$. We assume that $c(0) = 0$, $c'(q) > 0$ and $c''(q) > 0$. These costs can arise from network management and prioritization, or they can arise from other sources such as laying down new cables or improving old ones. Finally, to illustrate some of the propositions in more detail, we will sometimes invoke the following assumption:

Assumption 3 (Linearity): Consumers are uniformly distributed, $F(x) = x$, the value of QoS is $v_A(q_A) = v + w_A q_A$, $v_B(q_B) = v + w_B q_B$, costs of providing quality are $c(q) = cq^2$, and content provider profits excluding quality costs are proportional to sales, $\pi_A(x) = ax$ and $\pi_B(x) = b(1 - x)$.

We will consider the network operator's optimal business strategy, QoS investment choices and pricing in four regimes. **No Regulation** means that the network operator is free to set all three prices (price to consumers and a fee to each content provider), QoS levels, and to exclude one content provider if it so wishes. **No Exclusivity** means that the content provider is free to set all three prices and QoS levels, but cannot exclude a content provider. **No Fees** implies that the network operator can only set the price to consumers P and QoS levels, but fees to content providers are zero, $s_A = s_B = 0$. **No QoS** implies that QoS investments and thus variations in QoS are not possible ($q_A = q_B = 0$) and that the network operator can only set price P. Fees to content providers are zero, $s_A = s_B = 0$.

ANALYSIS

Pricing

We start by determining prices and fees set in stage 3. There are four possible cases to analyze: exclusive access, price discrimination, no fees, and no QoS variations.

Exclusive access. When exclusive access is implemented, the network operator sells exclusive access to its consumers to only one content provider. Given assumption 2, it is always more profitable to sell exclusive access to A. Hence, all consumers use A and we have that $x^* = 1$. The network operator chooses P and s_E to maximize $\Pi^E = P^E + s_E - c(q_A)$ subject to

$$v_A(q_A) - t - P^E \geq 0 \text{ (the market remains covered)} \qquad (6.3)$$

$$\pi_A(F(1)) - s_E \geq 0 \text{ (A prefers to purchase exclusive access).}^{[10]} \quad (6.4)$$

The monopolist network operator does best in raising the price and the fee until both inequalities become equalities. Its profits are then $\Pi^E = v_A(q_A) - t + \pi_A(F(1)) - c(q_A)$.

Price discrimination. When price discrimination is implemented, the network operator sells better QoS to content providers and charges them individual prices for access to "lanes" of different quality. Given that it is profitable to set prices such that both content providers purchase better QoS, the consumer indifferent between A and B is located at $x^*(q_A, q_B)$ defined above. The network operator maximizes

$$\Pi^{PD} = P^{PD} + s_A + s_B - c(q_A) - c(q_B) \text{ subject to}$$

$$v_A(q_A) - tx^*(q_A, q_B) - P^{PD} \geq 0 \text{ (the market remains covered)} \quad (6.5)$$

$$\pi_A(F(x^*(q_A, q_B))) - s_A \geq \pi_A(F(x^*(0, q_B))) \text{ (A prefers better QoS)} \quad (6.6)$$

$$\pi_B(1 - F(x^*(q_A, q_B))) - s_B \geq \pi_B(1 - F(x^*(q_A, 0))) \text{ (B prefers better QoS)} \quad (6.7)$$

Note that we assume that each content provider operates under the assumption that the rival always purchases better QoS. The network operator does best in raising all prices until the inequalities become equalities. The network operator profits are then

$$\Pi^{PD} = v_A(q_A) - tx^*(q_A, q_B) + \pi_A(F(x^*(q_A, q_B))) - \pi_A(F(x^*(0, q_B))) +$$

$$\pi_B(1 - F(x^*(q_A, q_B))) - \pi_B(1 - F(x^*(q_A, 0))) - c(q_A) - c(q_B) \quad (6.8)$$

No fees. In the case the network operator cannot set fees to content providers, it chooses just P^{NF} to maximize $\Pi^{NF} = P^{NF} - c(q_A) - c(q_B)$, subject to $v_A(q_A) - tx^*(q_A, q_B) - P^{NF} \geq 0$ (the market remains covered). Profits are $\Pi^{NF} = v_A(q_A) - tx^*(q_A, q_B) - c(q_A) - c(q_B)$.

No QoS. Finally, if there are no QoS improvements and fees to content providers, the network operator sets P^{NF} to maximize $\Pi^{NQoS} = P^{NQoS}$ subject to $v_A(0) - tx^*(0, 0) - P^{NQoS} \geq 0$ (the market remains covered). Profits in this case are $\Pi^{NQoS} = v_A(0) - tx^*(0, 0)$.

Investment

We now consider investments in improving QoS and the network operator's choice of business model. We can show the following proposition regarding the level of QoS under different business strategies.

Proposition 1. Equilibrium QoS levels can be ranked as follows: $q_A^{PD} \geq q_A^{NF} \geq q_A^{NQoS} = 0$, $q_B^{PD} \geq q_B^{NF} \geq q_B^{NQoS} = q_B^E = 0$ and $q_A^E \geq q_A^{PD}$ for $v_A'(q_A)/2 > \pi_A'(q_A)$, which under Assumption 3 reduces to $t > a$. The difference in QoS offered to A and B under Assumption 3 can be ranked as follows: $\Delta q^{PD} > \Delta q^{NF} > \Delta q^{NQoS} = 0$ and $\Delta q^E > \Delta q^{PD}$ for $bw_B + t(w_A + w_B) > aw_A$.

To see this, consider investments in each of the three cases outlined above that allow for QoS investments (investment is zero by assumption in case of no provision of QoS). QoS levels are determined by the equations $v_A'(q_A^E) = c'(q_A^E)$ in case of exclusivity, $v_A'(q_A^{PD})/2 + \pi_A'(q_A^{PD}) = c'(q_A^{PD})$ and

$v_B'(q_B^{PD})/2 + \pi_B'(q_B^{PD}) = c'(q_B^{PD})$ in case of price discrimination, and by $v_A'(q_A^{NF})/2 = c'(q_A^{NF})$ and $v_B'(q_B^{NF})/2 = c'(q_B^{NF})$ in case no fees are charged to A and B.[11] For the difference in QoS offered to A and B, under linearity we get $\Delta q^E = (1/2c)w_A$, $\Delta q^{PD} = \frac{w_A - w_B}{4c} + \frac{aw_A - bw_B}{4ct}$ and $\Delta q^{NF} = \frac{w_A - w_B}{4c}$, which, under assumptions 1 and 2, give the rankings in Proposition 1.

Exclusivity yields the highest investment in QoS for A if the effect of a quality increase in q_A on the profits of A is sufficiently small, price discrimination the second highest and no fees the lowest. Exclusivity allows the network operator to capture all gains from QoS increases in A that go to consumers. If the network operator implements price discrimination, there is an extra effect on QoS investment incentives that comes from the fact that increases in the QoS of A allows the network operator to not only raise the price to consumers but also to raise its fee to A. This implies that, if market share is very valuable to A, price discrimination can lead to higher QoS investments than exclusivity. Similarly, the value B places on buying better QoS also gives the network operator higher incentives to invest in QoS as the value to B of buying (compared to not buying) increases. Note also that the network operator will have incentives to improve QoS even if it does not charge content providers, as better QoS will allow it to raise the price consumers pay for access to content providers.[12]

Next, we compare the four different business models the network operator can implement: exclusive access, price discrimination, no fees and no QoS variation. We obtain the following proposition.

Proposition 2: Network operator profits can be ranked as follows:

i) $\Pi^{PD} \geq \Pi^{NF} \geq \Pi^{NQoS}$.

ii) $\Pi^E \geq \Pi^{PD}$, *for* $\underbrace{(P^E - P^{PD})}_{+/-} + \underbrace{(s_E - s_A)}_{+} - s_B - \underbrace{[c(q_A^E) - c(q_A^{PD})]}_{+/-} - c(q_B^{PD}) \geq 0$

iii) Under the linearity assumption the condition in ii) becomes

$$\Pi^E - \Pi^{PD} = -\frac{1}{16ct^2}(8ct^3 + a^2w_A^2 - 3t^2w_A^2 + 2at(w_A^2 - 8ct) + (b+t)^2w_B^2) \geq 0$$

(6.9)

which is increasing in w_A for $t > a$ and in a for $c > \frac{1}{8t^2}(a + t)w_A^2$. It is decreasing in w_B and b.

To see this, note that price to consumers, P, is increasing in both q_A

and q_B ($\partial P/\partial q_A = v_A'(q_A)/2 > 0$ and $\partial P/\partial q_B = v_B'(q_B)/2 > 0$). For Part (i), it is then easy to see that Price Discrimination is better than No Fees ($\Pi^{PD} \geq \Pi^{NF}$) since Price Discrimination both gives the network operator an additional source of revenues (the fees to A and B) and raises profits from consumers since q_A and q_B weakly increase (by Proposition 1). No Fees is also better than No QoS ($\Pi^{NF} \geq \Pi^{NQoS}$) since profits from consumers weakly increase with q_A and q_B (by Proposition 1). Costs of providing QoS also increase but, since the network operator is free to set QoS levels, it could always set them at zero or at the same level in each case. For part ii), we can decompose the difference in profits as follows

$$\Pi^E - \Pi^{PD} = (P^E - P^{PD}) + (s_E - s_A) - s_B - [c(q_A^E) - c(q_A^{PD})] - c(q_B^{PD}). \quad (6.10)$$

The first term is profit change from revenue from consumers, which can increase or decrease. It can also be expressed as

$$(P^E - P^{PD}) = (v_A(q_A^E) - v_A(q_A^{PD})) - (1/2)t + (1/2)(v_A(q_A^{PD}) - v_B(q_B^{PD})), \quad (6.11)$$

highlighting that it is more likely to be positive if the product differentiation parameter t is small so that A and B are less differentiated in the eyes of consumers, or if the quality difference between A and B is large and QoS of A increases under exclusivity. The second term in equation (10) is positive and is the increase in the fee to A that the network operator can implement since it now sells exclusive access instead of just better QoS. The third term is profit losses from not selling better QoS to B. The fourth term is cost increases from providing a higher level of QoS and the final term is cost savings from not investing in QoS for B. Under linearity, the comparative statics indicate that increasing the difference between the effects of QoS on consumers' valuation of content provider services or the difference between content providers' profitability increases the profitability of excluding one content provider instead of selling access to better QoS.

Hence, exclusive access to consumers will be favored by the network operator if the content providers are viewed as similar by the consumers (t is small); if the difference in quality between A and B is large; if exclusive access is very valuable to A; if A and B are heterogeneous in their ability to profit from consumers; and if cost savings from not improving the QoS of B are large.

Regulatory Regimes

Having established the network operator's preference over different business strategies, QoS improvement choices and pricing decisions, we now compare regulatory regimes from the point of view of consumers' surplus and total surplus. We assume that the regulator is concerned about total surplus (or total welfare), which we define as the sum of consumer surplus, network operator profits and content provider profits. Network operator profits and content provider profits are given above. Consumer surplus is given by

$$CS = \int_0^x (v_A(q_A) - ty - P)f(y)dy + \int_x^1 (v_B(q_B) - t(1 - y) - P)f(y)dy \tag{6.12}$$

and can be rewritten as

$$CS = v_A(q_A)F(x) + v_B(q_B)(1 - F(x)) - t\left(\int_0^x yf(y)dy + \int_x^1 (1-y)f(y)dy\right) - P, \tag{6.13}$$

where the first two terms are utility created from accessing content providers, the next term consumers' transportation costs arising from heterogeneity in consumer preferences, and the final term is the price that consumers pay for access to content providers.[13] For simplicity, we denote consumer surplus as $CS = V - T - P$, the sum of content provider profits from advertising (total profits minus potential fees to the network operator) as $CP = \pi_A(n_A) + \pi_B(n_B)$ and costs of improving QoS by $C = c(q_A) + c(q_B)$. Then, we can denote total welfare under each possible business strategy chosen by the network operator as

$$W^k = V^k - T^k + CP^k - C^k, \tag{6.14}$$

where k denotes the regulatory regime, $k \in \{E, PD, NF, NQoS\}$. This decomposition highlights that any effect on welfare from a particular regime or business strategy affects welfare either though its effect on i) consumers' common valuation of content provider services absent transportation costs, ii) transportation costs (consumers' preference distribution over content), iii) surplus created by content providers due to interaction with consumers and iv) costs of QoS improvements. Given this, we can now state the following proposition.

Proposition 3: Social welfare under the four regimes cannot be unambiguously ranked. The clear private profit rankings of proposition 2 suggest that it may not always be that the social and private incentives are aligned. The socially optimal form of regulation depends on parameter values such that

i) $W^{NF} \geq W^{NQoS}$, for $(V^{NF} - V^{NQoS}) - (T^{NF} - T^{NQoS}) + (CP^{NF} - CP^{NQoS})$
      $- C^{NF} \geq 0$.

ii) $W^{PD} \geq W^{NF}$, for $(V^{PD} - V^{NF}) - (T^{PD} - T^{NF}) + (CP^{PD} - CP^{NF})$
      $- (C^{PD} - C^{NF}) \geq 0$.

iii) $W^{E} \geq W^{PD}$, for $(V^{E} - V^{PD}) - (T^{E} - T^{PD}) + (CP^{E} - CP^{PD}) - (C^{E}$
      $- C^{PD}) \geq 0$.

The first term in i)–ii) is positive by assumption 1. The first term in iii) is positive only if QoS offered to A is higher under exclusivity than under price discrimination. The second term is either positive or negative depending on which x minimizes total transportation costs (for example, it is negative if that x is less than $(1/2)$ under assumption 3). The third term is positive by assumption 2 for i)–ii) and may be negative for iii), while the fourth term is always negative. Imposing assumption 3, parts i)–iii) in Proposition 3 reduce to

$$W^{NF} - W^{NQoS} = \frac{(w_A^2 - w_A^2)^2 + 4ct(w_A^2 + w_B^2)}{32c^2t} - \frac{(w_A^2 - w_B^2)^2}{64c^2t} +$$

$$\frac{(a - b)(w_A - w_B)(w_A + w_B)}{8ct} - \frac{w_A^2 + w_B^2}{16c},$$

$W^{PD} - W^{NF}$

$$= \frac{4act^2 w_A^2 + a(a+2t)w_A^4 - 2(-2bct^2 + (bt + a(b+t))w_A^2)w_B^2 + b(b+2t)w_B^4}{32c^2t^3}$$

$$- \frac{(aw_A^2 - bw_B^2)((a+2t)w_A^2 - (b+2t)w_B^2)}{64c^2t^3} + \frac{(a-b)(aw_A^2 - bw_B^2)}{8ct^2}$$

$$- \frac{a(a+2t)w_A^2 + b(b+2t)w_B^2}{16ct^2}$$

and

$W^{E} - W^{PD}$

$$= -\frac{4c(a-3t)t^2 w_A^2 + (a+t)^2 w_A^4 - 2(b+t)(-2ct^2 + (a+t)w_A^2)w_B^2 + (b+t)^2 w_B^4}{32c^2t^3}$$

$$- \frac{48c^2t^4 - ((a+t)w_A^2 - (b+t)w_B^2)^2}{64c^2t^3}$$

$$+ \frac{(b - a) - 4ct^2 + (a + t)w_A^2 - (b + t)w_B^2}{8ct^2}$$

$$- \frac{(t - a)(a + 3t)w_A^2 - (b + t)^2 w_B^2}{16ct^2}.$$

Thus, even under assumption 3, the optimal form of regulation depends on parameter values in a non-trivial way. Despite not giving a clear ranking of the regimes, Proposition 3 highlights the four different channels through which total welfare is affected.

POSSIBILITIES FOR FURTHER RESEARCH

There are several possible avenues for further research. First, our main analysis focused entirely on the incentives of the network operator to invest in improving QoS. One may also study content providers' investment incentives. One would expect investment incentives to be lower when the network operator can charge content providers. However, the ability to innovate and offer new services may depend on the level of QoS provided. Some innovations are not possible without a sufficiently high QoS level, which could imply that some content providers' innovation incentives could be higher when the network operator can charge fees to content providers because incentives to improve QoS levels then increase.

Second, our model is very flexible because it allows the network operator to freely invest in supplying capacity and QoS to each content provider separately and to potentially charge separate prices to each content provider. However, such a setup may not be optimal for an analysis of network congestion and prioritization. Our setup can be easily modified in this direction by assuming that QoS levels are dependent on each other, reflecting a situation where the capacity of the network is fixed and congestion occurs. To do this we can generalize the quality of service costs to $c_A(q_A, \mu q_B)$ and $c_B(\mu q_A, q_B)$ with $\partial c_A(q_A, \mu q_B)/\partial q_A > 0$, $\partial c_A(q_A, \mu q_B)/\partial q_B \geq 0$, $\partial c_B(\mu q_A, q_B)/\partial q_A \geq 0$ and $\partial c_B(\mu q_A, q_B)/\partial q_A \geq 0$, where the parameter μ is a measure of network capacity ($\mu = 0$ corresponds to our current case with no relationship between QoS levels). Then, increasing the QoS to A implies that the costs of providing better QoS to B increase because of congestion. An extension along these lines will presumably reduce the overall investment in QoS, but our results are likely to remain unchanged.

Third, an important issue often raised in the context of network neutrality is related to incentives of the network operator to vertically integrate into the supply of content and to use its position as a network operator to favor its own content. This issue can be analyzed in our framework by considering a merger between A (or B) with the network operator.

Fourth, our analysis is entirely focused on a monopolistic network operator. Introducing competition between network operators could potentially affect the result of the analysis.

Fifth, a crucial part of our analysis is assumption 2, stating that A is more efficient than B in generating revenue from consumers' attention. This assumption is important because it implies that A is more efficient while at the same time consumers value A higher than they value B. An equally plausible situation could involve consumers valuing A higher than B, while A would be less efficient than B in generating revenue from consumers.

CONCLUDING REMARKS

We have compared four different approaches to network neutrality and net management regulation: (i) no variations in QoS and no price discrimination allowed (No QoS variations); (ii) variations in QoS allowed but no price discrimination (No Fees); (iii) variations in QoS and price discrimination allowed but no exclusive contracts allowed between the network operator and a content provider (No Exclusivity); and (iv) no regulation: the network operator can sell exclusive rights to content providers. We found that:

- QoS offered to the two content providers will be highest if the network operator is allowed to price discriminate and charge content providers for access to better QoS. With an exclusive contract, the level of QoS offered may still be higher than with price discrimination if content providers do not profit much from increases in QoS but consumers value QoS highly.
- A private monopolist network operator will always prefer price discrimination to only variations in QoS or to no QoS improvements. The network operator will prefer to implement exclusive contracts if consumers view content providers as similar (low product differentiation) and if there is a large difference in the content providers' ability to profit from consumers so that exclusive access is very valuable for content providers.
- Ranking social welfare to determine optimal regulation yields ambiguous results dependent on parameter values. We identify four channels through which regulation affects total welfare: i) through the effect of QoS variations on consumer common valuation of the content providers, ii) through affecting total transportation

costs determined by consumer preferences over content providers, iii) through redistributing consumers among content providers and thereby changing total surplus created on the content provider side and iv) through changing the total costs of QoS provision.

The policy implication is that we should expect that network operators will have incentives to implement price discrimination and possibly also to exclude some content providers from reaching consumers absent any regulatory intervention. This can be prevented by implementing regulation, but it can come with costs in terms of reducing the network operators' incentives to invest in upgrading their network to achieve better guaranteed Quality of Service. A balanced path, for example as suggested by the FCC NPRM (FCC 2009), may be one way forward as it allows some quality of service variations and investment in improving quality of service that is driven entirely by payments from consumers, but shies away from allowing investments in quality of service to be driven by payments from content providers as well. It also has the benefit of preventing anti-competitive practices not modeled here, but that could potentially be important for welfare (see e.g. Economides and Tåg (2012) for a discussion).

NOTES

1. See Cerf (2006a, b) for a detailed explanation of the argument that innovation "at the edge" could be reduced.
2. See FCC, Report And Order, In the Matter of Preserving the Open Internet Broadband Industry Practices, GN Docket No. 09-191 & WC Docket No. 07-52, December 21, 2010, at paragraphs 1, 8.
3. See http://gigaom.com/broadband/heres-whats-hiding-behind-verizons-net-neutrality-suit/.
4. See http://www.informationweek.com/news/government/policy/229401316; http://thehill.com/blogs/hillicon-valley/technology/192899-senate-rejects-bid-to-overturn-net-neutrality-rules.
5. http://timwu.org/.
6. This regime is also in line with what was proposed in the "Internet Freedom Preservation Act" introduced to the United States Senate in January 2007. http://thomas.loc.gov/cgi-bin/bdquery/z?d110:S.215: . The summary states "Internet Freedom Preservation Act – Amends the Communications Act of 1934 to establish certain Internet neutrality duties for broadband service providers (providers), including not interfering with, or discriminating against, the ability of any person to use broadband service in a lawful manner. Allows providers to engage in activities in furtherance of certain management and business-related practices, such as protecting network security and offering consumer protection services such as parental controls. Prohibits a provider from requiring a subscriber, as a condition on the purchase of broadband service, to purchase any cable service, telecommunications service, or IP-enabled voice service. Requires a report from the Federal Communications Commission (FCC) to specified congressional committees on provider delivery of broadband content, applications, and services."
7. http://hraunfoss.fcc.gov/edocs_public/attachmatch/FCC-05-151A1.pdf.

8. Note that the explicit timing in stage 2 and 3 does not matter. The time structure is chosen for expositional purposes.
9. That the market is covered is essentially an assumption on that $v_A(q)$ and $v_B(q)$ are sufficiently large.
10. The ISP can always choose to sell exclusive access to B instead of to A, in which case A's profits are zero.
11. For second order conditions to hold, we impose $v_A'' - c'' \leq 0$, $(1/2)v_A'' + \pi_A'' - c'' \leq 0$, $(1/2)v_B'' + \pi_B'' - c'' \leq 0$, $(1/2)v_A'' - c'' \leq 0$ and $(1/2)v_B'' - c'' \leq 0$.
12. Comparing the case of exclusivity to the case of no fees, note that an increase in q_A under exclusivity implies that the network access price X can be increased more than under the no fees case. The reason is that under exclusivity QoS changes do not affect transportation costs since P is set by assumption such that they are always t for the marginal consumer (to ensure that the market remains covered).
13. Note that as we consider only the situation of a covered market, there are no welfare effects of changing the price for Internet access. Thus, we get no effect on welfare from monopoly pricing by the ISP.

REFERENCES

Cañón, C. I. (2009), 'Regulation Effects on Investment Decisions in Two-Sided Market Industries', *The Net Neutrality Debate*, http://ssrn.com/abstract=1374782.
Cerf, V. (2006a), 'Prepared Statement of Vinton G. Cerf', U.S. Senate Committee on Commerce, Science, and Transportation, Hearing on 'Network Neutrality', 7 February 2006.
Cerf, V. (2006b), 'Prepared Statement of Vinton G. Cerf', U.S. Senate Committee on the Judiciary, Hearing on Reconsidering our Communications Laws, 14 June 2006.
Chen, M. K. and B. Nalebuff (2007), 'One-Way Essential Complements', *mimeo*, Yale University.
Cheng, H. K., S. Bandyopadhyay and H. Guo (2010), 'The Debate on Net Neutrality: A Policy Perspective', *Information Systems Research*, **22**, 60–82.
Choi, J. P. and B. C. Kim (2010), 'Net Neutrality and Investment Incentives', *RAND Journal of Economics*, **41**, 446–71.
Economides, N. and B. Hermalin (2012), 'The Economics of Network Neutrality', *RAND Journal of Economics*, **43** (2), 602–29.
Economides, N. and J. Tåg (2012), 'Net Neutrality on the Internet: A Two-sided Market Analysis', *Information Economics and Policy*, **24**, 91–104.
FCC (2009), 'Notice of Proposed Rulemaking: In the Matter of Preserving the Open Internet Broadband Industry Practices', GN Docket No. 09-191, WC Docket No. 07-52.
FCC (2010), 'Report And Order, In the Matter of Preserving the Open Internet Broadband Industry Practices', GN Docket No. 09-191 & WC Docket No. 07-52, 21 December 2010.
Hermalin, B. and M. Katz (2007), 'The Economics of Product-Line Restrictions with an Application to the Network Neutrality Debate', *Information Economics and Policy*, **19**, 215–48.
Hogendorn, C. (2007), 'Broadband Internet: Net Neutrality Versus Open Access', *International Economics and Economic Policy*, **4**, 185–208.
Jamison, M. and J. Hauge (2008), 'Getting What You Pay For: Analyzing the Net Neutrality Debate', http://ssrn.com/abstract=1081690.
Krämer, J. and L. Wiewiorra (2009), 'Innovation through Discrimination!? A Formal Analysis of the Net Neutrality Debate', http://ssrn.com/abstract=1444423.

7. Policy and regulatory requirements for a future internet
Jonathan Cave

INTRODUCTION

Numerous experts and stakeholders have called for policy leadership to influence positively the development and impacts of the future internet. The current financial crisis and the accompanying belief that regulatory governance has failed have crystallised a growing realisation of the complexity and fragility of globally networked socioeconomic systems and of the need for a potentially profound rethinking of their governance. The implications go beyond the financial system – markets linked by high-speed networks and even higher-speed programme trading display new forms of instability, while financial markets' investment preferences and requirements for speed, security, etc. influence internet technologies and architecture and give force to arguments that appeal to infrastructure maintenance to justify particular forms of regulation (e.g. net neutrality). The crisis also helped focus minds on the interdependence of economic performance and other societal objectives, the absolute centrality of collaborative innovation to sustainable development and the need to balance healthy competition with constructive and collaborative engagement. This recognition finds political recognition in recent European-level initiatives ranging from the Recovery Plan[1] to Europe 2020[2] (and especially the Digital Agenda[3]), but builds on strong Information Society antecedents that emphasised linkage across: policy instruments (e.g. research and deployment support, standardisation, procurement and regulation); regions and sectors; government locations and levels; and stakeholder domains (administration, business and civil society). This chapter considers the need for and characteristics of internet-specific regulation and for changing existing regulatory and governance structures to accommodate the evolving internet.

The need for wide-ranging regulatory reform, if not the change needed, is agreed by a startlingly wide range of commentators including social and economic analysts of internet policy, technical experts, consumer groups, industry bodies, academics and MEPs. All call for clear leadership and evidence-based, rigorous, transparent and forward-looking planning.

With somewhat less unanimity, they support European proactive and explicit championing of equitable and transparent policy-making to enable fair, efficient and sustainable development.

A further element of context is provided by the adoption into policy of the 'future internet'. This goes beyond recognising that regulation and policy must continually adjust to the ever-changing internet. The future internet as a policy vision takes the present moment as a window of opportunity defined by the fortuitous combination of (in some countries) IPv6 transition, the global economic crisis and a tsunami of political and societal upheaval that is at least facilitated by social networking and many other elements.[4] There is widespread recognition that the future internet may have a very different architecture, players and (therefore) governance structures. It is clear to all that these changes reflect issues with the current internet and that today's institutional changes will determine tomorrow's balance of power. The future internet is meant to provide an *open* and *neutral platform* supporting both *cooperation* and *competition* through *interoperation* and delivering appropriate *quality of service* to a host of different applications and communities. But the definitions of the italicised terms are far from agreed and the future of the internet is hotly contested within and beyond the future internet. Regulation is, of course, only a small part of this complicated dialectic. But it may be more important than first appears.

This chapter considers the general forces affecting regulation of activity on the internet and the implications of internet-specific regulation for other forms. These derive from the migration online of activities that are (or are not) regulated offline. In an ideal world, this migration would be accompanied by a deliberative process of transposition; some regulated activities may no longer need regulation while others may need new or enhanced regulation. But the conditions do not favour deliberation. The pace of migration is rapid, convergence rewires linkages between activities and fundamental societal rights and objectives, the 'functional' aspects of online behaviour drag along off-line institutions, communities, cultures and empires and on-line counterparts rise up in contention. Section 2 briefly considers the general features of regulatory migration and the resulting questions facing regulatory reform. When tussle becomes conflict, everything of value may be placed at risk or changed utterly. There is therefore a need to develop 'portable' principles on which transitional forms of regulation can be based. These will need to cope with collisions; activities converging onto the internet bring in their train inconsistent or contradictory regulatory and other legacies. This can lead to fission (splitting off of 'internet-specific' theories and practices) or fusion (creation or emergence of new hybrids). Section 3 illustrates the interplay between theory and regulation using the example of network neutrality. More fundamentally, any analysis of internet regulation should recognise its complexity and that of the 'web' and other structures built upon it. Section 4 applies elementary models from complexity theory and the theory of games played on (and with) networks to identify specific features of relevance to regulation. Finally, the chapter argues that regulatory principles suitable to the internet domain should reflect the importance of the internet as a metaphor for a network-based view of human activity and the derivation of specific theories from stylised models of internet behaviour. This approach is used in Section 5 to develop some principles for regulatory reconsideration and reform.

A STYLISED VIEW OF INTERNET REGULATION

The desire to regulate on the internet may be symptomatic of the migration of ICT and internet impacts from the province of engineers, via the battlefield of the military-industrial complex to a global commons that touches almost every area of life in some parts of the globe and some aspects of life in almost every part of the globe. By no means everyone and everything is 'on the grid' but everything is within a few social, economic and political hops of the internet. In consequence, almost every area of policy is in some respects internet policy. This internet percolation makes the dynamics of change more complex and widens the range of government, business and civil society participants jockeying for power. This changes the case for regulation almost beyond recognition. There is no obvious reason to believe that incremental and independent changes by incumbent regulators and other stakeholders seeking to preserve the *status quo ante* will adequately meet the coming challenges.

Indeed, governance is already evolving in response to competitive and cooperative interactions among old and new players: sector-specific and general regulators at all levels; commercial actors throughout the rich and changing internet-affected 'value mesh' that pervades the economy; scientific expertise from a huge range of (previously separated) disciplines; and the 'bottom-up' influence of end-users, citizens, consumers, demographic and ethnic groups.

It may seem odd to place internet regulation so high on the policy agenda. The internet is not and, thanks to its global nature, cannot be directly regulated. Indeed, lack of regulation is part of its defining myth. But it has been the object of partial regulation from without – inherited rules for separate activities (content (broadcast); telecommunications; (e)commerce; privacy and security, etc.) – and within (e.g. self- and co-regulation and 'internet governance'). However, these rules are partial and often contradictory. They can have perverse rebound effects when applied to such a fluid and global system and are often formed and enforced by unrepresentative self-regulatory and governance bodies amid a tangle of unresolved linkages and resulting conflicts among e.g. technical, societal and economic interests and perspectives. There seems to be a clear need for a more comprehensive, coherent, transparent and accountable approach. This could also mitigate adverse impacts on 'home domain regulation' when parts of regulated activities migrate to the internet.

Regulation is often conflated with governance. Conventionally, regulation means that part of governance involving rules issued and enforced by state authority. But this definition covers instruments and powers rather than the regulated entities and activities. The 'internetisation' of governance inevitably shifts these between regulation (and formal bodies) and other forms of governance. Codes of conduct sit alongside statute law in domains such as content, privacy, etc. The future governance of the internet will be much influenced by how well governance institutions arise and pass away and take on or relinquish powers. This in turn depends on the degree to which structure and conduct changes are motivated by accountability pressures in the domain under consideration (e.g. content owners demanding state enforcement of intellectual property rights through service provider liability or political imperatives for state involvement with internet governance) as opposed to a search for efficient allocation of regulatory power in which such pressures are balanced with the organisation's competence to act effectively, transparently and proportionately. This can already be seen in the emergence of converged regulators covering all network industries or all aspects of communication. In time, they may give way to specialised internet regulators.

There is a second point of interpretation – 'regulated' may refer to the 'regular' (intended or evolved) operation of a system or device rather than to rules or constraints that enforce this regulation. In other words, it can – and in the perspective of this chapter should – be regarded as an end in itself rather than a necessary means to that end. This distinction separates the incentives of internet participants from their obligations and is especially important when they can evade or avoid obligations by moving online. The 'regulation' of the collective space of the internet can then be seen in teleological or deontological terms. Most of this chapter takes the teleological perspective, but many human actions are also constrained by a sense of duty. It is therefore appropriate to consider internet regulation as a matter of rights. Put simply it seems reasonable to construe the right to participate in internet governance as neither an individual nor a collective right, but as a *civic* right – an obligation participants owe to the internet itself (as a consensual social construct) to enable themselves to participate in a 'well regulated' internet; they take on this obligation by participating.

On the other hand, the migration of activity from traditional (commerce, broadcast, content distribution, personal data exchange, etc.) domains onto the internet may change regulation in those areas as well. For example, if multiple channels for internet connection provide voice telephony services, much (though perhaps not all) of the basis for utility regulation of telephone companies disappears. Similarly, globalisation of (e)commerce can reduce the *need* for competition rules (by enhancing competition) and certainly makes the *practice* of antitrust regulation harder (if only for jurisdictional and evidentiary reasons). Finally, as needs for regulation will continue to evolve, some organisations may (and most should) consider whether their current actions will encourage better governance in future or institutionalise perverse or ineffective ('Potemkin') regulation that stops progress without fixing the original problem.

Today's regulation for and of the internet is largely inherited from rules applying to separate activities converging on the internet: broadcast; telecommunications; (e)commerce; privacy and security, etc. Some regulatory principles translate directly. These include the potential of open access to prevent holdup and foreclosure and the known conditions favouring utility regulation versus facilities-based competition. The utility approach offers society direct influence over a wide range of policy objectives and critical impacts, by giving monopolies specific protections (e.g. entry regulation, investment and standardisation support, regulatory forbearance and voice in policy-making) in exchange for subjecting them to (investment, access, pricing, quality, etc.) controls and obligations (e.g. universal service and must-carry). By contrast, market-led approaches adapt general competition rules to harness competitive discipline in order to promote efficiency, affordability, quality, innovation – especially when the authorities cannot understand technology and demand well enough to identify optimal conduct, structures, etc. If this mixed regulatory legacy is to work coherently to improve outcomes throughout those parts of the economy dependent on the internet, competition and consumer protection must be seen as complements: effective competition forces firms to identify and serve consumer needs and desires while consumer protection enables users to seek out better offers from rival suppliers. The same synergy between competing suppliers and mobile demand works for *non-market* internet-based interactions as well; the global nature of the internet gives users some degree of choice over how and by whom they wish to be governed.

But these inheritances do not always play nicely together; rules sometimes conflict or are poorly understood. More importantly for the future of the internet, dominant incumbents with bottleneck power and legacy relations with their customary regulators may seek to influence rules, policies and other factors shaping the internet in order to preserve their market power. In particular, despite the policy recognition accorded to user needs and applications – especially in the future internet context alluded to above – disproportionate power is too often wielded by incumbent telecommunications service providers. This is somewhat mitigated by traditional regulation – especially in Europe, whose telecommunications services regulatory framework is founded squarely on competition principles and adapting to changes arising as a result of the internet. But even there the scope for applications and services to shape internet development is restricted, as can be seen in the dominance of the European internet by telecommunications service providers.[5]

This mix of different rules and conflicting interests might seem threatening and lead to calls for a 'world governance' approach. But this is not a consensus recommendation even among technocrats. There is as yet no single internet jurisdiction, no common legal foundation for regulatory powers, no agreed basis for regulation and no structure for enforcing even criminal law, let alone regulation. Equally, there is no obvious reason why a logically coherent 'convergence' of different regulatory approaches and powers onto the internet would be desirable. We should at least entertain the possibility of a positive and 'generative' chaos, capable of leading to improvements both in internet governance and of national and non-internet-specific regulations. Beyond this, the complex adaptive nature of the internet holds to promise of 'self-organised criticality' (Section 4) whereby the internet's functional effectiveness and self-regulating character emerge from the changing structure of the net itself.

Perhaps the fundamental policy questions are:

- whether cyberspace should be treated as a separate 'governance space'[6] or an extension of existing jurisdictions and markets – do we work towards making cyberspace self-governing or continue attempts (especially by governments and large commercial entities) to extend 'off-net' powers of compulsion, regulation and legitimisation into cyberspace; and
- whether we should seek to 'rescue' existing regulation (preserving powers and reshaping activities despite risks of institutionalisation and 'mission creep') or reconstruct the governance regime from the ground up, using e.g. a WTO-like consent mechanism to deal with issue linkage and coordination.

In any case, regulations and the challenges they address will continue to change; so, too will the appropriate mix of technical, economic, legal and societal *rules* and – this is crucial to the discussion in this chapter and current issues e.g. piracy – *instruments*. Just because a governance failure has a technological (or market or legal) solution does not mean that this is the best solution even if it may be the quickest, the cheapest, the most effective or the most appropriate in view of current definitions.

To illustrate, new regulatory issues (e.g. net neutrality) are making their way into policy before consistent definitions, an appropriate understanding of legacy regulatory principles and a sound basis for choosing among technical, economic and societal remedies have developed. Looking forward, we therefore need a clear framework to transpose inherited principles to the internet domain and to integrate them with available regulatory instruments in order to preserve clarity, provide necessary certainty and protect regulatory traction.

Such new issues raise a more practical question as well. Even off the internet, there are priorities among regulatory domains – for instance, security and law enforcement generally take priority over economic regulation. Therefore, it is appropriate to consider whether internet-specific rules should pre-empt or defer to general regulations and whether traditional priorities should be extended or modified in the internet domain. Several recent examples illustrate this conundrum. The spate of laws and treaties regarding the protection of digital intellectual property rights (IPR) raise troubling questions about the balance of economic ownership rights, basic rights of free expression and communication (internet access as a human right) and privacy (deep packet inspection as a technical means to facilitate enforcement). The standing of IPR as a legally-protected monopoly collides with commitments to free competition or open access to cultural legacies by means of public institutions in recent cases involving the wholesale scanning of books and other contents of libraries. This kind of collision, which can usefully trigger a re-examination of the technology-specificity of many basic rights and regulations, is becoming more prevalent as activities and business models converge onto the internet.

NEUTRALITY AS AN EXAMPLE OF COLLISION

Perhaps the most sharply suggestive such issue is 'net neutrality'. This was originally viewed as a specific problem arising in the context of a US market where competition among channels was limited and where local access monopolists and locally-dominant broadband service providers had potentially vast powers to control transactions between content owners and end-users. It applies in different form to technological 'platforms' associated with closed access devices. It is sometimes portrayed as a dispute between content owners and vertically integrated and oligopolistic service providers involving on one side the ability of the platform operators to expropriate gains from trade and on the other the presumed congestion and other external costs associated with content access. However, this simple dichotomy does not apply to the specific disputes and the impacts of proposed policies in fact involve a range of services – such as search (that creates only indirect gains from trade being itself a kind of platform with little or no congestion cost) or gaming (for which there is relatively little asymmetric connection and little scope for monetising peer-to-peer benefits). Despite these particulars, the discussion was recast as a matter of principle – the argument that discrimination of any form was *ipso facto* damaging to the public interest appealed to the guiding myth of the internet as an uncontrolled and unlimited commons, but flew in the face of technical reality. Bandwidth is not infinite, and different applications (and users) define quality of service in different ways – thus some rationing is inevitable, and simple rules of 'equal treatment' may have very unequal impacts on users. Moreover, this politicised version of the debate ignored basic economics – the 'right kind' of discrimination or differentiation is not only essential for efficiency, but even for the existence of some socially and commercially valuable services and facilities.[7] Since those early stages, net neutrality has crept into almost every aspect of internet regulation and internet governance. Although much of the rhetoric is simplistic, the debate has helped refine our understanding of the possible *basis* for mandatory net neutrality (prohibit discrimination against packets, applications, application classes, organisations, content types, etc.) and its underlying *objectives* (freedom of expression, freedom of commerce and IP ownership, QoS, etc.).

Differences of opinion can be seen by comparing different settings; the internet governance community discusses net neutrality as a norm or 'governance principle', European policy often describes it as a desirable policy outcome (like technological neutrality) and in the US finds expression as a specific regulation or legal provision (though a recent bill was defeated for political reasons).

The impact on regulation can be seen through this latter incarnation; as a regulation, net neutrality 'binds' previously-unregulated entities (e.g. ISPs), creating new regulatory relationships and possibly requiring changes in regulators' statutory remits. Finally, the 'generative' nature can be seen in its influence on new or adjusted types of economic/policy analysis. The balance of this section briefly considers some relevant collisions.

One of these is the 'war of theories'. Much competition and industrial organisation economics was shaped by the market failures of the day, from the great trusts of the 19th century to complex forms of interlocking coordination and facilitating practice in the 20th century. Net neutrality tussles based around the use of oligopsonistic platforms for delivering content to end-users – together with other examples derived from credit cards, travel agencies, newspapers and booksellers – have inspired a specific set of models that reflect a stylised value chain in which different users use a platform (provided by a third party for whose services they pay) in order to interact. Their demand for the platform service therefore derives from their demand for opportunities to interact with others using the same platform. If there are two kinds of user whose demand for the platform is derived from the need for appropriate pairings in order to engage in exclusive and mutually desired transactions, we speak of two-sided markets.[8] But the interposition of platform providers applies to a broader range of situations. As Weyl (2010) notes, users of a high-end credit card particularly value the chance to use the card at participating stores; because the credit card cannot price discriminate effectively, it under provides this matching service and will optimally subsidise the participation of particularly attractive merchants. In contrast, readers of a newspaper or subscription-based information service may wish to avoid advertising; the platform's limited price discrimination ability leads it towards more advertising and lower fees than would be optimal. The former version has tended to dominate the net neutrality debate; driven as it was by a tussle between providers of paid-for content and (vertically integrated) platform providers (typically with their own content to distribute). But of course, there are many possible extensions; it is quite reasonable, for example, to consider the platform as a club good with 'crowding types'[9] in which different types of users derive different types of (positive and negative) utility from the participation of different 'portfolios' of other users. In the above example, the merchants and the credit card users derive positive utility from each other's presence; the merchants prefer more high-value customers, but fewer rival merchants, while the customers value more high-end merchants for variety and for the economic benefits of competition and may also (up to the status value of an exclusive card) benefit from the presence of other users, to increase the range of outlets at which the card is accepted and to provide competitive pressure on which other cardholders can free-ride. Beyond this, the conventional model is concerned with *groups* of merchants or of customers; there may be advantages in considering specific networks or other (more than one-to-one) structures of repeated interaction. The advantage of this more general approach derives from the reductive nature of the collision – the tussle between content providers raised considerations of e.g. infrastructure investment, quality-of-service discrimination and traffic shaping, freedom of expression, etc. – but in a perspective that is highly focused on only one of the many uses of ISP platform services.

The implications of this debate for e.g. VOIP, peer to peer file sharing, online gaming, cloud computing, etc. are not developed in the same way as they would had a more general approach been used to frame the debate.[10] Thus the policy debate, the regulatory landscape, the applicable theory and the real-world outcomes all evolve together.

Behind this war of theories is a war of interests, of course. These interests are not all opposed. They include suppliers of proprietary and user-generated content (often platform providers in their own right[11]), cloud application providers, cloud platform providers, network service providers, ISPs, walled-garden providers, wireless and fixed-line transport service providers, providers of alternative or layered services, etc. They also include community interests that value connectivity, security, quality of service, reach, etc. in different ways. Beyond this are a range of policy interests, ranging over free trade, competitiveness of the creative sector, economic and technical efficiency, investment and innovation, inclusion of disadvantaged groups, etc. Establishing the need for regulation becomes extremely difficult when the underlying theory is strategically developed and deployed and when the theory and evidence evolve along with the market.

In evaluating competing theories, it is also useful to recall Einstein's possibly apocryphal maxim that theory should be 'as simple as possible – but no simpler'. A theoretical argument for (or against) net neutrality based on a model of end-users choosing a single ISP over which to perform a single transaction (downloading premium content) or set of transactions (search for premium content followed by downloading) is almost certainly too simple; policy based on such a theory is likely to have unintended consequences for other uses, patterns of connectivity and benefits arising outside the theoretical abstraction. Nor is it obvious that a collection of separate theoretical models for different uses or market arrangements can be integrated or aggregated without consequence. We therefore briefly consider the implications of complexity.

COMPLEXITY

It is almost a truism to observe that the internet and the socioeconomic networks constructed on it and operating over it form a *complex* system of linked subsystems. A 'layered' view is useful when considering how pricing, connectivity, quality of service, etc. affect the interactions among individuals and firms over the network that are the source of both individual demands and societal benefit (which may be different). It is slightly more useful to recognise the implications of that characterisation[12] for internet regulation. One typical feature of complex systems is strong emergence – the development of behaviour at the system level that cannot be understood or described in terms of the component subsystems. A related definition of strong emergence is behaviour that cannot be anticipated but can (given sufficient information) be predicted – and which must therefore be regulated (if at all) more in an ex post than an ex ante spirit, and more by principles-based than rules-based methods. Not all systemic behaviour is strongly emergent; a purely competitive market inhabited by rational economic agents (firms and individuals) will, in equilibrium, display the behaviour expected of a single 'representative' agent – the market acts as a sort of averaging device. In other cases, this 'scale-free' aspect fails; for instance, markets inhabited by poorly-informed or (modestly) irrational agents may behave like well-informed and rational agents (e.g. the wisdom of crowds[13]). Conversely, markets (or other systems) in which agents draw cues or inferences from others may behave like an irrational or psychotic 'person' even when the participants are as rational as their limited information and Bayes' Law will let them be ('rational herding'[14]). This happens as a result of mechanisms flowing from the part to the whole; it is the mechanism that allows the TCP/IP protocol to produce coherent and organised flows of data through the internet itself. Societal complex systems have another kind of emergence as well – 'reverse' linkages from the system to its component subsystems (e.g. when people receive and respond to signals about congestion, quality of service or security). This 'reverse emergence' can produce even more paradoxical effects. This is particularly important because most internet users did not even start out from a codified or regularised understanding of how the internet works or even how to make it work for them; instead, they felt their way, learning from the opportunities, threats and expressed beliefs of the day. Other complexity phenomena relevant to internet governance include synch[15] (the emergence of temporal, spatial or other kinds of order across the network as a whole), endogenous discrimination and self-organised criticality. These are briefly illustrated below. Taken together, they can point the way to an understanding of the 'mind of the net'. This is of vital importance to internet regulation; without it, it is impossible to determine what outcomes or behaviours are problematic, to separate those that will be self-limiting or self-governing from those needing explicit intervention, to separate 'signals' of something that breaks the rules from transitory or transitional 'noise' or to devise remedies for a problem once identified. The latter is particularly important; most forms of regulation rest on a combination of selection (inviting the participation of only the 'right sort') and incentives (encouraging 'good behaviour'). Without such a 'theory of mind' it is hard to predict how stakeholders will react. For instance, a net neutrality prohibition on price discrimination may lead to other forms of discrimination (e.g. quality of service discrimination or the injection of latency to discourage latency-sensitive uses such as gaming). This may be worse in terms of deadweight loss than profit-maximising price discrimination. On the other hand, if the coexistence of different patterns of use within a single ISP or part of the network produces congestion externalities that would be eliminated by efficient sorting into specialised or dedicated services, non-price discrimination may lead users with particular 'crowding types' (e.g. level and timing of use, costs of latency, etc.) to 'opt out' or self-associate with more compatible users in their own subnets or to arrange local peering or time-matching arrangements that eliminate troublesome congestion, etc. externalities.

To get a sense of how complexity-based models operate, consider three processes that may affect the structure and use of interactions among internet users:

- Contagion on networks – the spread of problems and solutions from one user to another, ranging from the prorogation of malware or compromised virtual machines to the diffusion of ethics of compliance, cooperation or opportunism.
- Games played on networks – this refers to strategic interaction among network users. In conventional game theory, players choose their strategies in response to the choices of all other players; in a network game, they pay particular attention to those with whom they are directly linked.
- Games of network formation – even though the internet in principle allows (almost) complete connectivity, in reality even potential connections are restricted and only a tiny fraction of these are actually used. This perspective considers the processes by which such effective geometries are chosen.

Each of these can be considered in its own right, and yields interesting and relevant insights for regulation that are valid in a world in which these processes are 'isolated' in the sense that their speeds can be strictly ranked (e.g. if contagion is very fast, changes of individual behaviour (games played on networks) are slower and changes of network structure are slower still). But even more interesting results are possible when the processes overlap and interact.

Contagion

The spread of problems, solutions, expectation or even behaviour through a network can be analysed from a 'mechanical' point of view as the result of contact rather than considered choice. This epidemiological point of view may be appropriate for an essentially risk-based approach to regulation, which treats e.g. security threats as contagious disease. A fairly typical result is the use of 'effective spreading rate' thresholds for classifying threats. Suppose that nodes in the network can be in either a healthy or a compromised state; the probability that a healthy node becomes compromised is proportional to the prevalence of the threat among that node's neighbours, while a compromised node recovers at an exogenous rate (e.g. the frequency of screening). The ratio of these two rates is the effective spreading rate; each network structure has a threshold above which a threat will propagate to the whole network. For scale-free networks, this threshold is effectively 0; such networks are therefore very good for detecting (eventually) problems and for motivating a common response, but involve much higher levels of adverse consequences than networks in which threats are localised and die out. Most scale-free networks include many 'peripheral' participants connected by highly-linked 'hubs'[16] – the contagion model suggests that surveillance and remedial measures targeted on these hubs will be highly effective in dealing with threats. Thus regulation can be efficiently limited to highly-central internet 'connectors' – indeed, the model can be used to justify a relaxed attitude to the accumulation and perpetuation of high degrees of centrality by major players. Moreover, there is likely to be some 'filtration' of issues by epidemiological fate – those that are persistent and/or widespread are likely to evoke regulation; thus the problem and the regulatory response (or institution) in effect stabilise each other.

Formation of Conventions

One simple form of interaction is the adoption or spread of conventions. Many economists[17] have modelled such situations as coordination games; each player plays the same binary game against all her 'network neighbours' – in effect choosing among various strategies a single one to be used in all interactions. The coordination aspect arises because a player whose neighbours all use the same strategy will copy them (e.g. standards adoption). Behaviour evolves through a random process; in each period, players chosen at random are allowed to reconsider their behaviour in light of their neighbours' actions. By assumption, they will attempt to do the best they can; with a small probability they make a mistake. The resulting Markov process – in a fully connected network – converges almost surely to a specific standard or convention. To understand which one it is, one needs to take into account that behaviour can change both by intention (adopting a best reply to one's neighbours' actions) and by mistake.

Starting from a uniform standard, if a sufficiently high proportion of one's neighbours change behaviour in response to their neighbours' actions or by mistake, a player with the chance to choose will try to switch. Associated with each standard, therefore, is a 'neighbourhood' within which behaviour will tend to return to the standard. Roughly speaking, the standard with the largest such neighbourhood will prevail in the long run. Again, network geometry matters; a small worlds network may support stable diversity, while simpler structures lead to uniformity. Another implication of relevance to regulation is that the stable standard may not be the best one from the players' point of view – in the case of two possible strategies, for instance, the stable one is the risk-dominant one (the one that would be best against an opponent who chose entirely at random); this need not be payoff-dominant (by assumption, one is better for both players than the other). A second observation is that group convergence to the 'better' outcome can be encouraged by (e.g. regulatory) changes to the payoffs of players who depart from the standard that are less invasive than those required to force each player to comply. However, convergence may take a very long time; networks with dense 'local' structures (e.g. Small Worlds networks in which a node's neighbours would not be far apart even if that node were removed) converge much faster than e.g. random networks (in which path lengths are short but there is little clustering. In other words, the density of interactions suggests whether light-touch (evolutionary) regulation will suffice.

Network Formation

Of course, internet participants can often choose with whom they wish to interact. A simple approach to strategic network formation is provided by the Jackson-Wolinsky[18] model. It starts from an 'allocation function' that associates to each network a payoff to each node. This need not be based solely on nearest-neighbour interactions; for instance, in a trading network it can reflect the net result of a pattern of direct and indirect trading opportunities. This may be important for extending e.g. competition or product liability regulation to networked markets in which traders have only indirect contact, as in the two-sided or *n*-sided market models discussed above or the network of service level agreements (SLAs) defining a cloud computing interaction network. The dynamics are simple; a link (which may or may not exist in the current network) is chosen at random; if it does not exist and both parties wish to be linked it is formed. If it already exists and either party wishes (on the basis of the allocation function payoffs) to break the link it is severed. Networks that do not change are called pairwise stable; networks that cannot be beaten by others that offer each participant at least a weakly higher payoff are not efficient. For many allocation functions, the stable and the efficient networks are completely different. In some cases, this inefficiency can result from myopia – there is therefore a case for regulation that limits or enforces certain linkages, or enforces long-term partnership or subscription arrangements. There is also a stochastic version of this model, in which the desired change (making or breaking a link) happens with sufficiently high probability; in this model, efficiency can sometimes be encouraged by enforcing a degree of inertia. But overall, the appropriate form of (any) regulation of network connection will need to reflect the incentives of the players, the current network and possibly the tension between what is good for the players involved (e.g. a collusive arrangement) and what is good for society as a whole. To take a mundane example, this kind of consideration can be used to scrutinise proposals for interoperability or IPR sharing in relation to the coordination patterns existing among other operators, or to extend a myopic analysis based on immediate changes in profits and consumer surplus to a 'competitive effects' analysis that takes into account the rearrangements that will logically follow if a given merger, partnership, etc. is approved.

Combined Effects

If these processes proceed at similar rates, highly interesting alternatives appear. For instance, in the epidemiological model, suppose that a healthy node responds to evidence of compromise among its neighbours by severing its links (with some probability) and replacing them with new, uncompromised partners. This dramatically changes the results described above; even a scale free initial network becomes (after an outbreak of troubles) much more heterogeneous – instead of a few hubs linking an ocean of peripheral participants, there are many nodes at each level of connectivity. Moreover, each node tends to be most intensely connected to similarly placed nodes, so targeted interventions or regulation are no longer effective. More interestingly, perhaps, the 'penetration threshold' is supplemented by a second threshold above which a problem switches from epidemic status (with isolated outbreaks) to endemic status (its effects may be managed, but the problem is never eradicated). More precisely, depending on the relation between the effective spreading rate and the rate at which nodes are able to 'require' their connections, the healthy state, the compromised state or either may be stable; there is even a region where the prevalence oscillates. Finally, in the zone where both states are stable, the network gradually separates into two loosely connected clusters, one of which is effectively free of the problem while the other is pervasively compromised. This endogenous emergence of a two-tier network is a robust result of contagion combined with freedom to make or drop links.

This is an example of a more general phenomenon of self-organisation. Many systems exhibit a degree of self-governance or self-regulation. Such arrangements are not always positive; Cave, Simmons and Marsden (2008) show that they often lead to mission creep, facilitated collusion or a toxic combination of stringent rules with deficient levels of compliance. However, these perverse outcomes are less likely if the participants are close to a disruptive change – for example if (as in a competitive economy) their profits are comparable and close to zero. Under these circumstances, they tend to react to threats before they become established in a coherent (if not always uniform) manner. This 'robust yet fragile' behaviour is found in many other systems. In financial markets, for instance, it might seem sensible to support institutions that are, if not too big, at least 'too connected to fail'. But this status brings its own (moral hazard) problems – institutions at the heart of the network have less incentive to take care than those on the periphery, but have more power and more information about systemic problems. Left to its own devices, such a system might correct structurally by evolving in the direction of a 'phase change' where small shocks could produce widespread responses (e.g. by institutions leaving the core and being replaced). Although this evolution keeps the system on the brink of collapse it also enables the system as a whole to detect and respond to threats. What threatens individual parts of the internet (or similar system) thus stabilises the functionality of the system as a whole. The lesson for regulation is to pay less attention to the position and health of individual nodes than to the structure and performance of the system as a whole, and to develop measures of self-organisation capable of distinguishing functional from destructive shocks and transients.

Principles for Reform

Such considerations suggest some general principles for reworking regulation in light of the continuing development of the internet and some practical considerations. In stating these, we are aware that some existing 'values' may be artefacts of particular times, places and types of internet use and may suffer destructive collisions.[19]

Four principles (in addition to the principles of Better Regulation[20]) are: openness, innovation-friendliness, smart regulation and leadership combined with humility and flexibility.

Openness ought to be self-evident but, as Zittrain[21] warns, tensions between commercial and public objectives and conflicting interests within these domains continually threaten to enclose parts of the internet. It is important to understand the principle; it is appropriate – even essential – to have separate internets, with different characteristics and sometimes-clear boundaries. But movement and interoperation should be, if not free, possible where there is a clear justification; the mutually-recognised basis for such justifications should form part of the constitutional infrastructure of the internet and the protection of openness and mobility should be an affirmative duty of all those involved with internet governance and especially with regulation. For example, licensing necessarily 'closes' part of the internet, but qualification should be – in principle – open to all and allocation should be non-discriminatory. In the TAFI study,[22] this finds particular expression in the somewhat utopian "power to the people" scenario in which offline government business and civil society power cannot be effectively (or at least directly) extended into the internet because its tendencies to enclose, to coerce and to exclude are limited by a commitment to openness of the internet for good or ill. This does not, of course, mean that there is no governance; the dynamic forces described in Section 4 are still in operation and a degree of self-organisation online is to be expected, with its own forms of discrimination, institutional creep, etc. In other words, there will surely be some form of cyber-militia; whether it will be 'well-regulated' in the sense of the 2nd Amendment to the US Constitution remains to be seen.[23] It is argued by some scholars (Finkelman 2000) that this Amendment protects the right of citizens to bear arms in order to protect their ability to constitute a 'well-regulated militia' as distinguished from a standing professional army or similarly 'official' body. The retention by internet users of a range of powers – e.g. to collect and share information about internet stakeholders' activities, to negotiate and agree to abide by standards, etc. – *can* thus help to preserve the self-correcting capabilities of the internet. This *may* be preferable to more formally-constituted and legally-backed forms of regulation, if only because such regulatory bodies – even if not captured by dominant – incumbents – may tend to view changes in light of existing rules and thus to miss emergent opportunities.

As noted above, perhaps the most essential characteristic of the future internet is support for ongoing innovation; technological, economic and regulatory, and both top-down and bottom-up. Regulation is part of 'innovation friendliness' (Aho 2006). In the globalised world, continuing innovation is necessary to the economic survival of those parts of the world – like Europe – whose only unique (and renewable) resource is intellectual and social capital. Societies wishing even to sustain current levels of welfare must therefore:

- Support well-thought-out risk-taking;
- Share risk, costs and benefits to ensure a societal portfolio that explores many avenues of development, is not restricted to a crowded competition for low-hanging fruit by individual fears of failure and ensures that the asymmetric fruits of innovation do not harden into a stratified society that ultimately loses flexibility; and
- Build in sufficient regulatory flexibility and neutrality to provide level playing fields for merit-based competition among technologies, architectures, services, applications and business models.

Smart regulation is a matter of mechanism design; governance is concerned with finding optimal actions for people and organisations and seeing to it that they are taken. Governance problems arise when regulators do not know what the stakeholders know (and thus cannot integrate their knowledge) and/or cannot (cost-effectively) observe (let alone compel) their actions. An 'incentive regulation' mechanism is designed to attract the right parties (e.g. to apply for licences) and to elicit relevant information (e.g. via regulatory submissions) and/ or provide incentives for them to take (individually or collectively) the actions that would be optimal if the information were known. 'Optimality' in this context balances static efficiency (minimising costs and maximising collective gains) and dynamic incentives for continuing innovation and investment, taking account of the costs and limited effectiveness of measures to induce stakeholders to reveal information or change their behaviour and the distortions caused by the mechanism itself. In some cases, the smartest regulation may be self- or co-regulation or even deregulation. In other words, it is often most efficient to involve key stakeholders directly in the regulatory process, because of their superior information, proximity to the actions requiring regulation, 'responsibility' (in the eyes of the public or the market) for the outcomes of such actions, ability to bear risks and/or ability to reduce the likelihood or severity of adverse impacts and/or to devise innovative and effective alternatives. This 'power sharing' can range from deregulation (laissez-faire) to statutory regulation.

Clear *leadership* and planning are needed, but so are history-aware and farsighted policies taking into account others' likely reactions and the need to accommodate and track future developments and respond accordingly. This entails a degree of *humility*: policy may need to 'nudge' internet development rather than attempting to force or control it, to reframe objectives at a feasible and meaningful level (e.g. setting quality of service targets in terms of reliable throughput rather than peak or average speed) and to engage a wide range of actors and stakeholders before objectives

Table 7.1   Varieties of self- and co-regulation

TYPE OF REGULATION	DESCRIPTION	
No regulation	No explicit controls on an organisation	
Self-regulation – also, broad categories of *embedded* self-regulation can be discerned as *subcategories* of regulation -	Regulations are specified, administered and enforced by the regulated organisation(s). However, the role of the state in such regulation is seen to be the most important factor.	
Self-regulation 1	Co-operative	co-operation between regulator and regulated on the operation of statutory regulation;
Self-regulation 2	Delegated	the delegation of the implementation of statutory duties by a public authority to self-regulatory bodies;
Self-regulation 3	Devolved	the devolution of statutory powers to self-regulatory bodies, often thought of as 'statutory self-regulation', i.e., the specification of self-regulatory schemes in statute;
Self-regulation 4	Facilitated	self-regulation explicitly supported by the state in some way but where the scheme itself is not backed by statute;
Self-regulation 5	Tacit	close to 'pure' self-regulation – self-regulation with little explicit state support, but its implicit role can be influential.
Co-regulation	Regulations are specified, administered and enforced by a combination of the state and the regulated organisation(s).	
Statutory Regulation	Regulations are specified, administered and enforced by the state.	

and instruments are defined and policies implemented. This must also involve *flexibility*:

- to recognise that policy issues frame, but do not capture, governance problems and market failures;
- to identify and continuously monitor a clear basis for regulation (e.g. market or other governance failure) and to ensure that regulators' objectives and powers follow basic principles (see endnote 20); and
- to construct and continuously to monitor multi-stakeholder governance discourse platforms and to support appropriate regulatory innovation and regulatory withdrawal where possible.

At a more practical level, both regulatory frameworks and strategies for advancing regulatory harmonisation in the global internet context should embody sound architectural principles, take the global context into account and find expression in a clear framework.

The architectural principles underlying the internet have ranged from ringing expressions of common or desirable values (of the form common in expressions of political will or as preamble to specific recommendations or Directives) to apparently limited technical principles such as the end-to-end principle. It is not necessary to rehearse these here and it would be presumptuous to pre-empt the societal processes needed to refine or integrate them. But two observations are worth emphasising. First, even political value declarations or statements of overarching objectives find direct structural expression because they help to coordinate the activities of many people, improve understanding of and appropriate compliance with regulations and other rules, and frame the processes of scrutiny, evaluation, protest and deliberation by which such rules are changed. Thus, they serve as a constitution for internet governance – a set of rules for making rules. Whether they are in fact universally accepted is less important for influencing the evolution (as opposed to the less-feasible 'design' or 'control') of the internet than the fact that they are clearly stated, accessible to reason and debate, and referenced in subsequent policy. The second observation is that societal norms like the end-to-end principle often operate indirectly, allowing complex and fecund socioeconomic and technological systems to emerge on top of the 'merely technical' internet. Moreover, the reason for their function should be separated from their justification. When the internet first emerged it was reasonable to suppose that the people at the ends of the network could be held responsible for their actions and trusted to act in their own interests (and to learn how to do so). At the same time, it was not technologically practical to imbue the network itself with the level of 'intelligence' needed to manage complex traffic flows, ensure quality of service, etc. Neither of these conditions holds today (botnets, irrationality and other factors have pre-empted individual control of 'end devices' but e.g. deep packet inspection and differentiated services enable far greater degrees of monitoring and control 'in the network'). But the value of the end-to-end principle still holds even if we must reinterpret 'trust' as responsibility, 'intelligence' as complexity and recognise that 'the network' is not limited to the physical network. In much the same way, copyright was an artefact of an age when legitimate use of others' intellectual property did not require copying, but theft did; neither of these is true of digitised content on the internet, but the value of clear and appropriate IPR remains important.

The *global context* is also vital for a value-based internet. There is broad support among experts and laymen alike for a regulatory system based on common and attractive architectural and policy principles [to be enumerated] and values, many of which are endorsed throughout the EC and other currently-dominant developed nations. But they are not universally supported in the developing world and do not in any case receive the same ranking.

- If 'our' future internet differs widely from the global internet or the internets of other global powers, we may lose purchase or find ourselves bypassed. Expressing our values and reaching our objectives may be frustrated or excessively costly.
- If we can protect 'our' internet, we need carefully to consider the incidence of costs on different groups within the EC. This has a dynamic aspect – flows of knowledge, human and social capital and economic activities may reroute themselves. Our sustainable development depends on networked interchange and continuing innovation and thus on our centrality to these flows.
- We can increase the odds of 'value-friendly' and 'competitiveness-enhancing' infrastructural change by strategic engagement in inter- and multi-national fora involved with internet architectures and governance and by supporting key research and standardisation endeavours that will drive the frontiers of internet development, but the most important drivers will not come from industrial policy attempts to pick technological winners – even if informed by a far-sighted view of how the world would change if Europe sets the pace of research. If such initiatives pay off, they will owe a great deal to an innovation-friendly[24] and internet-friendly environment to permit Europe to implement and explore pilot deployments and in this way to lead the world via the network externalities that lead to 'tipping' and clustering.

This requires a good measure of political courage. The priorities we set and even the approach we take must be chosen with an eye to the (discontinuous, uncertain) development of the global internet, not parochial issues and yesterday's problems.

Finally, it is worth noting that these changes should take place with all deliberate speed, but not faster. Rushing into what may be a mistake seems at odds with 'due process' protections in almost every democratic jurisdiction, especially when some of the constituent communities (especially the citizens and consumers) may take some time to realise, digest and articulate their concerns. From a structural point of view, temporal isolation of behavioural, regulatory and technological changes (very different speeds) allows decisions in each domain to anticipate responses in faster domains into account. On the other hand, such a regime should not be bound by the letter of possibly obsolete rules. Regulation reflects this in two 'architectural' choices:

- *ex post* vs. *ex ante* rules; and
- rule-based vs. effects-based (or 'black-letter' vs. 'rule of reason') regulation.

These choices also have implications for the regulatory platform – deliberative, court-like or administrative. In the same way, there are tradeoffs between architectural design and regulation – for instance, if the network does not use static IP addresses, responsibility, locational information and so on can only be imposed on the controllers of dynamic address assignment (like big ISPs).

In sum, national regulatory agencies and regional regulatory bodies must learn rapidly, but emphasise flexibility and foresight over speed. Improved understanding of how the internet works does not necessarily mean that the NRAs will take on more powers or directly regulate more entities and types of conduct: as mutual knowledge advances, the internet may become more effectively self-governing. Improved consumer information and mobility may largely remove the need for competition policy, access and net neutrality rules. The locus of regulation may shift; it may be necessary to regulate at one point to achieve a result in another. Finally, the inherent complexity of the internet itself, and its emergent properties (synchronisation, endogenous segregation, self-organised criticality, etc.) may let regulators restore light-touch and *ex post* approaches in order to avoid futile or counterproductive activities and to benefit from the 'intelligence' of the internet considered as an adaptive system.

NOTES

1. European Commission (2008).
2. European Commission (2010a).
3. European Commission (2010b).
4. In truth, these are not as coincidental as might appear; many elements of the 'perfect storm' have been visible for years and remain salient and vital thanks to persistent and widespread failure to respond at all levels. Some of this inertia doubtless reflects media peculiarities; the global reach and ostensibly low barriers to internet participation provide a massive audience on which (even if it is not listening) it is possible to free ride. The internet is a medium for communication, that blurs the lines between thought, expression and action. As a social technology, it subverts the reforming tendency by providing (possibly too-) easy access to evidence of injustice and even easier ways to 'respond'.
5. This is not helped by unclear demarcation of authority, responsibility and influence between regulators and other policy actors. It can be seen in the balance of revenues and profitability within the internet value chain; in Europe at least, the bulk of the monetised value added by directly-attributable internet activity is captured by the incumbent providers of the telecommunications services used to carry internet traffic. See e.g. Cattaneo et al. (2011).
6. Note that this may need to involve a form of multi-stakeholderism that does not try to wish away parochial interests. Governments have citizens, but the internet does not – it offers neither reciprocity nor democratic accountability (even in such remote and relatively unimportant areas as IP addressing and the DNS system). In a multi-stakeholder context, governments can speak for the interests of their citizens, businesses can speak for the interests of commerce, and NGOs and other parts of civil society can speak for people acting as communities, ethnic groups, customers, etc.
7. It has been pointed out that US telecom operators have never convincingly demonstrated scarce capacity justifying second-degree (customer self-selection on the basis of quantity) price discrimination. Nevertheless, there is compelling evidence of scarcity (e.g. induced by BBC iPlayer) and the efficiency argument for departures from neutrality does not depend on rationing. Note, too that profit-maximising and welfare-maximising price discrimination both imply inverse elasticity pricing, so proposed tariffs cannot necessarily be characterised as societally optimal or an undue exercise of market power simply on their form. Moreover, the firm and a benevolent regulator face different demand curves. As M. Cave (2003) notes: 'Firms also typically set their optimal (i.e. profit maximising) mark-ups according to the inverse of the elasticity of the demand they face. However, the firms' elasticities and the industry elasticities do not coincide. Hence, even if a firm privately sets prices with a Ramsey structure, this does not imply that it also sets them at the socially optimal Ramsey level.'
8. See e.g. Armstrong (2006) or Rochet and Tirole (2006).
9. Conley and Wooders (1997).
10. See e.g. Marsden and Cave (2007), which analyses 'next generation access to content' from the perspective of efficient market differentiation, or the contention that the internet is an n-sided rather than a two-sided market developed in Yahoo! UK & Ireland (2010) 'Traffic management and "net neutrality": A discussion document' (esp. section 4) Yahoo!'s response to the recent Ofcom consultation on traffic management and net neutrality: http://stakeholders.ofcom.org.uk/binaries/consultations/net-neutrality/responses/Yahoo.pdf.
11. For example, a publisher provides a marketing and development platform for its authors or artists; a social networking service like YouTube or Facebook – which has to buy internet access – provides a platform to users who supply content and to advertisers, profile scrapers and others who mine the network and provide additional services to users.
12. See e.g. Cave (2010) for a more complete treatment and references to the supporting literature.

13. Surowiecki (2004).
14. Hirschleifer and Teoh (2003).
15. Strogatz (2003).
16. This is not limited to the physical connectivity of the internet. Galeotti and Goyal (2010) use a model of dynamic network formation to show that 'a large majority of individuals get their information from a very small subset of the group'.
17. e.g. Jackson and Watts (2002).
18. Jackson and Wolinsky (1996).
19. The list is long and might include: free trade; the end to end principle; multi-stakeholderism; freedom of connection or expression (elaborated as basic rights); *droit morale* vs. economic forms of intellectual property right; rights to participate or not to be excluded from internet 'society'; and even, possibly, democracy.
20. Transparency, accountability, targeting, proportionality and consistency – see e.g. the European Commission's 2002 Action Plan on Better Regulation or Table 7 in Cave, Marsden and Simmons (2008).
21. Zittrain (2009).
22. Blackman et al. (2010).
23. See the discussion of regulation vs. governance in Section 2.
24. As recognised in Aho (2006), which include public procurement, regulation and standards and in the new instruments of Lead Markets initiatives and European innovation partnerships – see http://ec.europa.eu/research/innovation-union/pdf/innovation-union-communication_en.pdf.

BIBLIOGRAPHY

Aho, E. (2006), 'Creating an Innovative Europe Report of the Independent Expert Group on R&D and Innovation appointed following the Hampton Court Summit', http://europa.eu.int/invest-in-research/.

Armstrong, M. (2006), 'Competition in Two-Sided Markets', *RAND Journal of Economics*, **37(3)**, 668–91.

Bartle, I. and P. Vass (2005), 'Self-regulation and the Regulatory State – a Survey of Policy and Practice', *Research Report*, **17**, University of Bath, UK.

Blackman, C., I. Brown, J. Cave, S. Forge, K. Guevara, L. Srivastava, M. Tsuchiya and R. Popper (2010), 'Towards a Future Internet: Interrelation Between Technological, Social and Economic Trends', Final Report for the Towards a Future Internet (TAFI) Project, European Commission, **SMART 2008/0049**, http://www.internetfutures.eu/wp-content/uploads/2010/11/TAFI-Final-Report.pdf.

Cattaneo, G. et al. (2011), 'The European Internet Industry and Market', Report to European Commission DGINFSO, http://fi3p.mattisonline.co.uk/assets/pdf/FI3P%20D2%20%20EU%20Internet%20Industry%20and%20Market_Final.pdf.

Cave, J., S. Simmons and C. T. Marsden (2008), Options for and Effectiveness of Internet Self- and Co-Regulation Phase 3 (Final) Report (29 February), Report for European Commission, http://ssrn.com/abstract=1274571.

Cave, J. (2010), 'Who's Connected to Whom: the Impact of Liabilities and Network Structures on the Costs of Bad Behaviour Online', http://www.tprcweb.com/images/stories/2010%20papers/cave_2010.pdf.

Cave, J., C. Marsden and S. Simmons (2008), 'Options for and Effectiveness of Internet Self- and Co-Regulation', RAND Technical Report, **TR-566-EC**.

Cave, M. (2003), 'Remedies for Broadband Services', http://www.cullen international.com/cullen/telecom/europe/eurodoc/regsystem/addtexts/bb_cave.pdf.

Conley, J. and M. Wooders (1997), 'Equivalence of the Core and Competitive Equilibrium in a Tiebout Economy with Crowding Types', *Journal of Urban Economics*, 421–40.

European Commission (2008), 'A European Economic Recovery Plan' Communication

COM(2008) 800 final. 26 November 2008 http://eur-lex.europa.eu/LexUriServ/Lex UriServ.do?uri=COM:2008:0800:FIN:EN:PDF.

European Commission (2010a), 'EUROPE 2020: A European strategy for smart, sustainable and inclusive growth' Communication COM(2010) 2020 March 3 2010 http://ec.europa. eu/research/era/docs/en/investing-in-research-european-commission-europe-2020-2010.pdf.

European Commission (2010b), 'A Digital Agenda for Europe' Communication COM(2010) 245 final/2 August 26 2010 http://eur-lex.europa.eu/LexUriServ/LexUriServ.do?uri=COM: 2010:0245:FIN:EN:PDF.

Finkelman, P. (2000), 'A Well-regulated Militia: the Second Amendment in Historical Perspective', *Chicago-Kent Law Review*, **76(195)**, http://ssrn.com/abstract=1105369.

Galeotti, A. and S. Goyal (2010), 'The Law of the Few', *American Economic Review*, **100**, 1468–92.

Hirschleifer, D. and S. Teoh (2003), 'Herd Behaviour and Cascading in Capital Markets: a Review and Synthesis', *European Financial Management*, **9(1)**, 25–66.

Jackson, M. and A. Watts (2002), 'The Evolution of Social and Economic Networks', *Journal of Economic Theory*, **106(2)**, 265–95.

Jackson, M. and A. Wolinsky (1996), 'A Strategic Model of Social and Economic Networks', *Journal of Economic Theory*, **71**, 44–74.

Marsden, C. and J. Cave (2007), 'Beyond the "Net Neutrality" Debate: Price and Quality Discrimination in Next Generation Internet Access', http://web.si.umich.edu/tprc/ papers/2007/689/Netneutralitymarsdencavetprc2007c.pdf.

Rochet, J-C. and J. Tirole (2006), 'Two-Sided Markets: A Progress Report', *RAND Journal of Economics*, **37(3)**, 645–67.

Strogatz, S. (2003), *Sync: The Emerging Science of Spontaneous Order*, New York: Hyperion Press.

Surowiecki, J. (2004), *The Wisdom of Crowds: Why the Many Are Smarter Than the Few and How Collective Wisdom Shapes Business, Economies, Societies and Nations*, New York: Doubleday.

Weyl, A. G. (2010), 'A Price Theory of Multi-sided Platforms', *American Economic Review*, **100**, 1642–72.

Zittrain, J. (2009), *The Future of the Internet – And How to Stop It*, New Haven: Yale University Press.

8. Contract vs. statute in internet governance
Lee Bygrave

INTRODUCTION

This chapter is concerned with the following issue: what are the respective roles of contract and statute in governance of the internet and what are the reasons for each role? The chief catalyst for addressing the issue is the extensive reliance upon contract as the principal legal means for governing much of the internet and its virtual worlds. Coupled with this contractual predilection is fairly widespread reluctance to develop statutory measures in the field. How and why such a situation has arisen, and what its exact compass is, are questions worth considering, particularly given the internet's centrality to social, economic and political life. The importance of the questions is augmented by ongoing controversy over purported abuses of contractual power by the providers of internet-based services (see, for example, Fairfield 2008, de Zwart 2010, Suzor 2010a and Suzor 2010b). Any useful discussion over how such abuses ought to be remedied, or over the respective utility of contract and statute more generally, should be informed by a reasonably accurate picture of the roles that contract and statute currently play. This chapter goes a considerable way to providing that picture.

The term 'statute' is herein used in its extended sense as denoting more than simply domestic legislation; international codes in the form of treaties, pacts and conventions are embraced as well. Delegated legislation, such as ordinances and regulations, is embraced too. A key distinguishing feature of a statute for the purposes of this analysis is that it is formally agreed upon by national governments or government agencies acting alone or in concert. Further, a statute typically creates legal rights or obligations for a particular population without each member of the population first specifically assenting to it. Statutes tend accordingly to embody hierarchical, state-dominated power structures. Note, though, that formal differences exist between domestic and international statutes in the way they create and give effect to law. The main difference is that the rights and obligations created by an international statute—that is, a treaty or similar agreement under public international law—apply primarily to the states that are parties to the statute and will often not apply directly to, or be directly enforceable by, the populations of those states. However, the agreement may require each contracting state to transpose those rights and obligations in national law, thus making them (or elements of them) directly applicable to the populace. The Convention for the Protection of Individuals with regard to Automatic Processing of Personal Data, adopted by the Council of Europe in 1981, is one of numerous instances in point: it is not intended to provide, of itself, a set of rights directly enforceable in national courts (see its Explanatory Report, paras. 38 and 60), but requires contracting states to incorporate its principles into their national laws (Article 4(1)). Once so incorporated, those principles give rise to rights and obligations that are domestically justiciable.

In contrast to a statute, a contract may be hatched by any person or organisation (not just governments or their agencies) with the capacity to enter into legal relations, and it will only become legally binding upon a person or organisation once they specifically agree to its terms. Linked to the latter characteristic is the doctrine of privity of contract, which means that a contract normally only binds and benefits the contracting parties; a third party will thus be unable to sue or be sued on it. While inroads into the doctrine have been made in some jurisdictions, such as France (see, for example, Whittaker 1995) and England (see the UK Contracts (Rights of Third Parties) Act 1999), it remains a general point of departure in both common and civil law systems. Contracts are predominantly used in market and network modes of governance which purportedly embody flatter, less coercive forms of steering than a state-centric hierarchical mode of governance (for elaboration of these various modes as ideal types, see Meuleman 2008, pp. 329–50, 21ff). Yet, as shown further on in this chapter, contract can also be integrated in the latter type of governance mode.

The term 'internet governance' is herein used in line with the recent tendency to give it an expansive compass (see, for example, Mueller 2010, pp. 9–10). While one may query the desirability of that expansion—not least because it compounds the risk of 'internet governance' becoming a 'weasel' term—it is probably irreversible. How the term is defined affects assessment of the relative roles played by contract and statute. The preponderance of each type of legal instrument varies from context to context. A definition of internet governance that forecloses account being taken of a particular context will lead to a different perception of the balance between contract and statute than a definition that does not. In days past, internet governance was often treated as principally concerned with the setting of technical standards for data transmission networks based on the Transmission Control Protocol and Internet Protocol (TCP/

IP) suite, particularly the management of their naming and numbering system. As elaborated further below, statute does very little work in that context compared to contract. Nowadays, internet governance tends to be treated as concerned with a great deal more. Indeed, some would see it as now embracing pretty much 'the entirety of communication and information policy' (Mueller 2010, p. 10). This gives statute law potentially more importance relative to contract.

At the same time, it makes clearly identifying where the relevant corpus of statute ends very difficult. The same goes for identifying the relevant corpus of contract. It means, in principle, that any statute or contract that impinges—however remotely—on provision of, or policy on, electronic communications could be seen as relevant. Adopting such a broad approach is not particularly useful for the purposes of legal categorisation. For those purposes, it seems more useful to restrict the relevant corpus of law to statute or contract which has governance of electronic communications as its central remit or which otherwise affects such governance in a significant albeit incidental way. That type of law accordingly forms the focus of the chapter. One could further narrow the relevant corpus of law by restricting electronic communications to those based on TCP/IP networks, but this delimitation seems to be losing popularity as such networks merge with others. Thus, the delimitation is not strictly applied herein. Account is taken of the multiple levels at which the law in point may govern or affect electronic communications. These include the infrastructure for electronic communications, the services facilitated by that infrastructure, and the resultant data flows. In terms of the latter, relevant laws may affect or seek to affect either how data flows or what kind of data flows on the basis of the information content of the data.

Some caveats are necessary at the outset. First, while essentially a work of legal scholarship, the chapter is written for a generalist (though academic) readership with a view to summing up basic regulatory patterns in the field. It accordingly passes over some (but not all!) legal intricacies in the interests of presenting the 'big picture'.

A second caveat concerns the title of the chapter. While catchy, it is misleading insofar as it suggests that contract is necessarily at loggerheads with statute. While contract and statute can be in tension with each other, they are not intrinsically in conflict and they often work hand in hand—as illustrated further below. Moreover, many of the rules making up the law of contract are statutory. This is especially so in civil law systems where the principal rules of contract law are enshrined in the statutory law of obligations. The Civil Codes of Germany, Italy and France are prime examples in point. Yet also in common law jurisdictions large swathes of contract law that once were the preserve of the contracting parties and judiciary are now regulated by statute. For example, the UK Unfair Terms in Consumer Contracts Regulations 1999 apply mandatory rules to govern contracts between consumers and businesses; and the UK Employment Rights Act 1996 does the same for employment contracts.

Thirdly, the two types of legal instrument under investigation here are far from being the predominant tools of internet governance. This follows partly from the very concept of internet governance, which, as elaborated elsewhere in this book, encompasses a vast range of mechanisms for management and control—of which formal legal codes are but one instance. It follows also from the way in which the internet is actually governed. The bulk of everyday governance is extra-legal in the sense that it occurs without direct application of legal rules. And many of the normative codes in the field are not legally binding in themselves. In other words, neither contract nor statute does the core practical work of internet governance. Consider, for example, the internet standards developed by the IETF: such a standard is represented as 'not imply[ing] any attempt by the IETF to mandate its use, or any attempt to police its usage—only that "if you say that you are doing this according to this standard, do it this way"' (RFC 3935). This is a far cry from the formal force of contract, statute or a court decision. Moreover, the IETF consciously attempts to work outside the radar screen of lawyers by, for instance, never formally verifying or making claims about the details of patent agreements (Alvestrand 2009). This is not to say that an IETF standard or any other technical standard is incapable of gaining legal purchase. For instance, a statute might make reference to such a standard (see, for example, the EU Framework Directive on electronic communications (2002/21/EC) Article 17, which refers to certain technical standards and empowers the European Commission to mandate their implementation in particular circumstances). Alternatively, a court might find that adherence to a standard constitutes good business practice, thereby absolving a litigant from liability under a negligence claim. We must further remember that while much internet governance is extra-legal, it occurs in the shadow of law. Legal principles also constitute necessary (though not exhaustive) benchmarks for what is legitimate governance by both private and public actors.

Fourthly, the instruments considered herein do not constitute the entirety of the legal arsenal. Most notably missing from the following analysis is in-depth consideration of the role of the judiciary (case law) in internet governance. Additionally, with its focus on contract and statute, both of which are typically cast as core constituents of 'hard law', the chapter does not deal in detail with the many instruments that are typically cast as 'soft law'—namely, guidelines, declarations, recommendations, codes of practice and the like.

The division between 'soft' and 'hard' categories of law is usually depicted as a sliding scale based on several variables: obligation, delegation and precision (see, for example, Abbott and others 2000). In short, obligation concerns the degree to which an instrument is (commonly regarded as) binding. Delegation refers to the degree to which a third party, such as a court, is permitted to interpret and apply the instrument and resolve disputes over it. Precision concerns the degree to which the instrument stipulates clear, unambiguous rules. For present purposes, the latter variable is largely irrelevant to distinguishing the instruments that are the focus of this chapter from their 'softer' counterparts: numerous contracts and statutes are couched in vague terminology. Rather, the key variable herein is obligation: the more obligatory the instrument, the 'harder' it is. That criterion tends to translate into the degree to which the instrument is directly enforceable by a court (thus calling into play the delegation variable). In general, a court will be prepared to enforce contracts or statutes by providing remedies for their breach—assuming it has authority to do so. This will often not be the case with 'soft law' instruments. That the latter are nevertheless commonly seen as a type of law (though compare, for instance, Weber and Weber (2010, p. 24), who claim that such instruments are not law, only 'a social notion close to law') is because they are aimed at and capable of having some practical effect on conduct. Indeed, some scholars (for example, Abbott and Snidal (2000); Power and Tobin (2011)) argue that their effect may often be greater than that of 'hard law'. And, as noted above in relation to standards, they may be incorporated into 'hard law' or otherwise shape its application and development, through judicial, contractual or legislative processes (see, for example, Senden 2004, chs 8–11).

THE PROVINCE OF CONTRACT

The governance structure for the internet has been formed largely outside a treaty or other legislative framework that is internet-specific. Contractual mechanisms provide the legal mortar and bricks for much of the present structure, and they do so often without a direct basis in statute. Consider the internet's physical infrastructure, its naming and numbering system and the day-to-day provision of internet-based services: the management of all of these elements, from their construction to their deployment, is legally regulated primarily by way of a sprawling web of contracts. Concomitantly, the governance structure is relatively unencumbered by dirigiste ideology and has permitted a fairly high degree of self-regulation (Mifsud Bonnici 2008). While tentacles of government control are increasingly visible (Goldsmith and Wu 2006; Bygrave and Michaelsen 2009), private sector bodies have usually been allowed—and often encouraged—to lead the design and management of the internet. Governments have acted more as facilitative partners of these bodies than as heavy-handed regulators, at least in Western democracies. In other words, governance has been largely exercised by cooperative networks rather than decree.

Contract has been utilized from the internet's beginnings. It was the principal legal tool used by US government agencies to fund the efforts of the scientific research community in developing the internet and its precursor, the ARPANET (see generally Bing 2009). To be sure, the control that government thereby exercised over those efforts was distant and light-touch but it was, in legal terms, contractual at bottom. It was also capable of real bite. This was made clear when the internet technical community attempted to gain complete control over the internet naming and numbering system in 1997—the so-called 'gTLD-MOU' initiative. The Clinton–Gore Administration effectively killed the initiative by holding that its funding of internet development under a series of contracts gave it ultimate authority over the network (Mueller 2002, pp. 142–62; Goldsmith and Wu 2006, pp. 36–43).

Contract continued to be the US government's preferred legal tool when it formulated its general regulatory approach to internet-based commerce in the late 1990s. In 'A Framework for Global Electronic Commerce' (1997), the Clinton–Gore Administration stated that 'governments should establish a predictable and simple legal environment based on a decentralized, *contractual* model of law rather than one based on top-down regulation' (emphasis added).

Management of the internet's naming and numbering system is an important manifestation of that model. The legal relationships between the various actors involved in such management have been largely contractual. There are five main categories of contract: (i) agreements between the Internet Corporation for Assigned Names and Numbers (ICANN) and the US Department of Commerce (DOC); (ii) agreements between VeriSign (previously Network Solutions, Incorporated) and the DOC; (iii) agreements between ICANN and other bodies—domain name registries, domain name registrars and data-escrow providers; (iv) agreements between data-escrow providers and registrars or registries; and (v) agreements between registrars and registrants of domain names (see further Bygrave and Bing 2009: ch 5, section 5.1.3).

The private law character of this governance structure is reinforced by the fact that the central international body charged with managing the naming and numbering system—ICANN—is a private, non-profit corporation registered in California. The bulk of the other involved actors are also from outside the governmental sector. This is not to say that the role of government or of public law in this context is insubstantial (more on that further below). But it is plainly very different from, say, the traditional telecommunications sector where the central international governance body is a treaty-based intergovernmental organisation—the International Telecommunications Union (ITU)—and where there has long been extensive legislative activity. Moreover, much of the law that governs the internet naming and numbering system is formed outside the classical arenas of public international law. Its primary sources are accordingly found at the periphery of the traditional centres for law-making—namely, national parliaments and intergovernmental bodies, such as the ITU, EU, Council of Europe (COE) and World Trade Organization (WTO).

Much the same can be said for large tracts of the legal governance structure applying to other aspects of the internet and its transactional dimensions. Contract is used extensively to regulate the building and interconnection of the myriad communications networks that constitute the internet's physical layer or 'backbone'. It is also applied extensively to regulate access to that layer: consider, for example, the numerous access agreements entered into between Internet Service Providers (ISPs) and various types of end users (persons in domestic households, corporations etc) and between 'lower-tier' and 'upper-tier' ISPs.

Additionally, contract is extensively employed to regulate the dissemination and use of data at the internet's application and content layers. This is most salient with data in which intellectual property rights inhere. Software is an obvious example. The distribution and use of computer programs is governed principally by contract in the form of licence agreements—originally, 'shrink-wrap' licences for physical, off-the-shelf software packages; more recently and now more commonly, 'click-wrap', 'web-wrap' or 'browse-wrap' licences for purely online software distribution.

The digital environments created by software developers are also governed principally by contract, typically in the form of end-user license agreements ('EULAs') or Terms of Service ('ToS'). We see this exemplified particularly well with massively multiplayer online games ('MMOGs'), such as World of Warcraft, and with other popular virtual platforms, such as Facebook. For the millions of people participating in these environments, the formal rights, obligations and benefits attaching to their participation are legally dictated primarily by the respective EULA/ToS. The latter is thus a central means of governance in such environments, performing a function akin to the constitutional law of an ordinary country. Like such law, though, the EULA is rarely the sole means of governance. It will usually be one component of a digital rights management system

(DRMS)—that is, a technological-organisational infrastructure for managing online dissemination and use of data with the purported aim of protecting intellectual property rights in the data (Bekker and others 2003). The EULA rules will often be replicated and buttressed by technological measures, such as use of encryption and steganography ('digital watermarking'). In other words, the legal code of the DRMS will be integrated with, and reinforced by, its software code (de Zwart 2010, p. 608 and references cited therein; on the regulatory role of software more generally, see Reidenberg (1998) and Lessig (1999)).

Extensive use of contract is not unique to the field of internet governance. Summing up recent empirical evidence from a variety of fields, Edgeworth notes that '[r]ights are determined increasingly by reference to private contractual agreement rather than public regulation so that contract once more, as in the 19th century, "swallows up" much of the subject matter it was seen to "disgorge"' (Edgeworth 2003, p. 150). Indeed, he argues that this (re)ascendancy of contract is a hallmark of the 'postmodern' legal paradigm. In the field of internet governance, though, we need to keep in mind that this development is not so much a case of contract reclaiming lost territory as claiming new.

Care ought to be taken not to overstate the extent of this conquest. If we look more closely at the above-listed contractual frameworks, we find that they tend not to be based exclusively on contract but are also under the sway of statute or various types of 'soft law'. Although some of the latter resembles contract, it is not formally legally binding in the way that contract ordinarily is.

Governance of the internet naming and numbering system provides pertinent illustrations of these non-contractual dimensions. To begin with, some ccTLD governance regimes have a statutory footing. Norway is a case in point (Thunem and Lange 2009). Further, the role played by contract in governing the relationships between ICANN and ccTLD managers is more modest than for the relationships between ICANN and gTLD managers. Although ICANN has pushed for the creation of formal contractual agreements between itself and ccTLD managers, many of the latter have preferred to formalise their relationship with ICANN by an 'exchange of letters'. The latter mechanism has been characterised as contractual (Uerpmann-Wittzack 2008, p. 159 describing the exchange of letters between ICANN and the .de registry, DENIC, as a 'contract') but this is misleading. The parties enter into these exchanges in order to formalise their relationship in a way that avoids making them legally liable to each other. For example, ICANN's letter of 29 March 2006 to DENIC stipulates that 'nothing contained in this letter shall give rise to any liability, monetary or otherwise for ICANN'. This is hardly typical for an ordinary contract.

Another instrument that is hardly typical for an ordinary contract is the Affirmation of Commitments (AOC) concluded between ICANN and the DOC in late 2009 (for details, see Chapter 2 in this volume and Froomkin 2011). It is worth devoting some space to the legal status of this instrument, partly because it replaced an agreement that was clearly contractual (the Joint Project Agreement (JPA) of September 2006), partly because its own legal status is ambiguous, and partly because it now forms a central plank in the constitutional compact between ICANN and the DOC and, in a broader perspective, between ICANN/DOC on the one side and the rest of the world on the other. The AOC has definite contractual elements. In the first place, it is an agreement, as is made expressly clear in its clauses 1 and 11. And despite otherwise using the nomenclature of 'affirmation', both the DOC and ICANN are essentially agreeing to commit themselves to a particular course of action; the term 'affirms' equates with 'agrees to remain committed to'. Secondly, both parties make promises. Although ICANN makes far more promises than the DOC, it is wrong to suggest that the latter makes none. The DOC makes at least one fairly concrete promise, which is to keep participating in and support the Governmental Advisory Committee for the ICANN Board (AOC clause 6), and it makes a vaguer promise in terms of commitment to a 'multi-stakeholder, private sector led, bottom-up policy development model for DNS technical coordination' (AOC clause 4). Thirdly, a credible argument can be made out that the agreement is supported by proper consideration, which is a basic prerequisite for a valid contract under US law (and other common law systems, though not civil law systems).

The matter of consideration, though, is contestable, with at least one scholar claiming that the AOC probably does not qualify as a valid contract for lack of consideration (Froomkin 2011, p.199). Put somewhat simplistically, consideration is some action or thing undertaken or provided by a person (natural or legal) in exchange for, and at least partly because of, a promise by another person (for a classic exposition in terms of US law, see Farnsworth 2004, ch 2). Part of the doctrine of consideration is a rule that consideration cannot be 'past', which means that action undertaken prior to a promise being made cannot be valid consideration for the promise as it was not in response to the latter (see further, for example, Farnsworth 2004, pp.90–92). This rule seems to be the basis for the claim that the AOC is not supported by consideration. In Froomkin's view, ICANN and the DOC are simply doing what they have previously committed to doing; thus, the AOC is not supported by fresh consideration and thereby falls foul of the rule that consideration must not be 'past'. However, an argument can be made out that fresh consideration is provided. The argument would be that the lapse of the JPA caused a lapse of each party's legal commitments (at least as elaborated in the JPA) towards the other, thereby permitting each some leeway to change tack if they wanted. Through the AOC, the DOC effectively agreed not to change tack. This 'affirmation' of (or agreement to remain committed to) previous policy, in a situation in which the DOC was not legally required to do so, was something new and could thereby constitute fresh consideration for ICANN's promises. And ICANN—the argument would run—provided fresh consideration for the DOC's promises by agreeing to undertake review processes that go beyond what its Bylaws or Articles of Incorporation already required.

Yet regardless of the outcome of such an argument, any attempt to view the AOC as a valid contract faces more serious difficulties. One problem is lack of clear statutory authority enabling the DOC to bind itself, via contract, to the commitments it makes without violating US administrative and constitutional law—a similar problem has arguably afflicted the older ICANN/DOC contracts too (Froomkin 2000 and Froomkin 2002). Another difficulty concerns the agreement's probable lack of mutual enforceability given the vagueness of much of what each party promises. Accordingly, it would be foolhardy to assume that the AOC is a valid contract. Even if it is a valid contract, vestiges of the doctrine on sovereign immunity may limit remedies available for its putative breach.

WHY CONTRACT?

The growth in reliance on contract has a complex and multifaceted aetiology. It partly reflects dissipation of faith across much of the Western liberal sphere in the efficacy of state-run 'command and control' regimes—a tendency particularly salient over the past three decades (see, for example, Jänicke 1990, Moran and Prosser 1994, De Vries 2011). This loss of faith applies across many sectors but is especially acute regarding governance of rapidly changing technological infrastructures, such as the internet. Its corollary tends to be a belief in the ability of a competitive marketplace to deliver goods and services in the most appropriate manner. This gives relatively great latitude to private fiat and contractual mechanisms.

Thus, the roll out of the internet concurrently with growing loss of faith in the efficacy of 'top-down' regulation contributed to relatively extensive application of contract. This result was reinforced by the network's origins in the USA, where 'laissez-faire' ideology and commitment to freedom of expression have traditionally had a firmer grip on government than in many other countries. In light of that commitment, it is somewhat paradoxical that the USA was home to the first attempt to legislatively censor expression on the internet through enactment of the federal Communications Decency Act of 1996. That attempt, however, was ultimately thwarted by the strong place given to free speech in the US Constitution as interpreted by the US Supreme Court (see its decision in *American Civil Liberties Union v Reno*, 521 US 844 (1997)).

Other aspects of internet development have also engendered reluctance to apply extensive 'top-down' regulatory controls on the network. The informal, open, 'bottom-up' decisional culture of the network's technical pioneers—manifest most famously in their mantra of 'rough consensus and running code'—rapidly became a benchmark for subsequent governance regimes, such as that established by ICANN (see, for instance, Froomkin 2003). Its apparent embodiment of democratic ideals together with its spectacular success in fostering innovation with broad societal benefits gave such culture a high degree of legitimacy. It thereby placed a question mark against the propriety of more formal, hierarchical regulatory approaches, thus pre-empting knee-jerk recourse to them.

At the same time, governments have generally acknowledged the immense value of the payload created by the cooperative arrangements of the internet technical community and have been accordingly cautious about upsetting such arrangements. Indeed, one is tempted to suggest that legislators in this context—at least in the Western world—have taken heed of the lesson drawn by Ellickson in his classic account of *Order without Law*: 'lawmakers who are unappreciative of the social conditions that foster informal cooperation are likely to create a world in which there is both more law and less order' (Ellickson 1991, p. 286). Nonetheless, many governments have responded in relatively dirigistic fashion when the internet has threatened them or interests that they deem important. The most heavy-handed responses have tended to come from non-Western states, with China a salient case in point (see, for example, Sohmen 2001). Yet, as highlighted further below, Western governments too have been far from averse to attempting to subject aspects of the internet to legislative control.

The internet itself, though, poses serious challenges to the efficacy of any state-imposed regulation. As Mueller (2010, pp. 4–5) points out, one set of challenges arises from the global scope of internet communication and the 'quantum jump' in its scale. Another challenge arises from the way in which the internet distributes and disaggregates control. In particular, the internet has 'ensured that the decision-making units over network operations are no longer closely aligned with political units'. Linked to this, the internet has given birth to new institutions: '[d]ecision-making authority over standards and critical internet resources rests in the hands of a transnational network of actors that emerged organically alongside the internet, outside of the nation-state system'. Finally, the internet 'changes the polity' by facilitating 'radical changes in collective action possibilities'.

To this list of challenges one can add more generic problems, not least the slow pace in which legislative processes usually occur and the customary difficulties of reaching meaningful intergovernmental agreement on the details of any international regulatory instrument. The latter difficulties (elaborated further below) are especially problematic when the internet's global reach limits the purchase of purely national regulation.

All of the above-described factors have left public law and statute struggling to gain extensive traction in the field of internet governance. They have thereby helped to leave the field to a large extent the province of private ordering and contract. Yet it would be wrong to cast reliance on contract as simply a by-product of 'statutory default'. Contract has been actively promoted as a preferred legal tool on account of possessing certain purported strengths. When, as noted above, the Clinton–Gore Administration advocated use of contract in its policy paper 'A Framework for Global Electronic Commerce' (1997), it assumed that this would create a 'predictable, minimalist, consistent and simple legal environment for commerce'. Such assumptions are fairly commonplace. Other commonly assumed strengths of contract are the speed and flexibility with which it can usually be developed and amended, relative to statute. Some of these assumptions are contestable, others less so. For instance, the increasingly dense legalese of many EULAs along with the numerous changes they tend to undergo (Jankowich 2006 and Nino 2010), hardly make for a 'predictable, minimalist, consistent and simple legal environment'. Broader concerns exist too about the tendency of contract to cater for a narrow range of interests (typically just those of the contracting parties or often simply those of the party who drafted the contract) at the expense of the legitimate interests of others—a matter that is elaborated further below in respect of EULAs and the balance between contract and copyright.

Still, it is difficult to deny that contract is particularly well-suited to governing the digital world. Contract can be closely tailored to a particular technology and then quickly amended as the technology develops. It can operate across national jurisdictions relatively independently of them. It can be readily applied in ways that align with the market and network structures of the internet along with changes in those structures. And it can be applied in hierarchical, 'command and control' modes of governance along with more heterarchical modes.

All of these capabilities are nicely illustrated by the contractual web spun for the internet naming and numbering system. ICANN enters into a set of individual contracts with registries giving the latter rights to manage particular TLDs. The registries contract individually in turn with various registrars, which in turn individually contract with private legal or physical persons who then gain certain rights to the use of domains within the given namespace. The chain of bilateral agreements transmits obligations; the terms set by ICANN filtering down to the last link. The agreements have a dynamic element as they are revised on the adoption of new policies by ICANN. And they are frequently transnational, the parties often being based in different jurisdictions. Moreover, policy is developed and then cemented as law in essentially a legislative process, albeit with different formal outcomes, actors and procedures than in a traditional parliamentary system. ICANN functions as a legislative arena replete with its own set of lobbyists, constituencies and law-making procedures. Given its legal status, the 'legislation' ICANN produces must take the form of contract but the latter is employed similarly to the way in which ordinary statute tends to be employed—that is, to set down legally binding norms for an entire community or considerable sections of one.

The legislative role of contract in governance of ccTLDs is admittedly less significant than for gTLDs, with some governments using statute to lay down the ground rules for ccTLD management. Yet contracts are still employed at the lower end of the normative chain where they govern the relationships between registries, registrars and domain name holders. They function, though, as handmaidens of statute since they must faithfully reflect the statutory rules (along with other 'softer' norms, such as those documented in RFC 1591) further up the normative chain.

Governance of ccTLDs is but one of numerous areas where contract is integrated in and services a statutory 'top-down' regulatory structure—again showing the versatility of contract. Other such areas that are particularly pertinent to the internet include data protection law and law on provision of electronic communications services. Regarding the latter, statute requires, amongst other things, that the obligations it imposes on ISPs be followed up in contracts with end users (see, for example, the EU Universal Service Directive (2002/22/EC) Articles 20 and 30(5)). In the area of data protection law, statute mandates use of contract to ensure, for instance, that the outsourcing of data-processing operations remains subject to the relevant statutory rules (see, for example, the EU Data Protection Directive (95/46/EC) Article 17(3)).

Statute also sometimes services contract. In an internet context, this is evidenced particularly well by the recent round of legislative reform to promote electronic forms of commerce. An important element in that reform has been to give contractual transactions that are carried out electronically similar legal status to non-electronic transactions (see, for example, the 2006 UN Convention on the Use of Electronic

Communications in International Contracts, the E-Commerce Directive (2000/31/EC) and Electronic Signatures Directive (1999/93/EC)).

At the same time as contract is well-suited to governing the digital world, the latter is particularly conducive to use of contract. In the words of Hugenholtz (1999, pp. 308–09):

> The structure of the internet facilitates the establishment of a multitude of contractual relationships between information producers and end users, either directly or through intermediaries. The internet (or more precisely, the World Wide Web) is uniquely suited for this purpose. Both its 'textual' environment and its interactive nature are ideal conditions for a contractual culture to grow and flourish.

The burgeoning use of EULAs to govern interactive virtual worlds illustrates this point well.

Yet EULA proliferation highlights another important reason for the popularity of contract. This is that contract is an excellent means of control. It is particularly suited to micro-management and can be closely fitted to the particular needs of a virtual world provider. It can also be used to marginalise, if not lock out, public law norms that threaten those needs. These control possibilities become even greater when combined with technological measures. Not surprisingly, then, we find a considerable number of virtual worlds operating in effect as fiefdoms (Jankowich 2006; Mayer-Schönberger and Crowley 2006; Fairfield 2008; Fairfield 2009; de Zwart 2010).

THE PROVINCE OF STATUTE

Despite the popularity of contract, statute is far from absent in internet governance. Indeed, the range of legislation that we must regard as pertinent to the field has grown greatly as conceptions of what constitutes 'internet governance' have expanded. When internet governance is now (rightly or wrongly) treated as basically concerned with 'the entirety of communication and information policy' (Mueller 2010, p. 10), a large body of statute law becomes relevant. Such law can be seen as providing numerous ground rules for the provision of internet-related infrastructure and services, and for the resultant data flows. It does this for the most part through both international and national instruments. The regulatory intensity, though, varies considerably from context to context as does the degree to which the rules are internet-specific.

An exhaustive presentation of all relevant statute law would burst the boundaries of this chapter. Hence, the following paragraphs provide only examples of matters that have been the subject of relatively intensive statutory regulation and focus only upon relevant international agreements. Keep in mind, however, that most of the requirements laid down by those agreements have been or will be transposed into national laws. The actual number of statutory instruments is thus far greater than the number of instruments listed in the following.

Protection of intellectual property rights (IPR) is one matter that has long been singled out for energetic legislative effort. The Clinton–Gore administration signalled concern about the matter early on, stating already in its 1993 policy paper, 'The National Information Infrastructure: Agenda for Action', that it would 'investigate how to strengthen domestic copyright laws and international intellectual property treaties to prevent piracy and to protect the integrity of intellectual property' (principle 7). The plan thus constituted one exception to the 'decentralized, contractual model of law' otherwise championed by the administration. It helped give birth to several international agreements (most notably, the WTO TRIPS (Trade-Related Aspects of Intellectual Property Rights) Agreement of 1995 and two treaties under the auspices of the World Intellectual Property Organization (WIPO)—the Copyright Treaty and Performances and Phonograms Treaty, both of 1996) along with domestic legislation (primarily in the form of the Digital Millenium Copyright Act of 1998). These efforts were duplicated by governments elsewhere. The EU, for example, has enacted a raft of Directives with the aim of strengthening and harmonising European IPR regimes as they apply to the digital environment (see particularly the Database Directive (96/9/EC), Software Directive (2009/24/EC), Copyright Directive (2001/29/EC) and IPR Enforcement Directive (2004/48/EC)). The impact of some of these instruments is dealt with further below.

Cybercrime and information security are other matters attracting relatively intensive statutory regulation both nationally and internationally (for overviews focusing on international efforts, see Rutkowski (2011) and Williams (2010)). The chief international legal instrument on point is the COE Cybercrime Convention adopted in 2001. The Convention requires contracting states to make provision in their national laws not just for hacking and other standard 'CIA' offences (that is, activities impinging upon the confidentiality, integrity and availability of computer data and systems; see Articles 2–6) but certain content-related offences as well, namely dissemination of child pornography (Article 9), dissemination of racist and xenophobic material (Additional Protocol of 2003) and breach of IPR (Article 10). It is thus manifestation of a growing tendency for legislative measures on cybercrime to dovetail with legislative measures for protecting IPR, thereby helping to criminalise IPR violations. This is but one of many controversial sides to the agreement (see further, for example, Williams 2010, pp. 480–83). The Convention is otherwise noteworthy not just for being a rare instance of a treaty regime attempting to deal directly with internet-related activity but also for its impact beyond the circle of COE member states. It was prepared with assistance of states from outside that circle and is the only COE Convention to have been signed and ratified by the USA. It continues to constitute a significant point of departure for legal developments in other non-European states. Australia, for instance, has recently passed legislation allowing it to implement the Convention (see Cybercrime Legislation Amendment Act of 2012). As yet, though, the Convention hardly qualifies as a *global* agreement. It has been ratified by just 32 countries, the USA being the only non-European state in that group. A significant number of COE member states, including Austria, Belgium, Italy and Sweden, have not yet ratified.

Cybercrime and IPR aside, governments have shown much legislative zeal in the area of privacy and data protection (see further Chapter 10 in this volume). Even in the USA, where government has traditionally eschewed enacting comprehensive data protection legislation along the lines typical for Europe, we find a surprisingly great number of statutes on point. These tend to be narrowly circumscribed, and the coverage they offer, particularly with respect to processing of personal data by private sector bodies, is haphazard and incomplete (Schwartz and Reidenberg 1996, chs 9–14; Solove, Rotenberg and Schwartz 2011, chs 2 and 7). Yet when viewed in their entirety, they make up a hefty corpus of code. While some of the recent legislation on privacy and data protection takes specific account of the internet or digital environment (see, for example, the EU Directive 2002/58/EC on privacy and electronic communications), much of the seminal legislation does not and was adopted before the internet became widely used. This is especially the case with key international agreements (Bygrave 2008), such as the 1981 COE Convention for the Protection of Individuals with regard to Automatic Processing of Personal Data and the EU Data Protection Directive (95/46/EC). That does not mean the codes in question fail to apply to internet-related activity; they do apply, though not always with sensible results or a desirable degree of prescriptive guidance (Bygrave 2002, ch 18; Bygrave and Michaelsen 2009, pp. 120–21).

Academic discourse dealing specifically with internet governance now tends to devote considerable attention to legislation on cybercrime, IPR and privacy (see, for example, Goldsmith and Wu 2006; Mueller 2010). There is, however, a large body of other legislation which remains much less salient in that discourse but must now be regarded as fairly central to internet governance. The most glaring instance is legislation on deployment of electronic communications infrastructure and services. At the same time, discourse that does focus on such legislation has tended to pay scant attention to internet governance as such (see, for example, Walden 2009 and previous editions of that work). The disconnect has both technological and legal roots, the legislation in point being originally pitched at networks for 'telecommunication' which were not TCP/IP-based. It thus mirrors the gap that previously existed between the policy spheres of the ITU and the early governors of the internet, such as the IETF, ISOC and ICANN. The factual basis for the disconnect is now greatly weakened: the technological-organisational lines dividing TCP/IP networks from other forms of electronic communication have become less distinct; conceptions about the scope of the 'internet' and 'internet governance' have broadened; and much of the legislation previously dealing with telecommunication has been updated to cover TCP/IP networks. The EU regulatory framework on electronic communications, for instance, has undergone successive revisions partly in order to take better account of the internet environment.

The scope of that framework is worthwhile elaborating in detail as it demonstrates the considerable breadth of the impact it may have on internet governance. The framework is both extensive and dense. Its core alone comprises five Directives (2002/21/EC, 2002/19/EC, 2002/20/EC, 2002/22/EC and 2002/58/EC) and a Regulation ((EC) 1211/2009). These are supplemented by sector-specific recommendations, guidelines and notices along with rules of more general application (see generally Nihoul and Rodford 2011; Walden 2009). The immensity of the framework is testament to the fact that legal reform in the name of 'competition' and 'deregulation'—a central aim of the framework being to privatise and break up monopolized services in the telecommunications sector—sometimes does not so much decrease regulation as to reconfigure and augment it by establishing comprehensive legislative and policing schemes in order to ensure that competition actually occurs (see too Edgeworth 2003, p. 155).

The framework covers a wide range of matters. They include the obligations that state regulators may impose on ISPs and other providers of electronic communications services, use of radio spectrum, conditions for providing network access and interconnection, protection of personal data and end-user freedoms. An important limitation in coverage—at least in principle—is that the framework concerns only communications infrastructure, not the information content of the transmitted data (see Recital 5 in the preamble to the Framework Directive (FD) for electronic communications), though maintaining a strict separation between content and transmission is obviously difficult in practice. Content regulation is dealt with more directly by other sets of rules, including the E-Commerce

Directive and legislation on IPR, data protection and cybercrime as outlined above.

The severity of the framework's bite depends largely on the state of
market competition. The most stringent regulation is reserved for actors
who exercise 'significant market power'—that is, actors who are able 'to
behave to an appreciable extent independently of competitors, customers
and ultimately consumers' (FD Article 14(2)). Thus, 'ex ante regulatory
obligations should only be imposed where there is not effective competition, i.e. in markets where there are one or more undertakings with significant market power, and where national and Community competition law
remedies are not sufficient to address the problem' (FD Recital 27).

For the most part, the provisions of the framework are pitched at a high
level of generality. They also have little to say specifically about TCP/IP
networks. Governance of the internet naming and numbering system, for
example, is addressed obliquely. Aspects of that system may nonetheless
fall within the framework if references therein to 'number translation'
and 'numbering resources' extend to IP numbers. The framework fails to
clearly define what it means by 'numbers'; it also fails to clearly address
the extent to which IP numbers are embraced. It defines 'number translation or systems offering equivalent functionality' simply as elements of
an 'associated service' and thereby 'associated facility' (FD Article 2(ea)
and (e)), such services/facilities being covered by the framework. Further, it
covers use of 'geographic numbers' and 'non-geographic numbers', defining these in ways that link them to the 'national telephone numbering plan'
(Universal Service Directive (2002/22/EC) Article 2(d) and (f)) but without
excluding the possibility of IP numbers forming their basis. The framework also deals more generally with 'numbering resources' and 'numbering plans' (see below) though again fails to define these. On their face,
these terms are broad enough to encompass both IP numbers as such and
translations of IP numbers in the form of domain name addresses—a view
shared by UK legislators and reflected in the broad definition given to 'telephone numbers' in the UK Communications Act 2003 (see section 56(5)
and (10)). Such coverage may have long-term consequences for the use of
IP numbers and domain name addresses, particularly as the most recent
round of reform of the framework provides the European Commission
and national regulatory authorities with more explicit responsibility over
numbering schemes than existed previously. Whether it has also increased
the extent of their competence in the field is a matter of debate.

Prior to the reform, the Framework Directive stated that its provisions
'do not establish any new areas of responsibility for the national regulatory authorities in the field of Internet naming and addressing' (Recital
20 in its preamble). It went on simply to encourage EU member states,

'where ... appropriate in order to ensure full global interoperability of services, to coordinate their positions in international organisations and forums in which decisions are taken on issues relating to the numbering, naming and addressing of electronic communications networks and services' (Article 10(5)). Now the legislation requires member states to ensure that national regulatory authorities (NRAs) 'control the granting of rights of use of all national numbering resources and the management of the national numbering plans' (FD Article 10(1); see too Recital 20 in the preamble: '*All* elements of national numbering plans should be managed by national regulatory authorities, including point codes used in network addressing' (emphasis added)), and that NRAs 'establish objective, transparent and non-discriminatory procedures for granting rights of use for national numbering resources' (FD Article 10(1)). Moreover, the Commission is now empowered to 'take technical implementing measures using its executive powers' in situations where 'there is a need for harmonisation of numbering resources in the Community to support the development of pan-European services' (FD Recital 20; see too Article 19(3)(b)). And, following up FD Article 10(1), the Authorisation Directive (2002/20/EC) now lays down parameters for the procedures and conditions that member states may apply in authorising rights to use 'numbers'. Basically, authorisation procedures shall be 'open, objective, transparent, non-discriminatory and proportionate' (Article 5(2); see too Article 6(1)). They shall also be fairly prompt (Article 5(3)). Permissible conditions that may be attached to authorisations are set out in the Annex to the Directive.

As already indicated, whether these provisions are intended to apply to IP numbers or domain names is not clear. But if they do apply, they place—at least on paper—those parts of the traditional internet naming and numbering system which can be singled out as falling within the jurisdiction of the EU (and European Economic Area) under ultimate control of the public sector. Whether that control will lead to greater top-down regulation of the system remains, of course, to be seen. In some states, any push from, say, the European Commission for greater regulation will be met with resistance. The UK is one such state. While its central legislation on point extends to IP numbers and domain names (see the Communications Act 2003 section 56(5) and (10)), these have been removed from the jurisdiction of the main NRA (Ofcom) by secondary regulations (see the Telephone Number Exclusion (Domain Names and Internet Addresses) Order 2003 (SI No. 3281)). This was in line with the government's 'aim of promoting self-regulation and not applying additional regulation to cover the internet', along with its view that use of internet-related identifiers was subject 'to evidently effective self-regulation' (Timms 2003). However, the government has recently extended its powers to intervene in governance of the .uk namespace in the event of mismanagement by the Nominet-run scheme (see Digital Economy Act of 2010, sections 19–21).

CONTRACTUAL SUPREMACY IN GOVERNANCE OF INTELLECTUAL PROPERTY?

While contract and statute often work hand in hand, their relationship is not always friendly. This is the case when the one is used in an attempt to cancel out application of the other. The conflict arises typically when private fiat masquerading as 'freedom of contract' threatens to trump statutory-based public interests or to otherwise sideline use of statute. Protection of IPR is perhaps the most highly charged case in point. Conflict in that context occurs chiefly over how IPR is to be apportioned (between, say, original and subsequent developers of software) and the extent to which statutory limitations on IPR are to be respected.

Both types of conflict are present in the EULA-based governance regimes of particular virtual worlds due to systematic attempts by the providers of those worlds to supplant statutory rules on IPR through contract and software code (see, for instance, Fairfield 2008 and de Zwart 2010). Such attempts add credence to older fears that the ability of copyright legislation to meaningfully govern the exploitation of digital data risks redundancy due to a more potent regulatory combination of contract and technology (see, for example, Hugenholtz 1999 and references cited therein). In an early vision proffered by one scholar, '[t]here may be nothing for copyright to do, except perhaps to serve as a kind of *deus ex machina* justifying the use of technological and contractual means for protecting works in digital form' (Samuelson 1995, p. 125). Of greater concern, though, is the potential mental marginalisation of copyright and related public interests through extensive recourse to licensing. As Madison (2003, p. 277) has observed, 'there is the possibility that the licensing norm itself is internalized by the reader, listener, and user communities such that the world of information production and consumption is regulated informally, even in the absence of formal "legal" enforcement of particular licenses and of norms exogenous to the license itself'.

Fortunately, copyright legislation has not yet reached the point where it functions purely as symbolic code, and to claim that it definitely will reach that point would be overly presumptuous. It would also be overly presumptuous to regard copyright as lightweight law that contract can bowl over without resistance. There exist a large range of actual and potential legal restrictions on the ability to contractually derogate from particular end-user rights or freedoms for which copyright or neighbouring rights typically cater.

Some such restrictions are fairly concrete but narrowly tailored. For instance, the EU Software Directive stipulates that contract may not prevent a person having a right to use a computer program to make a back-up copy of the program (Article 5(2)). Users are given equivalent protection of their ability to analyse and decompile the software (Articles 5(3) and 6), with any contractual provisions to the contrary being deemed null and void (Article 8). Similarly, the EU Database Directive provides that contract may not prevent a database user from making normal usage of the database (Article 6(1)) or from re-utilising non-substantial parts of it (Article 8(1)), with contractual provisions to the contrary again being rendered nugatory (Article 15).

More general limits on contractual disposition over intellectual property exist too. For instance, restrictive licences giving rise to anti-competitive practices may be remedied through the imposition of compulsory licensing schemes whereby a holder of intellectual property is forced to grant individual licences for its use, at a price and under conditions that are determined jointly with the user or by the relevant state authorities when agreement cannot be reached. This involves, in effect, the state imposing and enforcing an involuntary contract between a willing buyer and an unwilling seller (Gorecki 1981). Provision for such schemes is made, for example, in the 1886 Berne Convention for the Protection of Literary and Artistic Works with respect to sound recordings and lyrics (Article 13) and broadcasting (Article 11bis (2)). For patented products, such schemes are permitted under the TRIPS Agreement (see Article 31; see too Article 40) and, more distantly, under the 1883 Paris Convention for the Protection of Industrial Property (see Article 5A(2)).

Courts in some jurisdictions have also applied similar sorts of remedies pursuant to general statutory rules on competition. Case law of the EU Court of Justice under Article 102 of the Treaty on the Functioning of the European Union (formerly Article 82 of the Treaty establishing the European Community) is perhaps the most ambitious in point (see especially Cases C-241/91P & 242/91P *Radio Telefis Eirean (RTE) and Independent Television Publication Ltd (ITP) v Commission* [1995] ECR I-0743, Case C-418/01 *IMS Health GmbH & Co OHG v NDC Health GmbH & Co KG* [2004] ECR I-5039 and Case T-201/04 *Microsoft v Commission* [2007] ECR II-03601; for discussion, see, for instance, Houdijk 2005 and Pereira 2011). That case law deals in part with the ability to access digital data (*IMS Health* and *Microsoft*) and thereby points to further potential use of compulsory licensing or equivalent remedies as a tool of internet governance. The flexibility and reach of such remedies under general competition law is augmented by their apparent ability to apply, at least in principle, independently of whether or not the undesired digital 'lock-up' is due to patent or other forms of IPR—a barrier created simply by contractual licence might well be sufficient in certain circumstances. Some scholars have even broached the possibility of using such remedies to break up ICANN's control over the internet naming and numbering system (Meyer and Utz 2007), but this would be an extremely long shot.

Restrictions on contractual freedom may be derived from other fields of law besides those dealing specifically with IPR and competition. These include rules on protection of fundamental human rights, consumer protection, abuse of rights and even rules in contract law itself. However, the purchase of many of these restrictions is blunted by uncertainty or dispute over the scope of their application (see generally Guibault 2002). Compulsory licences, for example, are frequently regarded as controversial remedies and their application is typically subject to stringent preconditions (see further, for instance, Harris (2004, pp. 134–36, 144–56) and Cotropia (2008) discussing restrictions on use of compulsory licensing under the TRIPS Agreement). Moreover, the strength and availability of the restrictions varies greatly from jurisdiction to jurisdiction. For example, doctrines on good faith and abuse of rights are most developed and readily applied in civil law systems (though rough equivalents are found elsewhere—see, for instance, Reid (2004) pointing to manifestation of doctrine on abuse of rights in Scots and English law). And common law systems seem generally most conducive to 'hard-headed' contractual freedom. This is indirectly evidenced by commercial actors' frequent preference for applying English or US law to govern transnational contracting.

All up, serious doubts must attach to the ability of statutory IPR regimes and more general law to prevent a combination of contract and technology from unilaterally dictating how intellectual property shall be used in the digital environment. The sway of the contract/technology combination over statutory IPR regimes is exacerbated by the general failure of such regimes to clearly establish the normative priority of their rules— including the statutory limitations they place on IPR—vis-à-vis contract (Guibault 2002 and Guibault 2006). It is further exacerbated by the fact that the contract/technology combination is no longer purely exogenous to such regimes but incorporated into them through the introduction of provisions on protection of 'technological measures' and 'rights management information' (see, for example, the 1996 WIPO Copyright Treaty Articles 11–12; EU Copyright Directive 2001/29/EC Articles 6–7). The ambiguity of those provisions, particularly over whether the protection they give technological measures must respect traditional end-user rights and freedoms (see further, for example, Bygrave 2003), compounds the above problems.

Future Statutory Overlay?

The final matter to be canvassed concerns the prospect of statute being accorded a significantly larger role in governance of the internet: will legislation be introduced in the field which dramatically overshadows or reduces the role of contract? The question is particularly pertinent in light of calls to develop new statutory schemes along a variety of fronts. At the domestic level, proposals for legislation establishing general principles, rights and obligations specific to internet use are being drafted in some countries. Brazil has perhaps come furthest in this regard with an expansively formulated draft Bill for a civil rights framework for the internet currently being considered by the national Congress (see *Marco Civil da Internet*; Bill no. 2126/2011). At the international level, there are proposals to develop a broad treaty-based regime to govern the internet generally (see, for example, Mueller, Mathiason and Klein (2007) arguing the merits of introducing a framework convention for internet governance akin to the 1992 UN Framework Convention on Climate Change). There are also proposals for international conventions of more limited scope (see, for example, Weber and Weber (2010) arguing in favour of a convention to govern the nascent 'Internet of Things'; Svantesson (2006) proposing a model convention to regulate cross-border internet defamation arising out of mass communication). And there are calls for greater government regulation of virtual worlds (see, for instance, de Zwart (2010) arguing that governments ought to develop a baseline of light-touch, internationally coordinated, regulatory standards for virtual world providers; Balkin (2004) proposing use of 'statutes of interration' to govern the legal relationships between providers and users of virtual worlds).

Much can be said in favour of the propriety of such proposals and they may find particularly fertile ground in some countries, such as Brazil. In other countries, however, their prospects of success are probably rather slim. Some of their proponents admit as much. Weber and Weber, for instance, state that the 'Internet of Things' is most likely to be subject to an industry-based self-regulatory regime due to the relative ease with which such a regime can be set up and subsequently adjusted to keep pace with technological developments (Weber and Weber (2010), p. 127).

Proposals for international conventions—especially multilateral initiatives—face particularly serious obstacles. One obstacle is the sheer clutter of the ideological landscape in which conventions must now be brokered. The horizons for regulatory policy are filled by cross-cutting sets of norms and interests—human rights, trade, national security, law enforcement, etc—about which it is increasingly difficult to reach broad consensus. Commitment to 'multistakeholderism' adds to these problems as does the lack of a sufficiently strong, dynamic and representative body to negotiate any multilateral convention let alone one with bite. The outcomes of the World Summit on the Information Society (see further Hubbard and Bygrave (2009)) are testimony to this. And the ITU still seems to have a long way to go in repairing its tattered reputation for potentially brokering a meaningful framework convention on internet governance— as MacLean (2008, p. 84) notes, '[i]f it continues on its present course, it now seems clear that progressive marginalization is the most the ITU can hope for, and that eventual disappearance "not with a bang but a whimper" its most likely fate'. It is hard to identify another organisation that is both able and willing to drive negotiations for a multilateral treaty forward. The World Trade Organization (WTO) is occasionally touted as such a body. Yet its ability to broker a broadly acceptable convention will be hampered by its commercial agenda. Its ability to broker such an agreement quickly and efficiently is also in doubt given its tardiness in crystallising policy on e-commerce (Wunsch-Vincent 2005). Another possible candidate is the Organisation for Economic Co-operation and Development (OECD) yet it seeks generally to generate guidelines and other instruments of 'soft law' rather than 'hard law'. The EU and COE are other possible candidates, and they are not averse to creating international 'hard law', but their ability to foster global consensus will be handicapped by their regional status and bias. The COE has recently sponsored development of a fairly comprehensive set of general principles on internet governance which could form the basis for a framework convention in the field (COE Ad Hoc Advisory Group on Cross-border Internet 2011) but has not (yet) taken concrete steps to initiate work on such an instrument and seems reluctant to do so. As for the EU, the current Vice-President of the European Commission who is responsible for the EU's Digital Agenda has aired the need for general governance principles in the form of a 'Compact for the Internet' yet emphasising at the same time that 'this is not about regulation' (Kroes 2011).

As for proposals to subject virtual worlds to greater statutory regulation, whether these will get off the ground will greatly depend on market dynamics. And it is very difficult to accurately predict how the market for virtual worlds will develop. As Mayer-Schönberger and Crowley (2006) show, the variables are numerous as are the possible trajectories. Two important variables are the degree to which EULAs affront the wishes of end users and the broader community, and the degree to which end users agitate for their wishes to prevail over EULA rules, thereby mobilising government to take action on their behalf.

It would be premature to assume that either variable is likely to play out strongly in ways that would favour legislative intervention. Although Fairfield (2008, p.433) labels EULAs 'anti-social' because 'they create confusion and litigation', it is remarkable that such contracts have rarely been the subject of litigation or vehement protest on a large scale, despite their massive deployment. While end users are not oblivious to the existence of EULAs—end users must usually formally accept such agreements prior to being admitted to the online service or platform in question—they are probably indifferent to the agreements' actual terms and, in the absence of untoward behaviour, they can generally enjoy the proffered service(s) without significant interference from the EULA drafter. The above-mentioned 'internalisation' problem identified by Madison (2003) might also contribute to end-user passivity. The increasingly dense legalese of EULAs no doubt contributes also to their marginal role for the bulk of end users: to paraphrase one commentator, EULAs appear not just to be written *by* lawyers but also *for* lawyers (Nino 2010; see too Jankowich 2006). It is instructive that in one of the few instances of EULA-focused litigation, the plaintiff was both a lawyer and an end user who got into trouble with the online community provider (Linden Labs) for allegedly purchasing virtual real estate in Second Life by improper means (*Bragg v Linden Research Inc.*, 487 F. Supp. 2d 593 (E.D. Pa., 2007); the case was ultimately settled out of court). Further, virtual world providers are not entirely free to make up and change the rules of their worlds at whim. If they are to survive commercially, they must go some way to respecting the wishes of the majority of end users (Grimmelmann 2006; Mayer-Schönberger and Crowley 2006). This blunts their ability to ride roughshod over end users and the broader public interest, thus helping to take some of the steam out of any possible end-user or legislator objections.

CONCLUSION

This chapter shows when and why contract enjoys a privileged position relative to statute in governing the internet. That position is due essentially to the fact that contract enables flexible micro-management of the digital world more easily than statute does. Whenever internet governors, particularly in the private sector, need 'hard law' to exercise fine-grained control which is tailored to the particular needs of a technological platform, service or online community and yet can be quickly adjusted as those needs change, contract will tend to be the tool of choice. Exacerbating this tendency is a fairly general ideological bias against developing new statutory forms of control except as measures of 'last resort'.

If we are to attempt to sum up in a single sentence the respective role of contract and statute in internet governance it is that the latter tends to play second fiddle to the former. Yet, like most such attempts, this is an oversimplification of reality. We can see from the foregoing analysis of copyright that contract may in some instances be threatening to relegate statute to a more marginal spot in the orchestra. In other instances, though, statute and public law may be jostling for a spot amongst the first violins—the case, for example, with EU legislation on electronic communications networks and services.

Indeed, the most important insight delivered by the chapter is that the relative roles played by contract and statute in internet governance are not frozen but fluid. How those roles change depends on numerous factors. They may change, for example, as conceptions of the parameters of internet governance change. They may change depending on the degree to which the internet facilitates behaviour posing a major threat to, say, established revenue streams (consider, for example, legislation on IPR) or basic human rights (consider, for example, legislation on privacy and data protection). They may change as political constellations change (consider, for instance, the replacement of the JPA by the AOC). Or they may change as conceptions of their respective degrees of legitimacy change in light of market behaviour (consider, for example, evolving views of the (un)fairness of EULA-based governance).

ACKNOWLEDGEMENTS

Thanks are due to Graham Greenleaf and Dan Svantesson along with my colleagues on the 'Igov2' project (http://www.jus.uio.no/ifp/english/research/projects/internet-governance/)—Emily Weitzenboeck, Tobias Mahler and Kevin McGillivray—for prompt feedback on an earlier draft of the chapter. Thanks go also to A. Michael Froomkin for discussing with me the legal status of the Affirmation of Commitments, and to Ian Walden for advising me on the scope of the UK Communications Act 2003. The bulk of the chapter was written in the latter half of 2011 when I was a Visiting Fellow at the Australian National University's College of Law. Research for the chapter has also been supported by EINS, the Network of Excellence in Internet Science (http://www.internet-science.eu/), which is funded through the European Commission's 7th Framework Programme.

BIBLIOGRAPHY

Abbott, K. W. and D. Snidal (2000), 'Hard and Soft Law in International Governance', *International Organization*, **54**(3), 421–56.

Abbott, K. W., R. O. Keohane, A. Moravcsik, A-M. Slaughter and D. Snidal (2000), 'The Concept of Legalization', *International Organization*, **54**(3), 401–19.

Alvestrand, H. (2009), 'The Internet Engineering Task Force', in L. A. Bygrave and J. Bing (eds), *Internet Governance: Infrastructure and Institutions*, Oxford: Oxford University Press, pp.126–38.

Balkin, J. M. (2004), 'Virtual Liberty: Freedom to Design and Freedom to Play in Virtual Worlds', *Virginia Law Review*, **90**(8), 2043–98.

Bekker, E., W. Buhse, D. Günnewig and N. Buhse (eds) (2003), *Digital Rights Management: Technological, Economic, Legal and Political Aspects*, Berlin and Heidelberg: Springer.

Bing, J. (2009), 'Building Cyberspace: A Brief History of the Internet', in L. A. Bygrave and J. Bing (eds), *Internet Governance: Infrastructure and Institutions*, Oxford: Oxford University Press, pp.8–47.

Bygrave, L. A. (2002), *Data Protection Law: Approaching Its Rationale, Logic and Limits*, The Hague, London and New York: Kluwer Law International.

Bygrave, L. A. (2003), 'Digital Rights Management and Privacy – Legal Aspects in the European Union', in E. Bekker, W. Buhse, D. Günnewig and N. Buhse (eds) (2003), *Digital Rights Management: Technological, Economic, Legal and Political Aspects*, Berlin and Heidelberg: Springer, pp.418–46.

Bygrave, L. A. (2008), 'International Agreements to Protect Personal Data', in J. B. Rule and G. Greenleaf (eds), *Global Privacy Protection: The First Generation*, Cheltenham, UK and Northampton, MA, US: Edward Elgar, pp.15–49.

Bygrave, L. A. and J. Bing (eds) (2009), *Internet Governance: Infrastructure and Institutions*, Oxford: Oxford University Press.

Bygrave, L. A. and T. Michaelsen (2009), 'Governors of Internet', in L. A. Bygrave and J. Bing (eds), *Internet Governance: Infrastructure and Institutions*, Oxford: Oxford University Press, pp.92–125.

Cotropia, C. A. (2008), 'Compulsory Licensing under TRIPS and the Supreme Court of the United States' Decision in *eBay v. MercExchange*', in T. Takenawa (ed.), *Patent Law and Theory: A Handbook of Contemporary Research*, Cheltenham, UK and Northampton, MA, US: Edward Elgar, pp.557–83.

Council of Europe, Ad Hoc Advisory Group on Cross-border Internet (2011), 'Draft Council of Europe Committee of Ministers Declaration on Internet Governance Principles 2011', (version 2.0; 11 April), http://www.coe.int/t/dghl/standardsetting/media-dataprotection/conf-internet-freedom/Internet%20Governance%20Principles.pdf, accessed 1 September 2011.

De Vries, P. (2011), 'The Resilience Principles: A Framework for New ICT Governance', *Journal on Telecommunication & High Technology Law*, **9**, 137–80.

De Zwart, M. (2010), 'Contractual Communities: Effective Governance of Virtual Worlds', *University of New South Wales Law Journal*, **33**(2), 605–27.

Edgeworth, B. (2003), *Law, Modernity, Postmodernity: Legal Change in the Contracting State*, Aldershot: Ashgate.

Ellickson, R. C. (1991), *Order without Law: How Neighbors Settle Disputes*, Cambridge, MA: Harvard University Press.

Fairfield, J. A. T. (2008), 'Anti-Social Contracts: The Contractual Governance of Virtual Worlds', *McGill Law Journal*, **53**(3), 427–76.

Fairfield, J. A. T. (2009), 'The God Paradox', *Boston University Law Review*, **89**(3), 1017–68.

Farnsworth, E. A. (2004), *Farnsworth on Contracts*, New York: Aspen Publishers.

Froomkin, A. M. (2000), 'Wrong Turn in Cyberspace: Using ICANN to Route Around the APA and the Constitution', *Duke Law Journal*, **50**(1), 17–184.

Froomkin, A. M. (2002), 'Form and Substance in Cyberspace', *Journal of Small & Emerging Business Law*, **6**(1), 93–124.

Froomkin, A. M. (2003), 'Habermas@discourse.net: Toward a Critical Theory of Cyberspace', *Harvard Law Review*, **116**(3), 749–873.

Froomkin, A. M. (2011), 'Almost Free: An Analysis of ICANN's "Affirmation of Commitments"', *Journal on Telecommunication & High Technology Law*, **9**, 187–234.

Goldsmith, J. L. and T. Wu (2006), *Who Controls the Internet? Illusions of a Borderless World*, New York and Oxford: Oxford University Press.

Gorecki, P. K. (1981), *Regulating the Price of Prescription Drugs in Canada: Compulsory Licensing, Product Selection, and Government Reimbursement Programmes*, Ottawa: Economic Council of Canada.

Grimmelmann, J. (2006), 'Virtual Power Politics', in J. M. Balkin and B. S. Noveck (eds), *The State of Play: Law, Games, and Virtual Worlds*, New York: New York University Press, pp. 146–57.

Guibault, L. M. C. R. (2002), *Copyright Limitations and Contracts: An Analysis of the Contractual Overridability of Limitations on Copyright*, The Hague: Kluwer Law International.

Guibault, L. M. C. R. (2006), 'Wrapping Information in Contract: How Does it Affect the Public Domain?', in P. B. Hugenholtz and L. M. C. R. Guibault (eds), *The Future of the Public Domain: Identifying the Commons in Information Law*, Alphen aan den Rijn: Kluwer Law International, pp. 87–104.

Harris, D. P. (2004), 'TRIPS' Rebound: An Historical Analysis of How the TRIPS Agreement Can Ricochet back against the United States', *Northwestern Journal of International Law & Business*, **25**(1), 99–164.

Houdijk, J. (2005), 'The IMS Health Ruling: Some Thoughts on Its Significance for Legal Practice and Its Consequences for Future Cases such as Microsoft', *European Business Organization Law Review*, **6**, 467–95.

Hubbard, A. and L. A. Bygrave (2009), 'Internet Governance goes Global', in L. A. Bygrave and J. Bing (eds), *Internet Governance: Infrastructure and Institutions*, Oxford: Oxford University Press, pp. 213–35.

Hugenholtz, P. B. (1999), 'Code as Code, or The End of Intellectual Property as We Know It', *Maastricht Journal of European and Comparative Law*, **6**(3), 308–18.

Jankowich, A. (2006), 'EULAw: The Complex Web of Corporate Rule-Making in Virtual Worlds', *Tulane Journal of Technology and Intellectual Property*, **8**, 1–59.

Jänicke, M. (1990), *State Failure: The Impotence of Politics in Industrial Society*, Cambridge: Polity Press.

Kroes, N. (2011), 'I propose a "Compact for the Internet"', blog of 28 June 2011, http://blogs.ec.europa.eu/neelie-kroes/i-propose-a-compact-for-the-internet/, accessed 1 September 2011.

Kuner, C. (2009), 'An International Legal Framework for Data Protection: Issues and Prospects', *Computer Law & Security Review*, **25**, 307–17.

Lessig, L. (1999), *Code, and Other Laws of Cyberspace*, New York: Basic Books.

MacLean, D. (2008), 'Sovereign Right and the Dynamics of Power in the ITU: Lessons in the Quest for Inclusive Global Governance', in W. J. Drake and E. J. Wilson (eds), *Governing Global Electronic Networks*, Cambridge, MA: MIT Press, pp. 83–126.

Madison, M. J. (2003), 'Reconstructing the Software Licence', *Loyola University Chicago Law Journal*, **35**, 275–340.

Mayer-Schönberger, V. and J. Crowley (2006), 'Napster's Second Life? The Regulatory Challenges of Virtual Worlds', *Northwestern University Law Review*, **100**(4), 1775–826.

Meuleman, L. (2008), *Public Management and the Metagovernance of Hierarchies, Networks and Markets: The Feasibility of Designing and Managing Governance Style Combinations*, Heidelberg: Physica-Verlag.

Meyer, L. and R. Utz (2007), 'Internet Revolution? Alternate Root Models in the Internet in the Light of Anti-trust and Trade Mark Law', *European Intellectual Property Review*, **29**(9), 362–70.

Mifsud Bonnici, Jeanne P. (2008), *Self-Regulation in Cyberspace*, The Hague: TMC Asser Press.

Moran, M. and T. Prosser (eds) (1994), *Privatization and Regulatory Change in Europe*, Buckingham: Open University Press.

Mueller, M. L. (2002), *Ruling the Root: Internet Governance and the Taming of Cyberspace*, Cambridge, MA: MIT Press.

Mueller, M. L. (2010), *Networks and States: The Global Politics of Internet Governance*, Cambridge, MA: MIT Press.

Mueller, M. L., J. Mathiason and H. Klein (2007), 'The Internet and Global Governance: Principles and Norms for a New Regime', *Global Governance*, **13**(2), 237–54.

Nihoul, P. and P. Rodford (2011), *EU Electronic Communications Law: Competition and Regulation in the European Telecommunications Market*, 2nd edn, Oxford: Oxford University Press.

Nino, T. (2010), 'The Virtual Whirl: The Emperor's New Terms', http://www.massively.joystiq.com/2010/04/03/the-virtual-whirl-the-emperors-new-terms, accessed 23 August 2011.

Pereira, A. L. D. (2011), 'Software Interoperability, Intellectual Property and Competition Law: Compulsory Licenses for Abuse of Market Dominance', *Computer Law & Security Review*, **27**(2), 175–79.

Power, A. and O. Tobin (2011), 'Soft Law for the Internet, Lessons from International Law', *SCRIPTed*, **8**(1), 32–45, http://www.law.ed.ac.uk/ahrc/script-ed/vol8-1/power.pdf, accessed 28 August 2011.

Reid, E. (2004), 'The Doctrine of Abuse of Rights: Perspective from a Mixed Jurisdiction', *Electronic Journal of Comparative Law*, **8**(3), http://www.ejcl.org/83/art83-2.html.

Reidenberg, J. R. (1998), 'Lex Informatica: The Formulation of Information Policy Rules Through Technology', *Texas Law Review*, **76**(3), 553–93.

Rutkowski, A. (2011), 'Public International Law of the International Telecommunication Instruments: Cyber Security Treaty Provisions since 1850', *info*, **13**(1), 13–31.

Samuelson, P. (1995), 'Copyright, Digital Data, and Fair Use in Digital Networked Environments', in E. Mackaay, D. Poulin and P. Trudel (eds), *The Electronic Superhighway: The Shape of Law and Technology to Come*, The Hague: Kluwer Law International, pp. 117–26.

Schwartz, P. M. and J. R. Reidenberg (1996), *Data Privacy Law: A Study of United States Data Protection*, Charlottesville: Michie Law Publishers.

Senden, L. (2004), *Soft Law in European Community Law*, Oxford: Hart.

Sohmen, P. (2001), 'Taming the Dragon: China's Efforts to Regulate the Internet', *Stanford Journal of East Asian Affairs*, **1**, 17–26.

Solove, D. J., M. Rotenberg and P. M. Schwartz (2011), *Information Privacy Law, fourth edition*, New York: Aspen Publishers.

Suzor, N. (2010a), 'The Role of the Rule of Law in Virtual Communities', *Berkeley Technology Law Journal*, **25**, 1817–86.

Suzor, N. (2010b), 'Digital Constitutionalism and the Role of the Rule of Law in the Governance of Virtual Communities', PhD thesis, Queensland University of Technology, http://eprints.qut.edu.au/37636/1/Nicolas_Suzor_Thesis.pdf, accessed 23 August 2011.

Svantesson, D. J. B. (2006), 'Borders *On*, or Border *Around* – The Future of the Internet', *Albany Law Journal of Science and Technology*, **16**(2), 343–81.

Thunem, H. and A. B. Lange (2009), 'The National Domain Name Regime for the .no Domain', in L. A. Bygrave and J. Bing (eds), *Internet Governance: Infrastructure and Institutions*, Oxford: Oxford University Press, pp. 179–201.

Timms, R. (2003), Statement by the UK Minister for Energy, E-Commerce and Postal Services to the House of Commons Standing Committee on Delegated Legislation, in conjunction with debate on the Draft Telephone Numbers Exclusion (Domain Names and Internet Addresses) Order 2003, 8 December 2003, http://www.publications.parliament.uk/pa/cm200304/cmstand/deleg1/st031208/31208s01.htm, accessed 1 September 2011.

Uerpmann-Wittzack, R. (2008), 'Multilevel Internet Governance Involving the European Union, Nation States and NGOs', in A. Follesdal, R. A. Wessel and J. Wouters (eds), *Multilevel Regulation and the EU*, Leiden: Koninklijke Brill NV, pp. 145–68.

Walden, I. (ed.) (2009), *Telecommunications Law and Regulation*, 3rd edn, Oxford: Oxford University Press.

Weber, R. H. (2010), *Shaping Internet Governance: Regulatory Challenges*, Berlin and Heidelberg: Springer-Verlag.

Weber, R. H. and R. Weber (2010), *Internet of Things: Legal Perspectives*, Berlin and Heidelberg: Springer-Verlag.

Whittaker, S. (1995), 'Privity of Contract and the Law of Tort: The French Experience', *Oxford Journal of Legal Studies*, **15**(3), 327–70.

Williams, K. S. (2010), 'Transnational Developments in Internet Law', in Y. Jewkes and M. Yar (eds), *Handbook of Internet Crime*, London: Willan Publishing, pp. 466–91.

Wunsch-Vincent, S. (2005), *WTO, E-Commerce, and Information Technologies: From the Uruguay Round through the Doha Development Agenda*, New York: Markle Foundation, http://www.iie.com/publications/papers/wunsch1104.pdf, accessed 24 August 2011.

9. Argument-by-technology: how technical activism contributes to internet governance
Alison Powell

INTRODUCTION

Who influences the future of the internet, and how? Internet governance literature has focused on discussing multistakeholderism, rulemaking, and sometimes design, but has difficulty considering the impact of technical activism that claims disruption of systems as part of its strategy. This chapter critically examines how and whether technical activism can contribute to internet governance. Drawing on Christopher Kelty's (2005) observation that persuasive arguments can be made both through language and by technology, it examines how existing definitions of governance, which are often focused on rule-making, engage with this broader set of 'arguments-by-technology'.

The concept of 'argument-by-technology' originally focused on the way that creating and debating the code that underpinned the internet (and hence, the platform on which code could be created and debated) created legitimacy through simple functionality. In other words, 'running code is rough consensus'. This legitimacy stemmed from the ability of participants to create the platforms upon which they engaged. More broadly, decision-making about the nature of the internet based on particular technical features of networks has remained a feature of the internet's history and kind of de facto 'governance by design'. Aligned with cyber-libertarianism, this perspective stresses the exceptional nature of the internet's centreless design, and hence the efficacy of making decisions about it by developing new technical standards.

Other spheres are also influenced by the idea that political or social purposes can be achieved through network design: alternative access networks such as community wireless networks hinge in part on the idea that new technical design principles will help to exemplify more egalitarian modes of communication. More recently, distributed cyber-vigilantism has re-emerged, including the recent actions of online collective Anonymous that are positioned as a 'defence' of WikiLeaks. Such arguments by technology can be understood as non-rule-based contributions to governance, but they may require a broader conception of governance that allows for an understanding not just on the efficacy of technical 'rhetoric' but on the substance of the argument and the culture in which it is embedded.

This chapter argues that:

1. technical activism or advocacy occupies an overlap between competing definitions of internet governance;
2. it is linked with an historical set of links between specific political or social values and features of internet design that configure expectations about technical action;
3. the assumed alignment between design and politics is only weakly communicated in situations when alternatives challenge existing institutions;
4. technical advocacy is best described as being part of a governance ecology.

The chapter concludes that a focus on this ecology provides a useful broadening of the analysis of internet governance processes, but that it must avoid the risk of overdetermining the impact of design decisions or technical exploits. The chapter begins by reviewing competing perspectives on internet governance.

ARGUMENTS-BY-TECHNOLOGY AND INTERNET GOVERNANCE INSTITUTIONS

Many existing definitions of internet governance focus primarily on the process of rule-making and decision-making, rather than the philosophical debates driving these decisions. Bygrave and Bing provide two contrasting definitions of internet governance. The first, derived from the WSIS working group on internet governance, focuses primarily on the development of principles, and fixes the roles of each of the participants. It reads: 'Internet governance is the development and application by governments, the private sector, and civil society, in their respective roles, of shared principles, norms, rules, decision-making procedures and programmes that shape the evolution and utilization of the Internet' (WGIG, cited in Bygrave and Bing (2009) p. 2). This definition is outcome oriented, in that it suggests that governance is the development of norms and rules to shape the internet.

A broader definition describes internet governance as: 'collective action by governments and/or private sector operators of TCP/IP networks, to establish rules and procedures to enforce public policies and resolve disputes that involve multiple jurisdictions' (Mueller, Mathiason, and McKnight 2004, cited in Bygrave and Bing (2009), p. 2). This broader defi-nition implies that a variety of persons and organizations are involved in making decisions about the internet, but again, rule-making appears as a central feature of governance.

Both of these definitions presented above – and indeed the entire enterprise of working out how to govern the internet – hinges on an assumption that the internet is unique, by virtue of its history, design, or capacity. The philosophical lever that permits this focus is the acknowl-edgement that the internet itself is the result of a collective negotiation among its original architects. Anthropologist of technology Christopher Kelty argues that in some technical cultures such as software produc-tion, arguments are made both by text and by technology. He describes how the shared international community of programming geeks is united by the extent to which they can influence the 'technical and legal conditions of possibility for their own association.' (Kelty 2005, p. 185). Thus, collaborating over the internet to create a network that works in an unexpected way could be considered as an argument about the ideal conditions of association of internet geeks. Kelty also identifies that these internet geeks, in addition to being engaged in collectively manu-facturing the technical conditions of possibility for their own association through code, are also collaborating globally at a scale never previously possible. These two features: the capacity to easily facilitate global and distributed collaboration, and the capacity to collectively design and manage the system supporting that collaboration, raise questions about the conventional rule-based definitions of governance. To what extent does 'argument-by-technology' contribute to internet governance? Does it challenge the frameworks that situate governance as primarily related to rule-making? The following section draws out two different outcomes for 'argument-by-technology' as it links with two influential perspectives on internet governance.

DESTABILIZING STATE-BASED GOVERNANCE

Mueller (2010) suggests that the ideologies of internet governance can be mapped on two axes from state to network and from transnational to national. He argues that the internet has introduced transnational aspects into communications regulation and governance, including more networks of transnational actors, such as civil society. This has nourished a move away from hierarchy and towards more networked forms of governance. This analysis of the shifting processes of governance argues that the global reach of the internet as well as its capacity to mobilize issue-based networks has presented a new set of issues for multistakeholder governance, one that challenges as well as integrates state-level forms of governance.

Some of the capacities of the internet thus influence existing governance processes. Mueller illustrates this by noting the shift from the state participation at the World Summits on the Information Society (WSIS) in the early 2000s to the broader participation in the later Internet Governance Forums. During the WSIS process, civil society actors, denied official voting status, pushed for the inclusion of issues beyond physical network access. At the conclusion of the WSIS process, the Internet Governance Forum, a 'talking shop', was meant to allow for the formation of dynamic coalitions to discuss emergent issues, with a more balanced participation between states and civil society. This process was originally meant to shift the form and the process of governance from one based on confined, state-level decision making towards negotiation across a variety of levels (Held and McGrew 2003). A range of stakeholders, many organized using the internet, participated. Raboy noted that these more open decision-making fora 'form[ed] the basis of a new model of representation and legitimation of non-governmental input to global affairs', and as a result, 'the rules and parameters of global governance . . . shifted' (Raboy 2004, p. 349).

The capacity of the internet to mobilize support and rally diverse stakeholders underpins, to a certain extent, these shifts in governance practice. However, as Mueller notes, this focus on the internet as a platform for political action fails to acknowledge the extent to which it is a site for political action as well. He identifies the nascent 'Access to Knowledge' movements (that include open source software advocacy, community networking, free cultures and copyright reform) as attempts to draw attention to the intrinsic politics of the internet. In these Access to Knowledge movements, digital communication platforms present a challenge to existing conventions of intellectual property and to existing state-level modes of governance.

The contributions to governance of such movements or quasi-movements are not always evident within framings of governance that focus on rule-making. Technology activist movements are often made up of practitioners rather than policy specialists, their organizational structures are often looser, and they often frame their interventions as concerned with process rather than outcome. As Hintz and Milan (2009) argue, for example, the multistakeholder processes of both WSIS and the IGF created barriers to participation of members of technology collectives whose loose, collective-based organizational structure was incompatible with the procedures for registering NGOs at these events, and who could not afford to participate. As well, while UN sponsored governance processes are one place where many internet stakeholders stake policy claims and 'talk shop', other decisions impacting internet governance issues take place through praxis.

The capacity for some technical experts to intervene in the function of internet networks also suggests that rebuilding the internet could be a form of governance in itself – an argument by technology, if you like. This capacity is alluded to in histories of the internet that focus on the ability of its users to contribute to its design, and in which deliberation is central to a design process that produces the internet itself. The potential of design and technology as arguments in themselves also underpins claims that technical design specifications can act as political interventions. These claims contribute to a contrasting perspective on internet governance that concentrates influence neither in rule-making nor in processes that contribute to rule-making, but instead in design and the positive or negative implications of design decisions.

DESIGN AND GENERATIVITY

If technology activism is difficult to square with a perspective on governance that is concerned with rule-making, it might be better understood from a perspective concerned with the relationship between the internet's design and its social influence. This strand of scholarship presumes that much of the influence of the internet has resulted from the capacities of its original design, and the social frameworks which became associated with these capacities. Jonathan Zittrain has developed this perspective by arguing that the internet, as well as the personal computer, are 'generative technologies'. Zittrain (2008) writes, 'generativity is a system's capacity to produce unanticipated changes through unfiltered contributions from broad and varied audiences' (p. 70). A descriptive concept grounded in the theories of technological affordances which analyzes the possible or likely uses of technologies, this concept is related to the normative ideals that also underscore Access to Knowledge movements. These include the ideas of sharing source code associated with the free software movement, and the theories of the informational commons.

Generativity can be advocated transnationally through open-source movements, locally through community networks, or in hybrid modes that also influence private sector actors, such as the development of filesharing sites like the Pirate Bay and the development of contribution-based news sites like Indymedia. Unlike the Access to Knowledge movements as described by Mueller, however, generativity is largely focused

on the capacities of a particular technology. Zittrain describes them as
the following: '1. how extensively a system or technology leverages a set
of possible tasks; 2. how well it can be adapted to a range of tasks; 3.
how easily new contributors can master it; 4. how accessible it is to those
ready and able to build on it; and 5. how transferable any changes are
to others' (p.71). Generativity, then, is a set of capacities inherent to a
design of a technology that permit it to make a range of tasks possible.
Generativity is at the heart of Kelty's original formulation of argument-
by-technology: the generative potential of computer code allows for the
contribution of internet geeks to the creation and maintenance of the
internet.

Zittrain argues that it is generativity that has influenced the development of the internet, and that the most significant challenge for the
future of the internet is the maintenance of generativity. This challenge
is made more difficult by the fact that the same generativity that invites
participation in and innovation of new applications for internet systems
also invites the development of spam, viruses and malware. Both benefi-
cent 'geeks' and malicious 'hackers' take advantage of this generativity
– exploiting either positively or negatively the capacities and weaknesses
of internet systems. This focus on the power of technical interventions
echoes discussions of the conceptual contributions of 'hacker culture'
– an empowered technical subculture sometimes associated with the
subculture of technical advocates who eventually designed and built the
early internet (see Turner 2005 and 2009). The hacker 'trickster' is often
described as enlivening the positive potential of computer networking:
'the hacker makes trouble for everyone, but this modern-day trickster
has a powerful purpose: the realization of a mythic utopia locked up
by our stagnating tendencies to freeze revolutionary technologies in the
ice of outdated social patterns' (Mosco 2004, p.48). This quotation is
typical of statements that delegate political or social influence to technical exploits. Zittrain, too, sees a politics in design, but acknowledges that
generativity can be negative.

The central governance problem, then, for Zittrain, is how positive
generativity can be maintained in the face of the problems of security,
privacy and neutrality that the internet raises. He is adamant that the
processes of WSIS and the IGF that he calls 'stakeholder governance'
don't include the geeks and hobbyists who are more interested in writing
code than participating in governance meetings. He writes, 'without
them we too easily neglect the prospect that we could code new tools and
protocols to facilitate social solutions' (p.243). Governance doesn't take
place among a new set of stakeholders engaged in discussion: it takes
place in code.

EXPECTATIONS ABOUT ARGUMENTS-BY-TECHNOLOGY: INTERNET HISTORY

So far, we have reviewed the contributions of two distinct perspectives on internet governance. The first states that the governance of the internet presents a challenge to existing state-based institutions, and that it has contributed to the rise of new institutions of governance. As well, a set of nascent social movements are beginning to politicize the internet. The second focuses on the extent to which the design of the internet is seen to be the primary force in its governance, for better or for worse. The point of contact between these two perspectives is, of course, an acknowledgement that the design of technology can be a political statement or express a set of political values.

The connections – or articulations – between values and technology are expressed in the internet governance field by the arguments made by different stakeholders about how to govern or regulate it. Cultural theorist Stuart Hall (1983) introduces the concept of articulation theory to describe how material elements, practices, and social groups are connected; articulations are 'lines of tendential force' linking political ideologies with particular cultural assumptions. These are not determined by the origins of the ideologies or assumptions. Thus, new ideas can be created through the connection of one set of ideas to another. This is evident in the connection of ideas about internet design with ideas about its politics. The next section looks historically at how these connections have been made.

The particular history of the internet's development is linked with expectations about the political aspects of technical developments. As computer historians and sociologists have noted, the cultural values of certain technical subcultures, like Californian internet geeks, have tended towards the individualist and libertarian (Turner 2005). Historically, there has been a close articulation between certain design features of the internet, and particular aspects of the political values shared by some members of this technical subculture. Take the classic example of John Perry Barlow's Declaration of Independence of Cyberspace:

> Governments of the Industrial World, you weary giants of flesh and steel, I come from Cyberspace, the new home of Mind. On behalf of the future, I ask you of the past to leave us alone. You are not welcome among us. You have no sovereignty where we gather . . . I declare the global social space we are building to be naturally independent of the tyrannies you seek to impose on us. You have no moral right to rule us nor do you possess any methods of enforcement we have true reason to fear. (Barlow 1996)

Barlow's focus on the specificity of the internet – its transactional nature, its basis in data – exemplifies an approach where the structure and architecture of the internet are taken as supporting a particular political or social philosophy. The manifesto likens the revision of the telecommunications policy laws undertaken by the US government to a parent out of touch with their children's culture. This associates the internet with youth, the future, and with a space outside of national regulation.

The idea that the internet has some features, for example its interlinked network architecture, that make it impractical or ideologically problematic to regulate, has been remarkably persistent. Hofman (2010) identifies it as part of a 'utopian vision of autonomy and creativity' (p. 2) associated with the early internet. This vision stressed the potential of the internet to delegitimize the existing modes of telecommunications operations by creating autonomous networks that could interconnect in a network of networks: an *inter*net. This network of networks was meant to oppose a centralized telecommunication network, the organization of which Hofman describes as a 'bureaucratic model which emphasizes collective security, stability and regularity' (pp. 5–6).

The political expectations of the development of an internetworked as opposed to centralized and switched network are expressed in a set of essays by David Isenberg in which he lauds the potential of a 'stupid network' where end-to-end trumps centralization. Isenberg thought of the stupid network as a philosophy, writing, 'a new network "philosophy and architecture"', is replacing the vision of an Intelligent Network. The vision is one in which the public communications network would be engineered for 'always-on' use, not intermittence and scarcity. It would be engineered for intelligence at the end-user's device, not in the network. And the network would be engineered simply to 'Deliver the Bits, Stupid', (Isenberg 1997). Isenberg's politicization of 'argument-by-technology' was shared by other internet pioneers. Lessig (1999) described how the 'minimalism by design' of TCP/IP protocols was intentional, noting 'it reflects both a political decision about disabling control and a technological decision about the optimal network design' (Lessig 1999, p. 32). Mitchell Kapor simply declared 'architecture is politics' (cited in Riedenberg 1998).

The assumption that there is some political or ideological salience in the design of a network has been surprisingly persistent, despite the potential negative consequences of its generativity. Isenberg's work for example, became even more explicit in its links between design and politics. In a 2002 update of the 'stupid network' idea, Isenberg, along with David Weisenberg, writes:

> In fact, the best network embodies explicit political ideals – it would be disingenuous to pretend it didn't. The best technological network is also the most

open political network. The best network is not only simple, low-cost, robust and innovation-friendly, it is also best at promoting a free, democratic, pluralistic, participatory society; a society in which people with new business ideas are free to fail and free to succeed in the marketplace. (Isenberg and Weinberger 2002)

The persistence of this political articulation to an argument-by-technology is fascinating, particularly as Zittrain and Hofman have identified that the libertarian ideals supposedly carried by the decentralized design of internet networks were equally available to the developers of spam, viruses, malware and cybercrime. Yet, in governance terms, the expectations established by original arguments-by-technology made by internet developers who shared a common culture have now landed in the realm of statecraft. US Secretary of State Hillary Clinton's 2010 'Internet Freedom Agenda' states, 'The internet has become the public space of the 21st century – the world's town square, classroom, marketplace, coffeehouse, and nightclub . . . The value of these spaces derives from the variety of activities people can pursue in them, from holding a rally to selling their vegetables, to having a private conversation. These spaces provide an open platform, and so does the internet. It does not serve any particular agenda, and it never should' (Clinton 2010). Within a decade, arguments specifically related to technical function became arguments for a foreign policy agenda, with the expectations originally related to technical function recast as political values that could be exported from America to the world. Despite the evidence to the contrary, that the same basic features of internet design could be used to limit the freedom of internet users, either by cybercriminals or by state-level actors themselves (Morozov 2011), the articulation between a particular libertarian type of democratic freedom and the design of the internet remains. In turn, these expectations shape the extent to which activism that either attempts to redesign networks or attempts to exploit certain technical features of networks can contribute to governance.

This section has illustrated how expectations established by the original 'arguments-by-technology' of internet architects configured the articulations between technology and politics that have been made. The next section examines the expectations and outcomes related to the creation, in the 2000s, of alternative access networks intended as critiques of the developing hegemony of network operators. These networks are broadly 'generative' in Zittrain's sense, but they are also described as being 'disruptive', particularly in their recapitulation of distributed – peer-to-peer – design modalities.

(RE)DESIGNING DISTRIBUTED NETWORKS: WIRELESS PEER-TO-PEER

Throughout the early 2000s various groups, including radio amateurs, open-source software practitioners and communication rights activists argued for a re-examination of wireless technology as an alternative mode of access to the internet, as well as a commons-based alternative to centralized control of communication. The need for this alternative was based on the decline of the promise of the non-commercial internet, the perceived inequalities of coverage perpetuated by commercial ISPs, and the enduring promise of an autonomous network built by its participants (Sandvig 2004). The community wireless networking (CWN) movement promised to design networks that could provide for increased local control of communication, or that could leverage the technical – and hence political – promise of peer-to-peer networking.

This promise was a recapitulation of the original attraction of a network built by its users. It promised to disrupt the process of increasing corporate control over the internet by building peer-to-peer networks governed by their users. Although the original design of the internet was indeed open to interconnection from a variety of devices and networks, and its routing algorithms designed to use networks to efficiently deliver packets, the idea of a peer-to-peer network was not defined in the IETF's Requests for Comments until 2009. The relevant RFC reads: 'We consider a system to be P2P if the elements that form the system share their resources in order to provide the service the system has been designed to provide. The elements in the system both provide services to other elements and request services from other elements.' What the RFC defines is the reciprocal data transfer relationships that characterize peer-to-peer filesharing as well as peer-to-peer wireless. By providing new modalities for transmitting data, these forms of sharing disrupt the increasingly hegemonic proprietary forms of internet access as well as network-based knowledge exchange. Cammaerts (2011) argues that these modalities reveal the increasingly complex relationship between hegemonic structures of market capitalism and alternative opportunities illustrated by specific technical arguments. Similarly, Mueller identifies peer-to-peer filesharing as an exemplar of a contrast between the networked organizations and practices that emerge online, and the legal frameworks aligned with existing perspectives on intellectual property. Peer-to-peer wireless networks, for their part, are perceived as challenging the centralizing control of corporate ISPs.

The expectation that peer-to-peer sharing of wireless signals could disrupt the process by which the internet became captured by commercial interests as well as the individualist rhetoric of intellectual property (or broadband network provision) animated the development of hundreds of community wireless projects in the decade to 2010. Empirical research conducted over the past five years reveals the extent to which some of these disruptive expectations were met, as well as how the more radical promise of peer-to-peer failed to be developed.

In 2003, a 'wireless commons manifesto' circulated on the internet suggested that the availability of mesh networking technology would provoke a social revolution. This nascent commons was understood by wireless geeks (much like internet geeks in culture and temperament) as both a technical and an organizational challenge, but one that would one day compensate for – or even replace – the increasingly corporate and hierarchical internet:

> Low-cost wireless networking equipment which can operate in unlicensed bands of the spectrum has started another revolution. Suddenly, ordinary people have the means to create a network independent of any physical constraint except distance. Wireless can travel through walls, across property boundaries and through a community. Many communities have formed worldwide to help organize these networks. They are forming the basis for the removal of the traditional telecommunication networks as an intermediary in human communication. (Wireless Commons Manifesto 2003)

The manifesto frames the wireless commons as disruptive to the 'traditional telecommunication networks' and their control of communications. Like the political screeds eliding the design of the internet with a transformative libertarian politics, it uses technical design metaphors to imply a social and political purpose. As an argument-by-technology, the wireless commons promises a decentralized alternative to existing communications infrastructures, one which was simultaneously disruptive and democratic. These two competing articulations are associated with different facets of networked communication, and they can be viewed as claims about different idealized forms of governance, made by the hackers and activists who have built wireless networks. These alternative networks are meant to present alternative arguments about how networks should operate, and to what extent their potential for democratizing communications should take precedence over their disruption of existing telecommunication industry practices.

THE WIRELESS COMMONS? EMPIRICAL EXAMPLES

Looking in detail at empirical studies of community networks, it is possible to see the way that advocates present their networks as disruptive to models involving corporate control or adherence to individual property rights. For example, as Forlano and Powell et al. (2011) report, the Funkfeur network of Vienna, Austria was founded as a way to highlight opposition to a proposed internet data retention law. This inspired a group of interested people to experiment with what they could do to create an ownerless, ad-hoc radio network that could distribute high-speed internet connectivity. Like other similar community networks, the idea was to create a meshed network that would provide both an alternative platform for experimentation, and an alternative means to connecting to the internet. Individual members establish radio links and experiment with improving and refining them in order, in theory, to build a commons and disrupt the capitalist model of internet service provision.

Carpentier (2008) identifies a similar set of claims made by the activists responsible for the Reseau Citoyen network in Brussels. Their website explicitly links the distributed commons-based network of radios with a political and social commons:

> We consider that equality between citizens is important and therefore some technical choices are excluded as they would imply that some systems would have to play a preeminent role. Each citizen is represented by a router, and no router should be able to control others. (cited in Cammaerts 2011, p. 56)

Architectural choices are also often elided with political or organizational choices on the part of network activists. The founder of the community wireless mesh network in Athens, Greece, reported that 'We have 1,000 administrators in the network. Everybody knows each other's ID and if someone abuses the network, other people push them out. It is a lot safer than the public internet,' (cited in Forlano and Powell et al. 2011, p. 17). The opportunities for autonomy proposed by these alternative and self-organized networks are described in this quotation as facilitating community control. The underlying assumption is that the openness provided on the CWN networks creates unique opportunities for autonomy and self-organization.

Yet many wireless collectives, despite their claims to be developing a commons, operate in practice through self-interested participation. For example, the Vienna network has purchased a direct link to the Vienna internet exchange for the benefit of its participants – but not necessarily the city's population in general. One of the founders of the network noted, 'The best motivation for people to build good links is so they have good capacity themselves.' (cited in Forlano and Powell et al. 2011, p. 45). This declaration of potential self-interest reiterates the complexity of an argument-by-technology in favour of communalism.

The Limits of the Wireless Commons

There is a thus a tension between the expectations about the potential of a technological alternative and the political and social consequences. Coleman (2011), for example, argues that disruptions to technical systems are forms of political resistance, even when they are not articulated as such. Similarly, Feenberg (1999) argues that technology is available for different political ends: its ambivalence permits both (or either) a conservation of hierarchy and/or a democratic rationalization of technology. Thus, it is not a given that a commons-based technology will disrupt a hierarchical and corporate industry structure. Still, CWN projects have had some transformative outcomes on local governance structures. Tapia et al. (2009) investigated how some CWN projects created partnerships with local governments that allowed the networks to be sustained, while Shaffer (2009) highlights how the long-term success of a local meshed network in Catalonia is due to participation in governance and network management by non-profits, local business, and government.

The thousands of community wireless projects established around the world are arguments in favour of commons-based access to knowledge, but their evolution after the initial enthusiasm for alternative access models faded has nuanced the potential significance of this particular argument-by-technology. Paralleling the alternative arguments made by internet advocates of previous decades, the argument in favour of commons-based access modes collapsed technical forms on to socio-political arrangements, promising a disruption and democratization of hegemonic control of communication. Overall, the arguments in favour of radical distribution and autonomous control have been weakened by the dominance of more conventional internet access modes. The social expectations of peer-to-peer sharing have not been widely met, although the development of some modes of hybrid partnership in local areas creates its own, more limited, contribution to alternative governance.

ANONYMOUS AND NETWORKED DISRUPTION

The practical technology activism advanced by proponents of CWN was a kind of positive recasting of technology's potential to disrupt an increasing corporatization and individualization of the internet. In terms of governance contributions, projects were successful in providing alternative modes of internet access and in developing various types of hybrid organizational partnerships with local institutions but the expectations of social or political transformation created by the technical metaphors employed in the Wireless Commons manifesto confronted with difficulty the hegemonic structures of the incumbent systems of ISPs. This contribution to governance is neither based only on rule-making nor fundamentally linked with design – it instead occupies a more complex space where attempts to exploit technical capacities to effect political and social transforms have unexpected and sometimes productive outcomes.

The two frames for internet governance reviewed at the beginning of the chapter suggest that the internet provides potential for newly networked, transnational forms of engagement, as well as suggesting that network designs could be carriers of politics. This chapter's final example concentrates on the activities of the hacker collective known as Anonymous. In particular, it considers how Anonymous contributed to a mediated drama involving state-level and corporate responses to the WikiLeaks release of US diplomatic cables in December and January 2010. In this drama, a 'swarm' of loosely affiliated participants appeared to exploit the opportunity to temporarily shut down web sites using distributed denial-of-service (DDoS) attacks, or 'mirror' websites themselves being blocked by such attacks.

These contributions to the 'WikiLeaks drama' (Coleman 2011) provide an illustration and a challenge to the expectations about networked activism employing technical exploits. The idea of an 'exploit' as a disruption of networked power is developed by Galloway and Thacker (2007). The exploit is the event, within a network, that takes advantage of the features of the network to undermine its power. The concept of the exploit again takes a technological and organizational structure as its central metaphor, linking to Mueller's (2010) identification of transnational advocacy networks as a new social formation contributing to internet governance. Yet the concept of the exploit captures an additional nuance of political action in an era of networked communication. It acknowledges that resistance is not necessarily organized, even when it takes advantage of organizational structures.

Previous theorizations of emergent social and ontological forms have included Deleuze and Guattari's (1980) understanding of rhizomatic forms of organization and cultural expression as emerging in contrast and challenge to hierarchical forms. The rhizomatic form has been used to explain tactical media and open-source movements, as well as other emergent social phenomena. However, Galloway and Thacker argue that control in a network society has shifted from oppositional force (involving state actors) to control via protocol (and the more complex set of actors that this introduces). Instead of the resistant block, or the rhizome, they suggest 'the swarm' as a metaphor for contemporary resistance. In a swarm, individual particles are interconnected but autonomous, and the direction of movement is influenced by a larger law or principle of collective intelligence.

Anonymous, as an apparently leaderless, loosely organized, and entirely internet-based group, provides an interesting case study to examine how expectations about swarms – and their tactics – might contribute to internet governance. Coleman (2011) provides an historical review of the organization and actions of Anonymous, noting that rather than describing an actual organization, the name acts as an 'improper name': 'The adoption of the same alias by organized collectives, affinity groups, and individual authors' (Deseriis 2010). This shared name was originally attached to online actions like trolling, and then to a series of actions taken against the Church of Scientology. Coleman describes how participants often describe themselves as being 'in it for the lulz' or for the pleasure of doing something disruptive and subversive online. She describes how a wing of Anonymous protesting Scientology began organizing protests outside of the internet, even if these still retained the 'grotesque, humorous, and offensive elements that are part and parcel of the lulz' (Coleman 2011). Eventually, some of these members also began to participate in other politically motivated actions. The makeup of Anonymous is more varied than descriptions of it as a 'hacker collective' suggest. It has very low barriers to participation, and a large diversity of types of members and types of participation. According to Coleman, some associated with Anonymous are 'hackers' with specific and deep technical skills, and a political philosophy dedicated to information freedom, and others are 'geeks' who are willing participants in technical culture with a more narrow range of skills. Others still may not self-identify as hackers or geeks but seek to contribute – or simply to observe.

Anonymous claimed credit for 'Operation Payback' – a set of politically motivated DDoS actions. In December 2010, after WikiLeaks released a set of US diplomatic cables, commercial organizations tried to shut down the WikiLeaks website, also using DDoS. Other online service providers such as PayPal, Visa and Amazon threatened to withdraw service and support to WikiLeaks. These actions, along with threats of legal ramifications, comprised what Benkler (2011) calls 'systemic threats' to WikiLeaks. These were performed in response to a call from Senate Homeland Security Committee Chairman Joe Lieberman. Anonymous contributed to the drama by staging DDoS counter-attacks, succeeding in shutting down Visa's website temporarily. Following these retaliatory actions, thousands of individuals – some claiming affiliation with Anonymous – set up mirror sites of all of the wikileaks.org content, defeating the purpose of cutting off access to the site.

The response to some of these 'systemic threats' by Anonymous, who had no formal connection with WikiLeaks and who appeared to take down websites effortlessly, were seized upon by mass media as an example of online anarchy. This particular action appears to align with the metaphor of the swarm. Instead of networked, organization-based resistance that directly countered state power, or rhizomatic political organization, Anonymous (as well as thousands of site mirrorers) came out of nowhere. It leveraged some of the functionality of a protocol-controlled network to disrupt entities with many more financial and material resources. Through these actions, and their representation in the media, Anonymous contributed to debates about the legitimacy of states in controlling their own information, the extent to which private companies should respond to state pressure, and the extent to which individuals and emergent entities could continue to disrupt internet function.

Did the actions of Anonymous and the WikiLeaks site mirrorers contribute to internet governance? The response depends on how such actors are positioned, especially relative to more conventionally constituted (or networked) organizations. Some commentators, like Crenshaw (2011) consider Anonymous to be a 'meme, rather than a group'. Others stress the potential political content of their actions: Morozov (2011) suggests that they might be a kind of social movement, likening DDoS to sit-ins intended to disrupt institutions. Yet based on empirical observation of the actions of people who identify themselves with Anonymous, Coleman (2011) claims there is more political agency at stake, arguing that participation in Anonymous actions can act as a gateway for geeks to become politicized. Certainly, the political action of such distributed organizations does not need to be labelled as 'politics' in order for it to be political. Events like the riots that took place across England in the summer of 2011 demonstrate that even seemingly chaotic actions are responses to underlying political situations. It is impossible to specify individual motivations for participating in a phenomenon such as Anonymous. This makes it very difficult to locate actions such as the DDoS within governance frameworks that focus on networked organizations or rule-making. Equally, while the actual DDoS actions exploit technical features of the internet, they are largely symbolic. The Anonymous DDoS in part helped to highlight questions about the legitimacy of DDoS as a tactic, especially when used by corporate or state-influenced entities against groups like WikiLeaks.

DISCUSSION

Technical activism contributes to internet governance by advancing competing articulations of values and technology. Existing perspectives on governance draw on these articulations, whether they focus on the development of networks of stakeholders, or on the ability of internet design to secure the positive benefits of the internet's generativity. These articulations also appear in the form of alternative modes of access such as CWN, or through exploits of the opportunities presented by the internet, such as the actions of Anonymous in response to the drama of WikiLeaks. Design does influence spheres beyond the technical. Furthermore, for members of technical subcultures like those mentioned in this chapter, the blurring between technology and politics may provide an entry point for greater political action. However, allowing technological arguments to stand in the absence of legal, political, or social arguments would be to permit anyone with the ability to control the technology – no matter how illegitimate – to set the terms of governance. It also demonstrates how the politicization of argument-by-technology could give rise to a subtle form of technological determinism – the belief that technology has autonomous influence on other spheres. It is thus essential not to overdetermine the influence of design on governance.

One way of accounting for the influence of technology activism on governance may be in broadening the scope of analysis. The frameworks currently available for understanding governance are limited in their ability to take into account the nuanced ways that different forms of technical advocacy contribute to governance. One alternative framework to consider is Dutton et al's (2004) evocation of an 'ecology of games' of internet governance. This framework considers governance not in terms of rule-making but instead as a set of games in which various actors negotiate their status as players. In any discussion, people might play roles as parents, business owners, taxpayers, or neighbours. To determine how to resolve a governance issue, they would have to negotiate among each other with reference to the various (and multiple) roles they might play. The advantage of this perspective is that it conceives of a much broader range of things as being 'governance', since all of the players are acknowledged as playing different roles simultaneously. Developing it further to reflect the influence of design and the impact of expectations about design could allow for descriptions of governance ecologies, rather than only governance processes. Governance ecologies would consist of a range of things including states, non-state actors like official 'civil society' and corporate entities, as well as technical designs and the features that they promise (for example, generativity). Ideally, it would also take into account the elements of culture and difference that are so often left out of discussions on technical activism or design.[1] Such a governance ecology would allow for a fuller consideration of how contexts for internet-related decision-making happen.

CONCLUSION

This chapter has attempted to illuminate the relevance for internet governance debates of arguments-by-technology, assessing the extent to which expectations about the potential of technical design influence political or social projects related to the internet. The chapter reviews how arguments by technology fuelled some of the political or philosophical arguments common to the technical subcultures associated with the original design of the internet. These arguments formed a basis through which many governance ideas were discussed. As the internet became an increasingly corporatized space, other arguments-by-technology attempted to counter this process. Community Wireless Networking projects built upon expectations about the relationship between peer-to-peer technologies and the reinvigoration of the commons. Finally, the actions of Anonymous and others in response to systemic threats to WikiLeaks appeared to constitute a swarm of resistance to forms of control executed through protocol. These examples illustrate a persistent expectation that technological designs can create political or social outcomes.

Of course, the expectations created by various technology designs and technological options do not necessarily result in the social transformations that a straightforward technological determinism might suggest. Instead, through various articulations between technology and politics, projects and actions influenced by the possibilities of various technologies create other outcomes. These can include new potential forms of local governance or draw into question the legitimacy of DDoS tactics used by corporations responding to pressure from parts of the US government. To better conceive of the relationship between these kinds of activities and other kinds of governance debates, it is important to consider the entire governance ecology. Within this ecology, argument-by-technology can be understood as making a contribution to governance, without overdetermining the social impact of design decisions.

NOTE

1. Technical cultures like the ones described here are noted for being culturally narrow: Dunbar-Hester (2010) reports on contemporary media activism including wireless communities, identifying that technology activism is deeply gendered: "'It is difficult to cultivate forms of technical affinity and expertise not associated with White masculinity, though the activists are more successful with regard to inclusion of women than of people of color'" (p. 121).

BIBLIOGRAPHY

Barlow, J. P. (1996), 'A Declaration of the Independence of Cyberspace', https://projects.eff. org/~barlow/Declaration-Final.html.

Benkler, Y. (2011), 'A Free Irresponsible Press: Wikileaks and the Battle over the Soul of the Networked Fourth Estate', *Harvard Civil Rights-Civil Liberties Law Review*.

Bygrave, L. and J. Bing (2009), *Internet Governance: Infrastructure and Institutions*, Oxford and New York: Oxford University Press.

Cammaerts, B. (2011), 'Disruptive Sharing in a Digital Age: Rejecting Neoliberalism?', *Continuum*, **25(01)**, 47–62.

Carpentier, N. (2008), 'The Belly of the City: Alternative Communicative City Network', *International Communication Gazette*, **70(3–4)**, 237–56.

Clinton, H. R. (2010), 'Remarks on Internet Freedom', Washington, DC: United States Government, http://www.state.gov/secretary/rm/2010/01/135519.htm.

Coleman, B. (2011), 'Anonymous: From the Lulz to Collective Action / The New Everyday', http://mediacommons.futureofthebook.org/tne/pieces/anonymous-lulz-collective-action.

Crenshaw, A. (2011), 'Crude, Inconsistent Threat: Understanding Anonymous', http://www. irongeek.com/i.php?page=security/understanding-anonymous.

Deleuze, G. and F. Guattari (1980), B. Massumi (trans), *A Thousand Plateaus*, London and New York: Continuum.

Deseriis, M. (2010), 'Improper Names: The Minor Politics of Collective Pseudonyms and Multiple-Use Names', *PhD Dissertation*, New York University.

Dunbar-Hester, C. (2010), 'Beyond "Dudecore"? Challenging Gendered and "Raced" Technologies through Media Activism', *Journal of Broadcasting & Electronic Media*, **54**, 21–135.

Dutton, W. H., S. E. Gillett, L. W. McKnight, and M. Peltu (2004), 'Bridging Broadband Internet Divides: Reconfiguring Access to Enhance Communicative Power', *Journal of Information Technology*, **19(1)**, 28–38.

Feenberg, A. (1999), *Questioning Technology*, London: Routledge.

Forlano, L., A. Powell, B. Lennett and G. Shaffer (2011), *From the Digital Divide to Digital Excellence: Global Best Practices for Municipal and Community Wireless Networks*, Washington, DC: New America Foundation.

Galloway, A. R. and E. Thacker (2007), *The Exploit: A Theory of Networks / Electronic Mediations*, Minneapolis: University of Minnesota Press.

Goldsmith, J. and T. Wu (2006), *Who Controls the Internet? Illusions of a Borderless World*, Oxford: Oxford University Press.

Hall, S. (1983), 'The Problem of Ideology – Marxism without Guarantees', in B. Matthews (ed.), *Marx 100 Years On*, London: Lawrence and Wishart, pp. 57–84.

Held, D. and A. McGrew (2003), 'The Great Globalisation Debate', in D. Held and A. McGrew (eds), *The Global Transformations Reader*, Cambridge: Polity Press, pp. 1–50.

Hintz, A. and S. Milan (2009), 'At the Margins of Internet Governance: Grassroots Techgroups and Communication Policy', *International Journal of Media and Cultural Politics*, **5(1&2)**, 25–38.

Hofman, J. (2010), 'The Libertarian Origins of Cybercrime: Unintended Side-Effects of a Political Utopia', *London School of Economics Discussion Paper*, **No. 62**, http://ssrn.com/ abstract=1710773.

Isenberg, D. (1997), 'Rise of the STUPID Network', *Computer Telephony*, **August 1997**, 16–26.

Isenberg, D. and D. Weinberger (2002), 'The Paradox of the Best Network', http://netpara-dox.com/.

Kelty, C. (2005), 'Geeks, Social Imaginaries, and Recursive Publics', *Cultural Anthropology*, **20(2)**, 185–214.

Lessig, L. (1999), *Code and other Laws of Cyberspace*, New York: Basic Books.

Morozov, E. (2011), *The Net Delusion: The Dark Side of Internet Freedom*, 1st ed., New York: Public Affairs.

Mosco, V. (2004), *The Digital Sublime: Myth, Power, and Cyberspace*, Cambridge, MA: MIT Press.

Mueller, M. (2010), *Networks and States: The Global Politics of Internet Governance*, Cambridge, MA: MIT Press.

Mueller, M. L., J. Mathiason and L. McKnight (2004), 'Making Sense of Internet Governance: Defining Principles and Norms in a Policy Context', Working paper published by the Centre for Convergence and Emerging Network Technologies, Syracuse University.

Proulx, S. (2007), 'Techno-Activism as Catalyst in Promoting Social Change', COST Action 298 Conference, Moscow.

Raboy, M. (2004), 'The WSIS as a Political Space in Global Media Governance', *Continuum: Journal of Media and Cultural Studies*, **18(3)**, 345–59.

Reidenberg, J. R. (1998), 'Lex Informatica: The Formulation of Information Policy Rules through Technology', *Texas Law Review*, **76(3)**, 553–84.

Sandvig, C. (2004), 'An Initial Assessment of Cooperative Action in Wi-fi Networking', *Telecommunications Policy*, **28(7)**, 579–602.

Tapia, A., A. Powell and J. A. Ortiz (2009), 'Reforming Policy to Promote Local Broadband Networks', *Journal of Communication Inquiry*, **33(4)**, 354–75.

Turner, F. (2005), 'Where the Counterculture Met the New Economy: The WELL and the Origins of Virtual Community', *Technology and Culture*, **46(3)**, 485–512.

Turner, F. (2009), 'Burning Man at Google: A Cultural Infrastructure for New Media Production', *New Media & Society*, **11(1–2)** (April), 145–66.

Wireless Commons Manifesto (2003), www.wirelesscommons.org.

Zittrain, J. (2008), *The Future of the Internet and How to Stop It*, Harrisberg, VA: Caravan.

PART II

HUMAN RIGHTS AND FUNDAMENTAL FREEDOMS

10. Data protection in a globalised network
Graham Greenleaf

INTRODUCTION: TECHNOLOGICAL CHALLENGES AND 'INTERNET GOVERNANCE'

This chapter[1] provides an overview of the state of global data privacy law (also called 'data protection' and 'information privacy') as at mid-2011, with an emphasis on the extent to which such laws are able to deal with new technological challenges associated with the networking of the world resulting primarily from the development of the internet, particularly since 1995. Special attention is given to two most likely indicators of the directions in which global data privacy will develop: the EU Commission's proposals for expansion of data privacy law set out in the report 'A comprehensive approach on personal data protection in the European Union' (EU Commission 2010); and the recent rapid expansion of new data privacy laws outside Europe.

The context of the new technological challenges is summarised in a report to the EU Commission (Korff, Brown and others 2010) as follows:

> We have seen dramatic technological change since the European Commission first proposed the Data Protection Directive in 1990. The internet has moved out of the university lab into 56 per cent of European homes and 95 per cent of OECD businesses. Computer processing power has continued to follow Moore's Law, with transistor density doubling every 18–24 months – around one thousand-fold in the last two decades. Computer storage capacity and communications bandwidth have both been increasing even more quickly, doubling every 12 months and hence a thousand-fold each decade. These exponential increases have radically increased the ability of organisations to collect, store and process personal data. The physical environment is now saturated with sensors such as CCTV cameras and mobile phones, with biometric and electronic identifiers used to link data to individuals. In the digital world almost every communication and Web page access leaves behind detailed footprints. The internet and mobile information appliances allow large quantities of personal data to be trivially moved between jurisdictions. Data mining tools attempt to find patterns in large collections of personal data, both to identify individuals 'of interest' and to attempt to predict their interests and preferences. New multinational companies have sprung up around these technologies to service a global customer base, with smaller enterprises outsourcing employee and customer data processing to developing world companies.

In a book dealing with 'internet governance', it is important to recognise that there is no global organisation 'governing' data privacy which is in any way equivalent to, say, ICANN in the field of domain names and numbers, nor as yet any global treaties equivalent to the importance of the Berne Convention or the WIPO Copyright Treaty in the field of copyright. Also, data privacy as a matter of national legislation and international agreements pre-dates the mid-1990s' rise to significance of the internet. Consequently, this chapter deals largely with national laws, and with pre-internet international agreements. To the extent that there is any consistent form of 'global governance' in relation to data privacy, we will see that it comes from a combination of various international agreements, a particular mechanism encouraging consistency (the 'adequacy' criterion in the EU data protection Directive, 1995), and the concomitant emulation of European standards outside Europe.

The focus of this chapter is on legal instruments (and to a lesser extent the agencies implementing them) at the national level, and the international agreements influencing them, and not with self-regulatory instruments or regulation by technology (code), acting outside of legislative structures (for which see Bennett and Raab 2006, Chs 6 and 7).

Data Privacy Laws: Effectiveness and Alternatives

Data privacy laws essentially comprise a set of enforceable data privacy principles (based on the 'life cycle' of personal data: collection, accuracy, security, use, disclosure, access, deletion etc) and an enforcement structure, almost always involving a data privacy authority (usually called a 'data protection authority' or 'privacy commissioner') as the first point of enforcement. The standard features of both principles and enforcement are discussed later. 'Privacy' is a broader interest than 'data privacy' and includes the protection of such interests as bodily integrity, solitude and freedom from observation, that do not necessarily involve issues concerning personal data, but the two increasingly overlap because of pervasive data collection.

Whether data privacy laws can sufficiently protect privacy in a networked world is an open question, but they are the legal instrument most capable of so doing. Other forms of legal protection (privacy torts, breach of confidence (both general principles and statutory rules), constitutional rights, surveillance limitation laws, consumer protection laws etc) give intermittent protection in some countries (and sometimes very effectively in specific cases) but do not provide the thorough and evolving protection provided by sets of data privacy principles. The fact that these alternatives are not discussed here does not diminish their importance in particular situations in particular countries.

Similarly, international human rights agreements sometimes create rights, or require creation of rights at national level, which sometimes protect privacy. Some general privacy rights have been employed by many courts in the protection of privacy and less frequently to specifically protect data privacy. The best examples are Article 17 of the International Covenant on Civil and Political Rights (ICCPR 1967) and particularly Article 8 of the European Convention on Human Rights. The effectiveness of these protections must not be ignored, and they do provide a basis in human rights law for data protection, but they have not yet been interpreted to encompass all aspects of data privacy, and often fall short of what is provided in specific data privacy instruments (Bygrave 1998, p. 247; 2010, p. 181). However, the EU's new constitutional instrument, the Charter of Fundamental Rights of the European Union, recognises a right to protection of personal data as a separate human right from the broader right of protection of privacy, the first time this has occurred in a human rights instrument (Bygrave 2010, p. 182).

The effectiveness of data privacy principles comes as much from their ideological effect and their global nature as from their enforcement (which is often lacking). Forty years of data privacy laws have created a language of data privacy, and a set of ethical standards to which most companies and governments feel obliged to at least give lip service. Attempts to break the power of this discourse by creation of alternative language/ethical standards, particularly the push for 'accountability' (discussed later), have failed as yet but are a continuing threat to the hegemony of conventional data privacy principles. Consequently, it can be argued that the most important form of 'self-regulation' in the area of data privacy is simply that many businesses and government agencies internalise the norms of data privacy principles once they are enacted and observe legislation to a significant extent even in the absence of effective enforcement activities. Survey data from Australia (cited in Greenleaf 2008a) and Hong Kong (cited in McLeish and Greenleaf 2008, p. 251) give some support for this proposition. In this fundamental sense there has indeed been a good deal of self-regulation in privacy protection.

There is very little evidence, from what we have seen in the last 40 years, that any non-legal constraints will prove effective against business and government self-interest in expanded surveillance: this applies to voluntary self-regulation (through codes of conduct, standard-setting, privacy seals, or spontaneous adoption of privacy-enhancing technologies (PETs) or privacy-by-design), the force of competition, or the adoption by consumers of PETs and counter-surveillance technologies. Bennett and Raab (2006, Chs 6 and 7) survey most of these approaches and find little significant evidence of their success unless they are integrated into a data privacy regime. In that case they become 'co-regulation' supported by legal requirements, not 'self-regulation', and may be more effective though studies are still lacking.

Evolution

The notion of data privacy, while it has held a consistent core for about 40 years, is not static. New principles continue to emerge and become absorbed in new or amended data privacy legislation, the most notable recent example being 'data breach notification'. Other emergent principles include data tracking restrictions, the anonymous transactions right, and the 'right to be forgotten', though they can usually be seen as specific implications of already existing general principles. New methods of enforcement have also become part of the 'standard kit' of DPAs and data subjects (eg representative complaint mechanisms are spreading; 'data breach notification' is as much an enforcement mechanism as a principle). But these occur within the framework of the accepted notion of 'data protection' (or 'data privacy' as used here).

PERSISTENCE, EXPANSION AND CONSISTENCY OF DATA PRIVACY LAWS

Since Sweden's *Data Act* of 1973 (the first national legislation to include most elements of what we now consider to be a data privacy law) legislation to protect privacy in relation to personal information has evolved in a largely consistent fashion across the world, with few major exceptions remaining.

Global Expansion of National Data Privacy Laws

The global rate of development of data privacy laws is accelerating, their geographical scope expanding, and their consistency increasing.[2] As at mid-2011 there are 75 countries (or otherwise independent legal jurisdictions) with data privacy laws, as detailed in the Appendix to this chapter. In a handful of cases (two Special Administrative Regions of China and five British dependent territories) these are not countries, but are largely autonomous entities with their own distinct legal systems (states or provinces of countries are not counted). By a 'data privacy law' is meant a law with a substantially complete set of data privacy principles which at least approximate minimal international standards (as in the OECD Guidelines (OECD 1980) or Council of Europe Convention (CoE 1981)), and a mandatory legal enforcement mechanism (not just self-regulation or guidelines). To be counted as such, a data privacy law must cover most of a country's private sector, not merely a few sub-sectors like credit reporting, health or financial information (eg Dubai), and not only the public sector (eg Thailand; USA). In almost all cases, data privacy laws do cover the national public sector as well as the private sector (Malaysia and India are exceptions). Some other countries (eg Canada) have separate laws for their public and private sectors. Almost all data privacy laws establish some form of specialised 'data protection authority' (DPA), variously named and with differing degrees of independence, with at least the power to investigate individual complaints (but with widely-varying powers of enforcement, or alternative avenues of enforcement), and the ability to have some input into the policy-making process. From 75 jurisdictions, Russia, Chile, Colombia, the Kyrgyz Republic, India, Japan and Taiwan are among the few remaining exceptions with no DPA.

The total number of new data privacy laws globally, viewed by decade, shows that their growth is accelerating, not merely expanding linearly: 7 (1970s), 10 (1980s), 19 (1990s), 32 (2000s) and 7 (1.5 years of 2010s), giving the total of 75. In the 1970s data privacy laws were a western European phenomenon (Sweden, Germany, Austria, Denmark, France, Norway and Luxembourg), and similarly in the 1980s (UK, Ireland, Iceland, Finland, San Marino and the Netherlands, and three UK territories), with Israel as the first non-European state in 1981 (Australia's 1988 legislation was public sector only). Acceleration commenced in the 1990s, as most remaining western European countries (EU and EEA) enacted laws (Portugal, Belgium, Spain, Switzerland, Monaco, Italy and Greece). More significantly, with the collapse of the Soviet Union many former 'eastern bloc' countries enacted data privacy laws as part of their protection of civil liberties (Slovenia, Czech Republic, Hungary, Slovakia, Poland and Albania), and the first ex-Soviet-republics (Lithuania and Azerbaijan) did likewise. The spread outside Europe also started, with the first laws in Latin America (Chile) and the Asia-Pacific (New Zealand, Hong Kong and Taiwan).

In the 2000s the acceleration continued, with dramatic expansion in the former eastern bloc and Soviet republic countries (Latvia, Bosnia & Herzegovina, Romania, Bulgaria, Croatia, Estonia, FYROM (Macedonia), Moldova, Serbia and Montenegro), plus the tidying up of the remaining European states (Cyprus, Malta, Andorra, Liechtenstein, Gibraltar). Outside Europe, expansion accelerated in the Asia-Pacific (Australia, South Korea, Japan, Macao SAR) and Latin America (Argentina, Colombia, Uruguay). In the Americas, Canada and the Bahamas added further new laws. Rapid development took place in Africa with new laws in Tunisia and Morocco (North African) and Mauritius, Cape Verde, Benin, Senegal and Burkina Faso (sub-Saharan Africa). The Kyrgyz Republic became the first country in Central Asia to legislate in 2008. In the first 18 months of this decade seven new laws have been enacted (Faroe Islands, Malaysia, Mexico, India, Peru, Russia – more accurately, brought into force – and Ukraine), making this the most intensive period of data protection developments in the last 40 years.

Geographically, almost two thirds of data privacy laws are in European states (48/75). EU member states now make up little more than one third (27/75), even with the expansion of the EU into eastern Europe. There are data privacy laws in all 27 member states of the EU, and a further 21 laws in other European jurisdictions. Only a few European states remain without such laws, such as Georgia and Belarus. There are six laws in Latin America, with Brazil set to become the seventh (Palazzi 2011). In the Americas are also the laws in Canada and the Bahamas (the only law in the Caribbean). In Asia there are now eight data privacy laws, with Singapore promising a ninth, and the other eight ASEAN states committed to improved privacy protection (but not specifically to legislate) by 2015 (Connolly 2008). Both Australia and New Zealand have data privacy laws, but none of the Pacific Islands do so (the only region with no such laws). In North Africa and the Middle East, there are three such laws, and five in sub-Saharan Africa. Further Acts are likely soon, with Bills progressing in South Africa and Ghana. The French-Speaking Association of Personal Data Protection Authorities (AFAPDP), and France's CNIL have both played key roles in developing expansion of data privacy in Africa. The Kyrgyz Republic law is the first in Central Asia, though Mongolia has laws covering many elements of data privacy (Greenleaf 2011a). So there are 27 data privacy laws outside Europe.

For over two decades the annual rate of adoption of new data privacy laws has been increasing steadily, from an average of 1.75 per year in the second half of the 1980s, to 3.5 per year for the last five years. The regions of the globe that have such laws have also been steadily expanding. If the current rate of expansion in the 2010s continues, 50 new laws will result in this decade. Even on the conservative (and probably unrealistic) assumption that the 2010s will see no more data privacy laws than the 2000s, the number of countries with data protection laws will exceed 100 by the decade's end, with the majority of data privacy laws by then coming from outside Europe. In addition, many existing laws are being strengthened to keep up with rising expectations of privacy protection, international agreements, and the examples set by other countries (see the 'Latest' column in the Appendix).

There are other ways that expansion could be measured, say by the populations of the countries concerned, or by their GNP. These could show different trends, but reflection on the size and economic significance of the countries so far included makes it obvious that data privacy laws are more common in the world's larger and more economically significant countries. The recent inclusion of India accelerates this trend, as will the likely inclusion of Brazil in the near future. By any measure, data privacy laws are of increasing and accelerating global significance.

Countries without Data Privacy Laws, and their Significance

The most economically significant countries still lacking data privacy laws (on the definition adopted here) are the USA, China and Brazil. India has now adopted a data privacy law (Greenleaf 2011b; 2011c; 2011d). The omission of Brazil is also expected to be remedied in 2011 (Palazzi 2011). Most other countries that do not yet have data privacy laws are of relatively low significance in international trade, though some countries with large populations are among them, particularly in sub-Saharan Africa (eg Nigeria), and in Asia (eg Indonesia). However, some regions of economic cooperation (eg ECOWAS, ASEAN, Mercosur) which have large populations in aggregate, may play an important role in international data privacy developments in future.

China is currently in what can be called the 'warring states period' of data protection, with numerous factions of the Chinese bureaucracy disputing the best way to deal with data protection issues. As yet it only has a limited patchwork of laws (including recent privacy protections in both criminal law and tort law), but there has been draft national legislation (Greenleaf 2008a) and recent draft 'guidelines' (Greenleaf 2011) both of which point in the direction of data privacy laws. What will eventuate in China, and whether it will influence others, are still questions to which no-one has a convincing answer.

There is a strong correlation between democracies and data privacy laws: most democracies have them (or are likely to soon), and most authoritarian regimes do not. The examples from eastern Europe in the 1990s show that data privacy laws can become aligned with democratic and post-authoritarian aspirations (Szekely 2008), as is also the case with South Korea (Park 2008). In the African region of greatest expansion of data privacy laws, the chairman of the Economic Community of West African States (ECOWAS) stated in 2011 that 'the region will never allow unconstitutional ascension to power', reflecting a 2001 regional declaration on democracy and good governance (ECOWAS 2011). It would not be surprising if data privacy as a form of human rights protection in North African states becomes a regional reality if the 'Arab Spring' of 2011 matures into newly democratic states. The high correlation is not surprising: democratic values help justify data privacy laws (Bygrave 2002, Ch. 7; 2010); and the 'watchdog' aspect of data privacy laws and institutions is a good fit for recent theories of 'monitory democracy' with its multitude of watchdogs monitoring the public sphere (Keane 2011, particularly Part III).

United States Exceptionalism and its Significance

The USA has many privacy laws and some effective enforcement, but no comprehensive privacy law in the private sector, nor much prospect of one, despite periodic calls for one from the major companies and Bills introduced into Congress. A recent report (Hoofnagle 2010) asserts that 'the US approach is incoherent, sectorally-based, and . . . legislative protections are largely reactive, driven by outrage at particular, narrow practices'. 'In [Federal] statutory law, privacy rights are found in the criminal code, the civil code, evidentiary law, family law, property law, contracts, and in administrative regulations. No single overarching statute even attempts to unify these interests in the diverse contexts in which "privacy" is used to frame some value'. However, says Hoofnagle, '[t]his has created a tension between state and federal governments, resulting in a levelling up of protections, because states (which tend to be more activist on privacy issues) can act where the US Congress is occupied with other issues'. As a result, there has been a profusion of innovative state laws in areas such as data breach notification and laws to limit effects of identity theft.

The key limits in the US approach to data privacy can be seen from Hoofnagle's analysis of the most important recent development in the USA:

> But most relevant to the new challenges [of technology] is the 'federal common law' being created on a case-by-case basis by the Federal Trade Commission (FTC). It is important to note that the FTC has adopted a more limited set of fair information practices than international authorities. The agency is concerned with notice, choice, access, security, and accountability. There has been almost complete inattention to the right of access, as the agency sees access as heightening security risks and potentially triggering a requirement to collect more personal data. In recent years, a heavy emphasis has been placed on security . . . Under it, a company can engage in maximum data collection, because the information is 'private' so long as it remains secret and secure within the company's systems.

He summarises the other main gaps in the privacy principles adopted across US laws as follows: 'US privacy law typically allows businesses to use personal information for different purposes, including for marketing, without the data subject's consent. This is because the sectoral system leaves many businesses unregulated ... Just a handful of laws create explicit purpose limitations'; and 'US privacy law generally does not have limitations on collection of personal information. Collection limitation runs counter to the notion of most enterprises, which attempt to collect as much information as possible in transactions.'

However, US exceptionalism should not be confused with a schism in global approaches to data privacy. Increasingly, the position is that the USA is the only significant outrider attempting to defend providing data privacy protection by a patchwork of sectoral laws (with significant limits to their principles) and no national DPA as a key means of enforcement. The rest of the world is increasingly adopting a generally consistent set of principles and establishing a DPA as part of the enforcement mechanism. Other countries that have previously taken an approach similar to the USA are changing course: Mexico, Malaysia and Peru have enacted laws which are both OECD and EU-influenced, with a DPA; Singapore and the Philippines are likely to do similarly (Greenleaf 2011). Japan and Taiwan have not yet adopted a DPA, but have enacted otherwise extensive data privacy laws. US attempts to impede the spread of data privacy laws in Asia and Latin America through APEC-supported alternatives (discussed later) largely appear to have failed.

The USA is best seen as a country with a unique, isolated and often inconsistent approach to data privacy, one that remains behind the rest of the world in some respects (particularly limits on collection and re-use), but which also often provides international leadership in relation to some principles (eg data breach disclosure, and other aspects of security) and in the deterrent effect of draconian examples of enforcement, particularly by the FTC. These differences are amplified by the core role it plays as the host or provider of numerous internet-based personal information services which have global reach. The attempt to make US-based services accommodate the data privacy approaches of most other countries will continue to be one of the defining features of global privacy developments for years to come. Similarly, attempts by US companies and the US government to use their combined economic and political influence to limit development of data privacy laws in other countries will continue to be important, but are probably now on the wrong side of history.

INFLUENCE OF INTERNATIONAL AGREEMENTS, AND 'EUROPEAN' STANDARDS

International agreements concerning data privacy have contributed a great deal to the development of consistency of national data privacy laws.

From the start of the 1980s the non-binding OECD privacy Guidelines (OECD 1980) and the first binding international agreement, the Council of Europe data protection Convention (CoE 1981), both embodied privacy principles with similar substance but expressed in somewhat different language.

The EU's Influence and its Future Intentions

From the mid-1990s the European Union's data protection Directive (EU 1995) embodied a set of privacy principles consistent with, but somewhat stronger than, those in the OECD and CoE agreements. However, the Directive added much stronger enforcement requirements, including establishment of an independent DPA and a right to have disputes heard by the courts. Unlike either of the earlier agreements, it also required limitations on data exports to countries outside the EU which did not have 'adequate' privacy laws (discussed in more detail later). All of these standards set by the Directive have become recognised as the strongest international standard for data privacy.

Fifteen years later, the EU's promotion of its standards is growing stronger, although it is not without critics. After reviewing the EU's current data privacy legal framework through conferences, consultations and commissioned reports (including Korff, Brown et al. 2010), the EU Commission has concluded that 'the core principles of the Directive are still valid and that its technologically neutral character should be preserved', although it should be strengthened in various ways (EU Commission 2010, 1), as discussed later. The European Commission is intent on expanding the global influence of its standards, and in fact seems to see them as 'universal principles' (EU Commission 2010, para. 2.4.2):

> Data processing is globalised and calls for the development of universal principles for the protection of individuals with regard to the processing of personal data. The EU legal framework for data privacy has often served as a benchmark for third countries when regulating data privacy. Its effect and impact, within and outside the Union, have been of the utmost importance. The European Union must therefore remain a driving force behind the development and promotion of international legal and technical standards for the protection of personal data, based on relevant EU and other European instruments on data privacy.

Furthermore, it is intent on strengthening both the principles and the enforcement mechanisms of EU data privacy (EU Commission 2010). 'The Lisbon Treaty provided the EU with additional means to achieve this: the EU Charter of Fundamental Rights – with Article 8 recognising an autonomous right to the protection of personal data – has become legally binding, and a new legal basis has been introduced allowing for the establishment of comprehensive and coherent Union legislation . . .'. The aim is to ensure 'that the fundamental right to data protection for individuals is fully respected within the EU and beyond' (EU Commission 2010, p. 1). The final two words indicate the significance for the rest of the world.

Outside Europe, something approaching 'European standard' data privacy laws is starting to become the norm in a number of parts of the world. This trend is most noticeable in Latin America, with Mexico recently joining Argentina, Colombia and Uruguay with EU-style laws. All the recent laws in West and North Africa show strong EU influence. In the last two years, revised laws in Taiwan and South Korea have moved further in the EU direction, as have new laws in India and Malaysia (while also showing influences of the OECD Guidelines). New draft guidelines in China also point in the EU direction. Japan, Macau, Hong Kong, New Zealand (soon to be the second Asia-Pacific country after Canada found to be 'adequate') and Australia (where protracted law reform should strengthen its law) all have laws which show EU influences to some degree. Nowhere in the new Asia-Pacific laws is there any strong evidence of APEC influence.

The Failing APEC Alternative

From the start of its development in 2003 the APEC (Asia-Pacific Economic Cooperation) Privacy Framework (APEC 2005) has been the only significant international attempt to break the influence of the EU Directive. APEC has 21 member 'economies' in Asia (including China but not India), the Americas (including the USA) and Australasia. Through its Framework, which is not legally binding, APEC advocated an alternative approach which falls short of the 'European' standards set primarily by the EU Directive in four respects: (1) its set of principles can be described as 'OECD Lite' (Greenleaf 2004), weaker than the Directive or most regional laws, and with no additions of value (Greenleaf 2008a); (2) a complete absence of any obligations to enforce the principles by law (self-regulation unsupported by legislation is acceptable for APEC), or even a recommendation for legislation; (3) no complementary obligation of free flow of personal data in return for adoption of basic standards (at best, an encouragement of development of mutually-acceptable cross-border privacy rules (CBPR) by companies); and (4) an 'Accountability' principle which is an incoherent substitute for data export limits (see later). However, it has stimulated regular discussion of data privacy issues between governments in the region, and more systematic cooperation between DPAs in the region on cross-border enforcement.

The APEC approach was initially enthusiastically supported by at least the USA, Australia, Canada and Mexico, and acquiesced to by other countries. However it has comprehensively failed to establish an alternative paradigm for data protection: almost no evidence of adoption of its principles in legislation in the region (the one obvious example, still not enacted, is discussed later under 'Accountability'); no increase in self-regulatory initiatives; and a faltering CBPR initiative (Greenleaf 2008a; Waters 2008; Waters 2011). New laws in the region are influenced more by the EU Directive than by the APEC Framework, as discussed throughout this chapter. APEC's attempt at establishing a regional form of CBPR with national endorsement seems to be on the verge of collapse, crippled by the lack of enforcement mechanisms in some jurisdictions, the opposite problem of stricter legal requirements in others, and a general decline in interest in involvement by most APEC economies (Waters 2008; 2011). Attempts are still being made at APEC meetings to finalise governance of the whole scheme. As discussed in the conclusion to this chapter, global analyses of data privacy developments still tend to accord too much significance to the APEC Framework as a brake on European influence. It is more likely that it will be seen as a dead-end: why pay attention to non-binding guidelines that no-one follows?

ECOWAS and Other Regional Agreements on Data Privacy

The Economic Community of West African States (ECOWAS), a grouping of 15 states under the Revised Treaty of the ECOWAS, agreed to adopt data privacy laws in 2008, and then adopted a *Supplementary Act on Personal Data Protection within ECOWAS* (ECOWAS 2010). This supplement to the Treaty establishes the required content of such data privacy laws, influenced very strongly by the EU Directive, and that each state is to establish a data protection authority. As noted earlier, four ECOWAS states have so enacted laws (Benin, Burkina Faso, Cape Verde, and Senegal), and a Bill is before Parliament in Ghana.

ASEAN (the Association of Southeast Asian Nations) has a much weaker agreement among its eleven members to increase their data privacy protection by 2015 (Connolly 2008; Munir and Yasin 2010), but three have legislation in progress (Thailand, the Philippines and Singapore), and one has legislated (Malaysia). In Latin America the four Mercosur countries have agreed to establish guidelines, but they are not completed (Palazzi 2011). The prospects for a 'regional bloc' of consistent data protection laws, similar to what has occurred in Europe, seem strongest in West Africa. It is possible though less immediately likely that such developments could also take place in other African sub-regions, Southeast

Asia or Latin America, although not in the Asia-Pacific as a whole or the APEC sub-set of countries.

CoE Convention 108 and Additional Protocol: a global agreement?

An adequacy finding from the EU does not impose any reciprocal obligations on the recipient country outside the EU to allow free flow of personal data from it to EU countries, but this reciprocal obligation can arise if the non-EU country becomes a party to the Council of Europe data protection Convention (CoE 1981).

Convention 108 (the *Convention for the protection of individuals with regard to automatic processing of personal data*) Articles 5–8 set out in 'broad brush fashion' a set of data privacy principles that 'were hardly ground-breaking at the time of the Convention's adoption' 30 years ago (Bygrave 2008). They are even more modest today. However, they did contain versions of almost all the elements we now recognise as core data privacy principles, and are similar to those found in the OECD Guidelines due to cross-influences between the drafters of the two instruments. The 2001 Additional Protocol (ETS 181) to the Convention adds a commitment to data export restrictions, to an independent data protection authority, and to a right of appeal to the courts, and brings the standards of the Convention approximately up to the same level as the Directive (thus showing how the Directive has also influenced other international instruments: Bygrave 2010). Thirty European countries have also ratified the Additional Protocol (see the Appendix). Twelve countries that have ratified the Convention (plus three territories on whose behalf the UK acceded to the Convention) have not ratified the Additional Protocol, but in almost all cases that does not matter because they are EU member states, or their laws have been found 'adequate' by the EU, and they already have the same obligations as the Additional Protocol would impose.

Convention 108 Article 12 always allowed in principle for non-European states to accede to the Convention (and thus to the Additional Protocol as well), by invitation of the Committee of Ministers under the Convention. But the Committee never issued any such invitations, and there was no means of applying. However, in 2008 the Committee explicitly agreed, in effect, that the Consultative Committee under the Convention could receive and assess applications to accede, and it would then consider such applications and issue invitations to accede where appropriate. The importance of this is that Convention 108 is the only realistic possibility for a global binding international agreement on data protection to emerge. In comparison, the likelihood of a new UN treaty being developed from scratch is miniscule, or as Bygrave puts it, 'realistically, scant chance' (2010, p. 181).

Because it has 42 existing members, there are significant advantages for non-European states to accede to Convention 108 and the Additional Protocol. These fall into three categories. In relation to EU countries, non-European states obtain a guarantee of free flow of personal data from the EU country (unless the EU country derogates from Convention 108 on that point), which the Directive does not give them. While Convention 108 accession will not automatically lead to a finding of 'adequacy' by the EU, it is hard to see the EU denying a finding of adequacy to a non-European state that accedes to the Additional Protocol as well as the Convention. Practically, it does not even seem necessary: none of the non-EU European countries that are Council of Europe members (and parties to the Convention) have even bothered applying for an adequacy finding (see the Appendix). In relation to other non-EU countries that are parties to the Convention, there arise mutual obligations of free flow of personal data between them, unless either derogates because of the other's lack of a data export restriction. Then there are more general advantages: it is a modest step towards a stronger international data protection regime, not a radical one; it involves voluntary acceptance as an equal party to a treaty of obligations concerning data, rather than by what can be seen as the unilateral imposition of a standard by the EU; and it avoids the necessity for individual countries to make decisions about which other countries have privacy laws which are 'adequate' or 'sufficient' to allow personal data exports to them. Depending on how long it takes the Committee of Ministers to make decisions, and whether those decisions are perceived to be fair and not unduly political, it could be a more attractive process than applying for an 'adequacy' finding to the EU Commission, and sufficient in practice even though not technically a substitute for that. However, it remains to be seen in practice if Convention 108 accession becomes either an alternative to, or a 'short cut' to, an adequacy finding for non-European countries. The process might also work in reverse, with the Council of Europe in effect 'rubber stamping' requests by non-European states that have received adequacy findings to accede to the Convention and Additional Protocol.

The main disadvantage to non-European countries could be that, if the Committee of Ministers allows countries outside the EU to accede to the Convention with laws of low standard, or without acceding to the Additional Protocol as well, this could result in an obligation (at least on non-EU countries) to allow data exports to countries with sub-standard laws. Only the practice of the Committee can resolve such questions. There is also a lack of mechanisms for citizens of countries outside Europe to enforce the Convention, including their inability to take cases to the European Court of Human Rights. Some of these matters could be dealt with in the current review of the Convention.

There is as yet little of substance to suggest that Convention 108 will become a key instrument of global governance of privacy. However, it has no realistic competitors as a global privacy instrument. Uruguay is apparently the first country to indicate its interest in accession (see CoE 108 accessions 2011, note under 'Non-member States of the Council of Europe'). A key factor may be whether members of a regional data privacy agreement such as ECOWAS see Convention 108 accession as a collective means of establishing free flow of personal data between their region and Europe, and other countries. Globalisation of Convention 108 could become one of the most important developments in privacy governance over the next decade, but it is too early to tell.

DATA PRIVACY PRINCIPLES

Why we value 'data privacy', and how we conceptualise the values that are served by the concept 'data privacy', are beyond the scope of this chapter, though of considerable importance, and matters of dispute (see Bygrave 2002, Chs 6–8; 2010, Parts 2–4 for an overview, or Bennett and Raab 2006, Ch 1 for a different approach). Instead, I will analyse the elements of 'data privacy' as it has emerged in international agreements and national legislation, and future directions.

Nature and Limits of Data Privacy Principles

The closest legal analogy to data privacy principles/rights is copyright. Both are bundles of rights which defy summation in a single phrase, but require precise enumeration of each right that makes up the 'bundle' we call 'copyright' or 'data privacy' in shorthand. We think we know intuitively what 'copyright' means, but technically it is a bundle of specific rights ('adaptation', 'reproduction', etc), which benefit authors (or other copyright owners), and differ between types of works. 'Data privacy' doesn't have a simple definition either, and is similarly a bundle of specific rights ('access', 'limited collection', 'security', etc), benefitting data subjects in this case, and which can differ between types of personal information. In both cases, enforcement differs between countries, and takes many forms.

The key distinction within data privacy principles is between those principles that do not significantly impede the expansion of data surveillance by organisations but may make them work more fairly ('efficiency' principles: Rule and others 1981) and those that do tend to limit expansions of surveillance (which we can call 'surveillance limitation principles'). As discussed, the USA has by-and-large limited its controls to the former (including access and correction in some areas, and security generally) and tried to ignore the latter (particularly the collection limitation principle), whereas the EU Directive, and laws influenced by it, include some elements which can be interpreted to impose significant limits on surveillance activities. This distinction is valuable for analysis of the extent to which a data privacy law assists, or impedes, the development (or legitimating) of expanded data surveillance. Another distinction is between principles that 'empower' individuals and those that 'impose obligations' on data controllers (Bennett and Raab 2006, pp. 121–5). Although not clear-cut, it helps to identify laws which enable individuals to exercise self-help rather than relying on 'paternalistic' enforcement (often absent) by DPAs or the state, and also to analyse where responsibility for initiating action lies (with the individual, the data controller, the DPA or the state).

All data privacy laws are based on some variant of a definition of 'personal data' or 'personal information', meaning that the individual who seeks protection must be identifiable from the information concerned, or from that information and (variously described) other information with which it can reasonably be assumed it may be combined. A range of legislative formulae express this common idea.

This definition of 'personal data' imposes two main limitations on the scope of data privacy laws. First, they do not extend to data which does not identify a person but does enable interaction with that person to take place in some way which is 'personalised'. Sometimes this will involve combining it with other information about the same (non-identified) person. Much new behavioural marketing does not require identification, it only requires increasingly sophisticated interaction. It is arguable whether the full panoply of data privacy principles should apply to all such interactions, or to only a sub-set, such as geo-location data. Second, if personal data is not stored in some material non-transitory form, data privacy principles will usually not apply (New Zealand is an exception, where case law has held that 'storage in the mind' suffices). Some forms of CCTV, for example, are therefore excluded. It is also arguable that this is an appropriate dividing line between data privacy laws and surveillance limitation laws.

Core Data Privacy Principles

With data privacy legislation in 75 jurisdictions (plus sub-national laws), it is not surprising that privacy principles are expressed in many differing forms, and that there are some principles which are only found in a few (or even one) piece of legislation. The most influential distinction between 'core' and 'non-core' principles is that of the Article 29 Working Party's interpretation of the EU Directive in order to operationalise the Article 25 'adequacy' criterion (A 29 WP 1997; 1998). Although their choice has not been contentious, the EU Commission is now proposing to 'define core EU data privacy elements' for the purposes of international agreements with the EU and the purposes of adequacy assessment (EU Commission 2010, para. 2.4.1).

The language and structure of data privacy principles fall into two main families, plus some hybrids. EU-influenced sets of principles tend to be organised around a broad requirement of 'fair and lawful processing', plus various other obligations, whereas laws with a stronger OECD influence (usually outside Europe) tend to avoid the broad 'fair and lawful processing' principle, unpacking it at the outset into a number of separate principles (including purpose specification, collection limitation, data quality, and use/disclosure limitation), but also adding others as does the EU. In substance, the result is much the same in what is covered, though not necessarily in the strength of coverage. If we look for the substantially common elements in the EU's 'core' elements and the 'Principle of National Application' in the OECD Guidelines, a common core of data privacy principles (expressed here in non-Eurocentric language), can be listed as follows (with some indication of significant variations):

1. *Collection* – limited, lawful and by fair means; generally with consent or knowledge (OECD 7; EU A 6(1)(a)); EU is more specific that collection must be minimum necessary (EU A 6(1)(b), (c)).
2. *Data quality* – relevant, accurate, up-to-date (OECD 8; EU A 6(1)(d)); EU adds requirement to de-identify or delete when use complete (EU A 6(1)(e)).
3. *Purpose specification* at time of collection (OECD 9; EU A 6); EU more explicit on legitimacy of purpose (EU A 7).
4. *Notice* of purpose and rights at time of collection (OECD ambiguous; EU A 10, 11).
5. *Uses* (including disclosures) limited to purposes specified or compatible (OECD 10)
6. Reasonable *security* safeguards (OECD 11; EU A 17).
7. *Openness* re personal data practices, including to persons other than data subjects (OECD 12); not specific in EU except in relation to data subjects (EU A 10, 11).
8. Individual rights of *access and correction* (OECD 13; EU A 12); EU adds right to object (EU A 14).

9.   Data controllers *accountable* for implementation (OECD 14; EU A 6(2)).
10. *Data export restrictions* (OECD says they may, but EU says they must, be limited to (a) countries which do not substantially observe these basic rules, and (b) do not prevent circumvention by re-exports) (OECD 17; EU A 25, 26).

The Article 29 Working Party's requirements for adequacy also adds what it considers to be core principles for specific types of processing including (1) additional safeguards for processing of sensitive data; (2) a right to opt out of direct marketing involving use of personal data; (3) additional safeguards for automated processing of personal data; and (4) special care in the operation of identifiers of general application (like national ID numbers or cards).

Data Export Limitations and 'Adequacy'

There are two main means by which countries can attempt to have their standards for data privacy continue to apply to information about their citizens or residents (or even those whose data has been processed on their territories): (1) give their own laws extra-territorial application under some circumstances; and (2) impose limitations on when personal data can be exported from their country to other countries.

Concerning extra-territorial application (the 'applicable laws' question) the aim of the EU Commission is to 'ultimately provide for the same degree of protection of EU data subjects, regardless of the geographic location of the data controller', through reforms to provisions concerning applicable law (EU Commission 2010, para 2.2.3). While their principal goal is to ensure that only one law applies within the EU internal market (and that it is clear which one applies), they also intend to apply this to 'data controllers established outside' the EU or the EEA. Jurisdictions outside Europe are equally enthusiastic about giving their data privacy laws extra-territorial effect, as can be seen in the laws of Australia, Hong Kong and India. There will inevitably be political and legal conflicts of considerable significance over this question of 'applicable laws'.

Concerning the second approach, data export limitations, the EU's 'border control' approach is to limit data exports unless 'adequate protection' can be demonstrated at the receiving end (EU Directive Articles 25, 26). In summary '[t]he effect of a Commission adequacy finding is that personal data can freely flow from the 27 EU Member States and the three EEA member countries to that third country without any further safeguard being necessary. However, the exact requirements for recognition of adequacy by the Commission are currently not specified in satisfactory detail in the Data Protection Directive.' There is a further problem that different EU member states make different judgments on adequacy (EU Commission 2010, para. 2.4.1).

As yet, the EU has only made 'adequacy' decisions in relation to nine jurisdictions as a whole (Andorra, Argentina, Canada, Switzerland, Faroe Islands, Guernsey, Israel, Isle of Man, and Jersey), a minority of which are of economic or political significance. Uruguay and New Zealand will soon be added to this list, following positive findings by the increasingly pragmatic A 29 Working Party (Greenleaf and Bygrave 2011). It is arguable that Colombia, Mexico and Peru also have adequate laws (Palazzi 2011), South Korea and India could each put forward a case after their 2011 reforms, as could Taiwan (with more difficulty), and Hong Kong and Australia might do so after their legislatures complete their reform processes (see generally Greenleaf 2011a). The new laws in Africa resemble the EU Directive in their principles, so arguments for adequacy would hinge largely on issues of effective enforcement. For European countries that have acceded to both Convention 108 and the Additional Protocol, an adequacy finding is not needed. But there could be significantly more adequacy findings outside Europe if the EU were more pro-active.

Despite the tardiness of the EU in making assessments, the desire to eventually obtain an 'adequacy' finding from the EU, or in a more amorphous form, to have one's law regarded as of the highest international standard (that the EU Directive is considered by many to embody) has been a significant influence on the development of laws outside Europe (as discussed above). The EU has been unwilling to make, and publicise, a sufficient number of decisions about what does and does not constitute adequate protection. Nor do European countries seem to have blocked particular data exports as frequently as occurred during the 1980s and 1990s, further reducing the impact of the adequacy requirement. Bygrave (2010, p.197) asserts there is considerable inconsistency and non-enforcement by EU members in relation to the data export provisions.

Outside Europe, 'border control' data export limitations are found in the majority of data privacy laws, and are sometimes added when there are revisions of existing laws. Various such limitations can now be found in the legislation of Australia, New Zealand, Taiwan, South Korea, India, and Macau, though their strength varies a great deal. There are provisions not yet in force in the laws of Malaysia and Hong Kong. Such restrictions already exist in the data privacy laws of the Latin American countries (except Chile), and the African countries.

The Contested Principle of 'Accountability'

Providing an alternative to the 'border control' approach is one objective of some proponents of the so-called 'accountability' principle, though they do not usually present it this way. Whether an 'accountability' principle strengthens or weakens data privacy depends very much on what you mean by 'accountability', because the term is ill-defined and fluid in the literature supporting it, which some of its proponents admit (Alhadeff, Van Alsenoy and Dumortier 2011).

The OECD Guidelines have an Accountability Principle (principle 14) but all it says is that a data controller 'should be accountable for complying with measures which give effect to the [other] principles', and the EU Directive has a similarly uncontentious provision (A 6(2)). The Article 29 Working Party's 'Accountability Opinion' of A 29 WP (2010) proposes 'a statutory accountability principle' which would add a new enforceable principle requiring data controllers to put effective measures into place to comply with other principles, 'and demonstrate this on request'. It suggests complementary specific requirements like privacy impact assessments (PIAs) 'for higher risk data processing'. Although the European Commission (EU 2010) says it will 'take account of the current debate on the possible introduction of an 'accountability principle', all it has as yet proposed under that heading are three improved methods of enforcement (discussed later): mandatory DPOs, mandatory DPIAs/PIAs in some situations; and promotion of PETs and 'privacy by design'. 'Accountability' should also not be confused with more precise notions of 'binding corporate rules' (BCRs) as a means of allowing data exports. The BCR approach of the A29 Working party opinion on BCRs (A29 WP, 2003) is all about exactly how legal liability is guaranteed in BCRs, and particularly 'third party beneficiary rights'. Here, 'accountability' has a strict meaning of 'legal liability'. None of these developments are objectionable.

The problem arises when proponents of 'accountability' present its elements without defining precisely what is their relationship to legal liability for breaches of privacy principles, by whom, and with what standards of proof. Abrams (2011), a leader of the 'Accountability Project', describes the 'two pieces to accountability' as a 'compliance program' and 'demonstration capacity', but without any reference to their relationship to legal liability, either to the regulator or data subject. Aladheff and others, while stating that 'accountability' is not a substitute for 'adequacy', want it to count toward an assessment of adequacy in a way that remains undefined (Alhadeff, Van Alsenoy and Dumortier 2011, p.25). Later, they refer to the possibility of 'accountability mechanisms' becoming 'a credible alternative to the existing mechanisms for international transfer' (p. 26), which seems to contradict their previous denial. This ambiguity is latent in the APEC Privacy Framework, which is completely silent on data export restrictions. Thus the APEC Accountability Principle (IX) becomes the only principle under which any liability for data exports could arise. All it says in clarifying that a data controller 'should be accountable' is that it should 'exercise due diligence and take reasonable steps to ensure' that overseas recipients 'will protect the information consistently with these Principles'. This APEC principle is translated in a Bill still before Australia's Parliament into a principle which allows exports of personal data to any country in the world, with the onus remaining on the data subject to prove that breaches of data privacy principles by the recipient occurred there, before the exporter suffers any 'accountability' at all. Gathering such proof would be a dangerous and expensive activity in many countries (Greenleaf 2010). The danger that 'accountability' is a Trojan horse for the replacement of data export restrictions based on 'border control' with a pseudo-restriction that is in practice meaningless is the reason that it requires this lengthy discussion. A satisfactory solution to the problem of data exports may be elusive, but 'accountability' is not it.

In a survey of the data protection accountability literature, Raab (2011) – neither proponent nor opponent – finds 'little help' in answering the crucial question posed by Bennett (2010), 'accountability for what and to whom', when it comes to defining the relationships between the bodies who are supposed to be involved in delivering accountability ('accounting firms, standards bodies, seal and trustmark programs [and] mediation and dispute resolution bodies': Bennett 2010), and 'the public whom they ultimately protect'. He is also particularly concerned that the Accountability Project suggests that some of its 'nine fundamentals' can be 'customised' (reduced) in particular, without explaining what 'accountability' will attach to the making of this decision. 'Accountability' is not gaining a precise meaning despite years of discussion, and should not play any significant role in data privacy beyond its possible value in making data processors legally liable for carrying out specific activities to implement data privacy principles, rather than just hoping that they will not be caught breaching them. It should not reduce or substitute for any other obligations.

Emergent Data Privacy Principles

The EU Commission is considering proposing the introduction of five new or expanded principles (EU Commission 2010, s. 2.1):

- *Transparency* – 'a general principle of transparent processing of personal data', including 'specific obligations for data controllers on the type of information to be provided', and 'one or more EU standard forms ('privacy information notices') to be used by data controllers';
- *Data breach notification* – 'a general personal data breach notification, including the addressees of such notifications and the criteria for triggering the obligation to notify', to apply when personal data is 'accidentally or unlawfully destroyed, lost, altered, accessed by or disclosed to unauthorised persons' is to be mandatory;
- *Improved means to exercise rights* – 'improving the modalities for the actual exercise of the rights of access, rectification, erasure or blocking of data' by deadlines, electronic exercise and access free of charge;
- *'Right to be forgotten'* – 'the right of individuals to have their data no longer processed and deleted when they are no longer needed for legitimate purposes', though perhaps only a clarification of the existing principle concerning deletion, is likely to be of particular importance in relation to social networks and the organisations with access to social network data for data mining;
- *'Data portability'* – 'providing the explicit right for an individual to withdraw his/her own data (e.g., his/her photos or a list of friends) from an application or service so that the withdrawn data can be transferred into another application or service, as far as technically feasible, without hindrance from the data controllers', is likely to be of seismic importance to the providers of social network services, who will be given an incentive to compete on data privacy as well as on other grounds. At present their services are not interoperable (it is not possible to have 'friends' etc on a different service), and while this proposal does not go as far as that, it would allow users to migrate in bulk to other services, taking all their personal data (User Generated Content) with them (provided the 'right to be forgotten' is also implemented.

The Commission is also considering other expanded rights including 'clarifying and strengthening the rules on consent' and may expand the categories of data to be considered as 'sensitive data', for example genetic data.

Outside Europe, many of these emergent international data privacy norms have already started to be incorporated in laws or legislative proposals. The USA has to some extent led the way with the development of data breach notification rights, but these are also now incorporated in the data privacy laws of Taiwan and South Korea (Greenleaf 2011a; 2011e), and in proposed legislation in Australia (Greenleaf and Waters 2010). South Korea also has an explicit 'no disadvantage in case of refusal' rule, requiring provision of services, with no extra costs, where data privacy rights are exercised. Australia has since 2001 had a specific principle requiring the option of anonymous transactions wherever this is feasible, whereas the EU's proposals for stronger data minimisation are not this explicit. Genetic data is already explicitly included in India's new law. Because of innovations like these at the national level in APEC economies, the EU Commission's proposals are unlikely to increase divergence in data privacy standards around the world in the long term. If they widen the gap between EU and APEC principles, that will only make APEC more irrelevant.

DATA PRIVACY ENFORCEMENT

In addition to privacy principles, the other requirement for a data privacy law is that it provides a means of enforcing them by law. In practice, as we have seen, almost all data privacy laws provide for an independent authority (a DPA) to be involved in their enforcement. But after that the common elements are more difficult to identify. And just because there are rising standards of data privacy principles, it does not necessarily follow that there will be a concomitant rise in levels of enforcement (Bennett and Raab 2006).

There are of course many other roles of a DPA that contribute to the governance of privacy, including their roles in influencing legislation, government policies, and business practices to develop in ways which are less privacy invasive. These are not the focus of this chapter but are analysed by Bennett and Raab (2006, pp. 133–43) as involving roles as ombudsmen, auditors, consultants, educators, policy advisors, and negotiators. However, they correctly state, their central role is as enforcers and the key question is the powers they have to order compliance with privacy principles (p. 143). It is more complex, because only some DPAs have an 'original jurisdiction' empowering them to make enforcement orders when they reach conclusions, rather than referring the matter to a court or tribunal for enforceable orders. In any event, there is almost always a right of appeal from a DPA's decisions to a court or tribunal (one exception is that the complainant has no appeal in Australia from a determination by the federal Privacy Commissioner: Greenleaf and Waters 2010).

Standards for Enforcement Mechanisms

There is no internationally accepted standard of what constitutes appropriate or sufficient enforcement of a data privacy regime. As with principles, the most widely accepted standard is the Article 29 Working Party's interpretation of what types of enforcement mechanisms and levels of effectiveness constitute 'adequate' enforcement in relation to the EU Directive (A29 WP 1997; 1998). These are (with quotations from the 1998 Opinion):

1. Delivery of a 'good level of compliance' with the content rules (data protection principles): 'A good system is generally characterised by a high degree of awareness among data controllers of their obligations, and among data subjects of their rights and the means of exercising them. The existence of effective and dissuasive sanctions can play an important [role] in ensuring respect for rules, as of course can systems of direct verification by authorities, auditors, or independent data protection officials.'
2. Provision of support and help to individual data subjects in the exercise of their rights: 'The individual must be able to enforce his/her rights rapidly and effectively, and without prohibitive cost. To do so there must be some sort of institutional mechanism allowing independent investigation of complaints.'
3. Provision of appropriate redress to the injured party where rules are not complied with: 'This is a key element which must involve a system of independent adjudication or arbitration which allows compensation to be paid and sanctions imposed where appropriate.'

Other international agreements have contributed little. The OECD Guidelines recommended legislation, but not a DPA, and the CoE Convention did not require a DPA until the Additional Protocol. The APEC Framework's approach to enforcement was completely non-prescriptive, allowing any method of enforcement (Greenleaf 2010), and this may be one of the reasons for its failure to date. Various APEC members have enacted laws which have enforcement mechanisms meeting EU standards, in some cases tailored to meet local needs (eg Korea's unique mediation system: Greenleaf 2011a).

The one other area in which separate international standards have emerged is for the independence of DPAs as a condition for their membership of international associations of DPAs (ICDPPC 2001) but details are beyond the scope of this chapter. Most DPAs established by data privacy laws meet these standards (the Macao authority can only be an observer at meetings because its enabling law has not yet been passed). The Malaysian DPA (not yet appointed) is likely to be an example of where the data privacy legislation fails to provide sufficient independence (it makes the DPA subject to ministerial direction), and is likely to result in accreditation being refused (Greenleaf 2010e; Munir and Yasin 2010). The European Commission has also taken action against Germany because of the lack of independence of some of its regional DPAs.

The Poor Enforcement Record of Most DPAs

It is not possible here to analyse the enforcement record of what are now nearly 70 DPAs, some of whose activities go back decades. There are no accepted evaluation criteria for the effectiveness of data privacy regimes as a whole (Bennett and Raab 2006, p. 235), and nor are there for assessing the overall effectiveness of DPAs. However, they rarely win accolades for effective enforcement. In Europe the EU Commission admits that '[t]here is consensus among stakeholders that the role of Data Protection Authorities needs to be strengthened so as to ensure better enforcement of data privacy rules' (EU Commission 2010, 1). There are a string of European studies since 2003 (summarised by Bygrave 2010, p. 197) documenting under-resourcing of enforcement efforts by DPAs, patchy compliance by data controllers (although they are generally supportive of data privacy objectives), and low awareness of data protection rights by individuals. Outside Europe, there is little evidence of a better enforcement record. In Asia and Australasia my own studies of Japan, Hong Kong and Australia give details of poor enforcement in those countries, due to a combination of inadequate enforcement powers (particularly Hong Kong and Japan), lack of appeal rights (Australia and Japan), and unwillingness to use those powers that are available (everywhere) (Greenleaf 2010a; 2010b; 2010c). The only DPA which is considered to enforce its legislation effectively is New Zealand (now endorsed by the A 29 Working Party finding of adequacy), with South Korea's enforcement having some credibility in the private sector but none in the public sector (Greenleaf 2011a provides a summary).

One near-universal contributor to the poor compliance record of DPAs is their failure to sufficiently document what they do about resolving complaints. There is a general under-reporting by DPAs of both the legal aspects of complaint resolutions and the outcomes of investigations. This results in a failure of 'responsive regulation' because of the lack of feedback loops concerning 'the tariff' that can be expected by complainants and respondents alike in relation to particular types of breaches (Greenleaf 2004). Lack of objective standards of what will/must be reported (both case examples and statistics) is a failure of accountability. It is one that has as yet been neglected by the European Commission, and by most DPAs whether European or not. However, the world's DPAs have recently resolved to report summaries of selected complaints, in a more consistent format, and to help make case law in their jurisdictions more readily findable (ICDPPC, 2009).

Emergent Mechanisms for Enforcement

New enforcement mechanisms are developing as standard tools of DPAs, but less coherently than emergent principles. In Europe, the EU Commission proposes, in light of its finding of the need to provide better enforcement, the following strengthening of European enforcement mechanisms (EU Commission 2010, ss. 2.2.4–5):

- *Representative actions* – 'extending the power to bring an action before the national courts to data privacy authorities and to civil society associations, as well as to other associations representing data subjects' interests';
- *Stronger sanctions* – 'for example by explicitly including criminal sanctions in case of serious data protection violations';
- *Mandatory independent data protection officers* – with harmonised rules related to DPO's tasks and competences;
- *Data protection impact assessment* – to be an obligation of DPOs in defined situations 'when sensitive data are being processed, or when the type of processing otherwise involves specific risks, in particular when using specific technologies, mechanisms or procedures, including profiling or video surveillance'.

Some EU Commission proposals are more in the nature of intended activities rather than new legal requirements, such as 'further promoting the use of PETs [privacy enhancing technologies] and the possibilities for the concrete implementation of the concept of "privacy by design"' and 'the possible creation of EU certification schemes (e.g. 'privacy seals') for "privacy-compliant" processes, technologies, products and services'.

Most of these proposed improvements are also found in at least some jurisdictions outside Europe. For example: representative actions are already provided for in Australia, Korea, Taiwan and (arguably) Hong Kong; collective mediation proceedings are a novel element in Korea; criminal sanctions for serious breaches of principles are included in pending Bills in Hong Kong and Australia; and privacy impact assessments (PIAs) are already mandatory in some circumstances for the public sectors in the US, UK and Canadian federal governments and will be in the Korean public sector. There is already a good deal of 'trading up' of remedies between jurisdictions in the Asia-Pacific, quite apart from influences from Europe.

NEW CHALLENGES OF A NETWORKED WORLD: CAN DATA PRIVACY LAWS COPE?

All the new technological challenges noted at the outset of this chapter are interconnected and multiply the effects and dangers of other changes. Take, for example, more ubiquitous data collection: 'The ubiquity of personal data and of data gathering means that the default position is shifting from state and private bodies having to decide to collect data to one in which they have to make an effort not to collect (increasingly sensitive) data' (Korff, Brown and others 2010). Where this occurs, then the privacy dangers of social networking services (SNS), or data mining, are multiplied accordingly.

The fact that the location of such a large proportion of internet services posing the most significant privacy threats (search engines, SNS etc) is in the USA makes American exceptionalism in data privacy far more significant than it would otherwise be. When that is coupled with the ease with which 'cloud computing' makes it technically possible for data to be transferred between servers and service providers (eg call centres) located in successive countries within a single day, the problem of data controllers being 'out of reach' of regulators concerned with protection of citizens of particular counties is clearly getting worse.

Under such circumstances, is it realistic to think that data privacy laws have any prospect of providing privacy protection? It is probably true that current laws (and enforcement practices) cannot and do not cope very well. But that is not the end of the matter, given the considerable strengthening of data protection laws proposed by the European Commission, and the legislative changes already taking place in the United States and in countries outside Europe. Perhaps one way of answering the question is to assess what are the main dangers posed by various new technologies, followed by assessing whether any of the proposed legal changes address those problems. So this chapter concludes with two examples of such juxtaposition, SNS and cloud computing.

The reader is invited to consider whether future data privacy laws may be able to cope with new technical and social developments such as these. It is arguable that data privacy laws are in a period of creative

Table 10.1   Social networking services (SNS)

Example 1: Social networking services (SNS)

Danger to privacy	Proposed reform
1 Default settings are anti-privacy	Mandatory defaults
2 Users don't know how to control privacy settings	Mandatory default re-sets
3 Data mining for marketing purposes	'Do not track' principle or explicit disclosures
4 3rd parties add personal data (photos etc) without permission	Simpler confidentiality / privacy actions between SNS users; 'take downs' by SNS operators would also assist
5 Tagging is out of user control	'No tagging' in 'Do not track'
6 Personal data can't be removed from SNS	'Right to be forgotten'
7 Non-interoperability of SNSs	'Data portability' but cannot mandate interoperability?
8 Facebook dominance reduces incentive for better privacy policies	More competition, such as Google+

Table 10.2   Cloud computing

Example 2: Cloud computing

Danger to privacy	Proposed reform
1 Data users lose control of physical location of data (data can go to locations with no privacy controls)	Data export laws based on physical destination; also improved notice
2 Other jurisdictions can impose legal control (eg USA Patriot Act can apply)	No answer once physical control lost
3 Individuals have no idea where their data is located	Disclosure of export locations; can also require consent
4 Security failures of cloud service providers (eg DropBox 4 hours with no passwords on accounts)	Vicarious liability of local data user

re-development, within Europe and elsewhere, including the USA, and that they may cope better in future than they are capable of at present. In addition, whatever their shortcomings, they are still the best regulatory response that we have, so we should use them.

CONCLUSION – THE TRAJECTORY OF GLOBAL DATA PRIVACY REGULATION

Bennett and Raab (2006), in the most systematic global review of data privacy regulation, presented their 'main research question' (p. xv) as whether there was a 'race to the bottom', a 'race to the top', or something else, in the global development of data privacy protection. They correctly caution that the existence and formal strength of a data privacy law is only one factor by which we should measure data privacy protection in a country, and two other key dimensions are the effectiveness of enforcement and the extent of surveillance (discussed below). Therefore, globally, there is more than one race to the top or bottom.

They noted that, in relation to legislation, the main conditions proposed by globalisation theories of regulation for a 'race to the bottom' (data mobility and wide national divergences in laws) were present in the case of data protection legislation (p. 276). Nevertheless, they found that 'there is clearly no race to the bottom', but nor did they find clear evidence of a 'race to the top', or global ratcheting up of privacy standards. In particular, they considered that the 'general suspicion that the APEC Privacy Principles are intended as an alternative, and a weaker, global standard than the EU' means that they 'may serve to slow and even reverse' the otherwise 'halting and meandering walk' to higher standards which the EU Directive had inspired (p. 283). They concluded that the most plausible future scenario (the Bennett-Raab thesis) was 'an incoherent and fragmented patchwork', 'a more chaotic future of periodic and unpredictable victories for the privacy value' (p. 295). So Bennett and Raab found some 'upward' global trajectory influenced significantly by the EU Directive, but sufficiently weak in the mid-2000s that the countervailing weakness of the APEC approach was enough to make the future quite unpredictable.

Half a decade later, it can be argued that there is now a clearer 'upward' global trajectory than Bennett and Raab found, provided we keep clear that we are only talking about the existence and formal strength of data privacy laws, not the other factors. Their analysis is based on the existence of only ten data privacy laws (on my definition) in countries outside Europe, plus two covering only the public sector. That was probably an under-estimate in 2006 because of some little-known laws, but in any event by mid-2011 there are 27 data privacy laws outside Europe (as many as there are EU member states), and a handful of Bills expected to be enacted soon.

Surprisingly, Bygrave's more recent global analysis of data privacy developments only assumes that 'well over 40 countries' have data privacy laws (Bygrave 2010, p. 166), even though he is aware of the new African laws in francophone countries (p. 193). This reflects the previous lack of availability of a catalogue showing that there are now more than 70 such laws. As argued above, the rate of expansion is greater than ever before. Of course, the number of data privacy laws can only be part of the measure, but in Africa, Latin America and even in Asia the European Directive has become the single most significant influence on the content of those laws, and leads to them embodying a relatively high standard of data protection principles. The lower standards of the APEC Privacy Framework have not served to 'slow or even reverse' this trend as Bennett and Raab and others (myself included) feared.

A handful of new data privacy laws across the globe each year, with EU-influenced privacy principles, and revisions of some existing weaker laws to strengthen them, does not constitute a 'race' in most uses of the term, but nor does it any longer look like such a 'halting and meandering walk' as Bennett and Raab found. It may not be a race, but data privacy laws do have a global trajectory, namely expansion at an increasing rate with principles more commonly influenced by the EU Directive than any other source.

Furthermore, the EU's own standards show every likelihood of strengthening, as do data privacy standards originating outside the EU. The global 'ratcheting up' of standards is likely to continue, at least in the near future. It is not possible to predict whether the Council of Europe Convention 108 and Additional Protocol will develop towards a global privacy agreement but if they do this will help accelerate global expansion (though perhaps not the strength of standards). The influence of some 'accountability' advocates (coupled with unchecked growth in 'cloud computing') is more likely to be a future countervailing factor than the APEC Privacy Framework.

As mentioned, Bennett and Raab counsel against any one-dimensional measure of data privacy laws, and their cautions must be heeded, though they are largely beyond the scope of this chapter. First, a strengthening of privacy standards (principles) does not in any way entail a corresponding increase in the enforcement of those standards (or its effectiveness). As discussed earlier, weak enforcement is a global problem for data privacy laws, and although there are valuable new enforcement mechanisms being developed, it is a separate question in every jurisdiction whether enforcement is improving. Second, there is no necessary correspondence between a rise in data privacy standards and a decrease in surveillance practices. In fact, in some countries the enactment or strengthening of privacy standards has been an explicit 'trade off' for new surveillance practices authorised or mandated by legislation. As Bennett and Raab conclude, there is not one race to the top or bottom that we must consider. It is better to say the various dimensions on which we must measure the health of privacy as a value, including data privacy principles, their enforcement, and surveillance practices. These dimensions, as they say, differ from place to place and time to time, and are not readily 'balanced' into one overall measure. Nevertheless, considered solely on the dimension of the global spread of EU-like data privacy laws, the Bennett-Raab thesis no longer appears correct. On the other dimensions of effective enforcement and limiting surveillance, there are no obvious global trajectories which could give rise to similar optimism.

NOTES

1. The assistance and contributions are acknowledged of Ian Brown, Lee Bygrave, Stewart Dresner, Marie George, Gus Hosein, Laura Linkomes, Jill Matthews, Charles Raab, Blair Stewart, and Nigel Waters. Responsibility for all errors and opinions remains with the author. This chapter was completed while the author was the Inaugural Common LII Fellow at the Institute of Advanced Legal Studies, University of London, July–August 2011, and was assisted by the opportunity to present some of its conclusions at the summer school of the Oxford Internet Institute in July 2011.
2. This part, and the table in the Appendix, is derived from my article Greenleaf, G. (2011), 'Global Data Privacy Laws: Forty Years of Acceleration' in *Privacy Laws & Business International Report*, **112**, which contains more details explaining the table.

BIBLIOGRAPHY

A29 WP (2010), 'Article 29 Data Protection Working Party – Opinion 3/2010 on the Principle of Accountability', WP 173, DG XV, 00062/10/EN, adopted on 13 July 2010.
A29 WP (2003), 'Article 29 Data Protection Working Party – Working Document on Transfers of Personal Data to Third Countries: Applying Article 26 (2) of the EU Data Protection Directive to Binding Corporate Rules for International Data Transfers', WP 74, DG XV, 11639/02/EN WP 74, adopted on 3 June 2003.
A29 WP (1998), 'Article 29 Data Protection Working Party – Transfers of Personal Data to Third Countries: Applying Articles 25 and 26 of the EU Data Protection Directive', WP 12, DG XV D/5025/98, adopted on 24 July 1998.
A29 WP (1997), 'Article 29 Data Protection Working Party – First Orientation on Transfers of Personal Data to Third Countries: Possible Ways Forward in Assessing Adequacy', WP 4, DG XV D/5020/97-EN final, adopted on 26 June 1997.
Abrams, M. (2011), 'Accountability 2011', Presentation at the Privacy Laws & Business Annual Conference, St Johns College, Cambridge, July 2011.
Alhadeff, J., B. Van Alsenoy and J. Dumortier (2011), 'The Accountability Principle in Data Protection Regulation: Origin, Development and Future Directions', 2011, https://lirias.kuleuven.be/bitstream/123456789/311284/1/Demystifying_accountability_JHA_BVA_JD_final_draft.doc.
APEC (Asia-Pacific Economic Cooperation) (2005), 'APEC Privacy Framework', http://publications.apec.org/publication-detail.php?pub_id=390, accessed 2 September 2011.
Bennett, C. (2010), 'International Privacy Standards: Can Accountability Ever Be Adequate?', *Privacy Laws & Business International Newsletter*, **106**, August 2010, 21–3.

Bennett, C. and C. Raab (2006), *The Governance of Privacy: Policy Instruments in Global Perspective*, Boston, MA: MIT Press.

Bygrave, L. (2010), 'Privacy and Data Protection in an International Perspective', *Scandinavian Studies in Law*, **56**, 165–200, http://www.uio.no/studier/emner/jus/jus/JUR5630/v11/undervisningsmateriale/, accessed 2 September 2011.

Bygrave, L. (2008), 'International Agreements to Protect Personal Data', in J. B. Rule and G. Greenleaf (eds), *Global Privacy Protection: The First Generation*, Cheltenham, UK and Northampton, MA, US: Edward Elgar, pp.15–49.

Bygrave, L. (2002), *Data Protection Laws: Approaching Their Rationale, Logic and Limits*, The Hague: Kluwer Law International.

Bygrave, L. (1998), 'Data Protection Pursuant to the Right to Privacy in Human Rights Treaties', *International Journal of Law and Information Technology*, **6(3)**, 247–84.

Connolly, C. (2008), 'A New Regional Approach to Privacy in ASEAN', http://www.galexia.com/public/research/articles/research_articles-art55.html, accessed 2 September 2011.

CoE (1981), *Council of Europe Convention for the Protection of Individuals with regard to Automatic Processing of Personal Data*, European Treaty Series No. 108, adopted 28 January 1981.

CoE 108 accessions (2011), 'Council of Europe CETS', No.108, http://conventions.coe.int/Treaty/Commun/ChercheSig.asp?NT=108&CM=1&DF=&CL=ENG, accessed 2 September 2011.

EU Commission (2010), 'A Comprehensive Approach on Personal Data Protection in the European Union', Communication from the Commission to the European Parliament, the Council, the Economic and Social Committee and the Committee of the Regions, December 2010.

EU Directive (1995), 'Directive 95/46/EC on the Protection of Individuals with Regard to the Processing of Personal Data and on the Free Movement of such Data', adopted 24 October 1995, *Official Journal of the European Communities (O.J.)*, L 281, 23 November 1995, pp.31 *et seq*.

ECOWAS (2011), 'Economic Community of West African States (ECOWAS) Press Release – ECOWAS reaffirms commitment to democracy', 12 August 2011.

ECOWAS (2010), 'Economic Community of West African States (ECOWAS)', Supplementary Act A/SA.1/01/10 on Personal Data Protection Within ECOWAS, 16 February 2010.

Greenleaf, G. (2011), 'Global Data Privacy Laws: Forty Years of Acceleration', *Privacy Laws & Business International Report*, **112**, 11–17.

Greenleaf, G. (2011a), 'Asia-Pacific Data Privacy: 2011, Year of Revolution?', *Kyung Hee Law Journal* (forthcoming), http://law.bepress.com/unswwps/flrps11/art30/.

Greenleaf, G. (2011b), 'India Attempts Data Protection by Regulations', *Privacy Laws & Business International Report*, **110**, April 2011, 11–14.

Greenleaf, G. (2011c), 'Outsourcing and India's New Privacy Law: No Cause for Panic' *Privacy Laws & Business International Report*, **111**, 16–17.

Greenleaf, G. (2011d), 'The Illusion of Personal Data Protection in Indian Law', *International Data Privacy Law*, **1(1)**, 47–69, http://idpl.oxfordjournals.org/content/1/1/47.full, accessed 2 September 2011.

Greenleaf, G. (2011e), 'Breach Notification and Diffused Enforcement in Taiwan's DP Act', *Privacy Laws & Business International Report*, **109**, 12–13.

Greenleaf, G. (2010), 'Taiwan Revises its Data Protection Act', *Privacy Laws & Business International Newsletter*, **108**, 8–10.

Greenleaf, G. (2010a), 'Country Studies B.3 – HONG KONG', in D. Korff (ed.), *Comparative Study on Different Approaches to New Privacy Challenges, in Particular in the Light of Technological Developments*, European Commission D-G Justice, Freedom and Security, http://ec.europa.eu/justice/policies/privacy/docs/studies/new_privacy_challenges/final_report_country_report_B3_hong_kong.pdf, accessed 2 September 2011.

Greenleaf, G. (2010b), 'Country Studies B.5 – JAPAN', in D. Korff (ed.), *Comparative Study on Different Approaches to New Privacy Challenges, in Particular in the Light of*

Technological Developments', European Commission D-G Justice, Freedom and Security, http://ec.europa.eu/justice/policies/privacy/docs/studies/new_privacy_challenges/final_report_country_report_B5_japan.pdf, accessed 2 September 2011.

Greenleaf, G. (2010c), 'Country Studies B.2 – AUSTRALIA' in D. Korff (ed.), *Comparative Study on Different Approaches to New Privacy Challenges, in Particular in the Light of Technological Developments*, European Commission D-G Justice, Freedom and Security, http://ec.europa.eu/justice/policies/privacy/docs/studies/new_privacy_challenges/final_report_country_report_B2_australia.pdf, accessed 2 September 2011.

Greenleaf, G. (2010d), 'Australia's Proposed Reforms (Pt II): Privacy Remedies', *Privacy Laws & Business International Newsletter*, **104**, 10–12.

Greenleaf, G. (2010e), 'Limitations of Malaysia's Data Protection Bill', *Privacy Laws & Business International Newsletter*, **104**, 5–7.

Greenleaf, G. (2010f), 'Australia's Proposed Reforms: Unified Privacy Principles', *Privacy Laws & Business International Newsletter*, **103**, 15–17.

Greenleaf, G. (2009), 'Twenty One Years of Data Protection in the Asia-Pacific', *Privacy Laws & Business International Newsletter*, **100**, 21–24.

Greenleaf, G. (2009a), 'Initial Enforcement of Macao's Data Protection Law', *Privacy Laws & Business International Newsletter*, **101**, 9, 27.

Greenleaf, G. (2009b), 'Rudd Government Abandons Border Security of Privacy', *Australian Policy Online*, 23 October 2009; [2009] ALRS 17.

Greenleaf, G. (2009c), 'Five Years of the APEC Privacy Framework: Failure or Promise?', *Computer Law & Security Report*, **25**, 28–43.

Greenleaf, G. (2009d), 'Macao's EU-influenced Personal Data Protection Act', *Privacy Laws & Business International Newsletter*, **96**, 21–22.

Greenleaf, G. (2008a), 'Non-European States May Join European Privacy Convention', *Privacy Laws & Business International Newsletter*, **94**, 13–14.

Greenleaf, G. (2008b), 'Privacy in Australia', in J. Rule and G. Greenleaf (eds), *Global Privacy Protection: The First Generation*, Cheltenham, UK and Northampton, MA, US: Edward Elgar.

Greenleaf, G. (2004), 'Reforming Reporting of Privacy Cases: A Proposal for Improving Accountability of Asia-Pacific Privacy Commissioners', http://papers.ssrn.com/sol3/papers.cfm?abstract_id=512782, accessed 2 September 2011.

Greenleaf, G. (2003), 'Australia's APEC Privacy Initiative: The Pros and Cons of "OECD Lite"', *Privacy Law & Policy Reporter*, **10(10)**, 1–6, http://www2.austlii.edu.au/~graham/publications/2004/APEC_V8article.htm, accessed 2 September 2011.

Greenleaf, G. and L. Bygrave (2011), 'Not Entirely Adequate but Far Away: Lessons from how Europe sees New Zealand Data Protection', *Privacy Laws & Business International Report*, **111**, 7–8.

Greenleaf, G. and N. Waters (2010), 'Australian Privacy Principles – Two Steps Backwards', *Privacy Laws & Business International Newsletter*, **106**, 13–15.

Hoofnagle, C. (2010), 'Country Studies B.1 – United States of America', in D. Korff (ed.), *Comparative Study on Different Approaches to New Privacy Challenges, in Particular in the Light of Technological Developments*, European Commission D-G Justice, Freedom and Security, http://ec.europa.eu/justice/policies/privacy/docs/studies/new_privacy_challenges/final_report_country_report_B1_usa.pdf, accessed 2 September 2011.

ICDPPC (2009), '31st International Conference of Data Protection and Privacy Commissioners – Resolution on Case Reporting', adopted 5 November 2009, Madrid.

ICDPPC (2001), '23rd International Conference of Data Protection Commissioners – Accreditation Features of Data Protection Authorities', adopted 25 September 2001, Paris.

Keane, J. (2011), *The Life and Death of Democracy*, London: Pocket Books.

Korff, D. and I. Brown et al. (2010), 'Final Report of the Comparative Study on Different Approaches to New Privacy Challenges, in Particular in the Light of Technological Developments', European Commission D-G Justice, Freedom and Security, http://ec.europa.eu/justice/policies/privacy/docs/studies/new_privacy_challenges/final_report_en.pdf, accessed 2 September 2011.

McLeish, R. and G. Greenleaf (2008), 'Hong Kong', in J. Rule and G. Greenleaf (eds), *Global Privacy Protection*, Cheltenham, UK and Northampton, MA, US: Edward Elgar.

Munir, A. and S. Yasin (2010), *Personal Data Protection in Malaysia: Law and Practice*, Selangor, MY: Sweet & Maxwell Asia.

OECD Guidelines (1980), 'Guidelines Governing the Protection of Privacy and Transborder Flows of Personal Data', OECD Doc. C(80)58/FINAL, adopted by OECD Council on 23 September 1980.

Palazzi, P. (2011), 'Data Protection Law in Latin America (PPTs)', Presented at the Privacy Laws & Business Annual Conference, Cambridge, July 2011.

Park, W. (2008), 'Republic of Korea' in J. Rule and G. Greenleaf (eds), *Global Privacy Protection*, Cheltenham, UK and Northampton, MA, US: Edward Elgar.

Park, W. and G. Greenleaf (2011), 'Korea Reforms Data Protection Act', *Privacy Laws & Business International Report*, **109**, 20.

Raab, C. (2011), 'The Meaning of "Accountability" in the Information Privacy Context' in D. Guagnin et al. (eds), *Managing Privacy Through Accountability*, London: Palgrave Macmillan (forthcoming).

Rule, J. and G. Greenleaf (eds) (2008), *Global Privacy Protection: The First Generation*, Cheltenham, UK and Northampton, MA, US: Edward Elgar.

Rule, J., L. Stearns, D. McAdam and D. Uglow (1981), *The Politics of Privacy: Planning for Personal Data Systems As Powerful Technologies*, New York: Elsevier.

Szekely, I. (2008), 'Hungary', in J. Rule and G. Greenleaf (eds), *Global Privacy Protection*, Cheltenham, UK and Northampton, MA, US: Edward Elgar.

Waters, N. (2011), 'The Asia Pacific Economic Cooperation (APEC) Privacy Framework – Implementation and Enforcement: Moving Forward or Treading Water' (PPTs), Privacy Laws & Business Annual Conference, St John's College, Cambridge, July 2011.

Waters, N. (2008), 'The APEC Asia-Pacific Privacy Initiative – a New Route to Effective Data Protection or a Trojan Horse for Self-regulation?', http://law.bepress.com/unswwps/flrps08/art59/, accessed 2 September 2011.

Appendix A.10.1   Global table of data privacy laws

This table lists known data privacy laws (as defined above) as at 30 July 2011.

Jurisdiction	Key Act	From[1]	Latest	Region	EU[2]	CoE[3]	Other Int.[4]
Albania	Act on the Protection of Personal Data	1999	1999	Europe	[I]	M; P	
Andorra	Law on the protection of personal data	2003	2003	Europe	A	M; P	
Argentina	Personal Data Protection Act	2000	2000	Latin Am	A		
Australia	Privacy Act 1988	2001	2001	Australasia			APEC; OECD
Austria	Datenschutzgesetz	1978	2009	Europe	M	M; P	OECD
Azerbaijan	Law on data, data processing and data protection	1998	1998	Europe		M	
Bahamas	Data Protection Act	2003	2003	Caribbean			
Belgium	Law on Privacy Protection in relation to the Processing of Personal Data	1992	1998	Europe	M	M	OECD
Benin	Loi sur la Protection des données personnelles	2009	2009	Africa			ECOWAS
Bosnia & Herzegovina	Law on the protection of personal data	2001	2001	Europe	[I]	M; P	
Bulgaria	Law for Protection of Personal Data	2002	2007	Europe	M	M; P	
Burkina Faso	Law on Protection of Personal Information	2004	2004	Africa			ECOWAS
Canada	Personal Information Protection and Electronic Documents Act	2002	2002	North Am	A		APEC; OECD
Cape Verde	Loi N° 133/V/2201 du 22 janvier 2001	2001	2001	Africa			ECOWAS

Appendix A.10.1 (continued)

Jurisdiction	Key Act	From[1]	Latest	Region	EU[2]	CoE[3]	Other Int.[4]
Chile	Privacy Law	1999	1999	Latin Am			APEC; OECD
Colombia	Data Protection Law	2008	2008	Latin Am			
Croatia	Act on Personal Data Protection	2003	2003	Europe	[I]	M; P	
Cyprus	The Processing of Personal Data (Protection of the Individual) Law	2001	2003	Europe	M	M; P	
Czech Republic	Personal Data Protection Act	1992	2000	Europe	M	M; P	OECD
Denmark	Act on Processing of Personal Data	1978	2000	Europe	M	M	OECD
Estonia	Data Protection Act	2003	2003	Europe	M	M; P	OECD
Faroe Islands	Act on processing of personal data	2010	2010	Europe	A		
Finland	Personal Data Act	1987	1999	Europe	M	M	OECD
France	Law relating to the protection of individuals against the processing of personal data	1978	2004	Europe	M	M; P	OECD
FYROM (Macedonia)	Law on Personal Data Protection	2005	2005	Europe	[I]	M; P	
Germany	Federal Data Protection Act	1977	2001	Europe	M	M; P	OECD
Gibraltar	Data Protection Act	2004	2004	Europe			
Greece	Law on the Protection of individuals with regard to the processing of personal data	1997	1997	Europe	M	M	OECD
Guernsey	Data Protection (Bailiwick of Guernsey) Law	1986	2001	Europe	A	M*	
Hong Kong SAR	Personal Data (Privacy) Ordinance	1995	1995	Asia			APEC

Country	Law			Region			
Hungary	Law on the protection of personal data and the disclosure of public information	1992	1992	Europe	M	M; P	OECD
Iceland	Law on the Protection and Processing of Personal Data	1989	2000	Europe	EEA	M	OECD
India	Rules under s43A (2008 Amendt), Information Technology Act 2000	2011	2011	Asia			
Ireland	Data Protection Act	1988	2003	Europe	M	M; P	OECD
Isle of Man	Data Protection Act	1986	2002	Europe	A	M*	
Israel	Privacy Protection Act 1981	1981	1981	M.East/N.Af	A		OECD
Italy	Consolidation Act regarding the Protection of Personal Data	1996	2003	Europe	M	M	OECD
Japan	Act on the Protection of Personal Information	2003	2003	Asia			APEC; OECD
Jersey	Data Protection (Jersey) Law	1987	2005	Europe	A	M*	
Kyrgyz Republic	Law on Personal Data	2008	2008	Central Asia			
Latvia	Law on Protection of Personal Data of Natural Persons	2000	2002	Europe	M	M; P	
Liechtenstein	Gesetz über die Abänderung des Datenschutzgesetzes (2002)	2002	2008	Europe	EEA	M; P	
Lithuania	Law on Legal Protection of Personal Data	1996	2003	Europe	M	M; P	
Luxembourg	Data Protection Law	1979	2002	Europe	M	M; P	OECD
Macao SAR	Personal Data Protection Act	2007	2007	Asia			
Malaysia	Personal Data Protection Act	2010	2010	Asia			APEC
Malta	Data Protection Act	2001	2001	Europe	M	M	
Mauritius	Data Protection Act	2004	2004	Africa			

Appendix A.10.1 (continued)

Jurisdiction	Key Act	From[1]	Latest	Region	EU[2]	CoE[3]	Other Int.[4]
Mexico	Federal Law on the Protection of Personal Data Held by Private Parties	2010	2010	Latin Am			APEC; OECD
Moldova	Law on Personal Data Protection	2007	2007	Europe	[I]	M; P	
Monaco	Act controlling personal data processing (2001)	1993	1993	Europe	[I]	M; P	
Montenegro	Law on Personal Data Protection	2008	2008	Europe			
Morocco	Data Protection Act	2009	2009	M.East/N.Af			
Netherlands	Personal Data Protection Act	1988	2000	Europe	M	M; P	OECD
New Zealand	Privacy Act 1993	1993	2010	Australasia	[A]		APEC; OECD
Norway	Personal Data Act	1978	2000	Europe	EEA	M	OECD
Peru	Law on Protection of Personal Data	2011	2011	Latin Am			APEC; US FTA
Poland	Act on the Protection of Personal Data	1997	2004	Europe	M	M; P	OECD
Portugal	Lei da protecçao de dados pessoais	1991	1998	Europe	M	M; P	OECD
Romania	Law on the protection of individuals with regard to the processing of personal data and the free movement of such data	2001	2005	Europe	M	M; P	
Russia	Federal Law Regarding Personal Data	2011	2011	Europe	S	M	APEC
San Marino	Law regulating the Computerized Collection of Personal Data	1983	1995	Europe			
Senegal	Act on the Protection of Personal Data	2007	2007	Africa			ECOWAS
Serbia	Law on Personal Data Protection	2008	2008	Europe	[I]	M; P	
Slovakia	Act on the Protection of Personal Data	1992	2005	Europe	M	M; P	OECD

Country	Law	From	Latest	Region	EU	CoE	Other
Slovenia	Personal Data Protection Act	1999	2004	Europe	M	M	OECD
South Korea	Data Protection Act	2001	2011	Asia			APEC; OECD
Spain	Ley Orgánica de Protección de Datos de Carácter Personal	1992	1999	Europe	M	M; P	OECD
Sweden	Personal Data Act	1973	1998	Europe	M	M; P	OECD
Switzerland	Data Protection Act	1992	1992	Europe	A	M; P	OECD
Taiwan	Personal Data Protection Act	1995	2010	Asia			APEC
Tunisia	Law on the protection of personal data	2004	2004	M.East/N.Af			
Ukraine	Law on Personal Data Protection	2011	2011	Europe	[I]	M; P	
United Kingdom	Data Protection Act 1998	1984	1998	Europe	M	M	OECD
Uruguay	Law on the Protection of Personal Data	2008	2008	Latin Am	[A]	M	OECD

Notes:

1 **Date columns:** 'From' = date original law enacted; 'Latest' = year of last significant amendment known

2 **European Union column:** M = country is an EU member state; A = country's protection of personal data has been held 'adequate' by the EU; [A] = Favourable Article 29 Working Party opinion on adequacy, but no final decision announced; EEA = country is a member of the European Economic Area; [I] = Adequacy finding is in practice irrelevant due to country acceding to both Council of Europe Convention 108 and Additional Protocol

3 **Council of Europe column:** M = country is a member state of the Council of Europe and has ratified the Convention; M* = United Kingdom has ratified Convention on behalf of sub-jurisdiction; P = country has also ratified the optional protocol; S = country has signed but not ratified Convention

4 **Other international commitments column:** APEC: 'economy' is a member of APEC; OECD; OECD = country is a member of OECD; ECOWAS = country is a member of Economic Community of West African States

11. Revisiting policy laundering and modern international policy dynamics
Gus Hosein

One of the challenges of modern policy-making, particularly for digital issues, is that policy-making is often done by national deliberative bodies, facing a global environment. Threats and challenges that are being responded to by national policies are often due to the rise of risks and opportunities that can be enabled anywhere in the world.

As academics and researchers we are accustomed to studying the policy process within a given political system. We look at a variety of issues and institutions, the actors, the stakeholders, the regulated, the regulators, and their interests. We look to the policy processes, the consultations, the consideration of various responses as policy-makers endeavour to create policy that best reflects the problems being faced and that is responsive to the consultative and deliberative processes (Baumgartner et al. 2002; Kingdon 1995).

Where academic research has been lacking in studies is in investigating how the dynamic global pressures influence national policy-making (Braithwaite and Drahos 2000). How can a government regulate an activity that is conducted using global vehicles and means? International law may apply but this is often beyond the remit of national parliaments, and oftentimes beyond the reach of national courts. Customs have emerged over time that sometimes regulate behaviour of global actors, and international regulatory practices have emerged more recently, but these are both slow to react to more recent developments.

If a global problem arises and exhibits itself locally, how is a deliberative policy-making institution supposed to respond? It could pass laws but this would require an in-depth understanding of global policy, international law, and in the case of policies that deal with science and technology, a detailed understanding of the particularities of each. Whether it is a response to environmental considerations in a country and its response to acid rain, or a response to terrorism exhibited locally but planned internationally, deliberative bodies have much to consider as they try to establish laws.

One answer would be for each deliberative body in each country around the world to establish their own research and consultative processes and try to reach the most equitable solution that reflects national culture and local needs. This is, after all, in theory what a democratic system would be expected to do.

Another answer would be for policy-making to go global: to search for best practices from around the world, seek out international agreements, and to find other means of ensuring the best outcome possible that may be harmonized around the world. The challenge with this model is that it is difficult for the parliaments of the world to come together to learn from one another and to come to agreements. Instead, this task is left to the executive arms of governments, who then bring these policies and experiences home to their legislatures.

This chapter is about this latter solution: the use of international policy dynamics to develop solutions to modern policy problems. In the 1990s researchers and policy experts noted that governments in North America and Western Europe had begun to use policy strategies and mechanisms that involved conducting policy-making at international fora. Actually, first they saw the results of use of these strategies and mechanisms: somehow the same policies were emerging around the world. They also noticed that deliberation in local parliaments was being superseded by the rise of international agreements on key policy areas. Quickly countries had the same draft laws, and shortly thereafter governments were pointing to other countries saying that we must follow their example.

The Clinton Administration and the European Union mastered this first phase of modern international policy dynamics. Policies on intellectual property and lawful access to personal information began appearing in legislatures around the world bearing similar language. Cognizant that globalization made it more challenging to enforce national laws and with the rise of jurisdictional challenges from global communications networks, the national and regional governments sought regional and global agreements.

Then in the 2000s, modern international policy dynamics were frequently used on security policy. Definitions of terrorism were being copied from Act to Act across countries; initiatives to gain access to personal information held on public and private sector data stores were spreading; and laws enabling new techniques of surveillance and data gathering were growing. Everywhere similar language emerged in law; and policy-makers delivered similar speeches. The narrative of 'global terror requires global solutions' was repeated in parliaments around the world as governments justified the passing of new laws where there was little understanding of local repercussions.

The challenge of engaging in the policy-making process became nearly insurmountable. Key stakeholders could not participate in international governmental organizations' meetings and negotiations. When these policies involved technologies and techniques, standards bodies became the meeting places – these organizations are often beyond the reach of non-industry stakeholders. Then, dealing with national policy initiatives meant understanding governments' claims of 'international obligations' and 'consensus', and understanding the effects of standards in technologies and practices.

This chapter is about these dynamics, but it is also about the lessons that policy researchers and civil society advocates learned as they tried to engage with international policy-making. It will discuss the dynamics in detail, identify some examples, but also identify some of the challenges in engaging in these policy processes. Some interventions by non-state actors were successful, however, and these stories are recounted. The chapter concludes by identifying emerging policy mechanisms that are used in modern deployments of globally-standardized policy-making.

MODELLING 'BEST PRACTICE'

Oftentimes when trying to counter a new policy proposal, we would be faced with the argument: most other governments have this power and they have not become police states, so we should be fine here. Whether it is the promotion of new surveillance laws or identity policy, governments have done their homework in assuring that they can point to other governments as examples.

Governments would model the practices of other countries, arguing that they needed to use the 'best practices' from around the world. This is by no means a new policy-making technique – laws are frequently copied, and often entire legal systems are adopted by other countries.

There is much in common between the legacy of British sedition and internal security laws in commonwealth countries, and the spread of modern anti-terrorism and security laws. In some cases this is because some governments lack the capacity to develop the sophisticated and delicate language required to pursue modern security threats. Another explanation is that governments find it easier to argue that harmonization is the primary purpose of legislative activity, and in turn, this can be used to minimize national discourse.

One instance arose when the Hong Kong government attempted to make changes to the Basic Law in order to deal with sedition. The changes were said only to be in an effort to harmonize the law with that of mainland China, harmonizing the list of groups that deserve special attention. When criticized about harmonizing with mainland China, the Hong Kong government argued that the earlier Basic Law was merely a harmonization with British law, and was in fact more severe. After protests, including one involving over 400,000 people, the government had to back down from these changes.

Another example is the policy discourse in Kenya. Following alerts from the United Kingdom and the United States, the Kenyan government released a Suppression of Terrorism Bill in June 2003. The bill provided for the power to detain any person in a place which is subject to an urgent search permit; any police officer above the rank of inspector may detain a suspect incommunicado for up to 36 hours without access to a lawyer, while also granting immunity to the police for application of 'reasonable force'. In broadening the list of those who can be identified as a terrorist, the bill provided that any individual who:

> (a) wears an item of clothing; or (b) wears, carries or displays an article, in such a way or in such circumstances as to arouse reasonable suspicion that he is a member or supporter of a declared terrorist organisation shall be guilty of an offence and shall be liable on conviction to imprisonment for a term not exceeding six months, or both.

As in Hong Kong, international policy dynamics were essential to this policy. Stories emerged of the United Kingdom and the United States pressuring Kenya to develop the legal regime to combat terrorism. They also noted that the law was an imitation of the USA PATRIOT Act 2001, the South African Terrorism Bill 2002 and Britain's Anti-Terrorism, Crime and Security Act 2001. Opponents to the bill in Parliament noted that:

> While the US Patriot Act (sic) is crafted in such a manner that targets foreigners and preserves the fundamental rights of American citizens, our own legislation seeks to reinvent the suppression of the fundamental rights and throws the bill of rights out of the window. (BBC 2003)

This relationship was denied by the Justice and Constitutional Affairs assistant minister Robinson Njeru Githae, as reported by Kenyan media, '[w]e have not to reinvented the wheel. What we have done is to pick the best of Suppression of Terrorism Act in the Commonwealth countries and given it a Kenyan outlook.' (Daily Nation 2003). That version of the bill failed after much controversy.

By merely stating that they are using 'best practices', governments are able to circumvent opposition. First, who would disagree with the august parliaments of Europe and North America, who must have thought through their policies with great care? And second, who has the capabilities to actually verify the content of these best practices to ensure local adherence?

For instance, when the UK government under Tony Blair was promoting ID cards, Blair often argued that the UK was out of step with the rest of Europe: 20 of 27 countries in the EU have ID cards. His argument was that these countries had ID cards, and so clearly those who were warning against ID cards on civil liberties grounds could not point to a single despotic EU country; and those who were opposing ID cards on feasibility grounds were clearly wrong in the court of European policy-maker opinion. It mattered little to Blair and the Labour government that the ID card being proposed in the UK was significantly different from the cards across Europe, and in fact the ID infrastructure he was promoting was likely to be illegal in some European countries such as Germany (Whitley and Hosein 2010).

LAUNDERING

Countries around the world copy laws not only from one another, but they use the guise of 'international conventions' as well. They do this by taking conventions from international bodies, signing on to them, ratifying and then implementing them into national law. This in itself is not a pernicious practice – these international bodies tend to be aligned to international legal principles such as human rights.

The United Nations places human rights at the core of its mission (UN Undated). The Council of Europe claims that its primary aim is 'to create a common democratic and legal area throughout the whole of the continent, ensuring respect for its fundamental values: human rights, democracy and the rule of law'. Language within these conventions is found in laws around the world, being a modern source of influence.

Other regional bodies are also sources of leadership. They are less duty-bound to human rights. The Association of Southeast Asian Nations (ASEAN) has as fundamental principles:

- Mutual respect for the independence, sovereignty, equality, territorial integrity, and national identity of all nations;
- The right of every State to lead its national existence free from external interference, subversion or coercion;
- Non-interference in the internal affairs of one another;
- Settlement of differences or disputes by peaceful manner;
- Renunciation of the threat or use of force; and
- Effective cooperation among themselves.

The African Union has extensive goals, of which human rights is indeed one, but one among many. The Commonwealth Secretariat also has many goals, grouped under two objectives of 'peace and democracy' (where we find human rights), and 'pro-poor growth and sustainable development (Commonwealth Secretariat, undated).

Many of the places where internet policy is being discussed most have even less of a focus on human rights. The Organisation for Economic Co-operation and Development (OECD), a modern source of strong influence on technology policy well beyond its membership, has as a mission to promote economic and social well-being but says nothing about human rights, liberty, or freedom. The G8 and the G20 also position themselves on economic issues, and make many political decisions, but are also silent on rights and liberties as they promote 'support growth and development' (G20 2010).

Governments have been known to use these international bodies to push policies. This is certainly not new – it is the art of statecraft and diplomacy in the post-World War II era. The difference with policy laundering is that governments sometimes push policies abroad on issues upon which they do not have consensus or approval at home. The most problematic practice arises when they then bring the policy home from the international body and convince their parliaments that the policy must be adopted because of 'international obligations'.

On a number of occasions we have seen liberally minded parliamentarians oppose a government surveillance policy until the government noted that it was merely adhering to international treaties and standards, at which point the liberally-minded internationalists would agree with the new policy. This technique also runs the risk of backfiring: an anti-internationalist parliamentarian would quickly raise the level of her opposition to a policy if it is seen as a foreign interference upon national policy-making.

It begins much as the 'modelling' policy dynamic, where governments copy international conventions and limit deliberation and debate. In the years after the terrorist attacks on the US in September 2001, governments around the world moved to ratify and implement into law the approximately 12 United Nations conventions on anti-terrorism. However, governments also added to and interpreted these conventions as they were adapted to national law. For example, according to the *New Zealand Herald*, Justice Minister Phil Goff stated in April 2003 that the new Counter-Terrorism Bill 'was the final step in adopting the last of 12 United Nations conventions aimed at fighting terrorism . . . It will give police and customs officers more powers to fight terrorism, including enabling police to use tracking devices, and will allow evidence found in the investigation of one crime to be used in the prosecution of another' (*New Zealand Herald* 2003).

These additional powers are not included within the standard conventions, however. Earlier the government minimized public consultation on a proposed law to freeze the financial assets of suspected terrorists because the government felt it was bound to act by these international agreements, which again was not a requirement of these conventions.

Human Rights and Cybercrime

Sometimes these can actually run counter to the very purposes of the international organizations. For instance, the Council of Europe has been busy promoting its Cybercrime Convention of 2001 around the world. Originally drafted for Council of Europe member states, proponents of the convention were reluctant to build too many safeguards into the Convention because they felt it was built upon the CoE's strong human rights foundation, and in particular the European Convention on Human Rights of 1950. But as it promotes the Cybercrime Convention in countries outside the CoE, it is not also promoting the Human Rights Convention. Governments are therefore seeing the Cybercrime Convention as a mechanism to increase their powers to combat cybercrime, but are not being compelled to question the human rights issues that are implicated.

It is therefore of little surprise that despite the Council of Europe's commitment to rights and freedoms, the Pakistani Ordinance on Cybercrime of 2007, promoted as being consistent with the CoE Convention on Cybercrime, goes well beyond the Convention. The 2007 version of the ordinance contended that: 'whoever commits the offence of cyber terrorism and causes death of any person shall be punishable with death or imprisonment for life' and for the criminalization of communicating 'obscene, vulgar, profane, lewd, lascivious, or indecent language, picture or image' (Pakistan 2007). One of the Council of Europe's primary goals is to end the use of the death penalty across Europe.

The above examples of policy laundering only show the mechanisms through which governments bring policies back home in misleading ways. Governments also push their policies through these international bodies. The leading examples of this practice are both from the UK.

Identity

The Blair government was very keen to implement its ID card programme as a response to the terrorist attacks on September 11 2001. The government knew that costs were a major consideration because what they had planned had never been trialled before on a national scale: a central register of an entire adult population's biometric information (fingerprints, iris scans, and facial scans). As above, first they argued that ID cards were in place in over 20 European countries. This was helpful in countering claims that ID cards were illiberal in principle. But the cost issue still loomed.

Next, the Labour government decided to claim that the biometrics were a necessary implementation due to US requirements for biometric passports. That is, in October 2001 the US Congress passed a law requiring biometrics in passports of countries that want to stay in the visa waiver programme. The US requirement was that the International Civil Aviation Organization (ICAO), a UN agency, would decide the biometrics to be included in the passport.

The negotiations then moved to ICAO meetings in Canada and Egypt. The natural choice for a biometric was facial recognition because the passport document already carried a photograph. As a result, in early 2003 ICAO approved the new standard for e-passports to include facial recognition (amongst other technologies such as RFID). European governments, including the UK government, pushed hard for the inclusion of additional biometrics, most notably fingerprints and iris scans. Though they were unable to gain approval for the mandatory inclusion of fingerprints and iris scans, they were able to reach a settlement: later in 2003 ICAO declared in a compromise that while the facial biometric would be the standard, countries may choose to add other secondary biometrics to the passport. ICAO remained concerned, however, by the idea of governments collecting these biometrics in a centralized register.

The result was that the US requirement for the visa waiver scheme countries was that in order to remain in the visa waiver scheme, governments would have to include digital photographs of the face of the passport holder. There was no requirement for a centralized register of biometrics, and no requirement for fingerprints or other biometrics.

This was not a satisfactory development for the Labour government as they needed to insist that there were international obligations to create a biometric register. They continued to point to the US as the external force for insisting on a centralized register of iris, fingerprint and facial biometrics, and few in Parliament knew otherwise to question the truth of that position.

Instead the UK government was amongst the leading governments that took the policy to Europe: unhappy with the exclusion of other biometrics in the international passport standard, these governments pushed the European Union to adopt a passport standard that required fingerprints to be included as well. The European Parliament eventually approved this standard, though it was never specified how many fingerprints were to be included, nor whether there would be a centralized register. One limitation however was that the passport standard would only apply to those countries that are members of the Schengen Agreement that removed internal borders across the EU. The UK government was not a member of this agreement.

Regardless, the UK government was now able to argue that there was an EU standard for biometric passports that would be required. The Blair government was then able to argue that the vast majority of the costs of the ID register in the UK (70 per cent) were to be covered by the mandatory biometric passport scheme; ID cards were merely a convenience on top of the required passport innovations.

Through policy laundering, Blair was now able to make the following statement:

> The case for ID cards is a case not about liberty but about the modern world. Biometrics give us the chance to have secure identity and the bulk of the ID cards' cost will have to be spent on the new biometric passports in any event. (Blair 2006)

There were three challenges to this approach. First, the US requirement did not include fingerprints. In fact, the US politicians who had promoted the original legislation to require biometric passports in 2001 grew concerned with the length of time it was taking European governments to develop the new passports because of their insistence on including fingerprints. US Representative James Sensenbrenner, then Chair of the Judiciary Committee (who had actually introduced the USA PATRIOT Act to the Congress in 2001) travelled to Europe to lobby governments to reconsider their insistence on fingerprints.

> While the added biometric element will strongly assist in confirming the identity of the passport holder, it further adds to the technical obstacles to completing the process and increases the cost of inspection infrastructure. . . . In my view, much expense and public consternation could have been avoided by a less technically ambitious approach, one that simply met the terms of the Act as written. (Sensenbrenner 2005)

The second challenge to the Blair government's approach was that the UK is not a member of the Schengen Agreement and therefore was not required to collect fingerprints. When this was eventually discovered in Parliamentary debates, the government responded that it did not want the British Passport to be a second-class document by not having additional security mechanisms – even though the US passport itself did not include fingerprints.

The third challenge was that none of these systems required a centralized register. Despite this, many politicians in the UK Parliament decided that because there were European requirements, then a fingerprint registry was necessary.

Academics, select journalists and advocates were able to disentangle the 'requirements', though it did take four years to convince politicians of the case. In December 2010 the newly elected Conservative–Liberal Democrat coalition government in the UK scrapped the identity card, and, importantly, also scrapped any requirement for the UK passport to implement the EU standard. The UK passport will not require fingerprints.

Other European countries have also faced some challenges in deploying the fingerprint passport standard. France tried to mimic the UK ID card plans but failed to achieve a consensus on how to build it. The German Parliament debated extensively the requirement to collect fingerprints and elected to only include two fingerprints in the passport but rejected the idea of creating a central store of fingerprints. In the spring of 2011, after 3000 citizens signed a petition opposing the collection of fingerprints for the Dutch passport, the Dutch government announced that it was also going to cease storing the fingerprint data from passport applications (Radio Netherlands Worldwide 2011).

Data Retention

Similar political mechanisms were used to require telecommunications service providers to retain personal information on their users. That is, for a number of years governments in the US and the UK were pushing for telecommunications data retention: a policy that required ISPs and telephone companies to retain information on individuals' usage patterns (websites visited, emails sent and received, phone calls made and received, and possibly locations at the time). These governments were unsuccessful at winning the national discourse. They both pursued the policy actively at the G8 in 2000 and 2001 but could not reach a settlement (Hosein 2008).

After 9/11 both governments considered including data retention policies in their legislative responses to the attacks. While the USA PATRIOT Act neglected to include retention (and it took until July 2011 for such a policy to be introduced into Congress), the UK government included a voluntary regime into the Anti-Terrorism, Crime and Security Act of 2001.

With little debate, in December 2001 the UK Parliament approved voluntary data retention. That is, telecommunications providers could voluntarily retain this information for up to two years. The law also empowered the government to make the requirement mandatory if it was unhappy with the industry response. So began years of negotiation with industry on how to successfully manage a voluntary regime.

There were two international gambits for the UK government to play, both at the European level. First, data retention was an illegal practice under the EU Data Protection Directive that requires that companies delete information that is no longer necessary. Laws that require retention on a mass scale are incompatible with this requirement. The UK government, alongside other governments, pushed successfully in 2003 for an amendment to EU law that permitted governments to allow for data retention in their laws.

The second challenge was that industry in the UK argued that they did not think that retention was an acceptable practice particularly when their European compatriots did not have to retain the data as the UK was nearly alone amongst EU countries in implementing retention policy. Following the Madrid bombings in 2004, some governments across the EU tried to implement a data retention requirement into EU law through a decision at the Council of the European Union. At the Council, governments themselves have voting rights. This was later deemed to be an illegal application of the Council's jurisdiction and it was then decided that any such European law would have to be approved as a Directive, through the European Parliament.

Following the London terrorist attacks in the summer of 2005, the UK government held the EU Presidency and lobbied the European Parliament to approve an EU-wide Directive mandating the retention of telecommunications data for two years. Promising the European Parliament greater powers, the governments of Ireland and Sweden also applied pressure. In December 2005 the European Parliament approved the EU Directive on Telecommunications Data Retention, requiring that by 2009 all EU member states deploy a mandatory data retention regime.

With data retention laws deployed across Europe, opposition to the practice has arisen in some quarters. Over 30,000 Germans signed on to a legal case opposing data retention that reached the Federal Constitutional Court. Courts in Romania and Bulgaria have ruled that data retention is incompatible with human rights law.

Despite this, retention continues unabated. For instance, following the Romanian Court decision against data retention (Romanian Constitutional Court 2009), the Romanian Parliament had to go back and reconsider the law. The Romanian Ministry of Information, Society and Communication (MSCI) is proposing a new data retention law, arguing that the EU Directive has equal legal status to Constitutional Court decisions:

> The Constitutional Court says you may not retain for 6 months the traffic data of a person that is not under penal investigation and we were retaining all citizens' data. On the other hand, this is against the EU directive, which asks to retain this data for a minimum of 6 months. Here, we are in a deadlock. (EDRI 2011)

In the UK, the opposition parties argued against data retention. In fact, when the two opposition parties created a coalition agreement to create a government following the elections of spring 2010, one of the clauses of the agreement included abandoning data retention (and ID cards and the EU passport standard). But no further action has taken place, despite all the action on other surveillance policy domains.

Dismantling data retention has proved to be more difficult as there is still a legal requirement at the European Union, and single court decisions in countries have yet to result in significant changes in law. This is a case of policy laundering that has stuck.

Consistent with the dynamics above, it is therefore of little surprise that the Pakistani Cybercrime Ordinance of 2007 included a data retention requirement. The government argued that this was merely an implementation of the Council of Europe Cybercrime Convention. However the Cybercrime Convention does not contain any reference to data retention. It took some convincing on our behalf to convince our partners in Pakistan that this was the case, as the government had been arguing adamantly otherwise.

EMBEDDING WITHIN STANDARDS

A final form of modern policy dynamics is to embed policy within mechanisms other than law. Much like how passport standards were used as political mechanisms to create national registries of biometric data, sometimes it is easier to get policies approved through technical standards committees rather than through combative and deliberative parliaments.

Iran and Nokia Siemens Networks

This is best illustrated with the example of the Iranian government's ability to spy on the opposition movements. In 2009 following the Iranian elections and the subsequent crackdown on protestors, the *Wall Street Journal* released a story about how the European company Nokia Siemens Networks had created the capability for the Iranian government to monitor communications in the country (Rhoads and Chao 2009).

The European Parliament responded in a resolution that it 'strongly criticises international companies, in particular Nokia Siemens, for providing the Iranian authorities with the necessary censorship and surveillance technology, thus being instrumental in the persecution and arrest of Iranian dissidents' (European Parliament 2010).

The roots of this practice go much deeper than a single company, and actually involve the complicity of European standards bodies. In the 1990s the Clinton administration introduced a law that would require telecommunications companies to develop technologies that allowed for lawful access to communications. Worried that innovations in traditional voice communications technologies would make it increasingly difficult for government authorities to use their lawful powers to intercept and monitor communications, the Communications Assistance for Law Enforcement Act provided an incentive and subsidy to US telecommunications companies to develop backdoors into their new technologies.

These companies were not immediately pleased with the requirement, and the half-billion dollar subsidy did not have the effect that the Clinton administration had hoped. Some within industry argued that because the law only applied to US companies it placed these companies at a disadvantage while competing globally.

The Clinton administration decided to push this policy internationally. With the support of other governments it sought to create a telecommunications standard for this lawful access requirement. It pursued this through the standard process at the European Telecommunications Standards Institute. At the same time, governments across Europe began implementing similar laws requiring access to modern communications infrastructures, but unlike the US these countries individually did not have jurisdiction over the telecommunications technology manufacturers. ETSI not only developed the standard in accordance with CALEA, but went beyond CALEA's reach and developed lawful access standards for mobile telephony, internet communications, and data retention (ETSI undated).

When Nokia Siemens was called to the European Parliament to explain their transactions in Iran, they stated that:

> Lawful Interception . . . is the name given to an internationally agreed approach for law enforcement authorities to intercept communications running over networks within their jurisdiction. It is a principle noted in the constitution of the International Telecommunications Union; addressed in several resolutions of the Council of the European Union; and firmly embedded in transparent technical standards, including those set out by the European Telecommunications Standards Institute (ETSI) and the 3GPP (3rd Generation Partnership Project). (French 2010)

Nokia Siemens Networks correctly pointed out that the practice was endorsed by the Council of the European Union, within the very same institution that was now questioning the ethics of the motives of a mere implementer.

It is therefore of little surprise that modern telecommunications kit sold in Europe and the US contains capabilities for law enforcement to conduct surveillance. And unless they are required otherwise, telecommunications technology will sell these same technologies to countries outside Europe. No simple change in law in a single country will restrict this practice now that it is embedded within technology standards, and in turn, into technology itself.

FAILING IN NEW WAYS

In many ways, our research in the early 2000s was successful at identifying the trend of modern policy dynamics to include modelling, policy laundering, and embedding. In some cases this research led to real policy change. The prime example emerged in the UK as policy-makers and politicians were compelled to understand the international policy dynamics of biometrics and passports, leading to the demise of the ID card and the requirement for fingerprints in UK passports.

In most cases, however, the policy objectives are well embedded in international conventions, 'best practices', and technological standards. Despite political upheavals that would normally result in policy change, many of the policies identified above are still in place.

Even where there have been some policy changes, the policies identified in this chapter continue to spread, but through new means. Interception laws are now becoming matters of debate in countries around the world, including Egypt (MacFarquar and Stack 2011), India (Arun and Subramani 2011), and Indonesia (Oktofani 2011). Identity cards and national registers are spreading throughout Africa, including Ethiopia (Anerbir 2010), Mozambique (Agencia de Informacao de Mocambique 2010), Nigeria (Babalola 2011), and even calls for regional IDs (Muramira 2011).

While there is some modelling, and the security agenda still dominates what little policy debate may be occurring, there are new dynamics at play. After all, how is it that these policies and technologies are spreading in developing countries that have far fewer resources? Why is it that national registries are spreading in countries where there is often a lack of essential resources? For instance, the largest identity project on earth is now taking place in India. The UID programme, now entitled 'Aadhaar', plans to fingerprint and iris scan the entire Indian population in the next few years to issue them all with unique identity numbers. Unlike in the UK where the primary argument was for national security, the Indian government is contending this is an aid project: if they can identify people, then development would occur more effectively.

This more noble development agenda is behind many of the schemes around the world. We are only now discovering that identity programmes and national patient records systems are being deployed with UNDP and World Bank funding. When we worked with the UN Refugee Agency in Djibouti we discovered that the UN agency's fingerprinting programme was being funded by Western governments including the Netherlands, while the Djiboutian government minister informed us that the Humanitarian Aid department of the European Commission (ECHO) was funding Djibouti's national ID infrastructure. Rather than the mere spread of ideas, we are now seeing the distribution of funds. These systems are being deployed without the safeguards that exist in the very countries and institutions that are funding them.

Now that the security policy agenda that followed the terrorist attacks in the US and Western Europe in 2001, 2004, and 2005 no longer has the saliency it once did, other policy agendas are the driving forces, using additional policy mechanisms. Just as advocates and researchers questioned the integrity of the claims of governments before in the war on terrorism, we will have to once again question the identified goals of development. My great worry is that in the first era of modern policy dynamics we risked appearing as though we were ignorant of the risks of terrorism; in this second era we will appear to be on the wrong side of humanitarian causes.

Ethics and morality aside, the greatest challenge that we had identified with modern international policy dynamics was that the quality of the policy discourse was being eroded. When parliaments are told that a government's new policy is merely an attempt to catch up with other countries or international conventions, politicians become less likely to question the details of the policy proposals. When these policies involve human rights and technological details, great attention and scrutiny is perhaps even more necessary. So the weakening of debate and scrutiny was the greatest casualty of modelling, policy laundering, and embedding policy quietly within technology. Now with foreign funding sources, governments are not compelled to question the value for money for policies, which is often the only debate that is inherent to all policy proposals. If the scrutiny fails at even that most basic stage, it will take considerable effort to ensure it does not fail on issues relating to technology, human rights, and whether we are building a better place while we try to solve problems we are not compelled to understand.

BIBLIOGRAPHY

Agencia de Informacao de Mocambique (Maputo) (2010), 'Mozambique: Biometric personal record card now in use', 13 December 2010.

Anerbir, Y. (2010), 'Diaspora asked to return for finger printing', *NewsDire*.

Arun, M. and L. Subramani (2011), 'India ahead in snooping: Google', *Deccan Herald*, 28 June 2011.

Babalola, J. (2011), 'Analysis of 67.7m fingerprints begins today', *The Nation*, 25 February 2011.

Baumgartner, F.R., B.D.Jones and J.D. Wilkerson (2002), 'Studying policy dynamics', in F.R. Baumgartner and B.D. Jones (eds), *Policy Dynamics*, Chicago: University of Chicago Press.

BBC News (2003), 'Kenya's terror bill rejected', 15 July 2003.

Blair, T. (2006), 'We need ID cards to secure our borders and ease modern life', http://www.telegraph.co.uk/comment/personal-view/3633979/We-need-ID-cards-to-secure-our-borders-and-ease-modern-life.html.

Braithwaite, J. and P. Drahos (2000), *Global Business Regulation*, Cambridge: Cambridge University Press.

Commonwealth Secretariat (undated), 'What we do', http://www.thecommonwealth.org/Internal/190957/what_we_do/.

Daily Nation (2003), 'Kenya: Anti-Terror Bill is not foreign, says Minister', http://allafrica.com/stories/200306300756.html.

EDRI (2011), 'Translation of MSCI's Expunere de Motive' in http://www.edri.org/edrigram/number9.13/new-draft-data-retention-romania, http://www.mcsi.ro/Transparenta-decizionala/24/ExpunereMotive (original).

ETSI (undated), 'Lawful Interception module', http://www.etsi.org/WebSite/Technologies/LawfulInterception.aspx.

European Parliament (2010), 'European Parliament resolution of 10 February 2010 on Iran', http://www.europarl.europa.eu/sides/getDoc.do?pubRef=-//EP//TEXT+TA+P7-TA-2010-0016+0+DOC+XML+V0//EN&language=EN.

French, B. (2010), 'Statement from Barry French, Executive Board Member and Head of Marketing and Corporate Affairs, Nokia Siemens Networks', European Parliament, Subcommittee on Human Rights Hearing on New Information Technologies and Human Rights, 2 June 2010.

G20 (2010), 'What is the G20', http://www.g20.org/about_what_is_g20.aspx.

Hosein, I. (2008), 'Creating Conventions', in W.J. Drake and E.J. Wilson III (eds), *Governing Global Electronic Networks*, Cambridge, Mass: MIT Press.

Kingdon, J.W. (1995), *Agendas, Alternatives, and Public Policies*, 2nd ed., New York: HarperCollins College Publishers.

MacFarquar H. and L. Stack (2011), 'Egyptians get view of extent of spying', *New York Times*, 9 March 2011.

Muramira, G. (2011), 'Rwanda: Mukaruliza calls for regional ID forum', *The New Times*, 2 June 2011, http://allafrica.com/stories/201106020037.html.

New Zealand Herald (2003), 'PM's war stance criticised as Parliament debates terrorism bill', *New Zealand Herald*, 2 April 2003.

Oktofani, E. (2011), 'Activists want wiretapping safeguards', *Jakarta Globe*, 26 March 2011.

Pakistan (2007), 'Cybercrime Ordinance of the Islamic Republic of Pakistan', 2007.

Radio Netherlands Worldwide (2011), 'Storage of passport fingerprints ends in July', 5 July 2011, http://www.rnw.nl/africa/bulletin/storage-passport-fingerprints-ends-july.

Rhoads, C. and L. Chao (2009), 'Iran's web spying aided by Western technology', *Wall Street Journal*, 22 July 2009, http://online.wsj.com/article/SB124562668777335653.html.

Romanian Constitutional Court (2009), 'Constitutional Court Decision', **no. 1258**, 8 October 2009.

Sensenbrenner Jr., F.J. (2005), 'Letter to His Excellency Luc Frieden, President of the European Council of Ministers and to His Excellency Franco Frattini, Vice President of the European Commission from F. James Sensenbrenner Jr., Chairman of the House of Representatives Committee on the Judiciary', 7 April 2005, http://www. privacyinternational.org/article.shtml?cmd[347]=x-347-234812.

UN (undated), 'Charter of the United Nations', http://www.un.org/en/documents/charter/ preamble.shtml.

Whitley, E. and G. Hosein (2010), *Global Challenges for Identity Policy*, London: Palgrave Macmillan.

12. Child abuse images and cleanfeeds: assessing internet blocking systems
T.J. McIntyre

INTRODUCTION

One of the most important trends in internet governance in recent years has been the growth of internet blocking as a policy tool, to the point where it is increasingly becoming a global norm. This is most obvious in states such as China where blocking is used to suppress political speech; however, in the last decade blocking has also become more common in democracies, usually as part of attempts to limit the availability of child abuse images. Numerous governments have therefore settled on blocking as their "primary solution" towards preventing such images from being distributed (Villeneuve 2010).

Child abuse image blocking has, however, been extremely controversial within the academic, civil liberties and technical communities, and this debate has recently taken on a wider public dimension. At the time of writing, for example, public pressure has forced the German Federal Government to abandon legislation which would have introduced a police run system while the European Parliament has also rejected Commission proposals for mandatory blocking (Baker 2011; Zuvela 2011).

Why have these systems been so controversial? Two lines of criticism can be identified, which might be termed the practical and the principled. The practical argument claims that blocking is ineffective, with ill-defined goals and easily evaded by widely available circumvention technologies (see e.g. Callanan et al. 2009). The principled argument, on the other hand, is that blocking systems undermine the norms associated with freedom of expression in democratic societies (Brown 2008). This latter argument stems from the fact that blocking sits at the intersection of three different regulatory trends – the use of technological solutions ("code as law"), a focus on intermediaries and the use of self-regulation in preference to legislation – which individually and all the more so collectively create a risk of invisible and unaccountable "censorship by proxy" (Kreimer 2006; McIntyre and Scott 2008).

This chapter introduces and evaluates these claims by examining three prominent examples of child abuse image blocking – the United Kingdom

Internet Watch Foundation ("IWF") Child Abuse Image Content ("CAIC") list, the European Union sponsored CIRCAMP system and United States hash value systems. It discusses the operation of each system and the extent to which the critics' concerns are borne out. It concludes by considering the lessons which might be learned for proposals to extend blocking to other types of content.

BACKGROUND AND REGULATORY CONTEXT

From the early days of the internet it was clear that the technology it embodied – in particular its possibilities for anonymity, decentralised distribution of content and regulatory arbitrage – threatened the ability of governments to control content such as child abuse images. Johnson and Post (1996) famously expressed this "cyber-libertarian" view when they argued that "efforts to control the flow of electronic information across physical borders – to map local regulation and physical boundaries onto Cyberspace – are likely to prove futile".

In response, however, "cyber-realists" argued that governments could adapt by shifting regulatory strategies. Three approaches in particular were identified and have since been widely adopted.

Regulation by Code

The first, most associated with Lessig (1999), stressed the role of code (software) as a means of regulation. Lessig noted that while the first generation of the internet was structured in such a way as to provide for anonymous speech, decentralised distribution and the use of encryption, there was no guarantee that this structure would persist. Instead, he pointed out, the architecture of the internet could easily be remade to facilitate governmental control – and to do so in an automated manner which could be much more efficient than more traditional means of enforcement.

Intermediary-based Regulation

The second, articulated by Boyle (1997) and Swire (1998), rejected the argument that the decentralised and international nature of the internet makes it difficult or impossible to control the conduct of users who may be anonymous or whose location might be uncertain. Instead, it was argued, regulators could simply resort to indirect enforcement, targeting intermediaries rather than end users. For example, Boyle presciently suggested that the state might target ISPs, pressuring or requiring them to "prevent copyright infringement through technical surveillance".

This argument relied on the fact that the effect of internet disintermediation was oversold – while there has certainly been a great deal of disintermediation, there has also been the creation of entirely new intermediaries with greater technical and legal powers to control the actions of their users. For example, as compared with the post office an ISP or webmail provider has greater technical capability to screen communications, and may not be covered by older laws prohibiting this. Consequently, the ISP, search engine, hosting provider and others have become the new gatekeepers or "internet points of control" and can be enlisted to stop the transmission of child abuse images (Zittrain 2003).

Self- and Co-regulation

Closely related to the use of intermediaries, the third approach involved the promotion by governments of industry self- and co-regulatory schemes, which became so common in the internet context that they have been described as the presumptive starting points for regulation of information technology (Koops et al. 2006).

These schemes appeared to offer substantial benefits for states and industry alike. By harnessing industry expertise and responsiveness, they dealt with the objections that governments lacked the knowledge necessary to regulate the internet and that legislation could not keep up with the pace of change online. Self-regulation also offered governments the possibility of outsourcing enforcement and minimising the accompanying costs, while industry was attracted by the promise of a flexible and light touch regulatory regime which might ward off more intrusive legislative intervention (Price and Verhulst 2005).

DEVELOPMENT OF CHILD ABUSE IMAGE BLOCKING

The three strategies mentioned above – a focus on intermediaries, regulation by code and the use of self- and co-regulation – neatly dovetail in the form of internet blocking which of its nature involves regulation by software and which generally (though not invariably) also involves ISPs and other intermediaries operating in a self- or co-regulatory context (McIntyre and Scott 2008).

Perhaps unsurprisingly, child abuse images have led the growth of blocking in democracies. Child abuse is a particularly abhorrent crime and as a result there has been a substantial degree of both domestic and international consensus as to the illegality of such images. Unlike many other types of content which governments seek to filter – such as adult pornography or file-sharing sites – the blocking of child abuse images has until recently generally provoked little public controversy (All Party Parliamentary Communications Group 2009, p. 9).

There is also an important practical aspect which has favoured this type of blocking. As compared with other types of content, there are fewer websites or images which are potentially illegal. The IWF CAIC list, for example, currently contains about 500 URLs at any one time (Internet Watch Foundation 2011a). In addition, judgments about child abuse images are easier to make than judgments about other types of content. Whether something "glorifies terrorism" contrary to the UK Terrorism Act 2006 requires a difficult assessment of the context, including how it is likely to be understood by members of the public (Banisar 2008, p.21). By contrast, the evaluation of child abuse images does not generally present the same difficulty. As a result, the systems required to monitor, blacklist, and ultimately block child abuse images present fewer administrative and technological difficulties.

In relation to child abuse images, blocking by ISPs also appeared to solve the problem that states could not control material hosted beyond their national borders – enabling them to take action on a domestic basis against material hosted abroad without the international cooperation necessary to have it removed at source. Children's advocacy groups therefore began to lobby for blocking as a form of situational crime prevention (See e.g. Carr and Hilton 2009).

These lobbying efforts have been remarkably successful, and during the last decade systems have been adopted in numerous jurisdictions including: the United Kingdom, Norway, Sweden, Denmark, Canada, Switzerland, Italy, Netherlands, Finland, New Zealand and most recently France (Villeneuve 2010; New Zealand Department of Internal Affairs 2010; La Quadrature du Net 2011).

In addition to these national systems, public and government pressure has led to many individual companies also adopting their own systems, with prominent examples including Google (search results), AOL (email attachments) and Facebook (uploaded images) (Office of the Attorney General 2010; Committee on Energy and Commerce 2006).

CASE STUDIES

These blocking systems all attempt to control the same basic subject matter. In almost every other way, however, they differ from each other.

Consider, for example, one of the most basic issues: who decides what material is to be blocked? The United Kingdom has pioneered an industry-led approach where decisions are made by a private body (albeit one with extensive links to the state), most European jurisdictions have adopted a police-led approach where a designated unit within the police force is responsible, while within the United States at least one major ISP (AOL) has preferred to create a blocking list entirely in-house, concerned that it would be treated as a state actor if it relied on a government provided list (Tambini et al. 2008; Dedman and Sullivan 2008).

Other aspects also differ greatly. While some blocking systems are purely preventive, others have been used for police intelligence gathering and even prosecution purposes. The channels which are filtered also vary, with some systems focusing solely on the web while others extend also to email, search engines and filesharing. Similarly, the technologies used vary from the crude (DNS poisoning) to the more sophisticated (hybrid URL blocking, hash value matching). Some systems operate at a purely national level, while others have an international effect. Perhaps most importantly, only a tiny minority of blocking systems are underpinned by legislation, with the majority operating on a voluntary or self-regulatory basis (Callanan et al. 2009).

This diversity of approaches makes it difficult to generalise about the issues presented. For example, a system which blocks at the domain name level (blocking all access to example.com) will certainly raise concerns as to proportionality and fears that significant quantities of innocent material will be blocked; while more granular systems which block at the level of the individual file may require much greater scrutiny of the actions of users, thus raising fresh concerns as to user privacy and function creep.

The following section will tease out these issues by examining three of the most prominent schemes. These systems – the IWF CAIC list, the EU funded CIRCAMP network, and the United States hash value blocking systems – cover a variety of different technologies and stages at which blocking can be deployed. Figure 12.1 (adapted from Ofcom 2008) illustrates this point by depicting the internet content chain and showing the stages at which these systems operate. Although blocking is most commonly associated with controlling *access*, we will see from the US hash value systems that it can also be used as a means of controlling *availability* also, by scanning and blocking files at the point of uploading.

IWF CAIC List ("Cleanfeed")

Since 1996 the UK has seen the development of an industry-led response to child abuse images. A private body funded by the internet industry and

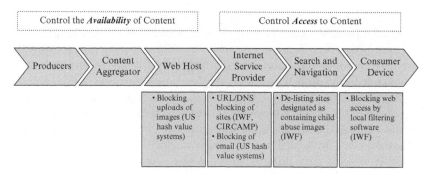

Producers	Content Aggregator	Web Host	Internet Service Provider	Search and Navigation	Consumer Device

| | • Blocking uploads of images (US hash value systems) | • URL/DNS blocking of sites (IWF, CIRCAMP) • Blocking of email (US hash value systems) | • De-listing sites designated as containing child abuse images (IWF) | • Blocking web access by local filtering software (IWF) |

Figure 12.1   Examples of blocking

the EU – the IWF – has acted as a hotline which works with police and government to receive public complaints and determine whether particular web pages contain potentially illegal material (including but not limited to child abuse images). If so, the IWF then forwards those complaints to the police and (where material is hosted in the UK) to the hosting provider in order to have that material removed (Walden 2010).

This approach has been remarkably successful at reducing the hosting of illegal material in the UK. It was, however, effective only in relation to domestic material. Where child abuse images were hosted abroad, takedown was dependent on the actions of local authorities and the material would remain available to UK users in the interim – or indefinitely where no local action was taken.

This limitation prompted British Telecom (BT) to develop a system which would block access to web pages hosted outside the UK. The technical system which they produced – dubbed "Cleanfeed" – represented a substantial step forward over the two main forms of web blocking then in use (IP address blocking and DNS poisoning). By using a two stage approach to blocking which combined redirection of traffic with the use of web proxies it filtered at the level of the full URL and appeared to minimise collateral damage. As compared with DNS poisoning, for example, it was capable of selectively blocking only http://example.com/users/johndoe/lolita.jpg, rather than all the material hosted at example.com (Clayton 2005). In addition, it should be noted that BT deliberately designed this system in such a way as to avoid logging data on users – effectively precluding its use for prosecution purposes and enabling them to present it as being solely for the protection of their customers (Hutty 2004).

Having developed this system, BT then persuaded the IWF to make its database of URLs available for blocking purposes. This was done in

2004, when the IWF first distributed its CAIC list to members. In mid-2004, therefore, BT began to trial the Cleanfeed system. Following the apparent success of this trial and the proof of concept it provided, there soon followed substantial pressure from politicians and children's advocacy groups for other ISPs to follow BT's example – including Home Office threats to introduce legislation compelling blocking unless ISPs "voluntarily" complied (Hargrave 2006).

This pressure convinced almost all UK ISPs to introduce filtering systems similar to BT's Cleanfeed, and government plans for legislation were ultimately abandoned in 2009 following an Ofcom survey which established that 98.6 per cent of home connections were subject to blocking systems. The UK government remains committed to 100 per cent coverage, however, and has relied on consumer pressure as well as its own purchasing power as a means of encouraging compliance amongst the remaining smaller ISPs (Williams 2009; O'Neill 2010).

At the time of writing, therefore, there is near universal coverage of UK users by blocking systems which filter against the IWF CAIC list. There is also a spill over effect to ISPs in many other jurisdictions (such as Ireland) where the IWF list is used in the absence of a local blocking system (GSMA Mobile Alliance Against Child Sexual Abuse Content 2008). In addition, the IWF list is widely deployed in home, workplace and school filtering software and is also used by search engines (including both Bing and Google) on a worldwide basis to remove URLs from search results (Internet Watch Foundation 2011b). When considered in terms of numbers of users covered, therefore, the IWF list may well be the most widely used blocking list ever. The UK model has also been influential elsewhere, and the name "Cleanfeed" has stuck as a generic term for UK blocking systems as well as related schemes in Canada and Australia (see e.g. Watt and Maurushat 2009).

It is striking, however, that this system has developed without any legislative basis, and has done so in a way which entrusts a private body with the role of determining whether content is "potentially illegal" with limited procedural safeguards and no judicial oversight. This became the subject of controversy in 2008, when the IWF added certain pages on Wikipedia to its URL list – before backing down and reversing its decision just five days later following a storm of public criticism (Davies 2009).

That episode focused public attention on the system and highlighted many issues raised by blocking. One of the first related to the blocked content itself. The pages blocked by the IWF did not match the public perception of child abuse images – instead, they contained a well known album cover from 1976 featuring a nude photograph of a prepubescent girl. While this image may well have been "potentially illegal" under

English law the overwhelming public view was that it should not have been blocked – not least because the album itself remained for sale in UK record shops. This in turn focused public attention on the basis of the power of the IWF to make censorship decisions for the entire UK internet (Edwards 2009).

Substantial collateral damage also emerged. Despite the claimed superiority of two stage URL blocking systems, it soon became clear that many users found themselves unable to edit Wikipedia – even pages completely unrelated to the block – due to the use of proxy servers as part of the blocking system (Clayton 2008).

The Wikipedia incident also demonstrated a remarkable lack of transparency and procedural safeguards. There was no notice given to Wikipedia either before or after its pages were blacklisted, and most ISPs presented deceptive error messages to users who attempted to access the blocked pages – with the notable exception of Demon Internet which notified users of the blocking via a stop page.

In addition, as Wikipedia soon discovered, the IWF system does not provide for any judicial appeal against its decisions – while there is an internal review procedure, the only external input into that system comes from the police (Internet Watch Foundation 2010a).

Some of the issues raised by the Wikipedia incident have since been addressed by the IWF – in particular, new policies allow it to use greater discretion in relation to borderline cases where blocking is likely to be counterproductive, while greater emphasis is now placed on seeking the removal of material at source where possible (Internet Watch Foundation undated). There remains, however, substantial controversy as to the role of the IWF. The majority of commentators would appear to share the views of Edwards (2009), who argues that if a blocking system is to be implemented then it should be put on a statutory basis. As against that, however, there is a strong minority view which argues that the IWF – precisely because of its industry-led nature – has served as a buffer against further state regulation of the internet (see e.g. Walden 2010).

CIRCAMP

Within Europe, the single most common type of blocking is based on the EU funded CIRCAMP (COSPOL Internet Related Child Abuse Material Project) model. As with Cleanfeed, this also focuses on blocking at the ISP level – unlike that system, however, the CIRCAMP approach relies on police to designate what material is to be blocked (McIntyre 2010).

CIRCAMP has its origins in Norway which, in 2004, paralleled the UK by adopting a national child abuse material blocking system.

Unlike Cleanfeed, however, the Norwegian system was police-led so that decisions as to which domains to block were made by the National Criminal Investigation Service. In addition, that system used DNS blocking only, rather than the hybrid URL based blocking associated with most Cleanfeed implementations (Deibert and Rohozinski 2010).

The experience of the Norwegian police in operating their domestic blocking system later led to Norway becoming the primary driver of the CIRCAMP project. From 2006 onwards this project has helped national police forces to adopt Child Sexual Abuse Anti-Distribution Filters (CSAADF) which are closely modelled on the Norwegian system. Currently eight countries – Denmark, Finland, Italy, Malta, Norway, Sweden, Switzerland and New Zealand – are using CSAADF blocking systems. This is generally done on a voluntary basis by ISPs, without any legislative underpinning.

The CIRCAMP project has followed the Norwegian approach by promoting the use of DNS blocking over other forms of blocking. Interestingly – and unlike most other blocking systems – it embraces the resulting overblocking by claiming that it serves as a deterrent to domain owners:

> The CSAADF focuses on blocking on domain level. We believe that this places the responsibility for the content of any domain or sub domain in the hands of the domain owner or administrator. If a domain owner places, accidental or willingly, child abuse material on his/her domain, and it is blocked by the police, the blocking will not be lifted until the material is removed. We believe that this will motivate content providers on the Internet to actively make an effort to avoid files with child sexual abuse on their systems/services. (CIRCAMP n.d.)

There is an exception, however, for certain hosting sites where CIRCAMP members will not block but will instead notify the owners seeking removal of the image:

> In cases where a hosting company has been taken advantage of, like free photo hosting companies – CIRCAMP members will inform the owner/administrator of that domain that they are hosting child sexual abuse material. In most cases this will result in the removal of the files very quickly. Such services are not blocked as the implications for legal users and services would be substantial. (CIRCAMP n.d.)

The CIRCAMP project also provides for information sharing between national police forces and in particular the sharing of black lists – though the decision as to which material is to be blocked remains a decision for national police forces, applying national law. CIRCAMP has also worked with INTERPOL on developing a "worst of" list of domains containing images of particularly serious sexual abuse that would be illegal in almost all jurisdictions.

As compared with the early Cleanfeed systems, CIRCAMP makes some advances in relation to transparency and procedural safeguards. While the IWF would not (until recently) notify a domain owner that a site had been blocked, the CIRCAMP model requires notification in respect of image hosting sites and also in situations where a "legal domain or home page/ company page of some sort" appeared to be compromised. In this case the site owner is contacted, told of the hacking or abuse and given the opportunity to stop the blocking by confirming that the child abuse material had been removed (CIRCAMP n.d.).

Similarly, while the IWF still does not require that users be notified about blocked pages the CIRCAMP system has from the outset emphasised the use of stop pages which contain "information about what kind of content the user's browser tried to access, links to national legislation, contact information to complain about the blocking and to the police" (CIRCAMP n.d.). Figure 12.2 provides an example of a stop page from Malta.

Also, as part of the CIRCAMP system EUROPOL now provides a web page for domain owners which enables them to seek a review of the blocking in each jurisdiction though a single request, rather than having to contact each jurisdiction individually (EUROPOL undated).

As with Cleanfeed, the system is not intended for prosecution purposes and CIRCAMP explicitly states that "the access blocking is purely preventive, no investigations against persons are initiated as a result of an Internet user being blocked and the 'stop page' displayed". However, the CIRCAMP model goes further and envisages that national police forces will also use blocking systems as an intelligence tool:

> In most participating countries the ISPs grant the police access to web logs that are generated when the "stop page" is displayed. The IP-address of the internet users has been removed from the logs, so they contain no identifying information. These logs are used for statistic purposes and will provide information about new sites that are unknown to the police. The statistics from these logs will also provide an overview of the Internet usage related to child sexual abusive material in addition to information about search words, type of operating system, browser, time of day that most Internet users are redirected to the "stop page" etc. (CIRCAMP n.d.)

The effect of this is made clear in a recent letter from Irish police to ISPs proposing the introduction of a CSAADF system. That letter acknowledges that users may have accessed a blocked site inadvertently, but goes on to request that in such cases the ISP should provide "details of other websites visited by the user" (Digital Rights Ireland 2011). This raises obvious privacy concerns, not least as it is often possible to identify users

Source: http://www.mpfstopchildabuse.org/ (accessed 20 July 2011).

Figure 12.2 CIRCAMP stop page, Malta

based on their internet history, and these are considered below further in the section on "Privacy".

United States Hash Value Blocking Systems

The systems discussed above focus on blocking access to particular web addresses and between them reflect the majority of blocking systems in Europe.[1] There is a similar system in the US – since 2008 the quasi-public National Center for Missing and Exploited Children (NCMEC) has operated a "URL Project" which provides participating ISPs with a list of URLs it has found to contain "the worst of the worst" forms of child pornography.[2] However that has not promoted blocking to the same extent as either the Cleanfeed or CIRCAMP models – while many ISPs subscribe to this list, the focus is on takedown of material hosted by those providers rather than blocking of material hosted elsewhere (Hakim 2008).[3]

Instead, a different form of blocking has been more prominent which focuses on the file itself rather than where it is located (see e.g. Anderson 2007). This approach relies on the use of hash values, which in effect serve as fingerprints to uniquely identify a particular file or photograph (for more detail see e.g. Salgado 2006). Where an internet intermediary has a database of hash values known to correspond to child pornography files then they can compare the hash values of files stored or transmitted by users and, if there is a match, they will be able to identify the file in question as constituting child pornography.[4]

AOL pioneered the use of this strategy through its Image Detection and Filtering Process ("IDFP") which it has run since 2004. Figure 12.3 (adapted from Colcolough 2009) illustrates how it works.

As Figure 12.3 shows, the IDFP scans all emails sent by AOL members, generating hash values for any images being transmitted. Those hash values are then compared with an internal database containing the hash values of child pornography images previously dealt with by AOL. If there

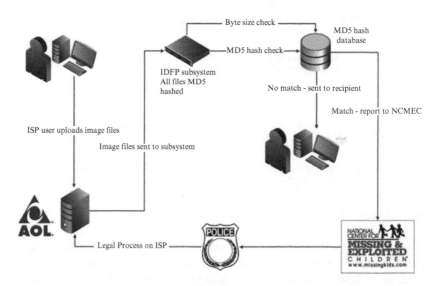

Figure 12.3   AOL's image detection and filtering process

is a match AOL will block the email. At that stage, having knowledge of the child pornography, it is obliged by US mandatory reporting rules to notify the Cyber Tip Line at the NCMEC by sending a report containing the image, username, email address and zip-code of the user.[5] The NCMEC will in turn notify the relevant law enforcement agency which can subpoena AOL for full details of the user.

This system has resulted in numerous convictions and has been influential in promoting other hash value blocking systems within the US. At the federal level, in 2008 Congress passed the PROTECT Our Children Act[6] which specifically authorises the NCMEC to provide hash values to ISPs for the purpose of detecting and blocking child pornography (but does not require that ISPs either monitor or block users' communications). Similarly, at the state level the New York Attorney General's office has established its own hash value database, which is now being used by Facebook, MySpace, isoHunt and others to detect and block uploads of child pornography images (Office of the Attorney General 2010).

These systems are, however, controversial and AOL's IDFP in particular has been criticised for the way in which it scans private emails. Although Fourth Amendment challenges to the AOL system have been unsuccessful (as the courts have not accepted that AOL should be treated as a state actor) it has been argued that this type of mass surveillance is a worrying development – one which is easily capable of being extended to other material which might be suppressed by government (Soghoian 2011, pp. 12–14).

As against that, however, there is also an opposing view that the use of hash value blocking is minimally intrusive (similar to spam filtering) in that such automated monitoring reveals nothing about the contents of communications beyond a binary determination: that the file is, or is not, known child pornography. Indeed, for this reason it has been suggested that hash value scans should not be treated as searches for the purpose of the Fourth Amendment (see e.g. Salgado 2006; Morrison 2011).

It should also be noted that there is a division of opinion within the US as to how blocking systems should be implemented – in particular, whether there is a role for the state in distributing hash values of known child pornography images. For example, AOL has publicly stated its concern about using a government supplied list, fearing that by so doing it would be considered an agent of the government (Dedman and Sullivan 2008). Conversely, the New York example shows that Facebook and others are content to block against hash values supplied by New York law enforcement authorities.

Leaving aside this debate for the moment, however, it will be apparent that hash value blocking may have several advantages over either the

Cleanfeed or CIRCAMP models. Systems such as those operated by the IWF or CIRCAMP members do not directly identify child pornography images, but instead point to locations. At best they can merely say that child pornography was found at a particular location at a particular time. Consequently, they require manual updating and review of each web address and will fail to detect the same image when moved to a new location. Each new location, therefore, will require fresh human intervention to block. Hash value blocking, on the other hand, does not rely on the image location and will correctly identify and block files even though they are being transmitted from a new location – and can also be applied in contexts (such as email or peer to peer) where DNS or URL based blocking will fail. While older forms of hash value matching (such as MD5 hashes) could be defeated by minor changes to files, newer "robust hashing" systems such as Microsoft's PhotoDNA are capable of identifying and blocking photographs even if they have been edited, resized or cropped (Whittaker 2009). Hash value blocking may also minimise concerns about overblocking – depending on the precise system used, false positives should be minimal.[7]

CRITICISMS OF BLOCKING SYSTEMS

Blocking systems have been questioned by many who fear that they may undermine freedom of expression online. The starting point for these critics is that internet blocking is, at its core, a form of restriction of freedom of expression and as such should comply with the democratic and constitutional norms associated with such restrictions. Instead, the argument runs, blocking may enable governments to sidestep these norms (Brown 2008). The following section considers these criticisms in light of the case studies above.

Transparency

A fundamental aspect of freedom of expression is that limitations of this right should be transparent and therefore subject to public oversight. Article 10 of the European Convention on Human Rights ("ECHR"), for example, states that any restrictions should be "prescribed by law" – which requires amongst other things that the legal basis for restrictions should be adequately accessible to the citizen.

However, blocking systems present significant challenges for transparency. Lessig has noted that regulation by code is inherently opaque, so in the case of internet blocking the user may not know that it is taking place, who is responsible or what material is being blocked. Consequently, he cautions that without "truth in blocking" these systems are likely to undermine free speech (Lessig 1999). Some blocking systems (such as CIRCAMP) have responded to this concern by introducing "stop pages" which notify users when their access to a web page has been blocked. Unfortunately others (notably the IWF) do not require this, permitting the deliberate deception of users as to why content is unavailable, and hindering any attempts to remedy wrongful blocking.

The focus on intermediaries presents its own problems. Unlike traditional systems for controlling content (which generally target either the speaker or the reader) blocking can be deployed in a covert manner unbeknownst to anyone but the intermediary. In the same vein, controls which are drawn up by self-regulatory systems generally escape the publicity which would attach to legislation or judicial decisions. As a result, Deibert and Villeneuve (2004) have noted that blocking systems are generally murky in their operation:

> as the practice of Internet content filtering and surveillance is largely new territory, the rules by which states implement such controls are poorly defined, not well known among the general public, and very rarely subject to open debate . . . as it stands now such decisions are typically taken behind closed doors through administrative fiat.

These concerns are all the greater in the case of child abuse images where regulators will understandably seek to keep the list of blocked material secret. While secrecy may be necessary to avoid blacklists becoming an index for paedophiles, it also makes it difficult to monitor the operation of such systems and forces society to take a great deal on trust. Unfortunately, this trust may not always be warranted. Instead, where blacklists have come to public attention this has often revealed that these systems have been poorly operated.

A recent example came from a CIRCAMP system in 2010 when a police blacklist shared between Sweden and Denmark was leaked. Volunteers from the German anti-blocking group AK Zensur confirmed that the domains on the list were currently blocked in Denmark, and then visited each website to assess whether it was correctly listed. Out of a representative sample of 167 websites, they found that 92 sites had already had their hosting accounts terminated, 66 domains had expired and six sites did not contain any illegal content, leaving only three sites which in fact contained child abuse images. This appeared to demonstrate a failure on the part of the Danish authorities to keep the blacklist current and, more importantly, to ensure that legal content was not blocked – a failure which would not have come to light otherwise (AK Zensur 2010).

It also, significantly, illustrated a further challenge for transparency. The volunteers who visited each website were not named in the study – reflecting their fears that simply visiting the blocked sites might constitute an offence. Where the law presents such risks for researchers it makes it all the more difficult to exercise informal oversight by civil society – even though the formal oversight mechanisms might themselves be deficient.

Legitimacy and Accountability

The IWF . . . is supported by the Police and CPS and works in partnership with the Government to provide a "hotline" for individuals or organisations to report potentially illegal content and then to assess and judge that material on behalf of UK law enforcement agencies.
– Crown Prosecution Service & Association of Chief Police Officers (2004)

I regret to inform you that the Home Office does not hold the information that you have requested regarding the relationship between the IWF and the Home Office. The IWF is a self regulatory, independent charity that has no formal links with the Home Office.
– Home Office, Response to Freedom of Information Act Request (2009)

Another common charge against blocking is that it lacks legitimacy and accountability. More precisely, the claim is that such systems – insofar as they can be adopted informally by private actors in response to government pressure – evade requirements that state measures which restrict freedom of expression should have a legislative basis, and avoid public law oversight mechanisms. As Marsden (2010) puts it "government favours more private censorship with loose – and therefore largely unenforceable – links to the government, but very strong policy and informal bonds". This is not an inevitable feature of blocking systems, some of which do have a legislative basis. It is, however, extremely common.

A particularly good example is the Dutch system, adopted in 2007, which involved ISPs voluntarily blocking access to domains designated by the police, using DNS blocking. A study commissioned by the government found that this was unlawful and contrary to Article 10 ECHR in that it lacked any specific legal basis – ultimately forcing it to be abandoned (Stol et al. 2008; Stol et al. 2009). Remarkably, however, when this system was found to be illegal, the response of the Dutch government was not to provide a legal basis, but instead to try to further privatise blocking. The tactic adopted was to seek to persuade ISPs to develop a purely self-regulatory scheme – in which the sites to be blocked would be designated by a private body rather than by the police – thus avoiding the safeguards which would apply to a state run system (Bits of Freedom 2011).

The Dutch experience illustrates the shifting focus of these blocking

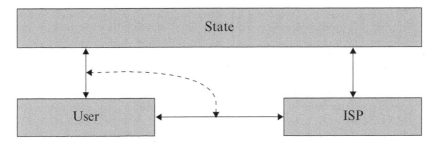

Figure 12.4   Lambers' model of "tilting"

systems: away from public bodies which are bound by constitutional constraints and towards private bodies such as ISPs which are insulated from judicial review. Lambers (2006) has described this approach as "tilting" where the "classical vertical state-citizen relationship on which . . . freedom of speech is founded, is short circuited since a second private party shifts between the state and the user: the ISP". He graphically represents this "tilt" in Figure 12.4 above.

Consequently, he argues, where non-legislative blocking is introduced the relationship between state and citizen becomes instead a relationship between ISP and user – one which is governed by private law only, deliberately displacing constitutional and public law rights.

This aspect of blocking has led critics such as Edwards (2009) to argue that if blocking systems are to be used then they should be reconstituted as public bodies – making them accountable to the ordinary mechanisms of public oversight and judicial review. As against that, however, there is a contrary view exemplified by Mueller (2010) which identifies the "saving grace of privatised governance" as the "ability of users and suppliers to vote with their feet", suggesting that if blocking is put on a statutory basis it is likely to become more rather than less pervasive. In practice, however, any significant customer response seems unlikely to happen for two reasons. First, the self-regulatory systems which we describe are often opaque in their nature, making it difficult for customers to understand what content is being restricted and by whom. Secondly, these systems are also often adopted on a universal or near universal basis, so that even where customers are aware of particular restrictions they may nevertheless have no realistic alternative. The UK example – where 98.6 per cent of the population are covered by Cleanfeed type systems – offers an example of a situation where exit is not a realistic option for most users.

It is, therefore, difficult to argue with the recent report commissioned by the OSCE Representative on Freedom of the Media which rejects the use of "voluntary" or self-regulatory systems, concluding that:

There is concern that voluntary blocking mechanisms and agreements do not respect due process principles within the states in which they are used. In the absence of a legal basis for blocking access to websites, platforms and internet content, the compatibility of such agreements and systems with OSCE commitments, Article 19 of the Universal Declaration and Article 10 of the European Convention on Human Rights is arguably problematic. Although the authorities' good intentions to combat child pornography and other types of illegal content is legitimate, in the absence of a valid legal basis in domestic law for blocking access to websites, the authority or power given to certain organizations and institutions to block, administer, and maintain the blacklists remains problematic. Such a "voluntary interference" might be contradictory to the conclusions of the Final Document of the Moscow Meeting of the Conference on the Human Dimension of the CSCE and in breach of Article 19 and Article 10 of the European Convention on Human Rights unless the necessity for interference is convincingly established. (Akdeniz 2011, p.24)

Fair Procedures

The complaint that internet blocking systems evade public law norms is particularly strong in relation to fair procedures – notably the right to be heard before a decision is made. This is not a facility which has been offered to site owners or users in most internet blocking schemes worldwide, despite the fact that blocking will operate as a prior restraint of speech – at best, the operators of internet filters generally provide (if at all) for review after the fact (Deibert and Villeneuve 2004). In response, it has been argued that the norms of administrative decision making may not always be appropriate in the context of child abuse image blocking. For example, it has been claimed that to notify a site owner may jeopardise criminal enforcement (see e.g. Walden 2010).

Whether this reasoning would resist legal challenge will depend on the standards of each national system. In the United States, for example, the court in *Centre for Democracy and Technology v. Pappert* (2004) found that a legislative scheme whereby websites could be blocked by court order on an *ex parte* basis, with no notice or opportunity to be heard, did not meet the procedural requirements which the First Amendment required for a prior restraint to be imposed (see e.g. the discussion in Kleinschmidt 2010).

Of course, not all jurisdictions share the US suspicion of prior restraints. But at a minimum, notice after the fact and an independent appeal mechanism would appear to be necessary to provide adequate procedural safeguards. Most systems, however, do not provide for any notification of the site owner – even where users attempting to visit a site are presented with a block page (see e.g. Internet Watch Foundation 2010b). Similarly, none of the systems described here includes any judicial oversight, and where appeal mechanisms are provided they do not always provide for an independent review or even a right to make submissions. For example, in 2008 when the IWF blocked a number of pages on Wikipedia, the review which was carried out excluded any input from Wikipedia itself, causing their lawyer to comment that:

> When we first protested the block, their response was, "We've now conducted an appeals process on your behalf and you've lost the appeal." When I asked who exactly represented the Wikimedia Foundation's side in that appeals process, they were silent. (Quoted in Davies 2009)

Overblocking

Internet blocking systems are often criticised as being disproportionate in their effect – that is, as being prone to causing collateral damage by blocking legal as well as illegal material. Both the IWF and CIRCAMP experiences bear this out – and it is striking that the CIRCAMP model deliberately adopts overblocking as a tactic to exert pressure on site owners.

The extent to which such overblocking takes place in any particular scheme will, of course, depend on a number of factors including the technological sophistication of the blocking system used and the diligence of those establishing and maintaining the blacklist. In general, however, the incentives faced by the ISPs and others who implement blocking systems favour overblocking. As Kreimer (2006) notes, the dominant motive of intermediaries is "to protect themselves from sanctions, rather than to protect the target from censorship". This reflects empirical evidence showing that internet intermediaries make decisions in a manner which minimises their own financial, legal and reputational risk (see e.g. Ahlert et al. 2004). Consequently, there is likely to be a structural tendency towards overblocking in many blocking schemes.

Mission Creep

> *Child pornography is great . . . Politicians do not understand file sharing, but they understand child pornography, and they want to filter that to score points with the public. Once we get them to filter child pornography, we can get them to extend the block to file sharing.*
> – Johan Schlüter, Chairman of the Danish Anti-Piracy Group (Quoted in Falkvinge 2011)

An important criticism of blocking systems is that they are prone to mission creep – that is, that once established for a particular purpose they may easily be extended to achieve a different goal. In relation to child abuse image blocking systems, this mission creep may take place in one of two ways.

The most commonly mentioned is that other material may be brought within their scope – for example, they may be extended to also block file-sharing, suicide, pro-anorexia, etc. sites. Edwards (2009) points out that the UK government has considered extending child abuse image blocking to sites which "glorify terrorism" and argues that the IWF system enables this to be done in a way which is invisible to the public. Indeed, Mueller (2010) goes further by arguing that mission creep is a feature rather than a bug, noting that "emotional appeals to 'the children' have deliberately been exploited as the entering wedge for a broader reassertion of state control over internet content".

It might be objected that mission creep is less likely in self-regulatory systems where ISPs have a financial incentive to minimise the scope of blocking. This argument is sometimes made in the UK in defence of the IWF-led system – Ozimek (2009) for example typifies this view when he expresses a preference for its "slightly quaint, non-governmental route" as being "rather less threatening . . . than the more 'efficient' [state-run] models used elsewhere".

There is undoubtedly some truth in this point, but it is significantly undermined by the fact that once a blocking infrastructure is in place it may be co-opted by others against the wishes of the ISP. Ironically, Cleanfeed itself illustrates this point. At the time of writing, the Motion Picture Association of America is suing BT, seeking an injunction requiring it to block access to a website (Newzbin) which is alleged to allow the illegal downloading of movies. According to a spokesman "BT was chosen because it's the largest and already has the technology in place, through its Cleanfeed system, to block the site" (Williams 2011).

A potentially more difficult (though less often discussed) aspect of mission creep is that the objective of blocking may be expanded from crime prevention to also take on an intelligence, investigation or prosecution role – for example, by using a particular system to identify and prosecute users who seek to access or transmit child abuse images. This will be especially true in jurisdictions such as the United States where there is mandatory reporting of offences related to child pornography – in those cases, by operating a blocking system an ISP will come under an obligation to report those users whose actions have been flagged (see Morrison 2011).

As we have seen, some ISPs (notably AOL) have embraced this expansion of blocking to encompass a prosecution role, while others (such as BT) have sought to avoid this possibility by minimising the data which they log about their users. However, the US experience shows that any blocking system can easily be repurposed as a prosecution tool by introducing mandatory reporting by ISPs where they have knowledge of child pornography. In this case, voluntary blocking coupled with mandatory reporting can become, in effect, ongoing surveillance of the entire user base.

This is especially so with hash value systems as compared with other forms of blocking. Cleanfeed or CIRCAMP web blocking systems do not easily facilitate prosecution. These systems are intended to stop access to material hosted elsewhere – outside the control of the user – and the IWF and others have been at pains to stress that the main goal of such systems is to prevent "inadvertent exposure". Consequently, if a user is prevented from accessing a site then there is little or no proof that they have committed or intended to commit a crime. Hash value blocking, on the other hand, can also be used for situations where a user attempts to make material available to others: for example, by scanning email attachments sent by a user (AOL) or images uploaded by a user to a shared group (Facebook). In these situations, if a blocking system detects a positive match then that in itself is evidence of the crime of possession on the part of the user and is likely to trigger any mandatory reporting requirement.

More generally, however, this type of mission creep presents significant risks for the criminal justice system. By introducing pervasive surveillance of all users – without any prior suspicion – even a low rate of false positives may result in the wrongful investigation, arrest and stigmatisation of many innocent users.

These risks can be seen by examining a previous large scale data-driven investigation of alleged child pornography offences. In 1999, a police investigation in the United States ("Operation Avalanche") led to the seizure by the US Postal Service of credit card records which appeared to implicate many tens of thousands of internet users in the purchase of child pornography. Of these, 7,272 records related to individuals in the United Kingdom. After these records were provided to the UK, in April 2002 the National Crime Investigation Service (NCIS) launched an investigation ("Operation Ore") which ultimately resulted in the investigation of 4,283 individuals. As these cases proceeded, however, it became clear that many of those individuals had not paid for child pornography – instead, they had either been the victims of credit card fraud, or had paid for legal (adult) pornography sites which shared the same billing service (Campbell 2005). This, however, came too late for many of the individuals concerned, at least some of whom committed suicide as a result of the wrongful accusations against them while others lost their jobs as a result (Leppard 2005).

PRIVACY

Blocking systems pose a special challenge to legal norms relating to privacy, confidentiality of communications and data protection. These systems, of their nature, often involve the monitoring of internet traffic generally with a view to deciding which particular messages to block. Except in a few cases – for example, where blocking software is run at a purely local level under the control of the end user – the operation of blocking can therefore involve third party pervasive surveillance of otherwise private communications (see e.g. Callanan et al. 2009, chap.6). There has, however, been relatively little examination of the issues this presents.

To the knowledge of this author, there have been no court cases which examine the operation of either the UK Cleanfeed system or the European CIRCAMP systems. In the United States there have been a number of defence challenges to prosecution evidence obtained as a result of the AOL IDFP system – in those cases, however, the challenges have invariably failed on the basis that the Fourth Amendment guarantee against "unreasonable searches and seizures" applies only against the state and not against an ISP acting in a private capacity. The most important case on point is *US v. Richardson* (2010) where the Fourth Circuit held that AOL was not acting as an agent of the government in scanning email, notwithstanding that it actively cooperated with law enforcement and was obliged by law to report any child pornography which it discovered to the NCMEC, based on a finding that there was "little evidence . . . to suggest that AOL intended to assist the Government" (see e.g. Morrison 2011).

In the US context, therefore, the voluntary nature of blocking may insulate it from judicial scrutiny.[8] It is probable, however, that a different result would be reached in a European context where both the European Convention on Human Rights and data protection guarantees recognise privacy rights which have horizontal effect so that they can be asserted against non-state actors. Indeed, a recent opinion of the European Data Protection Supervisor ("EDPS") suggests that such systems may be in breach of the Data Protection Directive[9] and Article 8 ECHR where they are introduced without a statutory basis:

> The EDPS underlines that monitoring the network and blocking sites would constitute a purpose unrelated to the commercial purpose of ISPs: this would raise issues with regard to lawful processing and compatible use of personal data under Article 6.1.b and Article 7 of the Data Protection Directive. The EDPS questions the criteria for blocking and stresses that a code of conduct or voluntary guidelines would not bring enough legal certainty in this respect. The EDPS also underlines the risks linked with possible blacklisting of individuals

and their possibilities of redress before an independent authority. The EDPS has already stated at several occasions that "the monitoring of Internet user's behaviour and further collection of their IP addresses amounts to an interference with their rights to respect for their private life and their correspondence ... This view is in line with the case law of the European Court of Human Rights". Considering this interference, more appropriate safeguards are needed to ensure that monitoring and/or blocking will only be done in a strictly targeted way and under judicial control, and that misuse of this mechanism is prevented by adequate security measures. (Hustinx 2010)

Despite these issues, however, privacy has often been overlooked in the literature on filtering. Bambauer (2009) for example has put forward a very useful four part metric for evaluating blocking systems which considers "openness, transparency, narrowness and accountability" – but leaves out of this metric any impact which particular systems may have on privacy of communications. Similarly Akdeniz's recent analysis of European blocking measures focuses on freedom of expression, leaving privacy issues aside (Akdeniz 2010).

This tendency to neglect privacy may reflect a focus on systems such as Cleanfeed and CIRCAMP where material targeted is publicly available on the web, creating fewer privacy problems. Privacy issues are becoming more important, however, with the growth of hash value blocking systems such as AOL's IDFP which – especially in conjunction with deep packet inspection – now make it feasible to target entirely private channels of communication such as email or instant messaging.[10]

It will be important, therefore, for future research to consider the privacy implications of these newer systems and whether indiscriminate and pervasive surveillance of this sort can ever be justified, however grave the material targeted. In particular, it would be desirable to assess individual measures with regard to their invasiveness and to reaffirm the principles of proportionality and necessity so that more invasive systems (such as the scanning of email) should only be used if it can be shown that less invasive systems (such as blocking of public web sites) would not achieve the desired goals.

EFFECTIVENESS

Are blocking systems effective? To answer this question we must first ask a preliminary question – effective in relation to what goals? This is a surprisingly difficult question to answer as few blocking systems set explicit objectives (see e.g. Stol et al. 2009). This (sometimes deliberate) vagueness reflects a tension between two competing factors – a political tendency to oversell what can be achieved and the technical realities which limit what can be done. However, we can take as our starting point the following summary from two prominent advocates of blocking:

- Blocking is a way of interfering with and disrupting the commercial trade of child abuse material
- Blocking helps to prevent accidental access to this illegal and harmful content by helping the public
- It helps to prevent deliberate access to child abuse material on the internet
- It helps to reduce the customer base of illegal websites
- It helps to prevent the re-victimization of those children who are or have been the victims of abuse. (Carr and Hilton 2011)

The distinction between deliberate and accidental access in this summary is significant – Carr and Hilton acknowledge that blocking can be circumvented, but go on to argue that it nevertheless has a role "in helping to prevent the casual, domestic consumer from stumbling across child abuse images by accident and in preventing those who might have a misguided sense of curiosity from gaining access". In this they echo a rationale common to most such systems – i.e. that they can serve to protect the innocent or inquisitive user even if they are ineffective at stopping the deliberate criminal.[11]

It is easy to see why this paternalist rationale has become the dominant argument of advocates of blocking. Circumvention methods are no secret, and research such as that of Eneman (2010) has demonstrated that sex offenders – even those without any formal education or experience in working with computers – already find it easy to defeat blocking systems. In addition, public awareness of circumvention tools is on the rise. The use of blocking and geolocation as means of enforcing copyright has ensured that users are increasingly familiar with the use of proxy servers, alternative DNS providers and services such as TOR – whether to access sites such as ThePirateBay which are blocked by their ISP or to view services such as the BBC iPlayer which are not available in their country (see e.g. Svantesson 2008). Consequently, arguments based on stopping accidental and casual access take on greater importance as it becomes clear that blocking is at best only weakly effective at stopping deliberate viewing.[12]

To what extent, then, are blocking systems effective at preventing accidental or casual access to child abuse images? Here, unfortunately, we are hampered by a lack of data. In the first place, there does not appear to be any evidence that accidental exposure has been a significant problem. In their recent Dutch study Stol et al. (2009) point out that:

> No interviewed expert, authority or other person involved was able to refer to a case in which a "decent" internetter was unexpectedly or incidentally confronted with child pornography on a website.

It may be that such systems are more effective at blocking casual viewing, but there is a lack of data in this regard also.[13] Few blocking systems have made statistics available as to the extent of access attempts which are blocked, and where data has been made available it has generally been unreliable.

A well known example comes from the UK where BT has published statistics from its Cleanfeed system claiming (most recently) that it has blocked up to 45,000 hits per day. While these claims have been uncritically reported by the mainstream media as demonstrating the success of blocking, closer analysis has revealed substantial issues with those figures. Notably, by counting "hits" rather than "page visits" it overstates the issue, as an attempt to visit a single page will almost always generate multiple hits for the files which make up that page. In addition, sources familiar with the system have acknowledged that a substantial portion of that traffic is likely to be generated by malware or foreign users seeking to abuse open proxies within the UK, something which again undermines the claims that casual viewing is being prevented. Ironically, the steps which BT has taken in designing the system (for example, not logging the IP addresses which attempted to reach a blocked site) ensure that no conclusive analysis of the figures can be carried out (Richardson 2004a; Richardson 2004b; Graham 2009).

Finally, it should be noted that there is a strong case that the use of blocking systems has been counterproductive, by distracting attention from international measures to achieve the removal of images at source. Villeneuve (2010), for example, has argued that "the introduction of filtering technology reduces the incentive for organisations with an already narrow conception of cooperation to further engage with relevant counterparts across international boundaries". German anti-blocking group AK Zensur illustrated this point in 2009, when using a leaked blocking list they succeeded in taking down 61 child pornography websites simply by contacting the hosting providers (Freude 2009). Research by Moore and Clayton (2008) has demonstrated that in relation to financial crimes it is possible to achieve effective cross-border cooperation without any need to resort to national blocking systems, supporting the argument that child abuse images could similarly be dealt with.

CONCLUSION

It has often been claimed that the "success" of internet blocking for child abuse content should be followed by extending blocking to other forms of internet content. When examined more closely, however, it is apparent that the claims made for blocking must be heavily qualified and do not support the further extension of these systems.

As we have seen, child abuse images represent probably the best case scenario for blocking. There is near universal agreement on the illegality of such material and considerable public support for countermeasures. From a practical perspective, such images are relatively straightforward to identify and the comparatively small number of sites involved makes it technologically and administratively more convenient to introduce blocking systems. These advantages do not, however, apply to the majority of other content which states seek to control, making the experience of child abuse blocking marginally relevant at best.

More generally, however, this chapter has also identified significant problems with child abuse blocking systems themselves. All three systems examined show very significant shortcomings in relation to legitimacy, transparency and accountability, while claims for the effectiveness of blocking have also been undermined. In addition, two of the systems appear to prove the truth of concerns about privacy and function creep, insofar as they have moved beyond their original goals of simple crime prevention and towards an intelligence gathering and even prosecution function. There is, therefore, a very real risk that by promoting blocking the constitutional values associated with freedom of expression and privacy of communications may be sacrificed – and worse, may be sacrificed for systems which are ineffective for their stated goal.

NOTES

1. Although hash value systems are most commonly associated with the US, there are also some European initiatives in this area. In particular, the Dutch Ministry of Justice and the Dutch Hotline have cooperated with hosting provider Leaseweb and Swedish company Netclean to trial MD5 hash value blocking of images uploaded to certain sites (Leaseweb 2009).
2. While this chapter generally uses the term child abuse images, in this and other sections the term child pornography is used to reflect the terminology used by US law.
3. A web based blocking system was mandated by legislation in Pennsylvania in 2002 but was ultimately ruled unconstitutional in *Center for Democracy and Technology v. Pappert* 337 F.Supp.2d 606 (2004). This experience appears to have influenced later US developments, and may be responsible for government strategies which promote voluntary and self-regulatory blocking systems which may escape similar judicial review.
4. This is a deliberate oversimplification of the issues associated with hashing and in particular does not address the issue of possible hash value collisions where different files generate the same hash value, generating false positives.
5. For an example of such a report see *United States v. Brent Terry* 522 F.3d 645 (2008).
6. Public Law 110-401, 122 Stat. 4229-4253.
7. The likelihood of hash value collisions may, however, increase where robust hashing

systems such as Microsoft's PhotoDNA are used. One Microsoft researcher has put the likelihood of false positives in PhotoDNA at one in 2 billion images (Richmond 2011).

8. There is an argument that scanning and blocking of emails may violate either the Federal Electronic Communications Privacy Act or state surveillance laws, depending on whether either or both the sender and recipient consent to scanning (see e.g. Metz 2008; Ohm 2009). Such violations would not, however, result in the suppression of evidence, which explains why these arguments have not been made in cases such as *US v. Richardson*.

9. Directive 95/46/EC.

10. A further application of hash values matching is in relation to private files which a user stores or backs up on a cloud computing service. With the move away from local storage and towards remote storage and backup this may result in all files stored by a user being scanned for contraband, irrespective of whether or not they are being sent to others. Although it is beyond the scope of this chapter, it is worth noting that in many jurisdictions there is lesser protection for remotely stored data than for data which is in the course of transmission, suggesting that hash value scanning of files stored remotely might be legally permissible even if blocking of those files in the course of communication would not be. On this point, see Soghoian (2010).

11. A variant of this argument is that blocking can prevent the accidental or casual viewer from developing a latent sexual interest in children, and can thereby prevent a progression to contact sexual offending (see e.g. Carr 2004). It should be noted that there is some debate as to whether viewing of child abuse images leads to "real world" offending. While some authors (e.g. Russell and Purcell 2005; Bourke and Hernandez 2009) suggest that it does, there appears to be no definitive study (compare the literature review in O'Donnell and Milner 2007).

12. In the United States in particular there is also a tension between different arms of government, with the State Department actively funding circumvention tools via its Global Internet Freedom strategy. Although intended for destinations such as China and Iran, such tools will undoubtedly also see a great deal of use domestically. See e.g. Figliola (2010).

13. This lack of data reflects the decentralised nature of most child abuse image blocking systems. Although the determination of what sites to block may be made by a central body, the implementation of that blocking is generally the responsibility of the individual ISP. As a result, there is no central repository of data or guarantee that any data is being logged. In addition, because individual ISPs may implement blocking in different ways any data which is logged may not be comparable with data from other sources.

REFERENCES

Ahlert, C., C. Marsden and C. Yung (2004), 'How "Liberty" Disappeared from Cyberspace: The Mystery Shopper Tests Internet Content Self-Regulation', http://pcmlp.socleg.ox.ac.uk/text/liberty.pdf.

AK Zensur (2010), 'Blacklists of Denmark and Sweden analysed', http://ak-zensur.de/2010/09/29/analysis-blacklists.pdf.

Akdeniz, Y. (2010), 'To Block or not to Block: European Approaches to Content Regulation, and Implications for Freedom of Expression', *Computer Law & Security Review*, **26(3)**, 260–72.

Akdeniz, Y. (2011), 'Freedom of Expression on the Internet: Study of legal provisions and practices related to freedom of expression, the free flow of information and media pluralism on the Internet in OSCE participating States', Organization for Security and Co-operation in Europe, http://www.osce.org/fom/80723.

All Party Parliamentary Communications Group (2009), 'Can we keep our hands off the net?', Report of an Inquiry by the All Party Parliamentary Communications Group, London, http://www.apcomms.org.uk/uploads/apComms_Final_Report.pdf.

Anderson, N. (2007), 'Image hash database could filter child porn', *Ars Technica*, http://arstechnica.com/tech-policy/news/2007/07/image-hash-database-could-filter-child-porn.ars.

Baker, J. (2011), 'European Parliament votes to remove offensive images at source', *Computerworld*, http://www.computerworlduk.com/news/public-sector/3261164/european-parliament-votes-to-remove-offensive-images-at-source/.

Bambauer, D. (2009), 'Cybersieves', *Duke Law Journal*, **59(3)**, 477.

Banisar, D. (2008), *Speaking of Terror*, Strasbourg: Council of Europe, http://www.coe.int/t/dghl/standardsetting/media/Doc/SpeakingOfTerror_en.pdf, accessed 12 May 2009.

Bits of Freedom (2011), 'Dutch providers abandon "ineffective" web blocking', https://www.bof.nl/2011/03/07/dutch-providers-abandon-ineffective-web-blocking, accessed 9 March 2011.

Bourke, M. and A. Hernandez (2009), 'The "Butner Study" Redux: A Report of the Incidence of Hands-on Child Victimization by Child Pornography Offenders', *Journal of Family Violence*, **24(3)**, 183–91.

Boyle, J. (1997), 'Foucault in Cyberspace: Surveillance, Sovereignty and Hardwired Censors', *University of Cincinnati Law Review*, **177**, 186.

Brown, I. (2008), 'Internet Filtering: Be Careful What You Ask for', in S.K. Schroeder, and L. Hanson (eds), *Freedom and Prejudice: Approaches to Media and Culture*, Istanbul: Bahcesehir University Press, http://ssrn.com/paper=1026597, accessed 4 October 2008.

Callanan, C. et al. (2009), *Internet Blocking: Balancing Cybercrime Responses in Democratic Societies*, Dublin: Aconite Internet Solutions.

Campbell, D. (2005), 'Operation Ore exposed', *PC Pro*, http://www.pcpro.co.uk/features/74690/operation-ore-exposed, accessed 6 May 2011.

Carr, J. (2004), 'Child Abuse, Child Pornography and the Internet', http://www.make-it safe.net/esp/pdf/Child_pornography_internet_Carr2004.pdf, accessed 12 September 2009.

Carr, J. and Z. Hilton (2009), 'Children's Charities' Coalition on Internet Safety Digital Manifesto', http://www.chis.org.uk/uploads/02b.pdf.

Carr, J. and Z. Hilton (2011), 'Combating Child Abuse Images on the Internet – International Perspectives', in J. Davidson and P. Gottschalk (eds), *Internet Child Abuse: Current Research and Policy*, Abingdon: Routledge.

CIRCAMP (n.d.), 'CIRCAMP overview', http://circamp.eu/index.php?option=com_content&view=article&id=11:circamp-overview&catid=1:project&Itemid=2, accessed 27 March 2010.

Clayton, R. (2005), 'Failures in a Hybrid Content Blocking System', http://www.cl.cam.ac.uk/~rnc1/cleanfeed.pdf, accessed 17 April 2009.

Clayton, R. (2008), 'Technical Aspects of the Censoring of Wikipedia', *Light Blue Touchpaper*, http://www.lightbluetouchpaper.org/2008/12/11/technical-aspects-of-the-censoring-of-wikipedia/, accessed 28 March 2009.

Colcolough, D. (2009), 'Investigating and Prosecuting Computer Facilitated Crimes Against Children', http://www.childrensmn.org/web/mrcac/handouts/184933.pdf, accessed 11 September 2009.

Committee on Energy and Commerce (2006), '*Making the Internet Safe for Kids: The Role of ISPs and Social Networking Sites*, Washington, DC: US Government Printing Office, http://ftp.resource.org/gpo.gov/hearings/109h/30530.txt, accessed 5 April 2011.

Crown Prosecution Service & Association of Chief Police Officers (2004), 'Memorandum of Understanding Between Crown Prosecution Service (CPS) and the Association of Chief Police Officers (ACPO) concerning Section 46 Sexual Offences Act 2003', http://www.iwf.org.uk/documents/20041015_mou_final_oct_2004.pdf, accessed July 24, 2009.

Davies, C. (2009), 'The Hidden Censors of the Internet', *Wired*, http://www.wired.co.uk/wired-magazine/archive/2009/05/features/the-hidden-censors-of-the-internet.aspx?page=all, accessed 20 September 2009.

Dedman, B. and B. Sullivan (2008), 'ISPs pressed to become child porn cops', *MSNBC*, http://www.msnbc.msn.com/id/27198621/, accessed 17 October 2008.

Deibert, R. and R. Rohozinski (2010), 'Beyond Denial: Introducing Next-Generation Information Access Controls', in R. Deibert et al. (eds), *Access Controlled: The Shaping of Power, Rights and Rule in Cyberspace*, Cambridge, MA: MIT Press.

Deibert, R. and N. Villeneuve (2004), 'Firewalls and Power: An Overview of Global State Censorship of the Internet', in A. Murray and M. Klang (eds), *Human Rights in the Digital Age*, London: GlassHouse.

Digital Rights Ireland (2011), 'Garda plans for web blocking referred to Data Protection Commissioner', http://www.digitalrights.ie/2011/03/29/garda-plans-for-web-blocking-referred-to-data-protection-commissioner/, accessed 16 May 2011.

Edwards, L. (2009), 'Pornography, Censorship and the Internet', in L. Edwards and C. Waelde (eds), *Law and the Internet*, Oxford: Hart Publishing.

Eneman, M. (2010), 'Internet Service Provider (ISP) Filtering of Child-abusive Material: A Critical Reflection of its Effectiveness', *Journal of Sexual Aggression: An international, interdisciplinary forum for research, theory and practice*, **16(2)**, 223.

EUROPOL (undated), 'Funnel Web Introduction', http://www.europol.europa.eu/index.asp?page=FunnelIntro&language=, accessed 21 March 2010.

Falkvinge, R. (2011), 'The Copyright Lobby Absolutely Loves Child Pornography', http://torrentfreak.com/the-copyright-lobby-absolutely-loves-child-pornography110709/?utm_source=feedburner&utm_medium=feed&utm_campaign=Feed:+Torrentfreak+(Torrentfreak)&utm_content=Google+Reader, accessed July 19, 2011.

Figliola, P.M. (2010), 'US Initiatives to Promote Global Internet Freedom: Issues, Policy, and Technology', Congressional Research Service.

Freude, A. (2009), 'Delete, Don't Block: It Works!', http://www.unpolitik.de/2009/05/28/delete-dont-block-it-works/, accessed July 16, 2010.

Graham, I. (2009), 'Statistics Laundering: False and Fantastic Figures', http://libertus.net/censor/resources/statistics-laundering.html, accessed 1 March 2010.

GSMA Mobile Alliance Against Child Sexual Abuse Content (2008), 'Implementation of Filtering of Child Sexual Abuse Images in Operator Networks', www.gsmworld.com/documents/GSMA_Child_Tech_Doc.pdf.

Hakim, D. (2008), 'Net Providers to Block Sites With Child Sex', *The New York Times*, http://www.nytimes.com/2008/06/10/nyregion/10internet.html?_r=2, accessed 14 September 2009.

Hargrave, S. (2006), 'Surfing with a safety net', *The Guardian*, http://www.guardian.co.uk/technology/2006/jun/29/guardianweeklytechnologysection, accessed 1 May 2009.

Home Office (2009), 'Response to Freedom of Information Request in relation to the relationship between the Internet Watch Foundation and the Home Office and network level blocking', http://www.whatdotheyknow.com/request/5357/response/18479/attach/html/2/ResponseT11%209.doc.html, accessed 27 February 2009.

Hustinx, P. (2010), 'Opinion of the European Data Protection Supervisor on the proposal for a Directive of the European Parliament and of the Council on combating the sexual abuse, sexual exploitation of children and child pornography, repealing Framework Decision 2004/68/JH', http://www.edps.europa.eu/EDPSWEB/webdav/site/mySite/shared/Documents/Consultation/Opinions/2010/10-05-10_Child_Abuse_EN.pdf.

Hutty, M. (2004), 'Cleanfeed: the Facts', *LINX Public Affairs*, https://publicaffairs.linx.net/news/?p=154, accessed 15 January 2010.

Internet Watch Foundation (undated), 'IWF URL List Policy and Procedures', http://www.iwf.org.uk/services/blocking/iwf-url-list-policy-and-procedures, accessed 15 February 2011.

Internet Watch Foundation (2010a), 'Content Assessment Appeal Process', http://www.iwf.org.uk/accountability/complaints/content-assessment-appeal-process, accessed 15 February 2011.

Internet Watch Foundation (2010b), 'IWF Facilitation of the Blocking Initiative', http://www.iwf.org.uk/public/page.148.437.htm, accessed 17 March 2010.

Internet Watch Foundation (2011a), '2010 Annual Report', http://www.iwf.org.uk/assets/
media/annualreports/Internet%20Watch%20Foundation%20Annual%20Report%20
2010%20web.pdf.

Internet Watch Foundation (2011b), 'IWF URL List Recipients', http://www.iwf.org.uk/
services/blocking/iwf-list-recipients, accessed 18 May 2011.

Johnson, D.R. and D.G. Post (1996), 'Law and Borders – The Rise of Law in Cyberspace',
Stanford Law Review, **48**, 1367.

Kleinschmidt, B. (2010), 'An International Comparison of ISP's Liabilities for Unlawful
Third Party Content', *International Journal of Law and Information Technology*, **18(4)**, 332.

Koops, B.-J. et al. (2006), 'Should Self-Regulation be the Starting Point?', in B.-J. Koops et
al. (eds), *Starting Points for ICT Regulation: Deconstructing Prevalent Policy One-Liners*,
The Hague: T.M.C. Asser Press.

Kreimer, S. (2006), 'Censorship by Proxy: The First Amendment, Internet Intermediaries,
and the Problem of the Weakest Link', *University of Pennsylvania Law Review*, **155**, 11.

Lambers, R. (2006), 'Code and Speech. Speech Control Through Network Architecture',
E. Dommering and L. Asscher (eds), *Coding Regulation: Essays on the Normative Role of
Information Technology*, The Hague: T.M.C. Asser Press.

Leaseweb (2009), 'LeaseWeb 1st Hosting Provider to Install Child Porn Filter', http://
blog.leaseweb.com/2009/03/16/leaseweb-1st-hosting-provider-to-install-child-porn-filter/,
accessed 20 July 2011.

Leppard, D. (2005), 'Child porn suspects set to be cleared in evidence "shambles"', *The
Sunday Times*, http://www.timesonline.co.uk/tol/news/uk/article539974.ece.

Lessig, L. (1999), *Code: And Other Laws of Cyberspace*, New York, NY: Basic Books.

Marsden, C. (2010), *Net Neutrality: Towards a Co-regulatory Solution*, London: Bloomsbury
Academic.

McIntyre, T.J. (2010), 'Blocking Child Pornography on the Internet: European
Union Developments', *International Review of Law, Computers & Technology*, **24(3)**,
209–21.

McIntyre, T.J. and C. Scott (2008), 'Internet Filtering: Rhetoric, Legitimacy, Accountability
and Responsibility', in R. Brownsword and K. Yeung (eds), *Regulating Technologies*,
Oxford: Hart Publishing, http://ssrn.com/abstract=1103030.

Metz, C. (2008), 'New York sends AOL "how-to-wiretap" slides', *The Register*, http://www.
theregister.co.uk/2008/10/20/cuomo_pron_crusade_continues/, accessed 30 June 2009.

Moore, T. and R. Clayton (2008), 'The Impact of Incentives on Notice and Take-down',
http://weis2008.econinfosec.org/papers/MooreImpact.pdf.

Morrison, S.R. (2011), 'What the Cops Can't Do, Internet Service Providers Can: Preserving
Privacy in Email Contents', *SSRN eLibrary*, http://papers.ssrn.com/sol3/papers.
cfm?abstract_id=1729000, accessed 23 February 2011.

Mueller, M. (2010), *Networks and States: The Global Politics of Internet Governance*,
Cambridge, MA: MIT Press.

New Zealand Department of Internal Affairs (2010), 'Digital Child Exploitation Filtering
System Code of Practice'.

O'Donnell, I. and C. Milner (2007), *Child Pornography: Crime, Computers and Society*,
Cullompton: Willan.

Ofcom (2008), 'Ofcom's Response to the Byron Review', http://www.ofcom.org.uk/research/
telecoms/reports/byron/, accessed 11 April 2009.

Office of the Attorney General (2010), 'Attorney General Cuomo announces expansion of
groundbreaking initiative to eliminate sharing of thousands of images of child pornography on social networking web sites', *New York State Attorney General*, http://www.ag.ny.
gov/media_center/2010/june/june21a_10.html, accessed 30 March 2011.

Ohm, P. (2009), 'The Rise and Fall of Invasive ISP Surveillance', *University of Illinois Law
Review*, 1417.

O'Neill, S. (2010), 'Government ban on internet firms that do not block child sex
sites', *The Times*, http://technology.timesonline.co.uk/tol/news/tech_and_web/the_web/
article7055882.ece, accessed 12 March 2010.

Ozimek, J. (2009), 'A censorship model', *The Guardian*, http://www.guardian.co.uk/commentisfree/libertycentral/2009/aug/02/internet-censor, accessed 21 September 2009.

Price, M.E. and S. Verhulst (2005), *Self-Regulation and the Internet*, The Hague: Kluwer Law International.

La Quadrature du Net (2011), 'French LOPPSI Bill Adopted: The Internet under Control?', http://www.laquadrature.net/en/french-loppsi-bill-adopted-the-internet-under-control, accessed 15 February 2011.

Richardson, T. (2004a), 'BT on child porn stats', *The Register*, http://www.theregister.co.uk/2004/07/22/bt_ispa_cleanfeed/, accessed 25 January 2009.

Richardson, T. (2004b), 'ISPA seeks analysis of BT's "Cleanfeed" stats', *The Register*, http://www.theregister.co.uk/2004/07/21/ispa_bt_cleanfeed/, accessed 25 January 2009.

Richmond, R. (2011), 'Facebook's New Way to Combat Child Pornography', *New York Times*, http://gadgetwise.blogs.nytimes.com/2011/05/19/facebook-to-combat-child-porn-using-microsofts-technology/, accessed 20 July 2011.

Russell, D.E.H. and N.J. Purcell, (2005), 'Exposure to Pornography as a Cause of Child Sexual Victimization', in N.E. Dowd, D.G. Singer and R.F. Wilson (eds), *Handbook of Children, Culture, and Violence*, London: Sage, pp. 59–84.

Salgado, R.P. (2006), 'Fourth Amendment Search and the Power of the Hash', *Harvard Law Review Forum*, **119**, 38.

Soghoian, C. (2010), 'Privacy and Law Enforcement: Caught in the Cloud: Privacy, Encryption, and Government Back Doors in the Web 2.0 Era', *J. of Telecomm. & High Tech. L*, **8**, 359–613.

Soghoian, C. (2011), 'An End to Privacy Theatre: Exposing and Discouraging Corporate Disclosure of User Data to the Government', *Minnesota Journal of Law, Science and Technology*, **12(1)**, 191.

Stol, W. et al. (2008), 'Filtering Child Pornography on the Internet: An Investigation of National and International Techniques and Regulations', http://www.wodc.nl/onderzoeksdatabase/internetfilters-tegen-kinderporno.aspx?cp=44&cs=6780.

Stol, W. et al. (2009), 'Governmental Filtering of Websites: The Dutch Case', *Computer Law & Security Review*, **25**, 251–62.

Svantesson, D.J.B. (2008), 'How Does the Accuracy of Geo-Location Technologies Affect the Law', *Masaryk University Journal of Law & Technology*, **2**, 11.

Swire, P.P. (1998), 'Of Elephants, Mice, and Privacy: International Choice of Law and the Internet', *The International Lawyer*, **32**, 991.

Tambini, D., D. Leonardi and C. Marsden (2008), *Codifying Cyberspace: Communications Self-Regulation in the Age of Internet Convergence*, London: Routledge.

Villeneuve, N. (2010), 'Barriers to Cooperation: An Analysis of the Origins of International Efforts to Protect Children Online', in R. Deibert et al. (eds), *Access Controlled: The Shaping of Power, Rights and Rule in Cyberspace*, Cambridge, MA: MIT Press.

Walden, I. (2010), 'Porn, Pipes and the State: Censoring Internet Content', *The Barrister*, **(44)**, 16–17.

Watt, R. and A. Maurushat (2009), 'Clean Feed: Australia's Internet Filtering Proposal', *Internet Law Bulletin*, **12(2)**, http://www.austlii.edu.au/au/journals/UNSWLRS/2009/7.html, accessed 6 May 2009.

Whittaker, Z. (2009), 'Microsoft develops image DNA technology for fighting child porn', http://blogs.zdnet.com/igeneration/?p=3655, accessed 22 February 2010.

Williams, C. (2009), 'Home Office backs down on net censorship laws', *The Register*, http://www.theregister.co.uk/2009/10/16/home_office_iwf_legislation/, accessed 16 October 2009.

Williams, C. (2011), 'Hollywood studios ask High Court to block film website', *The Telegraph*, http://www.telegraph.co.uk/technology/news/8597596/Hollywood-studios-ask-High-Court-to-block-film-website.html, accessed 20 July 2011.

Zittrain, J. (2003), 'Internet Points of Control', *Boston College Law Review*, **44**, 653.

Zuvela, M. (2011), 'Deleting trumps blocking in fight against online child porn', *Deutsche Welle*, http://www.dw-world.de/dw/article/0, 14968970,00.html, accessed 7 April 2011.

Cases

Center for Democracy and Technology v. Pappert 337 F.Supp.2d 606 (2004).
United States v. Brent Terry 522 F.3d 645 (2008).
United States v. Richardson 607 F.3d 357 (2010).

13. Privacy, law, code and social networking sites
Lilian Edwards

INTRODUCTION

> Giving the public details about oneself is a bourgeois temptation I have always resisted.
>
> Gustave Flaubert[1]

The Rise of Social Networking Sites (SNSs)

Times have changed somewhat since Flaubert wrote these words just before his death in 1880. Nowadays self-disclosure is not only socially acceptable, but also big business. The social networking boom has been going on for nearly a decade, a long time in internet history, with no sign of bust yet in sight.

Facebook, created in 2004 by Mark Zuckerberg, and perhaps the most iconic site in this field, reached, to media frenzy,[2] 500 million users[3] in 2010 – equivalent in "population" to the third biggest country in the world, with growth to one billion achieved in October 2012.[4] Half these users, Facebook claims, log on every other day and spend 700 billion minutes per month on Facebook. Facebook and other SNSs have stolen time (and advertising) from other better established entertainment media. A survey in the UK in April 2011 showed UK users spending two hours per day watching TV as opposed to two and a half hours on Facebook. Much of this access time is via smartphones rather than conventional computers, with half its users logging on via phone, and interestingly, 49 per cent of those surveyed said Facebook "was always on". In some countries such as Italy, it is anecdotally said that the younger generation regard Facebook as the whole of "the internet", using the platform to perform all their messaging, networking and content access tasks. To not be on Facebook is thus increasingly, at least in the US, EU and many non-Western wired markets a choice which is less a matter of idiosyncratic personal (or psychological, or parental) taste and more something that risks social exclusion, especially for the young. As we will see below, this has important consequences when thinking about the impact of Facebook and its kin on personal privacy, and how regulation should deal with this.

While the youth demographic is the most obvious class of SNS user (30 per cent of global users of Facebook in 2010 were aged 18–24), over a quarter of FB global users are aged 35 or older and the "silver surfer" demographic is one of the fastest growing.[5] 125 million people are counted as regular users of Facebook in the US and 26 million – half the population – in the UK, the second most vociferous Facebook-using nation; but the site is also widely used throughout the world, with only Russia, Japan and China outstanding as major SNS markets where Facebook is not the leading player.[6] In Europe, over a third of 9–12 year olds and three quarters of 13–16 year olds have their own SNS profile, despite the fact that Facebook's own rules ban under-13s from creating a profile and many SNSs have similar constraints.[7]

Facebook is not alone in the market. The social network phenomenon has spawned sites for every niche and social occasion: there are sites for students and seniors, Jews, gay people and Muslims, families and fetishists, and for every language and nationality imaginable. Some early success stories such as MySpace, Bebo and Friends Reunited are already bankrupt or in decline. Some new stars have emerged with new niche selling points, such as the phenomenally successful Twitter, which launched the idea of "micro-blogging" sites; or Foursquare, which has popularised the idea of social networking based around mobile users and locational data (a concept now taken up by, among others, Facebook Places and Google Latitude). Some such as Google-owned Orkut, are well known in certain countries – here, the Portuguese speaking world – and unknown in Anglophone circles. Some, such as LinkedIn, service a business rather than entertainment function. Some aim only at restricted age demographics such as Bebo, popular with the very young in the UK, and Club Penguin. Many services which started off to offer one type of entertainment, such as music streaming, or gaming, now also incorporate a social networking component, eg iTunes and Ping.

In Europe, a diverse pattern emerges of social networking uptake, fostered by differences in language, culture and history, especially among young people.[8] Although Facebook, with the market lead in 17 out of 25 EU markets, is overall the dominant player, especially among the very young (57 per cent of European 9–16 year olds use Facebook as their only or most popular SNS), in a number of European countries it is not the most popular SNS for youth overall; eclipsed eg by Hyves in the Netherlands and SchulerVZ in Germany. Livingstone et al (2011) working on the EU Kids Online project emphasise that this means understanding the social networking experience for the young in the EU is complex, driven not only by general factors such as age, gender and parenting style but also by the particular culture, rules and code of the most popular national SNSs.

For most SNSs, unlike Facebook so far, their popularity seems to be cyclical as the target audience moves on to the next big thing. The social networking phenomenon itself however so far seems to be resilient, with elements of social networking pervading other areas of the Web and other types of business. Social networking is used in education, to promote brands and advertise businesses, and famously, to help organise political movements and breed dissidence.[9] This is a long way from telling people what you had for breakfast. Inarguably, social networking is worthy of study from an economic, sociological, psychological, economic and political perspective. This chapter however will mainly restrain itself of necessity to a legal perspective, although work from these other disciplines will also be referred to, especially the extensive literature on children and social networking. It is also written from a primarily European legal perspective, although the phenomenon is of course, global.

Social networking sites (SNSs) can be characterised as "online social networks for communities of people who share interests and activities, or who are interested in exploring the interests and activities of others, and which necessitates the use of software".[10] SNSs differ enormously in their intended audience, numbers of users, business models, platforms (mobile, desktop, etc) and interfaces, but a number of structural points of similarity exist, with most containing some or all of:

- A facility to build "friends" or "buddy" lists, and to restrict some or all user personal data to only being visible by this group, or subsets thereof;
- disclosure of personal information via pre-structured "user profiles" including items such as name, picture of user, nickname, address, email address, birthdate, phone number, home city or town, school or college, pets, relatives etc;
- disclosure of some data in free form eg "status updates";
- A "news feed" or "timeline" ie, an amalgamated representation of data disclosed by different users at different times and in different contexts on the site (or, indeed, beyond it);
- non-explicit disclosure of personal data via eg user's navigation on site, user's clicking of images or text, user's location disclosed when accessing SNS by wireless or mobile internet connection.

As will also be seen below, most of these common features which enable and enhance social networking and allow the site to survive financially, are unfortunately also sources of concern when we turn to looking at user privacy. Newer features of SNSs which are allowing them to grow even more popular, such as smartphone access, locational data services (such as "check in" or "find your friends") and above all, the "app" economy – where a variety of third party services are delivered to the user via the main SNS platform – also inevitably turn out to involve even more ubiquitous privacy risks.

Business Model and Governance

SNSs do not all (yet) make money but some very clearly do. Facebook was valued at a peak capitalisation of $104 billion when it launched itself with great fanfare on the stock market in May 2012, although the shares issued have since been seen as initially overvalued and stock gain predictions have failed to materialise.[11] How these sites make money is crucial to understanding their relationship with privacy and personal data. Sites like Facebook monetise what appears to be a "free to users" service primarily by collecting the very rich vein of personal data subscribers disclose, adding it to other databases, mining it and turning it into anonymised profiles, and then selling these to marketers and advertisers so they can select which ads selected users with certain characteristics get to see (eg single; Christian; keen on football; certain geographical locations). These targeted or "behavioural" adverts command a premium in the ad economy because users are far more likely to click on them[12] than on standard "broadcast" adverts.

Other revenue streams exist for SNSs, such as the sale of merchandise, "virtual" gifts, brand sponsorship, etc, but these pale into insignificance beside the commodification of personal data. In some cases a fee paid by users is an alternative to the "free" service, which may provide premium services, such as relief from ads, extra functionality, loyalty bonuses etc. Such a "freemium" mixed economy has become the aspirational (if not yet always actual) model in the music online services world (eg Spotify, which has many social networking characteristics[13]) but in the mainstream SNS world, personal data remains the main price paid for services. As the EU Commissioner, Meglena Kuneva, famously said in 2009, personal data is the "new oil of the internet and the new currency of the digital world" (Kuneva 2009).

The relationship between SNSs, revenue and privacy protection is more complicated than the above simple equation between personal data and profit makes it sound. In a fascinating survey of 45 SNSs from all over the world, Bonneau and Preibusch 2009 found that the success of an SNS in the market is inversely correlated to the amount of attention it pays, and communicates to its users, concerning pro-privacy practices. Their conclusion was not just that SNSs try to maximise revenue by manipulating users to disclose as much data as possible but more subtly, that privacy as a user choice is positively excluded, and privacy conscious users are discouraged as non-profitable troublemakers. "Sites take care to avoid mentioning privacy . . ., because even mentioning privacy positively will cause them [other users] to be more cautious about sharing data. This phenomenon is known as 'privacy salience' and it makes sites tread very carefully around privacy, because users must be comfortable sharing data for the site to be fun" (Bonneau 2009). As a result, Bonneau and Preibusch suggest, SNSs intuitively adopt policies which are likely to alienate privacy fundamentalists and scare them away, eg demanding full real names rather than pseudonyms, and failing to implement secure protocols (for example, Facebook's recent dragging of feet on implementing the HTTPS protocol). They also find it in their best interests to keep privacy policies, even though demanded by law in the USA and elsewhere, as hard to find, read and understand as possible. We take up this point below.

Governance: Contract and Privacy/Data Protection Law

Both users (data subjects) and owners (data controllers) on SNSs are governed in their behaviour by a number of regulatory mechanisms. As Lessig's famous analysis suggests (Lessig 2006), regulation can be divided into law, norms, market and "code". This chapter will primarily look at the regulatory influence of law, and of "code" – the software and especially the privacy settings that an SNS employs. The influence of the market – primarily driving SNSs towards favouring disclosure over privacy – has been considered in part above. "Soft law" – norm creation by non-binding guidelines or standards – will also be considered, as will *social* norms.

Despite the best efforts of a flourishing vein of academic and libertarian commentary which has tried to redefine some SNS-like environments – notably gaming or "virtual world" environments such as World of Warcraft and Second Life – as "virtual states", which should bow in part or whole to the democratic wishes of their citizens or "netizens",[14] in reality, SNSs are largely commercially motivated dictatorships, with users governed unilaterally by the terms and conditions of the subscriber contract. These contract terms and conditions include privacy policies and acceptable use policies, and are also sometimes known (in software licensing parlance) as "end user license agreements" or EULAs. The fact that this contract is of course a standard term and non-negotiable instrument, imposed as classic consumer law would say, with a significant imbalance of power and asymmetry of information between the parties, on a "take it or leave it" basis – and in a marketplace where for various reasons, competition on terms of service such as privacy guarantees, does not flourish – will also be commented on below.[15]

Contract law is not the only law relevant here however. In Europe, data protection (DP) law is seen as the key legal regime regulating the collection, processing, sharing, selling and deletion of personal data on SNSs. In the US, despite the lack of an omnibus privacy protection law in the private sector, some governance is exercised over privacy policies and deceptive practices by the Federal Trade Commission (FTC), and some sectoral privacy protection law will be relevant, most notably the Children's Online Privacy Protection Act (COPPA).[16] In many other non EU states, national privacy laws will also be relevant eg in Canada, the PIPEDA (Personal Information Protection and Electronic Documents Act). In the section on law below, we will focus only on EU DP law, as by far the most stringent set of privacy rules operating in the developed world.

Contract law has of course its limits in that it binds only the parties privy to the contract. As discussed below in the section on social networking harms, some problems arise for users of SNSs (and, indeed, for persons who refuse to join social networks) not because of the actions of the site with whom they have contractual relations, but because of the acts of third parties: eg, other users on a site who tag their name on photos or in notes against their will; marketers or scammers who scrape personal details from public profiles. In these kinds of circumstances, general privacy laws such as DP law should provide protection; however in reality there are often insurmountable legal and practical enforcement difficulties.[17]

It should also be remembered that conventional laws relating to liability for defamatory, fraudulent, copyright-infringing, confidential[18] or obscene material may be invoked against SNS users, just as they can in more traditional publication arenas. Liability may also conceivably fall upon the owner or operator of the SNS platform as the "publisher" of the offending material, or under theories of authorisation, inducement, vicarious liability, etc. There is relatively little authority in Europe on the liability of the SNS in such circumstances, but it seems logical to assume that the immunity regimes or safe harbours of the EC Electronic Commerce Directive Arts 12–15 might apply to SNSs as to other hosts.[19] Such regimes typically give online hosts of third party content exclusion from any civil or criminal liability relating to that material, so long as material is removed expeditiously on notice of illegality. For these reasons as well as for good customer relations, it is common for SNSs which operate in Europe to provide a hotline or "abuse team" to receive complaints from users about content in breach of the acceptable use policies, so that prompt take down can provide a shield from liability.

In the US, by contrast, online services are rendered entirely immune from liability for publication torts under the Communications Decency Act s 230(c) (although liability for copyright infringement – dealt with by the Digital Millennium Copyright Act – and criminal material such as child pornography is excluded from this safe harbour). As a result it has been argued that SNSs in the US may be encouraged to be irresponsible in not adequately policing the content there accessible, especially to impressionable minors, since they are shielded from negligence actions.[20] One way of compelling SNSs to take user privacy seriously might be to hold them vicariously liable for privacy harms resulting from disclosures on their sites: however given the biggest SNSs are US-based, this total immunity would make this strategy impossible to enforce.

Young People and Social Networking

Finally, as already noted, there are specific privacy worries around the fact that SNS often target children and young persons as a key audience.[21] Early social networking websites, for example, included Classmates.com (founded 1995), focusing on ties with former school mates, and Facebook (founded 2004) originally built its audience by "capturing" entire school or undergraduate student years as a kind of digital class yearbook. Given the perceived vulnerability of young people in the online environment, their risk taking behaviour as recently documented by psychologists and neurologists, the lack of control over online life by parents and the general lack of life experience of children, this raises further concerns. It is stressed however that the problems with privacy associated with SNSs are often problems for all users, only exacerbated by youth demographic characteristics. We discuss this in the next section.

THE PROBLEM: SOCIAL NETWORKING HARMS vs BENEFITS

Harms

If law is to be invoked to regulate a social activity, it must, it is asserted, be shown to have demonstrable and sizeable risks or harms. Social networks have been accused in recent years of causing almost every possible social blight imaginable by the mass media, especially in relation to young people; encouraging sexual predators and grooming behaviour, encouraging suicidal behaviour and incitement thereto,[22] inciting and enabling fraud, deception, stalking, harassment, bullying, abuse and victimisation as well as encouraging young people to inflict antisocial behaviour on each other.[23] In one famous UK tabloid article it was even suggested that Facebook might cause cancer.[24] In the wake of the UK riots of summer

2011, social media have been widely accused of encouraging and inciting youth looting and violence, and Prime Minister David Cameron has threatened legislation to block, suspend or censor social media in ways previously mainly associated with non-democratic states.

The EU Kids Online survey (EU Kids Online 2011, p. 3), which surveyed children under 16 across all EU countries from 2006–2011, suggests children under 16 and even under nine do encounter risks online, but these do not always translate to harms, or are not always perceived as such by the children themselves. The EU Safer Social Networking guidelines[25] divide problems caused by SNSs into four categories: *contact* (inappropriate contact with children by adults); *conduct* (how young people themselves behave online and to each other (eg cyberbullying); access to *illegal* content; access to *age inappropriate content*. Interestingly there is no explicit mention of loss of *privacy* online. While there is clearly overlap within these categories (and harms not covered), the focus of the rest of this chapter is on regulation of privacy only, not on child protection as such.

Privacy harms arising out of the SNS phenomenon are not well defined in the literature, partly because of the constant intermixing of issues connected with child *safety* and child *privacy*. Similarly, because of the emphasis on child protection, the problems affecting the privacy of *all* users of SNSs, adult and child, are not as well researched as dangers specific to the young. There has however been extensive concern from adult users and the media about Facebook and its privacy settings since, particularly, redesigns of these in 2009 and 2010 in ways that were seen as covertly forcing users to share more and more personal data against their will.[26]

boyd and Hargittai 2010 trace a concern about Facebook privacy emerging and growing in US and global society through a series of privacy incidents or panics from around 2006 on. They trace successive user resistance to the introduction of the "newsfeed" in 2006, Facebook Beacon in 2007, redesign and complication of privacy settings in 2009 (which exposed much of a basic user profile to the public by default, unless steps were taken to "opt out" from disclosure), and another redesign featuring "Instant Personaliser" and "Social Plugins" in 2010, which again disclosed more data as a matter of "opt-out" rather than "opt-in" as well as displaying data drawn from other websites on Facebook. By 2010, EPIC had filed a complaint against Facebook with the FTC, the EFF had called for a Bill of Privacy Rights and 31 May 2010 was declared "Quit Facebook Day".

Outside the US, in Canada the Privacy Commissioner forced Facebook after formal investigation to make significant changes to its rules and settings in August 2009[27] and launched another investigation in 2010,[28] and the UK Information Commissioner investigated Facebook on the matter of whether profiles deleted were really terminated or merely deactivated with all personal data retained.[29] The European Commission (2010) in its proposals for reform of the Data Protection Directive (DPD) states as a ground for reform that "Data Protection Authorities, business associations and consumers' organisations [agree] that risks to privacy and the protection of personal data associated with online activity are increasing" (at p. 14). Similar actions and concerns have been expressed throughout Europe and elsewhere[30] and seem to convey an unmistakeable impression of concern by society and regulators with privacy harms arising from SNSs, especially, but not exclusively, in relation to children.

How then can we categorise these harms arising on SNSs and thus assess how best to prevent or reduce them? There are a number of ways to cut this cake. One approach might be to divide them into harms deriving from

- *explicit voluntary* disclosure of personal data then accessed or processed out of context in some way leading to harm (eg data disclosed in the belief friends only would see it, but later viewed by parents; data disclosed to world for networking purposes, but abused to commit crimes by ID thieves or burglars); and
- *non explicit involuntary* disclosure of personal data leading to harms (eg collection of user behavioural data to generate invasive targeted advertising).

Another approach is to distinguish *current* harms – eg, peer cyberbullying behaviour – from *future* or potential harms eg, possible discrimination by future employers on the basis of undesirable behaviour archived online and/or discoverable via search engines such as Google;[31] possible future social sorting on the basis of information disclosed about (say) income, age, gender, social class, ethnicity or risk taking behaviours;[32] possible damage to future relationships when prospective partners "Google" to pre-scan their date for problems.

Yet a third approach would distinguish harms inflicted or anticipated by parties who are *strangers* to the user concerned from harms inflicted by *known parties* – "friends", peers, relatives or teachers. The first is sometimes called "stranger danger" in the context of child protection, meaning stranger adults who are potentially abusers of children, but might actually embrace a wider range of actors. These "strangers" can themselves be divided into those who might be regarded as engaging in "legitimate", or justified, or beneficial surveillance – eg the police, private investigators, insurance or debt collection companies, civil litigators – and those whose surveillance is "illegitimate" ie motivated by illegal, harmful or anti-social purposes – eg ID thieves, burglars, fraudsters, spammers, phishers, stalkers, others engaged in harassment, and at the furthest extreme, potential abusers or predators. In the second category, peer harms are seen in contexts such as "cyberbullying", which is one of the most pressing current problems reported by young persons. Peer surveillance by parents, guardians or teachers is on the other hand normally regarded as socially beneficial and unproblematic; but for young persons themselves, it may be perceived as a particularly damaging intrusion into their privacy.[33]

Which if any of these "harms" need to be fixed by law or other remediating instrument? Is there always a correspondence between those harms most emphasised by the media, politicians or parents and those which inflict the most actual damage? The EU Kids Online survey assessment of risks and harms to children in EU countries suggests not. A social or policy consensus on this would make the task of the privacy-concerned lawyer in this area much easier.

We can examine these various types of harms using an illustrative case study.

THE OXFORD PHILOSOPHER AND THE UNIVERSITY PROCTORS

In July 2007, Oxford proctors in charge of discipline at the ancient university used Facebook to find evidence of students breaking university disciplinary rules. Students, who, in post-exam hilarity, had held wild parties, sprayed each other with champagne or shaving foam, or thrown flour bombs at each other, often posted photos of these incidents on Facebook. Proctors combed Facebook for evidence of such incidents and caught a number of students *in flagrante.* As a result, a number of students received disciplinary emails or more vigorous sanctions. The response from students was dismay and shock. The student union claimed that the incident was a "disgraceful" intrusion into the privacy of the students concerned. One caught perpetrator complained that she was "outraged":

> Alex Hill, 21, a maths and philosophy student, received an e-mail stating that three of her photos provided evidence that she had engaged in "disorderly" conduct. "I don't know how the proctors got access to it," the St Hugh's College student said. "I thought my privacy settings were such that only students could see my pictures."
> "They cited three links to pictures on my Facebook profile where I've got shaving foam all over me. They must just do it randomly because it would take hours and hours to go through every profile. I'm outraged. It's truly bizarre that they're paying staff to sit and go through Facebook. It must be extremely time-consuming."[34]

Although this case is now several years old (it was the first Facebook privacy incident to make major media headlines in the UK) similar incidents have been widely reported since. For example, boyd and Marwick (2011) note an incident where local police and teachers put together a slide show of images grabbed from Facebook profiles and showed these to the student body to encourage better online safety practices. Students were furious, one declaring that this was "a violation of privacy" (boyd and Marwick 2011). Similar outrage was stirred by a pro-privacy group which put together a site called "Openbook" in early 2010. Openbook merely displayed information which had been scraped from public profiles freely accessible on Facebook, but did it in an entertaining way as a specialised "Facebook search engine". Searches could be input such as "playing hookey", "pulling a fast one" and "duvet day" and the results displayed from profiles and status updates, complete with username and photos. Many searchers were horrified at the large-scale display of incriminating information to the world.[35]

The Privacy Paradox and Whether Young People Value Privacy on SNSs

These cases all concern voluntary disclosures of explicit data, which when taken out of the intended context – communication with a known set of peers – caused or had the potential to cause social and possibly legal embarrassment – harm – to the data subject. Such cases commonly inspire the common-sense reaction: "If they didn't want this to be seen, why did they disclose it?" or the more sophisticated version "Why didn't they restrict access to it using privacy settings?" Sociologically, this kind of example tends to lead to a belief that SNS users, particularly young people and children, do not value their privacy, and thus do not seek or need to have it protected. The most common policy derived is that if people, especially children, are educated that what they disclose on SNSs may have harmful consequences, they will cease to adopt such risky behaviour. Accordingly, there is no need for law to engage with disclosure on social networks and regulate the market. Such a conclusion is naturally not repelled by the SNSs whose profits, as noted above, are tied to disclosure and not to privacy protection; and is appealing to governments who fear over-regulating and alienating the new digital economies, and who have little money to spend on enforcing or creating legislation.

The reality disclosed by recent research is somewhat different. First, studies show repeatedly that just because young people regularly disclose personal and possibly damaging material on SNSs, this does not necessarily mean they do not value their privacy and do not wish it protected. Barnes 2006 and other researchers have called this the "privacy paradox" – the disconnect between "the way users say they feel about the privacy settings of their blogs and how they react once they experience unanticipated consequences from a breach of privacy" (Barnes 2006 citing Viegas 2005). Barnes' conclusion was that "on the Internet, the illusion of privacy creates boundary problems", for new users especially (see also Katz and Rice 2002). Students and young persons clearly wanted to keep information private from some persons, eg parents and teachers, but did not seem to realise Facebook was a public space.

Palfrey, Gasser and boyd (2010, p. 11) summarising recent research in February 2010, argue similarly and strenuously that despite the privacy paradox, teens "do in fact care about privacy". First, teens may be aware of the privacy risks but make a judgment call to risk them given the benefits of disclosing on social networks and their feeling that threatened harms are less risky than loss of social inclusion. Secondly, perceptions of young people as to what is private and what public may be different from those of older or less online-oriented users, and their behaviours are accordingly also different (though see to contrary, Hoofnagle et al 2010). Thirdly, especially in countries where users (including less technoliterate or educated users, as well as the young) are less sophisticated about online behaviour, it may mean that they were unaware of or unable to manipulate privacy settings, or were falsely confident that they had set their privacy controls to protect their disclosures of personal data, but had not in fact succeeded in setting them correctly.

Palfrey, Gasser and boyd (2010) justify this, first, from evidence that young people are in fact more vigilant about their privacy than older SNS users, being more likely to alter their privacy settings than older users, and engaging in a variety of activities to fool observers and defeat exclusionary policies eg volunteering fake ages, names etc; refusing to volunteer information; avoiding certain websites which make unreasonable demands or pass on information without permission.

Secondly, Palfrey, Gasser and boyd (2010), Steeves (2006) and many other researchers assert that young users regard SNSs not as a public space open to the world, but as a social space where they have, in legal parlance, reasonable expectations of privacy, not of absolute privacy but of sharing confidences only with a known and limited group. While adults often refer to their home or their bedroom as their most private space, for teenagers, in an age when parenting often closely resembles policing, such spaces are routinely invaded or surveilled by parents without permission or notice. Children's diaries are read, their bathrooms entered, their living spaces shared. Steeves (2006, p. 184) notes that children compare having online activity monitored to having their pockets searched or being stalked. Accordingly, SNSs become the private spaces of choice, free from the prying eyes of parents or teachers, but where disclosures are made to cement social bonds.

boyd and Marwick (2011) call this not-private not-public space a "networked public space", the modern equivalent of hanging out at the mall or the cinema, where group and individual social identities are worked out and social skills evolved. In such a context, Ms Hill's "outrage" at being stalked in an "underhand" fashion by Oxford proctors on Facebook seems understandable, rather than incomprehensible in an intelligent Oxford graduate: she believed she was operating in a peer group space technically open to the world but in fact of interest only to her selected peer group and was rudely awakened when external surveillance by law enforcement intervened. Her expectations of the *context* of her disclosures had been violated (see further Nissenbaum 2004).

Code, Privacy Settings and Defaults

The second theme that arises from the Oxford case study relates to the notion that teens and, indeed, possibly other SNS users (the old, the less digitally empowered) do have an understanding of and desire for privacy, and sometimes attempt to use SNS code to control access to their digital lives, but fail because they make mistakes when trying to adjust privacy settings on SNSs.

In the Oxford example above, it is very likely that Ms Hill was misled in this way (though the newspaper report does not make it clear). On Facebook, in the UK, in 2007, the default site setting was that profiles, including photos of events posted, were visible to everyone in the user's default "network". At the time this was relatively unknown to UK users.[36] For Ms Hill, an Oxford student with, one assumes, an *oxford.ac.uk* email address, her posts and photos would have been visible in their entirety to every member of the Oxford university network (unless she had deliberately altered these default settings – see below). While, from press reports, Ms Hill seems to have been aware that she belonged to a network and that this had disclosure implications, what she possibly failed to anticipate was that not only students but also staff on the Oxford University payroll (including proctors) might have *oxford.ac.uk* email addresses, and thus also have access by default to her profile and photos.

Privacy settings on SNSs can generally be altered by users, and Facebook has had an ever evolving set of user controls to change privacy settings since its inception. Two key points need to be made here. One, the defaults tend to be set to maximise disclosure and minimise privacy. Given the revenue stream of the SNS arises from disclosure of data, and that the success of the site is generally based on growth which is itself accelerated by the amount of disclosed as opposed to secret activity on site, this is hardly surprising.

Secondly, default settings are important because it is an effort to change them and this consumer inertia means that defaults often remain as they are even if their effects are harmful to the consumer (see Kesan and Shah 2006). The Oxford case shows this very well. If Ms Hill did nothing, then by default she shared her details with everyone in the Oxford University network, with, for her, unfortunate consequences.

Near the beginning of the SNS boom, privacy settings were often crude, making gross distinctions (eg either everyone in a group of friends could see all photos, rather than only one photo, or some members of the group) and the evidence was that few users were aware if these controls existed; even fewer took the time and energy to make changes. Gross and Acquisti (2005), for example, found that only 1.2 per cent of Carnegie Mellon students surveyed had changed their default settings to make their profile more private, and concluded that "only a vanishingly small number of users change the (permissive) default privacy preferences". There were good reasons for this: privacy settings were frequently hidden away as thoroughly as possible on the site, and site upgrades nearly always make privacy controls less not more visible. Instructions on how to use privacy controls were often difficult to understand or misleading, and controls were not consistent across different SNSs, or even within SNSs eg different rules for disclosure of photos than status updates.

More recent evidence however shows that the younger generation at least may have become relatively accustomed to changing privacy settings, whether as a result of media publicity, online safety education or peer sharing of expertise. The Pew Internet & American Life Project 2010 found that 71 per cent of 18–29 year olds reported changing their privacy settings, while only 62 per cent of those aged 30–49 and 55 per cent of those aged 50–64 had done so. boyd and Hargittai 2010 also reported that most Facebook users in their survey of 18–19 year old college students changed their privacy settings at least once in 2009 and engagement with changing settings increased significantly between 2009 and 2010 (table 5a) and 5b) in boyd and Hargittai 2010) when the media was filled with Facebook privacy scare stories. These findings suggest that the young have either become more aware of privacy risks or more adept at taking steps to manage their profile or, most likely, both.

The older generation, and those from cultures less "wired" than North America may still be doing less well. The UK's Ofcom 2008 study for example showed that almost half of all UK SNS users left their privacy settings on the default, including 44 per cent of adults surveyed.

But even if uptake on changing defaults is increasing, a large number of factors still mitigate against changing privacy default settings *successfully*. As privacy controls have become increasingly sophisticated and granular – ironically, partly in response to user complaints about privacy – both they, and the accompanying "legal code" – the privacy policy – have become complex and bloated. Bilton (2010a) writing in the *New York Times* noted that the Facebook privacy policy had gone from 1004 words in 2005 to nearly 6000 words in 2010, longer than the US Constitution. If the Privacy FAQ were added in, the length reached 45,000 words – half a novel. He noted further that to change all your privacy settings it was necessary to click through more than 50 buttons and choose from more than 170 options (Bilton 2010b).

More than simple complexity, as privacy settings become more complicated and change more frequently, policing one's privacy becomes a continuing process not a one-time decision. A number of campaigning websites have collected evidence that over time, Facebook's default settings have disclosed more and more personal data. In other words, a user would have had to be more and more practised at changing their settings and keeping up with these changes to maintain the same level of privacy/disclosure. Upsahl 2010 for the EFF noted that each historical change of privacy policy by Facebook had overall disclosed more *types* of data and to more *classes of audience*; McKeon (2010), an independent software engineer, then used this information plus personal knowledge to create a number of infographics visualising the increase in data disclosed and audience disclosure every time the site privacy policy changed.

This bias towards greater disclosure over time of the default settings on Facebook has been so well observed by regular users, that yet another change which requires users to opt out to maintain privacy, tends to be greeted more with resignation than surprise. Such familiarity breeds a certain degree of contempt, with regular users in boyd and Hargittai (2010)'s study reporting a higher degree of confidence in changing privacy settings than in many comparably skilled online activities eg uploading a video to YouTube (see Table 7 in boyd and Hargittai 2010). Given the complexity and opacity of these settings, the question however becomes, *even if* privacy settings are located and altered, is this done successfully? And is the user in a good position to assess with confidence if they have made changes successfully or are still making unwanted disclosures? Finally, are initially successful changes to privacy settings defeated by repeated modifications of defaults by Facebook and other SNSs?

Recent work by Madejski, Johnson and Bellovin (2011) shows for the first time empirical evidence that reported practice or confidence in making changes to privacy settings may be grossly misplaced. In a small study of 65 university students who regularly used Facebook, they found that every one had incorrectly managed their privacy settings, thus disclosing some amount of personal data by error to an unwanted audience. These violations were identified by the researchers but confirmed by the participants in the study, who had previously expressed 95 per cent confidence in their manipulation of settings. The researchers reported this as showing "a serious mismatch between intentions and reality" and that "the current approach to privacy controls is fundamentally flawed and cannot be fixed". Their reasoning was that the basic access control mechanism employed by Facebook was not only over complex but misconceived. Giving users a list of data held, and a set of permissions as choices for that data, does not map usefully to how most users think about their personal privacy. Instead their attitude to data disclosure is determined by the *context* in which disclosure takes place.

boyd (2010) similarly gives the example of a girl who allowed access to her Facebook profile to "friends of friends" but when asked if she wanted her mother to be able to see her profile, replied vehemently in the negative. It was then pointed out to her that she had friended her aunt, who had the girl's mother as a friend. boyd comments

> If Facebook wanted radical transparency . . . they could show [users] who . . . is included in "friends-of-friends" . . . They hide behind lists because people's abstractions allow them to share more. When people think "friends-of-friends" they don't think about all of the types of people that their friends might link to; they think of the people that their friends would bring to a dinner party if they were to host it. When they think of everyone, they think of individual people who might have an interest in them, not [third] party services who want to monetize or redistribute their data.

We return to this idea of context, and ways to specify privacy desires in code (including Madejski, Johnson and Bellovin (2011)'s proposed solution) below.

PROBLEMS OF LOSS OF CONTROL OVER DATA

A second set of problems associated with privacy and SNSs can be described as relating to a user sense of loss of control over data to third parties, via particular code innovations actively implemented by SNSs. Here we will briefly discuss apps; tagging by third parties; targeted advertising and profiling; and connections made between data disclosed on third party sites and SNSs.

Apps

One feature of Facebook which may have helped it become SNS market leader in several countries has been the opening up of the site to applications written by third parties who have entered licensing agreements – the so-called "apps" or Facebook Platform. Apps are used for near infinite purposes, including to play games like Farmville, patience, Tetris or Scrabble, to allow users to send virtual gifts to their friends; to interface with other popular sites such as Twitter, Flickr, Tumblr etc. Facebook claim around 20 million apps are installed per day.[37] What all these apps have in common is that (1) the contractual relationship between the app developer and the SNS site is normally unknown to the user (2) when the user attempts to use the application they are required to consent to a licence which almost invariably requires the user to share his or her own personal data, and sometimes to share the personal data of friends (3) the user's knowledge of their contractual rights against the app developer is often scanty or zero. The responsibility of the SNS platform itself for the app is uncertain, being based around uncertainties such as negligence law rather than codified in any specific way.

Users who sign up for apps rarely note how much personal information they are giving away when they say yes, especially because of their triviality, and as with Facebook itself, there is no option to negotiate on what data is disclosed. In the early days of apps, data disclosure often seemed entirely unrelated to what data was actually needed by the app to function. Edwards and Brown (2009) predicted that this would mean that apps would lure users into disproportionate privacy disclosures, and also become a conduit for collection for dishonest purposes of personal data. This prediction has now come to pass, with apps a regular source of ID theft, malware and other security alerts, leaking personal data both maliciously and accidentally. For example, in May 2011 Symantec announced that hundreds of thousands of apps had been "leaking" user data for years. These apps "could see your profile, photographs, chat messages and collect your personal information – even if you had set it to private".[38]

In early 2011, following the bad PR Facebook received about privacy in 2009–10[39] and an action brought against it by the Canadian Privacy Commissioner (2009a and 2009b) (settlement), Facebook revised its rules (Facebook Rules 2011) for developers of apps. The rules now state that "You will only request the data you need to operate your application" (rule II.1) and that "A user's friends' data can only be used in the context of the user's experience on your application" (at II:4). The result (judging unscientifically by ten random app invites this writer received) is that app requests are now more variable in the access to data they request, and requests are more proportionate to the task the app performs. All app developers still receive by default the user's "basic account information" which means: name, email, gender, birthday, current city, and profile picture URL (rule VII.3). The rules also require the app to have a privacy policy visible to users and forbid apps to share user data with advertising networks or to sell it to third parties. (This of course would interfere with Facebook's own monetisation strategies.) Apps are in principle forbidden to use a user's friends list outside the app. Users are to be given a route to request deletion of their data held by the app, and if an app is terminated by Facebook, all user data collected is to be deleted.

This all sounds good in principle. The question remains however, especially judging by the recent Symantec announcement, how much effort Facebook puts into policing and supervising the activities of its thousands of app developers and their compliance with its developer rules. It is also of course possible, as with the general privacy policy, for Facebook to change these developer rules at any time.[40]

Tagging and Third Party Data Disclosure by Users

On SNSs such as Facebook, photographs can be "tagged" with the names of the users who appear in them, and this tagging can be done not only by the data subject – the person in the photograph – but by any other SNS user. People who do not participate in the SNS itself can also be tagged, usually without their knowledge. It is quite possible that the students caught in the Oxford Facebook case (above) had not been so foolish as to tag themselves in photos depicting illegal acts, but that "friends" had done it for them. Photo-tagging has been one of the "killer app" features of Facebook and there is no community norm discouraging the tagging of other people's photos (although interestingly there do seem to be emerging norms that *deletion* of a tag must be respected). Again, it is possible on Facebook to amend the code defaults so that tagging cannot be done by third parties – but this option is buried in the privacy section and almost certainly entirely ignored by most users. We will return (again) to the issue of the setting of privacy defaults below.

Tagging is also, as noted above (see *Lindqvist v Kammaraklagaren* 2003), legally questionable in Europe where DP rules restrict the processing of the personal data of third parties without their consent, or other ground for processing (see fuller outline of DPO law below). Where persons not members of the SNS are tagged, it is hard to see how any theory of implicit consent could stand up and in the case of sensitive personal data, explicit consent is in any case required.

Loss of Control when Data Is Shared with, or by, Sites other than the SNS

In late 2007, Facebook announced that it had formed a partnership with certain third party retailers in an enterprise called "Facebook Beacon". Facebook took information about user's activities on these partner businesses, and published the details on Facebook for everyone to see. So, for example, a user might find a line on their profile saying "X went to Amazon and bought *The Joy of Gay Sex*" – something they might not want everyone to know, and certainly, in many cases, an embarrassing surprise. Many users complained. 50,000 signed a petition asking Facebook to "stop invading my privacy". Facebook succumbed to user and regulator[41] pressure in December 2007 and changed the system so that users had to explicitly "opt in" to having their details published by the Beacon system. Beacon was killed by the bad publicity and was officially abandoned in 2009.[42]

Facebook Beacon proved to be only the precursor to SNSs entering the world of online targeted or behavioural advertising (OBA). In 2007, both MySpace and Facebook announced their intention to target adverts at users using both explicit data collected from their user profiles, and non-explicit behavioural data (eg pages clicked on), combined with other sources of data, to create anonymised data profiles.[43] This followed in the wake of the enormous success of Google's targeted marketing programme using data gathered from user search terms to generate Google Adwords, and was quickly adopted as a strategy by other SNSs in the market (including Google's own) as well as by other "web 2.0" sites such as eBay.[44] SNSs give advertisers unprecedented access to a rich vein of personal data, often highly sensitive, in a context quite different from why that data was originally disclosed (unlike on Google Adwords). For many users, this produces an ill-defined feeling of distaste and surveillance, particularly where sensitive information disclosed to friends in private or even (as discussed above) in a semi-private "networked public", generates adverts which appear to the user to disclose that information to the world, even where that is not factually the case.

Legally, regulation of OBA is extraordinarily difficult, as the data profiles disclosed to advertisers are inevitably anonymised, and therefore arguably do not fall under the rules relating to either personal data (EU DP law) or Personally Identifiable Information (US) (see Schwartz and Solove 2011). Due to the degree of public and regulatory hostility aroused, however, on both sides of the Atlantic there are moves towards further regulation whether by soft law, hard law or code, with some concept of a "Do Not Track" option for users likely to emerge.[45]

For the moment, Facebook has come full circle from Beacon in 2010 with the introduction of "Social Plug Ins", otherwise known as the distributed "Like" button. What this means is that numerous websites have implemented the Facebook "Like" button, thereby allowing users browsing that site to show their support for, or interest in, that content. An item then appears in the user's Facebook profile and in the newsfeed of their friends (eg "Lilian liked the website Inappropriate Tarot Card Readings."). This has clear advantages for the participating websites in terms of publicity, with up to 80 per cent increases in readership reported, but it also allows Facebook to track where its users go even when they are not on Facebook, and to add that data to their database. This originally meant that Facebook also acquired data on non-Facebook users, who would probably be unaware that this was possible (Roosendaal 2011). These "social widgets", unlike Beacon, have been very successful: they appear on a third of the world's top 1000 websites, according to a 2011 *Wall Street Journal* investigation.[46]

Roosendaal suggests these buttons break basic expectations of European DP law and norms as (1) the user was unaware of the underlying Facebook data collection, merely wishing to express support for a service or content (2) even if aware, the data was given in one context and used in another (3) the purposes for which the data was given are unclear, thus breaking purpose limitation rules of EC DP law and (4) those who are not Facebook members are misled into participating in a site they have not joined. The *Wall Street Journal*, investigating these claims in May 2011, reported that Facebook had now ceased to collect data on non-members, describing it as a bug in the system. However it also reported that even if a Like button is not pressed, data about activity on that web page may sometimes be shared with Facebook (Roosendaal 2011).

BENEFITS

Having read the above, one might ask, hypothetically, if there is not a case to ban social networks. Leaving aside obvious impossibilities like defining SNSs to exclude the rest of the internet and ensuring uniform laws across the globe, this is a regulatory choice which would probably, despite Art 10 of the ECHR, be lawful in the EU if not under US First Amendment law. If SNSs are so full of risks, harms and pitfalls, what benefit is there to society in allowing them to exist? (I leave aside the motivation of industry profit here, as something which should be of only secondary significance to a public regulator.)

The answers have already been partly canvassed above. As boyd and many other researchers have noted, SNSs are vitally important to young people today as the place where they find their own kind of private space in which they can construct their identity, form communities, learn social skills and share valuable information. Marwick, Diaz and Palfrey (2010) point to studies which show that SNS users apply a "risk: benefit" approach to sharing personal data online (see Youn 2009) and yet still feel compelled to continue using them. As one user put it, "Like everyone says, get a Facebook. You need to get one." (boyd and Marwick 2011 at 8).

Livingstone (2008) working within the European experience, reports similarly that "optimistic accounts stress new opportunities for self-expression, sociability, community engagement, creativity and new literacies". Nor is this desire for social inclusion and self-expression via SNSs restricted to children. It was recently reported, eg, that even prisoners frequently have cellphones smuggled in so they can update Facebook from their cells.[47]

The benefits of social networking are societal as well as individual. boyd and Marwick (2011, p. 7) note that the SNS as "networked public" is a major venue for young people learning how to participate in civic and democratic society. For marginalised groups such as gays and lesbians, social networking is commonly used for political engagement and social relations with the mainstream, as well as negotiating personal identity.[48] Earlier, we mentioned the strong links that were publicised in 2010–11 between social networking and democratic activity in repressive regimes. While it would be more than foolish to say that Facebook or Twitter created the desire for democracy in Egypt (say), it has clearly been a useful tool both within and outside such regimes for political activism. In the developed world, many causes now depend for support and fundraising on Facebook pages, and an early stage in most controversies is now the creation of one or more Facebook Groups to rally supporters. The SNS Twitter has even recently been credited with "breaking" over-stringent UK privacy rules restricting freedom of the press.[49] Where these functions were once exercised in town halls or student common rooms, or via letter writing campaigns, now they happen online on SNSs (Shirky 2008).

Even in more privacy conscious Europe, the multiple benefits of SNSs are recognised. Viviane Reding, Commissioner for the Information Society and Media, spoke on the Safer Internet in 2008, noting the benefits of SNSs for cultural diversity, enhanced interactivity, minimal cost freedom of expression and "bringing about new economic opportunities for the European industry".[50]

If social networks are not to be banned then, how can they be made less harmful places for privacy? We consider below law, code and norms as regulatory mechanisms. The regulatory influence of the market, already discussed as primarily invidious to privacy, is discussed further within the section below on 'DP Law, SNSs and the Illusion of Consent'.[51]

REGULATORY STRATEGIES FOR DEALING WITH SNS-RELATED PRIVACY HARMS: LAW

EU Data Protection (DP) Law

EU DP law is commonly assumed to provide strong protection for the informational privacy of users both offline and online, and against both the state and private actors. It is, unlike in the US, an "omnibus" rather than sectoral privacy protection regime. The complex rules are found in the EC Data Protection Directive (DPD),[52] and its later extension in the EC Privacy and Electronic Communications Directive (PECD).[53] EU DP law was conceived long before the advent of the internet or social networking, and is explicitly founded on the right to respect for the private life of individuals protected by Art 8 of the European Convention on Human Rights (ECHR). It is consequently more concerned with human rights to privacy, than market effects, although the justification for the EU to intervene in this area was originally based on the removal of distortions across the Single Market by national laws relating to personal data. The Directive is required to be implemented in substance into the national laws of each EU state, though local legislatures have substantial autonomy in how they do this. Harmonisation of DP law across the EU is thus surprisingly low, although some uniformity is imposed, first, by the power of the European Commission to sue any state which does not in their view implement Directives correctly; secondly, by interpretation binding across Europe of the Directive by the European Court of Justice (ECJ), to which national courts may make a reference for clarification; and thirdly, by the opinions of the Art 29 DP Working Party. Although not binding, these opinions have considerable persuasive authority.

DP law aspires to give "data subjects" control over the "processing" of their "personal data". Personal data is defined in the DPD as "any information relating to an identified or identifiable natural person ('data subject')" where an identifiable person is "one who can be identified, directly or indirectly, in particular by reference to a identification number or to one or more factors specific to his physical, physiological, mental, economic, cultural or social identity".[54] Processing is defined very widely to include "any operation or set of operations performed upon personal data" including but not restricted to collection, recording, organisation, storage, alteration, retrieval, use, disclosure or deletion of personal data.[55]

Particular protection is given in the DP regime to "sensitive personal data" (SPD), which is defined in the DPD as "personal data revealing racial or ethnic origin, political opinions, religious or philosophical beliefs, trade union membership, and data concerning health or sex life".[56] The DPD states that particular conditions and safeguards must be observed when particularly "sensitive" personal data is processed; in particular in all but a few cases, *explicit* consent of the data subject is needed to justify the processing of SPD.

The DPD then goes on to prescribe a regime based on eight principles for the processing of personal data, which are based on but expand upon the OECD Privacy Principles[57] which themselves are related to the US's Fair Information Practices (FIPs). Duties are primarily placed on "data controllers" who are the agents who "determine the purposes and means of the processing of personal data".[58] Data controllers must notify their data processing activities with the supervisory authority. Key elements of the European DPD regime include that:

- processing is to be *fair and lawful*, with consent of the data subject as the primary (though not only) means of establishing that processing meets these conditions;
- processing is only to be undertaken for known and specified *purposes*;
- no more personal data is to be gathered than necessary and *relevant* to these purposes;
- data is to be kept *accurately* and if necessary updated;
- data is *not to be held longer than necessary* to fulfil these purposes;
- data is to be held *securely*;
- *rights of data subjects*, eg to access and correct their data, and prevent its use for direct marketing, are to be respected;
- *data is not to be exported* without consent to countries outside the EU where privacy protection is not "adequate".[59]

There are a number of significant exceptions to the ambit of most of these principles, including notably exemptions for national security and detection or prevention of crime, journalistic, artistic or literary purposes and users operating in the domestic or "household" sphere. Interestingly, the Art 29 DP WP takes the view that most SNS users are not themselves data controllers as their activities fall under the "household" exemption.[60]

Regulation and enforcement are key aspects of DP law: unlike in the US, for example, it is required that a "supervisory authority" independent of both government and commerce must enforce the DP rules, and that data subjects must have direct recourse to redress where their DP rights are infringed. A key problem in many EU states however is lack of resources for such enforcement, especially in a world of decentralised globalised data controllers, and connectedly, a lack of political will to rein in the privacy infringing activities of both state and the commercial sector.[61]

The question here then is whether these rules of law really protect the user of SNSs and deal with the problems we have outlined above. The answer, sadly, is a resounding no. Clearly, every user of an SNS discloses a great deal of personal, and indeed, sensitive, personal data (eg race, politics, sexuality or religious beliefs). They also involuntarily disclose data relating to their behaviour on the site (and sometimes, as discussed above, elsewhere). In theory, they should be protected from any *further* processing of this data by the SNS which may damage their privacy, by the giving or withdrawal of their consent to such activity. In reality, however, consent is no guarantee of protection on Facebook and its like, because the consent that is given by users is non-negotiable, non-informed, pressurised and illusory. In practice therefore, governance of privacy on SNSs is by contract and code, and barely if at all limited by DP law. Consent formally trumps DP law but the consent gained represents nothing about the wishes of the data subject.

DP Law, SNSs and the Illusion of Consent

The DPD, Art 2(h) prescribes that the data subject's consent means "any freely given specific and informed indication of [the user's] wishes by which data subject signifies his agreement to the personal data being processed". In reality, user consent is invariably obtained as part of registration before "admission" to the site is granted. Consent is usually obtained by displaying a link to the privacy policy (or terms and conditions, or equivalent) on the site and asking the user to accede to them by ticking a box. As there is no chance to negotiate and little or no evidence that users either read or understand these conditions, it is hard to see how this consent is either "free and informed" – yet business practice for the entire sector is to regard this consent as satisfactory.

Study after study indicates that (1) users do not read privacy policies; (2) that if they do, they do not understand them; (3) that even if they understand them, the fact that consent is the price of entry to the SNS outweighs all other considerations of risk; (4) that in any case, many SNS users, especially the young or less educated, have a faulty understanding of the privacy risks involved, due to asymmetric access to information and hard-wired human failure to properly assess future, intangible and contingent risks; and (5) that even when consent is considered in a free and informed way, constant vigilance is needed as privacy policies and practices are changed by site owners.[62] Because of all these factors, ticking a box to indicate "consent" to processing of data on SNSs is as random and fetishistic as jumping over a broom to indicate consent to marriage was in olden times.

For example, a recent UK survey by the OFT in 2010 found that 50 per cent of users never read privacy policies; 40 per cent seldom did; and 10 per cent always did (OFT 2010, para. 7.12). Such results have been roughly replicated time and again. A 2006 US survey based on Facebook found that 77 per cent had never read its privacy policy and that as a result large majorities had mistaken beliefs as to what those policies actually contained.[63] Meanwhile in a light-hearted experiment in April 2010, a games company in the UK found that 100 per cent of their customers in one day – 7500 people – agreed to download a game under condition that by doing so they transferred to the company their immortal soul. Not one queried the clause. This was reported under the title: "No-one reads terms and conditions – it's official" (Out-Law 2010a). Such results have led Grimmelman (2009, p. 1181) to describe the Facebook privacy policy as a "beautiful irrelevance".

Nor are these results simply a matter of reckless thoughtlessness by SNS users. By contrast, a 2010 EU Commission survey showed that 61.1 per cent of respondents regarded the right to manage online privacy as one of the three most important rights with which the EU should provide its citizens.[64] This is the privacy paradox revisited: users care deeply about their privacy but cannot be bothered to read privacy policies. Privacy policies are long, convoluted and unreadable, when users (all but a few freaks, like IT law professors) primarily want to get on with the fun bit of exchanging gossip and being invited to parties. SNS providers have taken advantage of the fact that the content of privacy policies is not prescribed, so long as one exists, and as a result have thrown into them "everything but the kitchen sink". As noted earlier, the Facebook privacy policy, as of 2010, reached a high water mark in 2010 of around 6000 words, longer than the US Constitution.

In terms of comprehensibility, such policies are sometimes, usually after regulatory pressure,[65] clarified for their potential audience, but more often still written, at least partly, in incomprehensible legalese.[66] In Europe, requests from the Article 29 Working Party (Art 29 WP 2010) for SNS providers to provide their users with clear and easy to understand information about the way in which their data will be processed seem to have made some, but not startling, headway, and do not of course address the point that privacy policies are in any case mostly not read.

None of this is enticing to users, but perhaps the even more compelling reason why users never read SNS privacy policies is that there is simply no advantage in doing so. Terms cannot be negotiated, and the service is offered as "take it or leave it". This is true in other consumer fields, of course, but in the SNS world there is no competition for users based on conditions of use in general, and privacy conditions in particular, and hence no "marketplace of choices" for users.

Why is this? As noted earlier, for many young people, to reject the market leader SNS is to risk substantial social exclusion. Even for adults, it is difficult to turn down the lure of Facebook, no matter what your privacy qualms (and increasingly, social networking is also part of business or educational advancement). This phenomenon is described as the "network effect" – ie, an SNS becomes more and more attractive as more and more of a potential user's social graph are based there. Network-based industries like SNS thus suffer in economics terms from market failure; there is no competition incentive to drive a race to the top in terms of privacy-protective policies, as users are reluctant to "shop around" if their friends are already based on one site. It also takes a great deal in such network economies to force a user to leave because the terms of service are invidious. boyd 2010, in an informal blog post, discusses this phenomenon of "lock in" (see also Brown and Marsden 2008) with some force:

> What pisses me off the most are the numbers of people who feel trapped. Not because they don't have another choice. (Technically, they do.) But because they feel like they don't. They have invested time, energy, resources, into building Facebook what it is. They don't trust the service, are concerned about it, and are just hoping the problems will go away.

Accordingly an SNS market for competition on privacy has signally failed to develop: indeed, as already noted earlier, Bonneau (2009) posits that the opposite is true, and that in fact, SNSs have business incentives to avoid any mention of privacy, let alone offering privacy incentives to carve out a niche in the market. This of course relates profoundly to the earlier discussion of how privacy practices which discourage disclosure are the polar opposite of what makes money for the SNS industry.

Furthermore, the consent given by most or many SNS users, especially young and inexperienced persons, is almost always based on a misapprehension of risks. It is in human nature to want jam today – fun and frivolity – over jam tomorrow – safety and security in some murky future where relationships, job opportunities and promotions may be pursued. Much sociological and criminological literature has indicated that, universally, consumer perceptions of future versus current risks are fundamentally flawed, something that is exacerbated in the young (see further Apgar 2006).[67] A one-time thought-free consent given today may also prejudice that user not just now but for an indefinite future time, given the persistence, recordability, dispersion and searchability of data disclosed on the internet via sites like Google and other types of archive (boyd 2007).

Last but not least, consent on Facebook is not a one-time deal. The rules of the privacy policy (as well as the privacy settings, discussed above) change constantly. Thus even the exceptionally rare informed, time-rich, and privacy-savvy consumer who seeks to read the privacy policy and contemplate its meaning, would have to remain in a constant state of vigilance to maintain a real sense of informed consent.

Solutions?

The law is used to dealing with consent as a faulty risk management process in the context of consumer law. Many laws require provision of pre-contractual information to consumers, and prejudicial terms in standard term contracts, which indicate a significant imbalance in bargaining power, can be struck down as unfair terms under UK and EU law.[68] Rules relating to unconscionability perform a similar role in some US state laws, though to a lesser extent. There are, perhaps unsurprisingly given the expense of consumer litigation, no cases in the UK as yet of online privacy policies, or user contracts generally, being attacked, though in the US, an arbitration clause that was part of the "rules" of an online virtual world has been successfully struck down (*Bragg v Linden Labs* (2007)). Such victories are rare however, and most users have neither the knowledge, funds nor desire to take court action against their favourite social network.[69]

A better approach might be to exercise control over SNS terms and conditions *proactively*, eg, by proposing model contracts for SNSs, which might *require* certain clauses, eg deletion of all data associated with the user when the user terminates their relationship, or *exclude* others, eg consent to sharing of personal data with targeted advertising and data profiling networks. Numerous voluntary industry or "co-regulatory" codes of conduct do already exist: eg, in the US, Facebook is signatory to TrustE, the industry privacy seal programme. In Europe, all but one of the market leader SNSs in the 25 EU members (EU Kids Online (1)) has signed up to the EU's guidelines (Safer Social Networking Principles for the EU; see EC Information Society 2009) although these seem concerned more with child safety, than with adult and child privacy. In the UK, leading good practice guidelines (though again, more oriented to safety than privacy) have been developed by UK Council for Child Internet Safety (UKCIS 2010).

However industry trust seals such as TrustE, being funded by the industry itself, are historically subject to "industry capture" and an unsatisfactorily lax level of enforcement (EPIC 2011). In Europe, enforcement of the Safer Social Networking Guidelines falls in part to industry to self-regulate and in part to the national supervisory authorities, which are in the main ill funded and already struggling to enforce general DP law. As a result, the Commission reported in its follow-up study in January 2010, that implementation of the guidelines had been unsatisfactory and in particular, that less than half of the signatories restricted access to profiles of minors to friends-only (Safer Social Networking Guidelines 2010; see also EC Information Society 2009).

A more radical and effective solution would be to move from voluntary to mandatory model contracts for SNSs. This idea is party modelled on the EC Unfair Terms Directive[70] and which suggests two types of restricted conditions: a blacklist of terms that are always deemed unfair and unenforceable, and a greylist of terms rebuttably presumed to be unfair. Interestingly the current draft includes in the second list, "terms enabling the trader to unilaterally alter the terms of the contract".

The draft proposals for reform of the DPD may go further still, with a suggestion of the drawing up of one or more EU standard privacy notices to be used by different sectors of data controllers (EC Communication 2010, para 2.1.3). Such forms unfortunately did not make it to the draft Regulation and even if they had, are still likely to concentrate on transparency, and perhaps to some extent on child protection, rather than restricting the powers of SNSs generally to engage in objectionable data gathering practices. This may be a precursor, though, to actually prescribing the substance of the terms on which SNSs can operate, rather than merely trying to clarify them to consumers.

This may seem heresy from a US market perspective, but a similar suggestion has very recently been floated by the EU with regards to cloud computing contracts (EC Consultation 2011b) which are also known by and large to set prejudicial terms against consumers on a "take it or leave it" basis (Millard et al 2010). Such clauses were provisionally proposed again in September 2012 (EC Communication 2012). What the impact of such a radical move would be in a market where the leading SNSs are mainly US-based, however, will be interesting to say the least. Can Facebook afford to abandon Europe? Or would the effect be as with the Canadian Privacy Commissioner intervention noted above, to extend European rules to the whole Facebook global audience? The French President Sarkozy asked the G8 nations in May 2011 to extend (inter alia) EU privacy law to the world (Huffington Post 2011): but even from a political as opposed to legal perspective, this seems a non-starter – even though recent months have seen a softening of the traditional US position and a more favourable attitude to EU style privacy principles (see US Consumer Privacy Principles 2012).

REGULATION OF SNSs BY CODE

As noted in the introduction, the second strand of governance on SNSs – and arguably the most important form – is what the software or "code" allows or compels the user to do. The international reach and power of code can be observed from the fact that when (Canadian Privacy Commissioner 2009a and 2009b) demanded changes to Facebook's settings in 2009, these changes operated to the benefit of every Facebook user across the globe.

Above, we already noted in detail how user privacy has become steadily less protected on Facebook, because changes in the default privacy settings have exposed more and more of a user's personal data to wider audiences. Kesan and Shah (2006, p. 596) note that software defaults of this kind disempower users because ". . . default settings will not be seen as defaults but as unchangeable. After all, if people don't know about defaults, they will assume that any alternative settings are impossible or unreasonable . . . Defaults are important not only in affecting a person's actions, but also in shaping norms and creating culture."

Grimmelman (2009, p. 184) thus opposes technical controls as a means of regulating privacy on SNSs for fear that left without market regulation they will produce an anti-privacy result. There is an obvious concern that SNSs will set all defaults at the least privacy-protective level, make changing the default obscure or complex, and then reap the benefits in data disclosure. As discussed above, many users will never change defaults, however unfortunate, and even those who are savvy enough to do so, may be falsely confident that they have succeeded in making the changes they desired. These issues are particularly worrying for the youngest SNS users. The EU survey of under 18s showed that almost half the younger age band of children surveyed, aged 9–12, said they were unable to change their privacy settings, compared to a quarter of children aged 13–16 (EU Kids Online 1). Children who left their profile as public were also more likely to give away key pieces of data than the ones who made them private or partly private. One fifth of public profiles displayed risky data such as phone number, address and school.

Given the extent to which users may be ruled by privacy defaults, how can law intervene to require that SNS "code" defaults are not actively harmful to user privacy?

One approach might be a general rule that software defaults in SNS sites are to be initially set at the most privacy-protective level. This idea, first floated by the European Parliament during the "cookie wars" of the early 2000s, seems at first sight the very opposite of social networking. Yet as the sociological work quoted earlier makes clear, networking, even for the young, is not about happy-go-lucky disclosure to everyone, but about carefully controlled and granular disclosures to selected publics. In such context, an initial default of disclosure to "no-one-but-friends" or even "no-one-at-all", followed by a clear start-up routine (akin to the step-by-step wizards followed to install software), where permissions could be allocated with the aid of prompts and time to think, could be remarkably sensible.[71]

However, for obvious reasons of economics and industry lobbying, it seems unlikely we will soon see anything approaching a start-up requirement of visibility to "no-one-at-all". Nonetheless, the Article 29 DP Working Party has recommended that SNSs should offer "privacy-friendly default settings" which allow users to opt in to giving access to data to more than their pre-selected friends (Art 29 WP 2009, para. 3.2). They also recommended that profiles should also by default not be available to search engines. Although there has been no immediate action in response other than the promulgation of guidelines, the findings of the EU Kids Online study quoted above have now led the European Commission to indicate its intention to press for mandatory automatic restriction of children's profiles to friends-only (Out-Law 2011).

A different way law might regulate defaults might be a general rule that *any* change in default privacy settings which increases disclosure must be achieved by positive assent (opt-in) not by default (opt-out).

This would address the problem of the way Facebook surreptitiously grabs more and more data from its most unaware and unskilled users, as shown in the infographs earlier. It would also have advantages for sites like Facebook in possibly restoring some of the trust between it and its users that has been lost in the last few years. Again, it would no doubt be opposed by the SNS industry but it is less obviously harmful to their revenues than the "zero-visibility" start-up approach floated above, and it has an element of fairness and transparency which should make it harder to oppose.

More Ways Law could Regulate Code

Code regulation is not just about defaults. Law might require certain positive features that SNSs have to implement to prevent privacy harms to users.

1. *A right to forget?* Mayer-Schoenberger (2009) points out that in the non-digital world, data naturally dissipated over time. Solove (2007), makes the same point, arguing that "gossip" had a natural shelf-life in the offline world, something not replicated online. On the internet,

instead, personal data persists, is duplicated, combined, disseminated, archived and rendered searchable, and often becomes inaccurate over time. This is particularly unfortunate for the young, as in the case study above, where harmless university pranks which would once have been forgotten, now are preserved to later become black marks for future employers etc. One of the most worrying aspects of the SNS phenomenon is the fact that many or most employers and other institutions now use them as a means to screen applicants.

The "right to forget" has now become a major part of the proposed draft reform of the DPD, where it is described as "the right of individuals to have their data no longer processed and deleted when ... no longer needed for legitimate purposes" (EC Communication 2010, para. 2.1.3). There has been severe criticism of this proposal on the grounds it is "foggy thinking", and might prejudice the historical record and freedom of speech (Fleischer 2011). One person's personal data may be another's account of their own life: which right, privacy or expression, should take precedence (Edwards 2011)? Technologists have pointed out the difficulty of identifying in advance what data a user wants to expire, and which to persist, given the contextual nature of privacy.

In the SNS environment however, a limited right to forget has attractions. Could personal data profiles on SNSs – or parts of them, such as status updates or relationship status – be set to expire by default after six months, say, or a year? Users could be warned by email that expiry was imminent and opt in to prevent that data being deleted if that was what they wished. This would address some of the problems of persistence of embarrassing personal data on the internet years after its hasty disclosure. On the other hand, for some users, expiry by default may be the opposite of what they want. The utility of the suggestion will again rest entirely with how the defaults are set.

A less sweeping version of the right to forget is simply the right to ensure deletion rather than mere deactivation of an SNS profile on request. In the first case, the personal data is actually deleted; in the second, the profile is merely hidden from view. After various publicised privacy incidents, Facebook promised to guarantee effective deletion of accounts after intervention by the Canadian authorities (Canadian Privacy Commissioner 2009a and b).[72]

Another variation is to consider not just the right to forget but the right to what might be called "obscurity", ie, for the contents of SNS profiles not to be spidered by search engines. Technically, this is easily achievable using the machine readable protocol robots.txt. Unsurprisingly, most of the guidelines relating to child safety suggest that a child's profile should be excluded from search engines eg UKCIS (2010, s. 6), as does Art 29 WP 2010. European DP law would suggest any user has the right to delete their data at any time, but in fact at present this right only exists where provisions of the DPD are being infringed.[73] In practice, when Facebook decided to allow its data to be searchable, users were presented with an opt-out choice rather than opt-in. As noted above, the reverse would have been more desirable.

2. *A right to take your data elsewhere: interoperability and portability.* Such a right enshrined in law would guarantee any SNS user the right to move all their data, including their friends list to another site. Why would this be privacy-promoting? As ENISA pointed out in 2007 (ENISA 2007), because, at present, SNS interoperability is almost zero, there is a very high overhead on users shifting to a new site. As a result users will put up with a bad deal rather than make the effort of replicating all their personal data and "friends" connections elsewhere. Effectively, lack of portability of data and interoperability between SNSs empowers the site owner and disempowers the user. Furthermore, because personal data has to be resubmitted every time a user decided to engage with a new software application providing social services (eg a photo blogging site; an instant messaging site; a calendar application) there is a strong tendency to make the "home" SNS site your "data warehouse" and use its functionality for all your needs. As a result, personal data is all placed, increasingly, in one basket and switching is hard. Finally when personal data is increasingly warehoused in one place, it becomes more vulnerable both to attacks by malicious hackers and "data grabs" by the government or litigators using subpoenas or equivalent. Regulatory drivers towards portability and interoperability in SNS code would thus be likely to both empower the user and reduce their privacy invasion and security risks.

    The market has created greater interoperability in recent years via open application programming interfaces (APIs) and projects such as Google's OpenSocial and Facebook Connect (Grimmelman 2009, p. 1194). Twitter initially shot to success partly by allowing third party developers almost complete access to the functionality of its core site. However these changes have not really achieved the core goal of allowing users to network effectively with other users on a proprietary platform, without staying tied to that platform themselves ("lock in"). Since that lock in to "walled gardens" is the heart of the SNS business model, it is doubtful the market will produce this without regulation. EC Communication 2010 notes explicitly that users on SNSs have "been impeded in exercising their rights of access, rectification and deletion" eg reporting inability to remove photos from sites. The proposal calls for these rights to be made more explicit, clarified and possibly strengthened. How this is to be done remains uncertain.

4.   *Longer term code solutions?*

   (a)   *Contextual privacy settings.* Madejski et al (2011) suggest that data should be automatically categorised with a predicted context, which would then generate a default privacy setting that should match users' intentions. The system would learn, using AI techniques such as natural language processing and image analysis, what privacy rules should be applied in what contexts. "For example, in the case of Facebook Places, if a user wishes to hide alcohol related information from everyone, it is reasonable to conclude that all location check ins at a bar should be hidden from everyone." This is a lovely idea and fits well with current notions of privacy and contextual integrity, but given the history of scaling AI to fit real world applications, one suspects it may be a while yet before we see a working system of this kind.

   (b)   *Privacy metadata.* Gelman (2009) suggests that users be given the opportunity to tag any piece of data with an icon which indicates their preferences as to how this data should be disclosed. Any site using that data should then respect these preferences. This should include sites even where the user is not a member. This model is partly drawn from the metadata of Creative Commons licences, and partly from the robots.txt files used to indicate opt-out from search engine spiders. The flaw in this attractive idea is that Gelman expects that sites will respect the privacy metadata out of a sense of social norms or "neighbourly respect". Her reasoning is that an automatic block imposed by code might chill free speech. From a European perspective, however this seems to have the disadvantage of any self-regulatory system relating to privacy and SNSs, in that market forces will drive the SNS towards disregarding privacy tags which interfere with its monetisation of personal data, whether explicitly or implicitly eg via installing competing privacy defaults which take precedence over the metadata. It is also somewhat reminiscent of the P3P (Privacy Preferences Platform) code of the dot.com boom era, which failed because of public inertia and hence lack of site uptake. Will SNS users be any more impelled to learn how to tinker with Gelman's tools than they were with P3P, especially if there is no guarantee sites will respect their choices?[74]

   (c)   *Decentralised SNS architectures.* Current leading SNSs, with their centralised architecture and proprietary access controls, in many ways reverse the open and decentralised model of the Web and mark an undesirable return to a mainframe model of computing. Such "walled gardens", as already extensively discussed, allow monetisation of audiences and have inspired innovation, but also encourage privacy violations. One solution already canvassed is to implement *legal* rights of portability of data and encourage interoperability. Another flavour of solution is to turn to code, and to build decentralised non-proprietary social networks, which arguably allow users full control of their content and their personal data, and hope they attract an audience (although network effects will make this very difficult). In one of the more intriguing responses to the Facebook privacy clashes of the last few years, a group raised $200,000 to build a "privacy-sensitive", decentralised architecture, open source social network, named Diaspora.[75] Diaspora's key elements are, first, that it is a distributed network – no one site "owns" or holds all the data; second, it is designed to allow users to separate information they want to share with various different groups eg work, family, close friends. (The latter, though not the former, model has also been adopted by Google + in its Circles concept – a system which has a fair stab at challenging Facebook's multi-million user network.) Such systems may depend on cheap local hosting by individual users rather than depending on free "cloud" storage by Facebook et al; conveniently such technology is also emerging, eg the Freedom Box project (http://wiki.debian.org/FreedomBox). Other decentralised solutions are also emerging at proof of concept level, such as peer to peer (P2P) network hosted social content.

CONCLUSIONS: LAW, CODE, MARKET AND NORMS

SNSs are currently governed as private spaces by contract, and their business model is based on maximising extraction of personal data from users, which can then be monetised in (hopefully) anonymised form. SNSs are not regulated as public spaces, by public regulation, with the public interest in mind, especially in the US where the most popular SNSs are based. Data protection law should perform the role of regulation in the public interest in Europe, but its safeguards are negated, first, by consents extracted from users which are neither free nor informed and, second, by the code of the SNS, in particular the default settings on the privacy controls. Accordingly privacy harms are caused to users of SNSs.

A classical laissez faire view would be that if privacy is viewed purely as an individual right, for individual benefit, then it could legitimately be left to the individual to assert and protect that right. However, if privacy is viewed, as it is far more in Europe than the US, as an aggregate social benefit (as asserted by Regan 1995; Bennett and Raab 2007, Ch. 2) then a strong case for public regulation of SNSs to preserve societal privacy can be made. This chapter has primarily argued for a middle ground European-style consumer protection model, based on proven harms, which suggests that in circumstances where users (adult and child) suffer significant harms, now or in the future, because of the exposure of and exploitation of their personal data, then mandatory protective measures should be extended to regulate the market, even though such disclosures are (sometimes) the users' own "choice".

The history of self-regulation in this field shows that voluntary progress on privacy on SNSs is slow, unsurprising given the market incentives towards disclosure. While some attempts will generally be made by operators to cater to the notion of child safety, given the heavy societal and law enforcement engagement in this notion, there is less long term PR loss in sidestepping the privacy rights of adults. Privacy scandals break out, but they also fade away as the next news story comes along. The history of Facebook's engagement with privacy and the slow creeping data grab of the last five years, as presented by inter alia boyd and Hargittai 2010; the *New York Times* (Bilton 2010); and McKeon (2010) is salutary.

Accordingly this chapter argues for mandatory legal controls over SNSs beyond those already theoretically available in some jurisdictions but rarely or never exercised, such as review of privacy policies as unfair consumer contracts. In particular, two approaches to reform were highlighted; laws which might mandate or ban certain clauses from the "legal code" of the SNS – its privacy policy; and laws which might mandate or ban certain features of its code – for example, requiring the privacy defaults to be set at the most privacy-protective level when a profile is first activated.

This is not the whole story. SNSs do not exist in a bubble of privacy regulation. A number of general issues being explored in the current DPD reform consultation will, if they come to pass, have immense impact on the SNS world. Three key issues under discussion are:

- *A general principle of transparency* (EC Communication 2010, para. 2.1.2) which might affect, as we have already seen, not just the way privacy policies are written, but what users get to know about what data is held about them, who it is shared with and how it is processed. Google Dashboard is an early and very basic (voluntary) attempt to give users some idea of what data is held about them by Google. European DP law may eventually require far more than this in the form of an online subject access right, which might begin to resemble the "publication plans" of public bodies under freedom of information laws.

- A general principle of limitation of the data a controller can collect and retain to that necessary for the purposes of processing – *data minimisation* (EC Communication 2010, para 2.1.3). Purpose limitation is already one of the key principles of DP law. However it fails to make much impact in a context such as SNSs where data is shared for no particular purpose with no clear end in sight. This is the area where the Commission is looking to new rules that might help restrain misuse of user data, such as the (already mentioned) "right to be forgotten" and "right to data portability".

- Promotion of *Privacy by Design* (PbD) (EC Communication 2010, para. 2.24). The aim here is to design systems to respect privacy and data security *ab initio*, rather than regarding privacy as a "bolt on after" feature, or even worse, as a bug, not a feature at all. Taken seriously, this might see steps taken to encourage more Diasporas and fewer Facebooks.

This chapter has talked little about norms, except in the negative sense of observing how little norm of privacy protection there is among those who own and control the code of SNSs. In Edwards and Brown (2009), we also speculated on whether the importance of privacy as a norm among users – especially young SNS users – had decreased, leading to less interest in self-protection against harmful disclosures. We argued that "the SNS phenomenon shows a clear shift of values from prizing privacy to prizing disclosure and visibility in the social online space". The research that has been carried out since, discussed above, shows things are not quite that simple. Young people still want privacy, even in a "reality TV" world; they just define it differently and find it in different places than their parents' generation. boyd and Marwick (2011, p. 26), put it this way: "Privacy is in a state of flux not because the values surrounding it have changed, but because the infrastructure through which people engage with each other has." Perhaps most importantly from a regulatory point of view, though, the new generation of users' sense of privacy does not seem to protect them well from the harms we have discussed – unlike Flaubert's resistance to "bourgeois" disclosure. Accordingly, unlike Flaubert, they need law to protect them from their own unwise privacy choices coming home to roost.

NOTES

1. See Barnes (2008). Famously, Flaubert guarded the privacy of his correspondence jealously for fear of biography, and burnt much of his lifetime correspondence in 1877 before his death in 1880.
2. See inter alia: the *Daily Telegraph* at http://www.telegraph.co.uk/technology/facebook/7902749/Facebook-reaches-500-million-members.html; the *Guardian* at http://www.guardian.co.uk/technology/2010/jul/21/facebook-500-million-users.
3. See http://www.facebook.com/press/info.php?statistics.
4. See http://www.bbc.co.uk/news/technology-19816709.
5. See http://www.viralblog.com/wp-content/uploads/2010/07/Facebooks-500-million-infographics.jpg.
6. See http://www.guardian.co.uk/media/2010/jun/23/mark-zuckerberg-facebook-cannes-lions.
7. See the EU Kids Online project work on age of EU children on SNSs (hereafter "EU Kids Online 1"; see Livingstone et al 2011 (see also EU press release, Reference: IP/11/479 Date: 18/04/2011) who report that evidence about the actual as opposed to reported (ie deceptive) ages of children online has been scarce until the EU Kids Online project.
8. These figures are taken from EU Kids Online 1, and therefore represent the pattern only for *children* under 16; a different pattern may well emerge from the entire EU population.
9. For a spirited rebuttal of the "cyber-utopian" notion that participation in the internet, and especially in social networks, necessarily breeds a greater spirit of democratic freedom in repressive regimes, see Morozow (2011).
10. http://en.wikipedia.org/wiki/Social_network_service.
11. See http://news.softpedia.com/news/Facebook-s-Profits-Soaring-Could-Be-Heading-Towards-a-100-Billion-Valuation-197913.shtml.
12. According to a 2010 US report by marketers NAI, "behaviorally-targeted advertising is more than twice as effective at converting users who click on the ads into buyers (6.8% conversion vs. 2.8% for run-of-network ads)": see http://www.webpronews.com/behaviorally-targeted-ads-get-more-conversions-2010-03.
13. See, for example, http://eu.techcrunch.com/2011/04/14/spotify-takes-the-axe-to-its-free-service-can-it-now-claim-to-slash-music-piracy/.
14. See (for example, and inevitably) Hunter and Lastowka (2004) and Lastowka (2010).
15. There have been minor efforts to placate the users of social networks with some impression of input into site policy, eg, notably Facebook's vote in 2009 on its new "Facebook Principles" (see press release at http://www.facebook.com/press/releases.php?p=85587) but these have in the main been cosmetic and used to smooth over bad PR (see attack on the entire process of the Facebook Principles by Anderson and Bonneau (2010).
16. See on US, EU and Canadian laws applicable to SNS privacy, a good survey in Marwick, Diaz and Palfrey (2010).
17. For example, Art 29 DP Working Party 2009 has suggested that a Facebook user tagging a photo without consent might be viewed as processing of a third party's personal (and sometimes sensitive personal) data, and thus in breach of DP law (see ECJ case of *Lindqvist v Kammaraklagaren* (2003)). This does not reflect accepted practice on SNSs, where the norm is to provide "opt-out" from tagging rather than by default a requirement for prior consent (though it is possible for a conscientious Facebook user to set up their privacy controls in this way).
18. See, for example, the first such reported English case of *Applause Store Productions v Firsht* (2008). In this case, a user created a fake Facebook profile which gave misinformation about the plaintiff's sexuality, business sense etc. Notably the courts awarded damages not only for libel but also for misuse of private information (breach of confidence).

19. Though see the notorious Italian case of *Italy v Google* (2010) where Google was held criminally liable for invasion of privacy for allowing the posting of a video on Google Video (a YouTube equivalent service) which ridiculed a Down's Syndrome schoolboy. No immunity was pleaded as the EC E-Commerce Directive excludes matters pertaining to DP law.

20. See, for example, *Doe v MySpace* (2008) (court held SNS immune from any liability in negligence relating to exposure of child online who had lied about her age to dangers of contact with predatory third party).

21. There is an enormous literature on this, some of which will be explored below. See especially two recent influential reviews, Marwick, Diaz and Palfrey (2010) and Hoofnagle et al (2010); see also forthcoming, Brown (2013). In the UK and EU, Livingstone et al 2011's work on UK Kids Online and EU Kids Online (list at: http://www2. lse.ac.uk/media@lse/whosWho/AcademicStaff/SoniaLivingstone/soniaLivingstone.asp x#generated-subheading3) is a key point of reference.

22. See in the UK, concerns about a Welsh "suicide cluster", BBC News (2008).

23. See for a fuller consideration of these risks, Livingstone et al (2011b); Schrock and boyd (2011).

24. See *Daily Mail*, "How using Facebook could raise your risk of cancer", 19 February 2009 at http://www.dailymail.co.uk/health/article-1149207/How-using-Facebook-raise-risk-cancer.html. The *Daily Mail* has also suggested Facebook spreads sexually transmitted diseases: http://www.dailymail.co.uk/news/article-1388719/Social-networking-linked-STD-rise-Facebook-blamed-making-casual-sex-easier.html.

25. Adopted February 2009 as voluntary industry guidelines across 17 of the 25 EU countries. (EC Information Society 2009).

26. See, for example, "Facebook Loses Friends as Privacy campaign grows" (*Guardian* 2010), http://www.guardian.co.uk/technology/2010/may/14/facebook-privacy-campaign-delete-account (noting "How do I delete my Facebook account?" had become a top Google search suggestion); "Beware: Facebook's Dr Evil wants to be your closest friend" (*Times* (2010)) (noting opposition to Social PlugIns), http://technology.timesonline. co.uk/tol/news/tech_and_web/article7113849.ece. See also discussion below of harms, and of problems with consent law.

27. See http://www.priv.gc.ca/media/nr-c/2009/nr-c_090827_e.cfm.

28. See http://news.bbc.co.uk/1/hi/technology/8484664.stm.

29. See http://news.bbc.co.uk/1/hi/technology/7196803.stm.

30. For example, action in July 2010 in Germany by the Hamburg data protection authority concerning processing of personal data on Facebook of third parties not signed up to the site: see http://news.bbc.co.uk/1/hi/technology/8798906.stm.

31. For examples of discrimination by employers, admissions officials etc, see 'Would be students checked on Facebook' (*Guardian* (2008)) (noting Cambridge University tutor admits to screening students via Facebook), http://education.guardian.co.uk/ universityaccess/story/0,,2238962,00.html; http://www.careerbuilder.co.uk/UK/share/ aboutus/pressreleasesdetail.aspx?id=pr28&sd=1/13/2010&ed=12/31/2010&siteid=cb pr&sc_cmp1=cb_pr28_ (2010 survey shows 53 per cent of UK employers use social networks to research applicants before hiring); "Did the Internet Kill Privacy?" (CBS News 2011) (noting 24 year old teacher fired in 2009 because pictures of her holding alcoholic drinks found on Facebook), http://www.cbsnews.com/stories/2011/02/06/ sunday/main7323148.shtml. Germany has passed a law banning employers from using Facebook profiles to research candidates before hiring them: see Out-Law (2010b). Google and LinkedIn searches are however allowed.

32. See Lyon (2003).

33. See Marwick, Diaz and Palfrey (2010) who emphasise that children are heavily surveilled in our society, at home and at school, and use SNSs extensively in their search for private spaces for social exploration away from the eyes of parents.

34. See "Caught on camera – and found on Facebook" (*The Times* 2007), http://techno logy.timesonline.co.uk/tol/news/tech_and_web/the_web/article2087306.ece.

35. The Openbook site is no longer up on the Web but see description at http://searchen-gineland.com/openbook-see-what-people-on-facebook-share-world-42139.
36. Partly as a result of the bad publicity around cases such as these, and partly because Facebook had outgrown the notion of being a "campus yearbook", regional networks (London, Cambridge, New York, etc) were dropped in 2009 – see boyd and Hargittai (2010).
37. See http://www.thesecurityblog.com/2011/05/facebook-applications-accidentally-leaki ng-access-to-third-parties/.
38. See http://www.zdnet.com/blog/igeneration/facebook-applications-leak-users-personal-data-to-third-parties/9906.
39. See also suggestions made by Art 29 WP 2009, which suggested, first, that the SNS operator should "have means to ensure that third party applications comply with the DPD" and secondly, that the APIs which allow the app access to user data held by the SNS should be written in a way that provided for granularity in data access requested.
40. For example, in January 2011, Facebook announced on a Friday that it would share the home address and mobile phone number of every user with app developers, even if these were kept private. This was said to be intended to help developers of locational data using applications. After public outcry, this decision was reversed. See Gustin (2011).
41. See settlement of FTC Privacy Beacon class action, December 2009 which required Facebook to establish a $9.5m privacy foundation in recompense for privacy violations.
42. See http://www.adbusters.org/blogs/blackspot-blog/myspacing-facebook.html.
43. See   eg   http://www.itnews.com.au/News/64502,facebook-and-myspace-monetize-friendship-with-targeted-ads.aspx.
44. See for a basic discussion of this complex subject Edwards (2009), especially at pp. 537–39.
45. The regulation of OBA specifically is too big a topic to be covered further in this chapter. See Schwartz and Solove (2011), especially part III; Ohm (2010) (raising doubts that data profiles are really successfully anonymised, given recent technical advances in de-anonymisation by the marketing industry). For European attitudes to OBA from privacy regulators, see Art 29 Opinion 2010. For a brief view of US FTC proposals on "Do Not Track" see http://wam.typepad.com/wam/2010/12/the-ftc-privacy-report-a-web-analytics-perspective.html.
46. See "Like Button Follows Users" (*Wall Street Journal* 2011), http://online.wsj.com/ article/SB10001424052748704281504576329441432995616.html.
47. Associated Press report, 20 March 2011, noting proposed legislative measure in South Carolina to make interaction on SNSs from prison a crime. See also BBC (2010), that Facebook pages taunting victims were taken down by FB in the UK: http://news.bbc. co.uk/1/hi/uk/8509774.stm.
48. Citing Warner (2005).
49. Though see more cynically the blog post http://blogs.channel4.com/gurublog/is-it-really-twitter-winning-the-injunction-war/1242 ("That isn't twitter or the internet making a mockery of the law, it is the few individuals who are breaking the injunctions in the first place.").
50. See transcript at http://europa.eu/rapid/pressReleasesAction.do?reference=SPEECH/ 08/465#_ftn1_ftn1.
51. For further dismissal of the market as sufficient regulatory guarantor of privacy on SNSs see Grimmelman (2009).
52. Directive 95/46/EC. For a longer introduction to the DP regime, see Edwards (2009).
53. Directive 2002/58/EC as amended October 2009, changes to be implemented in EU by 25 May 2011.
54. Art 2(a), DPD.
55. Art 2(b), DPD.
56. Art 8, DPD.
57. OECD Guidelines on the Protection of Privacy and Transborder Flows of Personal Data 1980.

58. Art 2(d), DPD.
59. Arts 6, 7, 12, 14, 16–17 and Chapter IV (data exports), DPD.
60. Although see to the contrary *Lindqvist* (2003).
61. See further, Edwards (2009).
62. See earlier account of successive attempts by Facebook to expand data disclosure, leading to successive privacy outrages: boyd and Hargittai (2010).
63. Zogby poll, "Most Americans Worry About Identity Theft" April 3, 2007 (cited by Grimmelman 2009, p. 1182).
64. Summary of responses to the public consultation, 'Priorities for a new strategy for European information society (2010–2015)', 19 May 2010, at 12.
65. See also Safer Social Networking Principles for the EU (EC Information Society 2009), which include as principle 1 that acceptable use policies should be "prominent, clear and age-appropriate". The UK ICO led a campaign in 2004–5 for "short" or "multi-layered privacy notices" as a supplement to full legal terms and conditions. It seems to have had little long term impact.
66. Note Facebook's attempt to make its privacy practices more acceptable by producing its plain English "Facebook Principles" (see http://www.facebook.com/principles.php, as of 23 May 2011); these however merely explain rather than override its full privacy policy.
67. In relation to poor risk analysis by young people especially, see EC Eurobarometer 2007, a Safer Internet for Children qualitative study concerning 9–10 year old and 12–14 year old children, which showed that children tend to underestimate risks linked to the use of internet and minimise the consequences of their risky behaviour.
68. See in the UK, the Unfair Contract Terms Act 1976 as amended, and the Unfair Terms in Consumer Contract Regulations 1999 SI No 2083, and at EU level, EC Unfair Terms Directive 1993 93/13/EEC: L 95/29.
69. The EU's plans to introduce something akin to US style class actions for consumer redress may help here: see EC Consultation 2011a.
70. Council Directive 93/13/EEC of 5 April 1993.
71. Though see to contrary Solove (2007, pp. 201–03), arguing it is "too authoritarian" to compel websites to change their code. This author begs to differ.
72. Even where the SNS co-operates in providing effective deletion mechanisms, disclosed data may still be available through repository sites such as the Internet Archive, http://www.archive.org/. It is unclear how a right to forget would cope with such third party mirroring.
73. Art 12, DPD.
74. Bonneau and Preibusch 2009 also argue for reducing information asymmetry by what they call standardised "privacy nutrition labels", which seem similar to Gelman's icons.
75. See http://maketecheasier.com/diaspora-the-open-social-network/2011/01/13/.

BIBLIOGRAPHY

Anderson, J. and J. Bonneau (2010), 'Facebook consultation as much of a sham as their democracy', http://www.cl.cam.ac.uk/~jra40/publications/2009-facebook-press-release.pdf.
Apgar, D. (2006), *Risk Intelligence*, Cambridge, MA: Harvard Business School Press.
Art 29 WP (2009), 'Article 29 Data Protection Working Party', Opinion on Social Networking, Opinion 5/2009, http://ec.europa.eu/justice/policies/privacy/docs/wpdocs/2009/wp163_en.pdf.
Art 29 WP (2010), 'Article 29 Data Protection Working Party', Opinion on Behavioural Advertising, 2/2010, http://ec.europa.eu/justice/policies/privacy/docs/wpdocs/2010/wp171_en.pdf.

Arthur, C. and J. Kiss (2010), 'Facebook reaches 500 million users', *The Guardian*, http://www.guardian.co.uk/technology/2010/jul/21/facebook-500-million-users.

Barnes, J. (2008), 'Gustave Flaubert's last letters', *The Times*, http://entertainment.timesonline.co.uk/tol/arts_and_entertainment/the_tls/article3537862.ece.

Barnes, S. (2006), 'A privacy paradox: social networking in the US', *First Monday*, **11(9)**, http://www.firstmonday.org/ISSUES/issue11_9/barnes/.

Barnett, E. (2010), 'Facebook reaches 500 million users', *Daily Telegraph*, http://www.telegraph.co.uk/technology/facebook/7902749/Facebook-reaches-500-million-members.html.

BBC News (2008), 'Web worries after suicide spate', *BBC News*, http://news.bbc.co.uk/1/hi/wales/7204172.stm.

Bennett, C. and C. Raab (2007), *The Governance of Privacy*, 2nd edn, London: Ashgate.

Bilton, N. (2010a), 'Price of Facebook privacy? Start clicking', *New York Times*, http://www.nytimes.com/2010/05/13/technology/personaltech/13basics.html.

Bilton, N. (2010b), 'Facebook privacy: A bewildering tangle of options', *New York Times*, http://www.nytimes.com/interactive/2010/05/12/business/facebook-privacy.html.

Bonneau, J. (2009), 'The Economics of Privacy in Social Networks', http://www.lightbluetouchpaper.org/2009/06/26/the-economics-of-privacy-in-social-networks/#comments.

Bonneau, J. and S. Preibusch (2009), 'The Privacy Jungle: On the Market for Data Protection in Social Networks, Eighth Workshop on the Economics of Information Security', http://www.cl.cam.ac.uk/~jcb82/doc/privacy_jungle_bonneau_preibusch.pdf.

boyd, D. (2007), 'Social Network Sites: Public, Private, or What?', *Knowledge Tree*, http://kt.flexiblelearning.net.au/tkt2007/?page_id=28.

boyd, D. (2010), 'Facebook and radical transparency', http://www.zephoria.org/thoughts/archives/2010/05/14/facebook-and-radical-transparency-a-rant.html.

boyd, D. and E. Hargittai (2010), 'Facebook privacy settings: who cares?', *First Monday*, **15(8)**, http://www.uic.edu/htbin/cgiwrap/bin/ojs/index.php/fm/article/view/3086/2589.

boyd, D. and A. Marwick (2011), 'Social Privacy in Networked Publics: Teens' Attitudes, Practices and Strategies', Draft paper for Privacy Law Scholars Conference, June 2011, Berkeley, CA.

Brown, I. (2013), 'Privacy Attitudes and Incentives', forthcoming in L. Edwards and I. Brown (eds), *Online Privacy Law: a European Perspective*, Cheltenham, UK and Northampton, MA, USA: Edward Elgar.

Brown, I. and C. Marsden (2008), 'Social Utilities, Dominance and Interoperability: a Modest Proposal', Third GikII Conference, Oxford.

Canadian Privacy Commissioner (2009), 'Report of Findings into the Complaint Filed by the Canadian Internet Policy and Public Interest Clinic (CIPPIC) against Facebook Inc.', PIPEDA Complaint #2009-008, http://www.priv.gc.ca/cf- dc/2009/2009_008_0716_e.cfm#sect2.

Canadian Privacy Commissioner (2009b), 'Facebook agrees to address Privacy Commissioner's concerns', http://www.priv.gc.ca/media/nr-c/2009/nr-c_090827_e.cfm.

EC (European Commission) Communication (2010), 'A Comprehensive Approach on Personal Data Protection in the European Union', Brussels, 4.11.2010 COM(2010) 609 final, http://ec.europa.eu/justice/news/consulting_public/0006/com_2010_609_en.pdf.

EC Communication (2012), 'Unleashing the Potential of Cloud Computing in Europe', September 2012, http://ec.europa.eu/information_society/activities/cloudcomputing/docs/com/com_cloud.pdf.

EC Consultation (2011a), 'SEC(2011)173: Towards a Coherent European Approach to Collective Redress', Brussels, 4 February 2011, http://ec.europa.eu/justice/news/consulting_public/0054/sec_2011_173_en.pdf, consultation closed 30 April 2011.

EC Consultation (2011b), 'Public Consultation on a European Cloud Computing Strategy', http://ec.europa.eu/yourvoice/ipm/forms/dispatch?form=cloudcomputing&lang=en.

EC Eurobarometer (2007), 'Safer Internet for Children report', http://ec.europa.eu/information_society/activities/sip/surveys/qualitative/index_en.htm.

EC Information Society (2009), 'Safer Social Networking Principles for the EU', Report, http://

ec.europa.eu/information_society/activities/social_networking/docs/sn_principles.pdf, also available at: http://www.europeandigitalmedia.org/uploads/documents/sn_principles.pdf.

Edwards, L. (2009), 'Privacy and Data Protection Online: The Laws Don't Work?', in L. Edwards and C. Waelde (eds), *Law and the Internet*, 3rd edn, Oxford: Hart.

Edwards, L. (2011), 'The right to forget or the right to spin', *Pangloss*, http://blogscript. blogspot.com/2011/03/right-to-forget-or-right-to-spin.html.

Edwards, L. and I. Brown (2009), 'Data Control and Social Networking: Irreconcilable Ideas?' in A. Matwyshyn (ed.), *Harboring Data: Information Security Law and the Corporation*, Palo Alto: Stanford University Press, pp. 202–27.

ENISA (2007), 'Recommendations for Online Social Networks', http://www.enisa.europa. eu/act/res/other-areas/social-networks/security-issues-and-recommendations-for-online-social-networks.

EPIC (2011), 'Social Networking Privacy', http://epic.org/privacy/socialnet/default.html.

European Commission (2010), 'Study on the Economic Benefits of Privacy Enhancing Technologies', http://ec.europa.eu/justice/policies/privacy/docs/studies/final_report_pets_16_07_10_en.pdf.

Facebook Rules (2011), 'Facebook Platform Developer's Policies', last revised 12 August 2011, http://developers.facebook.com/policy/.

Fleischer, P. (2011), 'Foggy thinking about the Right to Oblivion', http://peterfleischer.blog-spot.com/2011/03/foggy-thinking-about-right-to-oblivion.html.

Gelman, L. (2009), 'Privacy, Free Speech, and "Blurry Edged" Social Networks', *Boston College Law Review*, **50**, 1315, http://lawdigitalcommons.bc.edu/bclr/vol50/iss5/2.

Grimmelman, J. (2009), 'Saving Facebook', *Iowa Law Review*, **94**, 1137.

Gross, R. and A. Acquisti (2005), 'Information Revelation and Privacy in Online Social Networks (The Facebook Case)', ACM Workshop on Privacy in the Electronic Society, WPES.

Gustin, S. (2011), 'No Facebook, You May Not Share My Address and Phone Number With Developers', *Wired*, http://www.wired.com/epicenter/2011/01/no-facebook-you-may-not/.

Hoofnagle, C.J. et al (2010), 'How Different are Young Adults from Older Adults When it Comes to Information Privacy Attitudes and Policies?', http://papers.ssrn.com/sol3/papers.cfm?abstract_id=1589864&rec=1&srcabs=1588163.

Huffington Post (2011), 'French President Nicolas Sarkozy at eG8: Governments Must Regulate the Internet', http://www.huffingtonpost.com/2011/05/24/sarkozy-eg8-govern ments-regulate-internet_n_866065.html.

Hunter, D. and G. Lastowka (2004), 'The Laws of Virtual Worlds', *California Law Review*, **92**, 1.

Katz, J.E. and R.E. Rice (2002), *Social Consequences of Internet Use – Access, Involvement and Interaction*, Cambridge, MA: MIT Press.

Kesan, J. and R. Shah (2006), 'Setting Software Defaults: Perspectives from Law, Computer Science and Behavioral Economics', *Notre Dame Law Review*, **82**, 583–634.

Kuneva, M. (2009), 'Press Release: Brussels', http://www.europa.eu/rapid/pressReleases Action.do?reference=SPEECH/.

Lastowka, G. (2010), *Virtual Justice*, New Haven: Yale University Press.

Lessig, L. (2006), *Code Version 2.0*, New York: Basic Books.

Livingstone, S. (2008), 'Taking Risky Opportunities in Youthful Content Creation: Teenager's Use of Social Networking Sites', *New Media & Society*, **10(3)**, 393–411.

Livingstone, S. et al EU Kids Online, September 2011 at http://www2.lse.ac.uk/media@lse/research/EUKidsOnline/EU%20Kids%20II%20%282009-11%29/EUKidsOnlineIIReports/Final%20report.pdf

Livingstone, S., K. Olafsson and E. Staksrud (2011), 'Social Networking, Age and Privacy', EU Kids Online report, www2.lse.ac.uk/media@lse/research/EUKidsOnline/ShortSNS. pdf (in text, "EU Kids Online 1").

Livingstone, S. et al (2011b), 'Risks and Safety on the Internet: Key Findings from EU

Kids Online Survey of 9–16 year olds and their Parents in 25 Countries', http://www2.lse. ac.uk/. . ./EUKidsOnline/Executive_Summary_Full_Findings.pdf.

Lyon, D. (2003), *Surveillance as Social Sorting: Privacy, Risk, and Digital Discrimination*, London: Routledge.

Madden, M. and A. Smith (2010), 'Reputation Management and Social Media', Pew Internet and American Life Study, http://www.pewinternet.org/Reports/2010/Reputation-Management.aspx.

Madejski, M., M. Johnson and S. Bellovin (2011), 'A Study of Privacy Setting Errors in Online Social Networks', Draft Paper, Privacy Law Scholars Conference, June 2011, Berkeley, CA.

Marwick, A., D.M. Diaz and J. Palfrey (2010), 'Youth, Privacy, and Reputation', *Harvard Public Law Working Paper*, No. 10-29, http://papers.ssrn.com/sol3/papers. cfm?abstract_id=1588163.

Mayer-Schönberger, V. (2009), *Delete: The Virtue of Forgetting in the Digital Age*, Princeton: Princeton University Press.

McKeon, M. (2010), 'The Evolution of Privacy on Facebook', http://www.mattmckeon.com/ facebook-privacy/.

Millard, C., S. Bradshaw and I. Walden (2010), 'Contracts for Clouds: Comparison and Analysis of the Terms and Conditions of Cloud Computing Services', Queen Mary School of Law Legal Studies Research Paper, No. 63/2010, http://papers.ssrn.com/sol3/papers. cfm?abstract_id=1662374.

Morozow, E. (2011), *The Net Delusion: How Not to Liberate the World*, London: Allen Lane.

Nissenbaum, H. (2004), 'Privacy as Contextual Integrity', *Washington Law Review*, **79(1)**, 10, http://papers.ssrn.com/sol3/papers.cfm?abstract_id=534622.

Ofcom (2008), 'Social Networking: A Quantitative and Qualitative Research Report into Attitudes, Behaviours and Use', http://stakeholders.ofcom.org.uk/binaries/research/ media-literacy/report1.pdf.

OFT (2010), 'Online Targeting of Advertising and Prices', http://www.oft.gov.uk/shared_oft/ business_leaflets/659703/OFT1231.pdf.

Ohm, P. (2010), 'Broken Promises of Privacy: Responding to the Surprising Failure of Anonymization', *UCLA Law Review*, **57**, 1701.

OUT-LAW (2010), 'No-one reads terms and conditions – it's official', *OUT-LAW News*, http://www.out-law.com/page-10929.

OUT-LAW (2010b), 'German law bans Facebook research for hiring decisions', *OUT-LAW News*, http://www.out-law.com/page-11336.

OUT-LAW (2011), 'Social networks must automatically restrict children's profiles says EU Commission', *OUT-LAW News*, http://www.out-law.com/page-11881.

Palfrey, J., Gasser, U. and D. boyd (2010), *Response to FCC Notice of Inquiry 09-94*, *Harvard Law School, Public Law and Legal Working Paper Series*, *Paper* No. 10-19, http:// dash.harvard.edu/bitstream/handle/1/3745922/Palfrey_Gasser_boyd_response_to_FCC_ NOI_09-94_Feb2010.pdf?sequence=2.

Pew Internet & American Life Project (2010), http://www.pewinternet.org.

Regan, P. (1995), *Legislating Privacy: Technology, Social Values and Public Policy*, Toronto: University of Toronto Press.

Roosendaal, A. (2011), 'Facebook tracks and traces everyone: Like this!', *Tilburg Law School Legal Studies Research Paper Series*, No. 03/2011, http://papers.ssrn.com/sol3/ papers.cfm?abstract_id=1717563m.

Schrock, A.R. and D. boyd (2011), 'Problematic Youth Interaction Online: Solicitation, Harassment and Cyberbullying', in K.M. Wright and L.M. Webb (eds), *Computer-Mediated Communication in Personal Relationships*, New York: Peter Lang.

Schwartz, P. and D. Solove (2011), 'The PII Problem', Draft Paper for Privacy Law Scholars Conference 2011, Berkeley, CA.

Shirky, C. (2008), *Here Comes Everybody*, London: Allen Lane.

Solove, D. (2007), *The Future of Reputation: Gossip, Rumours and Privacy on the Internet*, New Haven: Yale University Press.

Staksrud, E. et al (2010), 'Evaluation of the Implementation of the Safer Social Networking Principles for the EU Part I: General Report', European Commission, January 2010 (Safer Social Networking Guidelines), http://ec.europa.eu/information_society/activities/ social_networking/docs/final_report/first_part.pdf.

Steeves, V. (2006), 'It's Not Child Play: The Online Invasion of Children's Privacy', *University of Ottawa Law and Technology Journal*, **3(1)**, 171.

UKCIS (2010), 'Good practice guidelines for the providers of social networking and other user-interactive services', http://media.education.gov.uk/assets/files/industry%20 guidance%20%20%20social%20networking.pdf.

Upsahl, K. (2010), 'Facebook's Eroding Privacy: A Timeline', http://www.eff.org/ deeplinks/2010/04/facebook-timeline/.

US Consumer Privacy Principles (2012), 'Consumer data privacy in a networked world: a framework for protecting privacy and promoting innovation in the global digital economy', http://www.whitehouse.gov/sites/default/files/privacy-final.pdf.

Viegas, F.B. (2005), 'Blogger's Expectations of Privacy and Accountability; An initial survey', *Journal of Computer-Mediated Communications*, **10(3)**, http://jcmc.indiana.edu/ vol10/issue3/viegas.html.

Warner, M. (2005), *Publics and Counterpublics*, Cambridge: MIT Press.

Youn, S. (2009), 'Determinants of Online Privacy Concern and Its Influence on Privacy Protection Behaviors Among Young Adolescents', *Journal of Consumer Affairs*, **43**, 389.

Cases

Applause Store Productions v Firsht [2008] EWHC 1781 (QB).

Bragg v Linden Labs, 30 May 2007, District Court for E. Pennsylvania, Civil Action No 06-4925.

Doe v MySpace, 528 F.3d 413 (5th Cir. 2008).

Italy v Google, (2010) reported in English, *OUT-LAW News*, 3 March 2010: http://www. out-law.com/page-10805.

Lindqvist v Kammaraklagaren (2003), ECJ, Case C101/101.

14. An internet bill of rights?
Rikke Frank Jørgensen

INTRODUCTION

The issue of a specific internet bill of rights has been a reoccurring topic over the past years, not least as part of the annual Internet Governance Forum.[1] From its emergence as an international policy topic, internet governance has been intersected by debates about human rights, not least the implications of article 19 (freedom of expression) and article 12 (the right to privacy) of the UN's Universal Declaration on Human Rights and how these and other human rights standards may be applied to the internet and the information society more generally. This chapter will argue that an internet bill of rights may in fact be a useful tool for 'translating' human rights standards to the online universe, presuming that such a bill is formulated within the framework of existing human rights standards.

The chapter will first provide a broad and historical account of the human rights regime, and second, will examine some of the attempts to relate human rights to internet governance during the WSIS and follow-up process, not least via a Charter of Human Rights and Principles on the internet. The latter will include examples of how information society principles may be derived from the human rights standards enshrined in the Universal Declaration of Human Rights. Concluding the chapter, the author will discuss some of the controversies related to the drafting of a Charter of Human Rights and Principles on the internet.

HUMAN RIGHTS BASIC[2]

The institutionalization of international human rights standards has constituted one of the major normative shifts in world politics since World War II. In December 1948, the United Nations General Assembly approved the Universal Declaration of Human Rights (UDHR) by a vote of 48 to zero, with eight abstentions. Later referred to by then-UN Secretary-General U Thant as the 'Magna Carta of Mankind', the UDHR comprised 30 articles dealing with two broad categories of human rights: civil and political rights; and economic, social and cultural rights. The General Assembly subsequently decided that the two categories would be detailed in separate treaty instruments—the International Covenant on Civil and Political Rights (ICCPR) and the International Covenant on Economic, Social and Cultural Rights (ICESCR), both agreed upon by the General Assembly in December 1966. Together, the UDHR, ICCPR, and ICESCR constitute the International Bill of Human Rights, which is the overarching framework for global human rights today.[3]

Civil and political rights are often referred to as first-generation rights because they were recognized at the national level in a number of eighteenth- and nineteenth-century constitutions, whereas economic, social and cultural rights were generally developed in national constitutions and international instruments in the post-World War II era. As such, the former are more deeply embedded in multiple legal systems and traditions. Moreover, political and civil rights have often been described as 'negative' rights in that they proscribe state interference with individual freedoms, whereas economic, social and cultural rights have been described as 'positive' rights that require states to create the conditions in which individuals and collectives can enjoy a certain quality of life, or to provide certain goods or services to that end. In operational terms though, the distinction is not so clear-cut.[4] The German sociologist Jürgen Habermas has argued that the catalogue of human rights is closely related to the liberal model of the public sphere and entails five broad categories of rights. The first three categories represent the basic negative liberties, membership rights, and due-process rights that together guarantee individual freedom of choice and autonomy. The fourth group entails the rights of political participation which guarantee public autonomy, whereas the fifth group represents social welfare rights which are necessary since the exercise of the other rights depends on certain social and material conditions to be met (Habermas 1996: xxvii).

Human rights are historically formulated in response to concrete experiences with human suffering, most notably revulsion against fascist atrocities during World War II, which played a catalytic role in expanding the scope and domain of human rights to be elaborated and enshrined in binding international agreements. Also, they traditionally concern the relationship between state and individual, thus protecting the individual against the arbitrary use of power by the state. The 'horizontal effect' however, is part of this relationship, implying that state obligations include a positive obligation to protect a private party against another private party by legislation and/or preventive measures or by investigating violations.[5]

While the International Bill of Human Rights provides the overarching foundation, the global human rights system also entails a range of other universal instruments. Four additional core treaties are the Convention on the Elimination of All Forms of Racial Discrimination

(1965); the Convention on the Elimination of All Forms of Discrimination Against Women (1979); the Convention Against Torture and Other Cruel, Inhuman or Degrading Treatment or Punishment (1984); and the Convention on the Rights of the Child (1989). In addition, there are many other universal instruments dealing with the interpretation and application of rights in particular areas or contexts. These take a variety of legal forms, ranging from 'hard law' covenants and conventions to 'soft law' declarations, guidelines, and recommendations.[6]

The global governance of human rights is substantively and architecturally very complex. Human rights is a deeply institutionalized field involving, at the global level, the UN Human Rights Council,[7] a multitude of monitoring mechanisms, interpretation guides (general comments on specific rights), special rapporteurs, and so on—working in a dense policy space to elaborate and interpret internationally agreed rights, build capacity, and promote compliance. The UN-based human rights system is supplemented by regional human rights mechanisms, which vary widely in constitution and effectiveness. The European regime is more 'legalized' than the international regime, and is based on the European Convention on Human Rights (ECHR), which was agreed upon by the Council of Europe in 1950. It includes a European Court of Human Rights to which unresolved cases may be presented for binding rulings. The Council of Europe also has adopted a series of additional human rights instruments. In parallel, within the European Union (EU), the European Court of Justice and other EU institutions have been progressively expanding the scope and strength of human rights protections and have reinforced the ECHR's influence. The most recent example is the Charter of Fundamental Rights,[8] which is included in the Treaty of Lisbon.[9]

The inter-American regime is also institutionally well developed, and shares broad commonalities with the European system. The Charter of the Organization of American States (OAS), signed in 1948, lists human rights as one of the organization's guiding principles. In 1959, the OAS created an expert Inter-American Commission on Human Rights, which later acquired the ability to receive complaints from individuals. The American Convention on Human Rights, which was agreed upon in 1969 and came into force in 1978, created an Inter-American Court of Human Rights that can issue nominally binding rulings. Regional regimes elsewhere are less developed and operate under far more constraining conditions. The African Charter on Human and Peoples' Rights, adopted in 1981, is supposed to extend protections not only to individuals but to collectives as well. It also contains an expansive menu of third-generation rights, including the rights to a healthy environment, development, and peace, and has bolder provisions on economic, social and cultural rights than its counterparts in Europe and the Americas. The Charter also created an African Commission on Human and Peoples' Rights, and more recently established an African Court on Human and Peoples' Rights, which entered into force in January 2004. Similarly, the League of Arab States adopted an Arab Charter on Human Rights in 1994, and has established an Arab League Human Rights Committee. In contrast, Asia still lacks a regional human rights regime, and given the cultural and political diversity of India, China and Japan, among others in the region, this is not likely to happen anytime soon. Finally, complementing the international and regional regimes and associated organizations are a variety of national mechanisms. These include national human rights institutions (NHRIs), which increasingly interact and cooperate on promoting human rights compliance and national capacity building. The NHRIs operate under a mandate established by the UN Paris Principles that were adopted by the UN General Assembly in 1993.[10]

In sum, the international community has made significant progress in establishing human rights standards and mechanisms for the ongoing monitoring of progress toward their realization. This is not to suggest that human rights are not consistently violated all around the world, often on a massive scale. However, the existence of a global framework for human rights provides mechanisms through which political and legal pressure can be applied to compel states toward greater conformity. Moreover, since the millennium, development agencies have increasingly adopted a human-rights-based approach in relation to development projects (Filmer-Wilson 2005).[11] A rights-based approach integrates the norms, standards and principles contained in international human rights treaties and declarations into the policies, plans, and processes in question. It is thus a way to provide the normative basis for a given policy area, and to use agreed human rights standards as benchmarks for measuring progress in relation to policy implementation. I have previously argued (Jørgensen 2011) that a rights-based approach has not fully been applied to global media and communication policy, despite numerous formal commitments to human rights standards, not least concerning the right to freedom of expression. In the following I focus on some of the specific attempts to address internet policy, including internet governance, from a human rights perspective.

THE INTERFACE BETWEEN HUMAN RIGHTS AND INTERNET GOVERNANCE

Human rights may be linked to internet governance in many ways as illustrated by several of the chapters in this book; however the relationship between the two is not always obvious. Broadly stated, there has been limited interaction between the communities of expertise and practice involved in human rights and internet governance respectively. Internet governance processes are often dominated by information and communication groups, scholars or policy-makers, which are typically not trained in the legal complexity of human rights, unsure how human rights standards might apply to the given policy issues, and are unclear on the practical implications of such an effort. As for the human rights communities, they have largely avoided delving into the full complexities of the global communication arena. At present, the WSIS follow-up process, particularly the Internet Governance Forum, represents one of the only arenas with ongoing dialogue between the human rights and information and communication communities. Let me briefly recapitulate the background for this encounter.

Human rights became a controversial issue already at the WSIS first phase, however mostly addressed at a very general level, as a reaffirmation of existing human rights standards within an information society context.[12] After the Geneva Summit in December 2003, the broad range of information society issues covered in the first phase of the WSIS was replaced by a narrower agenda of unresolved negotiation topics. These topics concentrated on internet governance, development financing, and WSIS follow-up and implementation, with internet governance to become the most contested issue. The WSIS second phase brought to a head the profound disagreement between the United States and many other governments and stakeholders concerning US control over the root zone file at the apex of the domain name system, and—via contractual relationships—over the Internet Corporation for Assigned Names and Numbers (ICANN).[13] Further, the WSIS process resulted in a rethinking of the character and scope of internet governance. Previously, the standard practice had been to equate the term 'Internet governance' with the social organization of internet identifiers and the root server system and, by extension, the functions performed by ICANN. This narrow vision overlooked the fact that there are various internationally shared private- and public-sector principles, norms, rules, procedures, and programmes that shape both the internet's infrastructure (physical and logical) and use for communication and commerce. As the WSIS discussions progressed, participants began to converge around the need for a broader, holistic conception that could encompass the full range of internet governance mechanisms and facilitate their systematic evaluation and improvement. This demand was met by a pair of reports issued in 2005 by the UN Working Group on Internet Governance (WGIG).[14] The WGIG developed a broadly framed 'working definition' of internet governance that was subsequently embraced by governments and other stakeholders. The effect of this broader definition was to put on the table a broad range of governance mechanisms and issues, including those pertaining to freedom of expression versus content regulation, privacy, 'information security' and network security, intellectual property, international trade, technical standardization, and other matters.[15]

Finally, and in consequence, the new understanding significantly increased the number of contact points between human rights standards and internet governance policies and programmes. As such, human rights received greater attention in the internet governance discussions of WSIS' second phase than they had in those of the first phase. For example, human rights standards were invoked in the WGIG's internal debates and the group's main report noted that 'Measures taken in relation to the Internet on grounds of security or to fight crime can lead to violations of the provisions for freedom of expression as contained in the Universal Declaration of Human Rights and in the WSIS Declaration of Principles.' The report also decried the lack of fully enforceable international standards on privacy protection (WGIG 2005b: 7). Similarly, the WGIG's background report made specific references to human rights. At the Tunis Summit in November 2005, the general human rights framing of the information society agreed upon in Geneva 2003 was reaffirmed, however human rights were also addressed more specifically in relation to internet governance.[16]

As a follow-up to WSIS, the first Internet Governance Forum (IGF) was convened in Athens in 2006, and resulted in the creation of a number of so-called dynamic coalitions. The dynamic coalitions address various topics related to the broader internet governance agenda and are multi-stakeholder in the sense that civil society groups, academics, business and government representatives alike participate. One of these coalitions is responsible for the most recent and substantiated attempt to 'translate' human rights standards to the internet; namely the Internet Rights and Principles Dynamic Coalition.[17] I next address the coalition's effort to create a Charter on Human Rights and Principles for the Internet in more detail.

A CHARTER ON HUMAN RIGHTS AND PRINCIPLES FOR THE INTERNET

At the Tunis Summit in 2005, former chair of the European Data Protection Agency Council, Stefano Rodotà authored an appeal that addressed the necessity of a 'Charter of the Rights of the Net'. The appeal highlighted the potential of the internet, and was formally presented at the Tunis Summit by the government of Italy. The appeal was endorsed by a number of prominent experts, and subsequently led to the creation of the Internet Rights and Principles Dynamic Coalition (IRPDC) at the first IGF in 2006 (originally called the Dynamic Coalition on an Internet Bill of Rights).

As formulated in the mission statement, the overall goal of the IRPDC is to specify rights on the internet and their related duties from the view-point of individual users, and to make those a central theme of the annual Internet Governance Forum agenda (IRPDC 2008: 1). The human rights point of departure is the International Bill of Human Rights consisting of the Universal Declaration of Human Rights, the International Covenant on Civil and Political Rights and its two Optional Protocols, and the International Covenant on Economic, Social and Cultural Rights. The IRPDC is currently (since 2009) led by London-based Global Partners and Associates, and comprises a steering committee, a human rights expert group, and the broader coalition consisting of more than 100 individual members.[18]

The IRPDC has worked via online collaboration and physical meet-ings at the annual IGFs starting in 2006. In 2009, the IRPDC appointed a small human rights expert group to advance the work on an Internet Charter and more specifically to secure that the Charter was firmly anchored in the existing human rights framework.[19] The following exami-nation of the content of such a Charter is inspired by the draft produced by this group (with Wolfgang Benedek as the main editor), plus the sub-sequent debates and revisions by the broader coalition.[20] The Charter on Human Rights and Principles for the Internet (hereafter referred to as the Internet Charter) is based on the following main sources of input; various draft sections produced by the IRPDC in the period 2006–2009, the Association for Progressive Communication's (APC) Internet Rights Charter from 2006, and the Universal Declaration of Human Rights and subsequent human rights law of the United Nations, including work done by regional human rights institutions. Further the Internet Charter is inspired by the WSIS Declaration of Principles of Geneva and the Tunis Agenda for the Information Society, which recognizes that Information and Communication Technologies (ICTs) present tremendous opportuni-ties to enable individuals, communities and peoples to achieve their full potential.

The Internet Charter consists of a preamble and two main sections. The first interprets human rights within an information society context, whereas the second defines principles and guidelines addressed to specific stakeholders and technologies. Below focus is on the rights and principles covered in section one, thus the application of existing human rights standards to the internet. This includes the following topics:

1.   Right to Access to the internet
2.   Right to Non-discrimination in internet Access, Use and Governance
3.   Right to Liberty and Security on the internet
4.   Right to Development through the internet
5.   Freedom of Expression and Information on the internet
6.   Freedom of Religion and Belief on the internet
7.   Freedom of Online Assembly and Association
8.   Right to Privacy on the internet
9.   Right to Digital Data Protection
10. Right to Education on and about the internet
11. Right to Culture and Access to Knowledge on the internet
12. Rights of Children and the internet
13. Rights of People with Disabilities and the internet
14. Right to Work and the internet
15. Right to Online Participation in Public Affairs
16. Right to Consumer Protection on the internet
17. Right to Health and Social Services on the internet
18. Right to Legal Remedy and Fair Trial for actions involving the internet
19. Right to Appropriate Social and International Order for the internet
20. Duties and Responsibilities on the internet
21. General Clauses

The Internet Charter opens with the right of everyone to access and make use of the internet as a right underpinning all other rights in the Charter. It is argued that access to the internet is indispensable for the full enjoyment of human rights; hence the right derives from its integral relationship to the enjoyment of other human rights. The right includes quality of service, freedom of choice of system and software use, ensuring digital inclusion, and net neutrality and net equality. These principles imply that means of access shall evolve in line with advancing technological possibilities, communication infrastructures and protocols shall be interoperable, using open standards, public internet access points shall be made available, and the internet architecture must be protected and promoted as a vehicle for free, open, equal and non-discriminatory exchange of information, communication and culture. Following internet access, the principles of universality and non-discrimination are addressed as laid down in article 2 of UDHR: 'Everyone is entitled to all the rights and freedoms set forth in this Declaration, without distinction of any kind, such as race, colour, sex, language, religion, political or other opinion, national or social origin, property, birth or other status. Furthermore, no distinction shall be made on the basis of the political, jurisdictional or international status of the country or territory to which a person belongs, whether it be independent, trust, non-self-governing or under any other limitation of sovereignty.'

The principles of universality and non-discrimination are used to specify that all rights in the Internet Charter are universal and that everyone is entitled to enjoy these rights, without distinction of any kind. The principles are specified in relation to equality of access, marginalized groups and gender equality. Regarding equity of access, the Charter stresses that certain groups have more restricted internet access than others, which can amount to de-facto discrimination; hence efforts to increase access must recognize and address these inequalities. Special attention must be paid to the needs of marginalized groups, and hardware, code, applications and content should be designed using universal design principles to ensure maximum accessibility. Further, there must be full participation of women in all areas related to the development of the internet.

Following these foundational principles, the Internet Charter continues with the specific rights of the UDHR and their application in an internet context. It should be noted that only those rights with specific relevance to the internet are included, excluding e.g. freedom from slavery and freedom from torture. Also, the Internet Charter does not follow the exact same structure as the UDHR.

The first topic addressed is the *Right to Liberty and Security on the Internet*, derived from article 3 of the UDHR: 'everyone has the right to life, liberty and security of person'. In the Internet Charter, this right is specified as the right to be protected against all forms of crime committed on or using the internet, as well as the right to secure connections on and to the internet. Recognizing that many security interventions may affect the right to liberty and security online, it is stressed that any security measure which affects the internet shall be consistent with international human rights laws and standards and that all restrictions must be precise and narrowly defined.

Next follows the *Right to Development through the Internet*, which is inspired by the UN Declaration on the Right to Development (1986), recognizing that all human rights require economic, social, cultural and political development in order to be fully realized. In the Internet Charter this is specified in relation to poverty reduction and human development as well as environmental sustainability. It is stressed that information and communication technologies shall be designed, developed and implemented to contribute to sustainable human development and empowerment, and that everyone has a responsibility to use the internet in a sustainable way, including disposal of e-waste and to use the internet for the protection of the environment.

The next topic: *Freedom of Expression and Information on the Internet*, represents one of the most debated human rights in relation to the internet. As enshrined in UDHR article 19; 'everyone has the right to freedom of opinion and expression; this right includes freedom to hold opinions without interference and to seek, receive and impart information and ideas through any media and regardless of frontiers'. Further, article 19 of ICCPR specifies that the right to freedom of expression may be subject to certain restrictions, but these shall only be such as are provided by law and are necessary for respect of the rights or reputations of others; for the protection of national security or of public order, or of public health or morals.

In the Internet Charter rights of expression are spelled out in relation to the right to use the internet to organize and engage in online and offline protest, the right to use the internet without censorship in any form, including freedom from blocking and filtering, the right to seek, receive and impart information and ideas through the internet, the right to access and make use of government information according to national and international law, freedom and pluralism of the media, and freedom from hate speech. The latter is specified with reference to CCPR article 20, which states that 'any advocacy of national, racial or religious hatred that constitutes incitement to discrimination, hostility or violence shall be prohibited by law'.

Next follows *Freedom of Religion and Belief on the Internet*, enshrined in UDHR article 18: 'Everyone has the right to freedom of thought, conscience and religion; this right includes freedom to change his religion or belief, and freedom, either alone or in community with others and in public or private, to manifest his religion or belief in teaching, practice, worship and observance.' The right also includes freedom from religion.[21]

The right to *Freedom of Online Assembly and Association*, is derived from UDHR article 20 stating that: 'everyone has the right to freedom of peaceful assembly and association. No one may be compelled to belong to an association.' The Internet Charter specifies this right as everyone's right to form, join, meet or visit the website or network of an assembly, group or association for any reason, as well as prohibition against blocking or filtering of access to those.

The *Right to Privacy* is one of the most debated human rights in relation to the internet. The right is enshrined in article 12 of the UDHR and reads: 'No one shall be subjected to arbitrary interference with his privacy, family, home or correspondence, nor to attacks upon his honor and reputation. Everyone has the right to the protection of the law against such interference or attacks.' In the Internet Charter the right is spelled out in relation to national legislation on privacy, privacy policies and settings, standards of confidentiality and integrity of IT-systems, protection of the virtual personality, right to anonymity and to use encryption, freedom from surveillance, and freedom from defamation. This implies that states must establish, implement and enforce comprehensive legal frameworks to protect the privacy and personal data of citizens, privacy policy and settings of all services must be easy to find, IT systems must be protected against illegitimate access, and that everyone has the right to a virtual personality, i.e. a personal identification in information systems. Further it implies a right to communicate anonymously on the internet and to use encryption technology, freedom to communicate without arbitrary surveillance or interception (including behavioural tracking, profiling, and cyber-stalking), including freedom from threat of surveillance or interception, and finally, no one shall be subjected to unlawful attacks on their honour and reputation on the internet.

Derived from the right to privacy (UDHR article 12), as well as privacy guidelines established at regional level (OECD Guidelines on the Protection of Data and Transborder Flows, 1980) is *the Right to Digital Data Protection*. The Internet Charter specifies the right to digital data protection in relation to the protection of personal data, obligations of data collectors, minimum standards on use of personal data, and monitoring by independent data protection authorities. First, fair information practices should be enacted into national law to place obligations on companies and governments who collect and process personal data, and give rights to those individuals whose personal data is collected. Second, collection, use, disclosure and retention of personal data must meet transparent privacy-protecting standards. Whoever requires personal data from persons should request the individual's informed consent regarding the content, purposes, storage location, duration and mechanisms for access, retrieval and correction of their personal data. Third, when personal information is required, only the minimum data necessary must be collected and for the minimum period of time for which this is required. Moreover, appropriate security measures shall be taken for the protection of personal data stored in automated data files against accidental or unauthorized destruction or accidental loss as well as against unauthorized access, alteration or dissemination. Finally, data protection should be monitored by independent data protection authorities, which work transparently and without commercial advantage or political influence.

The right to education is enshrined in UDHR article 26 and iterates that 'Everyone has the right to education. Education shall be free, at least in the elementary and fundamental stages. Elementary education shall be compulsory (. . .)'. In the Internet Charter this right is specified as the *Right to Education on and about the Internet*. This includes education through the internet and education about the internet and human rights. The right to be educated through the internet implies that publications, research, text books, course materials and other kinds of learning materials shall be published as Open Educational Resources with the right to freely use, copy, reuse, adapt, translate and redistribute them. Also, free or low-cost training opportunities, methodologies and materials related to using the internet for social development shall be promoted. Education about the internet and human rights includes raising awareness and respect for human rights (online and offline) and making digital literacy a key component of education.

Next follows the *Right to Culture and Access to Knowledge on the Internet*, based on the UDHR article 27. Article 27 addresses cultural rights stipulating that: 'everyone has the right freely to participate in the cultural life of the community, to enjoy the arts and to share in scientific advancement and its benefits' and that 'everyone has the right to the protection of the moral and material interests resulting from any scientific, literary or artistic production' of which he or she is the author. In the Internet Charter the right to enjoy your own culture includes the right to participate in the cultural life of the community, diversity of languages and cultures, the right to use one's own language, freedom from restrictions of access to knowledge by licensing and copyright, knowledge commons and the public domain, and free/open source software and open standards. It is stressed that the public service value of the internet shall be protected, including access to diverse information as well as different cultural content. Individuals and communities have the right to use their own language to create, disseminate, and share information and knowledge through the internet, with special attention given to minority languages. Creators have the right to be remunerated and acknowledged for their work and innovations; however this must be achieved in ways which do not restrict further innovation or access to public and educational knowledge and resources. Licensing and copyright of content must permit knowledge to be created, shared, used and built upon, using permissive licensing models. Publicly funded research and intellectual and cultural work must be made available freely to the general public, where possible. Finally, Free/libre and Open Source Software (FOSS) must be used, promoted and implemented in public and educational institutions and services.

The *Rights of Children and the Internet* is based on the UN Convention on the Rights of the Child (CRC), which calls for the provision of specific resources, skills and contributions necessary to ensure the survival and development of children to their maximum capability. As enshrined in article 25 of the UDHR: childhood is 'entitled to special care and assistance'. Related to the internet this means that children must both be given the freedom to use the internet, and also protected from the dangers associated with the internet. In the Internet Charter the rights of children are specified in relation to a right to benefit from the internet, freedom from exploitation and child abuse imagery, rights to have views heard, and the best interest of the child. First, children should be able to benefit from the internet according to their age and should have opportunities to use the internet to exercise their civil, political, economic, cultural and social rights. Second, children have a right to develop in a safe environment that is free from sexual or other kinds of exploitation. Measures should be taken to prevent the use of the internet to violate the rights of children, including through trafficking and child abuse imagery. However, such measures must be narrowly targeted and proportionate. Further, the effect of measures taken on the free flow of information online must be given due consideration. Third, children who are capable of forming their own views have the right to express them in all internet policy matters that affect them, and their views should be given due weight according to their age and maturity. Finally, the best interest of the child shall be the primary consideration in all matters of concern to children and the internet, as stressed in article 3 of CRC.

Next follows the *Rights of People with Disabilities and the Internet*. As enshrined in article 4 of the United Nations Convention on the Rights of Persons with Disabilities (CRPD), 'States Parties undertake to ensure and promote the full realization of all human rights and fundamental freedoms for all persons with disabilities without discrimination of any kind on the basis of disability'. In the Internet Charter this includes accessibility to the internet, and availability and affordability of the internet. First, it is stressed that persons with disabilities have a right to access, on an equal basis with others, the internet; hence standards and guidelines for accessibility should be promoted. Second, steps must be taken to ensure the effective use of the internet by people with disabilities.

The *Right to Work and the Internet* is derived from UDHR article 23, which states that 'everyone has the right to work'. In the Internet Charter the right to work is addressed in relation to respect for workers' rights, internet at the workplace, and work on and through the internet. Respect for workers' rights specifies that everyone has the right to use the internet to form trade unions, including the right to promote one's own interests and gather in freely elected organs of representation. Workers and employees shall have internet access at their work place, where available, and any restrictions on internet use in the work place shall be explicitly stated in staff or organizational policies. In case of surveillance of the internet use of employees, the terms and conditions for this must be clearly stated in work place policies and comply with the right to data protection. Finally, people shall have the right to seek employment and to work through or by means of the internet.

Next follows the *Right to Online Participation in Public Affairs* anchored in article 21 of UDHR, which stresses that 'everyone has the right to take part in the government of his country, directly or through freely chosen representatives' and that 'everyone has the right of equal access to public service in the country'. In the Internet Charter this is specified as a right to equal access to electronic services, and a right to participate in electronic government. Where electronic government is available, everyone must have the right to participate.

The *Right to Consumer Protection on the Internet* is inspired by the UN Guidelines for Consumer Protection (1999), which stress that consumers often face imbalances in economic terms, educational levels and bargaining power; hence governments should develop or maintain a strong consumer protection policy. In an internet context this implies that everyone must respect, protect and fulfil principles of consumer protection on the internet and that e-commerce must be regulated to ensure that consumers receive the same level of protection as they enjoy in non-electronic transactions.[22]

The *Right to Health and Social Services on the Internet* is derived from UDHR article 25, which stresses that '(1) Everyone has the right to a standard of living adequate for the health and well-being of himself and of his family, including food, clothing, housing and medical care and necessary social services, and the right to security in the event of unemployment, sickness, disability, widowhood, old age or other lack of livelihood in circumstances beyond his control.' In the Internet Charter the right to health is specified as a right to access health-related and social services on the internet.

The *Right to Legal Remedy and Fair Trial for Actions Involving the Internet* is based on articles 8, 9, 10 and 11 of the UDHR. Article 8 provides everyone with 'the right to an effective remedy by the competent national tribunals for acts violating the fundamental rights granted him (or her) by the constitution or by law', whereas article 10 entitles everyone in full equality to 'a fair and public hearing by an independent and impartial tribunal, in the determination of his rights and obligations and of any criminal charge against him'. Further, criminal trials must follow fair trial standards as defined by the UDHR (articles 9–11) and the ICCPR (articles 9 and 14–16) as well as other pertinent documents. In the Internet Charter these procedural rights are specified in relation to the right to a legal remedy, the right to fair trial, and right to due process. The Internet Charter stresses that it is increasingly common for the right to a fair trial and to an effective remedy to be violated in the internet environment, for example with internet intermediary companies being asked to make judgments about whether content is illegal and encouraged to remove content without a court order. It therefore reiterates that procedural rights must be respected, protected and fulfilled on the internet as they are offline. It further states that everyone has the right to due process in relation to any legal claims or possible violations of the law regarding the internet.

The *Right to Appropriate Social and International Order for the Internet* is derived from UDHR article 28, which reads, 'everyone is entitled to a social and international order in which the rights and freedoms set forth in this Declaration can be fully realized'. In the Internet Charter this includes governance of the internet for human rights, multilingualism and pluralism on the internet, and effective participation in internet governance. First, the internet and the communications system must be governed in such a way as to ensure that it upholds and expands human rights to the fullest extent possible. Internet governance must be driven by principles of openness, inclusiveness and accountability and exercised in a transparent and multilateral manner. Second, the internet as a social and international order shall enshrine principles of multilingualism, pluralism, and heterogeneous forms of cultural life in both form and substance. Finally, full and effective participation of all, in particular disadvantaged groups in global, regional and national decision-making must be ensured.

Next follows *Duties and Responsibilities on the Internet* anchored in article 29 of the UDHR, stressing that, '1) Everyone has duties to the community in which alone the free and full development of his personality is possible.' On the internet the duties of everyone to the community include respect for the rights of others, and responsibility of power holders. Everybody has the duty and responsibility to respect the rights of all individuals in the online environment and power holders must exercise their power responsibly, refrain from violating human rights and respect, protect and fulfil them to the fullest extent possible.

Finally, the Internet Charter provides some *General Clauses* related to interdependence of all rights in the Charter, limitations on rights in the Charter, the non-exhaustive nature of the Charter, and the interpretation of rights and freedoms of the Charter. First, it is stressed that all rights contained in this Charter are interdependent and mutually reinforcing. Second, all restrictions must be precise and narrowly defined, as well as the minimum necessary to meet a genuine need which is recognized under International law, and proportionate to that need. Third, the fact that certain rights and principles have not been included in the Charter or have not been developed in detail does not preclude the existence of such rights and principles. Finally, nothing in the Charter may be interpreted as implying for any State, group or person any right to engage in any activity or to perform any act aimed at the destruction of any of the rights and freedoms set forth in the Charter.

CONCLUSION

At the time of writing (spring 2011) the Internet Charter is in the process of wider consultation, and much debate has surrounded its format and substance. Some of the criticism that has been raised time and again concerns 1) the status of the rights in the Charter vis a vis excising human rights, specifically whether the Internet Charter may be used to downplay existing human rights standards, 2) disagreement on which topics and rights to include in the Internet Charter, and which not, and 3) concern that the Internet Charter may create confusion rather than be a useful vehicle to promote human rights in the information society.[23]

Regarding the first line of criticism, the appointment of the human rights expert group to assist the IRPDC has been one of the measures taken to ensure that the Internet Charter is firmly anchored in the existing human rights regime and terminology. Another measure has been to insert references to the UDHR in relation to each right and freedom in the Internet Charter, in order to clarify the human rights point of departure and to distinguish between long established rights and their possible application to the internet. As reiterated by the IRPDC, the idea of the Internet Charter is to translate existing human rights standards to an information society context,[24] thus to provide a convincing argument based on the evolving case law and practice, rather than to develop a legally binding document. The need for examples on what human rights standards may imply when translated to the internet era was iterated time and again during the WSIS process, and the Internet Charter may serve as a first step in this direction.

Regarding the format and substance of the Internet Charter, most sections have been up for debate, so the following topics represent just a few examples. First, it has been disputed whether to use the title and format of a Charter. Some have argued that the Charter title and format is misleading, and claimed that only legal documents may be called a Charter, while others argued that the notion often is applied to an important topical statement that is not legal by nature. So far, it has been decided to keep the title and format of an Internet Charter with reference to the latter argument and because many saw it as more 'punchy' than a policy paper format. Second, the relation between rights and principles has been contested, including whether to separate legally binding standards from more aspirational principles. In response, it was decided to open each article with the relevant UDHR reference, but to allow for both rights and principles when applying the given right or freedom to an internet context. This was, among others, based on the argument that in reality the two are mixed and constantly progressing, thus it is difficult to separate rights and principles which are in different stages of legal development without entering endless debates on the current status of either. As previously stressed, the Internet Charter is not a legal document, rather the strength of it is to present a persuading argument based on relevant belief and practice. Third, the 'Right to Access to the Internet' as a separate right has been disputed. In the first draft (1.0) access was placed as a separate theme under non-discrimination, in order to emphasize that the right to internet access is equal for all, and to keep with the original structure of the UDHR. In the revision process following the first draft, most people agreed that a right to access can be interpreted to flow from existing human rights, as a precondition for the enjoyment of many other rights. However many also argued that access should be presented as a separate human right, arguing that it has evolved into that status by common belief and practice, e.g. access having been the main issue at all IGFs so far. Following much debate, the Charter now opens with the right to access to the internet, emphasizing that the right underpins all other rights in the Charter. Finally, there has been debate on whether to include topics such as consumer rights, which are not part of the UDHR, however often debated in an internet context in relation to consumer protection vis a vis e-commerce, privacy etc. So far, it has been decided to keep the section on consumers rights, but to address some of the specific points in the section on Privacy and the section on Data Protection.

Another and more general line of criticism concerns whether the Internet Charter may create confusion rather than serve a useful vehicle to promote human rights in the information society, including in internet governance processes. Proponents of this criticism argue that plenty of standards already exist and that the real challenge is to implement existing standards rather than to produce new and non-binding text. Others argue that judging from the WSIS process and the evolving IGF debates, there has been a continuous call for advancing the debate on how human rights shall be respected, protected and fulfilled on the internet. As the development of relevant case law is slow, and the engagement of the wider human rights community in information society debates relatively limited, the Internet Charter may serve as a vision and an advocacy tool that is available to anyone interested in promoting human rights in the internet era.

In sum, human rights and internet governance have intersected on several levels during WSIS and beyond, most recently via the attempt to draft an Internet Charter. As illustrated above, the Charter addresses a wide range of issues pertaining to human rights in an internet context, and critics have argued that the Charter may downplay rather than advance long established human rights standards. In response, proponents of the Charter, including this author, have argued that as long as the Charter is framed within the existing human rights framework it might serve as a useful tool for advocacy and awareness raising for groups and policy makers concerned with promoting human rights as the basis for internet governance.[25] In the short term, a main challenge will be for IRPDC to finalize a text with broad agreement amongst the wider coalition, however in the longer term the relevance of an Internet Charter will need to prove its value via its actual uses and supporters.

NOTES

1. The Internet Governance Forum (www.intgovforum.org) was established as a follow-up to the UN World Summit on the Information Society (WSIS) in 2005 and has convened every year since 2006. In the following, I apply the understanding of internet governance that was developed during the WSIS process, thus 'Internet governance is the development and application by Governments, the private sector and civil society, in their respective roles, of shared principles, norms, rules, decision-making procedures, and programmes that shape the evolution and use of the Internet' (WGIG 2005b: 4).
2. The account of human rights in this section and the following is based on Drake and Jørgensen 2006.
3. The UDHR was drafted and approved in the short period of just two years. In contrast, negotiations over the two legal instruments dragged on for over a decade before concluding in 1966. The process of national ratification, thus getting binding commitment from states, has taken much longer and is still incomplete. The ICCPR and ICESCR build directly on the UDHR, reinforcing through codification, the strength of its injunctions.
4. For a discussion on the complexity of this distinction, see for example Koch 2005: 81–103.
5. Legal scholars speak of 'Drittwirkung' (effect by third party), which is used to stress that contracting states that have ratified human rights treaties must protect individuals' human rights in the realm of private parties as well. See Van Hoof and Dijk 1998: 23.
6. While many of the instruments amplify rights previously established in the International Bill of Human Rights, there are also additions. These sets of rights are often described as 'third-generation' rights. Leading examples include the rights invoked in the UN General Assembly's 1984 Declaration on the Right of Peoples to Peace and its 1986 Declaration on the Right to Development. The aspirational principles of these declarations have been affirmed in subsequent political statements or soft law, but they have not been embodied in binding treaties.
7. The Human Rights Council is a successor to the Human Rights Commission, which was replaced in 2006.
8. See http://eur-lex.europa.eu/en/treaties/dat/32007X1214/htm/C2007303EN.01000101.htm.

9. The Treaty of Lisbon came into force on 1 December 2009. It is available at: http://europa.eu/lisbon_treaty/index_en.htm.
10. For a global overview of NHRIs, see www.nhri.net. For a discussion on the role of NHRIs, see Kjærum 2003: 631–53.
11. According to the definition used by the Office of the High Commissioner for Human Rights, a rights-based approach is a conceptual framework for the process of developing policies that is normatively based upon international human rights standards and operationally directed to promoting and protecting human rights. See http://www.unhchr.ch/development/approaches.html.
12. See Marzouki and Jørgensen (2004) for a summary of the human rights issues raised during WSIS first phase.
13. See Marzouki and Jørgensen (2004).
14. The WGIG was a multi-stakeholder group appointed by former UN Secretary-General Kofi Annan in November 2004.
15. The definition of internet governance is the one applied in this chapter, cf. note 1. For a significantly more extended discussion of the issues, including the definition, see WGIG 2005a.
16. The role of human rights is linked to internet governance in paragraph 42 of the Tunis Agenda (subheading Internet Governance): 'We reaffirm our commitment to the freedom to seek, receive, impart and use information, in particular, for the creation, accumulation and dissemination of knowledge. We affirm that measures undertaken to ensure internet stability and security, to fight cybercrime and to counter spam, must protect and respect the provisions for privacy and freedom of expression as contained in the relevant parts of the Universal Declaration of Human Rights and the Geneva Declaration of Principles' (WSIS Tunis Agenda 2005).
17. See http://www.internetrightsandprinciples.org.
18. Please refer to the website (cf. note above) for further information on the IRPDC's structure and member base.
19. Members of the group are Wolgang Benedek (Austria), Meryem Marzouki (France), Rikke Frank Jørgensen (Denmark), Wang Sixin (China), Roberto Saba (Argentina) and Andrew Rens (South Africa).
20. The Internet Charter 1.0 was presented at the IGF in Vilnius on 13 September 2010. Based on feedback at the IGF and beyond the recent beta version 1.1 was published for further consultation. The current version of the charter is available at: http://irpcharter.org/charter/.
21. In version 1.0 of the Internet Charter the right was specified as everyone's right to express and practise their faith on the internet, however following some debate amongst the broader coalition on the precise implications of freedom of religion and belief on the internet, there is currently no specification of the right in an internet context.
22. In the review process, the inclusion of consumer protection has been a contested issue, as discussed below in the 'CONCLUSION'.
23. The following is based on the online debates that have occurred on the IRPDC mailing list in the period from November 2009 (IGF at Sharm-el-Sheik) to January 2011.
24. 'Based on the rights defined in the Universal Declaration of Human Rights, the IRPDC provides a platform to promote appropriate application and transposition of these rights to the online environment.(..).' FAQ answered by IRPDC, http://internetrightsandprinciples.org/node/13.
25. Most recently, IRPDC have produced a short version of 'punchy principles' (10 internet rights and principles condensed from the Internet Charter) which were launched on 31 March 2011 at the Expert Meeting on Human Rights and the Internet in Stockholm. The 10 Internet Rights and Principles, http://www.irpcharter.org/.

BIBLIOGRAPHY

APC (2006), 'Internet Rights Charter', http://www.apc.org/en/node/5677/.

Drake, W.J. and R.F. Jørgensen (2006), 'Introduction', in R.F. Jørgensen (ed.), *Human Rights in the Global Information Society*, Boston: MIT Press, pp. 1–49.

Filmer-Wilson, E. (2005), 'The Human Rights-based Approach to Development: the Right to Water', *Netherlands Quarterly of Human Rights*, **23(2)**, 213–41.

Habermas, J. (1996), *Between Facts and Norms*, Cambridge: Polity.

Jørgensen, R.F. (2011), 'Human Rights and their Role in Global Media and Communication Discourses', in R. Mansell and M. Raboy (eds), *The Handbook on Global Media and Communication Policy*, Oxford: Blackwell Publishing.

Kjærum, M. (2003), 'National Human Rights Institutions Implementing Human Rights', in M. Bergsmo (ed.) *Human Rights and Criminal Justice for the Downtrodden: Essays in Honour of Asbjørn Eide*, Leiden: Martinus Nijhoff, pp. 631–53.

Koch, I.E (2005), 'Dichotomies, Trichotomies, or Waves of Duties?', *Human Rights Law Review*, **5(1)**, 81–103.

Marzouki, M. and R.F. Jørgensen (2004), 'A Human Rights Assessment of the World Summit on the Information Society', *Information Technologies and International Development*, **1(3–4)**, pp. 86–88.

OECD (1980), 'OECD Guidelines on the Protection of Privacy and Transborder Flows of Personal Data', http://www.oecd.org/document/18/0,3343,en_2649_34255_1815186_1_1_1_1,00.html.

The Internet Rights and Principles Dynamic Coalition (IRPDC) (2008), 'Mission Statement', http://Internetrightsandprinciples.org/node/7.

United Nations (1948), 'The Universal Declaration of Human Rights', New York: United Nations, http://www.ohchr.org/EN/UDHR/Pages/Language.aspx?LangID=eng.

United Nations (1966), 'International Covenant for Civil and Political Rights', New York: United Nations, http://www2.ohchr.org/english/law/ccpr.htm.

United Nations (1966), 'International Covenant on Economic, Social and Cultural Rights', New York: United Nations, http://www2.ohchr.org/english/law/cescr.htm.

United Nations (1989), 'Convention on the Rights of the Child', New York: United Nations, http://www2.ohchr.org/english/law/crc.htm.

United Nations Department of Economic and Social Affairs (2003), 'United Nations Guidelines for Consumer Protection (as expanded in 1999)', New York: UN.

Van Hoof, G.J.H. and P. Dijk (1998), *Theory and Practice of the European Convention on Human Rights*, The Hague: Kluwer Law International.

WGIG (2005a), 'The Background Report of the Working Group on Internet Governance', Geneva: United Nations.

WGIG (2005b), 'The Report of the Working Group on Internet Governance', Château de Bossey, June 2005.

World Summit on the Information Society (2003), 'Declaration of Principles', Geneva: WSIS, http://www.itu.int/wsis/docs/geneva/official/dop.html.

World Summit on the Information Society (2003), 'Plan of Action' Geneva: WSIS, http://www.itu.int/wsis/docs/geneva/official/poa.html.

World Summit on the Information Society (2005), 'Tunis Commitment', Tunis: WSIS, http://www.itu.int/wsis/docs2/tunis/off/7.html.

World Summit on the Information Society (2005), 'Tunis Agenda for the Information Society', Tunis: WSIS, http://www.itu.int/wsis/docs2/tunis/off/6rev1.html.

15. Human rights, competition law, and access to essential technologies
Abbe Brown

INTRODUCTION

The internet is acquiring ever more prominence in daily lives. In turn, some companies – such as Apple, Microsoft and Google – seem to acquire more power in society, as a result of their control of the technologies which enable one to access to internet, or make use of some of its opportunities. Further, those who cannot have access to the internet are less able to participate in some aspects of society. This chapter explores how different legal tools may be combined to address these power imbalances. The key question will be whether or not products or technologies can be argued to be "essential"; and if so, is this a helpful label – what does this mean for those wishing to use the products or technologies? Competition and human rights will be used to explore these questions, and some reference will made to intellectual property rights ("IP") and to trade secrets, to the place they have in encouraging innovation and creativity, and their interaction with competition and human rights.[1] It will be argued that competition and human rights can play a role in identifying essential technologies and delivering and proposing access to them.

WHAT IS AN ESSENTIAL TECHNOLOGY?

Initial Points

Is anything really essential – much less a technology? Oxygen, water, basic food, shelter may be essential; perhaps even love, companionship and hope (Maslow 1943). These tangible and intangible things can be argued to be quite distinct from technology and the internet. For the first set of examples, this must be so. For the second set, one can argue that the internet and technology offer new forms of interaction and fulfilment – online dating sites such as http://www.match.com and http://www.mysinglefriend.com, Facebook, posting or "tweeting" on Twitter or being in virtual worlds (eg Second Life and World of Warcraft). Consider also voting online which is the subject of ongoing discussion by the Electoral Reform Society and the Open Source Digital Voting Foundation, if this is the only permitted form of voting; accessing health information when there is no doctor – or working with one in a new way, as is seen in the European Union funded project in National R&D Information Service in Estonia; or using a voice to text enabled eReader to provide new access to literature to the highly dyslexic (Kestrell 2010 and Switch11 2009). The technologies which enable all this could be argued to be essential.

The discussion so far comes with a strong element of subjectivity. As an avid reader, I value greatly the opportunities from eReaders; I am much more sceptical about arguments relating to social networking. Yet at the time of first preparing this chapter I was awestruck at the impact of social networking sites in circulating information, support and resistance in Tunisia and Egypt (Saez 2011). Others may not be.

So before we move on to consider the legal consequences of a technology being essential, is there a more objective means of identifying essential technologies? One could start with the activities enabled by a particular technology – or, more likely, a group of technologies which combine in a product or service – and the relationship between this, human rights and competition.

The Human Rights Perspective

Using human rights

As is explored elsewhere in this collection (see Chapter 14 by Jørgensen) there is a significant field of debate regarding the meaning of "human rights" and also regarding how human rights may be enforced (for an overview, see Symonides 2002). It is clear, however, that there is an existing body of human rights instruments, which has formed part of the work to transfer human rights into the internet arena (see the development of the Association for Progressive Communication Internet Rights Charter and also Jørgensen 2006), most recently through the Charter of Internet Rights and Principles (see Chapter 14 by Jørgensen).[2] Discussions are also ongoing regarding rights which some argue should be human rights – for example, a right of access to knowledge (Vadi 2008) or to use Facebook (Gurstein 2011). This will be considered in more detail later in this chapter.

The contemporary human rights instruments stem from the aftermath of the Second World War, as attempts were made to prevent a repeat of its atrocities by setting out rights which states were to accord citizens. The first step was the Universal Declaration of Human Rights of 1948. This is an aspirational document, not imposing obligations on states. It formed a base for two international treaties finalised in 1966 (see

Eide 2007) – the International Covenant on Civil and Political Rights ("ICCPR") and the International Covenant on Economic, Social and Cultural Rights ("ICESCR"). The website of the Office of United Nations High Commissioner for Human Rights states that most nations have ratified at least one of these.

Of present interest, the ICCPR includes protection of rights to life (article 6), against interference with privacy (article 17), to expression (article 19) and to vote (article 25) and the ICESCR has rights to health (article 2), to education (article 13), to take part in cultural life (article 15(1)(a)) and to enjoy the benefits of scientific progress (article 15(1) (b)). There is also the right to the protection of the moral and material interests of the author (article 15(1)(c)) – although General Comment No. 17 from 2005 of the Office of the High Commissioner for Human Rights Committee on Economic Social and Cultural Rights, "The right of everyone to benefit from the protection of the moral and material interests resulting from any scientific, literary or artistic production of which he or she is the author", considers that these rights do not create a human right to IP as a whole, particularly when it is owned by a company (see also Chapman 2001; Helfer 2003; and Dreyfuss 2010). Of present interest, however, is the relationship between the rights to expression and to vote and the right of an individual software developer to its material interests in respect of software – particularly when a government has required that that technology is the one which must be used to vote online.

Human rights can also be found in regional instruments, such as the European Convention on Human Rights and Fundamental Freedoms ("ECHR") 1951, the American Convention on Human Rights of 1969, the African Charter of Human and Peoples' Rights of 1981, the Asian Human Rights Charter 1998, the Revised Arab Charter of Rights of 2008, the European Union ("EU") Charter of Fundamental Rights ("EU Charter") and the doctrine of fundamental rights of the EU (see for example decisions of the European Court of Justice ("ECJ"), as it was then, in *Internationale Handelsgesellschaft v Einfuhr- und Vorratsstelle fur Getreide und Futtermittel* (1970: para. 4) and *Productores de Musica de Espana (Promusicae) v Telefonica de Espana SAU ("Telefonica")* (2008: paras 61, 64). Building on the discussion above of specific rights, there is a right to freedom of expression in the ECHR (article 10), the American Convention (article 13), the African Charter (article 9) and the Arab Charter (article 32); and the ECHR has a right to the protection of property (Protocol 1, article 1), which the European Court of Human Rights held, in *Anheuser-Busch Inc v Portugal* (2007), could encompass IP. The EU Charter provides in article 17(2) that "intellectual property shall be protected" (and see discussion in Geiger 2009). National constitutions also include human rights – for example, the Constitution of the United States has the well known First Amendment in respect of freedom of speech. Support for the growing importance of the internet in global society can also be identified from the recognition of access to the internet as a human right by courts in Costa Rica (Guadamuz 2010) and France (Jondet 2010). It should be borne in mind, however, that the rights are very rarely absolute, for example article 10 ECHR provides that states can limit the right to freedom of expression as "prescribed by law and [. . .] necessary in a democratic society . . . for the protection of health or morals".

A common theme across these instruments is that they impose responsibilities on states, as can be seen in the preambles of the ICCPR and ICESCR. This is consistent with the place of human rights in national constitutions, or their birth in the aftermath of the Second World War. Obligations of a state may appear of little relevance, however, if one is concerned at the power of the IP owner in the example discussed above. The implications of this are discussed below from the perspective of some court actions, and then later regarding attempts to impose human rights obligations on companies. For now, it is interesting to consider that in response to what was termed a "Twitter Revolution" (*The Economist* 2011), the government of Egypt asked that internet service providers (including large international companies such as Vodafone) remove internet access from Egypt. This was done (Cowie 2011). So in the end, does power really still remain with governments?

The discussion so far has noted that human rights which could be relevant to a discussion of essential technologies exist in a spread of national, regional and international instruments. But what are the consequences of this? How does the right interact with other human rights, which, as has been seen, may conflict? And what is their impact on disputes between private entities?

The contribution of human rights

IP and privacy cases in England and the EU provide useful examples. In England in *Ashdown v Telegraph* (2001), the Court of Appeal considered the publication of extracts from the diary of a politician and a claim for copyright infringement. Given the provisions of sections 3 and 6 of the Human Rights Act 1998, the court must avoid making decisions which are inconsistent with human rights. The Court of Appeal reviewed the relationship between freedom of expression, and its limits (including the right to property), and copyright and its limits, as set out in the legislation (*Ashdown v Telegraph* (2001: paras 13, 15, 24, 25, 29–34)). The Court of Appeal considered that there could be a conflict between copyright and freedom of expression. Given arguments, however, that copyright can aid expression, the court considered that this would be the case only rarely, when there was no other source of the information required; but that when there is a conflict, the relevant legislation meant that freedom of expression should prevail (*Ashdown v Telegraph* (2001: paras 43, 45)), see also Sims 2006, Birnhack 2003, and in the United States *Rosemount Enterprise v Random House* (1966), *Time Inc v Geis* (1968), discussion in Reis 2005 (pp. 272, 284 et seq, 304–5, 310). The rights to property – regarding jeans and a trade mark – and expression also formed part of the decision in England of the High Court in *Levi v Tesco* (2002). The dispute involved the parallel importing of jeans by a supermarket. The court took into account the spread of rights and the limits on them, and found that regard to human rights did not lead to a decision which differed from that which would have been reached using only the established IP principles (*Levi v Tesco* (2002: paras 22, 40–3).

The wide spread of human rights, and the potential for conflict, means that introducing them in an IP dispute does not guarantee a different outcome. Human rights had a more pronounced impact in England on privacy, when courts used articles 8 and 10 ECHR, and the existing action for breach of confidence, to create an action for misuse of private information. The landmark case is the decision of the House of Lords in *Campbell v MGN* (2002). When the House of Lords considered the relationship between the two human rights, it considered that neither right should be accorded precedence; it was a question of balance in each case (*Campbell v MGN* (2002: paras 17–19, 55, 86, 103,107, 110, 115–118, 119–124, 141)). Baroness Hale noted the challenge of this (*Campbell v MGN* (2002: para. 140)) and that this must become more difficult when more than two human rights are involved. In *Telefonica*, the ECJ considered states' need to impose legislation requiring the disclosure of the identity of downloaders of material, to comply with enforcement legislation. It found that there was no obligation to do so, and if states did impose legislation it must be consistent with EU privacy related legislation and with fundamental rights, including the rights in the EU Charter regarding property, judicial protection and respect for private life (*Telefonica* (2008: paras 6–27, 61–8)). The ECJ in *Telefonica* was not required to actually deliver a proportionate response in that case.

So what does the above discussion suggest in relation to the identification of essential technologies? International human rights law, supported by regional and national instruments, provides some objective guidance as to what could be considered an essential objective: expression, information privacy, life, health – and also property and in some cases, possibly IP. These rights may conflict, but after balancing them, the appropriate outcome may be apparent in a case. Yet even if a goal is argued to be essential, this does not in itself mean that any technology which can deliver this is essential. More than one technology/set of technologies could be used to deliver a particular right – for example a different blogging platform could be used to express views (which might suggest that there is no right to use Facebook, even as a forum for online discussions and assembly). But what if, as was argued in some of the IP cases, there is no alternative means by which to achieve the objective? The presence or absence of substitutes is at the heart of competition law; so its contribution to the identification of essential technologies will now be considered.

The Competition Perspective

A place for competition?[3]

A key part of competition law is the definition of a market. This involves consideration of a relevant alternative or substitute. The EU, which has a well developed competition law, will be taken as an example. In contrast with human rights, competition law exists at national and regional levels, not globally. There were attempts early in the Doha Round to introduce competition law to the World Trade Organization (which since 1994 has included the Agreement on Trade Related Aspects of Intellectual Property Law 1994, Annex IC to WTO Agreement). The Decision of General Council 1 August 2004 (WT/L/579 para. g) makes clear that this was not achieved, partly due to fears of the imposition of a capitalist approach (see Marsden 2003, pp. 15–16, 39, 42–43, 77–78, 136, 159 et seq, 186 et seq, 223, 236 et seq and Majoras 2008). There are some synergies between the substantive competition laws which do exist; for example the prohibition on the misuse of market power which in the EU now forms part of article 102 Treaty on the Functioning of the European Union, is addressed in the United States by section 2 Sherman Act, South Africa by section 8 Competition Act, Canada by sections 32 and 79 Competition Act and Australia by section 46 Trade Practices Act (Cth). The BRIC nations are making efforts to develop their own competition laws through their own collaboration and there is global cooperation through the International Competition Network.

Market definition

A market might be defined very narrowly (for example, the first product which enables music to be downloaded lawfully) or more widely (all forms of listening to music). In the EU, there is the European Commission's, the competition regulator's, Notice on the definition of the relevant market for the purposes of Community competition law of the EU. Key issues are firstly, the existence of actual substitutes from the supply and demand perspective and also the potential for them to be developed within a reasonable time, with the innovative and dynamic nature of suppliers and purchasers an important consideration; and secondly, the geographic parameters within which the market operates in a homogeneous manner.

Applying this within the internet context, the geographic element may well be global as was recognised by the Court of First Instance, as it was then, in *Microsoft Corp v Commission of the European Communities* (2007: para. 29). Yet if access to the internet from a particular locality, or access to educational materials in a particular language is considered, the geographic market may be narrower. The ability and willingness of countries to (attempt to) impose restrictions on access to online materials (for example the Great Fire Wall of China, see Branigan 2011) should also be borne in mind.

Regarding substitutability, relevant questions might be: is there another blog technology? How quickly could one be developed building on an established website technology? Are consumers able or willing to make an open choice as to the technology they use? How relevant is the old fashioned face to face conversation or phone call – or indeed Skype? Or is an entirely new form of communicating likely to be developed (for discussion on innovation, see Schumpeter 1943, p. 84, Geroski 2005, p. 427 and Glader 2006, pp. 135–37).

Further, are there other options to be pursued if one provider increased its price? Does regulation impose restrictions on options emerging – for example if there is a requirement that all online educational providers be licensed, a new one could not emerge immediately? Is there a standard – this can arise through formal agreement that a particular technology or technologies are to be used (eg the BluRay standard) or through the success of a particular product (eg *Microsoft*). A standard can lead to more products being interoperable – able to work together (see Mylly 2010) with more choice and less confusion for consumers. Yet this means that a technology which differs from or will not work with that other technology is unlikely to succeed, irrespective of its benefits.

A related point is that users may wish to use a technology which their peers use (like Facebook). Network effects exist where one technology is used widely and by a linked group, such that a better and cheaper technology which is incompatible cannot succeed. When there is a network effect, it is difficult to argue that there are potential substitutes (see Chapter 6 by Economides and Chapter 7 by Cave). Or does the ongoing success of new products, such as the eReader and texting, suggest that internet consumers are open to change (see discussion generally in Lemley and McGowan 1998)?

From the supply perspective, the question is how readily could one supplier provide the same technology/technologies? In more traditional industries, a key question might be how readily could the factory be adapted, or its products put to another use? Here, could the actual individuals and factories involved in making an eReader also make a mobile phone? Can software and hardware designers adapt their skills? And even if they could, is the technology in question the subject of IP, or is it secret, such that these skills cannot be used without the consent of another?

Within a competition analysis, the answers to these questions vary with the facts. Market definition is not a neutral, objective assessment – it is intertwined with reality, as is discussed in the European Commission's Notice (para. 12).

The Contribution of a Combined Approach

So far, human rights and competition have been seen, separately, to provide useful guidance to identify what might be an essential technology or technologies. Human rights can identify what might be an essential objective. Competition law can provide a means of identifying the technologies, in themselves or in combination with others, which can be used to deliver that essential goal. If there is only one technology or combination which meets that need, this would appear to be that essential technology.

What is achieved by this categorisation? One might argue essential objectives should be achieved, with greater access to an end product, or to technologies which would enable one new technology to work most effectively and deliver a better end product. This could be access both by consumers (for example a free download of an educational package), and also by businesses which wish to also sell the technology or product (for example by preparing and selling the required voting software/part of it). This is not problematic if the information about this technology is widely available and can be used by all. Yet the market definition discussion above suggests that if a technology has been assessed as being essential, it is quite possible that it will be protected by IP or is secret. What if the IP owner does not wish to share it – either at all, or only on payment of a reasonable fee? And what if a person cannot afford to pay? The possible wider contribution of human rights and competition to addressing this and delivering access to essential technologies will now be considered.

DELIVERING ACCESS

Using Competition Law to Create a Solution

When a national or regional competition law can be applied to a situation, it may provide a means for requiring that licences are granted of IP, or that information is shared even if it is a trade secret. The legal basis lies in the misuse of market power type legislation, introduced above. The EU is at the forefront of requiring licensing and information sharing, and EU case law and legislation will again be the example.

In the EU, the key provision is found in what is now article 102 TFEU: one should not abuse a dominant position.[4]

Dominance and Essential Technologies

For there to be a finding of abuse, once one has defined the market then one must assess whether or not a provider of a technology is in a dominant position. If the market definition tools led to the conclusion that one product, service or technology itself is essential, then there will be no alternative. There will be no one else in the market. Dominance can, therefore, be identified immediately. If there are other technologies in the market then none of the technologies can be deemed essential. It is still possible for the controllers of the technologies to be in a dominant position if they can act to an appreciable extent independently of others (see decision of ECJ in *United Brands Co v Commission of the European Communities* (1978: para. 65) – but dominant is not the same as essential.

Although this chapter will not develop arguments to limit the power of those who are merely dominant, it will draw on established principles relating to abuse of a dominant position. Dominance carries a burden and the controller of a technology will be subject to additional restrictions in respect of their dealings with it.

Abuse and Essential Technologies[5]

Through what has been termed the essential facilities doctrine (although this can be a controversial term), regulators have required that incumbent proprietors of traditional physical infrastructure (such as docks and railways, as discussed in the decisions of the European Commission in *B&I Line Plc v Sealink Harbours Ltd (IV/34.174)* (1992) and the Supreme Court of the United States in *USA v Terminal Railroad* (1912)) must provide access to competitors, in return for a payment, if they would otherwise be unable to compete with the operator of the facility and if the facility is of particular economic importance. The US Supreme Court considered, however, in *Verizon v Trinko* (2004) that the essential facilities doctrine does not exist (see Fox 2005) and the ECJ has never used the term in relation to IP and information (although there has been a cogent exposition of it in *Oscar Bronner GMbH v Mediaprint* (1998: AGO paras 33–53) by Advocate General Jacobs, in a case involving newspaper delivery services). Nonetheless, the doctrine has been referred to in scholarly discussion of the IP, information and abuse cases (eg Andreangeli 2009).

A line of European cases, from an undertaking provided by IBM to the European Commission in 1984 to the decision of the Court of First Instance in *Microsoft* in 2007, make it clear that in exceptional circumstances, dominant undertakings can be ordered to behave in a manner which seems inconsistent with their interests: supply goods, license IP, disclose confidential information. The first landmark case was of the ECJ in *Volvo v Veng* (1988) involving design rights and car spare parts, where the court held that it could, in principle, be abuse of a dominant position to refuse to license IP – in exceptional circumstances, with no exhaustive guidance as to what these might be (*Volvo v Veng* (1988: para. 9)). In this case and those that followed, courts sought to reconcile key principles for the European Union of unrestricted competition between member states, and of respect for the ownership of property, which includes IP (article 295 EC Treaty, now article 345 TFEU which had been discussed by the ECJ in *Volvo v Veng* (1988: paras 8 and 11) and *Etablissements Consten Sarl v Commission of the European Economic Community* (1966: para. 10)). As will be seen, the question remains, what are "exceptional circumstances"? And of present interest, should human rights be included, not least because of the importance of human rights in EU decision making, particularly since the Lisbon Treaty?

In the following ECJ cases, however, with *Magill* (1995) and *IMS v NDC* (2004) being of key importance, courts and regulators took a different stance when seeking to establish what exceptional circumstances might mean in a particular situation. It was established that there would be an abuse if there is a refusal to license material which is the subject of IP, which would be used to meet consumer demand, in a (possibly hypothetical) other market which would not otherwise be fulfilled; if there is a likelihood of elimination of competition if there was no licence; and if there is no objective justification for the refusal (see discussion in Ridyard 2004 and Meinburg 2006). The most important element of the test for present purposes is that the material sought was indispensable for the access seeker to be able to develop a new product.

This requirement makes sense in the light of the facts of, say, *Magill* (use of TV listings to make a new composite product). It is also consistent with the view of IP and competition as aiming to encourage innovation, by rewarding past and encouraging future innovation, by enabling the innovation which would not otherwise occur (see discussion in Scherer 2001, Mackaay 1990 and Merges 1994). In the position discussed here in relation to essential technologies, however, access will be sought by others to technology/technologies for use for their existing purpose. So it may be proposed not to develop a different communications tool, eReader or voting software but to make the existing one more cheaply, in areas where the IP owner has chosen not to operate or license early in the term of the patent;[6] or to make an existing product, which would not otherwise change, compatible with a technology so it could be of interest to more customers.

IMS, which involved IP protected structures of presenting data sets for use in the pharmaceutical industry, does leave some scope for future expansion of the test. It says that it is "sufficient" for the test to be met; sufficient, but not mandatory. Further, just before the decision of the ECJ in *IMS*, the European Commission took a quite different approach to the issue, in its *Commission Microsoft* (2004) decision. It referred to the existing tests and applied them to an extent (*Commission Microsoft* (2004: paras 573 et seq, 585–691, 694–708, 781–783, 1064)) but considered that it was not required to follow the rigid test which has been discussed; rather, the Commission looked at the entirety of the circumstances of the case (*Commission Microsoft* (2004: para. 558)). The European Commission made some interesting points regarding the need for an innovation balancing act – rewarding the investment, without the right to control for the full IP duration (*Commission Microsoft* (2004: paras 711–741)) and see Vezzoso 2006); but the most pertinent point is the suggestion that a new product may not be required.

The ongoing importance of this decision is unclear. When the Court of First Instance reviewed this decision in 2007 in the case discussed above, it did not consider whether or not the Commission's approach was correct, although it considered that no new approach had been taken to innovation balancing (*Microsoft* (2007: paras 690–691, 695, 697–698)); rather, in line with the court's role, it considered whether or not the *IMS* test which now existed could be met on the facts of *Microsoft*. The court found that it could (*Microsoft* (2007: paras 103–110, 118–153, 207–289, 337–422, 560–620, 621–703)) and made two extensions to the test which may also be of importance here: firstly, there need not be a new product, provided there was a technical development (a term included in article 102 as an example of abuse) (*Microsoft* (2007: para. 647)); and secondly there need only be a risk of elimination of viable competition, if the information is not obtained (*Microsoft* (2007: paras 421, 620)).

This test may be met more readily in the situations discussed here, for example if a product is being developed to make it compatible with others; but not necessarily always, if it is use of the existing technology which is proposed, just more cheaply and in a new area (see Howarth and McMahon 2008 and Anderman 2008). From the perspective of encouraging innovation, this requirement might be welcomed. From the perspective of delivering the essential human rights objective (even bearing in mind that in establishing this, regard will have been had to rights to property, IP and reward of the innovator) it may not be. In seeking a different approach, specific reference to human rights is highly unlikely in itself to give rise to a change, given that fundamental rights have been seen to have a role in decision making of the EU and its predecessors since well before the Lisbon Treaty. Support for a wider approach to abuse, consistent with that suggested in *Volvo* and in the *Commission Microsoft* decision, can come, however, from cases considering other aspects of IP and abuse.

Abuse and refusal to license and its corollary, raising of the infringement action, were discussed in IP infringement actions in the EU and in England. It has now been accepted, with the landmark case being the decision of the English Court of Appeal in *Intel v Via* (2002), that it can be a defence to an IP infringement action to argue that there was an abuse of a dominant position – but there must be a nexus between the abuse and the subject matter of the action. The court was reluctant to be clearer as to the test to be met for abuse. The *IMS* type restriction might not seem applicable, therefore, but there have not been any cases where evidence has been heard and a final decision made. A much narrower approach was taken by the Court of First Instance in *Promedia* (*ITT Promedia* 1998), determining when raising a court action could be abuse of a dominant position. The court required that there must, once again, be exceptional circumstances (and it referred to fundamental rights), more specifically that asserting the rights would, objectively, be manifestly unfounded, serve to harass the opposing party and be part of a plan to eliminate competition (*ITT Promedia* (1998: paras 30, 55, 56)). This was commented on favourably by the English court in *SanDisk v Philips* (2007), which involved steps taken prior to raising an action regarding MP3 patents.

Findings of abuse have also been made in cases involving regulatory behaviour and IP, where the *IMS* test is not suited. In 2005 the European Commission found that AstraZeneca had abused a dominant position by withdrawing marketing authorisations for a pharmaceutical product, so that others could not get regulatory clearance for a generic product, and also by providing misleading information to regulatory authorities regarding applications for supplementary protection certificates (*AstraZeneca Commission* (2005: paras 325–328, 741–749 and 602–862) and see Gunther and Breuvart 2005). The decision was upheld by the General Court in July 2010 (see *AstraZeneca AB v European Commission*; Galloway 2010). Further, an investigation was launched by the European Commission in 2007 into Boehringer, in respect of alleged misuse of the patent application system through an application argued to re-use information (also Straus 2010 and see European Commission Press Release 2011).

There have been investigations involving the setting of more formal standards – the classic proposition being that an IP owner has taken part in the setting of a standard but the IP owner did not disclose that to meet the standard, others would need to use technology over which they held rights (Lemley 2002 and Zhang 2010).[7] The failure to disclose the IP is argued to be an abuse of a dominant position. In 2007, the European Commission launched a competition investigation (case number COMP /38.636) into Rambus regarding the Dynamic Random Access Memory Chips standards and the alleged making of excessive royalty demands in respect of the patents (Rambus 2007). In 2009 Rambus agreed to provide undertakings that it would alter its behaviour in relation to licensing (Rambus 2009). It should be noted, however, that in parallel enquiries in the US, the US Court of Appeals for the District of Columbia Circuit in *Rambus v FTC* (2008) overturned a finding which the Federal Trade Commission had made in *Rambus FTC* (2007).

The potential for competition to interfere with the rights of the patent owner was also seen when a patent owner raised an infringement action in Germany in *Orange Book*. Technology which was the subject of a patent and also formed part of a formal standard, was used without a licence having been obtained. It was argued that an injunction should not be granted, on the basis that the failure to license was in breach of competition law. The German Supreme Court found that if the infringer had not made a binding offer to take a licence on a fair and non discriminatory basis (a term which will be discussed again later), then an injunction could be granted; if there was such an offer, there could be no injunction (see Ullrich 2010).

This brief discussion of findings of abuse makes it clear that there are different bases on which a court or regulator might find that there has been abuse when, in the broadest sense, restrictions are imposed on the access of others to technology. The more expansive approaches by English and German courts regarding competition defences, the *Astra* decision and *Boehringer* investigation suggest that the absence of a new product development plan by those seeking access may not be a problem; *Volvo* and *Microsoft* can be argued to support this.[8]

Even if this is so, the conclusion builds on a selection of cases from a small number of jurisdictions. Where would any complaint be made? Would these cases be relevant? Competition, which has been seen to have more interventionist capacity, will be considered first.

The Place of Action

Competition
From the competition perspective, if there is a law and conduct with which it would be concerned (eg, in the EU, conduct with impact on trade

between member states and a possible abuse)[9] a regulator may choose to investigate. It may then order that access is provided to others who seek information and technology, as was seen in *Microsoft*. The financial (fair, reasonable and non-discriminatory licence?) and practical (who should manage the process and protect information?) terms on which this is to be done is uncertain (*Microsoft* (2007: paras 1230–1279)). An enquiry involving formal standards may lead to undertakings which may include compulsory licensing or disclosure, as was seen in the European Union *Rambus* decision. *Microsoft* and *Rambus* suggest that licensing would be required on a fair, reasonable and non discriminatory licence basis. It remains unclear what this might mean, although the US Department of Justice did make some attempt to clarify this when it did not oppose the VITA standards (United States Department of Justice 2006). A regulator may also impose a fine, as was seen in the European Union in *Microsoft* (Microsoft and Europa 2008); but this will not deliver access to those requesting it or to others.

And it should be borne in mind that the regulator may not investigate. A European Commission enquiry into article 82, as it was then, led to discussion papers which suggested a wide approach to abuse (European Commission DG Competition Discussion Paper 2005, paras 227–240). In December 2008, Guidelines on the Commission's enforcement priorities in applying article 82 of the EC Treaty to abusive exclusionary conduct by dominant undertakings were issued, which placed a key focus on the *IMS* and *Magill* tests (European Commission Guidance on the Commission's enforcement priorities 2008, para. 78). Thus although the European Commission has been active in the information and communications field since the *Microsoft* case discussed here (Duns and Conboye 2010, Dolmans et al 2010 and also investigation into Google, see European Commission Google Press Release 2010) and its investigation in 2008 and 2009 into the pharmaceutical industry makes clear the concern with which competition regulators can view IP (see Pharmaceutical Inquiry 2008 and Batchelor 2010), intervention is not assured.

Competition could also be relevant when information can be obtained (for example, through patent specifications), just not the permission to use it. One could simply proceed and risk being sued for infringement and, as discussed above, try to use competition as part of the defence. Or one could be proactive like Nokia, and seek a declaration that a patent is not essential within a standard, and as such the standard (for third generation mobile telecommunications in Europe) can be met without infringement. The English courts were prepared to hear this case, and looked at the technology to determine if the patent is essential, rather than accepting the position of the standards body (*Nokia v Interdigital* (2007)).

Finally, regulatory investigation or court cases are unlikely to lead to a quick solution to that particular dispute, and may not have any impact on other decisions of IP owners or information controllers. The differences in decisions between jurisdictions, as seen in the Rambus experience, and the complexities involved in market analysis and assessment of abuse, also support this.

In summary, competition provides legal principles which can require the controller of a technology to provide it to others. But the legal principles, possible outcomes and the circumstances in which this can be used, are not clear. There are grounds, notably in the EU, for competition law to require that access be provided to what this chapter would term an essential technology; but it is more likely that this would be done if a new product or technology is developed, which will not always be the case. Competition has also not provided solutions when governments set a particular standard, or when those seeking access could not afford to pay a fair, reasonable and non discriminatory licence fee. There is also highly likely to be geographical variety regarding investigations made and decisions taken.

The discussion of human rights earlier revealed a broader spread of human rights instruments. Can this provide a more effective means of providing access – nationally, regionally and globally?

Human rights
Briefly, it cannot. The enforcement aspect of human rights law is incomplete, and varies throughout the world. Depending on national legislation, it may be possible to raise a direct action against a state for breach of human rights. One possibility could be failure to enable freedom of expression by providing reliable access to the internet (frequently not available in developing areas). The writer is not yet aware of any such action being raised, but it will be interesting to see what might develop in the light of the developments discussed in Costa Rica and France. But in the UK, a person could not use human rights to complain directly to a court in the UK regarding the level of provision of internet access or indeed its removal following any order made under the Digital Economy Act 2010 (which was passed after an application for judicial review in respect of the legislation failed, see *R (ex parte BT and TalkTalk) v Secretary of State for Business, Innovation and Skills* (2011) and see Chapter 16 by Matwyshyn).

As seen, it is possible for human rights in some countries to have an impact beyond states, and form part of the substantive element of disputes between private entities. Just as was seen in relation to competition (eg German *Orange Book* decision), it is also possible for human rights to form part of the court's consideration of remedies in IP infringement actions. In England in *Ashdown v Telegraph*, the Court of Appeal indicated that it would not be prepared to grant an injunction in the rare cases when freedom of expression should prevail over copyright, and would only award damages (*Ashdown v Telegraph* (2001: para. 46)); and the court of appeal indicated that in some cases, no payment would be appropriate (*Ashdown v Telegraph* (2001: para. 47)). Likewise, in the US regarding a parody of "Gone with the Wind" the Eleventh Circuit appeal court declined (again, unusually) to grant an injunction, noting that it should be "cognizant" of the First Amendment (*Suntrust v Houghton Miffin* (2001: 1265–1276) and see Netanel 2005 and Firth 2008).

Avenues might also exist at regional level. The ECtHR has heard several IP related actions (see Helfer 2008). For example, those concerned in the UK could, once they have exhausted local remedies in terms of articles 1 and 34 ECHR (and see the decision of the European Court of Human Rights in *Earl Spencer v UK* (1998)), make a complaint to the European Court of Human Rights (see Leach 2011, Chapter 2). This could argue that their rights to freedom of expression or to vote had been breached if their internet access is removed under the Digital Economy Act. Once again, this would be an innovative argument – it will be interesting to observe how this issue develops over time. It is also important to note that the ECtHR has been reluctant to impose positive obligations on countries – eg, return access, as would be sought here; decisions have rather been a mix of awarding damages and requiring that legislation be changed (Leach 2005 and Leach 2011, Chapter 3).

International level has seen more discussion of IP, technology and human rights. There have been resolutions of the UN Sub-Commission for the Promotion and Protection of Human Rights (2000/7 and 2001/21) regarding the impact of states' implementation of IP treaties on human rights. As noted above, there has also been a General Comment regarding the reward of the author (which it was considered did not constitute a right to IP), other human rights, their interrelationship and their contribution to education, development and health (General Comment No. 17 paras 1, 3, 4, 7, 10, 22–24, 35). There has not, however, been any consideration of access to technology by the international human rights monitoring and assessment bodies. It is understood that a complaint was made to the ICCPR Human Rights Committee regarding freedom of expression, following the High Court of Australia's decision in *Dow Jones and Company Inc. v Gutnick* (2002). The Australian court accepted jurisdiction and found there to have been defamation, by an article published in the internet version of a US newspaper. No details of the complaint and its status are available

(Ramasastry 2003). And even if a decision is made regarding technology by an international body, it would merely encourage change of conduct by and within a state, by agreement through a monitoring process (see discussion in Alfredsson 2009).

In summary, save in rare national cases, the human rights legislative framework does not provide a means of delivering access to technologies which has been determined, by competition law, to be the only means of meeting objectives which human rights law suggests are essential. It has also been seen that competition law could assist in delivering access to these technologies only in exceptional circumstances, and the weight of authority at present suggests the need for this to bring about a new development, rather than wider access to an existing solution. Once a technology has been identified as essential, therefore, human rights and competition can rarely be used to require the controller to provide wider access. But what of a less combative approach?

A NEW APPROACH

Using Human Rights

The UN monitoring process discussed above may help. Further, the World Summit on the Information Society ("WSIS") was established by the International Telecommunications Union, a United Nations body. It met in Geneva in 2003 and Tunis in 2005. The establishment of the WSIS attracted a range of views – was it a worthy attempt to address obstacles to the valuable contribution which information could make to society; or was it an example of regime shifting, moving information sideways into a new forum with no power to bring about real change (see Helfer 2004)? There was a Human Rights Caucus at the WSIS (see Jørgensen 2006, Introduction) and the outputs of Geneva seemed promising, eg recognising that "education, knowledge, information and communication are at the core of human progress, endeavour and well-being. Further, it was noted in Article 8 of the Declaration of Principles that Information and Communication Technologies (ICTs) have an immense impact on virtually all aspects of our lives" and targets were set in article 6 of the Plan of Action regarding connection to the internet. The key focus at Tunis, however, was the control of domain names. Yet Tunis did establish the Internet Governance Forum. This was established to meet annually for five years, and met in Baku in November 2012 (see Chapter 2 by Froomkin).

At the IGF meetings, there has been a growing focus on the involvement

390 Research handbook on governance of the internet

of a range of stakeholders, with non-governmental organisations, including human rights activists, attending alongside government representatives, large companies and UN staff. Although the IGF has no power, it enables initial discussions to take place, for example through dynamic coalitions including the Internet Rights and Principles Dynamic Coalition, which is working on the Internet Rights and Principles Charter discussed above (see also Brown 2009b). There has been growing discussion of human rights at the IGF, including of present interest in relation to government policy and open standards, which would be relevant to the voting example discussed above. Open standards is a broad term (see Fitzgerald and Pappalardo 2009) but will encompass situations when the standard focuses on the technical capacity to be met, rather than setting out a specific product (as discussed in the work of the IGF Open Standards dynamic coalition), when technology is made available royalty free, as with the W3C standards or (possibly) when it will be licensed to all who wish to use it at a reasonable and non-discriminatory licence fee, as proposed in the European Interoperability Framework (European Commission 2010, paras 2.10, 5.2.1).

Outside the IGF, there have been attempts to impose more human rights obligations on companies. It is states which are parties and have the responsibilities under human rights instruments (see also UN General Assembly 2010 "Human Rights Defenders"); yet if one is concerned at the power of Facebook (see Edwards 2009) over sensitive private information, or of an online health provider to charge high prices, then the rights to life, health and or against interference with privacy might not seem relevant. There have been steps taken to address this.

The key developments have been the United Nations Norms on the Responsibilities of Transnational Corporations and Other Business Enterprises with Regard to Human Rights of 2003 and the report of John Ruggie, United Nations Special Representative, of 2007 on "Business and Human Rights: mapping international standards of responsibility and accountability for corporate acts" (Ruggie 2007). This report concluded that although there was no legal basis for companies to have obligations under human rights instruments, there was a significant body of activity, for example through industry led codes, investor pressure and the initiatives of large companies, which were making regard for human rights a more central part of corporate activity (Ruggie 2007, paras 53, 80, 85, see also the resulting United Nations 2011 Global Guiding Principles). There have also been more focussed steps, for example in the EU the Article 29 Data Protection Working Party has been working with large companies, including Google, and this has led to some changes in practice (Schaar 2007).

A Human Rights Approach?

One might argue that relying on UN discussions, and hoping that companies will choose to follow unenforceable codes or respond to requests requiring a positive approach to society, is not reasonable. Yet enquiries by the US competition regulators, the Department of Justice and the Federal Trade Commission "Antitrust Enforcement and Intellectual Property Rights: Promoting Innovation and Competition", suggest that industries operate in different ways, and in the internet space there is much more openness, and less desire to control than in, say, pharmaceuticals and health (Department of Justice and Federal Trade Commission 2007, sections headed "IP and innovation", "Competition and innovation", "Business perspectives on patents: Software and the internet").

There are examples of new approaches to internet governance, technology and innovation. For example, it has been argued, building on the right to moral and material interests and the suggestion that IP may be a human right, that owners of IP may behave in a more equitable manner in terms of their use and sharing of technology (see Chapman 2001). There have also been challenges within the IP framework to the power of IP and attitudes of IP owners, for example with the establishment of the Development Agenda of the World Intellectual Property Organization and steps taken in relation to TRIPS and public health within the World Trade Organization.

In addition, corporate social responsibility has been seen to be entrenched in at least part of the corporate world (McBarnet et al 2007). Some IP owners are choosing to make their work available on a reciprocal or free licensing scheme – in addition to open standards discussed, consider the Eco-Patent Commons project and Creative Commons in relation to copyright software. There are also new forms of digitising and providing access to cultural know how, such as through the UK charity SCRAN. Further, although some companies seek IP, they are also willing to invest in different forms of funding and encouraging innovation, for example through the PATH Malaria Vaccine Project. Finally, although the vision of John Perry Barlow may have altered, it has not disappeared (see Chapter 1 by Ziewitz and Brown). There are new forms of behaviour and challenging incumbent power on the internet, as can be seen in virtual worlds in the Guilds of World of Warcraft (and see Jankowich 2006) and the Eve Council of Stellar Management and in the changes to the Facebook privacy policy in response to consumer revolt (see Chapter 13 by Edwards).

CONCLUSION – LOOKING BEYOND LAW

There are strong arguments for the existence of human rights. Human rights can identify essential objectives. Competition law also exists, although it is less widespread. Through market definition principles, competition law can enable a technology/set of technologies to be identified as the only means of delivering the essential objectives. This may occur rarely – but when it does, it is likely to be a problem as the uniqueness of the technology is highly likely to be supported by IP or regulation. Competition may provide a means of delivering access to these technologies, but will likely require the existence of a law, a payment, willingness to risk a court action or an interested regulator. Human rights does not provide a strong avenue for delivery of its goals.

So human rights and competition laws, where they exist, will take one only so far in requiring the delivery of greater access to technologies which are important to our developing internet society. States are restricted regarding the novelty of the approaches they can take to delivery of access, given that TRIPS includes enforcement powers (and see Pauwelyn 2010). In contrast, companies have been seen to be taking some innovative steps. This can be argued to be driven by external perspectives – eg Facebook and investor pressure.

But should those seeking change to forms of information and technology control prevail always? Given the arguments which can be made in favour of control of and payment for information and IP as part of a framework of encouraging and rewarding innovation, it should not. Rather, governments, IP owners and information controllers should have regard to some objective criteria when determining whether or not they should create essential technologies and accede to requests for access to them and on what terms. Coming full circle, there is a role here for human rights and competition. They cannot, or at least not always, require that access be provided, no matter how important the technology or goal might seem; but they provide a structure which can be used by states, companies and individuals as they seek to develop the future of internet governance.

NOTES

1. For more detailed discussion of these themes, see Brown (2012). See also climate change project, http://www.law.ed.ac.uk/essentialtechnologies/. All website addresses accurate as at 25 May 2011.
2. Note the author is a member of the Internet Rights and Principles Dynamic Coalition.
3. See also Brown (2009a).
4. Full relevant text "Any abuse by one or more undertaking of a dominant position within

the internal market or a substantial part of it shall be prohibited as incompatible with the internet market in so far as it may affect trade between member states . . .". Note this can apply to agreements (see decision of the ECJ in *Compagnie Maritime Belge Transports SA v Commission of the European Communities* (2000) even if other parts of competition law which deal with agreements (see following) would permit it. See article 101 TFEU, Commission Notice Guidelines on the application of article 81 of the EC Treaty to technology transfer agreements OJ C 101, 27 April 2004; and also Guidelines on the application of article 101 of the Treaty on the Functioning of the European Union to horizontal cooperation agreements OJ C 11, 14 January 2011. See also consultation webpage, http://ec.europa.eu/competition/consultations/2010_horizontals/index.html. Regarding standards and agreements, see Koenig and Spiekermann (2010).

5. For deeper discussions on abuse, see Spulber (2008).
6. Compulsory licensing regimes, eg section 48A UK Patents Act 1977, require a three year period of demand not met by supply – more urgent access might be sought.
7. Regarding work of International Telecommunications Union, see http://www.itu.int/en/ITU-T/ipr/Pages/default.aspx. The author is a member of the Intellectual Property Rights Ad Hoc Working Group of the ITU.
8. This chapter will not pursue the complex and evolving question of private competition action – see eg Bernard (2010).
9. This test is readily met, see Commission Guidelines on the effect on trade concept contained in articles 81 and 82 of the Treaty [2004] OJ C101/81.

BIBLIOGRAPHY

Alfredsson, G. et al (2009), *International Human Rights Monitoring Mechanisms: Essays in Honour of Jakob Th. Moller*, Netherlands: Martinus Nijhoff.

Anderman, S. (2008), 'Microsoft v Commission and the interoperability issue', *European Intellectual Property Review*, **30(10)**, 395–99.

Andreangeli, A. (2009), 'Interoperability as an "essential facility" in the Microsoft case – encouraging competition or stifling innovation?', *European Law Review*, **34(4)**, 584–611.

Batchelor, B. (2010), 'EC tones down its final report into the pharma sector, but ramps up enforcement activity', *European Competition Law Review*, **31(1)**, 16–20.

Bernard, K.S. (2010), 'Private antitrust litigation in the European Union – why does the EC want to embrace what the US FTC is trying to avoid?', *Global Competition Law Review*, **3(2)**, 69–74.

Birnhack, M.D. (2003), 'Acknowledging the conflict between copyright and freedom of expression under the Hunan Rights Act', *Entertainment Law Reveiw*, **14(2)**, 24–34.

Branigan, T. (2011), 'China's Great Firewall not secure enough, says creator', http://www.guardian.co.uk/world/2011/feb/18/china-great-firewall-not-secure-internet.

Brown, A.E.L. (2009a), 'Intellectual Property, Competition and the Internet' in L. Edwards, and C. Waelde (eds), *Law and the Internet*, London: Hart, p. 417.

Brown, A.E.L. (2009b), 'Towards access: the interface between intellectual property, competition and human rights', http://www.intgovforum.org/cms/index.php/component/chrono contact/?chronoformname=Workshopsreports2009View&curr=1&wr=26.

Brown, A.E.L. (2012), 'Intellectual property, human rights and competition: Access to essential innovation and technology', Cheltenham, UK and Northampton, MA, USA: Edward Elgar. See also climate change project, http://www.law.ed.ac.uk/essentialtechnologies.

Chapman, A. (2001), 'Approaching intellectual property as a human right: obligations related to Article 15(1)(c)', *Copyright Bulletin*, **35(3)**, 4–36.

Cowie, J. (2011), 'Egypt leaves the internet', http://www.renesys.com/blog/2011/01/egypt-leaves-the-internet.shtml#latest.

Department of Justice and the Federal Trade Commission (2007), 'Antitrust Enforcement and Intellectual Property Rights: Promoting Innovation and Competition', http://www.

ftc.gov/reports/innovation/P040101PromotingInnovationandCompetitionrpt0704.pdf, details of hearings.

Dolmans, M. et al (2010), 'Microsoft's browser choice commitments and public interoperability undertaking', *European Competition Law Review*, **31(7)**, 268–75.

Dreyfuss, R.C. (2010), 'Patents and Human Rights: Where is the Paradox?', in W. Grosheide (ed.), *Intellectual Property and Human Rights: A Paradox*, Cheltenham, UK: Edward Elgar, p. 72.

Duns, G. and J. Conboye (2010), 'IT and abuse of dominance', *Computers and Law*, **21(5)**, 19.

Edwards, L. (2009), 'Facebook and privacy', http://blogscript.blogspot.com/2009/09/facebook-and-privacy.html.

Eide, A. (2007), 'Interdependence and Indivisibility of Human Rights', in Y. Donders and V. Volodin (eds), *Human Rights and Educational, Social and Cultural Developments and Challenges*, Aldershot, UK and Burlington, VT, USA: UNESCO Publishing and Ashgate, p. 11.

European Commission Notice (1997), 'Commission Notice on the definition of the relevant market for the purposes of Community competition law, OJ C 372/03 9 December 1997.

European Commission (2005), 'DG Competition Discussion Paper', http://ec.europa.eu/competition/antitrust/art82/discpaper2005.pdf.

European Commission (2010), 'European Interoperability Framework', http://ec.europa.eu/isa/strategy/doc/annex_ii_eif_en.pdf.

European Commission (2010), 'Google Press Release, European Commission – Antitrust: Commission probe allegations of antitrust violations by Google', http://europa.eu/rapid/pressReleasesAction.do?reference=IP/10/1624&format=HTML&aged=0&language=EN&guiLanguage=en.

European Commission Press Release (2011), IP/11/842, 'Antitrust: Commission welcomes improved market entry for lung disease treatments' (6 July 2011), available at http://europa.eu/rapid/pressReleasesAction.do?reference=IP/11/842&type=HTML.

European Commission (2008), 'Guidance on the Commission's enforcement priorities in applying article 82 of the EC Treaty to exclusionary conduct by dominant undertakings', http://eur-lex.europa.eu/LexUriServ/LexUriServ.do?uri=CELEX:52009XC0224(01):EN:NOT.

Firth A. (2008), '"Holding the Line" – The Relationship between the Public Interest and Remedies Granted or Refused, be it for Breach of Confidence or Copyright', in P.L.-C. Torremans, (ed.), *Intellectual Property and Human Rights, Enhanced Edition of Copyright and Human Rights*, The Hague, the Netherlands: Kluwer Law International, p. 421.

Fitzgerald, A. and K. Pappalardo (2009), 'Moving towards open standards', *SCRIPTed*, **6(2)**, 467, http://www.law.ed.ac.uk/ahrc/script-ed/vol6-2/fitzgerald.asp.

Fox, E.M. (2005), 'A tale of two jurisdictions and an orphan case. Antitrust, intellectual property and refusals to deal', *Fordham International Law Journal*, **28**, 952.

Galloway, J. (2010), 'AstraZeneca v European Commission', *European Competition Law Review*, **31(12)**, 536–38.

Geiger, C. (2009), 'Intellectual property shall be protected!? Article 17(2) of the Charter of Fundamental Rights of the European Union: a mysterious provision with an unclear scope', *European Intellectual Property Review*, **31(3)**, 113–17.

General Comment No. 17 (2005), Office of the High Commissioner for Human Rights, http://www.unhchr.ch/tbs/doc.nsf/(Symbol)/E.C.12.GC.17.En?OpenDocument.

Geroski, P.A. (2005), 'Intellectual property rights, competition policy and innovation: Is there a problem?', *SCRIPT-ed*, **2(4)**, 422, http://www.law.ed.ac.uk/ahrc/script-ed/vol2-4/geroski.asp.

Glader, M. (2006), *Innovation, Markets and Competition Analysis*, Cheltenham, UK: Edward Elgar.

Grosheide, W. (2010), *Intellectual Property and Human Rights A Paradox*, Cheltenham, UK: Edward Elgar.

Guadamuz, A. (2010), 'Costa Rican court declares the Internet as a fundamental right', http://www.technollama.co.uk/costa-rican-court-declares-the-internet-as-a-fundamental-right.

Gunther, J-P. and C. Breuvart, (2005), 'Misuse of patent and drug regulatory approval systems in the pharmaceutical industry: an analysis of US and EU converging approaches', *European Competition Law Review*, **26(12)**, 669–684.
Gurstein, M. (2011), 'Is Facebook a human right? Egypt and Tunisia transform social media', http://gurstein.wordpress.com/2011/02/04/is-facebook-a-human-right-egypt-and-tunisia-transform-social-media/.
Helfer, L. (2003), 'Human rights and intellectual property: Conflict or coexistence', *Minnesota Intellectual Property Review*, **5**, 47.
Helfer, L.R. (2004), 'Regime shifting: The TRIPS Agreements and new dynamics of international intellectual property lawmaking', *Yale Journal of International Law*, **29**, 1.
Helfer, L.R. (2008), 'The new innovation frontier? Intellectual property and the European Court of Human Rights', *Harvard Journal of International Law*, **49**, 1.
Howarth, D. and K. McMahon (2008), '"Windows has performed an illegal operation": The Court of First Instance's judgment in Microsoft v Commission', *European Competition Law Review*, **29(2)**, 117.
Jankowich, A. (2006), 'EULAw: The complex web of corporate rule-making in virtual worlds', *Tulane Journal of Intellectual* Property, **Spring 2009**, 1.
Jondet, N. (2010), 'The French Copyright Authority (Hadopi): The graduated response and the disconnection of illegal file-sharers', http://ssrn.com/abstract=1664509.
Jørgensen, R.F (2006), *Human Rights in the Global Information Society*, Cambridge: MIT Press.
Kestrell (2010), 'The ePub format and why blind readers should care about it', http://kestrell.dreamwidth.org/65658.html.
Koenig, C. and K. Spiekermann (2010), 'Competition law issues of standard setting by officially-entrusted versus private organisations', *European Competition Law Review*, **31(11)**, 449–58.
Leach, P. (2005), 'Beyond the bug river. A new dawn for redress before the European Court of Human Rights', *European Human Rights Law Review*, **2**, 148–64.
Leach, P. (2011), *Taking a Case to the European Court of Human Rights*, Blackstone's Human Rights Series, 3rd edn, Oxford, UK: Oxford University Press.
Lemley, M.A. (2002), 'Intellectual property rights and standard-setting organizations', *California Law Review*, **90**, 1889.
Lemley, M.A. and D. McGowan (1998), 'Legal implications of economic network effects', *California Law Review*, **86**, 479.
Mackaay, E. (1990), 'Economic Incentives in Markets for Information and Innovation', *Harvard Journal of Law and Public Policy*, **13(3)**, 867–900, reprinted in R. Towse and R. Holzhauer (eds) (2002), *The Economics of Intellectual Property: vol I Introduction and Copyright, The International Library of Critical Writing in Economics*, Cheltenham, UK: Edward Elgar, p.145.
Majoras, D. (2008), 'Convergence, Conflict and Comity: The Search for Coherence in the International Competition Community', and 'Panel Discussion' in B.E. Hawk, (ed.), *International Antitrust Law and Policy*, Competition Law Institute, Fordham University School of Law, New York: Juris Publishing Inc.
Marsden, P. (2003), *A Competition Policy for the WTO*, London: Cameron May.
Maslow, A.H. (1943), 'A theory of human motivation', *Psychological Review*, **50(4)**, 370–96.
McBarnet, D. et al (eds) (2007), *The New Corporate Accountability Corporate Social Responsibility and the Law*, Cambridge, UK: Cambridge University Press.
Meinberg, H. (2006), 'From Magill to IMS Health: the new product requirement and the diversity of intellectual property rights', *European Intellectual Property Review*, **28(7)**, 398–403.
Merges, R.P. (1994), 'Of Property Rules, Coase, and Intellectual Property', *Columbia Law Review*, **94**, 2655–73, reprinted in R. Towse and R. Holzhauer (eds) (2002), *The Economics of Intellectual Property: vol I Introduction and Copyright, The International Library of Critical Writing in Economics*, Cheltenham, UK: Edward Elgar, p.145.
Microsoft and Europa (2008), 'Microsoft Fine Press Release, Europa Press Release – Antitrust:

Commission imposes E899 million penalty on Microsoft for non-compliance with March 2004 Decision', http://europa.eu/rapid/pressReleasesAction.do?reference=IP/08/318.

Mylly, U-M. (2010), 'An evolutionary economics perspective on computer program interoperability and copyright', *International Review of Intellectual Property and Competition Law*, **41(3)**, 284–31.

Netanel, N.W. (2005), 'Copyright and "Market Power" in the Marketplace of Ideas', in F. Leveque and H. Shelanski (eds), *Antitrust, Patents and Copyright*, Cheltenham, UK: Edward Elgar.

Pauwelyn, J. (2010), 'The dog that barked but didn't bite: 15 years of intellectual property disputes at the WTO', *J International Dispute Settlement*, **2**, 389–429.

Pharmaceutical Inquiry (2008), 'Sector Inquiry', http://ec.europa.eu/competition/sectors/pharmaceuticals/inquiry/.

Ramasastry, A. (2003), 'Should the U.N. Intervene in a Transnational Internet Defamation Case?', http://writ.news.findlaw.com/ramasastry/20030507.html.

Rambus (2007), 'Press Release: Antitrust: Commission confirms sending statement of objections to Rambus', http://europa.eu/rapid/pressReleasesAction.do?reference=MEMO/07/330&form.

Rambus (2009), 'Press Release: Antitrust: Commission accepts commitments from Rambus lowering memory chip royalties – frequently asked questions', http://europa.eu/rapid/pressReleasesAction.do?reference=MEMO/09/544&format=HTML&aged=1&language=EN&guiLanguage=en.

Reis, L.A. (2005), 'The Rodney King Beating – beyond fair use: a broadcaster's right to air copyrighted videotape as part of a newscast', *J. Marshall Journal of Computer & Info. Law*, **13**, 269.

Ridyard, D. (2004), 'Compulsory access under EC competition law – a new doctrine of convenient facilities and the case for price regulation', *European Competition Law Review*, **25(11)**, 669–673.

Ruggie, J. (2007), 'Business and Human Rights: mapping international standards of responsibility and accountability for corporate acts', http://www.business-humanrights.org/Documents/RuggieHRC2007.

Saez, C. (2011), 'US Panel puts Google, Facebook Communications Platforms on Human Rights Frontline', http://www.ip-watch.org/weblog/?p=14717&utm_source=daily&utm_medium=email&utm_campaign=alerts.

Schaar, P. (2007), 'Letter from Chair of Working Party to P. Fleischer', http://ec.europa.eu/justice/policies/privacy/news/docs/pr_google_16_05_07_en.pdf.

Scherer, F.M. (2001), 'The Innovation Lottery', in R.C. Dreyfuss et al (eds), *Expanding the Boundaries of Intellectual Property. Innovation Policy for the Knowledge Society*, Oxford: Oxford University Press.

Schumpeter, J. (1943), *Capitalism, Socialism and Democracy*, London: George Allen & Unwin.

Sims, A. (2006), 'The public interest defence in copyright law: Myth or reality', *European Intellectual Property Review*, **28(6)**, 335–43.

Spulber, D.S. (2008), 'Unlocking technology: antitrust and innovation', *Journal of Competition Law and Economics*, **4(4)**, 915–66.

Straus, J. (2010), 'Patent application: Obstacle to innovation and abuse of dominant position under Article 102 TFEU?', *Journal of Competition Law and Practice*, **2010**, 1.

Symonides, J. (ed.) (2002), *Human Rights: Concepts and Standards*, Vermont, USA: Dartmouth Publishing Co Ltd and Paris, France: UNESCO, Ashgrove.

Switch11 (2009), 'Intel Reader – eReader for Blind, Visually impaired', http://ireaderreview.com/2009/11/10/intel-reader-ereader-blind-visually-impaired/.

The Department of Justice and the Federal Trade Commission (2007), 'Antitrust Enforcement and Intellectual Property Rights: Promoting Innovation and Competition', http://www.ftc.gov/reports/innovation/P040101PromotingInnovationandCompetition rpt0704.pdf.

The Economist (2011), 'Briefing – The upheaval in Egypt', *The Economist*, 5 February 2011.

Ullrich, H. (2010), 'Patents and standards – a comment on the German Federal Supreme Court decision Orange Book Standard', *International Review of Intellectual Property and Competition Law*, **41(3)**, 337–51.

UN General Assembly (2010), '69th sessions Note: Human Rights Defenders', http://www2. ohchr.org/english/issues/defenders/docs/A-65-223.pdf.

United Nations Human Rights Council Guiding Principles on Business and Human Rights (2011).

United States Department of Justice (2006), 'VITA Standards Press Release: Department will not oppose proposal by standard-setting organization on disclosure and licensing of patents', http://www.usdoj.gov/atr/public/press_releases/2006/219379.htm.

Vadi V. (2008), 'Sapere Aude! Access to knowledge as a human right and a key instrument of development', *International Journal of Communications Law & Policy*, 345–68.

Vezzoso, S. (2006), 'The incentives balance test in the EU Microsoft case: a pro-innovation "economics-based" approach?', *European Competition Law Review*, **27(7)**, 382–90.

Zhang, L. (2010), 'How IPR policies of telecommunication standard-setting organizations can effectively address the patent ambush problem', *International Review of Intellectual Property and Competition Law*, **41(4)**, 380–410.

Cases

Anheuser-Busch Inc v Portugal (73049/01) [2007] E.T.M.R. 24 (2007) 45 E.H.R.R. 36.

Ashdown v Telegraph Group Ltd [2001] EWCA Civ 1142 [2002] Ch. 149.

AstraZeneca Commission Decision of 15 June 2005 relating to a proceeding under Article 82 of the EC Treaty and Article 54 of the EEA Agreement (Case COMP/A. 37.507/F3), http://ec.europa.eu/comm/competition/antitrust/cases/decisions/37507/en.pdf.

AstraZeneca AB v European Commission (T-321/05) [2010] 5 CMLR 28.

B&I Line Plc v Sealink Harbours Ltd (IV/34.174) (1992) [1992] 5 C.M.L.R. 255.

Boehringer EC Commission Opening of Proceedings COMP 39.246, http://ec.europa.eu/competition/antitrust/cases/dec_docs/39246/39246_951_10.pdf.

Campbell v MGN Ltd [2002] UKHL 22.

Commission of the European Economic Communities v International Business Machines [1984] 3 C.M.L.R. 147.

Compagnie Maritime Belge Transports SA v Commission of the European Communities (C- 395/96 P) [2000] E.C.R. I-1365.

Dow Jones and Company, Inc v Gutnick [2002] HCA 56.

Earl Spencer v United Kingdom (28851/95) (1998) 25 E.H.R.R. CD105.

Etablissements Consten Sarl v Commission of the European Economic Community (56/64) [1966] E.C.R. 299.

IMS Health GmbH & Co OHG v NDC Health GmbH & Co KG (Case C-418/01) [2004] 4 C.M.L.R. 28.

Intel Corp v VIA Technologies Inc [2002] EWCA Civ 1905 [2003] F.S.R. 33.

Internationale Handelsgesellschaft v Einfuhr- und Vorratsstelle fur Getreide und Futtermittel (11/70) [1970] E.C.R. 1125.

ITT Promedia NV v Commission of the European Communities (T111/96) [1998] ECR II-2937[1998] 5 C.M.L.R. 491.

Levi Strauss & Co v Tesco Stores Ltd [2002] EWHC 1625 (Ch) [2002] 3 C.M.L.R. 11 [2003] R.P.C. 18.

Microsoft Case COMP/C-3/37, http://www.microsoft.com/presspass/download/legal/euro peancommission/03-24-06EUDecision.pdf.

Microsoft Corp v Commission of the European Communities (T-201/04) [2007] 5 C.M.L.R. 11.

Nokia Corp v Interdigital Technology Corp [2007] EWHC 3077 (Pat) and [2007] EWHC 445 (Pat) and [2006] EWCA Civ 1618; [2007] F.S.R. 23.

Oscar Bronner GMbH & Co. KG V. Mediaprint (7/97) [1998] ECR 1-7791.

Productores de Musica de Espana (Promusicae) v Telefonica de Espana SAU (C- 275/06) [2008] 2 C.M.L.R. 17.
R (ex p BT plc and TalkTalk Telecoms Group plc) v Secretary of State for Business, Innovation and Skills, decision of 20 April 2011 [2012] EWCA Civ 232.
Radio Telefis Eireann v Commission of the European Communities (C-241/91 P) [1995] E.C.R. I-743 ('Magill').
Rambus, Inc, In the Matter of, Docket No. 9302, http://www.ftc.gov/os/adjpro/d9302/060802 commissionopinion.pdf.
Rambus Inc v Federal Trade Commission 522 F.3d 456.
Rosemount Enterprise v Random House 366 F.2d. 303, 309–311.
SanDisk Corp v Koninklijke Philips Electronics NV [2007] EWHC 332 (Ch) [2007] F.S.R. 22.
Suntrust Bank v Houghton Mifflin Co 268 F.3d 1257 (11th Cir. 2001).
Time Inc v Geis 293 F. Supp 130, 145–6.
United Brands Co v Commission of the European Communities (27/76) [1978] E.C.R. 207.
USA v Terminal Railroad 224 US 383.
Verizon Communications, Inc v Law Offices of Curtis V. Trinko, LLP 540 U.S. 398.
Volvo AB v Erik Veng (UK) Ltd (238/87) [1988] E.C.R. 6211.

PART III

NETWORKED CONTROL

16. The new intermediation: contract, identity, and the future of internet governance
Andrea Matwyshyn

INTRODUCTION

From early in the existence of the internet, users' interactions have been mediated by third parties – intermediaries.[1] But, just as internet content has evolved over time, so too has the role of intermediaries. Three trends in intermediation in particular are impacting the future of internet governance: invisibility, blended virtual-real space intermediation, and digital identity intermediation. The future of internet governance depends in part on recognizing these trends and generating a consensus on fairness in intermediary commercial conduct. In particular, we must consider the role of contract law as a tool of governance and user identity intermediation.

THE THREE SHIFTS

During the last 20 years, the role of online intermediaries has expanded, and the term "intermediary" now refers to a broader group of companies and information services than ever before. For example, social networks, which today functionally hold a critical role as intermediaries, did not exist in their current incarnation during the early stages of the internet: for example, when the key legislation providing intermediary liability protection was passed in the United States in 1996, none of today's most popular social networks had been founded.

Apart from these definitional changes, three important shifts are reflected by today's intermediaries. First, intermediation has progressively shifted from visible intermediation to invisible intermediation and from providing content *to* users in internet spaces to providing information *about* users. Second, it has shifted from internet intermediation to intermediation in both virtual and physical space. Third, the intermediation process has shifted from internet content intermediation to user identity intermediation. As a consequence, the types of harms implicated by intermediation today have also evolved.

401

The Shift from Visible to Invisible Intermediation

The first shift in intermediation involves a change from predominantly visible to predominantly invisible intermediation. In the early days of the internet, the primary open questions regarding the role of intermediaries involved whether intermediaries had any obligation to protect one user from another user's conduct online. In other words, did an intermediary have a duty to protect one third party from another equally-situated third party?

Because of the novelty and functional anonymity of the early internet, free speech became emboldened in virtual space, and, predictably, claims arose out of this emboldened speech (Sobel 2000; Cotter and Lidsky 1997). Traditional categories of these harms include tort, intellectual property, contract or criminal law based harms – defamation, copyright/trademark infringement, criminal content purveyance, and fraud (Scott 2011; Rogers 2009; Spurlin 2009; Gernat 2008; Preston 2007; Kende 2007; Peters 2007; Merlis 2005). Corporate claims in particular arose relating to alleged harms from various forms of internet speech – postings or emails of disgruntled or overzealous corporate insiders (Rowe 2005) or outside pump-and-dump fraudsters posting information to financial bulletin boards (Ballon and Eisenberg 2003) or other internet forums (Kramer 2005). In the United States, this set of questions regarding intermediary responsibility when one user allegedly harms another was the impetus for the passage of the Communications Decency Act including Section 230 (47 U.S.C. 230 2006; *Zeran v. Am. Online, Inc.* 4th Cir. 1997)[2] and the Digital Millennium Copyright Act Section 512 (17 U.S.C. § 512 2000), limiting intermediary liability for such speech.[3] In the EU, Article 12 of the Directive on E-Commerce similarly reflected these concerns (Council Directive 2000/31).

Over time, however, intermediation dynamics have shifted from visible to invisible intermediation. Now questions surround intermediary conduct not only with respect to filtering potentially harmful visible speech *from* users, such as posted defamatory comments, but also pertain to invisible filtering and resale of data *about* users, such as their clickstream data. Stated another way, visible intermediation of content (with a presumption against screening and reuse of user data) has become supplemented with invisible intermediation (with a presumption in favor of screening and reuse of user data). Intermediaries now frequently act as information aggregators, selling profiles of users or selling access to an audience of users based on internet histories.[4] Consequently, the legal analysis now must include not only questions of moderating user-on-user harm but also questions of whether intermediaries knowingly or negligently participate in causing harm. These new questions frequently involve privacy and information harms that are less transparent to the harmed user and have less available recourse at law.

For example, in trademark intermediary cases, the traditional debate has revolved around whether the intermediary had a duty to take down content known to advertise products that reflect trademark infringement. However, this visible question has evolved to include an invisible one as well – whether the intermediary is selling access to search keywords that are trademarked. As Professor Stacy Dogan has argued "in the typical trademark case against an online intermediary as an informational device to connect a third party – the advertiser – with potential customers . . . plaintiffs argue that the use of trademarks in keyword-based advertising causes confusion as to the source of the advertisers' goods or services and seek to hold the search engine legally responsible for that confusion" (Dogan 2010). The intermediary would argue that connecting a word with an advertiser's message and providing the information to an audience of users is simply a matter of contract – both the users and the advertisers have ostensibly provided contractual consent for the intermediary to connect them. The trademark owners would disagree.

It is this form of invisible intermediation through contract which warrants examination in particular. Using functionally unnegotiable form contracts intermediaries obtain "consent" from users to limitations on their speech in addition to collecting information about them. Perhaps most notable in this space of invisible intermediation is a trend toward intermediaries retaining the contractual right to deny users access to legal content that is deemed inappropriate in the sole discretion of the intermediary. This filtering dynamic can be viewed as a type of net neutrality concern; it is perhaps best described as net "content neutrality."[5] As such, questions exist not only of net neutrality in terms of service provision but also in terms of content neutrality with respect to invisible intermediation and censoring of lawful speech.

For example, the musical group Pearl Jam was recently angered when AT&T censored the group's political speech during a concert (Anderson 2007). AT&T asserted it had a discretionary contractual right to censor lawful speech per the agreement Pearl Jam had signed. In other words, the intermediary controlled the content of the internet broadcast in its sole discretion through its unexpectedly broad contract rights. Despite undoubtedly being represented by competent counsel during the transaction, Pearl Jam did not expect to be censored in their political speech in this manner. Their perturbation reflects the complicated nature of intermediaries' contracts. It also anecdotally reiterates what empirical studies appear to indicate about consumer contracting behavior in online spaces: users rarely read and perhaps even more rarely understand contracts about virtual spaces (Vu et al. 2007). Yet, when users perceive privacy invasive or "unfair" conduct on the part of an intermediary, they may nevertheless become upset.

Particularly when intermediary agreements reserve the right for intermediaries to filter legal content based on "network management" or, even more ambiguously, for "information security" reasons, a high degree of unsupervised discretion becomes concentrated in the hands of intermediaries. Though network management or information security concerns can include content neutral and technologically necessary measures, these rationales can also be used as a cloak for speech filtering by the intermediary and choosing to convey only some lawful content. As Professor Rebecca Tushnet has adeptly argued "if individuals' speech should not be attributed to intermediaries when it is unlawful, we should at least consider ways in which intermediaries could be deterred from interfering with it when it is lawful" (Tushnet 2008, p. 986).

The Shift from Virtual Space to Blended Space Intermediation

As the discussion of the shift from visible to invisible intermediation in the previous section began to illustrate, intermediation has become progressively more a creature of contract than of statute. In part because of this increased prominence of contract as a governance mechanism for internet speech, intermediation that was once limited to online spaces has also seeped into physical spaces. Users' ability to compartmentalize internet conduct from real space conduct is growing tenuous.

The ease of data mining and aggregation through intermediaries has meaningfully lowered the friction that once prevented easy blending of virtual and real space information. Due to these increased data mining capabilities and the financial incentives for user profiling, internet intermediaries now increasingly aggregate information from all possible sources into a "master" profile on each user that spans both virtual space and real space user identity. Consequently, a new information market has burgeoned. For example, by some estimates, approximately 45 percent of employers now incorporate social network information in background checks on employees (Guirola 2011) and the Federal Trade Commission appears receptive to such practices (Forbes 2011). Much anecdotal evidence exists regarding individuals who have been denied opportunities in real space based on (sometimes wrongly attributed) virtual space conduct (Forbes 2011). In the colorful words of one news report, "[p]ictures of an applicant on Facebook wearing a thong may be just as damaging for a job applicant as a criminal record" (Guirola 2011, para. 1).

A theoretical debate in technology legal theory revolves around equivalency of virtual and physical geography: should the internet be legally characterized as a separate space or merely as an extension of physical space for regulatory purposes (Goldsmith 1998; Johnson and Post 1996; Shapiro 2008; Fried 2000)? In other words, is technology best characterized as a limitation on or an extension of social control, sovereignty, and autonomy legal frameworks that exist in real space?[26] A clear divergence of opinion existed in the scholarly community over both the legitimacy of the internet as a separate space and the legitimacy of internet regulation as a separate field of legal study (Easterbrook 1996; Lessig 1999a, 1999b). Internet exceptionalists argue that activity on the internet can be regulated by internet community norms, not laws of territorial jurisdictions or globally harmonized laws. Critics on the other hand argue that the internet is simply a communications network that links people in different jurisdictions, whom governments can regulate, including through regulating intermediaries. Professors Goldsmith and Wu for example, argue in favor of a "bordered Internet," where regulations would be crafted to deal with the new internet dangers but basic domestic or international frameworks would remain (Goldsmith and Wu 2006). The rationale for a regulatory focus on intermediaries argues that intermediaries are in the best position to monitor their own systems in what Professors Mann and Belzley have called a "least-cost avoider" approach (Mann and Belzley 2005, p. 239). It can be argued, however, that even a bordered internet approach presumes some ability to compartmentalize harms between digital and real space contexts. On the other hand, the new intermediation harms with respect to user profiling – data privacy and information security harms – are inherently blended in their construction. They happen simultaneously in virtual space and real space. As such, they present a challenge to traditional internet governance paradigms.

Let us revisit the example Professor Lessig raises in *Code and Other Laws of Cyberspace* regarding a virtual rape in LambdaMOO, where a troubling internet exchange resulted in a virtual attack and sexual violation of one character by another inside a virtual space (Lessig 1999a). In the late 1990s, little recourse would have been available to the virtual victim. The moderators of the forum were arguably in the best position to defend the victim, punishing the perpetrator "in world." Apart from emotional distress, consequences of the virtual rape for the victim would also have likely stayed in world. Although this type of private contractual ordering may have been the hallmark of successful internet governance in the late 1990s, the shift toward blended intermediation has modified the dynamics of virtual spaces. Today, the situation and its consequences may play out differently; new laws exist that may cover the conduct. Though real space rape laws still do not extend to this type of conduct, updated laws on digital harassment likely do reach it in some cases (Fla. Stat. § 784.048). Similarly, whereas the intermediary's duty (or lack thereof) to monitor the conversations of these participants was the subject of the first generation of debate, the second generation of debate about intermediary conduct would involve subsequent information sharing about the incident. The intermediary may receive a request from law enforcement to cooperate in the investigation of the criminal harassment allegation; the intermediary, relying on its user contract permitting information sharing with police, would likely reveal the real space identity of the alleged harasser. Further, the victim's information may be resold by the intermediary; the intermediary who runs the forum may sell the activity logs and the (real space) identity of the virtual rape victim to marketers. The virtual rape victim may thereafter be flooded by advertisers selling violent pornography, and the user may now forever be part of a list of people allegedly interested in sadomasochism. Or, perhaps, the intermediary will include the details of the virtual rape as part of a broader user profile that combines the user's social network data and credit report information – the sort of data package that may be of interest to the user's prospective employers. It is these types of contractually permitted but potentially troubling information uses that are exacerbated by blended virtual and real space intermediation.

Particularly with respect to what have been termed "social intermediaries" (Kahn 2010) such as social networking websites, intermediation in virtual spaces seeps into, shapes and sometimes trumps real space interactions. As Professors Lilian Edwards and Ian Brown have argued, the success of the new generation of data-intensive social networking websites has created a verdant space for identity thieves to usurp user identities in real space through virtual space. These dynamics of social intermediaries should teach us that, although the law may provide some data control protections, aspects of the intermediaries' code itself provide an equally important piece of achieving data protection for users (Edwards and Brown 2009); virtual identity has become increasingly inextricable from real space identity. When we consider the evolution of product functionalities, the push by producers of technology appears strongly in the direction of blended virtual and real space intermediation. For example, Google's recent efforts to eliminate online anonymity and pseudonymity in their products demonstrate this type of blended intermediation: the company seeks to blend the virtual and the real space elements of user identity for purposes of better "knowing" its users (Tsukayama 2011). As a consequence, terms of use now frequently prohibit anonymous or pseudonymous use (Google 2011). In the words of Eric Schmidt, Google's CEO, a social network such as Google+ is not just a website, it is an "identity service" (Rosoff 2011).

In this manner, intermediaries are – both consciously and unconsciously – having an increasingly important impact on the processes of identity. Yet, when average users engage with a social network for the first time, they are rarely if ever capable of reasonably foreseeing the full possible consequences of their conduct: they ostensibly contractually consent to complex and non-negotiable digital agreements, which usually reserve the right of the intermediary to amend terms in its sole discretion. Thus, the process of intermediation and this connection between online and offline spaces has become progressively more opaque to average users. As such, this new condition of blended virtual-real space intermediation warrants consideration.

The Shift from Content to Identity Intermediation

The legal literature has explored primarily content intermediation – speech harm intermediation and product intermediation. However, as the two previous sections have discussed in different ways, it can be argued that internet intermediation has progressively shifted away from merely content intermediation in virtual spaces toward something far more sweeping and impactful: simultaneous intermediation of user identity in both online and offline contexts.

Because we have morphed from a world where intermediaries once provided information to users into a world where intermediaries increasingly provide information about users, intermediaries now construct the story – perhaps even the dominant or allegedly most "credible" story – about a user's identity. Who is this user as a person? What are his interests and background? How should he be perceived by others? As the first section argued, intermediaries increasingly opaquely control the information that users are allowed to both access and share, as well as the reach of that sharing. As the second section argued, the reach of this sharing and access involves unforeseen information from both virtual and real space interactions. In this section, I argue that the shift is coupled with intermediaries' increasing ability to control the *context* around available user information. As Professor Helen Nissenbaum has argued, information ought to be distributed and protected in a manner conscious of norms governing particular social contexts; when information systems function without regard for social norms and values, they weaken the fabric of social life (Nissenbaum 2009).

Intermediaries' ability to define the context of user information impacts users' ability to construct their own identities in both real and virtual space. When users' identities as constructed by intermediaries begin to trump users' own self-constructed identities, this rewrites the norms of human identity building. I have argued elsewhere that the role of technology such as the internet is critical to the way that humans develop and form identity (Matwyshyn 2007). Specifically, through the work of developmental psychology theorists such as Lev Vygotsky,[7] Urie Bronfenbrenner,[8] Albert Bandura,[9] and Erik Erikson,[10] we know that an individual interacts with and within a particular social context to generate development in an emergent manner. With respect to identity management, I have also argued elsewhere that the work of Erving Goffman offers us insights on the ways that individuals manage perceptions of self and stigma in internet spaces (Goffman 1986). Here, turning to insights from social psychology theory with respect to identity salience, roles and boundaries, I will argue that intermediaries increasingly usurp the power to manage users' identities away from users.

Some social psychology identity theorists[11] have argued that the self is composed of a group of role identities, each of which is connected to the self when embedded in a particular "role" (Stryker 2000). Roles can relate to work, family or other interpersonal relationships which come with and create a set of associated meanings and expectations for the person (Burke and Reitzes 1981), and may influence behavior (Burke and Reitzes 1981). Role identities can be organized hierarchically into a "salience hierarchy" of roles, with the most salient roles being most likely to be called upon in situations that involve different aspects of the self (Hogg, Terry and White 1995, pp. 255–69). In other words, the position of a particular role identity in this hierarchy – its salience[12] – explains the degree of prominence we attach to our various role identities and, potentially, the degree of effort we put into each role (Burke and Retizes 1981). However, because role identities have permeable boundaries and are interdependent, they sometimes conflict with each other (Kanter 1977, pp. 417–27; Pleck 1977). In those cases when role identities conflict, the self must either integrate or segment these role identities. Integration involves blending two role identities, while role segmentation is associated with large discrepancies in role identities.[13] Stated another way, a person is forced to negotiate the fit of their preferences, the salience of their various role identities, and the boundaries allowed by their social context to decide whether to integrate or segment their various role identities.

Role integration and segmentation is a continuum, and a person may select differently in different situations. For example, a person may hold a job as a high school teacher, and in this position he acts with decorum, setting a positive model for his students. But, on weekends our high school teacher may participate in a rock band that performs songs with adult themes. He enjoys both his roles as high school teacher and rocker but has chosen to firmly compartmentalize the two role identities and maintain

a sharp division between them. The two role identities are strongly segmented: he functions effectively in each situation independently without
reliance on the other role identity. He would not invoke his rock band
persona in the middle of teaching an algebra class.

In general, the research tends to indicate that maintaining firm boundaries on role identities makes it easier to manage borders of different roles.
Conversely, integrating role identities facilitates transitions across roles
(Clark 2000; Ashforth, Kreiner and Fugate 2000; Kreiner 2002; Nippert-
Eng 1996) because of increased flexibility[14] and permeability.[15] However,
more integrated roles increase the chance of role blurring (Desrochers 2002)
– a potentially undesirable result. Role blurring may trigger confusion and
anxiety about which role should be more salient in a particular situation.
When an individual chooses to maintain a highly segmented set of role
identities, the benefit is that each role is associated with a particular time
and place, allowing an individual to immerse completely in each role. The
individual controls the context: the high school classroom triggers a different set of behaviors from the teacher-rocker than being on stage at a show.
The downside is that the contrast between roles makes it more difficult to
transition between the two roles (Ashforth, Kreiner and Fugate 2000).

Internet intermediation of identity disrupts role salience and a user's
control of his role hierarchy. When identity is intermediated, this process
of controlling the extent of role integration and segmentation is taken
away from the user and instead placed in the hands of the intermediary. The user's desired salient role identity may become overshadowed
by the identity that the intermediary instead chooses to project for that
user. Intermediaries, particularly social network services, force all users
into a highly integrated identity hierarchy, sometimes against their will,
regardless of the user's actual salience hierarchy. In essence, segmented
role identity becomes almost impossible in a highly intermediated world
of information. For example, the intermediary will likely blur the high
school teacher-rocker role identities into one identity, despite the fact that
the individual in question had gone to lengths to maintain role separation.
Despite the high school teacher's utmost professionalism in the classroom,
perhaps because someone else tags him in a picture posted to a social
network during a weekend performance, a future employer may see the
photo, deem him unprofessional and reject him from consideration – a
rejection based on an integrated identity constructed by an intermediary
and not by the person himself.

Consequently, some users feel they have lost control of their salience
hierarchies to digital intermediaries (Madden and Smith 2010). However,
intermediaries would assert that even these users have given contractual
consent, and no problem exists. Here again with identity intermediation

contract law impacts internet governance. As mentioned previously, meaningful contractual consent becomes an increasingly tenuous construct in this circumstance as end user license agreements have become progressively more complex, (Matwyshyn 2008) unnegotiable and unilaterally amendable in the discretion of the intermediary (Facebook Terms of Use 2011). It comes as no surprise then that where intermediary conduct norms are governed solely by this user "consent," a spiral of progressively more aggressive intermediary conduct is likely. This spiral will likely result in increased loss of users' control over their identity management.

IMPLICATIONS FOR INTERNET GOVERNANCE

Professor Viktor Mayer-Schoenberger has stated that "studying the system of information privacy and copyright in particular, and of information governance in general, and examining what mechanisms of governance the various intermediaries employ may yield a richer, more accurate, and more effective strategy for information governance" (Mayer-Schonberger 2010, p. 1853). As the quote might imply, the three shifts in intermediation described in the previous section – increased invisibility, blended space intermediation, and increased identity intermediation – have important implications for broader questions of internet and information governance. Specifically, they caution us to pay attention to bottom-up forces shaping the internet. As I have argued elsewhere, two sets of forces govern the internet – top-down architectures of control and what I have elsewhere termed bottom-up "architectures of growth" (Matwyshyn 2008). Architectures of control refer to hierarchical impositions of social values that occur through legal code on the one hand, and computer code on the other hand, (Lessig 1999a, 1999b) what has been termed by Prof. Lawrence Lessig as "East Coast Code" and "West Coast Code." Both East Coast and West Coast Code impose a top-down order that, unless carefully constructed, can easily stifle innovation and the evolution of the technology-mediated marketplace of goods and ideas.

Architectures of growth, on the other hand, are constituted by bottom-up[16] regulatory forces that push back on architectures of control.[17] Stated another way, our ability to govern, particularly through internet governance, is impacted not only by top-down order but also by structures of order that are spontaneously arising out of the technology-mediated information exchanges of individual actors within our system.[18] The result of this evolution is a form of self-organization in which order in the system forms spontaneously and local rules govern the conduct of each actor. Numerous independent actors, acting in clustered groups (Barabasi

2002), frequently follow local rules[19] and demonstrate increasingly complicated visible patterns of organizational behaviors and norms – what might be termed "organizational code." [20] Legal behaviors can follow this pattern.[21] Law can be used to gently nudge the aggregate behaviors of the complex system toward more successfully harmonizing the competing legal, business, and social interests within it. This type of carefully built set of legal constructs that works to positively shift organizational code can be termed an "architecture of growth" (Matwyshyn 2008).

With respect to intermediaries, architectures of control to this point have focused on the "first generation" intermediary questions I identified previously – questions relating to one user of the service visibly harming another user. "Second generation" intermediation questions relating to invisibility, blended space, and identity intermediation instead implicate bottom-up dynamics – the strategic behaviors of various actors in the system. Global patterns are emerging (Johnson 2001) from the aggregation of these individual behaviors that could not have been forecast simply by understanding the behavior of one particular actor in the system. One set of such global patterns relates to intermediary contract norms in their terms of use.

As I have demonstrated empirically elsewhere, terms of use have progressively evolved over time in their terms in favor of their drafters in a statistically significant manner (Matwyshyn 2008). Intermediaries' terms of use are unlikely to demonstrate an exception. It is likely that the terms of use norms of intermediaries are changing to accommodate the three shifts in intermediation previously identified in this chapter; intermediaries are likely to be expanding the scope of their own contractual rights with respect to their users at the expense of user interests.

In the first generation of intermediary statutes and architectures of control, the conversation turned on whether one group of users possessed interests superior to other users. The Communications Decency Act Section 230 (47 U.S.C. § 230 2000), Digital Millennium Copyright Act Section 512 (17 U.S.C. § 512 2000) and Article 12 of the Directive on E-Commerce (Council Directive 2000/31) and similar statutory approaches, have focused on user to user harm and protecting intermediaries from being bound by unfair editorial and monitoring obligations. However, the current strategic business and contracting behaviors of intermediaries instead appear to indicate a volitional increase in monitoring: intermediaries monitor their users' conduct to be able to aggregate and commodify user data. In the current generation of intermediary behaviors, the tension exists not among interests of various users but between the interests of the intermediary itself and its users. While private ordering solutions may have worked in the late 1990s for internet spaces, internet governance today requires a fundamentally different approach with respect to intermediaries. These second generation intermediation questions are inadequately considered in existing architectures of control, and architectures of growth are needed.

In particular, five types of contractual reservations of rights now frequently appear in intermediary agreements and warrant analysis. First, intermediaries generally request blanket consent to bundle, aggregate and share user information with any party of the intermediary's choosing. Without the intermediary advising the consumer of the identities of these third parties or the full extent of data collection, the consent that a consumer can provide is crippled at best. A reasonable consumer cannot foresee consequences of material terms of the agreement and lacks the ability to negotiate them. Second, intermediary contracts evidence less focus on the user-user relationship and content provision, instead demonstrating a focus on maintaining maximum flexibility for intermediaries in the use and commodification of user information as a core revenue stream for the intermediary. In particular, they usually include the intermediary's ability to unilaterally amend terms. Third, intermediary agreements now sometimes contain contractual restrictions reserving discretion for intermediaries to censor otherwise lawful content. These restrictions present equity and content neutrality concerns. Fourth, contractual provisions requiring "real space" identity disclosure, such as prohibitions on anonymity and pseudonymity push toward blended virtual-real space intermediation and usurp users' control over identity management (Madden and Smith 2010). Finally, due to broad drafting of contracts by intermediaries and the technological evolution of data collection techniques used, users have difficulty conceptualizing the extent of identity intermediation and possible harm that the intermediary's conduct will trigger. In summary, current contract formation and drafting norms make it objectively impossible for a reasonable consumer to understand the consequences of her actions in online spaces.

These contractual concerns indicate that private ordering solutions through contract and market self-regulation in intermediation contexts are not proving successful. As such, additional architectures of growth are needed to rebalance the legally and developmentally undesirable contract imbalance between intermediaries and their users. Data stewardship obligations for intermediaries and stronger consumer information protection rights for users are needed. These rights can be constructed in various legal ways. Rights to delete (Mayer-Schonberger 2010), duties of reasonable care in data storage, notice obligations upon onward transfer, meaningful recourse for data breach and causes of action for negligent conduct in information security are all possible avenues; each can contribute to building more positive emergent structures in intermediated spaces.

However, the first step in building these new structures is simply recognizing the problem – the structural imbalance second generation intermediation concerns present – and that market self-regulation will not resolve this imbalance. By exploring the role of contract in contributing to this imbalance, this chapter has sought to start a new thread in internet governance inquiry – a thread focused on the emergent harms of content and identity control in second generation intermediation.

NOTES

1. When we talk about intermediaries and intermediation in digital spaces, we usually mean various types of information services companies that aggregate and filter content. We think of online marketplaces, search engines, and ISPs – those companies who exercise a degree of discretion over the internet content we see.
2. 47 U.S.C. § 230 (2006); *see also Zeran v. Am. Online, Inc.*, 129 F.3d 327, 330 (4th Cir. 1997) (barring claims against an online service provider under § 230 for interactive computer service provider alleged to have "unreasonably delayed in removing defamatory messages posted by an unidentified third party, refused to post retractions of those messages, and failed to screen for similar postings thereafter"). According to the preamble to the Communications Decency Act the purpose of the statute is "preserv[ing] the vibrant and competitive free market that presently exists for the Internet and other interactive computer services, unfettered by Federal or State regulation." 47 U.S.C. § 230(b)(2). For a discussion of the role of the CDA in entrepreneurship see, e.g., Goldman, E. (2010), 'Unregulating online harassment', 87 *Denver University Law Review Online*, **59**, 60, http://www.denverlawreview.org/how-to-regulate/2010/2/22/unregulating-online-harassment.html. See also e.g., Citron, D. and H. Norton (2011), "Intermediaries and hate speech: Fostering digital citizenship for our information age", *Boston University Law Review*, **91**, 1435 (arguing in favor of a nuanced approach to hate speech by intermediaries); Calo, M.R. (2010), 'Open robotics', *Maryland Law Review*, **70**, 571 (arguing in favor of borrowing a CDA-like approach in regulation of robotics); Seltzer, W. (2010), 'Free speech unmoored in copyright's safe harbor: Chilling effects of the DMCA on the First Amendment', *Harvard Journal of Law and Technology*, **24**, 171, 228 (noting that § 230 "specifically excludes intellectual property and criminal claims from its protections").
3. Statements by members of Congress appear to demonstrate a desire for broad intermediary immunity from tort claims in § 230, and the House Energy and Commerce Committee, where the bill originated, noted "[t]he courts have correctly interpreted section 230(c), which was aimed at protecting against liability for such claims as negligence." H.R. Rep. No. 107-449 (2002), 13.
4. Meanwhile, the user may not be aware that these particular third parties have access to her clickstream and other data.
5. While traditional net neutrality concerns revolve around invisible control over the internet "pipes," net content neutrality involves controlling the internet's "people."
6. Mosaic was developed in 1993 by two University of Illinois graduate students, Marc Andersen and Eric Bina. Immediately following the launch of Mosaic, use of the World Wide Web increased. Cassidy, J. (2002), *Dot Con*, New York: HarperCollins, 51.
7. Lev Vygotsky, the founder of contextualist developmental theory introduced the importance of analyzing development in a cultural context. The smallest unit of

analysis for Vygotsky is the child in a particular social context, an inherently variable construction across environments and individuals. Learning and development occurs on the person-society border through an individual interacting inside the "zone of proximal development." Help in development comes not only from humans in the environment but also from self-help using cultural tools such as computers. See, e.g. Vygotsky, L. (1978), *Mind in Society: The Development of Higher Mental Processes*, Cambridge, MA and London, UK: Harvard University Press, 84–91.

8.   An elaboration on Vygotsky and the evolving, nonlinear nature of social contexts that shape development can be found in the work of Urie Bronfenbrenner. Bronfenbrenner presents an ecological model that illustrates the importance of reviewing multiple levels of social context. Specifically, he identifies four levels of analysis: (1) macrosystem; (2) mesosystem; (3) exosystem; and (4) microsystem. See generally, Bronfenbrenner, U. (1971), *The Ecology of Human Development: Experiments by Nature and Design*, Cambridge, MA and London, UK: Harvard University Press.

9.   Albert Bandura's Social Learning Theory presents a consonant analysis to that of Vygotsky and Bronfenbrenner. The theory views the interaction between individuals and environments as a three way exchange in which the person, an entity with unique characteristics, performs a behavior in an environment which responds back to the person and the behavior in a process of reciprocal determinism; it is an idiosyncratic interaction. See, Bandura, A. (1986), *Social Foundations of Thought and Action: A Social Cognitive Theory*, Englewood Cliffs, NJ: Prentice-Hall; Bandura, A. (2002), 'Selective moral disengagement in the exercise of moral agency', *Journal of Moral Education*, **31**, 101.

10. Erikson frames development through identification of eight stages/dichotomies of human development and identity formation: (1) basic trust versus mistrust; (2) autonomy versus shame; (3) initiative versus guilt; (4) industry versus inferiority; (5) identity versus role confusion; (6) intimacy versus isolation; (7) generativity versus stagnation; and (8) ego integrity versus despair. See Erikson, E. (1963), *Childhood and Society*, New York and London, UK: W.W. Norton.

11. Two schools of thought exist in social psychology that are sometimes confused – on the one hand, identity theory, which emphasizes role behavior and on the other social identity theory, which emphasizes group process and intergroup relations. Identity theory focuses on the self as comprised of the various roles as the source of identity, and social identity theory focuses on the groups to which people belong as a source of identity. Hogg, M., D. Terry, and K. White (1995), 'A tale of two theories: A critical comparison of identity theory with social identity theory", *Social Psychology Quarterly*, **58**, 255–69.

12. Identities can be defined as the answer to the question 'Who am I?" Many of the "answers" are connected with the roles or jobs we perform. Stryker, S. and S. Serpe (1982) 'Commitment, identity salience and role behavior: Theory and research example', 206 in W. Ickes and E. Knowles (eds) (1982), *Personality, Roles, and Social Behavior*, New York: Springer-Verlag.

13. The questions examined in both the research on role identity salience and in boundary theory focus on how individuals value, negotiate and cross the lines of demarcation of their various role identities. Clark, C.S. (2000), 'Work/family border theory: A new theory of work/family balance', *Human Relations*, **53**(6), 47–770. Boundary theory, an offspring of identity theory, considers the blurring of these role identity lines and the outcomes that result, such as changes in meaning that people assign to roles and the ease of transition among them. Nippert-Eng, C. (1996), *Home and Work*, Chicago: University of Chicago Press. Ashforth, E.B., G. E. Kreiner, and M. Fugate (2000), 'All in a day's work: Boundaries and micro role transitions', *Academy of Management Review*, **25**, 472–91. Boundary theory is a general cognitive theory of social classification. Zerubavel, E. (1996), 'Lumping and splitting: Notes on social classification', *Sociological Forum*, **11**, 421–23.

14. Flexibility refers to the malleability of the boundary between two or more role/domains to accommodate the demands of one domain or another. Ashforth, E.B., G.E. Kreiner,

and M. Fugate (2000), 'All in a day's work: Boundaries and micro role transitions', *Academy of Management Review*, **25**, 472–91; Clark, C.S. (2000), 'Work/family border theory: A new theory of work/family balance', *Human Relations*, **53**(6), 47–770; Hall, T.D. and J. Richter (1988), 'Balancing work life and home life: What can organizations do to help?', *Academy of Management Executive*, **3**, 213–23.

15. Permeability involves the extent to which a boundary allows psychological or behavioral aspects of one role or domain to enter another. Ashforth, E.B., G.E. Kreiner & M. Fugate (2000), "All in a day's work: Boundaries and micro role transitions", *Academy of Management Review*, **25**(3), 472–491; Clark, C.S. (2000), "Work/family border theory: A new theory of work/family balance", *Human Relations*, **53**(6), 747–770; Hall, T.D. and J. Richter (1988), 'Balancing work life and home life: What can organizations do to help?' *Academy of Management Executive*, **3**, 213–23.

16. At least one noted legal scholar has highlighted the importance of considering bottom-up norms and legal emergence. See Radin, M.J. (2002), 'Online standardization and the integration of text and machine', *Fordham Law Review*, **70**, 1135–37. However, most internet regulation scholarly work to date has focused on top-down governance. See, e.g., Lessig, L. (2000), 'Foreword, cyberspace and privacy: A new legal paradigm?', *Stanford Law Review*, **52**, 987; Benkler, Y. (2002), "Intellectual property and the organization of information production', *International Review of Law & Economy*, **22**, 81; Zittrain, J. (2003), 'Internet points of control', *Boston College Law Review*, **44**, 653; Samuelson, P. (2000), 'Privacy as intellectual property', *Stanford Law Review*, **52**, 1125; Lemley, M. (2003), 'Place and cyberspace', *California Law Review*, **91**, 521.

17. For various applications of complex systems theory to other legal contexts see, e.g., Post, D.G. and D. Johnson (1998), '" Chaos prevailing on every continent": Toward a new theory of decentralized decision-making in complex systems', *Chicago-Kent Law Review*, **73**, 1055 (arguing that legal theory would be enriched by paying attention to algorithms derived from the study of complex systems in contexts such as competitive federalism and the "patching" algorithm). See also, e.g., Crawford, S.P. (2003), 'The biology of the broadcast flag', *Hastings Communication and Entertainment Law Journal*, **25**, 603; Werbach, K. (2004), 'Supercommons: Toward a unified theory of wireless communication', *Texas Law Review*, **82**, 863; Brenner, S.W. (2004), 'Toward a criminal law for cyberspace: Distributed security', *Boston University Journal of Science and Technology*, **10**, 1; Creo, R.A. (2004), 'Mediation 2004: The art and the artist', *Penn State Law Review*, **108**, 1017; Chen, J. (2004), 'Webs of life: Biodiversity conservation as a species of information policy', *Iowa Law Review*, **89**, 495; Hughes, S.H. (2004), 'Understanding conflict in a postmodern world', *Marquette Law Review*, **87**, 681; Farber, D. (2003), 'Probabilities behaving badly: Complexity theory and environmental uncertainty', *U.C. David Law Review*, **37**, 145; Beecher-Monas, E. and E. Garcia-Rill (2003), 'Danger at the edge of chaos: Predicting violent behavior in a post-Daubert world', *Cardozo Law Review*, **24**, 1845; Ruhl, J.B. and J. Salzman (2003), 'Mozart and the Red Queen: The problem of regulatory accretion in the administrative state', *Georgetown Law Review*, **91**, 757; Goldberg, D. (2002), 'And the walls came tumbling down: How classical scientific fallacies undermine the validity of textualism and originalism', *Houston Law Review*, **39**, 463; McLean, T. (2001–2002), 'Application of administrative law to health care reform: The real politik of crossing the quality chasm', *Journal of Law and Health*, **16**, 65; Salzman, J. et al. (2002), 'Regulatory traffic jams', *Wyoming Law Review*, **2**, 253.

18. The internet has demonstrated itself to be a complex system. Complex systems are characterized by a large number of similar but independent actors who persistently move, respond, and evolve in relation to each other in an increasingly sophisticated manner. For various applications of complex systems theory to other legal contexts see, e.g., Post, D.G. and D. Johnson (1998), '"Chaos prevailing on every continent": Toward a new theory of decentralized decision-making in complex systems', *Chicago-Kent Law Review*, **73**, 1055 (arguing that legal theory would be enriched by paying attention to

algorithms derived from the study of complex systems in contexts such as competitive federalism and the "patching" algorithm).

19. For example, outside of User Agreements, online communities often have additional community rules of conduct. *See, e.g.*, AOL Instant Messenger Web Chat Rules & Etiquette, http://www.aol.com/community/rules.html.

20. Organizational code includes the behavioral, strategic, and legal norms of actors in response to changes in substantive law, the role of the transactional bar in shaping the comparative power and strategies of actors within the system, and evolving contracting norms. For a discussion see, e.g., Matwyshyn, A. (2008), 'Mutually assured protection: toward development of relational internet data security and privacy contracting norms', in A. Chandler et al. (eds.), *Securing Privacy in the Internet Age*, Stanford, CA: Stanford University Press. Borrowing terms from Eric Raymond, organizational code can be said to be order developing through a babbling "bazaar," which permits norms to percolate to widespread acceptance, while legal code and, frequently, computer code develop order through a "cathedral" style where norms are hierarchically imposed. *See*, Raymond, E. (2004), 'The Cathedral and the Bazaar', http://www.catb.org/~esr/writings/cathedral-bazaar/cathedral-bazaar/.

21. The behavior of complex adaptive systems frequently cannot be accurately predicted and can naturally evolve to a state of self-organization on the border between order and disorder. *See*, Williams, P. (1997), *Chaos Theory Tamed*, London, UK: Taylor & Francis Limited.

BIBLIOGRAPHY

Anderson, N. (2007), 'Pearl Jam censored by AT&T, calls for a neutral "Net"', *Ars Technica*, http://arstechnica.com/old/content/2007/08/pearl-jam-censored-by-att-calls-for-a-neutral-net.ars.

Ashforth, E.B., G.E. Kreiner, and M. Fugate (2000), 'All in a day's work: Boundaries and micro role transitions', *Academy of Management Review*, **25**, 472–91.

Ballon, I. and J. Eisenberg (2003), 'Poison pen: Chat board liars may be vulnerable to lawsuits', *Practicing Law Institute/Patent*, **754**, 163.

Barabasi, A.L. (2002), *Linked: How Everything is Connected to Everything Else and What It Means*, New York: Penguin Group, p. 49.

Burke, P.J. and D.C. Reitzes (1981), 'The link between identity and role performance', *Social Psychology Quarterly*, **44**, 83–92.

Clark, C.S. (2000), 'Work/family border theory: A new theory of work/family balance', *Human Relations*, **53**(6), 47–770.

Cotter, T. and L. Barnett Lidsky (2007), 'Authorship, audiences, and anonymous speech', *Notre Dame Law Review*, **82**, 1537.

Council Directive 2000/31, 2000 O.J. (L 178) 3, recital 5–7 and Article 12, http://europa.eu.int.

Desrochers, S. (2002), 'Measuring work-family boundary ambiguity: A proposed scale', Bronfenbrenner Life Course Center Working Paper #02-04.

Dogan, S. (2010), 'Trademark remedies and online intermediaries', *Lewis & Clark Law Review*, **14**, 467.

Easterbrook, F. (1996), 'Cyberspace and the law of the horse', *University of Chicago Legal Forum*, **1996**, 207.

Edwards, L. and I. Brown (2009), 'Data control and social networking: irreconcilable ideas?', in A.M. Matwyshyn (ed.), *Harboring Data: Information Security, Law and the Corporation*, Stanford, CA: Stanford University Press, pp. 202–28.

Facebook (2011), 'Terms of Use, Section 13', https://www.facebook.com/terms.php.

Forbes (2011), 'Employees can't be fired for Facebook complaints, Judge says', *Forbes*, http://blogs.forbes.com/mobiledia/?p=426.

Fried, C. (2000), 'Perfect freedom or perfect control?', *Harvard Law Review*, **114**, 606, 618.

Gernat, R.K. (2008), *Strategies for Prosecuting Internet Pornography Cases: Leading Prosecutors on Interviewing the Suspect, Developing a Trial Strategy, and Negotiating the Charges; Avoiding the Pitfalls of Prosecuting Internet Crimes against Children*, Boston, MA: Aspatore.

Goffman, E. (1986), *Stigma: Notes on the Management of Spoiled Identity*, New York: Simon & Schuster, Inc.

Goldsmith, J. (1998), 'Against cyberanarchy', *University of Chicago Law Review*, **65**, 1199–200.

Goldsmith, J. and T. Wu (2006), 'Digital borders', *Legal Affairs*, **Jan-Feb**, 40.

Google (2011), 'Google Plus terms of use', http://www.google.com/accounts/TOS.

Guirola, J. (2011), 'FTC approves social media reports, Channel 8 News, Las Vegas', http://www.8newsnow.com/story/15190651/ftc-approves-social-media-reports.

Hogg, M., D. Terry, and K. White (1995), 'A tale of two theories: A critical comparison of identity theory with social identity theory', *Social Psychology Quarterly*, **58**, 255–69.

Johnson, D. and D. Post (1996), 'Law and borders – The rise of law in cyberspace', *Stanford Law Review*, 48, 1367.

Johnson, S. (2001), *Emergence: The Connected Lives of Ants, Brains, Cities and Software*, New York: Scribner.

Kahn, D. (2010), 'Social intermediaries: Creating a more responsible web through portable identity, cross-web reputation and code-backed norms', *Columbia Science & Technology Law Review*, **11**, 176.

Kanter, R.M. (1977), *Work and Family in the United States: A Critical Review and Agenda for Research and Policy*, New York: Russell Sage Foundation, 417–27.

Kende, M. (2007), 'Regulating internet pornography aimed at children: A comparative constitutional perspective on passing the camel through the needle's eye', *BYU Law Review*, **2007**, 1623.

Kramer, D. (2005), 'The way it is and the way it should be: liability under §10(B) of the exchange Act and Rule 10B-5 thereunder for making false and misleading statements as part of a scheme to 'Pump and Dump' a stock', *University of Miami Business Law Review*, **13**, 243.

Kreiner, G.E. (2002), 'Boundary preferences and work-family conflict: A person-environment fit perspective', Paper presented at the annual meeting of the Academy of Management Conference, Denver, CO.

Lessig, L. (1999a), *Code and Other Laws of Cyberspace*, New York: Basic Books, 63.

Lessig, L. (1999b), 'The law of the horse: What cyberlaw might teach', *Harvard Law Review*, **113**, 501.

Madden, M., and A. Smith (2010), 'Reputation management and social media', *Pew Internet and American Life Project*, http://www.pewinternet.org/~/media//Files/Reports/2010/PIP_Reputation_Management_with_topline.pdf.

Mann, R. and S. Belzley (2005), 'The promise of internet intermediary liability', *William & Mary Law Review*, **47**, 239.

Matwyshyn, A. (2008), 'Mutually assured protection: Toward development of relational internet data security and privacy contracting norms', in A. Chandler et al. (eds.), *Securing Privacy in the Internet Age*, Stanford, CA: Stanford University Press.

Matwyshyn, A. (2007), 'Technology, commerce, development, identity', *Minnesota Journal of Law, Science & Technology*, **8**, 515.

Mayer-Schonberger, V. (2010), 'Beyond privacy, beyond rights – Toward a "systems" theory of information governance', *California Law Review*, **98**, 1853.

Mayer-Schonberger, V. (2009), *Delete: The Virtue of Forgetting in the Digital Age*, Princeton, NJ: Princeton University Press.

Merlis, S. (2005), 'Preserving internet expression while protecting our children: Solutions following Ashcroft v. ACLU', *Northwestern Journal of Technology & Intellectual Property*, **4**, 117.

Nippert-Eng, C. (1996), *Home and Work*, Chicago: University of Chicago Press.

Nissenbaum, H. (2009), *Privacy in Context*, Palo Alto: Stanford Press.
Peters, R. (2007), 'It will take more than parental use of filtering software to protect children from internet pornography', *NYU Review of Law & Social Change*, **31**, 829.
Pleck, J.H. (1977), 'The work-family role system', *Social Problems*, **24**, 417.
Preston, C. (2007), 'Zoning the internet: A new approach to protecting children online', *BYU Law Review*, **2007**, 1417.
Rogers, A. (2009), 'Protecting children on the internet: Mission impossible?', *Baylor Law Review*, **61**, 323.
Rosoff, M. (2011), 'Google+ isn't just a social network, it's an "identity service"', *Business Insider*, http://www.businessinsider.com/google-isnt-just-a-social-network-its-an-identity-service-2011-8.
Rowe, E. (2005), 'When trade secrets become shackles: Fairness and the inevitable disclosure doctrine', *Tulane Journal of Technology & Intellectual Property*, **7**, 167.
Scott, J. (2011), 'The internet and protection of children online: Time for change', *Canadian Journal of Law & Technology*, **9**, 1.
Shapiro, A. (1998), 'The disappearance of cyberspace and the rise of code', *Seton Hall Constitutional Law Journal*, **8**, 703, 709.
Sobel, D. (2000), 'The process that "John Doe" is due: Addressing the legal challenge to internet anonymity', *Virginia Journal of Law & Technology*, **5**, 3.
Spurlin, C. (2009), 'Does filtering stop the flow of valuable information? A case study of the Children's Internet Protection Act (CIPA) in South Dakota', *South Dakota Law Review*, **54**, 89.
Stryker, Sheldon (2000), 'Identity competition: Key to differential social movement involvement,' in S. Stryker, T. Owens and R. White (eds), *Identity, Self, and Social Movements*, Minneapolis: University of Minnesota Press.
Stryker, S. and Burke, P. (2000), 'The past present and future of an identity theory', http://www.scribd.com/doc/16210252/Stryker-Identity-Theory.
Tsukayama, H. (2011), 'Schmidt: Google Plus is for those who want to use their real names', *Washington Post*, http://www.washingtonpost.com/blogs/faster-forward/post/schmidt-google-plus-is-for-those-who-want-to-use-their-real-names/2011/08/29/gIQAcPiCnJ_blog.html.
Tushnet, R. (2008), 'Power without responsibility', *George Washington Law Review*, **76**, 986.
Vu, K.-P. et al. (2007), 'How users read and comprehend privacy policies', Proceedings of the 2007 Conference on Human Interface: Part II.

Statutes

17 U.S.C. § 512 (2000).
47 U.S.C. § 230 et seq. (2000).
Fla. Stat. § 784.048.

17. Network neutrality: a research guide
Christopher T. Marsden

INTRODUCTION

Network neutrality is a growing policy controversy, which must be traced in its policy history, examined and defined, and its two elements separated: the present net neutrality 'lite' debate and the emerging net neutrality 'heavy' concerned with fibre access networks in future. In this guide, I explain its past, explore the legislation and regulation of its present, and explain that economics and human rights will both play a part in its future. There are net neutrality laws in the Netherlands, Chile and apparently Finland, regulation in the United States and Canada, co-regulation in Norway, and self-regulation in Japan, the United Kingdom and many other European countries. It is a debate which has existed since at least 1999, and which will grow in importance as internet access matures and service quality increases with the demand on the network for more attractive fixed and mobile/wireless services.

HISTORY: TRUST-TO-TRUST AND CONTROL OF COMMUNICATIONS

Network neutrality is the latest phase of an eternal argument over control of communications media. The internet was held out by early legal and technical analysts to be special, due to its decentred construction, separating it from earlier 'technologies of freedom' (de Sola Pool 1983) including radio and the telegraph. Spar (2001) argues that control is a historical evolutionary step in communications media development, while Wu (2010) following Lessig (1999a) argues that closure need not be an inevitable outcome.

The internet had never been subject to regulation beyond that needed for interoperability and competition, building on the Computer I and II inquiries by the Federal Communications Commission (FCC) in the United States (Werbach 2005), and the design principle of End-to-End (E2E) that was first described by Saltzer, Reed and Clark (1981). That principle itself was bypassed by the need for greater trust and reliability in the emerging broadband network by the late 1990s, particularly as spam email led to viruses, botnets and other risks. As a result, E2E has gradually given way to trust-to-trust mechanisms, in which it is receipt of the message by one party's trusted agent which replaces the receipt by final receiver (Clark and Blumenthal 2011). This agent is almost always the Internet Service Provider (ISP), and it is regulation of this party which is at stake in net neutrality. ISPs are not only removing spam and other hazardous materials before they reach the (largely technically uneducated) subscriber, ISPs also can remove other potentially illegal materials on behalf of governments and copyright holders, to name the two most active censors on the internet, as well as prioritising packets for their own benefit. As a result, the E2E principle would be threatened were it not already moribund.

The legal policy and regulatory implications of rapidly standardising innovation on the communications ecology was well understood by Benkler, who was concerned with the need to maintain interoperability and openness to ensure a 'commons' in which unaffiliated and non-commercial innovation could flourish (Benkler 1998a, 1998b). The internet's core values of openness and democracy have been established by accident as well as design. Noam (2008) states: 'There is nothing especially new about [media law's] recent round – net-neutrality – as a conceptual issue, or in terms of its policy options, except for the terminology.' Benkler (2006) and Lemley and McGowan (1998) have argued that though network effects may tend to closure of the network, regulatory scrutiny may not be the only outcome that will result in greater openness.

It is not novel to claim that protocols regulate user behaviour on the internet ('Code is law' as Lessig (1999a) put it), but legal commitment to freedom of speech means that law can regulate the internet, by enforcing conditions to enable free speech. As Wu (2003a) explains, laws can regulate the internet as surely as vice versa, and with more constitutional authority if less technical virtuosity (Mayer-Schonberger 2008; Reidenberg 2005). By 1998, the innovation-control argument hinged on Microsoft's leveraging of its operating system monopoly into browser and video software, and by 2000 this had led to scrutiny of AOL-Time Warner, notably the potential for foreclosure of Instant Messaging and video (Faulhaber 2002), and of cable-telephony horizontal merger such as that between AT&T and MediaOne (Lemley and Lessig 1999). This moved on to control over WiFi, an unlicensed spectrum technology capable of providing Local Area Network connectivity and opening the control over end-users exerted by fixed and wireless ISPs (Croxford and Marsden 2001). Net neutrality as a description was first applied to the debate about internet traffic management practices (ITMP), or Quality of Service on the internet in 2003 (Lessig and Wu 2003; Wu 2003b), though the debate began when academics feared that cable TV's closed business model would overtake the open internet in 1999 (Lemley and Lessig 1999; Lessig 1999a, 1999b).

Initial treatment of network neutrality discussed ensuring four 'Net Freedoms' (FCC 2005) for end-users: freedom to attach devices, run applications, receive the content packets of their choice and to receive 'Service Plan Information . . . meaningful information' (on which see the section on transparency). Even in 2011, scholars are suggesting freedom to innovate can be squared with design prohibitions (van Schewick 2010), despite over a decade of multi-billion dollar protocol development by the ISP community resulting in the ability to control traffic coming onto their networks (Waclawsky 2005), and wholescale rationing of end-user traffic (see the second section, 'REGULATION AND LAW OF NET NEUTRALITY'). Berners-Lee (2006) explained: 'There have been suggestions that we don't need legislation because we haven't had it. These are nonsense, because in fact we have had net neutrality in the past – it is only recently that real explicit threats have occurred.' Berners-Lee was particularly adamant that he does not wish to see the prohibition of QoS because that is precisely the claim made by some US net neutrality advocates – and opposed by the network engineering community.

History: Definition and Development

Net neutrality may be seen to comprise two separate non-discrimination commitments (Marsden 2010a), one of universal service and another of common carriage. Backward-looking 'net neutrality lite' claims that internet users should not be disadvantaged due to opaque and invidious practices by their current ISP. The argument is that a minimum level of service should be provided which offers open internet access without blocking or degrading of specific applications or protocols – an updated form of universal service (Mueller 1998), generally proposed at 2Mbps. That provides a basic level of service which all subscribers should eventually receive.

Forward-looking 'positive net neutrality' describes a practice whereby higher Quality of Service (QoS) for higher prices should be offered on fair, reasonable and non-discriminatory (FRAND) terms to all-comers, a modern equivalent of common carriage (Noam 1994). The type of service which may be entitled to FRAND treatment could result in short-term exclusivity in itself, as for instance wireless/mobile cell towers may only be able to carry a single high-definition video stream at any one point in time and therefore a monopoly may result. As common carriage dictates terms but not the specific market conditions (Cherry 2006, Marsden 2011), transparency and non-discrimination would not automatically result in a plurality of services. I argue against social or economic justifications for either barring any proprietary high-speed traffic at all, or for strict versions of net neutrality that would not allow any traffic prioritisation. There is too much at stake either to expect government to supplant the market in providing higher speed connections, or for the market to continue to deliver openness without the most basic of policy and regulatory backstops to ensure some growth (Meisel 2010, p. 20).

The net neutrality problem is complex and far-reaching: attempts to dismiss it as a problem that can be overcome by local loop (last mile) telecoms competition (Cave et al. 2009; Renda 2008) do not fully acknowledge persistent problems with market failure. Economic analysis can provide useful analysis of problems emerging in positive net neutrality, but throttling and blocking at the basic internet service level is generally straightforward anti-competitive discrimination in competition law, and unjustified censorship in communications law. The physical delivery of internet to consumers is subject to a wide range of bottlenecks, not simply in the 'last mile' to the end-user. There is limited 'middle mile' (backhaul) competition in fixed ISP markets, even in Europe where the commitment to regulation for competition remains, as wholesale backhaul is provided by the incumbent privatised national telecoms provider (in the UK, British Telecom). Even if platforms did compete in, for instance, heavily cabled countries, there would remain 'n-sided' market problems in that there is no necessary direct (even non-contractual) relationship between innovative application providers and ISPs (Economides and Tåg, 2007), so that platforms may set rules to 'tax' data packets that ultimately impoverish the open innovation value chain, so ultimately causing consumer harm. Thus the archetypal garage start-ups such as Facebook (founded 2003) and YouTube (founded 2005) would have had less opportunity to spread 'virally' across the internet, as their services would be subject to these extra costs. Many commercial content providers, such as Google, use Content Delivery Networks (CDN) and other caching mechanisms to accelerate the speed of delivery to users, in essence reducing the number of those 'hops'. Content is therefore already delivered at different speeds depending on the paid priority the content provider assigns to it, but not the ISPs' policies.

History: How Traffic Management has Changed Common Carriage

Network congestion and lack of bandwidth at peak times is a feature of the internet. It has always existed. That is why video over the internet was until the late 1990s simply unfeasible. It is why voice over the internet has patchy quality, and why engineers have been trying to create higher QoS. 'End-to-End' is a two-edged sword, with advantages of openness and a dumb network, and disadvantages of congestion, jitter and ultimately a slowing rate of progress for high-end applications such as High Definition video. E2E may have its disadvantages as compared with QoS, and in this it has obvious parallels with 'common carriage'. Common carriers who claim on the one hand the benefits of rights of way and other privileges, yet on the other claim traffic management for profit rather than network integrity, are trying to both have their cake and eat it (Frieden 2010b).

It is worth stating what common carriage is not. It is not a flat rate for all packets. It is also not necessarily a flat rate for all packets of a certain size. It is, however, a mediaeval non-discrimination bargain between Sovereign and transport network or facility, in which an exchange is made: for the privileges of classification as a common carrier, those private actors will be granted the rights and benefits that an ordinary private carrier would not. As Cherry (2006) has written, common carriers are not a solution to a competition problem, they far predate competition law. They prevent discrimination between the same traffic type – if I offer you transport of your high definition video stream of a certain protocol, then the next customer could demand the same subject to capacity, were the internet to be subject to common carriage.

Deep Packet Inspection and Other Traffic Management Techniques

In order to manage traffic, new technology lets any of the ISP routers (if so equipped) look inside a data packet to 'see' its content, via what is known as Deep Packet Inspection (DPI) and other techniques. Previous routers were not powerful enough to conduct more than a shallow inspection that simply established the header information – the equivalent of the postal address for the packet. An ISP can use DPI to determine whether a data packet values high-speed transport – as a television stream does in requiring a dedicated broadcast channel – and offer higher-speed dedicated capacity to that content, typically real-time dependent content such as television, movies or telephone calls using VOIP. Most voice calls and video today use a dedicated line, your copper telephone line or cable line: tomorrow they may use high-speed fibre lanes on your internet connection. That could make a good business for ISPs that wish to offer higher capability for 'managed services' via DPI (not all ISPs will do so, and it is quite possible to manage traffic less obtrusively by using the DiffServ protocol to prioritise traffic streams within the same internet channel). Waclawsky (2005) stated in regard to ISP traffic management protocols that 'This is the emerging, consensus view: [it] will let broadband industry vendors and operators put a control layer and a cash register over the Internet and creatively charge for it.'

DPI and other techniques that let ISPs prioritise content also allow them to slow down other content, as well as speed up content for those that pay (and for emergency communications and other 'good' packets). This potentially threatens competitors with that content: Skype offers VOIP using normal internet speeds; uTorrent and BBC's iPlayer have offered video using peer-to-peer (P2P) protocols. Encryption is common in these applications and partially successful in overcoming these ISP controls, but even if all users and applications used strong encryption this would not succeed in overcoming decisions by ISPs simply to route known premium traffic to a 'faster lane', consigning all other traffic into a slower non-priority lane (a policy explanation simplifying a complex engineering decision). P2P is designed to make the most efficient use of congested networks, and its proponents claim that with sufficient deployment, P2P could largely overcome congestion problems.

Traffic management techniques affect not only high-speed, high-money content, but by extension all other content too. You can only build a high-speed lane on a motorway by creating inequality, and often those 'improvement works' slow down everyone currently using the roads. The internet may be different in that regulators and users may tolerate much more discrimination in the interests of innovation. To make this decision on an informed basis, it is in the public interest to investigate transparently both net neutrality 'lite' (the slow lanes) and net neutrality 'heavy' (what rules allow higher speed content). For instance, in the absence of regulatory oversight, ISPs could use DPI to block some content altogether, if they decide it is not to the benefit of ISPs, copyright holders, parents or the government. ISP blocking is currently widespread in controlling spam email, and in some countries in blocking sexually graphic illegal images.

One of the main claims by ISPs wishing to traffic manage the internet is that internet traffic growth is unmanageable by traditional means of expansion of bandwidth and that therefore their practices are reasonable. In order to properly research this claim, regulators need access to ISP traffic measurement data. There are several possible means of accessing data at Internet Exchange points, but much data is private either because it is between two peers who do not use an exchange, or because it is carried by a CDN. The delays to the network may make it unreliable for video gaming or VOIP (Thinkbroadband 2009): 'users received on average 24% of the maximum "up to" headline speeds advertised ... During peak hours (6 pm to midnight) speeds dipped by approximately 20% ... Ping times, an important metric for online game playing came in at around 150 ms which is too high for acceptable gaming performance.' Regulators are beginning to engage with measurement companies to analyse real consumer traffic (for instance in the UK and US regulators have employed SamKnows to conduct wide-ranging measurement trial, while Akamai and Cisco issue quarterly 'state of the internet' traffic aggregation studies), and more research into the reality of the consumer broadband experience is much needed.

Rural Digital Divide

The upgrading of consumer internet connections from copper to fibre broadband is a gradual process, with urban areas and new build/multi-occupier households faster and cheaper to upgrade than rural areas and older as well as single-dwelling properties. This partially explains the rapid deployment of fibre in capital cities such as Stockholm and Paris, as well as Tokyo, Hong Kong, Taipei and Seoul (Marsden 2010a, pp. 56–58). Even in these early adopter nations, the deployment of fibre outside urban areas, and especially in areas with no cable networks, is patchy. Countries with high cable build such as South Korea, the Netherlands, Germany and the United States should achieve urban and suburban roll-out rapidly. There will remain a prominent policy question regarding rural and semi-rural access to high-speed broadband, as a copper telephone line with more than 3km distance to a local exchange will not achieve high speeds with ADSL, ADSL2 and ADSL2+ technologies (the theoretical maximum at 3km on a perfect copper line is 8Mb/s with all three technologies). Therefore, rural households will depend on a combination of satellite and mobile technologies, though the possibility of higher performance remains theoretical.

These rural households may therefore prove the most resistant to significant breaches of network neutrality for basic services such as Skype, and empirical research is needed into the types of service held most valuable by these households. The Netherlands and United States evidence is that it is services which offer price competition to the vertically bundled products of the ISP, notably voice and text services, which are most valued by customers. As higher speed services develop, more than price discrimination may distinguish ISP from other services, and research into consumer revealed preference is needed (Marsden et al. 2006). Finland in 2010 offered a guarantee of universal access to 1Mb/s broadband for all households on non-discriminatory terms by 2012, a minimum QoS guarantee backed by law, making it the world's first country to offer such minimal neutrality (Akdeniz 2011). Other countries may soon follow, and Australia is building a wholesale fibre to the home network, supplemented by rural satellite which will offer much higher speed universal service, though conditions of retail access remain to be negotiated. However, the more common current response by most developed countries is to seek voluntary agreement on consumer transparency and degrees of traffic management to be permitted.

REGULATION AND LAW OF NET NEUTRALITY

In this section, I focus on net neutrality regulation and law in the European Union, as the United States has announced regulatory action, but its legal status is likely to be the subject of continued uncertainty, whereas Europe passed minimal net neutrality legislation in 2009, which had to be implemented by member states by May 2011.

Although net neutrality was the subject of FCC regulatory discussions and merger conditions from 2003 (Frieden 2010b, 2011), its status was unsure at the start of 2013 with no legislation passed by Congress, and FCC actions reserved to isolated examples of discrimination that were to be litigated early in that year. President Obama was committed to net neutrality regulation from his Senate career in 2006 (Marsden 2010a, p.1). A Notice of Proposed Rule Making (NPRM) by the FCC extended a consultation on net neutrality over 2009–10. This process was finishing just as the Court of Appeal in April 2010 judged that the FCC's regulatory actions in this area were not justified by its reasoning under the Communications Act 1996 (Ammori 2010; *Comcast v. FCC* (2010)). The successful *Comcast* appeal meant that the FCC had three legal choices: reclaim Title II common carrier authority for ISPs under the 1996 Telecommunications Act, ask Congress to re-legislate to grant it Title I authority, or try to assert its own Title I authority subject to legal challenge (Marsden 2010a). It adopted this last course in its Order of 23 December 2010 (FCC 2010), which was published in 2011 and is to be challenged before the courts with a hearing in 2013 (Frieden 2011, pp.6–15; Marsden 2010b; Donahue 2010).

The European institutions in late 2009 agreed to impose transparency and net neutrality 'lite' conditions on ISPs, in directives that had to be implemented in national law by May 2011. BEREC (2010) note that legal provisions in the Directives permit greater 'symmetric' regulation on all operators, not simply dominant actors, but ask for clarification on these measures: 'Access Directive, Art 5(1) now explicitly mentions that NRAs are able to impose obligations "on undertakings that control access to end-users to make their services interoperable"'. The new wider scope for solving interoperability disputes may be used:

Revised article 20 of the Framework Directive now provides for the resolution of disputes between undertakings providing electronic communications networks or services and also between such undertakings and others that benefit from obligations of access and/or interconnection (with the definition of 'access' also modified in Art 2 AD as previously stated). Dispute resolutions cannot be considered as straightforward tools for developing a regulatory policy, but they do provide the option to address some specific (maybe urgent) situations. The potential outcome of disputes based on the transparency obligations can provide a 'credible threat' for undertakings to behave in line with those obligations, since violation may trigger the imposition of minimum quality requirements on an undertaking, in line with Art 22(3) USD.

The European Commission was in 2011 consulting on the future of the Universal Service Obligation (EC 2010) which may be extended to 2Mbps broadband (impacting member state law some years later), which will mark a new 'line in the sand' in Europe for minimum service levels. That may also require commitments to offering that access to the open internet, not a throttled, blocked, walled garden area.

National Regulatory Responses

Net neutrality has been most effectively carried into legislation or regulation in Japan and the European Union, as well as Norway and Canada (where it is called ITMP: De Beer 2009).

Norway: European Economic Area (not full EU) member, Norway, dealt with net neutrality in 2008–9. A complaint first arose due to a dispute between an ISP, NextGenTel, and the Norwegian state broadcaster NRK in mid-2006 (Marsden 2010a, 172–73). The regulator in Norway persuaded the ISPs and cable companies to sign a co-regulatory pact on transparency and consumer rights in 2009. The Norwegian Code (2009) states:

- Internet users must be given complete and accurate information about the service they are buying, including capacity and quality.
- Users may send and receive content of their choice, use services and applications of their choice and connect any hardware and software that does not harm the network.
- The connection cannot be discriminated against based on application, service, content, sender or receiver.

At national level, most EU member states have been slow to recognise net neutrality problems, despite strong anecdotal evidence arising (Dunstone 2006).

Netherlands: in June 2011 the government introduced a net neutrality provision into Parliament, following controversy over KPN Mobile's intention to charge extra for VOIP and text messaging by alternative providers. The vote was postponed twice, on 14 and 21 June, and was approved by the Netherlands Senate in July 2011. It offers a basic prohibition on blocking and throttling of content, a form of net neutrality for existing services, without guidance on what may be the rules for high speed content on next generation access networks (Bits of Freedom 2011). It must be implemented from 1 January 2013.

United Kingdom: Ofcom has confined itself to measuring ISP broadband performance, and making it easier for consumers to switch to rival providers (Kiedrowski 2007), and carrying out research on the levels of speed and latterly service quality that consumers receive. The government itself has tried to encourage some form of self-regulation by industry for minimal consumer information provision (see section 'Transparency and "Reasonable Traffic Management" below).

Canada: Net neutrality is politically controversial in Canada, where a celebrated breach took place in 2005 (De Beer 2009). The regulator announced an evidence-based inquiry into net neutrality held in 2009. As a result, new principles of transparency and non-discrimination were declared; these await cases and regulatory decisions in which to add detail to the broad declarations (Geist 2011a). Bandwidth caps have been the subject of extensive regulatory hearings and political controversy in 2011 in Canada, and these are discussed in the next section.

Bandwidth Caps

Usage based billing (UBB), to use the Canadian expression, is not new in internet policy, being the default in most countries prior to the introduction of broadband modems in the late 1990s. Only in countries with unmetered local calls, such as Canada and the United States, was internet use 'all you can eat' (Oftel 2000). UBB became a headline issue in 2010 in both the United States and Canada. Different practices have been identified by Geist (2011a). With the introduction of broadband cable in Canada, its regulator the Canadian Radio-television and Telecommunications Commission (CRTC) permitted UBB with monthly download caps on users. This was justified by the shared resource used by cable modem subscribers in the local loop. The CRTC (2011) reiterated its permission for UBB, justified by reference to its responsibilities to ensure competition under Section 7 of the Telecommunications Act 1993. Comcast in the US created a 250GB cap (Burstein 2008), which was considered more transparent than its previous usage of DPI and other techniques led by its subcontractor Sandvine to prevent Peer-to-Peer transfers.

Most UBB relates to maximum download capacity, and is assessed independently of the maximum download speeds which users can receive, the latter being the 'headline rates' that are generally used in broadband advertising to consumers. OECD (2008) shows that of 215 broadband packages sampled, almost half would result in users exceeding their monthly caps within three hours at advertised maximum speeds. OECD (2010) shows that while two countries (Japan, South Korea) have replaced almost half of their copper lines with fibre, the vast majority are still copper-based. There is wide variation in practices between countries, though comparisons are difficult to put into context (Bauer 2010). Countries which were bottom of the OECD tables for bandwidth provision in 2008, Australia and New Zealand have adopted the radical step of commissioning a national fibre local loop to replace their incumbent telephony monopoly. Public intervention is by no means a taboo in broadband investment, and the European Commission has repeatedly approved all non-urban public investment in fibre deployments proposed by member states. Broadband is not an investment to be left wholly to the private sector, and investment incentives such as permitting UBB will not of themselves ensure national fibre to the premises.

The deployment of fibre to the local exchange is in itself no major current constraint on capacity: it is the backhaul cost from the telephone exchange to the internet that is the constraint here (and in future, the cost of fibre from exchange closer to the customer). All broadband users share the backhaul capacity from the local exchange to the internet, capacity which must be bought wholesale from the incumbent in most cases. Therefore, incumbents can control the capacity available to competitive ISPs. Burstein (2011) has stated his belief that current caps are designed to prevent 'over-the-top' (OTT) video to be delivered via broadband, competing with the triple-play offers of ISPs which want subscribers to pay for a telephone line, broadband service and cable or internet delivered video programming. OTT video would compete with the last of these services, and degrading or capping the broadband service can protect the incumbent's video service. Burstein estimates the backhaul costs to ISPs as under $1/month, whereas Ofcom (2006) estimated the costs of backhaul for BBC's iPlayer video catch-up service to UK ISPs as in the order of £4–5/ month. Prices have fallen rapidly with increases in transmission efficiency in that period (Moore's Law alone will have decreased prices by 75 per cent over five years). Much more research is needed into backhaul costs and other constraints on UBB.

Transparency and 'Reasonable Traffic Management'

One of the several principles of network neutrality promulgated by both the FCC and European Commission is that only 'reasonable network management' be permitted, and that the end-user be informed of this reasonableness via clear information (Faulhaber 2010). Both the FCC in the US and the European Commission have relied on non-binding declarations to make clear their intention to regulate the 'reasonableness' of traffic management practices. In Canada, the CRTC has relied on inquiries to the dissatisfaction of advocates, while in Norway and Japan non-binding self-regulatory declarations have been thus far non-enforced.

Transparency is a work in progress, and best regulatory information practices have yet to emerge – without such practices, any commitment to net neutrality is specious. Faulhaber (2010) has suggested four basic principles based on examination of other industries' information regulation: '1) disclose all information relevant to customer choice, 2) to which customers have easy access, 3) clearly and simply, and 4) in a way that is verifiable'. He argues that Comcast would not have been reprimanded by the FCC had its traffic management been more transparent. I suggest a fifth principle: information should be cross-compared by an accredited independent third party that is not reliant on broadband industry funding, such as a consumer protection agency. This could be carried out at arm's length via a self- or co-regulatory agreement.

From May 2011, both European regulators and the European Commission have begun to attempt to define 'reasonable traffic management' for the purposes of the European law on internet traffic. This is likely to produce more robust guidelines for both ISPs and consumers (Sluijs 2010), with a BEREC work group which reported in 2012. The European law was in 2009 amended to include the following:

> 19. Transparency obligations on public communications network providers providing electronic communications services available to the public to ensure end-to-end connectivity, . . . disclosure regarding any conditions limiting access to and/or use of services and applications where such conditions are allowed by Member States in conformity with Community law, and, where necessary and proportionate, access by national regulatory authorities to such information needed to verify the accuracy of such disclosure.[1]

In the UK, Ofcom has tried to encourage industry self-regulation via transparency Codes of Conduct. It has also carried out measurement of ISP practices in collaboration with SamKnows, a consultancy that has also worked with the FCC. SamKnows is measuring 17 metrics over 2010–12.[2] It has worked with Ofcom since 2008, and the FCC since 2010 (with the latter it is conducting 11 tests over a three year period). US FCC-SamKnows tests with project name TestMyISP are also supported by the Measurement Lab, notably the New America Foundation. The Canadian CRTC made rules in 2009, but there is little evidence of enforcement of

CRTC principles of reasonableness, which are to be made on a case-by-case basis (Geist 2011a).

Implementing Regulation of Net Neutrality

Net neutrality regulatory solutions under the 2009 European Directives had to be implemented by May 2011. They can be classified by the 'degree of self-regulation' involved, from basic informal communication through to formal regulation. The general trend is towards an expansion of scope of co-regulation, often at the expense of statutory regulation. A wide variety of models of co-regulatory tools exist, for those actions that require coordinated or joint implementation (Marsden et al. 2008; Tambini, Leonardi, Marsden 2008). Without co-regulation responsive to constitutional protection of freedom of expression at national levels, measures cannot be self-sustaining (Marsden 2011).

In the UK, Ofcom has continually attempted since 2008 to reach a self-regulatory solution. By 2011, with the timetable for implementation of EC Directives growing near, the government-funded Broadband Stakeholder Group (BSG) produced a Code of Conduct, upon which UK government minister Vaizey indicated that Sir Tim Berners-Lee would play an oversight role (Vaizey 2011). Whether such a ramshackle arrangement satisfies the European Commission, which is legally obliged to monitor implementation, remains to be seen in the course of 2013. It is likely to first ask the 27 member states for details of their detailed implementations, before a further information request can be made which would be a prelude to a possible case for a preliminary ruling before the Court of Justice of the European Union (CJEU). Such a case would be unlikely to be heard before 2014.

In the US, implementation of the technical means for measuring reasonable traffic management are to be tested in a self-regulatory forum, though with FCC blessing, the Broadband Industry Technical Advisory Group (BITAG), under Executive Director Dale Hadfield. Its specific duties include that to offer 'safe harbor' opinions on traffic management practices by parties making formal reference for an advisory technical opinion: 'Specific TWG functions include: (i) identifying "best practices" by broadband providers and other entities; (ii) interpreting and applying "safe harbor" practices; (iii) otherwise providing technical guidance to industry and to the public; and/or (iv) issuing advisory opinions on the technical issues germane to the TWG's mission that may underlie disputes among discrete parties' (BITAG 2011, s. 7.1). BITAG has a broad multi-stakeholder constituency and is therefore far from simply an industry self-regulatory solution, but charges companies for testing of their solutions and is not currently mandated by law, therefore continuing to act as a self- rather than co-regulatory forum.[3] As a Delaware-incorporated entity with published bylaws and an antitrust policy to formally exclude government activity, BITAG is a classic self-regulatory organisation in structure. The FCC under its 2010 Order must establish a multistakeholder Open Internet Advisory Committee. US legal and policy scholars may wish to research the extent to which this offers advantages and costs in constitutional oversight and regulatory flexibility as compared with more administrative law supported bodies in Europe. Weiser has proposed that a co-regulatory mechanism be supported (Weiser 2009).

Unsurprisingly, net neutrality regulation has been fiercely resisted by the ISPs who wish to discriminate and charge non-affiliated content providers higher prices or throttle popular existing services, and its implementation has relied on a series of declarations and merger conditions prior to full implementation via regulations and legislation. Mergers afford regulators the opportunity to introduce such relatively minor adjustments as merger parties are eager to conclude the overall deal, and trade off the relatively minor inconvenience of controls on traffic management in the interests of successful approval. In the same way as consumers – even with perfect information – may not view traffic management as the primary goal of their subscription to broadband (and are thus easy targets for restrictive conditions so long as industry standards prevent real choice between ISPs), so ISPs may make strategic choices to accept some limited traffic management conditions as a price of approval. The failed 2011 merger of AT&T Wireless and T-Mobile could also illustrate the propensity to enforce net neutrality via merger conditions, as could the merger of Level 3 and Global Crossing, important Tier 1 backbone providers with extensive Content Delivery Networks.

The Special Case of Wireless or Mobile Net Neutrality?

Mobile remains a poor substitute for the fixed internet, and mobile smartphone users (the most advanced mobile users) in 2010 only downloaded an average of 79 Megabytes per month (Cisco 2011). It is misleading to use headline percentage growth to suggest there is a major congestion issue – people are finally using the internet on mobile networks via dongles and smartphones, so absolute usage is increasing slowly compared to growth. Mobile data traffic was in 2010 a total of 237 Petabytes, which Cisco states is three times greater than the entire internet in 2000. More relevant is that it was 1 per cent of the internet in 2010, a global total of 21 Exabytes. If mobile data grows twice as fast as the global internet for the next decade, it will amount to 11 per cent of the entire internet by 2020. At that point, it will become more than a statistical insignificance in global terms. Mobile claims should be met with robust scepticism as mobile is such a minute part of the entire internet traffic measured, and indeed a substantial part of mobile 'traffic' is intended in future to be handed off to femtocells, WiFi cells, and other fixed wireless infrastructure, piggybacking on the relatively stable and mature fixed internet that is expanding at approximately its historical growth rate of 50 per cent per annum to meet capacity (Cisco 2011). Mobile is a trivial proportion of overall internet traffic by volume, but commands massive premiums over fixed traffic for the services provided.

European regulators' group BEREC (2010, p. 11) explained: 'mobile network access may need the ability to limit the overall capacity consumption per user in certain circumstances (more than fixed network access with high bandwidth resources) and as this does not involve selective treatment of content it does not, in principle, raise network neutrality concerns'. They explain that though mobile will always need greater traffic management than fixed ('traffic management for mobile accesses is more challenging'), symmetrical regulation must be maintained to ensure technological neutrality: 'there are not enough arguments to support having a different approach on network neutrality in the fixed and mobile networks. And especially future-oriented approach for network neutrality should not include differentiation between different types of the networks.' BEREC (2010, p. 3) concluded that mobile should be subject to the 'net neutrality lite' provisions available under Directives EC/136/2009 and EC/140/2009, listing some breaches of neutrality: 'blocking of VoIP in mobile networks occurred in Austria, Croatia, Germany, Italy, the Netherlands, Portugal, Romania and Switzerland'.

Regulations passed in licensing mobile spectrum can affect network neutrality at a fundamental level. Interoperability requirements can form a basis for action where an ISP blocks an application. Furthermore, wireless ISPs may be required to provide open access, as in the FCC auction of 700MHz Upper Block C frequencies in 2008 (Rosston and Topper 2010, pp. 115–16), or in more general common carriage requirements traditionally imposed on public communications networks since before the dawn of modern communications, with railways and telegraphs.

The FCC specifically asked for answers to regulation of managed 'specialized' services (see the third section 'THE FUTURE: PUBLIC POLICY CONSIDERATIONS IN NET NEUTRALITY') and wireless net neutrality in 2010, and announced that they were prepared not to enforce their proposed regulation on wireless services in the near future (FCC 2010). This means that the faster growing and more competitive US market will be less regulated than the more sluggish and less competitive European market.

THE FUTURE: PUBLIC POLICY CONSIDERATIONS IN NET NEUTRALITY

Net neutrality is a more politically important issue than telecommunications regulators are legally bound to explore, as at stake are technologies of censorship (La Rue 2011). BEREC (2010, p. 20) explains:

> Freedom of expression and citizens rights, as well as media pluralism and cultural diversity, are important values of the modern society, and they are worth being protected in this context – especially since mass communication has become easier for all citizens thanks to the Internet. However intervention in respect of such considerations lies outside the competence of BEREC.

Forms of private censorship by intermediaries have been increasing throughout the last decade even as the law continues to declare those intermediaries (mainly ISPs, but increasingly also video hosting companies such as YouTube, social networks such as Facebook, and search providers such as Google) to be 'Three Wise Monkeys'. These intermediaries are not subject to liability for their customers' content under the EC/2000/31 Articles 12–14 so long as they have no actual or constructive knowledge of that content: if they 'hear no evil, see no evil and speak no evil' (Marsden 2010a, pp. 105–49). Any net neutrality solution needs to be holistic, considering ISPs' roles in the round.

DPI and other advanced traffic management techniques will permit much more granular knowledge of what an ISP's customers are downloading and uploading on the internet. ISPs could filter out both annoying and illegal content. For instance, they could 'hear' criminal conversations, such as those by terrorist sympathisers, illegal pornographers, harassers, those planning robberies, libellous commentary and so on. They could also 'see' illegal downloading of copyrighted material. They would be obliged to cooperate with law enforcement or even copyright industries in these scenarios, and this could create even greater difficulties where that speech was legal in one country but illegal where it was received (Deibert et al. 2010). Net neutrality is therefore less unpopular with smaller ISPs that wish to avoid a legal liability morass, which Directive 2000/31/EC (E-Commerce Directive) and other national ISP non-liability 'safe harbor' [sic] laws are expressly designed to prevent.

In the discussions to amend the E-Communications Framework via Directives 2009/136/EC and 2009/140/EC, large well-resourced European incumbent ISPs saw the opportunity to make common cause with mobile operators (Wu 2007) and others, in an alliance to permit filtering. Politicians in 2013 are reviewing the E-Commerce Directive (COM 2010, pp. 10–11), having passed local laws that favour, for instance, their copyright industries, such as the Digital Economy Act 2010 in the United Kingdom or the HADOPI law in France (EC 2011), implementation of both of which is highly politically controversial. The regulation of the internet is erecting entry barriers with the connivance of the incumbent players, with potentially enormous consequences for free speech, for free competition and for individual expression (Akdeniz 2011). This may be the correct policy option for a safer internet policy (to prevent exposing children to illegal and/or offensive content), though it signals an abrupt change from the open internet (Zittrain 2008). It is therefore vital that regulators address the question of the proper 'lite' approach to net neutrality to prevent harm to the current internet, as well as beginning to address the heavier questions of positive – or tiered – breaches of network neutrality.

Privacy inquiries can also impact on regulatory control of traffic management, with the UK government taken to the door of the European Court by the European Commission for approving the both secret and invasive behavioural advertising practices of British Telecom and PHORM (Marsden 2012). The introduction of network neutrality rules into European law was under the rubric of consumer information safeguards and privacy regulation, not competition rules, and the US Congress is in 2013 actively exploring privacy rules and controls on ISP behavioural advertising activities.

The Future Development of Net Neutrality and the Internet

The future of the internet is a non-trivial issue; in fact it is central to the future of productivity in most industries. It is an enabling technology, which means that the exchange of information on this open platform promises (and delivers) real efficiencies in the economy and society generally, as it helps collaboration and improvement (Carnoy et al. 1993). It is also socially enabling 'Web 2.0' or 'the participative web' (Schrage 2000; Seely Brown and Duguid 2000). That is, it has become a virtual playground, classroom, laboratory and chat room (Palfrey and Gasser 2008; Tapscott 1999). Moreover, small businesses and solo home-based workers depend on the internet. The promise of virtual worlds and massive online collaboration is to extend this impact even further by 2020.

The 'Wealth of Networks' analysis of Benkler (2006) thinks of the internet as a giant experiment, combining laboratory with user innovation and feedback, while Boyle (2008) describes a wider movement 'Enclosing the Commons of the Mind' and Post (2009) extends a comparison with Jeffersonian America. The open internet is a commons for all to enjoy. That is the basis for claims that it should be preserved and regulation induced to prevent any more enclosure of that commons, while at the same time ensuring that the commons is not ruined by free-riders – that there is no 'Tragedy of the Commons'. The open internet is by no means the only or necessarily the most important place for public opinion to be formed, but it is the open public space that gives legitimacy to all these private or semi-private spaces.

Digital Divides and Developing Countries

The problems of development and the global Digital Divide are intimately connected to net neutrality. Internet connectivity is still very expensive for most developing countries, despite attempts to ensure local internet peering points (exchanges) and new undersea cables, for instance serving East Africa. To flood the developing world's ISPs with video traffic, much of which came from major video production countries such as India, Nigeria and of course Hollywood, could place local ISPs in serious financial peril. Casualties in such undertakings include, for instance, countries blacklisted by major ISPs for producing large amounts of spam: Nigerian consumers have previously discovered that their email was blocked because the ISP was also used by spammers.

The second development problem that net neutrality debate centres on is the wireless or mobile internet. Most developing countries' citizens have much lower bandwidth than the West, and most of their connectivity is mobile: India is probably the poster child for a country with at least ten times more mobile than fixed phone subscribers. In the next several years, the developing world internet user will test the limits of mobile networks, and capacity as well as price might determine the extent to which they can expect a rapidly developing or a Third World internet experience. I flag up development issues because they are critical. Universal service is still a pipe dream for many in the developing world, and when that arrives, the definition it is given will determine the minimum threshold that ISPs have to achieve. As Mueller (2007, p. 7) states, net neutrality 'must also encompass a positive assertion of the broader social, economic and political value of universal and non-discriminatory access to Internet resources among those connected to the Internet'.

The types of non-net neutrality employed in West Asia/North Africa in winter 2010–11 were politically rather than economically motivated, that is, political censorship designed to prevent citizens' access to the internet. Mueller (2007, p. 8) argues that the tendency of governments in both repressive and traditionally democratic regimes to impose liability on ISPs to censor content for a plethora of reasons argues for a policy of robust non-interference. That is especially valuable in countries where there is much less discussion of how government deployment of ISPs as censors can endanger user privacy and freedom of expression. Mueller suggests that the net neutrality metaphor could be used to hold all filtering and censorship practices up to the light, as well as other areas of internet regulation, such as domain name governance. Network neutrality has become an important policy issue discussed at the United Nations Internet Governance Forum (IGF). The IGF discussion of net neutrality has substantially increased (IGF 2008, 2009), and was a cause of much controversy in the renegotiation of the International Telecommunications Regulations in Dubai in December 2012.

We may expect to see more protest behaviour by 'netizens' who do not agree with net neutrality policies, especially where ISPs are seen to have failed to inform end-users fully about the implications of policy changes. Regulators and politicians are challenged publicly by such problems, particularly given the ubiquity of email, Twitter and social media protests against censorship, and there are two Pirate Party MEPs elected to the European Parliament. Research into social activism against corporate control of the internet is a growing research field (Hart 2011).

Internet Interconnection, CDNs and 'Managed Services'

It is not only in the last mile or in the consumer's ISP that net neutrality may be affected by policy decisions to differentiate between traffic. Much work has previously disclosed that internet peering has been largely replaced by paid interconnection (Faratin et al. 2008), and in 2010 a dispute between Comcast and Level 3 was claimed by the latter party to involve a net neutrality dispute disguised as an interconnection dispute (a European dispute between Orange and Cogent in connection with Megavideo traffic involved similar claims). The timing of the dispute as Comcast was bidding to buy the television network NBC caused some suspicion that Level 3 was leveraging the political pressure on Comcast at a critical stage of the merger review. There have also been claims that Comcast may leverage its internet access business to stream NBC programming at a discount to non-affiliated programming, which led to a specific merger condition prohibiting such differentiation. A recent dispute in Canada regarding the conduct of Shaw Communications, a west coast ISP, has revived these concerns, as the company appeared to indicate that its online movie subscribers would not exceed bandwidth caps with its affiliated service as opposed to competitors such as NetFlix. Shaw put out a statement explaining that the initial marketing material was in error, and that internet streaming of its own service would contribute to the bandwidth cap, but a dedicated cable-only service would not, much as the AT&T uVerse uses the same physical fibre to deliver video service and data service, the former as 'managed services', the latter as non-managed IP (Anderson 2011). The difficulty for the regulators will be to identify which data is a managed service and which is the straightforward IP stream.

Further questions for regulators will include whether ISPs can provide CDN services to content providers in competition with third party CDNs. CDNs such as Akamai provide a 'virtual' ISP access service by locally caching content for content customers close to the local telephone exchange, by investing in tens of thousands of servers distributed across networks and geographies. This is sometimes described as OTT (over the top) video service. Google has built a very large proprietary CDN for its own traffic, notably its video YouTube service, and other large content carriers such as the BBC and Facebook may follow suit. A further question arises, as these CDNs are almost entirely downloading content to customers rather than acting as peers, and therefore creating a very large traffic imbalance. As a result, we can expect to see paid interconnection increasing, and peering decrease (Marsden 2010a, pp. 95–114).

It should be stressed that current telecommunications laws typically allow for disputes between public carriers, which essentially means ISPs. Search engines, video hosting sites and CDNs are not public carriers, but private carriers, and therefore their relations with ISPs are regulated by contract law rather than regulators, with the latter having no legislative mandate to affect those private parties' relations. Calls for search neutrality or regulation of CDNs may therefore be effective lobbying discussion, but do not relate to telecoms regulation as currently constituted (Frieden 2011).

CONCLUSIONS: FUTURE POLICY RESEARCH

The internet's evolution is dynamic and complex. The availability and design of a suitable regulatory response must reflect this dynamism, and also the responsiveness of regulators and market players to each other. Therefore, national legislation should be future proof and avoid being overly prescriptive, to avoid a premature response to the emerging environment. The pace of change in the relation between architecture and content on the internet requires continuous improvement in the regulator's research and technological training. Regulators can monitor both commercial transactions and traffic shaping by ISPs to detect potentially abusive discrimination. An ex ante requirement to demonstrate internal network metrics to content provider customers and consumers may be a practical solution, via a regulatory or co-regulatory reporting requirement. The need for better research towards understanding the nature of congestion problems on the internet and their effect on content and innovation is clear (Marsden et al. 2008). These conclusions support a light-touch regulatory regime involving reporting requirements and co-regulation with, as far as is possible, market-based solutions. Solutions may be international as well as local, and international coordination of best practice and knowledge will enable national regulators to keep up with the technology 'arms race'.

The European legal basis for regulatory intervention is an enabling framework to prevent competition abuses and prevent discrimination, under which national regulators need the skills and evidence base to investigate unjustified discrimination. Regulators expecting a 'smoking gun' to present itself should be advised against such a reactive approach. A more proactive approach to monitoring and researching non-neutral behaviours will make network operators much more cognisant of their duties and obligations. A consumer- and citizen-orientated intervention depends on preventing unregulated non-transparent controls exerted over traffic, whether imposed by ISPs for financial advantage or by governments eager to use this new technology to filter, censor and enforce copyright against their citizens. Unravelling the previous ISP limited liability regime risks removing the efficiency of that approach in permitting the free flow of information for economic and social advantage.

NOTES

1. Annex to Directive 2002/20/EC Authorisation Directive by Directive 2009/140/EC at OJ L337/68 18 December 2009.
2. For more details and methodology, see http://www.samknows.com/broadband/ofcom_and_samknows for Ofcom and https://www.testmyisp.com/faq.html for the FCC tests.
3. For details see http://members.bitag.org/kwspub/BITAG_Membership/.

BIBLIOGRAPHY

Akdeniz, Y. (2011), 'Study on legal provisions and practices related to freedom of expression, the free flow of information and media pluralism on the Internet, Organisation for Security and Cooperation in Europe', http://www.osce.org/fom/80723, accessed 23 July 2011.
Ammori, M. (2010), 'How I lost the big one bigtime', http://ammori.org/2010/04/07/how-i-lost-the-big-one-bigtime/, accessed 23 July 2011.
Anderson N. (2011), '"Very bold or very dumb": data caps don't apply to ISP's own movie service (updated)', *Ars Technica*, July 15, http://arstechnica.com/tech-policy/news/2011/07/very-bold-or-very-dumb-data-caps-dont-apply-to-isps-own-movie-service.ars, accessed 23 July 2011.

Ayres, I. and J. Braithwaite (1992), *Responsive Regulation: Transcending the Deregulation Debate*, Hartford, CT: Yale University Press.

Bauer, J.M. (2010), 'Learning from Each Other: Promises and Pitfalls of Benchmarking in Communications Policy', *Info*, **12:6**, 8–20.

Benkler, Y. (1998a), 'Communications Infrastructure Regulation and the Distribution of Control over Content', *Telecommunications Policy*, **22:3**, 183–96, http://www.benkler.org/PolTech.pdf, accessed 23 July 2011.

Benkler, Y. (1998b), 'Overcoming Agoraphobia: Building the Commons of the Digitally Networked Environment', *Harvard Journal of Law and Technology*, 11, 287–400, http://www.law.nyu.edu/benklery/agoraphobia.pdf, accessed 23 July 2011.

Benkler, Y. (2006), *The Wealth of Networks: How Social Production Transforms Markets and Freedom*, New Haven, CT and London: Yale University Press.

BEREC (2010), '42 BEREC Response to the European Commission's consultation on the open Internet and net neutrality in Europe', http://www.erg.eu.int/doc/berec/bor_10_42.pdf, accessed 23 July 2011.

Berners-Lee, T. (2006), 'Net neutrality: This is serious', http://dig.csail.mit.edu/breadcrumbs/node/144, accessed 23 July 2011

BITAG (2011), 'By-laws of Broadband Industry Technical Advisory Group', http://members.bitag.org/kwspub/background_docs/BITAG_Bylaws.pdf, accessed 23 July 2011.

Bits of Freedom (2011), 'Netherlands launches internet freedom legislation', https://www.bof.nl/2011/06/22/netherlands-launches-internet-freedom-legislation/, accessed 23 July 2011.

Boyle, J. (2008), *The Public Domain: Enclosing the Commons of the Mind*, New Haven, CT: Yale University Press.

Burstein, D. (2008), 'Comcast's Fair 250 Gig Bandwidth Cap', http://www.dslprime.com/docsisreport/163-c/53-comcasts-fair-250-gig-bandwidth-cap, accessed 23 July 2011.

Burstein, D. (2011), 'Wireline costs and caps: A few facts', http://www.dslprime.com/dslprime/42-d/4148-costs-and-caps, accessed 23 July 2011.

Carnoy, M., M. Castells, S.S. Cohen and F.H. Cardoso (1993), *The New Global Economy in the Information Age; Reflections on Our Changing World*, New York: Macmillan.

Cave, M., R. Collins, N. van Eijk, P. Larouche, L. Prosperetti, A. de Streel, et al. (2009), 'Statement by European Academics on the Inappropriateness of Imposing Increased Internet Regulation in the EU', 8 January 2009, http://papers.ssrn.com/sol3/papers.cfm?abstract_id=1329926, accessed 23 July 2011.

Cherry, B.A. (2006), 'Misusing Network Neutrality to Eliminate Common Carriage Threatens Free Speech and the Postal System', *Northern Kentucky Law Review*, **33**, 483.

Cherry, B. (2008), 'Back to the Future: How Transportation Deregulatory Policies Foreshadow Evolution of Communications Policies', *Information Society*, **24:5**, 273–91.

Cisco (2011), 'Visual Networking Index (VNI) Global Mobile Data Traffic Forecast', http://www.cisco.com/en/US/solutions/collateral/ns341/ns525/ns537/ns705/ns827/white_paper_c11-520862.html, accessed 23 July 2011.

Clark, D. (1988), 'The Design Philosophy of the DARPA Internet Protocols', *Computer Communications Review*, **18:4**, August, 106–14.

Clark, D.D. and M.S. Blumenthal (2011), 'The End-to-End Argument and Application Design: The Role of Trust', *Federal Communications Law Journal*, **63:2**, 357–90.

COM (2010), '245: A Digital Agenda for Europe', European Commission, Brussels, http://ec.europa.eu/information_society/digital-agenda/documents/digital-agenda-communication-en.pdf, accessed 23 July 2011.

Crowcroft, J. (2011), 'The Affordance of Asymmetry or a Rendezvous with the Random?', *Communications and Convergence Review*, **3:1**, 40–56.

Croxford, I. and C. Marsden (2001), *WLAN Standards and Regulation in Europe*, London: Re:Think!

CRTC (2011), 'Telecoms Decision 2011-44, Usage-based billing for Gateway Access Services and third-party Internet access services', Ottawa, 25 January 2011, File number: 8661-C12-201015975, http://www.crtc.gc.ca/eng/archive/2011/2011-44.htm, accessed 23 July 2011.

De Beer, J. (2009), 'Net Neutrality in the Great White North (and its Impact on Canadian Culture)', *Telecommunications Journal of Australia*, **59:2**, 24.1–24.19.

De Sola Pool, I. (1983), *Technologies of Freedom*, Cambridge, MA: Belknap.

Deibert, R.J., J.G. Palfrey, R. Rohozinski and J. Zittrain (eds) (2010), *Access Controlled: The Shaping of Power, Rights, and Rule in Cyberspace*, Cambridge, MA: MIT Press.

Donahue, H. (2010), 'The Network Neutrality Inquiry', *Info*, **12:2**, 3–8.

Dunstone, C. (2006), 'Presentation by Carphone Warehouse/TalkTalk CEO at the 2006 Ofcom conference', http://www.ofcom.org.uk/event/2006conference/presentations/sessi on3, accessed 23 July 2011.

EC (2010), 'Consultation on the Future of the Universal Service Obligation', http://ec.europa. eu/information_society/policy/ecomm/library/public_consult/univeuniv_service_2010/ index_en.htm, accessed 23 July 2011.

EC (2011), 'Synthesis Of The Comments On The Commission Report On The Application Of Directive 2004/48/EC Of The European Parliament And The Council Of 29 April 2004 On The Enforcement Of Intellectual Property Rights (COM/2010/779 final) of July 2011', http://ec.europa.eu/internal_market/consultations/docs/2011/intellectual_property_rights/ summary_report_replies_consultation_en.pdf, accessed 23 July 2011.

Economides, N. and J. Tåg (2007), 'Net Neutrality on the Internet: A Two-Sided Market Analysis', *Working Paper*, NYU Center for Law and Economics, New York.

European Union (EU) (2003), 'Inter Institutional Agreement', http://eur-lex.europa.eu/ LexUriServ/LexUriServ.do?uri=OJ:C:2003:321:0001:0005:EN:PDF accessed, 23 July 2011.

Faratin, P., D.D. Clark, S. Bauer, W. Lehr, P.Q. Gilmore and A. Berger (2008), 'The Growing Complexity of Internet Interconnection', *Communications & Strategies*, **72**, 51, http://ssrn.com/abstract=1374285, accessed 23 July 2011.

Faulhaber G.R. (2002), 'Network Effects and Merger Analysis: Instant Messaging and the AOL–Time Warner Case', *Telecommunications Policy*, **25:5–6**, 311–33.

Faulhaber G.R. (2010), 'Transparency and Broadband Internet Service Providers', *International Journal of Communication*, **4**, 738–57.

FCC (2005), 'Appropriate Framework for Broadband Access to the Internet Over Wireline Facilities et al., Policy Statement', FCC, **20**, Rcd 14986.

FCC (2010), 'In the Matter of Preserving the Open Internet Broadband Industry Practices', GN Docket No. 09-191 WC Docket No. 07-52, REPORT AND ORDER, adopted: 21 December 2010.

Frieden, R. (2010a), *Winning the Silicon Sweepstakes: Can the United States Compete in Global Telecommunications?*, Hartford, CT: Yale University Press.

Frieden, R. (2010b), 'Invoking and Avoiding the First Amendment: How Internet Service Providers Leverage Their Status as Both Content Creators and Neutral Conduits', *University of Pennsylvania Journal of Constitutional Law*, **12**, 1279.

Frieden, R. (2011), 'A Layered and Nuanced Assessment of Network Neutrality Rationales, Tilburg TILEC Workshop on Law and Economics', http://www.tilburguniversity.edu/ research/institutes-and-research-groups/tilec/pdfs/events/20-21june2011/paper-robert-frieden.pdf, accessed 23 July 2011.

Gaines, S.E. and C. Kimber (2001), 'Redirecting Self-Regulation', *Environmental Law*, **13:2**, 157–84.

Geist, M. (2011a), 'Unpacking the Policy Issues Behind Bandwidth Caps & Usage Based Billing', http://www.michaelgeist.ca/content/view/5611/99999/, accessed 23 July 2011.

Geist, M. (2011b), 'Canada's Usage Based Billing Controversy: How to Address the Wholesale and Retail Issues,' http://www.michaelgeist.ca/component/option,com_ docman/task,doc_download/gid,53/, accessed 23 July 2011.

Harris, S. and E. Gerich, 'The NSFNET Backbone Service: Chronicling the End of an Era', *Connexions*, **10**, (April 1996), http://www.merit.edu/networkresearch/projecthistory/ nsfnet/nsfnet_article.php, accessed 23 July 2011.

Hart, J.A. (2011), 'The Net Neutrality Debate in the United States', *Journal of Information Technology & Politics*, **1**, 1.

Haßlinger, G., G. Nunzi, C. Meirosu, C. Fan, and F. Andersen (2011), 'Traffic Engineering Supported by Inherent Network Management: Analysis of Resource Efficiency and Cost Saving Potential', *International Journal of Network Management*, **2:25**, DOI: 10.1002/ nem.770.

Internet Governance Forum (IGF) (2008), 'Network Neutrality: Examining the Issues and Implications for Development', Co-hosted Workshop, 4 December, http://www.intgovfo rum.org/cms/index.php/2008-igf-hyderabad/event-reports/72-workshops/370-workshop-58 -network-neutrality-examining-the-issues-and-implications-for-development, accessed 23 July 2011.

Internet Governance Forum (IGF) (2009), 'Programme, Format and Schedule for the 2009 Meeting, Revision of 4 June 2009', http://www.intgovforum.org/cms/2009/postings/ ProgrammePaper.04.06.2009.rtf, accessed 23 July 2011.

Kiedrowski, T. (2007), 'Net Neutrality: Ofcom's View', http://www.wwww.radioauthority. org.uk/media/speeches/2007/02/net_neutrality, accessed 23 July 2011.

La Rue, F. (2011), 'Report of the Special Rapporteur on the promotion and protection of the right to freedom of opinion and expression', Human Rights Council Seventeenth Session Agenda item 3, A/HRC/17/27 of 17 May 2011, http://www2.ohchr.org/english/bodies/ hrcouncil/docs/17session/A.HRC.17.27_en.pdf, accessed 23 July 2011.

Labovitz, C., et al. (2009), 'ATLAS Internet Observatory Annual Report, and their presenta- tion to the North American Network Operators Group', http://www.nanog.org/meetings/ nanog47/presentations/Monday/Labovitz_ObserveReport_N47_Mon.pdf, accessed 23 July 2011.

Lemley, M.A. and L. Lessig (1999), 'Ex Parte Declaration of Professor Mark A. Lemley and Professor Lawrence Lessig in the Matter of: Application for Consent to the Transfer of Control of Licenses of MediaOne Group, Inc. to AT&T Corp, CS Docket No. 99-251, Before the Federal Communications Commission'.

Lemley, M.A. and D. McGowan (1998), 'Legal Implications of Network Economic Effects', *California Law Review*, **86**, 479–611.

Lessig, L. (1999a), *Code and Other Laws of Cyberspace*, New York: Basic Books.

Lessig, L. (1999b), 'The Limits in Open Code: Regulatory Standards and the Future of the Net', *Berkeley Technology Law Journal*, **14:2**, 759–70.

Lessig, L. and Wu, T. (2003), 'Letter to the FCC Ex parte', 22 August 2003, http://www. timwu.org/wu_lessig_, accessed 23 July 2011.

Malik, O. (2010), 'Nov. 7: U.S. Mobile Data Traffic to Top 1 Exabyte', http://gigaom. com/2010/11/07/in-2010-us-mobile-data-traffic-to-top-1-exabyte/.

Marsden, C. (2001), 'The Start of End-to-End? Internet Protocol Television', *Intermedia*, **29**, 4–8.

Marsden, C. (2010a), *Net Neutrality: Towards a Co-regulatory Solution*, London: Bloomsbury Academic.

Marsden, C. (2010b), 'Appeals Court Demolishes FCC Legal Argument for Ancillary Jurisdiction without Title I Argument in Comcast', http://chrismarsden.blogspot. com/2010/04/appeals-court-demolishes-fcc-legal.html.

Marsden, C. (2011), *Internet Co-regulation: European Law and Regulatory Legitimacy in Cyberspace*, Cambridge: Cambridge University Press at http://www.cambridge.org/gb/ knowledge/isbn/item6445008/?site_locale=en_GB, accessed 23 July 2011.

Marsden, C. (2012), 'Regulating Intermediary Liability and Network Neutrality', Chapter 15 in Ian Walden (ed.), *Telecommunications Law and Regulation*, 4th edn, Oxford: Oxford University Press, pp. 701–50.

Marsden, C., J. Cave, et al. (2006), 'Assessing Indirect Impacts of the EC Proposals for Video Regulation', TR-414, Ofcom, Santa Monica, CA: RAND.

Marsden, C., S. Simmons, I. Brown, L. Woods, A. Peake, N. Robinson et al. (2008), 'Options for and Effectiveness of Internet Self- and Co-regulation Phase 2: Case Study Report', 15 January 2008, prepared for European Commission from, http://ssrn.com/ abstract=1281374, accessed 23 July 2011.

Mayer-Schonberger, V. (2008), 'Demystifying Lessig', *Wisconsin Law Review*, **4**, 713–46.

Meisel, J.P. (2010), 'Trinko and Mandated Access to the Internet', *info*, **12:2**, 9–27.

MINTS (2007), 'Methodology', http://www.dtc.umn.edu/mints/methodology.html, accessed 23 July 2011.

MINTS (2009), 'MINTS pages updated, many new reports, further slight slowdown in wireline traffic growth rate', http://www.dtc.umn.edu/mints/news/news_22.html, accessed 23 July 2011.

Mueller, M. (1998), *Universal Service: Competition, Interconnection, and Monopoly in the Making*, Washington, DC: AEI Press.

Mueller, M. (2007), 'Net Neutrality as Global Principle for Internet Governance', *Internet Governance Project Paper*, IGP07-003, http://internetgovernance.org/pdf/NetNeutralityGlobalPrinciple.pdf, accessed 23 July 2011.

Noam, E.M. (1994), 'Beyond Liberalization II: The Impending Doom of Common Carriage', *Telecommunications Policy*, **18:6**, 435452.

Noam, E.M. (2008), 'Beyond Net Neutrality: Enduser Sovereignty', *Columbia University Draft Paper for 34th Telecoms Policy Research Conference*, 14 August.

Norwegian Code (2009), 'Guidelines for Net Neutrality', http://www.npt.no/iKnowBase/Content/109604/Guidelines%20for%20network%20neutrality.pdf, accessed 23 July 2011.

Odlyzko, A. and D. Levinson (2007), 'Too expensive to meter: The influence of transaction costs in transportation and communication', http://www.dtc.umn.edu/~odlyzko/doc/meteringexpensive.pdf, accessed 23 July 2011.

OECD (2008), 'OECD Broadband Portal, Table 5(m): Time to reach bit/data caps at advertised speeds', http://www.oecd.org/dataoecd/11/15/39575302.xls, accessed 23 July 2011.

OECD (2010), 'OECD Broadband Portal, Table 11: Percentage of fibre connections in total broadband among countries reporting fibre subscribers', http://www.oecd.org/dataoecd/21/58/39574845.xls, accessed 23 July 2011.

Ofcom (2006), 'Market Impact Assessment: BBC new on-demand video proposals', http://stakeholders.ofcom.org.uk/market-data-research/tv-research/bbc-mias/ondemand/bbc-ondemand/, accessed 23 July 2011.

Oftel (2000), 'Draft Direction under Condition 45 of the Public Telecommunications Licence granted to British Telecommunications plc of a dispute between BT and MCI Worldcom concerning the provision of a Flat Rate Internet Access Call Origination product (FRIACO)', http://www.ofcom.org.uk/static/archive/oftel/publications/internet/fria0400.htm, accessed 23 July 2011.

Palfrey, J. and U. Gasser (2008), *Born Digital: Understanding the First Generation of Digital Natives*, New York: Basic Books.

Post, D. (2009), *In Search of Jefferson's Moose: Notes on the State of Cyberspace*, New York: Oxford University Press.

Reidenberg, J. (2005), 'Technology and Internet Jurisdiction', *University of Pennsylvania Law Review*, **153**, 1951.

Renda, A. (2008), 'I Own the Pipes, You Call the Tune: The Net Neutrality Debate and its (Ir)relevance for Europe', CEPS Special Reports, Centre for European Policy Studies, Brussels.

Rooney, B. (2011), 'Net Neutrality Debate in Europe Is "Over"', http://blogs.wsj.com/tech-europe/2011/02/28/net-neutrality-debate-in-europe-is-over/?mod=google_news_blog, accessed 23 July 2011.

Rosston, G.I. and M.D. Topper (2010), 'An Anti-trust Analysis of the Case for Wireless Net Neutrality', *Information Economics and Policy*, **22:10**, 103–19.

Saltzer, J.H., D. Reed and D. Clark (1981), 'End to End Arguments in System Design', Second International Conf. on Distributed Computing Systems, 509–12.

Schrage, M. (2000), 'The Debriefing: John Seely Brown', *Wired*, August, S.8.08.

Seely Brown, J. and P. Duguid (2000), *The Social Life of Information*, Cambridge, MA: Harvard Business School Press.

Sluijs, J.P. (2010), 'Network Neutrality between False Positives and False Negatives:

Introducing a European Approach to American Broadband Markets', *Federal Communications Law Journal*, **62**, 77.

Spar, D. (2001), *Pirates, Prophets and Pioneers: Business and Politics along the Technological Frontier*, London: Random House.

Tambini, D., D. Leonardi and C. Marsden (2008), *Codifying Cyberspace: Communications Self-Regulation in the Age of Internet Convergence*, London: Routledge.

Tapscott, D. (1999), *Growing Up Digital: The Rise of the Net Generation*, New York: McGraw Hill.

Teubner, G. (1986), 'The Transformation of Law in the Welfare State', G. Teubner (ed.), *Dilemmas of Law in the Welfare State*, Berlin: W. de Gruyter.

Thinkbroadband (2009), 'Average mobile broadband speed clocks in at 0.9 meg', http://www.thinkbroadband.com/news/p/2.html.

United Kingdom Parliament (2010), 'Digital Economy Act', http://www.opsi.gov.uk%2Facts%2Facts2010%2Fukpga_20100024_en_1&ei=LxwMTOCE56V4gaanIGbAQ&usg=AFQjCNH1_aWgbfrLbgPyhm8lpQDOpaa_ww&sig2=UOKxFp6oDeyxFexURnrn3A, accessed 23 July 2011.

Vaizey, E. (2011), *Hansard HC Deb*, 5 April 2011, c259WH, http://www.publications.parliament.uk/pa/cm201011/cmhansrd/cm110405/halltext/110405h0002.htm#11040557000591, accessed 23 July 2011.

Van Schewick, B. (2010), *Internet Architecture and Innovation*, Cambridge, MA: MIT Press.

Waclawsky, J.G. (2005), 'IMS 101: What You Need to Know Now', http://www.oplan.org/documents/articles/IMS_need_to_know/fss_download/file, accessed 23 July 2011.

Weiser, P. (2009), 'The Future of Internet Regulation', *University of California Davis Law Review*, **43**, 529–90.

Werbach, K. (2005), 'The Federal Computer Commission', *North Carolina Law Review*, **84**, 21.

Werbach, K. (2010), 'Off the Hook', *Cornell Law Review*, **95**, 535.

Wu, T. (2003a), 'When Code Isn't Law', *Virginia Law Review*, **89**, 679, http://papers.ssrn.com/sol3/papers.cfm?abstract_id=413201, accessed 23 July 2011.

Wu, T. (2003b), 'Network Neutrality, Broadband Discrimination', *Journal of Telecommunications and High Technology Law*, 141–72, http://ssrn.com/abstract=388863, accessed 23 July 2011.

Wu, T. (2007), 'Wireless Net Neutrality: Cellular Carterfone and Consumer Choice in Mobile Broadband', *International Journal of Communication*, **1**, 389; *Columbia Public Law Research Paper*, No. 07-154, http://papers.ssrn.com/sol3/papers.cfm?abstract_id=962027, accessed 23 July 2011.

Wu, T. (2010), *The Master Switch: The Rise and Fall of Digital Empires*, New York: Knopf.

Yoo, C. (2010), 'The Changing Patterns of Internet Usage', *Federal Communications Law Journal*, **63**, 67–90, http://www.law.indiana.edu/fclj/pubs/v63/no1/2010-Dec.-Vol.63-05_Yoo.pdf, accessed 23 July 2011.

Zittrain, J. (2008), *The Future of the Internet and How to Stop It*, New Haven, CT: Yale University Press.

Cases

Comcast v. FCC (2010), No. 08-1291, delivered 6 April 2010, http://pacer.cadc.uscourts.gov/common/opinions/201004/08-1291-1238302.pdf, accessed 23 July 2011.

18. Enhancing incentives for internet security
Michel van Eeten and Johannes M. Bauer

INTRODUCTION

The devices and software constituting the internet are maintained by numerous players with very different incentives to provide for security. Hardware and software vendors, Internet Service Providers (ISPs), application and service providers, various types of users, security service providers, as well as government and non-government actors involved in governing the internet, interact in a trans-national, multi-level system. This system is continuously attacked by players with increasingly malicious and criminal motives (OECD 2009; Hogben et al. 2011). The proliferation of new network architectures and services such as cloud computing, mobile internet, and social networks raises additional security concerns (e.g., Blumenthal 2011). Highly distributed with hierarchical elements, the internet is best described as a nested system with subsystems that are more closely connected than others. Security at the system level is an emergent property, influenced but not fully determined by security decisions of individual participants. Even at the level of individuals or organizations security is partially affected by decisions of other players. Enhancing the incentives for internet security requires a clear understanding of the factors that shape security decisions of the many players involved in the internet and of the forces that relentlessly seek to breach information security, often in pursuit of fraudulent and criminal purposes. As the struggle for acceptable information security unfolds as a technology race between attackers and defenders, designing better incentives also has to grasp the co-evolutionary dynamics of the realms of information security and cybercrime.

Information security is not easy to define and can be operationalized at different levels from individual users to nations and possibly the global internet as a whole. Not all information stored and processed in subsystems is equally sensitive. As security is costly, it is economically rational to accept a certain level of vulnerability. Furthermore, whereas protection might make sense in some cases, in others it might be more cost-effective to enhance the resilience of the system rather than reinforce its defenses. Thus, addressing information security requires a differentiated approach. Due to the interrelatedness of players in the internet ecosystem, even a differentiated approach requires considerable coordination among the many participants on the supply and demand side. Some of this coordination can and will arise from decentralized decisions, based on market and non-market relations. However, due to the unique character of information industries one cannot assume that such coordination will lead to socially desirable outcomes, in other words, that private incentives are well-aligned with broader social objectives.

To improve the governance mechanisms influencing security, a systemic understanding of their direct and indirect effects on the internet ecosystem is necessary. Ideally, this would be based on a comprehensive analysis of the security decisions of the participants in the value network and their interactions. Due to the great complexity and dynamic of the internet and its many uses, such a full model is currently beyond reach. The main goal of this chapter is therefore more modest: to assess the likely effects of existing and possible alternative forms of governance on specific classes of players and to identify measures that will likely improve the situation compared to the status quo. Given the centrality of economic considerations for information security decisions but also the behavior of attackers, the next section briefly reviews the characteristics of the internet economy that render information security such a hard problem. The following section discusses in greater detail the security incentives of key players and the final section draws conclusions for governance.

SECURITY FROM AN ECONOMIC PERSPECTIVE

Information security is the outcome of decentralized decisions of the various players in the internet ecosystem. These decisions are influenced by the incentives perceived by each player. Incentives can be defined as the economic and non-economic factors that are seen as relevant for a decision by a player. Factors that are security-enhancing will be referred to as positive incentives and those that tend to reduce security as negative incentives. Depending on how strong the positive or negative relation between a factor and security is, incentives fall on a spectrum between high-powered and low-powered. Every player is typically operating under multiple, positive and negative, high- and low-powered incentives. A set of incentives will be referred to as a governance mechanism or a governance arrangement. It may be difficult to assess the net effect of conflicting incentives theoretically. Given the multiplicity of forces and the dynamic interrelations in the internet, it will often only be possible to determine the direction of an incentive assuming that everything else remains unchanged, in other words, to assess partial effects. For example, costs of investing in security will be, other things being equal, a negative incentive (disincentive) to provide security: the higher the cost, the lower security investment.

All agents in this system, including hardware vendors, software vendors, ISPs, security service providers, and different types of users, make security decisions based on the perceived incentives. Many agents will use economic rationales when making security decisions, explicitly assessing the costs and benefits of alternative courses of action. As will be discussed in more detail in subsequent sections of this chapter, important incentives for defenders are the costs of improving security, the expected direct and indirect costs of security breaches, and the benefits of security measures. For cybercriminals, relevant economic incentives will be the cost of carrying out attacks, the expected costs of being caught, and the potential rewards from the fraudulent or criminal activity (Schipka 2007; Moore et al. 2009). Even if the choices of players are driven by non-economic motives, such as idealistic or political motives, they can be expressed in terms of costs and benefits. Agents will typically be heterogeneous, with relevant information on these issues unevenly and asymmetrically available among them. The outcomes of decentralized security decisions will depend on the degree to which the private costs and benefits deemed relevant by the each agent sufficiently well reflect the social costs and benefits. If there are deviations between private and social costs and benefits, uncoordinated decentralized security decisions will yield suboptimal overall levels of security. Forms of governance may be able to correct such deviations, either by altering incentives for individual players or by mandating certain outcomes. Research in the economics of networks helps identify conditions when decentralized decisions work and when they will not work well.

Private and Public Good Characteristics

Information security can be assessed at the level of an individual agent, an organization, the level of a sector, or the information system as a whole. For individual players, the level of information security will depend to a considerable degree on private actions such as the amount of investment in security and the procedures adopted to support it. However, in distributed systems, either at the level of organizations, an industry, or the entire internet, it also depends on the efforts of other agents. Security therefore is a hybrid good with both private as well as public good aspects. The recent literature on security management has developed criteria for private efforts designed to enhance security (e.g., Gordon and Loeb 2006). With regard to the public good aspects, characteristics that have been shown for the provision of public goods in general also hold for system-level information security (Varian 2004). The level of security that can be achieved in an information system may depend on total effort, best effort, or on the level of effort exerted by the weakest link. Using a simple game-theoretic modeling framework with two players, Varian (2004) illustrates the varied outcomes of security decisions made by decentralized agents. Compared to coordinated decisions aimed at maximizing the social optimum, several forms of market failure emerge if agents make security decisions unilaterally. These include free rider behavior and sub-optimally low efforts to provide for security. Varian's work also illustrates that the outcomes in a technology race between defenders and adversaries will depend on the relative magnitude of costs and benefits. If the benefit-cost ratio for the defender is higher than for the attacker, the latter will give up and the defender will exert minimum effort to fend off further attacks. In the opposite case, the defender will be pressed by the attacker and will have to exert maximum effort to keep security breaches at bay (Varian, 2004, p. 13). Although a variety of outcomes is possible, in general, decentralized decisions will lead to under-provision of security.

Network Effects and Externalities

In interconnected information systems many forms of interdependence between actors exist that affect the incentives to provide security. Widely recognized interdependencies are network effects and network externalities (Liebowitz and Margolis 2003). Network effects exist if the benefits and/or costs of being part of a network are influenced by the total size of the user base. In a competitive market with network effects, suppliers will try to capitalize on first-mover advantages and therefore accelerate the speed with which products and services are brought to the market. Other things equal, they may be willing to trade off speed to market for higher security (Anderson and Moore 2006). However, there are boundaries to such behavior, as firms with a reputation for poor products may not be able to capture first-mover advantages. Suppliers of hardware and software will also utilize commercial strategies to increase network effects to their advantage. For example, they may use pricing strategies, such as termination fees or bundled offers that increase customer lock-in and switching costs. They may seek alliances with providers of complementary hardware and software to further enhance network effects. The presence of network effects explains the relatively concentrated structure of many information markets. Network effects also influence the level of security threats experienced by users, as a larger installed base renders it more appealing for types of cybercrime that utilize untargeted attacks, such as fraudulent sales and phishing. Furthermore, whereas a good security record may provide advantages for firms seeking to expand their customer base, in the presence of lock-in and switching costs, these incentives will be reduced once a customer has joined the network.

Network externalities are a different type of interdependence in information systems. Whereas many types of network effects are reflected in market transactions (e.g., in discounted prices to attract new customers), network externalities remain uncompensated unless some collective measure is adopted to "internalize" them (Bauer and van Eeten 2009; OECD 2009). Because they are uncompensated, network externalities bias the incentives of agents compared to the socially optimal choice. With regard to information security, positive externalities exist if an agent's security decision reduces the security risk of other agents. For example, improved protection against malware also benefits other users, as the protected machine or device is less likely to be abused for the further dissemination of malware. Negative externalities exist if a security decision increases the security risk of another agent. For example, in the case of targeted attacks such as hacking, security improvements by one agent may result in a redirection of attacks to other agents, thus increasing their breach probability, other things equal. One key result in the economics of information security literature is that in the presence of negative security externalities, decentralized security decisions will result in overinvestment in security compared to the social optimum. In contrast, if positive externalities are present, decentralized security decisions will lead to underinvestment in security compared to the social optimum (Shim 2010).

Path Dependence

Information networks and service are highly complex systems that evolve over time in an incremental fashion. New systems and features coexist with legacy systems or aspects thereof. Technological, economic, and policy decisions made at any point in time typically constrain and shape subsequent choices, resulting in forms of path dependence (Arthur 2009). An example is the internet's open end-to-end architecture. It was put into place when the few participants in the network were trustworthy and security was not a primary concern. Replacing this legacy architecture faces several obstacles. For one, much of the technical infrastructure is still rooted in this original design, with efforts such as DNSSEC only gradually being implemented. At the same time, the norms and conventions of players making these decisions place a high value on openness and therefore create additional hurdles for tighter security approaches (Hoffman 2010). Similar forms of path dependence and problems with legacy systems exist across all users, applications, and services.

Nature of Security Risks

The incentives of agents to respond to security risks depend on the perceived nature of the risks. Attacks may be targeted or untargeted and the risks associated with different types of attacks may be independent or interdependent. Targeted attacks are aimed at one particular individual or organization and may include hacking or whaling. Untargeted attacks, such as the dissemination of Trojan horses or keyloggers, seek to harm any vulnerable system on the network. On the internet, risks are typically interdependent, meaning that the security risks of an individual or organization are not only dependent on own measures to mitigate threats but also dependent on the security decisions of other participants and the state of the network in general. However, the effects of interdependence vary with the type of attack. In case of targeted attacks, security investment by one organization may lead to redirection of attacks and hence increase the information security risks of other organizations. Thus, security investment is afflicted with negative externalities. In the case of untargeted attacks, increased security investment by an organization may actually lower the security risks of other organizations. Security investment goes hand in hand with positive externalities. As mentioned, the first case is prone to overinvestment in security and the second to underinvestment.

Gordon and Loeb (2002) further pointed out that the probability distributions of security threats vary and may require different best responses. Their paper distinguishes two classes of vulnerabilities: one in which optimal security investment increases monotonically with the threat level and a second class in which the cost of defense against certain security risks becomes prohibitively high so that, above a certain threat threshold, it is better to invest in recovery and resilience. The state of information of agents on the specific type of risks faced and their information on actions by others will therefore affect responses to threats. If such information is not common knowledge, decentralized, uncoordinated decisions may not yield best response strategies.

Moral Hazard and Adverse Selection

Information security often requires joint technical, economic, and behavioral efforts. Measures undertaken in one of these dimensions may influence the others. In situations where a principal cannot fully observe the security efforts of an agent and the consequences of the agent's behavior are not directly attributable to this agent, undesirable behavior may result. Moral hazard exists, if an agent's effort to maintain desirable levels of security is reduced by the presence of technical security means or of cyberinsurance.

For example, an employee may be careless in following security protocols on the assumption that technical security measures are more than sufficient. Likewise, if an organization has taken out insurance against information breaches, security personnel may behave less diligently knowing that potential losses will be covered by the insurance (Kunreuther and Heal 2003; Böhme and Kataria 2006; Shetty et al. 2010). Adverse selection is also related to problems of incomplete and asymmetric information. It implies that individuals and organizations with a higher security risk may seek insurance more frequently than those with a lower risk profile. An insurer may not have sufficient information to assess the risk profile of an applicant. Both moral hazard and adverse selection create undesirable effects for information security. In the case of cyberinsurance, moral hazard may be reduced or even overcome with requirements to invest in protection or with insurance premiums that are contingent upon the effort by the insured. It is more difficult to overcome within organizations relying on technical means of defense; even in that case, there is some evidence that systematic training programs may mitigate the problem (Shim and Bauer 2011).

Network Topology and Propagation of Malware

Recent research in network science has generated promising new insights as to how the topology of networks is related to economic and social processes, including the propagation patterns of infections (Easley and Kleinberg 2010, chapter 21). These approaches typically model the state of nodes on a network (e.g., "susceptible to infection", "infected", "recovered") and the transition probabilities between these states. Nodes are heterogeneous and the probabilities of state changes are influenced by the graph of the network (Bokharie et al. 2010). Although this research is still in a highly abstract state, it suggests that critical thresholds exist that determine whether an infection will propagate further or not (Draief et al. 2008; Mieghem et al. 2009). As the topology of networks is influenced by economic and policy choices, these insights may eventually be useful in designing more effective defenses against cybersecurity threats. One of the possible conclusions is that intervention at choke points may be an effective way of mitigating certain forms of threats, lending credibility to a claim that was advanced on more intuitive grounds by Anderson et al. (2008).

Formal and Informal Norms

Information security decisions are also influenced by formal and informal norms. Some of these norms emerged from repeated interactions of the participants in the information ecosystem but many are deliberately designed.

Appropriate design and modification of these rules, regulations and other norms is a core aspect of governance. Most countries have laws that target various forms of computer-based fraud and crime as well as related privacy issues, (even though some of them may need updating to reflect the present nature of threats and recent developments of the internet, such as mobile computing). Formal norms regulating cybersecurity are less widely available although they could, in principle, be powerful tools to address some of the incentive problems identified in earlier paragraphs. Whereas such laws are relevant, other forms of governance are of great importance in internet security. An increasing number of countries rely on public-private partnerships such as Computer Emergency Response Teams (CERTs), Computer Security Incident Response Teams (CSIRTs), and other initiatives to promote information security. There are also mechanisms among the supplier industries that create security-enhancing incentives, including voluntary blacklists, such as Spamhaus, peer pressure among Internet Service Providers and a vigilante culture that is widespread among their security staff. Numerous initiatives are also underway within the internet governance system (DeNardis 2009; Knake 2010; Mueller 2010).

Legal and regulatory rules as well as other forms of governance affect information security in two principal ways. First, they change the costs and benefits of decisions and therefore the outcome of the strategic interactions. Varian's (2004) analysis suggests that liability rules can help overcome the free rider problem in the total effort scenario and that negligence rules could help address security issues that arise in the weakest link scenario. Likewise, Anderson (2001) has pointed to the problem of "liability dumping", the transfer of liability to other agents in the value net. Liability is contested because of the many complications of deciding which party should bear which types of liability, the difficulty of establishing fault or negligence, and the associated enforcement problems (Spindler and Recknagel 2008). Moreover, there are concerns that improper liability rules would decelerate innovation, particularly in the software industries. Nonetheless, economic analysis suggests that carefully designed legal rules constitute powerful security-enhancing incentives. Second, successful governance also defines a focal point for behavior of agents, therefore generating a nudge toward an envisioned outcome or goal (Basu 2011). This second aspect is often misunderstood but is an important channel through which governance processes and mechanisms affect a socio-technical system.

Co-evolution of Cybercrime and Security

The realms of cybercrime and cybersecurity are coupled in a co-evolutionary manner. Events in one domain affect the other but they are also influenced by developments within the domain. The motives of cyber-criminals are complex and affected by many factors, including peer pressure (e.g., Holt et al. 2012). Attackers primarily driven by economic motives will expand the level of effort if either the costs of attacks decrease or if the potential rewards of attacks increase. In contrast, they will reduce criminal activities if the costs increase (e.g., because of tighter security measures or stricter law enforcement) or if the rewards decline. Information security decisions will likewise respond to developments in the realm of cybercrime. Other things equal, if the level of attacks increases, it will be rational to increase security efforts or to improve resilience. If the costs of providing a certain level of security decrease (e.g., because of advances in security technologies), players may be able to increase the level of security with the same security expenses, spend less on security while maintaining the original security level, or combine the two options (improve security somewhat, lower expenses somewhat).

Bauer and van Eeten (2009) identified an asymmetry between the two realms: increased security efforts will result unanimously in higher costs for cybercriminals, at least in the short run. On the other hand, a reduction in cybercrime has ambiguous effects on security as it may either increase, decrease, or leave the existing level of security unaffected. Higher levels of cybercrime may not lead to a reduction on the overall security level but they may increase the direct and indirect costs of defenses and thus generate a burden for society. On the other hand, lower levels of cybercrime may not increase the level of security but rather manifest themselves in lower security costs. In the long run, increased defenses may trigger further innovation in attack technology that may be more difficult to avert. A technology race between attackers and defenders may therefore lead to steadily increasing costs for society. How strong these effects are is influenced by the characteristics of the available security technology. If it is a constant or even decreasing-cost technology, the cost escalation may be limited; if it is an increasing-cost technology, because additional security efforts are more expensive, the cost escalation may be accelerated.

ENHANCING INTERNET SECURITY

Common Policies

Over the past decade, most industrialized countries have developed policies aimed at improving internet security. Notwithstanding national differences, they share a core of similar elements. First, most countries launched multi-year publicity campaigns to raise awareness of security issues among consumers and small and medium-sized enterprises (SMEs). Large enterprises were assumed to have specialized staff capable of identifying and managing security risks.

Second, governments improved information sharing and collaboration among market players and government organizations, typically by setting up public-private collaboration in information exchanges. Such exchanges bring together key players in a specific area, e.g., energy companies and other critical infrastructure operators or banks and other financial service providers. Public and private actors also established CSIRTs that enable information sharing and collaboration at the operational level.

Third, governments have invested in more effective law enforcement against cybercrime. The expertise and capabilities within the organizations of the police and the public prosecutor to investigate and prosecute cybercrime have been increased. Complementary to these investments, cross-border cooperation among law enforcement agencies has been strengthened, for example, by signing and ratifying the Council of Europe's Convention on Cybercrime.

These policies expressed the underlying approach to internet governance, which relied heavily on self-regulation and public-private partnerships (Lewis 2005). More recently, a fourth common element has emerged, which fits less comfortably within this approach: policies to deal with the threats to national security (e.g., Kramer et al. 2009; Clark and Knake 2010). We discuss this new element in the next subsection. The potentially devastating impact of certain attacks has led to doubts about whether self-regulation is still a viable approach – i.e., whether the private sector has sufficient incentives to invest in mitigating these threats – or whether it needs to be complemented by mandatory policies.

Expansion of Policies to Include National Security

The fourth common element has emerged more recently than the others: investing in military cyberdefense capabilities. In recent years, a variety of internet attacks against states have transformed the way in which governments understand internet security. They used to understand it first and foremost as a crime problem and, thus, as an economic phenomenon. Recent attacks, however, have led governments to also view certain threats as problems of national security.

An influential incident that has propelled this development occurred in April and May 2007. Members of a Kremlin-backed youth movement used a variety of botnets to effectively disconnect the country of Estonia – "the most wired country in Europe," according to *Wired* magazine – from the internet (Davis 2007; Kirk 2008; Clover 2009). It was a crude type of attack, called a Distributed Denial-of-Service (DDoS) attack, which aims to overwhelm targets with bogus traffic from thousands or millions of different sources, so that they can no longer handle legitimate traffic. Estonia called in NATO for assistance.

In July 2008, preceding a Russian military invasion, botnets were used to render Georgian governmental and news websites inoperable (Markoff 2008). During the prolonged attacks, some of the victims moved their operations to other locations, outside of the country. One newspaper set up a Blogspot account, which was hosted on Google's massive infrastructure and therefore more resilient to attacks. Other sites moved to Estonia, which offered to help, having experienced a similar fate the year before. One security expert observed that Georgia was in effect "cyberlocked," as it relied heavily on connections to the rest of the world that ran through hostile territory – i.e., Russia (Shachtman 2008).

In a technical sense, the attacks on Estonia and Georgia were quite modest in size. The effects were so severe because of the limited connectivity of both countries. However, given the large-scale criminal computing infrastructure currently available, it is not difficult to see how such attacks could be scaled up to a level that worries countries with more advanced internet infrastructure. The Estonia attacks were estimated to have cost a few thousand US dollars, should they have been executed through rented botnets (Lesk 2007). In other words, even with limited financial means, large-scale attacks appear possible.

In 2010, a much more sophisticated and resource-intensive attack was discovered that raised the prospect of damaging attacks against more industrialized countries. The attack was dubbed Stuxnet – after the Stuxnet worm that made up one part of the overall attack – and it ended up successfully penetrating and sabotaging Iranian nuclear facilities (Markoff 2011). Many experts have argued that all countries, also those with the most advanced infrastructure, are vulnerable to attacks with this level of sophistication (Markoff 2010).

It turns out to be very difficult to identify who is behind the attacks, as evidenced by the recent attacks on US governmental resources coming out of Chinese networks (Reid 2007). They could be state-sponsored or not. In the case of Stuxnet, however, the sheer amount of investment needed to develop the attack points to state-sponsorship (Halliday 2010). Most experts assume Israel was behind the attack, perhaps in collaboration with the United States (Broad et al. 2011).

All these developments have given rise to a wide range of speculation about impending large-scale attacks, including, but not limited to: massive crime waves that thwart the growth of the online economy; sweeping DDoS attacks rendering critical internet resources inoperable; malware pandemics that, like the large worm outbreaks of the early 2000s, cause widespread damage to businesses around the world; targeted attacks by terrorists or enemy states that cause large-scale disruption of critical infrastructures, including power grids, communication networks and banking systems (e.g., CSIS 2008).

In the US, as elsewhere, cybersecurity has moved up the policy agenda. As part of his Comprehensive National Cybersecurity Initiative (CNCI), President Obama announced a new military command for cyberspace within the Pentagon, as well as a White House office responsible for coordinating private-sector and government defenses against the daily cyberattacks mounted against the United States (Sanger and Shanker 2009). In 2011, the Administration sent a legislative proposal to Congress that places high emphasis on sharing of information on data security breaches, empowers the Department of Homeland Security to develop and implement coordinated cybersecurity policies by establishing a new National Cybersecurity Protection Program, and suggests measures to increase the security of critical infrastructures (White House 2011). In addition to national initiatives, intergovernmental organizations have also become more active in this area (see Sommer and Brown 2011 for an overview). For example, in 2008 NATO established a Cyber Defence Centre of Excellence, mandated to provide assistance to allied countries suffering internet attacks. Tellingly, it is located in Tallinn, Estonia.

Emerging New Policies: Shift from End Users to Intermediaries

Internet security threats are highly varied and constantly changing. Existing policies are challenged to adapt and catch up with the developments. One area has received a lot of attention over the past few years: the rise of so-called botnets. Malicious software, such as worms, viruses and Trojans, has been used to infect tens of millions of computers worldwide, often without the owners of those machines being aware of the infection.

Many of these machines are recruited into networks of thousands or even millions of computers that can be used for criminal purposes. They are currently the main vehicle for global spam distribution, for hosting phishing websites to commit fraud at financial institutions, for click fraud, for denial-of-service attacks that try to extract ransom from their victims, and other forms of perpetration (OECD 2009). Estimates of the total annual damage of internet security incidents vary wildly and need to be looked at with great caution. Taking into account the direct and indirect costs, they are often estimated in the tens of billions of US$ per year for the US alone (e.g., US GAO 2007).

Botnets are predominantly used for criminal purposes rather than for terrorist or state-sponsored attacks. That said, botnets increasingly blur the boundary between criminal risks and national security risks. The attacks on Estonia and Georgia used botnets, as did the attacks on Visa, MasterCard and others, in the wake of WikiLeaks' release of the diplomatic cables. The spread of the worm that built the cryptic Conficker botnet paralyzed parts of the British and French military as well as government and health institutions in other countries (Clover 2009; Soper 2009). More importantly, these attacks employed existing criminal botnets to attack nation states, turning a problem of crime into one that potentially impacts national security.

Botnets are typically associated with the infected personal computers (PCs) of end users. But malware can be used to infect all kinds of internet-connected machines and recruit them into botnets. In addition to PCs, botnets have been found to consist of web servers, routers, mobile devices and recently even supervisory control and data acquisition (SCADA) systems, used to control energy systems and other infrastructural equipment. Notwithstanding this diversity, a large portion of the machines in botnets presumably belong to end users, in particular home users and small and medium-size enterprise (SME) users. Compared to larger corporate users, these groups often do not achieve adequate levels of protection (van Eeten and Bauer 2008).

Security measures that address end users directly – including awareness raising and information campaigns – are useful, but they have proven to be insufficient to reduce the overall problem. Not because end users are incorrigible. Some surveys suggest that they do, in fact, increasingly adopt more secure practices, such as using anti-virus protection, a firewall, and automatic security updates for their software (e.g., Fox 2007). The attackers, however, also adapt and innovate their strategies. The net result is an inadequate defense against malware infections: while the capabilities and practices of end users are improving, they lag behind the increasingly sophisticated threats of attackers (e.g., Wash 2010).

Many experts have pointed out the flaws associated with a focus on end users. In 2007, a review by the UK House of Lords (2007a, p. 80) summarized the now dominant critique of this approach: "The current emphasis of government and policy-makers upon end-user responsibility for security bears little relation either to the capabilities of many individuals or to the changing nature of the technology and the risk."

In light of these shortcomings, the focus has recently shifted from end users to other market players. This is not to say that end users are now absolved of responsibility. The shift merely signals that the efforts of other players are also necessary for an adequate response against botnets. Special attention is being paid to internet intermediaries – market players who could function as natural "control points" for end user activities. A recent report by the OECD (2010, p. 9) defines internet intermediaries as follows: "Internet intermediaries bring together or facilitate transactions between third parties on the internet. They give access to, host, transmit and index content, products and services originated by third parties on the Internet or provide Internet-based services to third parties."

A variety of intermediaries can help to mitigate the impact of botnets. High on the list are the ISPs. Since ISPs – in the sense of access providers – are the gateway between their customers and the wider internet, they are in a unique position to detect and mitigate the malicious activity of their customers' machines. An increasing number of proposals and initiatives are being launched aimed at mobilizing ISPs in the fight against botnets. A variety of policy measures have been introduced in different countries, from binding self-regulation that requires ISPs to act on infected machines (e.g., Australia, the Netherlands) to national call centers to help infected customers (e.g., Germany, South Korea). More controversial proposals have emerged that try to move beyond the current voluntary efforts, asking governments to force ISPs to assume more responsibility. For example, Anderson et al. (2008, pp. 50–54) propose that liability for infected machines should be assigned to the ISPs, rather than to the consumers who own the machines. The authors also suggest imposing statutory damages on ISPs that do not respond promptly to requests for the removal of compromised machines. Another proposal has been to subsidize the clean up of infected machines, in what the author calls a public health approach to cybersecurity (Clayton 2010). The possible effects of these proposals are not yet fully understood. They will have to be investigated in more detail before these ideas can be transformed into realistic policy options.

Botnets and, more generally, malicious software, are at the heart of many of the security threats that currently plague the internet. In the next section, we focus on this area to explore the existing incentives for internet intermediaries. In the last part of the chapter, we ask how these incentives might be modulated.

INCENTIVES OF INTERNET INTERMEDIARIES

Internet security is a highly interdependent phenomenon. As a result, many market players influence, in one way or another, the threat of botnets. Here, we focus on three internet intermediaries that arguably are the most influential players: ISPs, software vendors and financial service providers.

This section draws substantially on the findings of a qualitative empirical field study (van Eeten and Bauer 2008). We conducted 41 in-depth interviews with 57 professionals of organizations operating in networked computer environments that are confronted with malware. Interviewees represented a stratified sample of professionals from different industry segments (e.g., hardware, software, service providers, and users) in six countries (Australia, Germany, the Netherlands, United Kingdom, France, and the United States). Moreover, we interviewed experts involved in the governance of information security issues such as CERTs and regulatory agencies. Based on this data, we identified and analyzed the consequences of the incentives of intermediaries.

Internet Service Providers

While the term ISP is used to cover a variety of businesses, typically ISPs are defined as providers that offer individuals and organizations access to the internet. What incentives do ISPs have to reduce the problem of malware? One view is: very few incentives, if any. Recently, the UK House of Lords Science and Technology Committee published a report which states (House of Lords 2007a, p. 30): "At the moment, although ISPs could easily disconnect infected machines from their networks, there is no incentive for them to do so. Indeed, there is a disincentive, since customers, once disconnected, are likely to call help-lines and take up the time of call-centre staff, imposing additional costs on the ISP."

Notwithstanding such claims, most ISPs are in fact increasing their efforts to fight malware. A survey from the EU's European Network and Information Security Agency (ENISA) found that 75 percent of ISPs report that they quarantine infected machines (ENISA 2006). All ISPs we interviewed described substantial efforts in the fight against malware, even though they are operating in highly competitive markets and most countries do not have governmental regulations requiring them to do so. Several incentives help explain why the ISPs see these efforts as being in their own interest.

Costs of customer support and abuse management
A key incentive for ISPs is the cost of customer support and abuse management. A medium-sized ISP reported costs of eight euros on average for an incoming call to their customer center while an outgoing call – for example, to contact a customer regarding an infected machine – was estimated at 16 euros. The incentive here is that security incidents generate customer calls, thus quickly driving up the costs of customer care. An interviewee at a large ISP emphasized that the customer support desk was a substantial cost for the company and that the number of calls was driven up by infections of their customers' machines.

Similar to customer contact, dealing with abuse notifications drives up costs because it requires trained staff. Tolerating more abuse on the network raises the number of notifications that the ISP receives. Abuse notifications can come through different channels, most notably through email sent to the abuse desk – typically abuse@provider.com – and through the informal networks of trusted security professionals that exist across ISPs, CSIRTs and related organizations.

As with customer complaints, not all malware infections will result in abuse notifications. One ISP reported internal research which found that only a small percentage of the compromised machines it saw on its network showed up in the notifications. For the interviewed ISPs, customer contact and abuse notifications constituted a positive incentive to invest in security both at the network level and at the customer level. There is another way of responding to these incentive mechanisms, however: don't respond to abuse notifications and avoid customer contact altogether. This attitude does save the ISP direct costs related to security. Indeed, there is a class of so-called "grey" or "rogue ISPs" doing exactly this. However, non-response also has negative repercussions such as the direct and indirect costs of being blacklisted, which makes it a less attractive strategy for legitimate ISPs.

Costs of blacklisting

Blacklisting is a loosely used term typically referring to ISP's practice of using so-called DNS Blacklists (DNSBL) to filter incoming traffic. Mail servers, for example, may be configured to refuse mail coming from specific IP addresses, IP ranges or whole networks listed on a DNSBL. Virtually all ISPs nowadays use blacklists. Each DNSBL has its own criteria for including an IP address in the list and its own procedure for getting an address off the list. Spamhaus, an international non-profit organization funded through sponsors and donations, maintains several well-known blacklists – though they prefer the term block lists – which Spamhaus claims are used to protect over 600 million user inboxes.

Blacklisting provides an incentive to invest in security because it ties in with the incentives mentioned earlier. It directly impacts the ISP's business model. A security officer at a large ISP explained that the expectation of being blacklisted led to a much more proactive approach to remove bots from the network, including the purchase of equipment that automates the process of identifying infected machines on the network. That ISP contacted around 50 customers per day and, if a customer did not resolve the problem, the connection was suspended. When asked how they got the business side of the company to approve this policy, he answered: "They hated it at first. But at the end of the day, the media fallout by being cut off by AOL and MSN was too big. The big ISPs, they use very aggressive [DNSBL] listings. They take out whole IP ranges. We used to be hit hard and entire ranges of our IP addresses were blacklisted."

Costs of brand damage and reputation effects

The "media fallout" mentioned by the interviewee points to a more general concern with brand damage that was mentioned by many interviewees as an incentive to invest in security. With few exceptions, these ISPs want to present themselves as responsible businesses (Arbor Networks 2007) providing safe services for their customers. A related incentive is the reputational benefits of offering secure services. It is unclear how strong this incentive is. Even if customers care about security, most will find it very difficult to assess the security performance of one ISP relative to its competitors. Nevertheless, the more significant finding here is that whether or not ISPs really care about bad publicity, being blacklisted has direct effects on their operating costs as well as their quality of service. The latter may in fact drive customers away. As one industry insider described it: "A high cost action is to investigate each complaint rigorously. A different kind of high cost action is to do nothing."

Costs of infrastructure expansion

An incentive that was more difficult to gauge is the effect of malware on the capital expenditures of the ISP – that is, the need to invest in infrastructure and equipment as more spam or malware comes through the network. Interestingly, malware-related infrastructure expenditures – apart from the costs of security equipment – were mostly seen as unimportant during our interviews. Infrastructure costs do not gradually increase with the amount of malware and spam, but rather as a step function when capacity runs out. It is very difficult to relate these expenditures, decided upon by other parts of the organization than the security staff, back to specific traffic patterns of spam and malware infections. In terms of incentives, this lack of awareness suggests that infrastructure cost is not a strong driver of the attempts of ISPs to reduce the impact of malware.

Benefits of maintaining reciprocity

All interviewees mentioned the informal networks of trusted security personnel across ISPs, CSIRTS and related organizations. When describing how their organization responded to security incidents, interviewees would refer to personal contacts within this trust network that enabled them, for example, to get another ISP to quickly act on a case of abuse. These contacts are reciprocal. They are also contacted about abuse in their own network and are expected to act on that information. To maintain reciprocity, an ISP has to treat abuse complaints seriously, which is costly. The more abuse takes place on its network, the more other contacts in the network will ask for intervention. Maintaining reciprocity not only establishes the informal network as a security resource, it also reduces the likelihood of being hit with blacklisting or other countermeasures. As one interviewee explained: "What enforces security on a service provider is threats from other service providers."

Costs of security measures

So far we have discussed incentives that reinforce the benefits of security for ISPs with regard to malware. The incentive structure is mixed, however, and includes disincentives as well. An obvious disincentive is the costs of additional security measures. Typically, the tradeoff is between the direct costs of additional measures which are visible in the short term versus the more diffuse costs caused by increasing security problems, such as customer support and abuse management. We should mention, however, that the ISP's decisions often were not shaped by formal economic assessments or detailed analysis of their own cost structures. As one insider phrased it, "ISPs very much drive by the seat of their pants. Except for a very few of the largest ones, they are not actually examining the figures." The ongoing consolidation of the ISP industry might contribute to a gradual change toward more deliberate practices, although most likely the informal practices will continue to play a role, if only because the data needed for formalization is difficult to collect.

Legal risks and constraints

Another disincentive is related to legal constraints. During the interviews, the European ISPs had different answers to the question of how much maneuvering space the "mere conduit" provision of the EU E-Commerce Directive allowed them. Monitoring their network more closely for security reasons could potentially lead to liability issues. If the ISP's monitoring reveals, for example, file sharing traffic of pirated materials, they may be forced to act upon this information to avoid legal claims from holders of intellectual property rights.

In some EU countries, interviewees reported that privacy regulations that potentially treat IP addresses as private data had led their legal departments to set boundaries which limited the ability of security staff to track malicious activity on their network – for example with regard to tracking individual IP addresses. One interviewee reported that security staff sometimes were not allowed to use information on malicious activity that was detected on the network. Some legal experts argued that these legal risks are non-existent, that they are based on an incorrect understanding of current legislation. While that might be true, the reality is that the ISPs' legal departments tend to be rather risk averse in dealing with this ambiguity.

Cost of customer acquisition
Some security measures may impose restrictions on what customers can do on the network. This provides a disincentive. Anything that might turn people away is a problem, because the cost of acquisition of new customers is high. The burden of proof fell on the security staff to convince management that the proposed measures were protecting the brand.

Overall assessment
The balance between incentives and disincentives will vary depending on the ISP. On the whole, recent years have witnessed increased efforts by ISPs in dealing with malware, even in the absence of regulation or other forms of public oversight. The incentive mechanisms we discussed strengthen the ISP's interest to internalize at least some security externalities originating from their customers as well as from other ISPs. In short, the current incentive structure seems to reward better security performance for legitimate market players – though it is sensible to keep in mind that in many countries price competition is intense, which is a disincentive with regard to security, other things equal.

Some of the security-enhancing incentives discussed above work as disincentives under different business models than those of the ISPs we interviewed. Another business model is sometimes referred to as "rogue ISP" or ISPs that are, in the words of one interviewee, "decidedly grey." These attract customers precisely because of their lax security policies. While these ISPs have more disincentives for improving security than the ones we interviewed, they are not fully immune to some of the security-enhancing incentives we discussed earlier, most notably blacklisting. An additional incentive for non-responsive ISPs is the pressure put on them by their upstream providers – the ISP "who feeds them the internet," as one respondent phrased it – or by the providers with whom the ISP exchanges traffic at peering points. If an ISP were de-peered, the disconnected ISP would have to buy transit service for its traffic, and therefore incur much higher operating costs.

Financial Service Providers

The multitude of companies that buy and sell products or services over the internet operate on a wide variety of business models each with different incentive structures for security. We have chosen to focus particular attention on online financial services as they have been an important target of malware attacks, arguably more than any other sector (Counterpane and MessageLabs 2006). This includes bricks-and-mortar banks offering part of their service portfolio online, credit card companies, as well as online-only service providers such as PayPal. The sector has been confronted with a wide range of threats ranging from botnet-assisted phishing spam runs and phishing websites to keyloggers and trojans that enabled man-in-the-middle attacks during secured banking sessions.

Benefits of increased online transaction volume
A key incentive for all these companies are the benefits they derive from processing online financial transactions, resulting in a strong interest to enable a growing volume of online transactions. Credit card companies and online financial service providers typically charge a fee per transaction. The situation is somewhat different for bricks-and-mortar banks. Their incentive to pursue online banking is the considerable cost savings that it enables, compared to branch offices, mail or phone channels. Beyond fixed infrastructure costs, the marginal cost per transaction essentially nears zero. Given the incredible volume of financial transactions, costs savings of that magnitude translate into a very powerful incentive to move online as much volume of these services as possible.

How does this incentive affect security decisions? To answer that question, we need to understand how transaction volume interacts with several other incentives: the benefits of trust in the online services, the benefits of usability, the costs of security measures and the costs of fraud.

Benefits of trust
Within the sector, it is assumed that trust of consumers in the security of these services is a necessary condition for their uptake. That rewards investing in security. Beyond this generic consensus, however, views quickly diverge. Surveys typically find that consumers turn away from online banking because of fear of security problems. (e.g., GetSafeOnline 2006). On the other hand, many online financial services still report strong growth rates (e.g., PayPal 2007). An industry study of trust in e-commerce (Lacohée et al. 2006) tried to bridge these seemingly conflicting findings: "People use specific services not because they trust them, but because they in some way provide a benefit to the individual and they know that if something goes wrong, restitution will be made." In other words, from a customer's perspective, it seems more important that financial service providers assume liability for online fraud than that they achieve a certain level of – perceived – security.

Benefits of usability

If increased security would increase trust, then, other things being equal, it may raise the uptake of online services. But increased security may also affect the usability of a service. In some countries, two-factor authentication is the norm, while in others, fewer security technologies are in place. One of the reasons why some banks do not introduce two-factor technology is that it might significantly raise the threshold for people to do online banking. That would directly impact the volume of online transactions – and would influence decision making against such measures, even if this means that fraud losses are higher. By balancing usability and security, these companies try to maximize the growth of online financial transactions, while keeping the level of fraud at manageable levels.

Costs of fraud

Fraud losses provide another incentive for security. In the US, banks are liable for direct fraud losses under the Electronic Funds Transfer Act of 1978. Under this regime, customers are compensated for such losses, unless the bank can prove that the customer's claims are false. In many other jurisdictions, banks are strictly speaking not liable for such losses. In practice, however, the banking sector has often adopted voluntary codes which specify that customers who suffer losses are compensated – unless there are clear indications that they have colluded in the fraud.

Over the past years, fraud losses have risen. But these figures have to be seen in their context. The United Kingdom has arguably the best statistics available, based on actual banking data. Industry reported that card-not-present fraud losses rose by 350 percent in the period of 2000–2008. Over the same time period, the total value of online shopping alone increased by 1077 percent. So relative to the transaction volume, the level of fraud decreased.

Credit card companies do publish such numbers. In 2006, Visa Europe reported that their overall fraud rate was at "an all-time low" of 0.051 percent (fraud to sales by cards issued). However, card-not-present fraud, which includes online fraud, was the fastest growing type of fraud and now accounted for 40 percent of cases. PayPal reported direct losses to fraud of 0.41 percent of overall transactions, but could not give information on the trend of their losses (House of Lords 2007b, p. 196).

Costs of security measures

While exact figures are hard to come by, the companies we interviewed all claimed that their security investment levels are much higher than the direct yearly losses, often by one or two orders of magnitude. They do not see direct losses as being representative of the overall problem. It would be much more devastating, for example, if online fraud were to erode customer trust or slow down the uptake of online financial services.

In general, the incentives are to keep fraud at acceptable levels and compensate victims, rather than to eliminate it. The latter would be economically inefficient, not only in terms of direct cost, but also because it might require security measures that raise the threshold of using online financial services for customers. A reduction in the growth of the online transaction volume is likely to imply higher costs for the banks than the current damage of online fraud.

Overall assessment
The incentives of financial service providers are such that in many cases they compensate customers for damages suffered from online fraud. They are willing to internalize these costs because the benefits far outweigh them. In that sense, they internalize the externalities of sub-optimal security decisions of their customers as well as those of others, such as the software vendors whose software is exploited to execute the attacks. If compensation is indeed the norm, then the security level achieved by the whole value network may not be too far from the optimum. The financial institutions bear the externalities, but they are also in a position to manage the risk through their security measures around online financial services.

However, there are several important considerations to take into account. First, one could argue that there are still externalities in the sense that important social efficiencies could be gained if people had higher trust in these services and would adopt them more quickly. Second, not all fraud-related costs of customers are compensated. In cases of identity theft, victims may struggle for years with the consequences of having their personal information abused, such as blemished credit reports (TechWebNews 2005). Third, in several countries the banking sector is reconsidering the existing liability regime, which might lead to liability dumping. In New Zealand, for example, the banking association introduced a new code which has shifted at least part of the liability to the customers (South 2007).

The development of what one could call "re-externalizing" fraud losses to the customers is not without risks to the banks themselves, as part of customer trust in internet banking is partly based on the expectation that fraud losses are compensated. If customers experience more liability for their online transactions, it might reduce the uptake of these services that directly affects the banks' major incentive: the growth of online transaction volume. For this reason, a security official in the financial sector called the attempts to shift part of the liability to the customers "a very dangerous path to follow."

Software Vendors

The very nature of malware focuses attention on software vendors. Malicious code can compromise machines in different ways. Attackers may use social engineering – i.e., tricking users into voluntarily installing software that includes malware. They may also exploit software vulnerabilities. The software market is highly differentiated. Each market segment has somewhat different characteristics and hence different incentives for software vendors to improve security before and after release and for malware writers to exploit vulnerabilities.

In recent years, much has been written about the incentives for software security, mostly in pessimistic terms. First, some authors claim that security is a "market for lemons," as consumers cannot tell secure from less secure software (Anderson and Moore 2006). Second, in many segments all software is vulnerable, so there might not be a "secure" alternative. Third, many segments of the software market tend to have dominant firms because of the combination of high fixed and low marginal costs, positive network externalities and customer lock-in because of interoperability and compatibility issues. "So winning market races is all important," Anderson and Moore conclude (2007, p. 7). "So platform vendors start off with too little security, and such as they provide tends to be designed so that the compliance costs are dumped on the end users."

This analysis provides a powerful explanation for how we got to the current state of affairs. Recent years have seen substantially increased efforts of many vendors to improve the security of their software. The development and deployment of vulnerability patches has improved. Arguably more important, the development of the software itself is increasingly focusing on security issues. Most of our interviewees agreed on this. They disagreed over the effectiveness of these efforts – some argued it was too little too late, others thought the market was moving in the right direction. Notwithstanding the different business models of software vendors, a number of incentives may explain why this trend reversal took place.

Costs of vulnerability patching
Developing patches for discovered vulnerabilities is costly, even if the fix itself is not hard to write. As one senior software security professional explained: "It's like the MasterCard commercial—two line code change, 20 minutes, finding every other related vulnerability of that type on every affected product version and all related modules, fixing it, testing it, 3 months. Giving the customers a patch they can use that does not break anything, priceless." Anecdotal data suggests that an ongoing process of

patch development, testing and release for a complex piece of software – like an operating system or an enterprise database system, which consists of tens of millions lines of code – is easily measured in millions of dollars per cycle. Even more important, some interviewees argued, are the opportunity costs of tasking good software developers with vulnerability patching.

Patching also imposes costs on the customer who applies the patch. This may include the cost of testing the patch before deploying it within the organization, the actual deployment for all the relevant systems, as well as the costs of remediation when the patch turns out to "break something" – e.g., introduce system instabilities. Several studies have shown these costs to be substantial (e.g., August and Tunca 2006). Strictly speaking, the vendor does not experience these costs and some have suggested that these costs should be regarded as externalities that the vendor shifts onto its customers (e.g., Schneier 2007). But there are indirect effects that do affect the vendor. First, it raises the maintenance costs of the software. Many enterprises assess the so-called "total cost of ownership" of software. It is not uncommon for maintenance costs to be much higher than the price of the license itself. Second, if patching is too costly for customers, they may not keep their machines adequately patched. The resulting security problems may tarnish the reputation of the software itself – we return to brand damage and reputation effects shortly.

In response to these effects, many vendors have set out to reduce the costs of patching for their customers. For enterprises, patching is a different issue than for home users. The former need to have more control over the deployment of patches as patches potentially disrupt critical systems. In some cases, they might opt to not apply certain patches. The vendors we spoke to described efforts to better support their business customers in this regard. Microsoft, for example, introduced Windows Server Update Services (WSUS) which allows IT administrators to control the deployment of patches across the computers in their network. Furthermore, vendors try to improve the information they provide with patches, so that businesses can make an informed risk assessment regarding if, when and how to deploy a patch.

For home users, reducing the costs of patching has mainly consisted of developing easier, more user-friendly mechanisms to deliver and install patches. Microsoft developed "Automatic Updates" and turned these on by default in Windows XP SP2. In the environment of open source software, Firefox – an internet browser with the second-largest market share, after Microsoft's Internet Explorer – has enabled automatic updates by default since version 1.5. Rather than bundling patches, the developers of Firefox release the patches as soon as they are ready. The default setting of the browser is to download and install them at the earliest opportunity.

The developers reported that under this new model, 90 percent of Firefox users installed a recent security patch within six days (Snyder 2007).

The costs of patching could also work as a disincentive for security for those vendors that seek to avoid these costs. As a result vulnerabilities remain unpatched for too long, if they ever get patched, or the quality of patches might be too low. The urgency of this issue increases if attackers are indeed, as has been reported, moving away from exploits in the operating system and toward third-party applications and hardware drivers (Lemos 2006). If a vendor's market position requires them to perform costly patch development, then these costs might incentivize more investments in security early in the development process, in the hope of reducing the number of vulnerabilities after release.

Costs of secure software development

While vulnerability patching is generally seen as desirable, many have argued that it does not solve the underlying problem. Finding and patching vulnerabilities might not make the software product itself more secure (Rescorla 2004). Furthermore, patch development consumes resources that are not used to make software more secure before it is released.

This is a valid criticism. However, several interviewees made the case that costly patching procedures still provide an incentive for more up-front investments in secure software development. One argued that the more powerful incentive for secure software development is the fact that back-end patching costs are much higher than the costs of preventing the vulnerability during development.

We did not come across economic analyses that directly compare the costs of secure development with those of patching. It seems clear, however, that the costs of secure software development are substantial. It requires more resources and can affect time-to-market of a new product – a critical factor in many software markets though here too the effect may be tempered by customer lock-in. Furthermore, secure development often involves costly assurance processes. One interviewee described the so-called "Common Criteria" evaluations for major releases of their products. These evaluations are done by external consultants and were estimated to cost between US$0.5–1.0 million each – not including the time-consuming involvement of internal staff.

Even in the absence of hard numbers, the interviewees were adamant that there are significant cost savings to be made by investing in secure software development. After Microsoft started its "Security Development Lifecycle" initiative, it published numbers which suggest that it resulted in significant reductions in the number of vulnerabilities found after release (Microsoft 2008).

Cost of brand damage and reputation effects
Reputation effects are another incentive for security. The strength of these effects is notoriously difficult to estimate. Some have suggested that they provide a fairly weak incentive (Schneier 2007). Whether that is true or not, it does seem to play a role. The major security-related changes within Microsoft were driven by the major worm and virus outbreaks in 2002 and 2003. The key difference between those security incidents and ones that preceded them was scale and the resulting damage. Neither affected Microsoft directly. The reputation effect of those incidents seems to be the most plausible explanation for the changes in the company's course.

As mentioned earlier, Microsoft has invested in mechanisms to make it easier for its customers to patch their machines, even though they do not suffer the customer's patching costs directly. Furthermore, so far Microsoft has allowed pirated versions of Windows to download security patches. This appears to value the reputation of the platform higher than denying services to non-customers. The incentive of reputation effects might be stronger in open source communities, where reputation is a very valuable resource (e.g., Watson 2005). It might help to understand why early in the development of what would become the Firefox browser, the developers made a number of security-conscious choices. The security performance of the browser played a key role in marketing the browser, as well as in receiving the positive evaluations of software reviewers.

Benefits of functionality
Even vendors with an established market position will at some point want customers to buy a newer version of their product or a complementary product. Developing new functionality in software is one way of selling new versions. The drive of the market to produce ever more powerful software has generated numerous innovations. At the same time, it has made it much harder to build secure software.

Functionality versus security is not necessarily a zero-sum tradeoff. New functionality can be security related, for example, or it might be implemented securely. In practice, however, they can be difficult to reconcile. The history of software development is rife with examples where tradeoffs in the design of software have often favored functionality over security. Many of the much-maligned features of Microsoft's Internet Explorer, such as its deep integration into the Windows platform, started out as functionality. There have been many beneficial uses of this functionality, but it also has turned out to be a huge security risk. In response, starting with IE7, many of these design decisions were reversed.

There is an intrinsic tension between adding functionality and making software more secure. Security benefits from simplicity and a limited amount of code (e.g., Barnum and Gegick 2005; Bernstein 2007). Many of today's major software products have neither. The need to expand functionality with each release only exacerbates the situation. Of course, secure software development practices set out to mitigate this problem, by reducing the "attack surface" of a certain functionality and managing the remaining risks or, if the functionality is inherently insecure, by excluding it from the product.

One could argue that as the security-related costs of users go up, the market will reward security-related functionality that can reduce those costs. There are several well-known counterarguments to this – including lock-in effects, lack of alternatives, weak market signals for security and the information asymmetry between vendor and customer. That said, there appears to be a market demand for certain security improvements, most notably those that reduce the total cost of ownership. Whether the market over time can distinguish between empty claims and security improvements that actually achieve cost-savings is not yet clear.

Benefits of compatibility

As discussed above, software products benefit from positive network externalities. The value of a software platform – such as an operating system – increases non-linearly with the number of users. There are two sides to this: the more users there are, the more vendors will want to develop software for that platform; and the more software there is for the platform, the more users will want to adopt it. Anderson and Moore (2007, p. 5) concluded that all of this implies that platform vendors will impose few security restrictions so as to appeal to third party software vendors – i.e., to maintain compatibility and inter-operability of software. How these incentives play out for a specific vendor depends on the type of product they provide and the position they have in the market.

For a dominant platform, maintaining compatibility is key when moving from one version to the next. As one industry insider told us: "The only thing [Microsoft] cared about in the transition from Windows 95 or Windows 98 to Windows XP was application compatibility, otherwise people would never move to XP." This had all kinds of effects on security and the problem of malware. To achieve maximum compatibility, the default installation of XP set every user up with administrator privileges, which means that people typically operated their machine under a user account that allowed unrestricted control over the machine. From a security standpoint, this is undesirable, because it means that once a machine is successfully attacked during use, malware has full access to the machine.

In response to the default user setup of XP, third-party vendors assumed that all users would run with administrator privileges and they designed their programs accordingly. In turn, because so much software assumed the user to run with administrator privileges, running the system as a regular user with limited privileges was not really viable. Large organizations did sometimes set up the desktops of their employees with restricted regular user accounts. This is a costly set up, however, because it requires a lot of support staff to manage these installations. Even minor changes needed administrator privileges and thus a support staff action. Of course, if you set up your users as administrators, the support costs are also high, because of the increased security risks.

The only way to break out of this self-reinforcing path dependency is for everyone to adapt their behavior. During the development of Vista, Microsoft decided to change the default way user accounts were set up. This required Microsoft developers to create a viable standard user mode with restricted privileges. They introduced User Account Control (UAC) for this purpose. Their enterprise customers, many of whom wanted to run their desktops under standard user accounts, applauded this development, as it promised to reduce their total cost of ownership. The problem was that it created serious compatibility issues with the existing third-party software, much of which still presumed administrator privileges. While vendors were informed about the upcoming changes, many did not actually adapt their code to work with these features. One interviewee explained that it was not attractive for vendors to comply with the new restrictions, because they had to invest in changing their code just to get the same functionality that they already had before Vista.

When Vista was released, a substantial number of these compatibility issues were unresolved, even though Microsoft itself developed auto-mitigation measures to deal with many application compatibility problems that the vendors did not resolve themselves. Microsoft anticipated these problems to a certain extent. They felt that the compatibility problems of end users were worth the price in moving the software industry to build software that could operate under a standard user model. But without a way to force the third-party vendors to adapt their software, this would be "a dangerous game to play," said one interviewee, as Microsoft itself will receive part of the blame for these problems. UAC is one example. Other security improvements in Vista suffer from the same incentive problem: they only work if the independent software vendors adapt their code. Just how painful these lessons have been, is illustrated by Vista's successor: Windows 7. Microsoft reverted back to the same default as Windows XP by setting up the default user account with administrative privileges. It is less secure, but also much less susceptible to problems with third-party software.

On the whole, the benefits of compatibility and inter-operability create strong path dependencies that can only be broken away from at high cost.

Benefits of user discretion

An issue that runs throughout the challenge of software security is user discretion – that is, key decisions about how to configure and operate the software product are left to the user. The user – or in enterprise contexts, the IT administrator – decides whether or not to install vulnerability patches, the user decides whether to operate within User Account Control or to turn it off, the user decides how to configure a firewall, and so on.

User discretion allows a software product to be adapted to a wide variety of contexts and preferences of those that use it. That means the product can reach a wider market and can create more benefits for its users, making it more valuable. Perhaps more importantly, user discretion touches on property rights. Software runs on machines that are not owned by the vendor. In principle, it is the owners who should be able to decide how to balance tradeoffs among functionality, performance, availability and, yes, security – as well as any other value that is relevant to them. After all, the owners are the first to bear liability for what their system does – whether this affects them when patch deployment breaks critical business applications, for example, or others, when their systems are compromised and used to attack other users. "We are not in the business of telling our users what to do," was how one interviewee summarized it. "We can inform them, educate them and provide them with the appropriate tools, but we cannot make these decisions for them."

With user discretion comes user responsibility. This is a blessing and a curse for software vendors. The blessing is obvious: many of the current security problems fall within the realm of user behavior rather than within the realm of software production. This shields vendors from part of the responsibility to resolve these problems. Of course, it is also a curse. The decisions that users make affect the security performance of a product, which in turn affects the reputation of the product and its vendor. There is plenty of evidence demonstrating that in many cases, users lack the information or expertise needed to make rational security tradeoffs or that their decisions do not account for the costs they impose on others – including, but not limited to, reputation damage of the software vendor.

There are limits to user discretion. There are hard limits, where software simply does not enable or allow you to take certain actions, and softer limits, where the default configuration of a product tries to guide behavior in a certain direction. For example, when Microsoft introduced UAC, it turned the feature on by default, but it did include the possibility to turn it off by changing the system settings. Preliminary feedback indicates that, so far, over three quarters of the users keep UAC turned on.

Where and how to set such limits is a difficult balancing act for vendors. It implies many tradeoffs between user discretion and protecting the integrity and reputation of the product. As one interviewee explained: "That debate raged on for four years straight, from the team level to the senior VP level and we rehashed that debate fifty times in those four years. You know – what should the defaults be and how much pain can we put the users in to get through to the independent software vendors? Are we being too aggressive with this plan or are we not aggressive enough? It was a huge engineering decision that really took a lot of guts at the VP level to support because we knew we were going to generate some customer dissatisfaction. But the alternative is to say: I hope anti-malware engines can keep up with malware."

Overall assessment
Software vendors work under a mixed set of incentives which may vary for different market segments. They do experience increasing costs as a result of growing security problems, most notably the direct and indirect costs of patch development and reputation effects. That explains why many vendors have substantially increased the efforts to improve the security of their software. The vendors also experience incentives that make it costly and difficult to introduce more secure software, even if they are willing to invest in development. The net effect of the mixed set of incentives is dependent on the product and the market segment in which the vendor operates. Assuming all other things being equal, the increased efforts mitigate software-related security problems. However, at the same time as security efforts are being increased, malware is becoming more sophisticated, adapting to the new defenses. Notwithstanding the efforts of software vendors, many of our interviewees expected that the situation would get worse still, before it would get better.

Vendors do not bear the full costs of software insecurity – i.e., there are externalities. Schneier (2007) has repeatedly argued that all the money that consumers of software products are spending on additional security products and services should be counted as externalities generated by those software products. That might not be fully correct and overestimate the size of the problem. To a certain extent, security problems are connected to users' decisions and behaviors – as is inevitable, given user discretion over the configuration and use of software, as well as social engineering attacks which do not need software vulnerabilities to compromise a system. If somebody decides to buy a cheap or highly functional software product with known security problems plus separate security software, it is the consumer's choice and should not be treated as an externality. In theory, a well-functioning market would offer software with different degrees of protection and let consumers choose. However, that assumes that everybody has full information and that there are no externalities on the consumer side. As we know, in many software markets consumers experience lock-in effects or a lack of alternatives. So there are externalities generated by the vendors' decisions, but they are probably lower than the total cost of security measures.

IMPLICATIONS FOR POLICY

The potential of large-scale internet attacks has intensified the debate on appropriate policy responses. Until now, government policies have focused on user awareness campaigns, better international collaboration among law enforcement agencies, public-private information sharing and better data collection on security problems. Measures at the national level are complemented with international formal and informal collaboration (see Bauer and van Eeten 2009, for a more detailed discussion). While useful, these measures have proven to be ineffective to lastingly reduce the threats posed by botnets and other forms of security threats. Whereas these measures might have contributed to preventing an escalation of security incidents, a recent series of high-profile breaches such as the attacks against Sony PlayStation Network, Epsilon, RSA SecureID, and Google have raised renewed concerns.

The last few years have witnessed a controversial debate over additional policy measures. Proponents of an economic approach to internet security have advocated measures like publishing data on the security performance of ISPs, introducing product liability for software vendors, regulating minimum security standards for hardware vendors, and imposing statutory fees on ISPs that do not act against compromised machines (e.g., Anderson et al. 2008).

All of these measures set out to re-align the market incentives to internalize or mitigate security externalities, so as to enhance internet security. While these proposals are an important and innovative contribution to moving beyond the current ineffective policies, there are many possible complications associated with most of these measures. Researchers in this area have a tendency to treat issues of institutional design as rather trivial. That is to say, they assume that the models indicate what market design is optimal, that this design can be brought into existence at will and that actors will behave according to the model's assumptions. If the past decade of economic reforms – including privatization, liberalization and deregulation of network-based industries – has taught us anything, it is that designing markets is highly complicated and sensitive to the specific context in which the market is to function. It cannot be based on formal theoretical models alone. Institutional design requires an in-depth empirical understanding of current institutional structures and their effects on outcomes.

If this debate was not already complicated enough, botnets are increasingly portrayed as a threat to national security (e.g., CSIS 2008). Rather than treating them as a versatile tool for criminal activity, which has been the dominant approach until recently, the threat environment is extended to include botnets as an important weapon for military and terrorist purposes. This is only logical, in light of the events we described in the introduction. Botnets are being used for purposes that threaten the security of nation states. These two perspectives – crime and national security – are not mutually exclusive. In fact, the national security perspective often implicitly subsumes the threats posed by crime by arguing that there are even worse scenarios to take into account.

To a certain extent both perspectives can be correct at the same time. Incidents like those in Georgia and Estonia inextricably combine criminal resources and military, even terrorist, purposes. What makes this overlap so problematic is that they lead to very different and conflicting policies, both in terms of goals as well as means. Fighting crime acknowledges that it is economically rational to tolerate a certain level of insecurity. All markets are afflicted with a certain level of crime. The costs of higher security have to be weighed against the benefits. This can lead to counter-intuitive outcomes.

A brief example will have to suffice (for a more detailed discussion, see van Eeten and Bauer 2008). For several years there have been ongoing and successful malware-based attacks against banks and credit card companies. It would not be difficult or necessarily very costly for financial institutions to raise the security of online payment services. The problem is that the opportunity costs are estimated to be much higher than the fraud that is prevented through such measures. The financial institutions have a strong incentive to increase their online transaction volume – banks because of cost savings associated with having customers conduct transactions online rather than through other channels; credit card companies because each transaction earns them a fee. Any security measure that would raise the threshold for consumers to use these services would reduce these benefits. Financial institutions have found that it is currently more efficient to compensate the losses of customers who are a victim of fraud, rather than increase the security in ways that would impede the usability of these services. Society as a whole also benefits from these substantial efficiency gains, as long as financial institutions can compensate the actual damage while still improving their profits. In short, from this perspective, the goal of policies should be to reach the optimal level of insecurity in light of the actual damage and the costs, including opportunity costs, of reducing it further. The way to find these levels is to make sure the market incentives are aligned appropriately. This logic assumes without further examination that all risks are appropriately accounted for by the stakeholders.

Contrast this to the national security approach. Here, potential not actual damage is the leading concern – where potential typically implies thinking in terms of worst case scenarios. And the worst case scenarios are pretty bleak – as in massive economic and social destabilization. So bleak, in fact, that the only possible response is to prevent such events. Where fighting crime allows for trial-and-error, national security typically requires us to prepare for the worst. Where fighting crime can look at averages or a run of cases, the military mindset is to ensure national security meets every last threat. Of course, the current status quo is by no means prepared for the worst. No wonder, then, that proponents of this view are quick to call the governance model of self-regulation a failure and to dismiss "the market" for having failed to ensure security. A closely related argument is to point out that cybersecurity is a public good, which implies that without government intervention, it will not be produced (e.g., Lewis 2005). Of course, fighting crime also implies government involvement, but the subtext here is that the government needs to intervene in much more consequential ways than mere law enforcement.

Underlying these two approaches are two different views on what it means to ensure security. The difference between them is analogous to a critical distinction from the field of reliability theory, namely between marginal reliability and precluded-event reliability. Adapting these two approaches to the realm of cybersecurity, we can see why the issue of botnets leads to such controversy when it comes to their implications for policy (see Table 18.1).

Both approaches imply their own problems. Treating botnets as a problem of national security (precluded-event security) tends to militarize issues that, so far, primarily concern organizations and individuals, not nations. It subordinates the interests of these organizations and individuals to rather unbounded notions of national interests. To put it differently, rather than interventions based on actual costs and benefits of (in)security for societal actors, the interventions would be driven by the potential costs to society of attacks that have not yet occurred. The word "benefits" is conspicuously absent from the last part of that sentence because they rarely seem to play a role in assessments of national security issues. Yet,

Table 18.1   Marginal and precluded-event security

Variable	Marginal Security	Precluded-Event Security
Context	Efficiency	Social dread
Risk	Localized	Widely distributed
Damage	Actual damage	Potential damage
Standards	Average or run of cases	Every last case
Learning	Trial & error learning	Formal learning with limited trial & error
Calculation	Marginal (variable cost)	Non-fungible (fixed requirement)
Orientation	Retrospectively measured	Prospectively focused
Control	Probabilistic	Deterministic

Source: Adapted from Roe and Schulman (2008, p. 53).

we know that there are dramatic benefits associated with precisely those properties of the internet that have made it so vulnerable.

In more general terms, this argument has been developed by Zittrain (2008, p. 8). It is precisely the ability of current PCs to run "arbitrary code" that makes them a generative technology while at the same time rendering them vulnerable to malicious code. He states: "[T]he same qualities that led to [the success of the Internet and general-purpose PCs] are causing [them] to falter. This counterrevolution would push mainstream users away from the generative internet that fosters innovation and disruption, to an appliancized network that incorporates some of the most powerful features of today's internet while greatly limiting its innovative capacity – and, for better or worse, heightening its regulability." Not without hyperbole, he calls this scenario "the end of the internet."

On the other hand, the Achilles' heel of an approach based on fighting crime (marginal security), is the scenarios of low probability and high consequence. Given the dependence of all aspects of global society on the internet and electronic communications in general, widespread and extended failure would have catastrophic consequences. That such a pervasive failure or technological terrorism has not yet happened and has a low probability complicates the formulation of a response. Like other events with a low but non-trivial probability, it could be considered a "black swan event" (Taleb 2007). Cost-benefit analysis of such catastrophic events would help in shaping more rational responses but it is extremely difficult. Complications include the choice of an appropriate time horizon, the quantification of the risk in question, problems of monetizing a wide range of qualitative impacts, and the determination of social discount rates applied to monetized future events (Posner 2004).

Nonetheless, devising an overall internet security policy would greatly benefit from such an exercise.

Risk and disaster researchers are divided on the question of how to deal with "black swan events." One group of authors emphasize that we tend to underestimate the possibility of "black swan events" (Perrow 1999; Perrow 2007). As a consequence, we tend to under-invest in prevention and preparation for such events. While this is a valid point, these arguments typically do not adequately take into account the aggregate costs of such a risk management strategy. These have first been pointed out by Wildavsky (1988). The damage of each individual event may be so enormous, that the costs of trying to preclude it often seem justified. But this logic runs into problems in two ways. First, there is an endless supply of possible events that we would have to preclude. Adding up the cost for all those efforts easily overwhelms the available resources. Furthermore, such a strategy of preparation sucks up resources for risks that may never materialize. These resources are then no longer available to respond to actual events. Also, the opportunity costs of such risk averseness are enormous and may impose a higher burden on society than the disasters themselves.

A broad assessment of the costs and benefits of cybersecurity will need additional work. However, it is possible to ask whether decentralized stakeholder decisions are the most effective way of dealing with the problem. The case studies in van Eeten and Bauer (2008) have revealed many instances in which the responses of individual players in the ICT value net are only partially effective at best. Feedback mechanisms, such as blacklisting and reputation effects, do improve security, but in many cases they are insufficient to fully internalize the costs and broader societal risks into private security decisions. This internalization is most effective in cases where most costs and benefits are borne by the parties involved, as discussed in the case of financial institutions. Even in those cases, though, the costs of achieving a desired level of security are increased by actions or omissions by players in other segments of the value chain.

A multiplicity of parallel collective efforts that complement decentralized security incentives will be necessary to address the diverse security needs and attack strategies. These range from strengthened voluntary cooperation to improved public-private partnerships and formal legal and regulatory actions, possibly using critical intermediaries in the value network (van Eeten et al. 2010; Levchenko et al. 2011). In addition to national measures, international and global efforts will have to be expanded in these different institutional forms. Many such initiatives are already under way, including the framework provided by the Cybercrime Convention (which, while ratified only by about two dozen countries, has provided a blueprint for many others) and the London Action Plan (LAP).

In addition to these government-led programs, important co-regulatory and self-regulatory initiatives have emerged, including the steps to enhance security undertaken within ICANN and the Internet Governance Forum (IGF), international collaboration of CERTs and CSIRTs within the international Forum of Incident Response and Security Teams (FIRST), and private sector initiatives such as the Anti-Malware Testing Standards Organization (AMTSO).

Over the next few years, as new security policies for the internet take shape, a balance will have to be struck between these competing approaches. Internalization by individual players is more difficult in the generative areas of the internet that provide general-purpose platforms for a plethora of applications and services. In these cases, both benefits and costs of actions are disseminated widely and a matching of social costs and benefits via individual decisions is unlikely. Such balancing is also unlikely in the case of catastrophic risks that might affect cyberspace. Some form of collective action may hence be needed to augment the existing resilience of the internet. However, great care has to be undertaken that any such measure does not inadvertently reduce the existing level of resilience. The challenge will be to find ways to enhance security while protecting the aspects of the internet that are fueling its innovative prowess. Ways to improve the security of the core infrastructure are well known but will not be implemented unless some form of collective agreement is found and enacted. Likewise, complementary ways to strengthen the legal and regulatory environment to more effectively act against perpetrators will likely be needed. In all these cases, carefully designed policies might be able to improve the incentives of the players to make decisions closer aligned with a societal optimum.

REFERENCES

Anderson, R. (2001), 'Why Information Security is Hard – An Economic Perspective', Proceedings of the 17th Annual Computer Security Applications Conference, New Orleans, Louisiana IEEE Computer Society, http://www.acsac.org/2001/papers /110.pdf.

Anderson, R., R. Böhme, R. Clayton and T. Moore (2008), 'Security Economics and the Internal Market', ENISA (European Network and Information Security Agency), http:// www.enisa.europa.eu/doc/pdf/report_sec_econ_&_int_mark_20080131.pdf.

Anderson, R. and T. Moore (2006), 'The Economics of Information Security', *Science*, **314**, 610–613.

Anderson, R. and T. Moore (2007), 'Information Security Economics – and Beyond', Computer Laboratory, University of Cambridge, http://www.cl.cam.ac.uk/~rja14/Papers/ econ_crypto.pdf.

Arbor Networks (2007), 'Worldwide Infrastructure Security Report', **Volume III**, http:// www.arbornetworks.com/report.

Arthur, W.B. (2009), *The Nature of Technology: What It Is and How It Evolves*, New York: Free Press.

August, T. and T.I. Tunca (2006), 'Network Software Security and User Incentives', *Management Science*, **52(11)**, 1703–20.

Barnum, S. and M. Gegick (2005), 'Economy of Mechanism', https://buildsecurityin. uscert.gov/daisy/bsi/articles/knowledge/principles/348.html?branch=1&language=1, 25 November 2007.

Basu, K. (2011), *Beyond the Invisible Hand: Groundwork for a New Economics*, Princeton, NJ: Princeton University Press.

Bauer, J.M. and M. van Eeten (2009), 'Cybersecurity: Stakeholder Incentives, Externalities, and Policy Options', *Telecommunications Policy*, **33(10–11)**, 706–19.

Bernstein, D.J. (2007), 'Some Thoughts on Security after Ten Years of qmail 1.0', 1st Computer Security Architecture Workshop in conjunction with 14th ACM Conference on Computers and Communication Security, Fairfax, Virginia, http://cr.yp.to/qmail/ qmailsec-20071101.pdf.

Blumenthal, M.S. (2011), 'Is Security Lost in the Cloud?', *Communications and Strategies*, **81(1st Quarter)**, 69–86.

Böhme, R. and G. Kataria (2006), 'On the Limits of Cyber-Insurance', Fischer-Hübner, S.E.A. (ed), *Trust and Privacy in Digital Business*, Berlin, New York: Springer, pp. 31–40.

Bokharie, V. S., O. Mason and F. Wirth (2010) 'Spread of Epidemics in Time-Dependent Networks', in *19th International Symposium on Mathematical Theory of Networks and Systems-MTNS 2010*, Budapest, Hungary.

Broad, W.J., J. Markoff and D.E. Sanger (2011), 'Israeli Test on Worm Called Crucial in Iran Nuclear Delay', *New York Times*, http://www.nytimes.com/2011/01/16/world/ middleeast/16stuxnet.html.

Clark, R.A. and R.K. Knake (2010), *Cyber War: The Next Threat to National Security and What to Do About It*, New York: Ecco.

Clayton, R. (2010), 'Might Governments Clean-up Malware?', Ninth Workshop on the Economics of Information Security (WEIS 2010), Harvard University, http://weis2010. econinfosec.org/papers/session4/weis2010_clayton.pdf.

Clover, C. (2009), 'Kremlin-backed Group Behind Estonia Cyber Blitz,' *The Financial Times*, http://www.ft.com/cms/s/0/57536d5a-0ddc-11de-8ea3-0000779fd2ac.html.

Counterpane & MessageLabs (2006), '2005 Attack Trends & Analysis', http://www.counter pane.com/dl/attack-trends-2005-messagelabs.pdf.

CSIS (2008), 'Securing Cyberspace for the 44th Presidency: A Report of the CSIS Presidency', http://csis.org/files/media/csis/pubs/081208_securingcyberspace_44.pdf, accessed 14 March 2013.

Davis, J. (2007), 'Hackers Take Down the Most Wired Country in Europe', *Wired*, **15**, http:// www.wired.com/politics/security/magazine/15-09/ff_estonia.

DeNardis, L. (2009), *Protocol Politics: The Globalization of Internet Governance*, Cambridge, MA: MIT Press.

Draief, M., A.J. Ganesh, and L. Massoulié (2008), 'Thresholds for Virus Spread on Networks', *Proceedings of the 1st International Conference on Performance Evaluation Methodologies and Tools*, New York.

Easley, D. and J. Kleinberg (2010), *Networks, Crowds, and Markets: Reasoning About a Highly Connected World*, New York: Cambridge University Press.

ENISA (2006), 'Provider Security Measures Part 1: Security and Anti-Spam Measures of Electronic Communication Service Providers – Survey', European Network and Information Security Agency, http://www.enisa.europa.eu/doc/pdf/deliverables/enisa_ security_spam.pdf.

Fox, J. (2007), 'Consumer Reports: Putting Consumers Back in Control', http://www.ftc. gov/bcp/workshops/spamsummit/presentations/Consumers.pdf.

GetSafeOnline (2006), 'The Get Safe Online Report', http://www.getsafeonline.org/media/ GSO_Cyber_Report_2006.pdf.

Gordon, L.A. and M.P. Loeb (2002), 'The Economics of Information Security Investment', *ACM Transactions on Information and System Security*, http://portal.acm.org/citation. cfm?id=581274.

Gordon, L.A. and M.P. Loeb (2006), *Managing Cybersecurity Resources: A Cost-Benefit Analysis*, New York: McGraw-Hill.

Halliday, J. (2010), 'Stuxnet Worm is the Work of a National Government Agency', *Guardian.co.uk*, http://www.guardian.co.uk/technology/2010/sep/24/stuxnet-worm-national-agency.

Hofmann, J. (2010), 'The Libertarian Origins of Cybercrime: Unintended Side-effects of a Political Utopia', London School of Economics, Centre for Analysis of Risk and Regulation (CARR), Discussion Paper No. 62, available at http://ssrn.com/abstract=1710773.

Hogben, G., D. Plohmann, E. Gerhards-Padilla and F. Leder (2011), 'Botnets: Detection, Measurement, Disinfection & Defence', European Network and Information Security Agency (ENISA), http://www.enisa.europa.eu/act/res/botnets/botnets-measurement-detection-disinfection-and-defence.

Holt, T.J., A.M. Bossler, and D.C. May (2012), 'Low Self-Control, Deviant Peer Associations, and Juvenile Cyberdeviance', *American Journal of Criminal Justice*, **37(3)**, 396–412.

House of Lords (2007a), 'Science and Technology Committee, 5th Report of Session 2006–07, Personal Internet Security, Volume I: Report', Authority of the House of Lords, http://www.publications.parliament.uk/pa/ld/ldsctech.htm.

House of Lords (2007b), 'Science and Technology Committee, 5th Report of Session 2006–07, Personal Internet Security, Volume II: Evidence', Authority of the House of Lords, http://www.publications.parliament.uk/pa/ld/ldsctech.htm.

Kirk, J. (2008), 'Student Fined for Attack Against Estonian Web Site', http://www.infoworld.com/article/08/01/24/Student-fined-for-attack-against-Estonian-Web-site_1.html.

Knake, R.K. (2010), *Internet Governance in an Age of Cyber Insecurity*, Washington, DC: Council on Foreign Relations Press.

Kramer, F.D., S.H. Starr, and L. Wentz (eds) (2009), *Cyberpower and National Security*, Dulles, VA: Potomac Books, Inc.

Kunreuther, H. and G. Heal (2003), 'Interdependent Security', *Journal of Risk and Uncertainty*, **26(2)**, 231.

Lacohée, H., S. Crane and A. Phippen (2006), 'Trustguide: Final Report', BT Group Chief Technology Office, Research & Venturing / HP Labs / University of Plymouth, Network Research Group, http://www.trustguide.org.uk/Trustguide%20-%20Final%20Report. pdf.

Lemos, R. (2006), 'Attackers Pass on OS, Aim for Drivers and Apps', http://www.securityfocus.com/news/11404.

Lesk, M. (2007), 'The New Front Line: Estonia under Cyberassault', *IEEE Security and Privacy*, **5(4)**, 76–79.

Levchenko, K., et al. (2011), 'Click Trajectories: End-to-End Analysis of the Spam Value Chain', http://cseweb.ucsd.edu/~savage/papers/Oakland11.pdf.

Lewis, J.A. (2005), 'Aux Armes, Citoyens: Cyber Security and Regulation in the United States', *Telecommunications Policy*, **29(11)**, 821–30.

Liebowitz, S.J. and S.E. Margolis (2003), 'Network Effects', M.E. Cave, S.K. Majumdar and I. Vogelsang (eds), *Handbook of Telecommunications Economics*, Amsterdam: North-Holland/Elsevier, pp. 75–96.

Markoff, J. (2008), 'Cyber Attack Preceded Invasion: Georgia's Web Infrastructure Hit, but Was It Russia?', *Chicago Tribune*, http://archives.chicagotribune.com/2008/aug/13/business/chi-cyber-war_13aug13.

Markoff, J. (2010), 'A Silent Attack, but Not a Subtle One', *New York Times*, http://www.nytimes.com/2010/09/27/technology/27virus.html.

Markoff, J. (2011), 'Malware Aimed at Iran Hit Five Sites, Report Says', *New York Times*, http://www.nytimes.com/2011/02/13/science/13stuxnet.html.

Microsoft (2008), 'Microsoft and the Adoption of the Security Development Lifecycle (SDL)', http://download.microsoft.com/download/Microsoft_and_the_Security_Development_Lifecycle_Oct08.docx.

Mieghem, P.V., J. Omic and R.E. Kooij (2009), 'Virus Spread in Networks', *IEEE/ACM Transactions on Networking*, **17(1)**, 1–14.

Moore, T., R. Clayton, and R. Anderson (2009), 'The Economics of Online Crime', *Journal of Economic Perspectives*, **23(3)**, 3–20.

Mueller, M. (2010), *Networks and States: The Global Politics of Internet Governance*, Cambridge, MA: MIT Press.

OECD (2009), *Computer Viruses and Other Malicious Software*, Paris: Organisation for Economic Co-operation and Development.

OECD (2010), 'The Economic and Social Role of Internet Intermediaries', OECD, http://www.oecd.org/dataoecd/49/4/44949023.pdf.

PayPal (2007), *Key Financial Facts*, http://www.pppress.co.uk/Content/Detail.asp?ReleaseID=5&NewsAreaID=22&SearchCategoryID=-1.

Perrow, C. (1999), *Normal Accidents: Living with High-risk Technologies. With a New Afterword and a Postscript on the Y2K Problem*, Princeton, NJ: Princeton University Press.

Perrow, C. (2007), *The Next Catastrophe: Reducing Our Vulnerabilities to Natural, Industrial, and Terrorist Disasters*, Princeton, NJ: Princeton University Press.

Posner, R.A. (2004), *Catastrophe: Risk and Response*, New York, NY: Oxford University Press.

Reid, T. (2007), 'China's Cyber Army is Preparing to March on America, says Pentagon', *Times Online*, http://technology.timesonline.co.uk/tol/news/tech_and_web/the_web/article2409865.ece.

Rescorla, E. (2004), 'Is Finding Security Holes a Good Idea?', Workshop on Economics and Information Security, http://www.rtfm.com/bugrate.pdf.

Roe, E. and P. Schulman (2008), *High Reliability Management: Operating on the Edge*, Palo Alto: Stanford University Press.

Sanger, D.E. and T. Shanker (2009), 'Pentagon Plans New Arm to Wage Cyberspace Wars', *New York Times*, http://www.nytimes.com/2009/05/29/us/politics/29cyber.html?_r=3&ref=us.

Schipka, M. (2007), 'The Online Shadow Economy: A Billion Dollar Market for Malware Writers', White Paper, MessageLabs Ltd.

Schneier, B. (2007), 'Information Security and Externalities', NSF/OECD Workshop Social & Economic Factors Shaping The Future Of The Internet, Washington, DC, http://www.oecd.org/dataoecd/60/8/37985707.pdf.

Shachtman, N. (2008), 'Estonia, Google Help "Cyberlocked" Georgia', *Wired*, http://www.wired.com/dangerroom/2008/08/civilge-the-geo/.

Shetty, N. et al. (2010), 'Competitive Cyber-Insurance and Internet Security', T. Moore (eds), *Economics of Information Security and Privacy*, New York: Springer.

Shim, W. (2010), Impact of Interdependent Risk on Cyber Security: An Analysis of Security Investment and Cyber Insurance, Ph.D. Dissertation, East Lansing, MI, Michigan State University.

Shim, W. and J.M. Bauer (2011), 'Effective Implementation of Technical Security Controls in the Presence of Moral Hazard', Unpublished Manuscript, East Lancing, MI, Michigan State University.

Snyder, W. (2007), 'Time to Deploy Improvement of 25 Percent', http://blog.mozilla.com/security/2007/06/18/time-to-deploy-improvement-of-25-percent/.

Sommer, P. and I. Brown (2011), 'Reducing Systemic Cybersecurity Risk', *OECD Working Paper*, No. IFP/WKP/FGS(2011)3.

Soper, M.E. (2009), 'Conficker Worm Shuts Down French and UK Air Forces', http://www.maximumpc.com/article/news/conficker_worm_shuts_down_french_and_uk_air_forces.

South, G. (2007), 'Web Issues over Banking Code', *The New Zealand Herald*, http://www.nzherald.co.nz/topic/story.cfm?c_id=126&objectid=10458545.

Spindler, G. and E. Recknagel (2008), 'Legal Aspects of Internet Banking in Germany',

D. Seese, C. Weinhardt and F. Schlottermann (eds), *Handbook on Information Technology in Finance*, Berlin, Heidelberg: Springer, pp. 731–52.

Taleb, N.N. (2007), *The Black Swan: The Impact of the Highly Improbable*, New York: Random House.

TechWebNews (2005), 'One In Four Identity-Theft Victims Never Fully Recover', *Information Week*, http://www.informationweek.com/showArticle.jhtml?articleID=166402700.

US GAO (2007), 'Cybercrime: Public and Private Entities Face Challenges in Addressing Cyber Threats', United States Goverment Accountability Office, http://www.gao.gov/new.items/d07705.pdf.

Van Eeten, M. and J.M. Bauer (2008), 'Economics of Malware: Security Decisions, Incentives and Externalities', OECD STI Working Paper, 2008/1, http://www.oecd.org/dataoecd/53/17/40722462.pdf.

Van Eeten, M., J. Bauer, H. Asghari and S. Tabatabaie (2010), 'The Role of Internet Service Providers in Botnet Mitigation: An Empirical Analysis Based on Spam Data', *STI Working Paper*, 2010/5, http://www.oecd.org/officialdocuments/displaydocument/?doclanguage=en&cote=dsti/doc(2010)5.

Varian, H. (2004), 'System Reliability and Free Riding', in L.J. Camp and S. Lewis (eds), *Economics of Information Security*, Dordrecht: Kluwer Academic Publishers, pp. 1–16.

Wash, R. (2010), 'Folk Models of Home Computer Security', Paper presented at the Symposium on Usable Privacy and Security (SOUPS), Redmond, WA, July 14–16, 2010.

Watson, A. (2005), 'Reputation in Open Source Software', http://opensource.mit.edu/papers/watson.pdf.

White House (2011), 'Cybersecurity Legislative Proposal', http://www.whitehouse.gov/the-press-office/2011/05/12/fact-sheet-cybersecurity-legislative-proposal.

Wildavsky, A. (1988), *Searching For Safety*, New Brunswick, NJ: Transaction Books.

Zittrain, J. (2008), *The Future of the Internet: And How to Stop It*, London: Allen Lane.

Index

no longer publisher-
     rightsholder but
     rightsholder-user 89
  see also contract; standards
Licklider, JCR 4
Liechtenstein
  data protection 225, 257
LinkedIn 310
Linux 13
Literary works *see* Google Books
Lithuania
  data protection 225, 257
Luxembourg
  data protection 225, 257

Macau
  data protection 225, 231, 239,
     257
Malaysia
  data protection 225, 226, 229, 231,
     232, 239, 245, 257
Malta
  child protection 285
     'stop pages' 286, 287
  data protection 225, 257
Mauritius
  data protection 226, 257
Mercosur 227, 232
'mere conduit' 462
Mexico
  data protection 226, 229, 231, 232,
     239, 258
MFNET 6
Microsoft 188, 379, 373, 382–6, 420,
     468–73
  Internet Explorer 470
  IE7 470
  PhotoDNA 290
  Security Development Lifecycle
     initiative 469
  Windows
     7 472
     98 471
     Vista 472
     XP 471, 472
mobile *see* wireless
Moldova
  data protection 225, 258
Monaco
  data protection 225, 258

Mongolia
  data protection 226
monitoring
  Google, data collection 83
  see also interception; surveillance
monopolies 129, 130–33, 147
  see also
Montenegro 225, 258
Morocco
  data protection 226, 258
Motion Picture Association of
     America 296
movies 296, 437
Mozambique 273
MSN 126, 461
music 312, 403
MySpace 47, 289, 310, 327

NATO 455, 456
NCMEC (National Center for
     Missing and Exploited Children)
     287–9
'net effects' 155–6
NetFlix 437
Netherlands
  child protection 280
     DNS blocking 292
  data protection 225, 258
  fingerprint data 269, 274
  network neutrality 419, 425, 427–8,
     433
  social networks 310
networks
  contagion 154–5
  content delivery networks 422, 424,
     437–8
  'Intergalactic' 4
  'network effect' 379
  network formation 156
  neutrality 121–41, 145, 149–52
     definition 421
     effects
       of regulations 127, 130, 136–9
       on quality of service 129, 130
     four net freedoms 421
     'lite' v 'heavy' 424, 433
     mandatory 150
     pioneer jurisdictions 425
     pricing 121–41
     two-sided 126